THE HUMAN RESOURCE FUNCTION IN EDUCATIONAL ADMINISTRATION

Sixth Edition

William B. Castetter
Professor Emeritus
Graduate School of Education
University of Pennsylvania

Merrill,
an imprint of Prentice Hall
Englewood Cliffs, New Jersey   Columbus, Ohio

Library of Congress Cataloging-in-Publication Data
Castetter, William Benjamin
    The human resource function in educational administration / William B.
Castetter. — 6th ed.
        p. cm.
    Rev. ed. of: The personnel function in educational administration. © 1992.
    Includes bibliographical references and indexes.
    ISBN 0-02-320201-7
    1. School personnel management—United States.   I. Castetter, William
Benjamin. Personnel function in educational administration. II. Title.
    LB2831.58.C37 1996
    371.2′01′0973—dc20
                                      94-40074
                                               CIP

Editor: Debra A. Stollenwerk
Production Editor: Stephen C. Robb
Cover Designer: Proof Positive/Farrowlyne Associates
Text Designer: Ed Horcharik
Production Buyer: Patricia A. Tonneman
Electronic Text Management: Marilyn Wilson Phelps, Matthew Williams, Tracey B.
    Ward, Karen L. Bretz
Illustrations: Ed Horcharik

This book was set in ITC New Baskerville and Swiss 721 by Prentice Hall and was
printed and bound by R. R. Donnelley & Sons Company. The cover was printed by
Phoenix Color Corp.

© 1996 by William B. Castetter
Prentice-Hall, Inc.
A Simon & Schuster Company
Englewood Cliffs, New Jersey 07632

Earlier editions, entitled *The Personnel Function in Educational Administration,* © 1992,
1986, 1981, 1976, and 1971 by William B. Castetter.

Printed in the United States of America

10 9 8 7 6 5 4 3 2 1

ISBN: 0-02-320201-7

Prentice-Hall International (UK) Limited, *London*
Prentice-Hall of Australia Pty. Limited, *Sydney*
Prentice-Hall of Canada, Inc., *Toronto*
Prentice-Hall Hispanoamericana, S. A., *Mexico*
Prentice-Hall of India Private Limited, *New Delhi*
Prentice-Hall of Japan, Inc., *Tokyo*
Simon & Schuster Asia Pte. Ltd., *Singapore*
Editora Prentice-Hall do Brasil, Ltda., *Rio de Janeiro*

To Roberta, with gratitude and affection

Preface

If modern school systems are to function well in this society, one of the necessities, surely, is to keep pace with the educational imperatives thrust upon them as the twilight of the twentieth century draws near. The flood of contemporary problems that are pounding at the floodgates of educational institutions—and the forces by which they are impelled—are reshaping the work settings, work and work technology, and the behavior of people who render service for educational institutions.

Recognition of and developing initiatives for dealing with the forces of change in both the internal and external environments that are affecting teaching and learning are at the heart of contemporary school system realities. Failure to understand and to cope with today's change-driven educational problems will, in all likelihood, prevent school systems from shedding a currently unfavorable image and their organizational infirmities.

The purpose of this text is to emphasize the emerging significance of the human resources function in educational administration—how the function is planned, organized, led, and controlled in the interest of organizational effectiveness. More importantly, special consideration is given to the quality of a system's human resources—how members are recruited, selected, inducted, developed, appraised, compensated, informed, and protected through the justice and bargaining processes.

The text is organized into four parts, containing thirteen chapters, a glossary, and two appendices. A summary of the four parts and the introductory chapter follows:

- Chapter 1. *Purview of the Human Resources Function.* Chapter 1 is designed to present a broad view of the nature, significance, and scope of the human resources function and its relationship to other organizational functions within a public institutional setting.
- Part I. *Shaping the System's Future Through Strategic Planning.* Part I (which contains Chapter 2) focuses on the first of eleven processes included in

the text. It is concerned with strategic planning and its linkage to the human resources function.

- Part II. *Human Resources Processes: Recruitment, Selection, Induction, Development, and Appraisal.* The underlying intent of the five chapters comprising Part II is to extend understanding of the key activities involved in school system staffing.

- Part III. *Human Resources Processes: Justice, Continuity, and Information Technology.* The three chapters included in Part III are devoted to protection of system members through the continuity and justice processes, as well as the importance of information technology in influencing individual, group, and system performance.

- Part IV. *Human Resources Processes: Compensation and Bargaining.* Part IV addresses two human resource processes: compensation and collective bargaining. Both chapters offer models for linking the processes to the strategic aims of the system.

Special Features of the Sixth Edition. The major changes in this edition are described below:

- Three chapters (appraisal, collective bargaining, and problem personnel) have been eliminated, parts of which have been blended into single chapters.

- Each chapter contains an overview, review, and preview. Each contains a set of chapter terms, chapter objectives, chapter exercise(s), review and discussion questions, notes, and supplementary reading.

- The text contains 140 figures and 58 tables, the intent of which is to portray significant chapter points as they pertain to chapter content.

- The introductory chapter (Purview of the Human Resources Function) presents a broad view of the human resources function by focusing on six function dimensions: *mission, human, organization, cultural, ethical,* and *environmental.*

New and Updated Features. Each chapter contains a Chapter Exercise in the form of class and individual assignments to elicit responses to selected problems in the chapter. Chapter exercises can be shaped to fit various class settings, teaching styles, course objectives, and individual projects or seminar instructional approaches.

Special attention has been given to the regulatory aspects of the human resources function. A digest of major regulatory provisions has been updated, as well as references in each chapter where related regulatory conditions are involved.

The glossary has been expanded to include new terms designed to aid and add to the user's understanding of the extension of human resources knowledge, which is accompanied by new words, new meanings, and new symbols.

The chapter on information technology has been expanded because of the demand for and accumulation of school system information. Invention of the computer in the middle of the twentieth century, as well as other cybernetic machines, has provided organizations with useful tools to gather, store, recall, utilize, and extend system capability through information technology.

Each of the process chapters contains a hypothetical illustration of a chapter-related human resources school system policy (the Riverpark school system). The guiding premises illustrate the importance of system commitment to certain values to which it intends to adhere in the management of its human resources.

Acknowledgments. The author wishes to acknowledge the contributions of those who have helped to shape past and present editions of this text. This includes graduate students, colleagues, critics, editors, reviewers, and librarians. I am indebted particularly for assistance in preparation of the sixth edition to Dr. Richard S. Heisler, Dr. Mark C. Nagy, Dr. John Baillie, Dr. Hinda R. Bornstein, and Susan C. Owens, who in various ways provided information and guidance as the text evolved through several drafts. I gratefully acknowledge the invaluable contributions of the reviewers: Robert E. Anderson, Wichita State University; Kenneth J. Murray, University of Central Florida; Gary M. Crow, Louisiana State University; Robert H. Decker, University of Northern Iowa; and Carol B. Furtwengler, Wichita State University. Finally, I offer my sincere appreciation to Debbie Stollenwerk, my editor, whose support and encouragement have been vital elements throughout preparation of this edition.

William B. Castetter

Contents

PART II

HUMAN RESOURCES PROCESSES: RECRUITMENT, SELECTION, INDUCTION, DEVELOPMENT, AND APPRAISAL   83

CHAPTER 3
Recruitment   85

CHAPTER 4
Selection   131

CHAPTER 5

Induction   181

CHAPTER 6

Development   225

CHAPTER 7

Performance Appraisal   269

PART III

HUMAN RESOURCES PROCESSES: JUSTICE, CONTINUITY, AND INFORMATION TECHNOLOGY   321

CHAPTER 8

Employment Justice   323

CHAPTER 9

Employment Continuity   367

CHAPTER 10

Information Technology and the Human Resources Function   415

PART IV

HUMAN RESOURCES PROCESSES: COMPENSATION AND BARGAINING   455

CHAPTER 11

Compensation: Fundamental Concepts   457

Chapter 1

Purview of the Human Resources Function

CHAPTER OVERVIEW

- Contemporary Human Resources Problems
- Function Purpose and Organizational Setting
  Function Significance
- Dimensions of the Human Resources Function

  Mission Dimension
  Human Dimension
  Organizational Dimension
  Environmental Dimension
  Culture Dimension
  Ethics Dimension

CHAPTER OBJECTIVES

- Develop an appreciation of the nature, significance, and scope of the human resources function in a public institutional setting.
- Focus on the potential influence of the human resources function on organizational effectiveness and the forces that affect that influence.
- Present a preview of eleven human resources subsystems (processes) and how they are linked to the system's infrastructure.
- Lay the strategic and operational planning foundation in order to make the kinds of decisions that will lead to desired performance of individuals, work units, and the system at large.

CHAPTER TERMS

Culture	Infrastructure
Ethics	Mission
External environment	Organization structure
Human resources function	Regulatory environment
Internal environment	Values

This chapter presents a broad framework for viewing the management of the **human resources function** in school systems. Its intent is to:

- Place in perspective the nature, dimensions, and significance of the function.
- Stress the considerable impact of the endless and sometimes dramatic rapidity of change and the role of the human resources function in the resolution of challenges it represents.
- Consider the proposition that everything that goes on in a school system is linked to its human resources.
- Identify major current and emerging problems confronting contemporary school systems and associated environmental forces that both enhance and hinder organizational change.
- Provide a foundation for conceptualizing, developing, administering, correcting, and improving effectiveness of the human resources function.

This final decade of the twentieth century is marked by ferment created by sociocultural, political, governmental, economic, and technological forces. These circumstances will continue to pose ever-increasing challenges for those who design and administer the human resources function.

Subsequent chapters will elaborate upon various aspects of the broad outlines of this chapter. They will deal with the translation of concepts into functions, processes, subprocesses, policies, programs, practices, and procedures essential to implementation of system strategic aims.

CONTEMPORARY HUMAN RESOURCES PROBLEMS

Those responsible for managing today's human resources affairs face diverse pressures. These pressures include union power; regulatory controls; personnel litigation; competition for qualified people; career development issues; pay packages; affirmative action; comparable worth issues; performance appraisal reform; restructuring; modernizing information systems; and changes in the work, the worker, and the work environment.

Tomorrow's personnel managers (regardless of school system size) will face additional challenges as they address pressing social needs. Judging from early indications, the closing years of the twentieth century are shaping up as a period in which educational systems will be forced to deal with a host of problems that have extensive implications for the human resources function. Examples include legislated learning, greater investment in staff development, modification of vocational education, shortages of qualified staff members in early childhood education, empowerment of teachers, more effective use of educational technology, incentive pay plans, and alternative approaches to teacher certification and tenure.

Given these challenges, consider some major people problems confronting contemporary school systems. These problems, listed in Figure 1.1, are foremost among those cited in educational reform literature.[1] Figure 1.1 provides a point of departure for (a) understanding the forces, factors, and conditions involved in giving direction to the human resources function; (b) emphasizing the importance of appreciating the nature, extent, and causes of workplace problems; and (c) establishing a supportive framework on which to fashion strategies, policies, and processes that enable the function to contribute more capably to a school system's established purposes.

Although the list of problems in Figure 1.1 must be considered incomplete, it helps to illustrate that the challenges are compelling enough to warrant redesigning of functional strategies directed toward greater resource productivity. Among various criticisms leveled at current human resources management, one gaining credence is that traditional models have yet to develop comprehensive approaches to cope satisfactorily with changing internal and external environments. In large measure, present models fail to reflect the degree to which emerging developments are shaping the nature and needs of a human resources function whose force is vital to achieving organizational purpose. For example, changes in the internal and external environments have outstripped our full understanding of their organizational implications. Most current models have yet to bring together two elements critical to improving the human resources function. The first element consists of plans to cope with political, economic, and technological forces; regulatory provisions; collective bargaining movements; generational culture; and an increasingly litigious society. The second element includes incorporation of new ideas, strategies, policies, and processes generated by academicians from a variety of disciplines, as well as those developed by practicing administrators.

The sections that follow extend this discussion of current school personnel problems by identifying key factors inherent in and having considerable influence on the design of contemporary models of the human resources

Abridgement of human and civil rights
Academic, personal, and professional freedom
Access to personnel files
Affirmative Action
AIDS
Americans with Disabilities Act
At-will employment
Automatic annual salary increments
Benefit program adjustments
Certification legislation
Class size reduction and enrollment decline
Community residence requirements for system members
Court-ordered desegregation
Court-ordered reduction of property tax assessments
Drug testing
Educator competence
Electronic information applications
Employee personal assistance programs
Employment law
Equal employment obligations
Family and Medical Leave Act
Inclusion of enforceable codes of ethics in bargaining agreements
Mandated salary schedules based on preparation and seniority
National health insurance
Negligent hiring
Nepotism
Personnel empowerment
Personnel seniority
Polygraph testing
Power equalization between system and human resources
Professional standards and practices
Reduction in staff, "bumping"
Rights and responsibilities of educators
School choice
Sexual harassment/abuse by school employees
Site-base management
Strikes in school entities
Union protection of its monopoly position
Use of uncertified personnel
Vouchers and tax credits
Year-round schooling

FIGURE 1.1
Illustrative issues related to the contemporary domain of the human resources function.

function, the interaction of these factors, and their implications for resolution of human resources problems typified by those in Figure 1.1.

FUNCTION PURPOSE AND ORGANIZATIONAL SETTING

What is the meaning of the human resources function? What are its goals? What specific activities comprise the function? Is there a difference between the human resources function and personnel administration? What major factors influence the function? Considering these matters is the principal purpose of this section.

Underlying an analysis of the human resources function is the notion that organization presupposes existence of interrelated parts. This concept is illustrated in Figure 1.2, which portrays administrative functions and subfunctions of the hypothetical Goodville school system.

The purpose of a scheme such as that in Figure 1.2 is to identify, classify, and interrelate major functions and subfunctions that must be performed somewhere in the system if its mission is to be fulfilled. The human resources function, it should be noted, is divided into 11 areas: *planning, bargaining, recruitment, selection, induction, appraisal, development, compensation, justice, continuity,* and *information.*

The goals of the human resources function in any educational system are to attract, develop, retain, and motivate personnel in order to (a) achieve the system's purposes, (b) assist members in satisfying position and group performance standards, (c) maximize personnel career development, and (d) reconcile individual and organizational objectives. These goals must be translated into operational terms to give direction to those responsible for their implementation.

In sum, the human resources function is an essential factor in the operation of a school system, but the manner in which the activities are implemented (frequently referred to as *personnel administration*) varies widely from system to system. All school systems structure tasks and authority relationships, such as that portrayed in Figure 1.2.

Function Significance

From the preceding definitions of the function, one can examine the significance of this important subsystem of a school organization. Function significance can be viewed from several perspectives:

* In contrast to other major functions, human resources is concerned primarily with activities related to people.

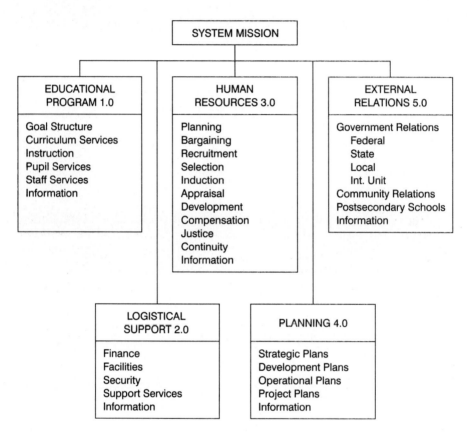

FIGURE 1.2
Major administrative functions and subfunctions of the Goodville school system.

- The scope of the function, as illustrated in Figure 1.3, is extensive. Function activities can have a pervasive effect on the careers of system personnel.
- Design and operation of the function can have positive or negative effects on the individual, the group, and the system. Individuals' behaviors, as well as combined behaviors, influence organizational effectiveness. An important task of the function is to develop a structure within which individuals and groups are able to work cooperatively and perform productively.
- Effects of the external environment are crucially important to system personnel. Thus, function design involves monitoring the environment for changes to which the system must be prepared to respond.

The following sections examine five elements of the school system **infrastructure** and their relationship to the human resources function.

These elements include the system mission, human resources, organization structure, environment, culture, and ethics.

DIMENSIONS OF THE HUMAN RESOURCES FUNCTION

Any attempt to understand the scope and significance of the human resources function and its role in facilitating individual, group, and system effectiveness requires some understanding of its *dimensions.* The text that follows highlights key dimensions of the human resources function and their implications for designing, implementing, controlling, and correcting courses of action so that desirable results are achieved within the bounds of established standards.

Figure 1.3 identifies major dimensional elements that have an impact on the operation of the human resources function. It is clear that management of a school system involves many interdependent activities, governance of which is influenced by various forces, factors, and conditions. Because each of those forces have potential for affecting organizational performance, each must be understood to appreciate fully how they pervade the decision-making process. In the context of decision making, the dimensions noted in Figure 1.3 can be considered as a framework for bringing about school system improvement in a mission-oriented and *ethically appropriate* manner. The first of these dimensions—the *system mission*—is the subject of the following discussion.

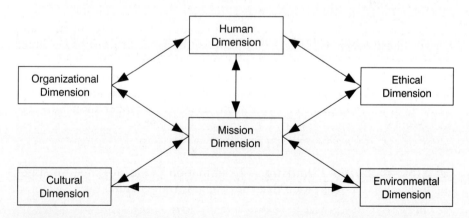

FIGURE 1.3
Dimensional elements that define and influence the design and operation of the human resources function.

Mission Dimension

The **mission** of a school system identifies the purposes for which it has been created, its boundaries and activities, as well as the governmental and collateral purposes it is expected to satisfy. The mission represents the foundation for providing an educational program and supporting services that will enhance the mental, moral, social, and emotional development of children, youth, and adults served by the school district. By way of illustration, Joyce, Hersh, and McKibbin define system mission as follows:

> The mission of the school can be defined by how it enters into the lives of students. Formal education is an organized attempt to enter into and change students' lives to help them develop the capacity to respond to reality in new ways. The primary task in selecting the mission is to identify how the school can enter the lives of students in order to change their responses to living in the world. Three domains that can be greatly enhanced by organized schooling include:
>
> • Personal domain—personal capabilities such as creativity, intelligence, and motivation.
> • Social domain—interactive social and economic skills.
> • Academic domain—skills that comprise an academic subject area such as mathematics or English.[2]

To some educators developing a mission statement to guide school system planning and choosing from the multitude of underlying choices that must be made to coordinate diverse system activities represents a meaningless exercise in academic nonsense. As we examine mission statements, however, such as those in Figure 1.4, mission is arguably the most basic property of a school system, and one possessing considerable practical utility.

Mission is the system's overarching plan from which a set of subplans derive. These subplans include definition of the kinds of work to be done, division of labor, specification of the number and kinds of jobs needed and how they are structured, how resources are allocated, and articulation of system **values** and their content through such processes as personnel involvement, goal acceptance and commitment, as well as member induction and socialization.

Mission-anchored Planning.   Examination of various mission statements leads to the realization that they embody the potential for:

• Clarifying the core purpose for school system existence.
• Identifying services that the public expects the system to deliver in exchange for financial support.

The Sierra Club

Before   The mission of the Sierra Club is to influence public, private, and corporate policies and actions through Club programs at the local, national, and international levels.

After   Building on generations of success, the Sierra Club inspires people to join in protecting earth's natural treasures and vitality. Through the club, individuals magnify their power to restore the places where they live and preserve the places they love.

Berryessa Union School District

Before   The Berryessa Union School District is dedicated to serving the educational needs of pupils within the community. The board of trustees, staff members, and the state share in the responsibilities for the education of pupils. The commitment is to provide a free public education to main a literate populace, which is the basis for a democratic society.

After   In Berryessa Union School District, we are committed to providing the necessary resources and inspiration for each student to develop

- A command of learning
- Social responsibility
- Critical thinking

We are dedicated to motivating students to achieve their maximum potential and to value lifelong learning.

FIGURE 1.4
Illustration of the reworking of an organization mission.

Source: Cynthia D. Scott, Dennis T. Jaffe, and Glenn R. Tobe, Organizational Vision, Values, and Mission, p. 66, © 1993 Crisp Publications, Inc., 1200 Hamilton Court, Menlo Park, CA, 94025; 800-442-7477.

- Providing a framework for judging the extent to which the mission is being realized.
- Creating a focus for defining the scope and limitations of the system's endeavors.
- Establishing a point of departure for deciding which key activities need to be performed.
- Deciding how financial, technical, human, and organizational resources will be allocated.
- Focusing on the end state rather than on the means of getting there.
- Bringing into being a frame of reference by which controls are generated to implement the mission (strategies, policies, programs, projects, rules, and regulations).

Another important value of a clearly defined mission statement is that it serves as a boundary guide as to what it should not do as well as to state what it intends to do. There is, for example, a hierarchy of laws, rules, and decisions in each state that have operational meaning for school systems. These include such elements as the state constitution statutes; state board of education rules; department of education regulations; court decisions; and system policies, contracts, and rules.

Consequently, these governing influences eliminate discretionary consideration of certain decisions while also leaving important permissive decisions to the school system. A reality-based mission statement serves as an important contemporary base for defining the scope of acceptable choice regarding such current education issues as fitting religion into the public schools, sex education, preschool day care, pressures for extensive extracurricular programs, the extent of special education and pupil disability arrangements, various types of age–group plans, continuing education classes for pregnant teenagers, desegregation, bilingual education, and issues relating to cultural diversity, quality of work life, and restructuring the system.

System Mission and School Reform Assumptions.   It has been noted previously that public education in the United States is the responsibility of individual states. Day-to-day administration is the responsibility of individual states. The official curriculum is what state and district officials set forth in curricular plans and courses of study. There is more to education, however, than the official curriculum, including those indirect entities such as the family, church, social institutions, television, and work settings. Moreover, the official curriculum is not necessarily one that is adhered to in individual school systems, schools, and classrooms.

It is against this curricular background that contemporary education reform movements have been initiated. It is also this curricular reform background that involves *underlying assumptions* that influence the design of the school system mission. The school system mission is about purpose. Mission designers make decisions that convert the system mission into educational programs and that have direct and indirect effects on teaching processes, learning experiences, system policies, classroom practices, and operational procedures.

It is especially important, then, at this juncture in our history, that mission designers give serious attention to addressing the underlying assumptions upon which the school system mission should be structured. *Following are some illustrations of assertions, assumptions, and hypotheses that have been advanced as part of the reform movement in education.* These premises create a difficult conundrum for mission planners: how to avoid basing decisions and derivative plans on postulates advanced as fact. Mission elements, from which building blocks such as strategies, tactics, policies, plans, and projects are derived, need to be looked at critically and searchingly to assess their significance in furthering the design of a master plan.

- Every pupil can be given the best education we can offer if we double the current per pupil expenditure.
- The best education reform strategy is to change the curriculum.
- Schools can and should be organized to address all missions that serve the interests of the community.
- A high positive correlation exists between pupil expenditure and school quality.
- Passage of the Goals 2000 Educate America Act in 1994, by establishing federal academic guidelines, will create conditions conducive to the intellectual, physical, moral, and aesthetic development of pupils.
- Changing the internal organization of schools will result in greater student learning because contemporary school structures prohibit learning.
- Incompetent teachers and undemanding curricula are responsible for the current infirmities in American education.
- A changing society and a changing economy has no relationship to demands for school reform.
- By revamping or restructuring the internal organization of a school system, the purpose or mission of schooling will take care of itself.
- Outcome-based education is the one best way to improve student achievement.
- General education goals, as expressed in a mission, should be reduced to a high level of specificity so that they can be structured, measured, and serve as indicators of school performance effectiveness.
- School choice (12 different contemporary plans) is the one best way to improve teaching and learning.
- Giving principals sole responsibility for firing teachers will improve teaching and learning.
- State mandates governing curriculum content, including genocide, duty to vote, the evils of tobacco, drugs, social diseases, lessons in driver education, religion, cultural diversity, environmental education, and bilingual classes, have helped students to know and do the right things.
- Studies have shown that adherence to Deming's management principles will improve the total quality of a school system.[*]

Viewed in the context of this discussion, the mission plan is important because it provides a focal point for debating, discussing, and arriving at a consensus among system members as to their personal expectations and

---

[*] See note 1 for sources relative to the mission statements, as well as to school reform assumptions in Chapter Exercise 1.1.

beliefs, as well as to their expressed wishes about what the organization's common purpose should be.

For all of these considerations, the system mission, if clearly understood, can be conducive to internalizing commitment, even dedication to an explicit set of values. The school system is ill served when officials fail to appreciate the interactive potential of a system mission and to use it consistently as a standard in making decisions regarding transformation from the present to a desired state. Creation and application of a unified purpose through a mission statement is frequently hindered by short-term perspectives and being blinded by the business at hand.

Human Dimension

Human resources refers to those individuals who comprise the school staff and contribute to the operation of the school system. This includes members who vary in such characteristics as quantity and quality of position preparation; gender, age, and personality; work experiences, learning styles, work expectations, and assignments; temperaments, attitudes, aptitudes, and stress tolerance levels; and skills, interests, and motivation.

As we strive to learn about the human dimension and its significance for school system effectiveness, one actuality is worth recognizing: *individual performance is the core element fundamental to any organizational endeavor.* Individuals carry out the instructional process; decide what, when, where, how, and by whom school work is done; and decide which employees enter and leave the system.

In the following discussion, several aspects of the human dimension are included to illustrate how they fit into the context of meeting expectations of individuals, groups, and the system.

Humanistic Perspective. Humanism is defined as an expression of human values and a means to developing the free responsible individual. Humanism is based on the incontestable principle regarding the inalienable and sacred rights of the individual.[3] For centuries the rights of the individual have been given compelling expression through (a) the Magna Carta (1215); (b) the Declaration of the Rights of Man and the Citizen adopted by the French National Assembly (1789); (c) the U.S. Bill of Rights and Amendments (1791); (d) the Emancipation Proclamation (1863); (e) the Women's Suffrage Act (1920); and (f) the Universal Declaration of Human Rights adopted by the United Nations General Assembly (1948).[4] How the force of these documents are relevant to the shaping of the human resources function of a school system is exemplified in Article 23 of the Universal Declaration of Human Rights.[5]

Article 23

1. Everyone has the right to work, to free choice of employment, to just and favorable conditions of work and to protection against unemployment.

2. Everyone, without any discrimination, has the right to equal pay for equal work.

3. Everyone who works has the right to just and favorable remuneration ensuring for himself and his family an existence of human dignity, and supplemented, if necessary, by other means of social protection.

4. Everyone has the right to form and to join trade unions for the protection of his interests.[6]

"Other means of social protection" currently include a canopy of safeguards for educators that have evolved over time. Illustrative are academic freedom; tenure; formal grievance and concern-complaint procedures; union contracts; personnel policies; codes of ethics; various local, state, and federal regulatory provisions; and the judicial system of the United States (see Chapter 2).

Figure 1.5 depicts a personnel bill of rights whose intent is to define the human standards the system aspires to and intends to observe in the individual-organization relationship. They set forth expectations the system has for its personnel and provide a foundation for maintaining modes of thought or action in which human interests, values, and dignity predominate (see Figure 1.2).

If the ideals of human dignity and worth are to permeate organization culture, it is clear that they must have a significant role in the conduct of the human resources function. Adoption of and adherence to a set of guidelines that are ethically oriented is a way of committing system authorities to a posture for enhancing individual-organization relationships. Their intent is to represent a guarantee to members that they will enjoy the same rights as position holders as they do as ordinary citizens. They create a framework for gaining commitment of individuals to pursue their personal, position, group, and organization goals. In addressing the value of the individual personality, the system is extending to the workplace the principles of fair and reasonable treatment in exchange for outcomes such as high productivity and improvement in work motivation.

Organizational Dimension

The formal organization, as represented in Figure 1.2, is one of the forces in the system infrastructure influencing the design and operation of the human resources function. Organization derives from the system mission, which in turn emanates from the external environment (state system of education). Key elements of an educational institution include system purpose, leadership, structure, incentives, and culture.

- The right to give and receive feedback.
- The right of fair treatment in every area of work experience.
- The right to basic dignity, respect, and personal identity as a human being.
- The right to a style of management that enhances self-esteem and dignity as a person.
- The right to have the opportunity for a meaningful job for which they are qualified.
- The right to be consulted and involved in those decisions that relate to the employee's job.
- The right to be involved in social action programs.
- The right to set their own work goals.
- The right to set their own lifestyle.
- The right to be creative in the performance of the task and in the fulfillment of the daily goals.
- The right to fair compensation for their efforts.
- The right to work hard to develop in a way that enables them to meet new challenges.
- The right to be coached, assisted, and helped in the achievement of their goals.
- The right to an optimistic, trusting, and caring relationship in their work environment.

FIGURE 1.5
A personnel bill of rights.

Source: Reprinted, with permission of the publisher, from Tough-Minded Leadership, by Joe D. Batten © 1989 AMACOM, a division of the American Management Association, New York. All rights reserved.

Purpose.   As noted previously, a well-developed and extensively promulgated sense of common purpose is fundamental to unification of the talents, education, experience, and motivation of individuals and groups to achieve the reason for the system's existence. Statements of mission take their origin from various sources, including state education laws, state mandates requiring school systems to establish a mission statement, or from strategic plans developed independently by local school districts.

Because a mission statement represents the system's strategic aim and provides a means of establishing outcomes it intends to achieve, the educational impact it intends to create, and client expectations it aims to satisfy, its articulation and communication are highly important. The following text focuses on the role of leadership in organizing the school system to carry out its mission effectively.

Leadership. A number of leadership elements enter implementation of the system mission, but the single most important requisite is deciding multiple issues on the basis of the extent to which they support and enhance values and expectations set forth in the mission statement. Because missions are stated in broad terms, they are frequently subjected to various interpretations by various interest groups. Securing mission acceptance and adhering to its sense of purpose, however, is fraught with issues and pressures from religious groups, politicians, and social activists to incorporate their interests within the framework of broad system purpose. Hard as it may be, every decision made by leadership needs to be viewed in terms of whether its impact will be instrumental in furthering strategic intent.

In seeking to remedy selected system negative circumstances, leadership is constantly faced with challenges from both internal and external sources. In advancing school system interests as well as the status of the human resources function to a more desirable state, these complex problems are among the more compelling to be noted:

• Finding solutions to problems associated with the growing diversity of the work force.

• Dealing with the question as to whether the system's present priorities are those that should be its basic priorities in the future.

• Resolving internal, external, and professional issues that are barriers to desired personnel performance.

• Deciding how best to employ structure, leadership styles, rewards, money, power, authority, recognition, incentives, and controls to improve the productive contribution of individuals and groups.

• Fostering union-system relations in a manner that collective bargaining becomes a positive force for system unity and goal orientation.

What is important to remember is that to challenges such as the foregoing, few proven solutions are universally applicable in large, medium, and small school systems. With these thoughts in mind we move to consider ways in which the **organization structure,** an inescapable characteristic of organizations, is shaped to meet challenges posed in implementing the system mission in the milieu of contemporary society.

Every organization has a structure—a plan for linking positions and people to purposes. The structure may be one that has been formally adopted by the board of education and described by organizational charts, position guides, and organizational manuals. Or it may be an informal structure, without documentation or evidence of any kind to describe its characteristics. In any case, organizations are comprised of people who occupy positions, interact with each other, and are vitally concerned that they be compensated, both in responsibilities inherent in the work they perform and in their individual contributions to organizational effectiveness.

As illustrated in Figures 1.6 and 1.7, elements of a structure include purposes, people, activities, and relationships. One of the inferences that can be drawn from analysis of an organization structure is that its design and implementation involve individual and group participation through which system purpose is transformed into policies, functions, processes, activities, operations, and control mechanisms aimed at achieving perceived organizational outcomes. Another inference is that there are compelling questions to be resolved about the design of the organization structure such as:

- What are the key activities that need to be performed to serve the interests of our students, human resources, regulatory agencies, community groups, parents, and the school system?
- What is the most appropriate way to group these key activities into positions?
- How shall positions be grouped into attendance units, departments, administrative and supervisory groups, support services, and temporary personnel requirements?
- What number of positions should be in the structure? What major tasks, authority relationships, and performance criteria should be established for each position?
- To what extent should the system be decentralized for decision-making purposes? Centralized?
- What integration devices such as communication and coordination are most suitable for bringing together positions, position holders, and work units into a cohesive whole for system betterment?
- What chain of command should be established? How many levels of management are needed in large systems? Small? Medium?

Structural questions such as these force designers to focus on how best to utilize the structure to consider among the feasible options that are most likely to result in improving individual, group, and system performance. One of the inescapable circumstances of school management in the late years of the twentieth century is that the complexity, as well as the politically and intellectually demanding tasks associated with school restructuring, require an appreciation of a host of factors that must be taken into consideration.

Despite all the criticism about school system structures that has surfaced in the long-running debate about "restructuring schools," especially regarding hierarchies, levels of management, close supervision, and top-down decision making, some mode of procedure, of fusing human and nonhu-

Purposes	Every organization has a structure—a plan for linking positions and people to purposes. The purposes of an organization form the starting point of structural planning because all activities flow from purpose.
Activities	Activities are divided into positions; positions are grouped into major functions; functions are grouped into organizational units.
Superior–subordinate	Every structure has a hierarchy to coordinate organizational activity. The essence of a hierarchy is the superior–subordinate system in which certain positions are granted authority to direct the work of subordinate positions. The number of subordinates reporting to a superior is referred to as the span of control. Degrees of responsibility and authority are referred to as levels or layers of administration in the hierarchy.
Line and staff relationships	Most organizations have line and staff positions. Line positions are those that have the authority to initiate and carry through the basic activities of the organization that are essential to goal attainment. Collectively, line positions form the chain of command in an organization through which decisions are made, information communicated, and activities coordinated and controlled. Staff positions are those responsible for rendering advice, service, and counsel to individuals and groups within the organization.

FIGURE 1.6
Elements of an organization structure.

man resources into a cohesive effort toward purpose attainment, is inescapable. An arrangement of authority is essential to implement system improvement through direction and coordination. Without a chain of command, power becomes unbridled.

Controls. Control mechanisms are essential to any and all forms of human resources planning. One compelling reason is that every plan that the school system initiates, and allocates resources for, should have built-in means for judging its effectiveness. Indeed, there are numerous other justifications for control mechanisms, such as preventing and correcting deviations from standards; curbing turnover, absenteeism, sick leave, and other benefit abuses; and minimizing behaviors that are antiorganizational, self-serving, defiant, rebellious, or in violation of the system's code of ethics.

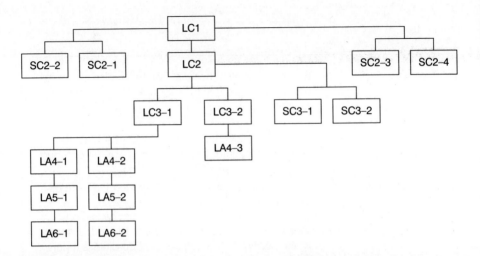

Central Administration

A. Line Positions

LC1	Superintendent
LC2	Deputy Superintendent: Instruction
LC3–1	Director: Secondary Education
LC3–2	Director: Elementary Education

B. Staff Positions

SC2–1	Assistant Superintendent: Business
SC2–2	Assistant Superintendent: Personnel
SC2–3	Assistant Superintendent: Research
SC2–4	Assistant Superintendent: Planning
SC3–1	Coordinator: Pupil services
SC3–2	Coordinator: Curriculum Services

Attendance Units

A. Line Positions

LA4–1	High School Principal
LA4–2	Middle School Principal
LA4–3	Elementary School Principal
LA5–1	Assistant Principal
LA5–2	Assistant Principal
LA6–1	Department Head
LA6–2	Department Head

Explanation of Position index

First Letter Indicates Line or Staff Position
- L = Line Position
- S = Staff Position

Second Letter Indicates Location of Position
- C = Central Administration
- A = Attendance Unit

First Number Indicates Structural Level of Position
1. Superintendent
2. Assistant Superintendent or Deputy Superintendent
3. Director or Coordinator
4. Principal
5. Assistant Principal

Second Number Indicates one of several similar positions at same level

Example: LA4–3 indicates a line position in an attendance unit at fourth level, elementary school principal.

FIGURE 1.7
Position index system designed to clarify school system organization structure and to develop a uniform system of titles (see also Figure 12.3).

Two kinds of controls should be mentioned: system and functional. System controls are focused on the total organization and include policies, position descriptions, strategic plans, and mission statements. Functional controls pertain to those measures that guide the human resources function, such as the eleven personnel processes identified in Figure 1.2.[7]

Employing this discussion as background for a broad view of the organization structure, the reader is advised that each of the remaining chapters contain content relating to the significance of the structure within the various processes of the human resources function.

Environmental Dimension

School systems are created by and intended to serve the society that creates and sustains them. Those engaged in or aspiring to managerial roles in school systems need an effective working knowledge of the relationship of the environmental dimension to the operation of the human resources function. Consequently, a model for understanding the interaction of the school system environment and its influence on individual, group, and organizational behavior is presented in Figure 1.8. This schematic portrayal of the environmental dimension consists of two types of environments: external and internal. To give the reader more specific insights into the pervasive influence of environmental forces on social, organizational, functional, and

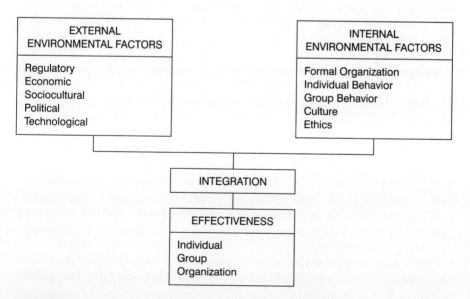

FIGURE 1.8
Environmental interactions that influence performance effectiveness.

position-holder objectives, the following discussion provides a brief summary of their significance.

External Environment.   Much of the evolution of the human resources function, both in public and private sectors, has been brought about more by the **external environment** than by practitioners. Major external forces that affect the human resources function have been grouped arbitrarily into five clusters (as outlined in Figure 1.8) in order to establish a framework for analyzing the complex interaction between environmental factors and the human resources of a school system. Environmental-organizational interaction suggests that there are constraints, forces, and options to which a system must respond in order to achieve stability and viability. The human resources function plays a vital role in helping the system to live within economic strictures, meet legal mandates, honor contractual obligations, deal with pressures of special-interest groups, adapt to emerging technologies, and uphold ethical standards while maintaining centrality of purpose. Striking this balance requires organizational effort of considerable magnitude. For this reason, the aim of the discussion that follows is to (a) note the political, economic, technological, and environmental forces referred to earlier about the human resources function; (b) indicate the importance of understanding their potential for strategic and operational planning for human resources (to be discussed in Chapter 2); and (c) point out the organizational significance of forging proactive personnel policies in response to evolving social phenomena, such as changing environmental patterns, educational retrenchments, an environment of fewer resources, and evolving ethics of the work force.

   Regulatory factor.   Education in the United States operates within a framework of regulatory controls of varying degrees. As indicated in Figure 1.9, these elements include the Constitution; federal laws; state, county, and municipal laws; court decisions; executive orders; administrative agency rulings; legal challenges; and employment contracts. It is generally agreed that provisions governing employment in both the public and private sectors have far-reaching influence on the operation of the human resources function. Each state system controls the school curriculum and supporting services, who shall teach, how schools are financed, and school board policy-making authority. In addition, there are regulatory controls governing taxation limitations, salaries, benefits, collective bargaining, performance appraisal, tenure, grievance procedures, and budgetary requirements.

   This **regulatory environment** extends to the federal government and the judicial system, which influences virtually every aspect of the human resources function, including discrimination, hiring practices, compensation, benefits, and unjust dismissal. Beckham and Zirkel, in their analysis and review of legal issues in public school employment, indicate that the relationship between public schools and their employees is one of the most frequently litigated aspects of American education. Prominent employment disputes include discrimination, First Amendment rights, due process, collective bargaining, performance appraisal, dismissal, and staff reductions.[8]

A 1988 study of United States Supreme Court decisions affecting education brings into focus the regulatory influence regarding employee rights and responsibilities. Decisions relate to compensation, residency requirements, strikes, age of retirement, due process, right to teach, involuntary transfer, leaves of absence, continuing education, loyalty oaths, union-related matters, tenure, contract renewal, and at-will dismissal.[9]

Because school systems operate within an environment external to their existence, and over which they exercise little control, knowledge of the present environment, especially its direction and organizational impact, is an essential aspect of human resources management. In addition to the regulatory factor, there are four other factors noted in Figure 1.8 (economic, political, sociocultural, and technological) that affect conditions in the workplace. Following are some indicators illustrative of the external environmental impact on people, positions, and direction of the human resources affairs.

Economic factor. Virtually all funds needed to operate a public school system stem from public education policy in the external environment. About four-fifths of the annual school budget is devoted to system member requirements. Economic conditions shift rapidly with governmental actions, which in turn influence the extent to which school systems are able to realize organizational and human resource goals.

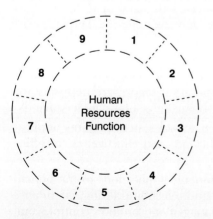

FACTORS
1. Constitutional Guarantees
2. Federal Laws
3. State Laws
4. Court Decisions
5. Executive Orders
6. Administrative Agency Rulings
7. County-Municipal Laws
8. Legal Challenges
9. Employment Contracts

FIGURE 1.9
Regulatory environment of the human resources function.

Political factor. Numerous groups in the external environment (political, religious, ethnic, antitax, reformist, business, and governmental) have the potential to influence public education policy regarding school reform, discrimination, desegregation, health care, sexual harassment, gay rights, bilingual education, teacher certification, vouchers, school choice, and so forth. Among the foremost issues in recent local, state, and federal elections (crime, taxation, health, and schools), the crisis in public education has been one of high profile for electorate consideration.

Sociocultural factor. Included in the extending challenges facing those who manage the human resources function are those stemming from a combination of social and cultural elements. Worthy of note are such matters as political correctness, pressures for religious accommodation, drug/alcohol testing, AIDS, taxpayer resistance to the elevating costs of education, changing values of system members, assaults on school personnel, privacy rights, Family Rights Act of 1991, employees speaking out, and external demands for school reform.

Technological factor. Technology, in terms of the human resources function, refers to the sum of ways in which the school system provides itself with the material means needed to carry out its process, mechanisms, and techniques employed by the system to deliver educational services and to extend its potential for doing so. Among the emerging challenges for the human resources function created by the advent of modern technology and the quickening pace of its development are these pressing agenda items:

- *Technology assimilation*—Ensuring that technology is available for and used to best advantage by the system and its members.
- *Comprehensive information system*—A modern systematic plan designed to acquire, store, maintain, protect, retrieve, and communicate data in a valid and accurate form, employing computer and noncomputer approaches.
- *Staff development*—With advances in electronic technology, a critical shortage of computer-literate support staff has developed. Programs for assisting personnel, especially those in the temporary category, are necessary for computer users to acquire skills to satisfy burgeoning information demands.
- *Office operations*—An information-driven school system requires application of new technology to increase efficiency and effectiveness of office operations.
- *Computer applications*—Examples of computer applications to the human resources function include recruitment and selection tracking, attendance tracking, training and development management, position control, compensation (including benefits), regulatory adherence, payroll, forms management, record center operations, and computer-assisted instruction.

Internal Environment. Internal as well as external forces affect the human resources function in overt and covert ways. Interaction of these influences creates administrative challenges, especially their impact on individual and group behavior, as well as strategies needed to cope with the inexorable tendency to environmental change. Among the key *internal environmental* factors in Figure 1.8, the five that follow are noteworthy.

Formal organization. The formal organization of a school system, identified in Figure 1.8 as one of the forces influencing the design and operation of the human resources function, derives from the system, which in turn emanates from the external environment. These forces also include the organization structure, ends for which the school system exists, work (roles) to be performed, and technology for performing the work such as curriculum, instructional system, teaching-learning tools, and facilities.

Individual and group behavior. Dealing with personnel problems in the workplace is something all administrators have to do. How it is done may eventuate in productive, nonproductive, or counterproductive behaviors. Individual and group behaviors are two forces that shape human issues in every organization and give such matters system, legal, social, and economic significance. Implications for those responsible for dealing with behavioral problems are considerable. The following points are relevant:

- Mention has been made previously that modern school systems employ personnel whose mental, physical, intellectual, and emotional characteristics vary extensively. Approaches for dealing with human diversity involve system orientation to understanding the psychological makeup of individuals so that the underlying needs of the system and its members can be accommodated.
- Leadership style employed to relate to varying personalities depends upon characteristics of the leader, the followers, and the situation. These factors influence which of the several leadership styles (directive, participative, free-rein, or a combination of these) will enhance personnel cooperation and performance.[10]
- Grouping is an integral component of any organization. Groups have been categorized as formal (command and task) and informal (interest and friendship). Unions are accorded formal status because they are officially and legally organized.
- Work involved in implementing the school system mission is divided into segments or units to which work groups are assigned. Work is usually organized by functions (finance, human resources); programs (preschool, elementary, intermediate, secondary, postsecondary); geography (school

attendance units); departments (mathematics); and committees (standing, such as board of education finance committee).

- Productive groups share several characteristics: members tend to make valuable contributions to group effort; formal and informal goals of the group are achieved; group members share a sense of satisfaction and high morale; and productive groups have an appropriate mix of skills and background, an effective group structure, and a good communication process.[11]

- Work expectations are created not only by the individual and the organization but also by group norms, standards, structure, and goals.

The reader should note that Figure 1.8 includes two internal environmental elements, namely **culture** and **ethics,** which are linked to group behavior. Such terms as *norms, values, sanctions, disciplinary action, behavior patterns, shared meanings,* and *habits of thinking* are commonly used to describe group and organization culture. Ethics of individuals, groups, and organizations are intertwined with group culture because they involve concerns about rights, obligations, expectations, and justice. Leadership implications of culture and ethics are several and form the basis for the sections that follow.

Culture Dimension

Every school system has a culture—a set of interrelated values and priorities, norms and expectations, and ideas and ideals. Norms, according to Smither, serve a variety of useful functions, such as (a) establishing standards and shared expectations that provide a range of acceptable behavior for group members; (b) providing guidelines for unsocialized individuals to fit into the ongoing group; and (c) establishing standards for behavior that facilitate interaction between members and are a means of identifying with one's peers.[12]

The culture of an organization encompasses many factors and forces, and according to Ellis, most of them are transitory or intangible. Examples include changing values, social trends, authority, needs, rights, obligations, and expectations of both system and its personnel groupings.[13]

One of the important questions about school system culture is, What is its relationship and significance to the human resources function? One response is that to a considerable extent culture is tied to the impact of change in the workplace. There are shifting human values and changes in the demographics of the work force (in ethnic background, in cultural diversity, and in graying of the instructional cadre).

There is another set of forces that are culture laden with the potential for affecting individual and group behavior. This category includes regulatory agencies, community groups, boards of education, school management, unions, standing committees, work units (such as elementary schools), and support groups (maintenance, operation, clerical, food service, security, and transportation). In one way or another, each of these system entities and their constituents are affected by changes that have personal, organizational, legal, state, national, and international causes.

Culture and Need Satisfaction.   The need to balance organizational imperatives with individual and group expectations has always been a challenging managerial endeavor. Contemporary forces of change have rendered traditional approaches to resolving workplace problems irrelevant.

One way of viewing employment in a school system is as an exchange between the individual and the organization in which each gets something in return for giving something. Figure 1.10 conceptualizes the exchange theory of employment (referred to in the literature as a psychological or social contract).[14] The psychological or social contract is unwritten, but it is constantly in operation as the means through which both parties seek to have certain conditions of work satisfied.

In summary, both workers and management recognize that job satisfaction hinges on *nonmonetary* rewards, as well as the actual paycheck. So, smart managers offer those intangibles as relatively cost-free incentives to maintain a happy, productive work force.

Cultural factors in the human resources function that can be changed by those in leadership positions include envisioning, bringing to life, reinforcing, rewarding, and embedding constructive behavior. Beyond helping members to understand their culture, creating means to enhance its positive features aids in neutralizing tendencies toward system instability, breakdown of standards and values, as well as alienation and uncertainty that comes from a lack of purpose or ideals. A set of indicators derived from several human resources processes creating and managing culture include:

The system agrees to ←——→	The individual agrees to
• Equitable compensation	• Join
• Rights and privileges	• Stay
• Position security	• Exceed role expectations
• Assist in improvement	• Work independently
• Proper placement	• Self-improvement
• Fair treatment	• Cooperate
• Opportunity for advancement	• Adhere to system expectations

FIGURE 1.10
Conceptualization of the employment exchange theory.

- *Induction*—Develop socialization programs focusing on system culture.
- *Appraisal*—Change traditional performance culture from a measurement process to a communication process.
- *Planning*—Focus on neutralizing change-restraining forces.
- *Justice*—Maintain justice system for prompt and effective treatment of personnel rights and responsibilities.
- *Recruitment*—Locate and attract candidates suitable by nature to accept, commit, and further system desired culture.

Consideration of cultural aspects inherent in each of the eleven personnel processes will be given in succeeding chapters as they pertain to understanding and nurturing a proactive cultural foundation.

Ethics Dimension

It is an inescapable fact that decisions give life to a school system and that most decisions are permeated by ethics. Consequently, a broader understanding of ethical behavior in the workplace, and especially as it applies to the human resources function, is one step toward dealing with personnel problems and enhancing system betterment.

Ethics, according to a dictionary definition, refers to the rightness or wrongness of certain actions, and to the goodness or badness of the motives and ends of such actions. What is or is not ethical, however, lends itself to personal interpretation.

According to Karp and Abramms, all decisions are determined by values; and these values are revered, freely chosen, and must be expressed.[15] Three identifying characteristics of the relationship between values and ethics, as depicted in Figure 1.11, are that they are value driven, action oriented, and situational.

Ethics and Decision Making.   For those who run school systems, including board members, superintendents, principals, supervisors, department heads, and other instructional leaders, the ethics dimension has some clear implications. The relationship between ethical sensitivity and the human resources function is an intimate one, as can be derived from the following:

- Leadership is intrinsically involved with decisions about such matters as organizational purpose, goals, objectives, strategies, and their implications.
- Ethical considerations, when factored into the decision-making process, uphold human dignity as a contributor to positive personal and organizational behavior.

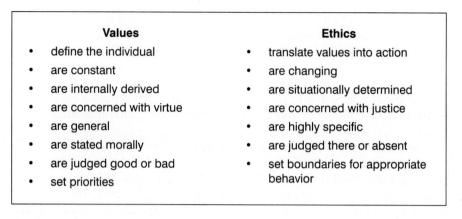

Values	Ethics
• define the individual	• translate values into action
• are constant	• are changing
• are internally derived	• are situationally determined
• are concerned with virtue	• are concerned with justice
• are general	• are highly specific
• are stated morally	• are judged there or absent
• are judged good or bad	• set boundaries for appropriate behavior
• set priorities	

FIGURE 1.11
The relationship between values and ethics.
Source: H.B. Karp and Bob Abramms, "Doing the Right Thing," in Mary F. Cook, Editor, The Human Resources Yearbook, 1993–1994 Edition (Englewood Cliffs, NJ: Prentice-Hall Inc., 1993), 8–19. © 1993, reprinted by permission of the publisher, Prentice Hall/A Division of Simon & Schuster.

- Decisions made by leaders have direct impact on both the internal and external environments.
- Task orientation of individuals and groups is influenced by ethical sensitivity to their expectations, aspirations, well-being, conditions of work, compensation equity, and the reward system.
- Decisions and power are inseparable. Those who have authority to make decisions are able to exert control over others, either directly through position power or indirectly through various forms of expertise.

From the foregoing points it can be assumed that power to decide represents a form of capability for influencing member behavior. As we examine the eleven personnel processes in forthcoming chapters, attention will be focused in part on decisions with ethical connotations, especially in such areas as recruitment, selection, appraisal, compensation, development, and justice.

Exercise of authority through the decision-making process includes consideration of its ethical implications. Some of the reasons for providing a foundation for judgments based on organizational values and implemented by ethical actions are the subject of the discussion that follows.

Guidelines for Ethical Standards. It is generally assumed that educators and educational systems are the principal guardians of the nation's culture. Enhancement of this assumption by a school system requires various underlying strategies for strengthening and maintaining standards of ethical behavior among those in its employ. Following are some suggestions.

Social change and ethics issues.   Social change and its evolving generational attitudes have brought the matter of ethical conduct in public organizations to the forefront of leadership concerns. Emerging regulatory plans and practices, the power of human resources to contest management actions, and the changing composition of school staffs are illustrative of forces influencing greater attention to policies and other plans that define ethical standards to aid personnel in understanding and avoiding unethical situations.

Identification of system ethical issues.   Reports of unethical behavior by school employees is commonplace. One action for dealing with personnel misconduct is through identification of the presence, nature, and extent of current unethical situations. In brief, leadership in resolving unethical practices requires the presence of an information base for planning and deciding the system's approach for resolving behavioral dilemmas.

Ethical standards.   Ethical standards to which a school system is committed need to be clearly and extensively communicated. Mechanisms for this purpose include personnel handbooks, policy manuals, codes of ethics, adherence to the psychological contract, enforcement provisions governing unethical behavior, and staff development programs for all categories of personnel. Such approaches are among those aimed at communicating, interpreting, and enforcing ethical and legal behavioral standards that will lead to emergence of organizational settings conducive to improving workplace behavior.

Categories of ethical concern.   Issues of ethical concern for the school system include obligations as well as various kinds of responsibilities. For example, system and member obligations, such as those following, have the inherent potential for unethical conduct when behavioral obligations and responsibilities are unfulfilled:

- Member ethical obligations to the school system.
- System ethical obligations to its members.
- Teacher ethical obligations to students.
- System ethical obligations to the public.
- Personnel obligations to the profession.
- System and personnel obligations to adhere to the psychological contract.
- System and member commitment to professional employment practices.
- System and member obligations and responsibilities to *claimants* in the external environment such as taxpayers, creditors, suppliers, governments, unions, accrediting agencies, and recruitment sources (colleges and universities, other school systems, and placement agencies).

• System and member obligations to adhere to contract requirements (employment, compensation, tenure, construction, benefits, and dismissal).

It is worth noting here that system indifference and inattention to as well as nonenforcement of behavioral rules generate organization disrupters that undermine cultural stability and the ability to carry out the system's mission effectively. Some examples of common behavioral dysfunctions are typified by individuals who engage in off-duty crime, cover up discriminatory employment practices, condone gender discrimination, engage in sexual harassment or sexual relationships with students, abet employment intrusion by political interests, are addicted to lateness and absenteeism, or abuse leave and workers' compensation benefits.

The human resources approach to resolving improper conduct by members of the system, according to Levesque, is to recognize and use three action stages:

• *Prevention*—To work toward proactive measures that resolve potential problems before they occur.

• *Control*—To establish specific, realistic, and understandable standards that reinforce mutual needs between employees and the organization, and thereby reduce the likelihood of serious discontinuities.

• *Correction*—To initiate timely, effective, and appropriate measures when deviations arise that might otherwise create a detrimental organizational consequence.[15,16]

In sum, there is considerable support for the proposition that prevalence of moral rectitude contributes to the desired image, wellness, and effective operation of the entire school system. Establishment of a set of rules governing member behavior, and utilization of a model for applying performance standards, are indicative of approaches needed in the quest for rightness of principle or practice in the workplace.

REVIEW AND PREVIEW

One of the main purposes of studying the human resources function of a school system is to develop a broader understanding of the forces, factors, conditions, and circumstances that shape its role as a contributor to organizational effectiveness. The fundamental intent of this chapter is to convey the viewpoints that follow.

Social change and educational reform movements brought about by a combination of sociological, political, economic, regulatory, technological, and human resources forces require changes in models for enhancing the potential of the function to clarify problems and to develop plans for their solution.

Evolving models of the human resources function extend well beyond traditional tasks of record keeping, social work, and collective bargaining. Today's designs consider the human resources function to be a vital unit in any organization entity. The organized and unified array of system parts interact through human performance to establish a productive public institution. The eleven personnel processes within the human resources function (Figure 1.2) are linked to the organization infrastructure (Figure 1.3). Dimensions of the infrastructure include system mission, human resources, regulatory requirements, environmental factors, and ethical presence.

The chapter that follows examines the planning process as a component of the human resources function and its linkage to the elements in the organization infrastructure referred to in this chapter.

REVIEW AND DISCUSSION QUESTIONS

1. From the perspective that school systems are influenced by the internal and external environments, respond to the following:

   a. List three examples, drawn from your personal experience, of the influence of the external environment on the school system.

   b. List three examples of the influence of the school system on the internal environment.

   c. List three examples of the influence of the school system on the external environment.

   d. List three examples of the influence of the internal environment on the school system.

2. Allusion is made in this chapter to the psychological contract, which is viewed as an unwritten understanding between the system and its members as to what each expects to give and receive from the other. In what manner is this contract established? To what working conditions does the understanding apply? Is the contract similar in certain ways to that of a marriage agreement? What is the linkage between a collective bargaining agreement and a psychological contract?

3. Develop a one-page description of the five most important contemporary challenges for those who administer the human resources function.

4. Write a response to these statements: (a) among the least productive workers are those employed in school system offices; and (b) technological breakthroughs in the office environment justify increased capital expenditures per office worker, thus improving their productivity.

5. List five court decisions that have influenced administration of the human resources function (see notes 8 and 9 for references).

6. Would you defend or refute each of the following statements?

   • Today's classroom model has not changed discernibly since the Venetians taught fractions to groups of mercantile students in the mid-fifteenth century.

   • We can create schools for the twenty-first century by tinkering with the ones we have.

   • Regulation and regimentation are essential to the success of our educational enterprise.

- Most graduates of schools of education feel unprepared to use new instructional technologies.
- Today's schools are preparing people for the workplace of 1953.
- We should ask whether the text-book should continue to be the organizing force that determines what goes on in our classrooms.
- We can no longer assume that schools are exempt from changes or can stay the same and still produce graduates who can succeed in tomorrow's workplace.

7. As the school system director of human resources, you are requested to submit an outline of a personnel ethics policy. Which of the following items should be considered?

- Regulatory requirements (federal, state, and local) governing ethical behavior.
- Categories of personnel in the policy.
- Definition of ethical practices.
- Corrective action to be taken for ethics violations.

- A code of ethics to supplement system policy.

8. Describe the organization structure of a school system, drawn from your personal experience. Does the structure differentiate between line and staff positions? The number of structural levels? The reporting relationships of each position? Base compensation on the structural levels? Contain a uniform system of titles?

9. If one defines culture as those personnel values that generate standards or norms for individual and group behavior, how is culture relevant to discipline? Individual socialization? Personnel selection? Culture communication? Rewards and punishment? Union membership? Behavior of the central administration?

10. The author avers that the system mission is arguably the most basic property of a school system. Do you believe this to be a credible statement? Why or why not?

CHAPTER EXERCISE 1.1

Directions: This exercise contains statements from textbooks, articles, newspapers, and other published materials relating to educational reform assumptions and their implications for designing and implementing the school system mission. Determine whether you completely disagree, somewhat disagree, somewhat agree, or completely agree with each of the following statements:

- Private school vouchers will resegregate society and destroy the common school.
- National curricular standards will make American schools productive.

- To change the curriculum is to manipulate traditional values in American culture.
- Team teaching and reduced departmentalization are conducive to higher pupil achievement.
- Educational outcomes are dependent primarily on the leadership of school administrators.
- One strategy for reforming public education is to ban teacher unions from striking.
- According to Deming's systemic approach to Total Quality Management (TQM), 85 percent of the prob-

lems in any organization are within the system, not with individuals.

- According to Deming, the output of a system is primarily influenced by the process rather than by individuals.
- Shifting the locus of control from the central office to school attendance units (site based) produces systemic change.
- The primary unit of change (school attendance units) and those closest to the student have the greatest opportunity for affecting student outcomes.
- Family backgrounds, socio-economic status, and related variables are the keys to student achievement and are beyond the school to control or impact.
- Restructuring and reform initiatives concentrating on individual schools or school districts fail to meet the needs of special education.
- Meeting the needs of minority and at-risk youth is a paramount concern among educators.
- Restructuring requires one to be willing to act beyond the data and without benefit of guidance from empirical research.
- Creating commitment to change is not the same as overcoming resistance to change.
- The school, not the school district, is the primary focus of improved instructional practice and staff development.
- School boards and administrators are good at doing more of what they are already doing.

- School boards fail to provide far-reaching or politically risky leadership for reform.
- States bear a great deal of responsibility for the current problems in local school governance.
- Systemic reform in public schooling will not be accomplished without corresponding restructuring of school boards.
- School boards should not become involved in individual personnel decisions.
- Teacher unions are increasing their control of school boards by influencing school board elections.
- School boards are controlled by the interests of those they employ.
- A new political dimension is developing between board members who owe support to a union and board members with a broader constituency.
- A thousand studies and ten thousand reports about what is necessary is nothing fancy: decent classrooms, good libraries, devoted teachers, small classes, committed teachers, and low tuition. If these were in place, hostilities over schooling, curriculum, affirmative action, racism, and free speech would shrink; pools of acrimony would drain away.

NOTES

1. For timely works on education reform and implications for the human resources function, see S. B. Bachrach, Education Reform: Making of Sense of it All (Boston: Allyn and Bacon, 1990); G. Bracey, "The Condition of Public Education," Phi Delta Kappan 74, 2 (1990), 104–117; A. Collins, "The Role of Computer Technology in Restructuring Schools," Phi Delta Kappan (September 1991), 28–36; S.C. Conley, "Who's on First? School Reform, Teacher Preparation, and the Deci-

sion-making Process," Education and Urban Society 21, 4 (1990), 366–379; Stanley Elam, Editor, The State of the Nation's Public Schools: A Conference Report (Bloomington, IN: Phi Delta Kappa, 1993); D. E. Kinnaman, "Strategic Planning for a New Generation of American Schools," Technology and Learning (1990), 20–30; Mary Anne Raywid, "The Evolving Effort to Improve Schools: Pseudo Reform, Incremental Reform, and Restructuring," Phi Delta Kappan (October 1990), 140–143; Seymour B. Sarason, The Culture of School and the Problem of Change (Boston: Allyn and Bacon, 1982); Edgar H. Schein, Organizational Culture and Leadership (San Francisco: Jossey-Bass, 1985); and Michael J. Schmoker and Richard B. Wilson, Total Quality Education: Profiles of Schools that Demonstrate the Power of Deming's Management Principles (Bloomington, IN: Phi Delta Kappa, 1993).

2. From The Structure of School Improvement by Bruce R. Joyce, Richard H. Hersh, and Michael McKibbin. © 1983 by Longman Publishing Group.

3. Grolier, Inc., Encyclopedia Americana (The Author, Vol. 14, 1982), 553.

4. World Book Inc., The World Book Encyclopedia (Chicago: The Author, Vol. 9, 1990), 415.

5. Ibid.

6. Ibid.

7. Adapted from Joseph D. Levesque, The Human Resource Problem Solver's Handbook (New York: McGraw-Hill Inc., 1991), III.3.86.

8. Martha M. McCarthy, "Discrimination in Employment," in Joseph A. Beckham and Perry A. Zirkel, Editors, Legal Issues in Public School Employment (Bloomington, IN: Phi Delta Kappa, 1983), 46–47.

9. Perry A. Zirkel and Sharon N. Richardson, A Digest of Supreme Court Decisions Affecting Education (Bloomington, IN: Phi Delta Kappa Educational Foundation, 1989), Chapters 4–6.

10. See John M. Ivancevich and Michael T. Matteson, Organizational Behavior and Management, Third Edition (Homewood, IL: Irwin, 1993), 451.

11. See Dennis Middlemist and Michael A. Hitt, Organizational Behavior (St. Paul, MN: West Publishing Company, 1988), Chapters 3–4.

12. Robert D. Smither, The Psychology of Work (New York: Harper and Row, 1988), 368.

13. Robert J. Ellis, "Using Human Resources Programs to Support Cultural Change," in Mary F. Cook, Editor, The Human Resources Yearbook, 1993/1994 Edition (Englewood Cliffs, NJ: Prentice-Hall Inc., 1993), 2.2.

14. For a detailed treatment of the psychological contract, see Mary Coli Meyer, "Motivation," in William R. Tracey, Editor, Human Resources Management and Development (New York: AMACOM, 1985), 201–204.

15. H.B. Karp and Bob Abramms, "Doing the Right Thing," in Mary F. Cook, Editor, The Human Resources Yearbook, 1993 / 1994 Edition (Englewood Cliffs, NJ: Prentice-Hall Inc., 1993), 8.19.

16. From Joseph O. Levesque, The Human Resource Problem Solver's Handbook (New York: McGraw-Hill Inc., 1991) III.3.81.

SUPPLEMENTARY READING

Backes, John S. "Charting Future: Developing Vision and Mission Statement." National Forum of Educational Administration and Supervision Journal 9, 3 (1992-93), 39–48.

Business Week 3346. "The Future of Technology in Education." (November 15, 1993, Special Advertising Section).

Carson, C. C.; R. M. Huelskamp; and T. D. Woodall. "Perspectives on Education in America." Final Draft. Albuquerque, NM: Sandia National Laboratories, April, 1992.

Clune, William H. "Educational Government and Student Achievement." In William H. Clune and John F. Witte, Editors, Choice and Control in American Education. Vol. 2: "The Practice of Choice, Decentralization and School Restructuring." New York: Falmer, 1990, 391–423.

Dansberger, Jacqueline P.; Michael W. Kirst; and Michael D. Usdan. Governing Public Schools: New Times, New Requirements. Washington: Institute for Educational Leadership, 1992.

Galbraith, Jay R.; and Edward E. Lawler III & Associates. Organizing for the Future. New York: Jossey-Bass, 1993.

Goodlad, John I. What Schools Are For. Second Edition. Bloomington, IN: Phi Delta Kappa, 1994.

Ivancevich, John N.; and Michael T. Matteson. Organizational Behavior and Management. Third Edition. Homewood, IL: Irwin, 1993.

Journal of Staff Development. 15, 2, (Spring, 1994), 2–20. Four articles devoted to altering the culture of schools appear in this issue ("What Leaders Need to Know About School Culture"; "Changing the School Culture through Transactional Education"; "Improving School Culture Through Study Groups"; and "Taking Small Steps to Improve Collaboration").

McDonnell, Lorraine; and Anthony Pascal. Teacher Unions and Educational Reform. Santa Monica, CA: RAND Corporation, 1987.

Phi Delta Kappan. "Special Section on School Boards." 75, 5 (January 1994), 366–402.

Webb, L. Dean; Paul A. Montollo; and M. Scott Norton. Human Resource Administration: Personnel Issues and Needs in Education. Second Edition. New York: Macmillan, 1993.

PART I

Shaping the System's Future Through Strategic Planning

Chapter 2
Strategic Planning for Human Resources

Part I, the first of 11 human resources processes included in this text, is concerned with strategic planning and its linkage to the human resources function. Chapter 2 addresses the formidable management task of developing, implementing, and evaluating the human resources planning process that takes the following basics into account:

- A concept of planning.
- The strategic planning connection to the human resources process.
- A strategic planning process.
- Planning and the information system.
- Present and future positions and position holders in strategic planning.
- Individuals, groups, and system effectiveness.

Chapter 2

Strategic Planning for Human Resources

CHAPTER OVERVIEW

CHAPTER OBJECTIVES

- Introduce strategic planning, the first of 11 human resources processes employed in administering the human resources function; illustrate the importance of forming visions, values, goals, ideas, and actions to implement human resources plans; and highlight salient events in the planning sequence, the major planning components, and their interrelationships.
- Emphasize the importance of identifying goals before seeking them.
- Stress the conviction that strategic plans are temporary and are subject to change as environments and strategies change; that an imperative leadership role is to translate the system's mission, goals, and values into meaningful terms for enhancing individual, group, and total system performance.
- Emphasize that attainment of school system quality cannot be left to chance or tradition; that a planning process is vital to reaching the system's expectations.

CHAPTER TERMS

Effectiveness	Planning
Human resources goals	Position guide
Human resources policies	Position specifications
Information system	Program structure
Organizational chart	Staff ratio
Organizational manual	Strategy
Organizational structure	Work analysis

IMPORTANCE OF PLANNING

Planning is humanity's way of projecting intentions. Because it deals with concepts of the future, problems requiring imagination and choice, deliberate forethought, and attainment by design, it represents a most appealing and challenging endeavor. It is recognized as an organization's most reliable way of realizing goals. It is the antithesis of expediency, laissez-faire, and indirection. It is an effort to set a course of action to guide the action toward a set of expectations. Ackoff, in defining the nature of planning, notes that although planning is a decision-making process, it is a special kind of decision making: (a) planning is something we do in advance of taking action, that is, it is anticipatory decision making; (b) planning is required when the future state that we desire involves a set of interdependent decisions, that is, a system of decisions; and (c) planning is a process directed toward producing one or more future states that are desired and are not expected to occur unless something is done.[1]

Plan preparation for a school system's human resources is not difficult to demonstrate. Examination of the analytic framework shown in Table 2.1 indicates that considerable organizational confusion and uncertainty would prevail without a system of plans and means by which activities related to each of the personnel processes can be directed and controlled.

TABLE 2.1
Analytic framework for redesigning the human resources function.

What is the planning connection of each of the human resources processes to these considerations:	Human Resources Processes										
	A	B	C	D	E	F	G	H	I	J	K
Systematizing plans to resolve current and emerging practices and problems?											
Improving the linkage between the human resources function and organization purpose? Between the human resources function and other management functions? Among the processes of the human resources function?											
Anticipating the ramifications of new educational programs, new personnel, new roles, and new technologies for the human resources function?											
Contriving plans to deal with changes in the internal and external environments?											
Contributing to personnel need fulfillment?											
Concentrating human resources processes in areas where they will have the greatest impact on the school system's future?											
Attracting, developing, retaining, and motivating the quality and quantity of personnel committed to the system's performance culture?											
Shaping the human resources function to assist the system to make the transition from where it is to where it wants to be?											

Note: Human resources processes designations are A, planning; B, recruitment; C, selection; D, induction; E, development; F, appraisal; G, justice; H, continuity; I, information; J, Compensation; K, bargaining.

Clearly, the range of human resources processes shown in Table 2.1, as well as the questions linked to those processes, suggests that some form of planning, regardless of system size, is an administrative imperative for coping with the emerging complexity of problems related to human resources management activities.

Questions shown in Table 2.1 provide the context around which the textual material in this chapter is woven. Although there are a variety of factors that affect the extent to which any school system engages in a planning process—what kinds of plans are developed and who participates in the planning—some form of organizational planning process is indispensable to the system's stability, viability, efficiency, and effectiveness. Use of a planning process enables school planners to put means and ends into proper perspective, identify system and attendance unit priorities, review alternative plans, choose the appropriate alternative and **strategy** for solutions, and revise plans on the basis of errors or detected failures. The process is applicable to both systemwide and unit planning. It is conceivable, for example, that the system will develop policies for the continuing education of all personnel and will include funds in the annual budget for that purpose. However, the manner in which planning is undertaken and plans made for development of personnel in individual schools as well as expenditure of funds for that purpose may be partially or completely decentralized.

It is anticipated that one of the outcomes of the organizational planning process will be a system of plans that will structure objectives and subordinate goals, that is, convert broad purposes of the whole organization into objectives for each of the units in the central administration and for each individual school and position. The planning process and derivative plans are designed to minimize random behavior and dysfunctionalism and to facilitate coordination of goal-directed activity. It is worth noting that a school system's human resources needs are linked to its strategic objectives. The planning process, both short- and long-term, is a crucial component in helping to articulate the system's future direction, in underscoring the changes and mix of human resources needed, and in developing a framework within which these resources are utilized effectively. The development of a system of plans as antecedent to improving human resources performance is treated in the following section.

HUMAN RESOURCES PLANNING PROCESS

The observation has been made previously that strategic or long-range planning should set broad direction for achieving system aims, including a comprehensive, long-range plan for their accomplishment. Operational planning, on the other hand, should focus on component plans needed to implement strategy. A practical way to facilitate development of the system mission through human resources planning is to utilize planning tools most appropriate for this purpose. Let us look at one kind of planning tool, referred to here as a *process,* and see how it can be employed in dealing with the complexities of strategic planning as the system is being guided from the present into the future.

Process, as the term is used here, refers to a series of progressive and interdependent steps designed to (a) enhance actions to bring about positive change in the human resources function, (b) establish a systematic approach for coping with routine and nonroutine human resources problems, and (c) improve human resources problem solving.

An example of a planning process for the school system's human resources is illustrated in Figure 2.1. It should be noted that the process consists of a series of steps or activities that serve to systematize the manner in which managerial judgments are made relative to people plans and people planning. The ultimate ends toward which the process is directed include (a) heightening the impact of the human resources function on organizational purpose, (b) contriving ways that will bring about desired changes in system performance, (c) orienting the planning process beyond short-term needs, and (d) assessing the internal and external environments likely to influence planning choices. The first step in the process, articulation of a mission statement, is the subject of the discussion that follows.

PHASE ONE: DEFINING SYSTEM EXPECTATIONS, STRATEGY, AND VALUES

In an age of shrinking budgets, an increasingly diverse society, changing social mores, confusion regarding means and methods of improving public education in the United States, as well as a growing chorus of school system

Phase	Activity
One	Define, clarify, articulate, and communicate expectations for the system's human resources.
Two	Assess the overall state of the human resources function in the context of the current school system's needs and aspirations.
Three	Develop a strategic plan.
Four	Implement the strategic plan.
Five	Monitor, evaluate, and adjust the strategic plan.

FIGURE 2.1
Sequential model of the human resources planning process.

critics, the task of developing plans for educational reform appears to be a rather daunting undertaking. It is essential, however, for every institution seeking to improve teaching and learning through the human resources function, to develop a set of plans and administer its affairs in an orderly and humane manner in accordance with a set of beliefs and values to guide its human resources planning efforts.

As noted in Figure 2.1, Phase One of the human resources planning model includes definition and articulation of the system's expectations for its human resources.

Articulation of Mission Statement

A mission statement, as well as the entire human resources planning process, involves consideration of the following questions:

• What is the school system *expected to do*?
• What is the system *currently doing or not doing* to achieve its expectations?
• What *should the school system be doing* to achieve its expectations?

The question of what the school system is expected to do provides the source from which the system creates its strategy to carry out the mission. In giving thought to the school system's expectations, the following statement by Lawrence Cremin, as well as the examples provided in Chapter 1 (mission dimension), are helpful:

> [The] aim of education is not merely to make parents, or citizens, or workers, or indeed to surpass the Russians or the Japanese, but ultimately to make human beings who will live life to the fullest, who will continually add to the quality and meaning of their experiences and their ability to direct that experience, and who will participate actively with their fellow human beings in the building of a good society.[2]

Mission as a Frame of Reference.   The mission statement can be conceived as a frame of reference by which to assess program options, communicate ideas, shape system performance culture, and coordinate system functions such as human resources with system strategic aims.

In establishing school system expectations on the basis of a mission statement, it is important to consider several factors for incorporation into strategic planning for human resources. These factors include claimant interests, strategy levels, scope, and school system individuality.

Claimant Interests.   There are various interests that human resources planning must satisfy, including societal interest (governmental); system interest (strategic aims); functional interest (human resources); and personal interest (economic, social, and psychological objectives of position holders).

Strategy Levels.   System strategy is designed to accomplish broad system purposes; functional strategy, such as human resources, is created to serve, support, and enhance system strategy.

Scope.   The scope of the mission is to provide a foundation for systemwide planning and to implement plans aimed at achieving primary expectations; to set planning boundaries; to alter, remove, add, or extend existing programs and practices; and to channel available resources into plans most likely to produce intended results.

School System Individuality.   *Individuality* refers to the set of characteristics that should be taken into consideration in utilizing the mission for school improvement purposes. School systems differ profoundly from other organizations. Schools are, for example, small, medium, and large; urban, suburban, and rural; year-round and academic year; those whose student population is largely African-American or white; those where most students' first language is not English; those where a dozen or more languages are spoken; and those for children of military personnel. Thus, the human resources planning process, in concert with the system mission, are tools through which plans are made to accommodate the unique and special characteristics that form the fabric of a particular school system.

Strategic Planning

A strategic school system plan may be described as a planning tool to do the following:

- Move the system from its current to a desired state.
- Establish basic system purpose, goals to be sought, and the general means (tactical plan) by which they will be sought.
- Address fundamental questions about structures needed to develop system purpose, direction, and future generations of educational programs and services.
- Make planning and tactical decisions within the framework of system mission, goals, policies, and human resources values.
- Provide a point of departure to assess the impact of future environments on strategic plans.
- Link functional goals (e.g., educational programs and services, human resources, logistics, and external relations) to the goals of the strategic plan.

• Assess social, legal, technological, political, economic, educational, and governmental factors that may create opportunities for or obstructions to strategic plans.

Figure 2.2 provides an illustration of the anatomy of the strategic planning process as conceived by the Riverpark school system. Through this process the system intends to address and explore the range of options, opportunities, and strategies through which to enhance the system's future condition.

What is perhaps the most appealing aspect of strategic planning is that it provides a unique opportunity to pull back from the immediate details of everyday school system life, important though they are in their own terms, in order to examine what is at stake in efforts to move the system from where it is to where it should be. Contemporary times are full of animation and activity regarding the resolution of problems confronting educational systems. Redesign efforts through instructional and organizational reform, restructuring, decentralization, comprehensive care for children from birth to graduation, and site-based management are commonplace. The appeal of strategic planning is a mechanism for weaving the fabric of a school system, through an ongoing process, involving position holders working with each other in some way to make school improvement an aggressive movement for dealing with a critical societal infirmity.

Values and Human Resources Planning

Assuming that a strategic plan is a framework that sets forth what a school system is expected to do, what it chooses to do, and what it intends to be like in a desired future strategic position, a set of value-driven influences is essential to guide decisions aimed at having a positive effect on the performance of the system's human resources. Figures 2.3 and 2.4 are illustrative of tools that serve a most important function in this regard. The intention of these goals and policies of human resources is to define the human standards the system intends to observe in managing the human resources function; to create a conditional covenant, declaration, or promise between two parties to develop certain conditions regarding work, workers, and working conditions; and to provide the moral impetus for doing the right thing in resolving matters relating to those who serve the system.

Given ideals for system personnel relating to dignity and worth such as those proposed in Figures 2.3 and 2.4, it can be seen how important they are to administration of the human resources function. They commit school leadership to a set of values for guidance in relationships among individuals. They represent an obligation to organization members that they will enjoy the same rights as they do as ordinary citizens.

Knowledge gained of broad system and human resources function goals is used to engage Phase Two of the human resources planning process (as

The future status Riverpark school system desires for its human resources is based upon these common premises for action:

Goals. The primary aim of the system is to achieve teaching and learning outcomes beyond those established by state regulations and those proposed by the federal government.

Planning focus. The underlying intent of the system's strategic planning process is to identify conceivable opportunities, favorable and unfavorable relevant changes, regulatory trends, economic conditions, union initiatives, and sociocultural factors that impact on attainment of our desired future status.

Planning priorities. The following priorities have been identified through systemwide review and given primacy as human resources objectives during the time frame portrayed below:

- Develop and implement a strategic planning model to serve the system's interests effectively and efficiently.
- Take steps to achieve our strategic aims through the collective bargaining process.
- Enhance the recruitment process to attract and retain the quality of personnel needed to improve teaching and learning outcomes.
- Identify anticipated changes in the educational program and their impact on the future work force.

Time frame. The time frame shown below represents one of the components of the strategic planning process. Current and strategic plans are reviewed, revised, and recast each year and adjusted as necessary.

	Strategic Planning Time Frame					
Current	2	3	4	5		
	Current	2	3	4	5	
		Current	2	3	4	5
			Current	2	3	4	5
				Current	2	3	4	5

Planning involvement. A planning council is established to ensure systemwide participation for developing current and strategic plans. Council members are representative of and accountable to work units (central, teaching, support) for input regarding decisions affecting their work and working conditions. One aim of the planning process is to avoid management exclusivity—unwritten, temporal, and intuitive approaches borne of individual experience rather than of system implications of current developments and trends.

FIGURE 2.2
Elements of Riverpark school system's strategic *planning process* for its human resources.

With respect to human resources, the aspirations of the Goodville school system are to:

- Employ personnel whose abilities, skills, experience, training, character, and mental and physical fitness will contribute maximally to attainment of the system mission and nurture the optimum development of individual personality.

- Provide fair, courteous, and considerate treatment to all personnel.

- Create and maintain a hospitable environment that will respect the dignity of and avoid discrimination against personnel because of membership in any religious order, society, association, or union.

- Establish machinery to settle grievances.

- Provide safeguards to protect personnel from arbitrary treatment.

- Maintain equality of opportunity for current personnel or applicants, irrespective of race, religion, age, or sex.

- Provide opportunity for advancement to qualified personnel.

- Clarify internal and external position relationships and provide career development programs.

- Enable personnel to pursue career development programs through leaves of absence.

- Maintain opportunities for retired personnel to perform services on a part-time basis.

- Endeavor to maintain stability of employment for all personnel whose internal performance meets system expectations and whose external behavior is not contrary to the system's mission.

- Provide economic security in the form of salaries, wages, incentives, and benefits that are competitive with systems in the region.

- Develop and maintain a performance appraisal plan to improve personnel effectiveness, estimate individual potential, and determine appropriate compensation action.

- Place personnel in positions to make the best of their abilities.

- Deal properly with personnel unions on all matters of mutual interest.

- Require those who are responsible for personnel supervision to be tolerant, fair, and patient with subordinates.

- Furnish personnel with full information on matters affecting their positions as well as those matters having to do with system policies, plans, and programs.

- Appoint a system ombudsman—responsible only to the chief executive—with whom personnel may confer on matters encompassed in the human resources function. This official should investigate personnel complaints or perceived violations of rights and initiate recommendations for their resolution.

FIGURE 2.3
Human resources goals for the Goodville school system.

The Foxcroft Board of Education recognizes that:

- The quantity and quality of the human resources in its employ directly affect attainment of the aims of the school system.
- Emphasis in organizations on individual achievement and effort is conducive to goal performance.
- An organization is more likely to be effective if the conditions and climate of work are both stimulating and satisfying to personnel.

We further recognize our responsibility to provide an effective educational program that will benefit the children, youth, and adults of the City of Foxcroft. To implement this acknowledgment of its responsibility, the Board of Education has established the following policies relating to personnel in its employ.

It is the policy of the Foxcroft Board of Education to:

1.0   Attract to the system people with growth potential, capable of performing competently in the positions established by the system's human resources plan.

1.1   Make selections for positions solely on the basis of ability to fullfill responsibilities as defined in the position guide.

1.2   Place each member of the staff in a position for which he/she is qualified and in which he/she has an opportunity to advance.

1.3   Establish a balanced and equitable compensation system for all personnel that is related to the person and position requirements specified in the position guide.

1.4   Provide a comprehensive program of collateral benefits.

1.5   Provide position security to the greatest extent possible, consistent with satisfactory performance.

1.6   Assist each individual to perform effectively in his/her present position and in other assignments by providing internal and external opportunities for development.

1.7   Appraise the performance of all personnel with a view to assist them in improving their present capability and future potential.

1.8   Negotiate fairly and realistically with union representatives.

1.9   Insist that the rights and privileges guaranteed to individuals in our political system will prevail in the Foxcroft school system.

1.10   Maintain an effective information system to facilitate administration of the function.

Note: Numbers to the left are policy index numbers.

FIGURE 2.4
A statement of **human resources policies**.

shown in Figure 2.1). This step is frequently referred to as organizational diagnosis. As detailed in the section that follows, Phase Two involves formation of data bases relating to key planning areas in the internal and external environments. This derivative information provides a context within which to arrive at what is known about the present condition of the system's human resources, and to consider options and develop assumptions about conditions that need to be created to achieve the desired end results.

PHASE TWO: ASSESSMENT OF THE HUMAN RESOURCES CONDITION

As the educational reform movement becomes a reality, there is little disagreement about the conditions of schooling in the United States:

- School systems, whether small, medium, or large, are in need of considerable improvement, in both efficiency and effectiveness.
- All systems engage in some form of planning, whether sophisticated or unsophisticated, formal or informal, piecemeal or holistic.
- A systematic approach to planning enhances the likelihood of educational improvement.
- School systems with the biggest problems tend to be located in large cities with poor populations, to have entrenched bureaucracies, and to have a pervasive union influence.
- There is no best approach to human resources planning. Each system, regardless of size, must develop its own blend of strategies, purposes, policies, programs, and practices that work within the context of system culture and the realities of meeting current and future expectations.
- Small school systems can expect planning advantages deriving from either short-term fixes or long-term overhaul.

Probing for Strategic Direction

The planning process model shown in Figure 2.1 indicates that Phase Two is aimed at assessing the current condition of the system and its linkage to the human resources function. This step is basic to enabling the function to play a pivotal role in creating a performance potential to confer desired outcomes on the system, its members, and those for whom it renders service. This responsibility means shaping the system to be able to perform effectively under conditions of continuous change, unanticipated schooling requirements, scarcity of resources, as well as demographic, political, and governmental uncertainty. Meeting these requirements will require close scrutiny of questions such as:

- How can human resources planning be linked more closely to the school system's strategic plan?
- What is the system's current situation regarding attainment of our educational expectations?
- Which are our strongest educational programs? Our weakest?
- What informational inputs are needed to develop the strategic plan?
- What will the future external environment represent in terms of demand for school system services?
- What conditions must the system create to meet present infirmities and anticipated future conditions?
- What priorities should be established for the allocation of anticipated resources? What current basic priorities should be questioned?
- What factors, both internal and external, might inhibit attainment of system education aims?

Strategic Planning Considerations

Assuming that a school system has settled on its *educational goals*, as well as the *social purposes* (often in the form of laws) it is called upon to serve (see Chapter 1), the focus of Phase Two of the human resources planning process is to provide a forum for the system to examine questions such as those mentioned in the preceding list, resolution of which requires dealing with challenging, complex, and unapparent issues. One of the key organization resources essential to examination of the current state of the system is *information,* because selected forms of this planning mechanism are basic to decisions for bridging the gap between *standards* and *norms.* Closing the breach between practice and purpose involves balancing the system's ideological commitment with omnipresent political, governmental, and special interest demands, which when in imbalance is fraught with the potential for diminishing educational expectations.

Although development and maintenance of a human resources **information system** will be addressed in Chapter 10, the role of information in the conduct of an evaluation of organization strengths and weaknesses is the centerpiece of the discussion that follows.

As indicated in Figure 2.5, determination of the school system's current condition in relation to its strategic aims involves delineation of key factors that need to be evaluated. Moreover, decisions regarding the conduct of the evaluation include such matters as what is to be evaluated; means of evaluation; information needed; membership participation; and how data will be collected, refined, stored, communicated, and utilized to implement the strategic plan.

FIGURE 2.5.
Guidelines for evaluating current system conditions.

Adequacy of current system strategic aims.
Adequacy of human resources function aims.
Analysis of present system and function per-
formance.
Analysis of past system and function perfor-
mance.
Adequacy of mechanisms for strategic
review plans.
Problems with current system and function
goals.
Adequacy of current programs, policies, and
structures.
Adequacy of current planning information.

We have already described some of the broad strategic questions that need to be examined in the evaluation of the human resources function and its compatibility with the purpose and goals of the organization. Performance discrepancies and their causes lead to the matter of tapping into information sources that can provide clues for determining types of changes and actions needed to bring about intended reform. Generally speaking, all data in the information system pertaining to the human resources function, as well as data bases that can be developed, are applicable to a human resources evaluation.

Strategic Planning Areas and Data Sources

In recent years many school systems have come to realize that information is one of their key assets, along with building and equipment, human resources, and fiscal resources. Various terms are used to describe information, such as *computer-based* and *nonautomated; external* and *internal;* and *centralized* and *decentralized* data bases. The term *human resources information system* refers to the integration of a variety of data bases that have a bearing on the human resources function. For example, managing the 11 subprocesses of the human resources function effectively and efficiently requires information from both the internal and external environmental forces that influence human resources decisions. Among the major classes of information essential to human resources planning are:

- *Purpose information*—Includes the system purpose hierarchy of mission, objectives, goals, strategies, and policies.
- *Program structure information*—Components of the educational program that interact with the human resources function.

- *Pupil information*—Present and future school enrollees for whom the educational program is designed.

- *Position information*—Number, types, work content, and structural location of present and future positions.

- *Position-holder information*—Information about present and future position occupants.

- *Organization structure information*—Assignment of tasks, responsibility, and authority of the human resources function.

- *External environment information*—Economic, governmental, legal, union, and public influences affecting personnel decisions.

- *Internal environment information*—Work force, negotiated contracts, budgets, audits, structure, technology use, planning efforts, legal compliance, and system culture.

The foregoing classes of system information underscore the need for a comprehensive set of information-gathering tools to collect data for improving strategic planning and performance. The most common mechanisms for gathering strategic planning data are listed in Figure 2.6. With such data at hand, the system can focus on plans to upgrade priority activities. In the text that follows, each of the classes of information noted in the preceding list will

FIGURE 2.6.
Sources of data for human resources planning.

Accounting reports	Plans
Accrediting agencies	policies
Audits	programs
Budgets	projects
Computer bases	Self assessments
Contracts	Services (personnel)
Enrollments (system)	System culture
Environmental data	Technology use
Files (personnel)	Statistical data
Forecasts	absenteeism
Interviews (exit)	deaths
Inventories (skill)	grievances
Job analyses	polls
Job specifications	promotions
Observation	questionnaires
techniques	recruitment
Organization	retirement
charts	selection
documents	surveys
records	transfers
structure	turnover

be examined to illustrate its importance in identifying effective programs and practices and for improving those less than satisfactory.

Purpose Information

We have observed that the human resources function, like all broad administrative functions, is determined largely by the school system purpose structure. Purpose determines the **program structure,** the number and types of positions, the quantity and quality of persons needed to implement the educational program, and administrative processes and relationships employed to maintain the system. Hence, determination of educational aims and expectations is an imperative planning task, one that precedes all other organizational activities. It is evident to even the most casual observer that the abilities and values that enrollees are expected to acquire under the guidance of the school affect the size and characteristics of the school staff. Purposes are the ends toward which the educational program structure is directed. They determine which educational opportunities are provided, and in turn affect the size and composition of the school staff. It is worth restating here that purposes have little value unless they can be translated into attainable objectives. As the purpose structure is shaped and clarified, the likelihood increases that better decisions can be made on what should be taught, how it is to be taught, who should do the teaching, what outcomes are anticipated, and how they should be measured.

After the overall purposes of the school system have been established, additional planning decisions need to be made before the organization structure best suited to meet future institutional needs can be visualized. These include assumptions or premises derived from the broad purpose hierarchy, which are essential to preparation of specific forecasts, master plans, policies, programs, and budgets. Figure 2.7 contains a series of questions that will elicit the types of purpose-related information on which planning assumptions can be based. Planners need to know, for example, the bases on which pupil forecasts will be made, the number of school attendance units needed, the educational programs and supporting services each school will accommodate, and the professional and supporting staff arrangements that are envisioned. The implication of this line of analysis is that projection of the future organization begins not with the status quo, but instead with purpose information that clarifies educational and human problems and ways in which they can be solved.

The reader is advised to review the idealized personnel objectives shown in Figures 2.3 and 2.4 in conjunction with Figure 2.7. Figures 2.3 and 2.4 present purpose-related illustrations, providing an overview of the nature of current purpose information that is gathered and analyzed in order to form a data base for strategic planning.

- What persons in what age groups should be educated at public expense? Within what age limits should pupils be compelled to attend school? What pre- and postcompulsory age groups should be included in the educational program?
- What purposes are schools expected to achieve? What should be the range and nature of educational experiences provided by the school system to achieve its purposes?
- How should the educational program be structured? Should it be similar to or different from the following pattern?

	Age Groups
Prekindergarten	1–5
Kindergarten	5–6
Elementary school	6–12
Middle school	12–15
Senior high school	15–18
Junior college	18–20
Adult education	16 years and more

- What are the most effective ways of organizing instructional groups?
- What methods, materials, and services should be used to make educational experiences meaningful to learners?
- What should be the size and composition of the professional instructional staff? The administrative staff? The support staff? To what extent should the staffing of each attendance unit be decentralized?
- What special services should be provided in each of the school attendance units? In the central administration?
- What systemwide services to teachers—for example, continuing education, supervision, professional library, and curricular and instructional aids—should be provided?
- What central administrative services—for example, pupil personnel, staff personnel, logistics, plant, research, planning, external relations, and coordination—are necessary?
- What should be the size and deployment of the support staff—for example, custodial, maintenance, transportation, food, clerical, and security services?
- What positions should be retained in the future organization structure? Added? Dropped? Modified?
- To what extent should existing personnel comprise the future organization structure? New personnel?
- How can the future structure be organized to satisfy member needs more effectively?

FIGURE 2.7
Critical considerations involved in developing human resources planning assumptions.

Program Structure Information

It is reasonable to assume that school officials who make personnel decisions will be better equipped to do so if they are fully versed in the organizational ramifications of two key aspects of the educational program: *organization of instruction* and *instructional grouping*.

Organization of Instruction. Broad goals of the system are implemented through some form of instructional organization. Assumptions are made by the system as to the breadth and depth of learning experiences to be included in the curriculum, where the experiences will be provided, when they will be offered, by whom, in what manner, in what grouping arrangements, and for what purposes. Decisions such as these have considerable influence on the quality and quantity of personnel needed to staff the educational program. Arriving at such decisions is no easy matter because it involves consideration of conflicting philosophies of education; theories of curriculum development; psychologies of learning; and needs of the individual learner, the local community, the state, the region, and the nation. One of the inferences to be drawn from Table 2.2 is that the choice of alternatives relating to the instructional program affects the number, types, and levels of sophistication of personnel employed. An instructional program organized around the assumption that the subject matter of the past is the basis for developing a satisfactory curriculum will be staffed differently than one based on the assumption that encourages the fullest development of every individual for whom the school is responsible.

Instructional Grouping. Class or group size refers to pupil membership in a group organized for instructional purposes. The question of how many pupils should be assigned to an instructional group has been and still remains the subject of serious concern by all who are interested in the nation's schools. It should be noted that assumptions regarding class size are of vital significance to human resources planning. There are several reasons why so much significance is attached to the question of class size. The first is the educator's quest to provide grouping arrangements most conducive to learning and study. Although it is clear that a given class size is no absolute guarantee of the educational progress of all children, many educators are convinced that the grouping plan is an important contributor to educational attainment.

The second reason is cost. There is a considerable difference between the budgetary requirements of a school system that decides it needs one classroom teacher for every 20 pupils and one that sets the class size at 40 pupils.

The major share of current expenditures in a school budget for any fiscal year is allocated to staffing requirements. In searching for the maximum return for every dollar invested, assumptions about class size are always open

TABLE 2.2
Illustration of instructional program options that influence human resources plans.

Program Component		Illustration of Alternatives
Program focus	*or*	Central purpose is development of the intellect. Central purpose is to develop individuals for effective social living.
Program content	*or*	Rigid, grade-sequenced learning experiences. Flexible-sequenced learning experiences determined by learner readiness, interest, and/or needs.
Program breadth and depth	*or*	Program limited to time-tested elements of our social heritage. Program planned to encompass breadth and depth of educational opportunities.
Program location	*or*	Within attendance units of system. Within and outside of system.
Program staff	*or*	Conventional: one instructor per group. Nonconventional: variable staffing at different levels of system, including volunteers, part-time personnel, aides, and peer instructors.
Program time	*or*	Uniform schedules (day only). Variable schedules (day—evening—summer).
Program flexibility	*or*	Pupil moves through program experiences at uniform rate (one grade per school term). Pupil moves through system depending on achievement.
Pupil grouping	*or*	Graded (learning groups closed). Nongraded (learning groups open).
Program control	*or*	Program decisions restricted to professionals. Program decisions unrestricted (staff, parents, pupils, and/or community groups).
Program instructional methods	*or*	Conventional forms of instruction. Augmented forms of conventional instruction.

to question. If a class of 25 is as effective for educational purposes as a class of 20, is adherence to the latter figure educationally and fiscally defensible?

The rapid growth of collective bargaining in public education is another reason why planning assumptions must include consideration of class size. The matter of class size has become a negotiable item in many contracts between teachers and boards of education, a development that, some observers suggest, may prove to be an impediment to new forms of instructional grouping and staff utilization.

Despite experimentation with new forms of instructional grouping, educational technology, and staff utilization and deployment, the question of class size cannot be dismissed as irrelevant when developing human resources planning assumptions. In making assumptions, consideration must be given to the purpose for which instructional groups are formed (the type of learning desired), the intellectual and emotional needs of pupils, the skills of the teacher, and the nature of the subject matter.

Research into the class-size question and related policy and budgetary implications began late in the nineteenth century. Since then, through periods of declining and expanding enrollments, researchers have tried to resolve relevant questions such as: Is there an optimum class size? Do small classes make an impact on teacher morale? Does class size affect the kinds of instructional procedures used in the classroom? Recent reports on these questions are contradictory and do not answer conclusively many of the important questions relating to the effects of class size on pupil learning, the teaching process, teacher morale and job satisfaction, and cost-quality relationships.[3]

Resolution of critical issues relating to class size (including the economics of achieving smaller instructional groups, increasing teacher contact with pupils, and schedule reorganization) involves, directly or indirectly, most of the personnel processes. So central and pervasive is the matter of class size to improvement of pupil performance that the design and operation of the personnel function should be considered as a key factor in increasing the learning level of students and their effectiveness in learning in terms of time and effort expended.

Grouping schemes, it should be noted, should not be viewed as substitutes for excellence in teaching, for adjusting methods and materials of instruction to individual pupils, or for making provisions for those children whose adjustment will be difficult under any organized plan of instruction. It is equally plain that regardless of the grouping plan, every school system needs a staff that is adequate in size and composition—one that is deployed and balanced properly—to provide all pupils with essential instructional services. Although *class size* is important, a concept of equal significance in developing human resources planning assumptions is *staff size*.[4]

Pupil Information

Pupil information is of major importance to school organizations, especially when viewed from the standpoint of specific effects of declining or increasing enrollments. A survey by the National School Boards Association indicated the following aftereffects of declining enrollments: reduced state aid; hiring freezes or reductions in force; smaller class sizes; redistricting of school boundaries; and closing, modifying, leasing, or selling of school facilities. Increasing enrollments, from another point of view, may create double sessions, overcrowded classrooms, and a need for rapid staff expansion.[5]

Consequently, accurate enrollment projections are vital to staff planning strategies. Literature models employed by school districts to project enrollments are numerous and varied. A review of enrollment projection models indicates that at least four practical methods are available: *census class projection, ratio retention projection, housing projection,* and *total population forecast.* Of the various techniques employed in enrollment projections, the most commonly used procedure is the *ratio retention* or *cohort survival* method.[6] A 1989 report by Phi Delta Kappa on enrollment projection concluded that the cohort survival method, when adapted to a specific environment, provides results that are sufficiently accurate to permit planning for school staff requirements.[7]

Appendix A contains an illustration of the retention ratio projection (cohort survival) technique. It should be noted that in addition to birth and enrollment data such as those shown in Appendix A, external environmental information is essential to making enrollment projections as consistent as possible. Examples of such information include:

- Local and statewide birth rates
- Ethnic composition of community population
- Emerging communities
- Changing community population patterns
- Nonpublic school enrollments
- Changing transportation patterns
- Integration mandates
- Open school enrollment policies
- School census data
- National census data
- Zoning regulations
- Utility connections and plans
- Bank deposits
- Building permits
- Initiation of voucher plans
- A material event, such as the loss by a city or town of a major employer
- External pressure for school system adoption of a "multiracial, multicultural—gender—education" policy
- Industry mobility
- Changes in employment patterns
- Family mobility
- State, regional, and community planning data

Investigations of the reliability of enrollment forecasts indicate that the following guidelines deserve consideration:

- Adopt two separate forecasting methods: one at the district level and one at the building level.
- Employ a district level method, such as the cohort survival technique, to account for enrollment trends and community variables.
- For comparative purposes, develop enrollment forecasts for each school attendance unit.
- Take into account rapid enrollment changes. This kind of development may require a housing survey or a school census in addition to or in combination with standard projection procedures.[8]

Position Information

After the system goal structure has been established, the task of categorizing the work evolving from the structure into work units, job categories, positions, position descriptions, and **position specifications** can be undertaken. The foundation of any educational enterprise is the work or input needed to accomplish the purpose for which it exists. Accordingly, the system's long-term educational and human resources aims represent the basis on which a host of personnel-related activities are determined. Among this needed information are the number and types of positions to be included in the budget; who does what kinds of work, in what groups, and in what locations; who coordinates the work; how the work is to be done; and how the work expectations are to be judged.

Work Analysis. The concept of **work analysis,** or task specialization process, is further elaborated on in Table 2.3, which shows the nature and scope of school system work, positions evolving from required work activities, and the structural settings in which the work is performed.

As indicated in Table 2.3, instructional and related tasks are assigned to *attendance units* (individual schools), whereas the general administrative work is allocated to the *administrative unit*. Various types of positions are created at both the central level and in attendance units.

Among the questions to be raised in analyzing school system work for organization renewal purposes are:

- How many jobs will be needed in the future (groups of positions such as teaching, administration, clerical, transportation, maintenance and operation, food service, and security arrangements)?
- What are the position responsibilities for each job (e.g., computer programmer)?

TABLE 2.3
Nature and scope of school system work, positions, and structural settings.

Types of System Work	Types of Positions	Structural Setting	Hypothetical Proportion of Total System Personnel (%)
Planning, organizing, leading, controlling total system.	Professional administrative: superintendent, assistant superintendent, associate superintendent, directors, assistants to higher-level positions.	Central administration.	1
Planning, organizing, leading, controlling individual school attendance units.	Professional administrative: principals, assistant principals, department heads, team leaders.	Individual client service units (schools).	3
Instructional programs (regular, special).	Professional teaching: classroom teachers. Professional specialists: art, health, library, guidance, music, physical education, psychological service, reading, speech correction, home–school visits, audiovisual.	Individual client service units (schools).	62
Instructional support programs: operation, maintenance, food service, transportation, health, security, secretarial, clerical.	Classified: skilled, semiskilled, unskilled.	Certain personnel work under direction of central administration; others work in attendance units under direction of principal.	34

- What are the strengths needed for each position? Do position incumbents have the strengths necessary to perform effectively in the position?

Information derived from work analysis is usually formalized and set forth in the school system organization manual. The importance of this step cannot be overemphasized, especially the inclusion of position descriptions and position specifications.[9]

A *position description* includes these elements: (a) general functions of the position, (b) specific position responsibilities, and (c) position relationships. A *position specification* identifies the qualifications (personal, educational, and experiential) required of persons who hold or seek system positions (see Figure 2.9 for illustration).

Position information in the school system organization manual that describes the job evaluation system can provide a framework for addressing matters relating to a variety of personnel processes; for example, position specifications help to ensure that persons performing the same job will receive the same salary. When properly designed, job evaluation systems help the school system to arrange a legal defense and rationale for dealing with claims of system bias relating to age, sex, and race. Moreover, position information establishes the basis for managing personnel activities such as recruitment, selection, induction, compensation, career development, performance appraisal, grievance resolution, and reshaping the organization structure. Additional terminology relating to work analysis, developed by the Bureau of Intergovernmental Personnel Development Programs, can be found in the Glossary.[10]

Much importance is attached to the role of positions in the human resources function, as indicated by the objectives listed in Figure 2.8. These objectives signify, too, why position information is so vital for managing virtually all human resources activities.

Position Projection

Table 2.4 illustrates one of several methods that can be employed to transform planning information into professional positions that will be required in the future organization structure. Using the set of numerical transactions proposed, staffing assumptions can develop an idea of the kind of **organizational structure** that should be established for a specific time span under a given set of conditions. The approach shown in Table 2.4 is not difficult to initiate—any school district can use it to undertake an analysis of staffing objectives and policies needed for their attainment. Advantages can be derived from the type of personnel projection illustrated in Table 2.4. These include:

- Extending the range of planning activities in a school administrative unit beyond a single year.

- Ensure present and future work requirements of system are met.
- Specify position context, primary function, work content, responsibilities, authority, accountability, and relationships.
- Determine position classification.
- Establish basis for position holder requirements.
- Set position performance standards through results-oriented descriptions versus activity-oriented position descriptions.
- Provide basis for compensation administration, recruitment, selection, induction, appraisal, development, and legal compliance.
- Establish strategic importance of rank order of each position.
- Create basis for designing, redesigning, and clarifying organization structure.
- Develop foundation for projecting future staff size, position characteristics, roles, skills, and technology requirements.
- Expand quality and quantity of position information in computer data base.

Note: The terms *position description* and *job description* are often employed interchangeably. (See Figure 2.9 for illustration of position guide.)

FIGURE 2.8
Objectives of position descriptions.

- Identifying future trends in enrollments on which to base personnel needs.
- Developing an inventory of present personnel components.
- Projecting the present numerical staff adequacy into the staff size ultimately desired in each of the system's operating units.
- Quantifying personnel needs for budgetary purposes.
- Translating planning assumptions into a future organizational structure.
- Linking personnel planning with other systemwide planning efforts.
- Determining the priority order of personnel needs.
- Identifying obstacles to realization of the total personnel plan and developing methods for surmounting them.

In preparing projections of professional positions, it is important to note that effective results depend on both accuracy of enrollment projections and proper representation of the desired ratio between pupils and professional personnel. There is no standard ratio applicable to all districts. Each district, through careful examination of relevant internal and external variables, must determine the ratio that will work most effectively for it. This involves consideration of the various economic, political, and social

TABLE 2.4.
Projection of professional positions required in the future organization structure of the Cloudcroft school system.

	Base Year	Base Year + 1	Base Year + 2	Base Year + 3	Base Year + 4	Base Year + 5
1. Enrollments						
K–6	6,819	7,153	7,228	7,195	7,083	6,829
7–9	2,583	2,983	3,208	3,457	3,630	3,861
10–12	2,308	2,337	2,449	2,485	2,634	2,839
Total	11,710	12,473	12,885	13,137	13,347	13,529
2. Personnel ratio objectives						
a. Pupil–teaching personnel	28:1	28:1	27:1	26:1	25:1	24:1
b. Pupil–instructional specialist personnel	213:1	211:1	211:1	190:1	178:1	169:1
c. Pupil–administrative personnel	532:1	480:1	460:1	438:1	417:1	423:1
d. Pupil–total professional personnel	24:1	24:1	23:1	22:1	21:1	20:1
e. Professional staff per 1,000 pupils	41	41	42	44	46	48
3. Ratio objectives expressed as staff size						
a. Teaching personnel	420	445	477	505	534	564
b. Instructional specialists	55	59	61	69	75	80
c. Administrative personnel	22	26	28	30	32	32
d. Total professional personnel	497	530	566	604	641	676
4. New positions						
a. Teaching personnel		25	32	28	29	30
b. Instructional specialists		4	2	8	6	5
c. Administrative personnel		4	2	2	2	0
d. Total professional personnel		33	36	38	37	35

Assumptions: Pupil–Teacher ratio will be reduced from 28:1 in base year to 24:1 in base year + 5. Professional staff will increase from 41 per 1,000 pupils in base year to 48 per 1,000 pupils in base year + 5. Pupil-instructional special- ist ratio and pupil–administrative personnel ratio will increase as shown above. *Note:* See Figure 2.11 for method for computing professional staff ratio (2e above).

concerns that influence such a policy decision. Once established, this ratio is then used to methodically ascertain professional personnel requirements of the individual system.

It may well be that some systems facing a period of declining enrollments may not choose to permit the number of pupils per professional staff member to decline, but would rather hold the ratio constant through staff attrition. Regardless of which decision is made regarding the desired staffing ratio, care must be taken to ensure that the intended change is gradual and attainable over the proposed period of time. In assessing the level of the overall professional staffing ratio, attention should be focused also on existing ratios among teaching, instructional, and administrative personnel. It may be that new ratio objectives would more properly serve the educational mission.

The reader should recognize that the approach suggested in Table 2.4 is not offered as the ultimate solution to long-term human resources forecasting. For example, the technique employed to project professional personnel requirements could be broadened to include data on support personnel to make the planning more comprehensive. Moreover, techniques can be refined to quantify planning requirements for each school attendance unit prior to consolidating the data for systemwide forecasts. Planning tools for this purpose have been illustrated in the section on personnel information.

Structure Projection

Completing the forecast of the long-term human resources requirements for the system makes it possible to project the organizational structure in detail. The model of organization structure is projected in terms of redefined objectives, including positions, functions, and reporting relationships best calculated to achieve them. Existing organizational functions, functionaries, and methods of operation are ignored in developing the model structure. Several types of planning tools that can be of assistance to school officials in redesigning the organizational structure should be mentioned. These include the position guide, the organizational chart, and the organizational manual.

The Position Guide. The **position guide,** an example of which is shown in Figure 2.9, can be used to specify the work or expectations of each position in the organization, relationships of the position, and qualifications needed to perform the work allocated to the position. It is also useful in the recruitment, compensation, development, position analysis, and control processes.

The Organizational Chart. Although it is perfectly clear that an **organizational chart,** such as the one shown in Figure 2.10, has limitations in

---

Goodville School District
Position Guide

Part A: Position Requirements

Position Title: Instructor of Mathematics, Senior High School

Position Code: T68

Primary Function: To participate, as a member of the instructional staff, in directing learning of all students in the area of mathematics. Such participation shall be directed toward attainment of general and specific behavioral objectives of each course, of the school, and of the school district.

Major Classroom Responsibilities: (1) Planning for teaching, (2) motivating pupils, (3) developing classroom climate, (4) managing the classroom, (5) interacting with pupils, (6) evaluating pupils.

Illustration of Key Duties: (1) *Planning for teaching:* within the framework of goals established by the school system, plans the long- and short-range objectives for each assigned course; collects and utilizes a wide variety of information to aid in guiding the growth and development of individual pupils; selects meaningful subject matter and related learning experiences appropriate to various stages of pupil's development; selects and utilizes teaching procedures appropriate to attainment of short- and long-range objectives; selects teaching materials considered to be conducive to attainment of intended goals; (2) *Motivating Pupils:* establishes standards for individual pupils in terms of ability level of each; uses a variety of activities to develop pupils' curiosity and discoveries; (3) *Developing a classroom climate:* creates a classroom climate conducive to pupils' intellectual, social, emotional, and moral development; (4) *Managing the classroom:* controls pupils' behavior and activities so that they contribute positively to accomplishment of goals; (5) *Interacting with pupils:* utilizes concept formation, principles, and generalization in helping pupils understand subject matter; (6) *Evaluating pupils:* evaluates pupils' performance continuously to determine nature and extent of direction needed to attain goals.

FIGURE 2.9
Illustration of position guide for teaching position.

portraying the realities of an organizational structure, it is an extremely useful planning tool for establishing and appraising formal relationships. It helps to establish the organization's views as to the functions, relationships, and levels of various positions in the administrative hierarchy. It provides a skeletal view of the total organization, its position composition, and a general picture of the relative importance and status of the several positions comprising the structure. It can be used, too, as a working hypothesis to test position guides and position responsibility charts.[11]

Special Assignment: Sponsor of the Square Club, a voluntary organization designed for students who wish to further their knowledge, interest, and skill in mathematics.

Organizational Relationships: (1) is accountable to department chair for performance of assigned responsibilities; (2) coordinates work with members of mathematics department; (3) relates role to building systemwide programs and objectives.

Performance Standards: Performance in this position is considered satisfactory when: (1) *in-class behavior:* there is evidence that the pupils assigned to courses for which the instructor is responsible have achieved the established behavioral objectives as specified by course criteria for acceptable performance; (2) *out-of-class behavior:* there is evidence that the instructor has developed out-of-class behavior that results in effective cooperation with colleagues and laypersons, and in effective self-development.

Part B. Position-Holder Qualifications

Position-Holder Qualifications: (1) *Education:* (a) graduate of a four-year accredited college; (b) professional preparation; (c) academic major in mathematics; (2) *Skills, knowledge, abilities:* (a) functions effectively as a member of an instructional team; (b) organizes and works effectively with small seminar groups; (c) maintains strong commitment to mathematics program and to team teaching; (d) has ability to develop program plans in cooperation with students, parents, staff; (e) works effectively with laypersons in community; (f) has ability to adapt to differences and changes in pupil characteristics, program characteristics, leadership characteristics, colleague characteristics, and community characteristics; (g) has desire and ability to make decisions that go beyond directions from curriculum and instruction guidelines; (h) has desire and ability to achieve close relations with students without emphasis on the authority relationships; (3) *Experience:* three years of experience in teaching mathematics in a secondary school.

The Organizational Manual. An **organizational manual,** as noted previously, is a document that describes the formal organizational structure. It contains charts and statements relating to position authority and responsibility. The advantages of an organizational manual are numerous. Most important, however, is that the manual represents a formal commitment by the organization to a structure. In addition, the organizational manual helps to identify line and staff responsibilities, communicate to all members of the organization the nature of the structure, minimize overlapping of functions, enable the organization to allocate responsibilities, and improve the human resources function.

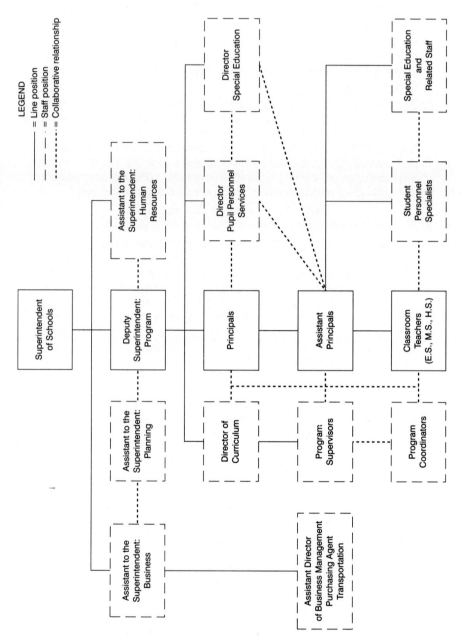

LEGEND

—— = Line position

— · — = Staff position

········· = Collaborative relationship

FIGURE 2.10
System organization chart of the Cloudcroft school district.

Planning activity involved in developing the foregoing tools is of considerable importance in that it can help to enhance personnel's role fulfillment, create better role understanding, lead to wiser use of the structural tools, and make a more effective organization.

External Environment Analysis

If a school system is to function well in contemporary society, it must understand and make plans to cope with dynamic temporal movements in the *external environment*. External factors, such as those identified in Figure 1.8, influence the organization as a whole as well as its components and its effectiveness.

Assessment of external variables that affect the system mission, as well as the informational inputs derived from such assessments as assumptions, forecasts, and projections, are important elements that must be integrated into the strategic planning process.

Because the number and types of variables in the external environment influencing the system and its functions are virtually limitless, a choice must be made as to which appear to be most critical in planning the system's future. Examples of potentially relevant variables include:

- Extension of regulatory legislation and procedures generated by federal, state, county, and municipal agencies.
- School enrollment trends (short- and long-term).
- Educational reform movements (federal, state, county, and municipal).
- Extension or curtailment of state-mandated educational programs.
- Extension or curtailment of financial support for education.
- Community pressures for educational change.
- Personnel costs under varying economic conditions and contract negotiations.
- Personnel composition and skill-level demand under varying employment conditions.
- Trends in judicial rulings affecting the human resources function.
- Emerging educational technology and its potential for improving teaching and learning.
- Emerging technology for improving organization information systems, and its application to strategic planning.

Variables selected for analysis and projection should be chosen on the basis of assumed relevance to achieving both system and human resources function aims. The preceding list of variables, as well as emerging issues pertinent to the human resources function, merit continuous monitoring in order to enhance more systematic approaches to strategic decision making.

Internal Environment Analysis

Internal as well as external forces, as noted in Chapter 1, affect the effectiveness of a school system. Interaction of multiple elements creates a variety of administrative concerns, especially the impact on individual and group behavior. Formal organization strategies are needed to cope with the inexorable tendencies of internal and external environmental change. Examination of Figure 1.8 brings into focus influential internal environmental factors that need to be considered in developing strategic plans.

Internal factors such as *formal organization, individual and group behavior, system culture,* and *work force diversity* in school systems are not readily measured. Although their influence on *strategic* plans is, for the most part, intangible, they are factors affecting organizational performance and must be considered in gaining an understanding of the causes of and ways to enhance individual, group, and system effectiveness. The following questions are those included in focusing the analytic spotlight on the internal environment:

- What organization characteristics promote or impede the system's ability to increase its responsiveness to current and future demands (policies, programs, processes, procedures, practices, rules, and regulations)?
- What is the quality of authority relationships as perceived by the system's individuals and groups?
- Is the system's division of labor efficiently structured?
- How satisfactory is the current approach to rewards and punishment?
- Does our present leadership promote change and innovation?
- What are our strengths and weaknesses in each functional area (program, logistics, planning, human resources, and external relations)?
- Are the system's values, expectations, and attitudes being communicated effectively to the membership?
- How effective are the system's efforts to bring about in an ethnically diverse work force an understanding and appreciation of the values, norms, expected behaviors, abilities, and social knowledge needed to carry out position and performance standards, career development, and interpersonal relationships?

PHASE THREE: DEVELOPMENT OF A STRATEGIC PLAN

Phases One and Two of the human resources planning process include (a) identification of organizational and human resources objectives and (b) formation of data bases for use as tools in planning how to achieve future system goals. Phase Three involves drawing inferences, considering planning options, and making personnel decisions based on information derived from Phases One and Two.

Many factors are involved in and complicate decision making for human resources planning. For example:

- What are the planning implications of the pupil enrollment forecasts?
- Will there be a shortage or surplus of system personnel to meet future needs?
- To what extent do incumbents have the skills, abilities, and attitudes to fill projected positions?
- What assumptions should be made about professional staff size? Support staff size? (Staff size is the number of staff members per 1,000 students. See Figure 2.11 for a computation illustration.)
- To what extent should existing jobs be redesigned? New jobs designed?
- What decisions should be made about various kinds of staff balance (system; work unit; staff category; staff utilization; staff load; staff competency; and racial, ethnic, gender, age, and instructional balance)?
- How can the system redesign the organizational structure to clarify (a) the nature and location of each position, (b) the relationship of this position to other positions, (c) role specifications, (d) position level, (e) types of position interactions, (f) position authority and responsibility, (g) position status and importance, and (h) position expectations and rewards?
- How can the system make more effective and efficient use of its human resources?
- What changes should be made in personnel plans as a result of anticipated developments in the external environment?
- To what extent should existing instructional, administrative, support, specialist, and temporary positions be redesigned? New positions designed?

In brief, making the transition from an existing to a more desirable human resources condition requires systematic planning. The planning process described in this chapter should help to chart managerial direction, reduce uncertainty, and minimize random behavior in efforts to achieve both the aims of the school organization and its members.

PHASE FOUR: IMPLEMENTATION OF THE STRATEGIC PLAN

Introducing changes in the human resources function involves a variety of activities to improve existing arrangements, as well as to develop new

A. Goodville School District has the following pupil membership:

Grades	Resident Membership	Nonresident Membership	Total Membership	Resident Pupils for Whom Tuition Is Paid in Another District	Staffing Pupil Units
K	939	1	940	0	470.0
1–6	4,065	39	4,104	0	4,104.0
7–12	3,397	25	3,422	1	3,764.2
Total	8,401	65	8,466	1	8,338.2

B. The district has 392 professional employees, including superintendent, principals, teachers, administrative assistants, special teachers, psychologists, nurses, teachers of special subjects (who are not counted as regular teachers), and librarians.

C. To compute the number of staffing units in the system, use the average daily membership, which includes pupils sent by other districts; exclude resident pupils sent to other districts.

1. Divide total half-day kindergarten membership by 2 ($940/2 = 470$).
2. Multiply total secondary membership by 1.1 to account for the difference in secondary over elementary school staffing ($3,422 \times 1.1 = 3764.2$).
3. Compute total staff units $470.0 + 4,104.0 + 3764.2 = 8,338.2$.

D. Professional staff size:

$$\frac{\text{Professional employees} \times 1,000}{\text{Staffing pupil units}} = \frac{392 \times 1,000}{8,338.2}$$

$$= 47 \text{ professional staff members for every 1,000 pupils}$$

Note: Staffing ratio is defined as the number of staff members per 1,000 students.

FIGURE 2.11
Method for computing professional staff ratio.

approaches and capabilities based on review of external-internal environmental conditions, threats, and opportunities. Phase Four of the human resources planning process presumes that there is organizational commitment to implement the design of the strategic development plan. As illustrated in Figure 2.12, implementation strategy takes into account objectives, strategies, programs, projects, timing of activities, delegation of responsibilities, and allocation of resources to undertake specified courses of action.

School systems differ in many ways including size, location, leadership, resources, quality and quantity of personnel, instructional technology, complexity, stability, and internal–external environments. Each school system must determine how the process can be performed most effectively and efficiently. The planning process model shown in Figure 2.1 provides a framework for analyzing problems related to the function and the steps involved in developing approaches to achieve long-term objectives.

Table 2.5 illustrates a format employed in the Goodville school system to plan, manage, and monitor various activities associated with positions in the organizational structure. Worthy of note are (a) approaches employed to govern the creation, specifications, elimination, recruitment, selection, appraisal, forecasts, and relationships relevant to all positions in the budget; (b) allocation of authority and responsibility; (c) control guidelines; and (d) structural relationships.

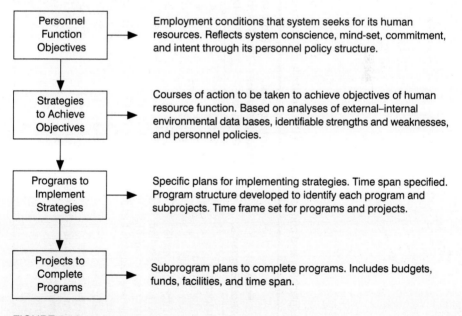

FIGURE 2.12
Sequential implementation of change strategies.

TABLE 2.5
Position planning and control network of the Goodville school system.

Position Network Elements	Professional Administrative Positions	Professional Teaching Positions	Professional Specialist Positions	Instructional Support Positions	Noninstructional Support Positions
Position location	C-A	A	C-A	A	C-A
Position reports to	5	5	5	5	5
New position route	5-3-2-1	5-3-2-1	5-3-2-1	5-3-2-1	5-3-2-1
Position abolition route	3-2-1	3-2-1	3-2-1	3-2-1	3-2-1
Request for new position route	5-3-2-1	5-3-2-1	5-3-2-1	5-3-2-1	5-3-2-1
Temporary replacement route	5-3-4	5-3-4	5-3-4	5-3-4	5-3-4
Permanent replacement route	5-3-4	5-3-4	5-3-4	5-3-4	5-3-4
Transfer route	5-3	5-3	5-3	5-3	
Dismissal route	5-3-2-1	5-3-2-1	5-3-2-1	5-3-2-1	5-3-2-1
Position guide route	6-5-3-2-1	6-5-3-2-1	6-5-3-2-1	6-5-3-2-1	6-5-3-2-1
Performance appraisal process	5-R	5-R	5-R	5-R	5-R
Recruitment process	1-3-4-5	1-3-4-5	1-3-4-5	1-3-4-5	1-3-4-5
Internal	4-R	4-R	4-R	4-R	4-R
External	4-R	4-R	4-R	4-R	4-R

Position Network Elements	Professional Administrative Positions	Professional Teaching Positions	Professional Specialist Positions	Instructional Support Positions	Noninstructional Support Positions
Selection process	4-R	4-R	4-R	4-R	4-R
Participation route	7	7	7	7	7
Recommendation route	7-3-2-1	7-3-2-1	7-3-2-1	7-3-2-1	7-3-2-1
Nomination responsibility	3	3	3	3	3
Appointment responsibility	1	1	1	1	1
Rejection resolution route	1-3-1	1-3-1	1-3-1	1-3-1	1-3-1
Position forecasts	6-3-2-1	6-3-2-1	6-3-2-1	6-3-2-1	6-3-2-1
Position relationship within organization structure	6-3-2-1	6-3-2-1	6-3-2-1	6-3-2-1	6-3-2-1

Code
1 = Board as a whole
2 = Personnel committee
3 = Chief Executive
4 = Asst. Supt., Human resources
5 = Unit head (see administrative almanac)
6 = Planning office
7 = Selection committee
C = Central administration
A = Attendance unit
R = Responsibility for administering

Guidelines elaborating position control concepts:
- Central recruitment, decentralized selection
- Position guides for each position, reviewed annually
- All positions open to internal application
- Unit heads (5) notify Asst. Supt., Human resources (4) of position vacancy (temporary or permanent))
- Selection committees have joint responsibility of (1) and (2)
- (4) Responsible for forms, documentation, processes in position, control plan
- Positions created or abolished in adoption of annual budgets; interim position replacement route specified above
- Chief Executive makes nomination to Board for each position
- If Board rejects nomination, Chief Executive nominates another candidate

Both internal and external organizational environments change and, in turn, generate system changes. Central and unit administrators are responsible for improving the function not only by resolving those problems inherent in existing plans but also by developing new policies and innovative ways of meeting old and new problems. New approaches to personnel motivation, new designs for feedback systems, application of emerging instructional technologies, and more effective use of personnel time are matters that are the responsibility of and should be of vital concern to those involved in administration of the function.

PHASE FIVE: MONITORING, ASSESSING, AND ADJUSTING THE STRATEGIC PLAN

The final phase in the human resources planning process is to determine the appropriateness of plans to meet projected conditions and the extent to which performance conforms to plans. Inherent in the control function are three closely related steps that form the basis of this phase: (a) reviewing plans (including goals, objectives, programs, and standards); (b) checking results against expectations; and (c) adjusting to correct deviations from plans. Ideally, every plan that the school system puts into operation should have *built-in means* for judging its effectiveness. Viewed in this manner, monitoring and evaluating the effectiveness of plans is an omnipresent function of school administration, an aspect of the administrative process designed to keep means and ends in balance. Human resources planners need to know:

- How feasible are the planning assumptions on which the function is based?
- Is the current organizational structure conducive to system effectiveness?
- Are positions being filled according to position guides?
- What steps have been taken to implement systemwide development and career paths for personnel?
- Are the numbers and quality of personnel satisfactory?
- Are personnel deployed, balanced, and utilized effectively?
- What initiatives are needed to adjust differences between actual and expected planning outcomes?

The foregoing questions address the importance of *judging the effectiveness* of the human resources function. **Effectiveness,** as the term is used here, means the extent to which goals of the function are achieved. One way to sharpen goal statements is to establish *effectiveness criteria* by which to measure progress toward goals or actual goal achievement. For example, What criteria should be used to measure the effectiveness of the recruitment program? The performance appraisal process? Personnel selection outcomes? When goals are stated in precise terms, the task of developing criteria by which they can be measured becomes more feasible.[12] In evaluating function outcomes, the effects of some changes are readily discernible while others are less apparent. For example, for the goal, "To create a problem-solving environment to cope with continuing and emerging personnel problems," what criteria should be employed to judge its effects? In this case the goal statement must be amplified before effectiveness criteria can be developed. Moreover, concrete effects will probably not be perceptible for some time after the program is initiated.

Finally, it should be noted that human resources planning is a cyclical operation that probably will never attain perfection. Periodic revisions of plans and the assumptions on which they are based will always be necessary. Nevertheless, if the planning process is carefully structured, implemented, and controlled, chances are good that the school system will have sufficient personnel available to meet its personnel requirements and that it will not have to endure constant organizational crises created by the lack of qualified people to perform the variety of tasks essential to its purposes.

REVIEW AND PREVIEW

The purpose of this chapter has been to present a human resources planning process—the first of 11 processes that comprise the structure of this text. Five phases of the planning process shown in Figure 2.1 include (a) establishing goals for the system's human resources, (b) assessing the present status of the human resources condition, (c) developing a strategic plan to project what the human resources function aims to accomplish in the long run, (d) stressing the importance of initiating courses of action to implement planning strategies, and (e) monitoring and evaluating the strategic plan to check program performance against goals. Three planning concepts were highlighted as important components of the planning process: (a) viewing human resources planning as a framework for integrating all human resources activities; (b) developing a human resources information system to be utilized to facilitate the planning process; and (c) monitoring and evaluating the planning process to assess progress toward goals, identify performance discrepancies, reexamine goals, and modify courses of action where evaluation indicates justifiable change.

Chapter 3 takes up the human resources recruitment process and its linkage to achievement of organizational strategy.

REVIEW AND DISCUSSION QUESTIONS

1. In determining the effectiveness of a *school system,* list five *evaluative criteria* that should be employed for this purpose. In evaluating the

human resources function, suggest five *criteria* you consider to be applicable. In each case, identify the kinds of *data* that would be needed.

2. Interview a superintendent of schools or an executive in charge of the human resources function. Pose the following questions: Has strategic (long-range) planning been attempted in your system? Has it been a success? In what respects? What do you see as its shortcomings? What hurdles need to be overcome to improve strategic planning?

3. What do the school code or state agency regulations in your state have to say about school system planning? How do the systems concepts discussed in Chapter 1 relate to strategic and operational planning? To the human resources function?

4. Develop a graphic representation of an actual school organization structure. Write a critique of the formal structure and of the manner in which the human resources function is arranged.

5. The author states that staff balance is an important aspect of the human resources function. Do you agree? Disagree? On what grounds?

6. What are your views on the information given in this chapter on class size?

7. Describe several decision-making situations in a school system in which strategic information could be usefully employed.

8. Read the following three quotations from a news release, and state your reactions regarding (a) the system mission and strategic planning, (b) the apparent misunderstanding of the importance of the system mission in school system planning, and

(c) contemporary school system infirmities:

- "The crisis in American education starts with this fact: The teachers, principals, and superintendents who run our schools don't know exactly what it is that the nation expects them to do."
- "We must eliminate this terminal confusion over our mission."
- "Give us some goals and then get out of the way."

9. Why do all types of organizations encounter difficulty in formulating a mission statement? Specifying the conditions relevant to achieving the mission? Creating and adhering to programs based on the mission? Evaluating the formal organization and its functions based on the mission?

10. Would you defend or refute each of the following statements?

- The most important policy document in any school system is the school budget.
- The following internal and external forces are impediments to both operational and strategic planning:
  a. Conflict among board of education members.
  b. Racial and ethnic differences among board members.
  c. Relationship between board and superintendent.
  d. Demands for specific school policies from religious and other interest groups.
  e. Political intervention in school system policies.
  f. Desegregation issues.
  g. Redistricting issues.

CHAPTER EXERCISE 2.1

Directions: Form the class into five committees and designate a chairperson for each group. Then, have the committees perform the following assignments:

Group A—Secure data from a school system and project school enrollment for a ten-year period using the method illustrated in Appendix A or the one cited in this chapter, note 7.

Group B—Using the enrollment data compiled by Group A, project the number of professional positions needed for a five-year period. Consider the school system's intentions and expectations for the period under consideration.

Group C—Project the number of support positions (all positions on the payroll not classified as professional) needed by the school system used by Group A.

Group D—Design a research project aimed at identifying the strengths and weaknesses of the human resources function in a hypothetical school system.

Group E—Develop a set of effectiveness criteria for the human resources function to assist Group D in shaping its research project. Consider control standards such as human resources policy, professional staff per 1,000 pupils, consistency of human resources practices, position specifications, person specifications, the overall state of the human organization, the quality of supervision, and the quality of planning outcomes in key long-term areas.

CHAPTER EXERCISE 2.2

Directions: Each member of the class is assigned to defend or refute one of the following statements (student presentations should be based on supporting information):

- Strategic planning is applicable to any situation so long as it is directly related to overall organizational purposes.
- A decision to hire a new school superintendent or someone with unique talents could be considered a strategic decision.
- A poor strategy is better than no strategy at all.
- The difference between operating decisions and strategic decisions is that the latter is concerned primarily with risks and uncertainties.

- Every major decision in a school system should be tested by this criterion: How might this decision affect the system's future?
- Evaluation of system planning implies that both the human resources function and the results derived from human resources processes (recruitment, induction, etc.) should be reviewed periodically.
- We already have a de facto national curriculum and a national testing system imposed by textbooks and nationally standardized, norm-referenced tests.
- Three major federal legislative initiatives concerning public education (Goals 2000: Educate America Act;

Improving America's Schools Act of 1993; and School-to-Work Opportunities Act of 1993) rely heavily on local district plans to guide local school system planning.

• Federal government education initiatives recognize the family and the church as educational institutions.

• Of the three factors that influence student learning (classroom culture, school attendance unit, and school district), classroom culture is considered to be the most influential.

• Schools cannot fulfill their mission to educate students by addressing the social, physical, and emotional needs of all students.

• The *official* and *tested curricula* reveal the least amount of usable information about what actually happens in the classroom and what students are learning.

NOTES

1. Russell L. Ackoff, A Concept of Planning (New York: Wiley-Interscience, 1970), 2–4.

2. Lawrence A. Cremin, Popular Education and Its Discontents (New York: Harper and Row, 1990), 125. For a viewpoint about what education is, what it should be, and where it can be most productively advanced, see John I. Goodlad, What Schools Are For (Bloomington, IN: Phi Delta Kappa Educational Foundation, 1994). For more viewpoints on educational goals, see Phi Delta Kappa, Educational Goals and Objectives (Bloomington, IN: Phi Delta Kappa, 1972); Stanley L. Elam, "The Second Gallup/Phi Delta Kappa Poll of Teachers' Attitudes toward the Public Schools," Phi Delta Kappa 70, 10 (June 1989), 793–794; and George S. Counts, Education and American Civilization (New York: Teachers College, Columbia University, 1952), 311–430.

3. For summaries of research on class size, see Educational Research Service Inc., Negotiating the Class Size Issue (Arlington, VA: Educational Research Service, 1978); Educational Research Service Inc., Class Size: A Summary of Research (Arlington, VA: Educational Research Service, 1978); Gene Glass and Mary Lee Smith, Meta-Analysis of the Research on the Relationship of Class Size and Achievement (San Francisco, CA: Far West Laboratory for Educational Research and Development, 1979), 45; James W. Guthrie, Do Teachers Make a Difference? (Washington, DC: Bureau of Educational Personnel Development, 1970); Helen Pate Bain and C. M. Achilles, "Interesting Developments on Class Size," Phi Delta Kappan, 67, 9 (May 1986), 663–665; Paul T. Sindelar and Cynthia O. Vail, "Class Size," Encyclopedia of School Administration and Supervision (Phoenix, AZ: Oryx Press, 1988), 58; and Tommy M. Tomlinson, Class Size and Public Policy (Washington, DC: U.S. Department of Education, 1988).

4. Class size refers to the number of pupils enrolled in a class or in an instructional group. Average class size is the average number of pupils enrolled in a school attendance unit or in a school administrative unit.

Teacher-pupil ratio is the number of pupils enrolled per full-time teacher. **Staff ratio** is the number of staff members per 1,000 students. (See Figure 2.11 for a computation illustration. Caution: Users of staffing indices should use care in developing ratios to make assumptions about staffing policy. The following observations are relevant: Staffing ratios are norms indicative of how schools are presently staffed. They are not to be conceived as standards as to how schools should be staffed. Staffing indicators can best be employed comparatively to determine reasons why a system's staffing patterns are the same as or different from those of other systems. Research studies do not identify models of staffing patterns that have gained acceptance in the educational community, probably because of the variety of factors that influence decisions governing the number and types of personnel to be employed. If, for example, a school system has a ratio of 60 professionals for each 1,000 pupils, there is no assurance that this staffing ratio will provide the necessary instructional, administrative, and support competence needed to provide an outstanding instructional program for which the staffing ratio has been computed. Optimum staffing ratios do not guarantee that individualization of instruction will be enhanced, that instructional processes will be improved automatically, that teacher behavior will be instantly more effective, or that pupil achievement will increase dramatically.)

5. National School Boards Association, Declining Enrollment (research report) (Evanston, IL: National School Boards Association, 1976).

6. Wallace H. Strevell, "Techniques for Estimating Future Enrollment," American School Board Journal (March 1952), 35.

7. Phi Delta Kappa, Enrollment Projections (Bloomington, IN: Phi Delta Kappa, 1989).

8. Joyce King-Stoops and Robert M. Slaby, "How Many Students Next Year?" Phi Delta Kappan 62, 9 (May 1981), 658.

9. For a comprehensive study of job descriptions, see JoAnn Sperling, Job Descriptions in Human Resources (New York: American Management Association, 1985).

10. Terminology defining jobs, positions, and related terms is contained in the glossary. For sources of definitions, the process of job evaluation, and pitfalls to be avoided, see Gundars E. Kaupins, "Lies, Damn Lies, and Job Evaluations," Personnel 66, 11 (November 1989), 62; U.S. Civil Service Commission, Job Analysis: Developing and Documenting Data (Washington, DC: Bureau of Intergovernmental Personnel Development Programs, 1972); U.S. Department of Labor, Dictionary of Occupation Titles (Washington, DC: Bureau of Employment Security, U.S. Government Printing Office, 1972; updated supplement, 1982); and U.S. Department of Labor, Handbook for Analyzing Jobs (Washington, DC: U.S. Employment Training Services, Manpower Administration, U.S. Government Printing Office, 1972).

11. Descriptive materials for developing organization manuals are presented in Leo Lunine, How to Research, Write, and Package Administrative Manuals (New York:

American Management Association, 1983); and William S. Hubbartt, Personnel Policy Handbook (New York: McGraw-Hill, 1993).

12. Personnel control systems are analyzed in Dale Yoder and Herbert G.

Heneman, Jr., ASPA Handbook of Personnel and Industrial Relations (Washington, DC: Bureau of National Affairs, Inc., 1979), Chapter 22.

SUPPLEMENTARY READING

Anson, Edward M. III. How to Prepare and Write Your Employee Handbook. Second Edition. New York: American Management Association, 1988.

Bennis, Warren. On Becoming a Leader. Reading, MA: Addison-Wesley, 1978.

Brodinsky, Ben. Defining the Basics of American Education. Bloomington, IN: Phi Delta Kappa, 1977.

Burack, Elmer H. Creative Human Resources Planning and Application. Englewood Cliffs, NJ: Prentice-Hall Inc., 1988.

Cuban, Larry. The Managerial Imperative and the Practice of Leadership in Schools. Albany: State University of New York Press, 1988.

Dorio, Marc. Personnel Manager's Desk Book. Englewood Cliffs, NJ: Prentice-Hall Inc., 1989.

Kellogg, John B. "Forces of Change." Phi Delta Kappan 70, 3 (November 1988), 199–205.

Kemper, Richard E.; and John N. Mangieri. "America's Future Teaching Force: Predictions and Recommendations." Phi Delta Kappan 68, 5 (January 1987), 393–396.

Levesque, Joseph. Manual of Personnel Policies, Procedures, and Operations. Englewood Cliffs, NJ: Prentice-Hall Inc., 1986.

McCune, S. Guide to Strategic Planning for Educators. Alexandria, VA: Association for Supervision and Curriculum Development, 1986.

McPartland, James M. "Staffing Decisions in the Middle Grades: Balancing Quality Instruction and Teacher-Student Relations." Phi Delta Kappan 71, 6 (February 1990), 465–469.

National Staff Development Council. The School Improvement Planning Manual. Oxford, OH: National Staff Development Council, 1991.

Orstein, Allan C. "Administrator/Student Ratios in Large School Districts." Phi Delta Kappan 70, 10 (June 1989), 806–808.

Pogrow, Stanley. "On Technological Relevance and the Survival of U.S. Public Schools." Phi Delta Kappan 63, 9 (May 1982), 610–611.

Ricks, James D. "Strategic Planning for Educational Settings." National Forum of Educational Administration and Supervision Journal 7, 3 (1990-91), 289+.

Rothwell, William J.; and H. C. Kazanas. Strategic Human Resources Planning and Management. Englewood Cliffs, NJ: Prentice-Hall Inc., 1988.

Stakenas, Robert G.; and Roger Kaufman. Technology in Education: Its Human Potential. Bloomington, IN: Phi Delta Kappa, 1981.

Taylor, Raymond G. "Forecasting Teacher Shortages." National Forum of Educational Administration and Supervision Journal 7, 2 (1990-91), 70–85.

Thomas, J. E. Strategic Management: Concepts, Practices, and Cases. New York: Harper and Row, 1988.

Tracey, William R. The Human Resources Glossary. New York: American Management Association, 1991.

Tracey, William R. Human Resources Management & Development Handbook. New York: American Management Association, 1985.

Werther, William B.; and Keith Davis. Human Resources and Personnel Management. Fourth Edition. New York: McGraw-Hill, 1993.

PART II

Human Resources Processes: Recruitment, Selection, Induction, Development, and Appraisal

Chapter 3
Recruitment

Chapter 4
Selection

Chapter 5
Induction

Chapter 6
Development

Chapter 7
Performance Appraisal

Part II examines five major human resources processes: recruitment, selection, induction, development, and appraisal. The underlying intent of Part II is to expand our understanding of those key activities that make up organizational staffing. These activities include generating applicant pools, matching individual talents with present and future position requirements, and adjustment and development of system members.

- Chapter 3 discusses the nature of the recruitment process in its strategic focus on present and future positions and position holders; recruitment policy guidelines; and strategies needed to identify, attract, and retain persons with potential for enhancing individual, group, and system effectiveness.

- Chapter 4 examines the selection process, public and system employment policies, and selection practices.

- Chapter 5 deals with characteristics of the induction process, including purposes, programs, and practices essential to enhancing individual retention, socialization, performance, and position and personal satisfaction.

- Chapter 6 analyzes the development process and its constituent activities designed to improve present performance and career enhancement.
- Chapter 7 provides a set of beliefs about the appraisal process and its potential for performance improvement through communicating, teaching, disciplining, and rewarding staff members.

Chapter 3

Recruitment

CHAPTER OVERVIEW

- The Recruitment Contexture

  Integration of Human Resources Planning and the Recruitment Process
  Recruitment Planning: Design Elements
  Public Employment Policy and Recruitment
  System Employment Policy and Recruitment
  Recruitment and System Commitment
  Recruitment and Human Resources Information

- The Recruitment Process

  Recruitment Process Factors
  Developing Applicant Sources
  Coordinating the Applicant Search
  Recruitment Control and Effectiveness

CHAPTER OBJECTIVES

- Develop and describe a model for recruitment of human resources.
- Describe the relationship between public and system employment policies.
- Examine the regulatory aspects of the recruitment process.
- Demonstrate the linkage of the recruitment process with the selection, induction, and development process.

CHAPTER TERMS

Affirmative action   Recruitment contexture

Discrimination   Recruitment control

Employment disadvantages   Recruitment effectiveness

Equal employment opportunity (EEO)   Recruitment process

The foremost and perhaps most challenging problem of any organization is to identify from its pool of human resources those individuals who fit position requirements or who can be developed to fit them. This central task has become more difficult in recent years for educational systems because of technical advances, inflation, shortages in certain types of teaching positions, and the contemporary image of teaching as a career. As the competition increases for qualified talent to conduct the work of educational systems, the processes involved in locating, attracting, selecting, and socializing human resources become ever more critical for organizational effectiveness.

The term *recruitment* as used here refers to those activities in personnel administration designed to make available the numbers and quality of personnel needed to carry on the work of the school system. As such, the recruitment facet of the human resources function has both short- and long-range implications. The short-range plan involves those activities needed to meet current demands for personnel that continually exist in every organization when positions are vacated and cannot be filled from internal sources. The long-term plan is designed to ensure a continuous supply of qualified professional and support personnel. The theme of this chapter is that an extensive and aggressive program of recruitment, directed toward placing and keeping a qualified and satisfied individual in every position in the system, is critical to organizational effectiveness. With this in mind, we shall first discuss *integration of human resources planning with the recruitment process,* especially the manner in which the system goes about developing specific recruitment plans to close the gap between the positions to be filled in the *future organization structure* and the *projected* profile of the *existing* personnel force. Then we shall turn to a discussion of coordination of public employment policy, system policy, and recruitment. The intent is to stress the point that modern recruitment does not take place in a social or organizational vacuum. Discussion of policy integration leads to a description of the recruitment process itself. It is through activities comprising this process that the system actually goes about the business of attracting candidates from various sources to fill anticipated position vacancies. Each of these activities or subprocesses is examined as an interdependent element along with other components of the planning system. Emphasis is given to the proposition that effective direction of the recruitment function will minimize problems that ensue in the *selection* of personnel, in the *placement* of personnel so that they can perform effectively, and in the career *development* of personnel so that they are eventually assimilated into the system. The **recruitment process** is viewed as a unified staffing effort involving an *internal* dimension (moving qualified individuals up from within), an *external* dimension (moving outside personnel sources into the system), and an *integrative* dimension ensuring that recruitment activities function harmoniously to reinforce each other.

THE RECRUITMENT CONTEXTURE

There is a set of internal and external environmental circumstances, facts, and events—the **recruitment contexture**—that must be considered in developing recruitment strategies and the programs and processes by which they are implemented. Arrangement, weaving, and union of these constituent parts into an effective recruitment process represents the substance of this chapter. These parts include the strategic plan, public and system employment policies, system size, the information system, and the recruitment process. These factors must be taken into account in developing a recruitment strategy, as must the entire set of activities designed to attract job candidates who have the abilities and attitudes needed to help the school system in its quest for continuous improvement.

Long before the recruitment process reaches the individual applicant, various ramifications engage the attention of recruitment planners. External and internal environmental factors play a part in recruitment decisions. It is not certain which one or which set of influences affect the recruitment process at any given time, nor which ones affect an individual's decision to become an applicant. What is clear, however, is that the recruitment process can be an important contributor to school system effectiveness. Research has demonstrated that well-designed recruiting programs result in greater employee commitment, higher productivity, and higher quality of work.[1] The recruitment process has the potential to attract to the school system its future leaders, career devotees, high achievers, problem solvers, and innovators. Unplanned, haphazard, and casual approaches to recruitment frequently create costly personnel problems such as position-person mismatches, ineffective performance, undue supervision, absenteeism, lateness, turnover, antiorganization behavior, unwarranted tenure, and personnel litigation.

Integration of Human Resources Planning and the Recruitment Process

Figure 3.1 demonstrates the link between the human resources planning process (discussed in Chapter 2) and the satisfaction of personnel demand

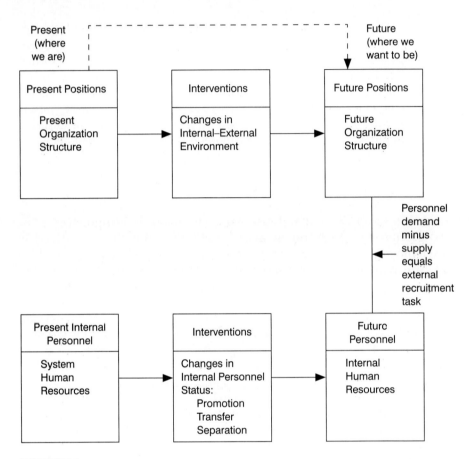

FIGURE 3.1
Perspective of multiyear human resources planning for an educational system.

developed through the implementation of that process. Examination of Figure 3.1 indicates that there are two key elements in human resources planning: *positions* and *people*. Both elements change over time because of changes in the individual as well as in the internal and external environments of the system. Also apparent in Figure 3.1 is the fact that there are two phases to human resources planning: short run and long run.

Short-run human resources planning, as illustrated in Figure 3.2, is concerned with (a) affecting a high degree of compatibility between *existing* positions and people and (b) filling current position openings with *existing* personnel. From an administrative standpoint, these short-run staffing problems involve changing the position, changing the position holder, and removing the position holder. Modification of the position is usually undertaken when the position holder does not possess the necessary qualifications to perform up to position expectations.

Long-run human resources planning differs from short-run planning in these ways: (a) the planning focus is on the more remote future, the totality of positions in the future organizational structure, and personnel required to staff those positions; (b) the planning process is interdependent with other long-term functional planning, such as that required for nonhuman resources, instructional programs, and instructional support programs; (c) present personnel must be evaluated and, when possible, placed in an ideal position; and (d) the gap between present and anticipated personnel must be realized through the recruitment process. Moreover, long-term human resources planning is also different from short-run planning in that the former organization takes time to devise creative ways in which to seek congruency between the work system and human system components of the school organization.

Figure 3.3 illustrates how the human resources planning process leads into and is extended by the recruitment process. Employment of the model shown in Figure 3.3 is based on the premise that position vacancies occurring annually in every personnel category would be filled by a combination of methods: transfer, promotion, recruitment, and development (which includes formal training, planned work experience, performance appraisal, counseling, and coaching).

Recruitment Planning: Design Elements

Recruitment may be viewed as one aspect of system planning designed to facilitate recruitment aims through three concomitant activities: determination of personnel need, satisfaction of need, and maintenance and improvement of service. In this context, recruitment becomes an important phase in the satisfaction of personnel need. There must be an awareness by authori-

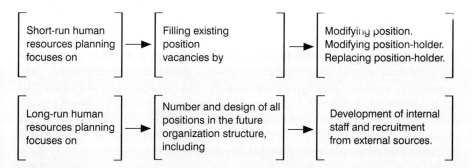

FIGURE 3.2
Focus of short- and long-run human resources planning.

FIGURE 3.3
Integration of human resources planning and recruitment.

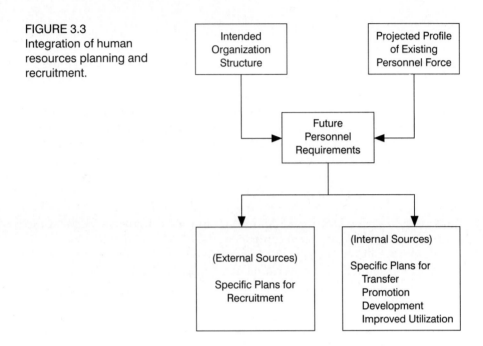

ties, however, that recruitment should not be considered as the first step in the human resources function. Rather, it is one of several subprocesses undertaken to *implement personnel policies and previously established plans*. How, for example, can the chief executive and staff develop a systematic approach to recruitment if the board of education has not clarified its intentions with respect to the number and quality of personnel to be employed? How can those responsible for recruitment answer questions of a prospective applicant if decisions concerning the compensation structure are not made? As a matter of fact, the recruitment program stands or falls as a consequence of policies previously initiated for all aspects of personnel planning.

Among the premises on which an effective recruitment plan rests are:

• Activities in recruitment planning are guided by and coordinated with previously established human resources, personnel development, and selection plans. The human resources plan establishes the number of positions to be filled throughout the planning period, the development plan indicates the potential of current personnel to fill certain vacancies in the system, and the selection process eliminates those who do not meet position and organizational requirements.

• Recruitment is conceived as an essential but not isolated aspect of the total human resources function.

- Recruitment is viewed as a carefully planned, organized, directed, controlled, continuous, and ongoing operation.
- Staff participation is encouraged in formulating and implementing recruitment plans.
- The board of education is the prime mover in recruitment planning. This implies a complex of positive attitudes and actions on the part of this body, leading to the development of employment conditions calculated to attract and retain qualified personnel.
- The board of education delegates responsibility for implementation of recruitment policy to its executive officer.
- Specific duties of the board's executive officer in the recruitment process include determination of immediate and long-term quantitative and qualitative personnel needs, establishment of qualification standards for all personnel, preparation of current and long-term budgetary plans that embrace provisions calculated to satisfy personnel needs, development of a systematic plan to locate and attract qualified persons for service in the system, and appraisal of the effectiveness of recruitment plans.
- Nomination of all persons to positions of employment in the system is a responsibility of the chief executive officer; the board makes all appointments.
- The search for qualified personnel is broad based, not restricted to specific institutions of geographic areas.
- The number of personnel applying for each position in the system is maximized. The application ratio is the number of applicants applying for each position (10:1, 20:1, etc).
- Recruitment methods influence the number of applicants for a particular position.
- The number of applicants recruited affects the caliber of those finally selected.
- Recruitment activities are not abandoned during periods when personnel supply is abundant and demand is low. Competent personnel are not necessarily found nor recruited easily.
- Recruitment is the key tool for meeting the requirements and the spirit of public employment policy as well as for dealing with the human resources assumptions discussed in Chapter 2, such as position design and redesign, staff development, balance, and utilization.
- Utilization of computer technology significantly enhances the system's ability to improve the recruitment process. This includes collection of internal data on the quantity and quality of personnel needed, particular types of skills and backgrounds required, and matching position requirements with applicant characteristics and capabilities.

- A well-designed recruitment plan is closely integrated with (a) overall human resources planning; (b) other major functions, such as the educational program and support services, finances, and external relations; and (c) other processes of the human resources function, such as selection, induction, development, compensation, and information.

This concept of recruitment excellence, which emphasizes the necessity for all units within an educational system to work toward locating, employing, and retaining quality personnel, requires a specific description of the activities involved in its implementation. This is the purpose of the following sections.

Public Employment Policy and Recruitment

Various kinds of employment **discrimination** that exist in our society have brought about extensive legal reforms embodied in legislation, guidelines, regulations, court decisions, and interpretive rulings aimed at correcting abuses of individual employment rights. Consequently, recruitment and selection of personnel under a public policy framework require school officials to do more than simply cope with accelerating changes occasioned by legalisms. Extensive changes have been required in the modification of behavior of system personnel and alterations in organizational roles and exercise of these roles.

The essence of legislation that shapes public employment policy is *antidiscrimination*. Types of employment discrimination are listed in Table 3.1. A substantial portion of educational employment litigation pertains to allegations of unlawful discrimination.[2]

Major legislative action by the federal government to enforce public employment policy is outlined in Table 3.2, the intent of which is to curtail and ultimately eradicate discrimination in employment practices on the basis of race, color, age, religion, gender, and national origin.

It has been said that an individual entering the educational marketplace does so under a canopy of government protection. This observation is borne out by the information contained in Table 3.2. Analysis of the information shown in Table 3.2 indicates that government protection of the individual employee is extensive. Although not all of the federal and state legislation directly affects the public school employee, the indirect influence of federal and state employment policy is considerable. Public personnel policy reflects, by and large, protection deemed necessary for individuals associated with public and private organizations. In effect, resolution of problems of public employment involve *adherence to existing federal, state, and local employment policies;* such policies call for new strategies, attitudes, and techniques in development and application of processes that comprise the personnel function. This observation of public employment policy is especially pertinent to the recruitment process. Federal and state employment policy

TABLE 3.1
Sources of employment discrimination.

• Racial discrimination	• Employment rights
Assignment	Age discrimination
Dismissal	Alcohol control
Hiring	Drugs
Promotion	Handicap discrimination
	Health rights
• Gender discrimination	National origin discrimination
Compensation	Obesity
Conditions of employment	Performance appraisal
Pregnancy-related practices	Privacy rights
Retirement benefits	Religious discrimination
Sexual harassment	Wrongful discharge
Workplace romance	

Notes: For a detailed treatment of the ever-increasing body of law that serves to protect human resources interests, see Mary F. Cook, Editor, *The Human Resources Yearbook, 1993–94 Edition* (Englewood Cliffs, NJ: Prentice-Hall, 1993); Melanie C. Geyer, *Human Boundaries and Personal Abuse: A Christian Perspective on Personal Boundaries, Boundary Violations, and Abuse* (Denville, NJ: Dimension Books, 1992); Joseph D. Levesque, *The Human Resource Problem Solver's Handbook* (New York: McGraw-Hill, 1992); William R. Tracey, *The Human Resources Glossary* (New York: American Management Association, 1991); Wake Forest University School of Law, *Personnel Law Issues Handbook*, Revised Edition (Winston Salem, NC: Wake Forest School of Law, 1992).

Sources dealing with affirmative action plans are identified in Chapter 3, note 5.

is designed to ensure that all Americans will be considered for hiring on the basis of their ability and qualifications without regard to race, color, religion, gender, or national origin. Thus, one of the responsibilities of human resources managers is to develop policies, procedures, attitudes, and behaviors generally accepted in the culture and in the world of work.

Affirmative Action. The intent of **affirmative action** plans initiated by the federal government has been to accord preferential treatment in recruitment, hiring, promotion, and development to groups against whom discrimination has been practiced. Since the inception of affirmative action policy, its goal has been given various interpretations. For example:

- Recruiting groups that are underrepresented in the employer's work force.
- Changing management attitudes toward underrepresented groups.
- Removing discriminatory obstacles that work to the disadvantage of underrepresented groups.
- According preferential treatment in hiring and promotion decisions to underrepresented groups.[3]

TABLE 3.2
Relationship of public employment policy and the human resources function.

Federal Employment Policy

Listed here are major laws enacted by the federal government in the nineteenth and twentieth centuries that constitute national public employment policy and, directly or indirectly, influence the employment policies of public and private educational institutions. Employment policy has been influenced and shaped by a variety of social, political, economic, and ethical factors over the course of two centuries. This policy represents the codified value judgments of society regarding relations between personnel and institutions.

Year Enacted	Legislation	Planning	Recruitment	Selection	Induction	Appraisal	Development	Compensation	Collective Bargaining	Justice	Continuity	Information
1866	Civil Rights Act of 1866									X		
1871	Civil Rights Act of 1871									X		
1883	Pendleton Act (Civil Service Commission)			X			X	X		X	X	
1923	Federal Civil Service Classification Act					X	X					
1931	Davis-Bacon Act							X				
1932	Anti-injunction Act								X			
1935	National Labor Relations Act								X			
1935	Social Security Act							X				
1936	Walsh-Healey Public Contracts Act							X		X		
1938	Fair Labor Standards Act								X	X		
1947	Labor-Management Relations Act								X			

Personnel Processes Affected

Federal Employment Policy

Year Enacted	Legislation	Planning	Recruitment	Selection	Induction	Appraisal	Development	Compensation	Collective Bargaining	Justice	Continuity	Information
						Personnel Processes Affected						
1959	Labor-Management Reporting and Disclosure Act	X							X			
1962	Work Hours Act of 1962							X				
1963	Equal Pay Act of 1963							X				
1964	Civil Rights Act of 1964		X	X		X	X	X		X		
1966	Freedom of Information Act									X		X
1967	Age Discrimination in Employment Act of 1967									X		
1967	Reemployment of Veterans									X	X	
1968	Garnishment Provisions, Consumer Credit Protection Act							X		X		
1972	Equal Employment Opportunity Act of 1972									X		
1972	Title 9 of the Education Amendments of 1972									X		
1973	Rehabilitation Act of 1973	X	X							X		

TABLE 3.2, *continued*

Federal Employment Policy

Year Enacted	Legislation	Planning	Recruitment	Selection	Induction	Appraisal	Development	Compensation	Collective Bargaining	Justice	Continuity	Information
									Personnel Processes Affected			
1974	Employee Retirement Income Security Act							X		X		
1974	Privacy Act		X							X		X
1974	Vietnam Era Veterans Readjustment Assistance Act of 1974	X										
1978	Age Discrimination in Employment Act Amendments					X		X		X		
1978	Civil Service Reform Act							X	X	X		
1978	Pregnancy Discrimination Act							X		X		
1984	Retirement Equity Act									X		
1986	Age Discrimination in Employment Amendments Act of 1986									X		
1988	Age Discrimination Claims Assistance Act of 1988									X		
1988	Employee Polygraph Protection Act					X	X			X	X	X
1990	Americans with Disabilities Act		X	X						X		X

Federal Employment Policy		Personnel Processes Affected										
Year Enacted	Legislation	Planning	Recruitment	Selection	Induction	Appraisal	Development	Compensation	Collective Bargaining	Justice	Continuity	Information
1991	Civil Rights Act of 1991	X	X	X		X	X	X		X	X	
1993	Family and Medical Leave Act of 1993		X	X		X		X		X	X	

Notes: Federal controls also include Presidential Orders. These are Executive Orders such as 10988 (1962), 11141 (1964), 11246 (1965), 11375 (1967), 11478 (1969), 11491 (1970), 11616 (1971), 11625 (1971), 11758 (1974), 11830 (1975), 11838 (1975), 11935 (1976), 12067 (1978), 12106 (1978), 12125 (1979), 12138 (1979), and 12250 (1980). They affect organizations that hold government contracts.

Various states and cities have enacted employment legislation (state certification laws, state fair employment practices acts, special state labor laws) that exerts a significant impact on the recruitment and related personnel processes listed in the columns to the right. In addition, school systems and unions have developed policies, procedures, and practices that, taken together, help to shape the administration of the human resources function. State, city, institutional, and union employment policies are in force that influence to a greater or lesser extent all the human resources processes here listed (unemployment compensation, tenure, leaves, antidiscrimination, age discrimination, minimum wage, working conditions, pay periods, evaluation, collective negotiations, transfer, dismissal, retirement, promotion, and resignation). For details see Commerce Clearing House, Inc., *Guide to Fair Employment Practices* (Chicago: Commerce Clearing House, Inc., latest edition).

The most controversial interpretation, and the one that continues to be constantly litigated, is that pertaining to preferential treatment. The controversial nature of the preferential treatment aspects of affirmative action may be judged from major civil rights rulings by the United States Supreme Court.

These rulings have been viewed by some observers as "judicial revisionism"; others note that "long-settled cases have no degree of finality or certainty."[4] Moreover, new law suits can be anticipated, because the court has widened the right to fight affirmative action plans.

System Affirmative Action Program. Affirmative action as it applies to the personnel function in educational institutions is considered here as those plans developed and actions taken by the system to comply with **equal employment opportunity (EEO)** regulations. Consequently, an affirmative action program includes the following components: (a) policy statements, (b) allocation of responsibility, (c) communication, (d) work-force utilization analysis, (e) goals and timetables, (f) linkage of goals to personnel processes, and (g) program control.[5]

System Employment Policy and Recruitment

Recruitment is an essential part of a comprehensive plan to develop and maintain a staff capable of contributing maximally to attaining the institution's purpose. The more today's school administrators consider the educational problems they are expected to solve, the more clearly they realize that their organizations cannot function successfully unless they are fully and competently staffed. They also recognize that an effective school staff is not a matter of luck. Indeed, they understand the close association between planning and educational returns, and they view their primary task as one of developing plans and devising means for their realization.

Effective solution of modern recruitment problems depends to a large extent on the policy posture of the board of education. Although attention has been drawn previously to the social and organizational importance of employment policy, the matter is reemphasized at this time because it is considered to be the key element in the recruitment process as modeled in Figure 3.4. Policy is the keystone of a series of designs (purposes, policies, programs, procedures, and processes) developed to facilitate implementation of human resources plans. Recruitment planning, which is a part of system planning, is future oriented and, therefore, has as its central purpose *minimization of uncertainty and organizational aimlessness.* The point of concern here is that policies can be translated into action in an orderly way only if organizational planning for recruitment precedes individual planning by those responsible for recruitment operations. Individual administrators or recruiters within the organization should not unilaterally decide answers to numerous personnel problems encountered during recruitment. If the sys-

1. Are hiring restrictions based on sex, national origin, age, or religion bona fide occupational qualifications?

2. Are prerequisites to employment valid indicators of success in the specific jobs which they are used?

3. Is there a legitimate business necessity for policies that adversely affect certain classes of employees?

4. Are questions used in the job interviews directly related to the candidate's ability to perform the job?

5. Are hiring, promotion, compensation, and job-assignment decisions based on considerations that relate to qualifications, merit, and performance rather than stereotypic assumptions?

6. Is pregnancy treated like any other temporary disability in terms of sick leave, seniority, and disability benefits?

7. Have reasonable accommodations been made to enable qualified handicapped employees to perform adequately?

8. Have reasonable accommodations been made to the religious beliefs of employees?

9. Have precautions been taken to ensure that current practices do not perpetuate the effects of past discrimination?

10. Are employment policies and internal grievance procedures well publicized to all employees?

FIGURE 3.4
Criteria for evaluating system employment practices.

Source: Martha M. McCarthy, "Discrimination in Employment," in Joseph A. Beckham and Perry A. Zirkel, Editors, Legal issues in Public School Employment (Bloomington, IN: Phi Delta Kappa, 1983), 46–47.

tem does not decide in advance what courses of action will be pursued throughout all phases of recruitment, it is doubtful that any individual member involved in recruiting can act consistently or provide ready answers to questions posed by applicants.

It goes without saying that if personnel policies are to be meaningful, they should be written. Clear-cut written statements on recruitment, for example, will indicate to applicants the intent and attitudes of the system with regard to employment. Written policies also make it possible to inform every individual and agency concerned with the recruitment process of system standards, to give the administrative staff guidelines to work with in making recruitment decisions, to provide means of standardizing certain recruitment procedures, and to minimize uncertainties in the recruitment process for those responsible for its implementation.

The nature of recruitment policies will certainly have a profound effect on *planning*. For example, if greater stress is to be placed on recruiting only personnel who can meet high standards, increases in budgets may have to be projected, different recruitment techniques may be needed, and sources for locating such personnel may be quite different from those used if qualifications for personnel are lowered. Because unit and individual plans stem from those of the organization, recruitment plans and procedures adopted by a school organization have systemwide ramifications. It is primarily for this reason that recruitment is not exclusively a personnel function. Although major responsibility for informational and operational aspects of recruitment is usually assigned to the individual in the central administration charged with performance of the human resources function, other administrators, both line and staff, frequently have important roles to play in the process. Human Resources policy is a statement of the system's intent with regard to the treatment of the people in its employ.

Figure 3.5 illustrates an employment policy and procedures for its implementation. Analysis of the content of Figure 3.5 indicates that the policy contains at least three components: (a) system intent, (b) procedures for implementing policy, and (c) authority to implement policy. Reasons for establishing and maintaining policy on personnel matters are not difficult to discern. First, there are numerous and continuing personnel decisions made in the system by a variety of administrators. Without policy guidelines for decisions and actions on personnel matters, inconsistencies that develop would generate dissatisfaction and defeat the aims of the human resources function. Moreover, consistent action is impossible unless personnel decisions are made within a policy context. Finally, policy guidelines provide for continuity of the personnel process despite the mobility of administrators and school board members. In short, policy is essential to system stability, growth, and survival.

Table 3.3 illustrates the relationship between recruitment policies and procedures in the Foxcroft school system. The example brings into focus the nature of recruitment policies, the need for procedures to implement them, and the variety of factors to be taken into account in their development. It should be apparent that the numerous recruitment-related decisions suggested in Table 3.3 must flow from policy so that consistency and common purposes are enhanced. It is also manifest from examination of the policies enumerated in Table 3.3 that recruitment policy is influenced by a host of internal and external factors, including public employment policy (referred to previously), union policy, community mores, board and administrative values, general cultural values, and economic condition of the system.

Analysis of the environmental factors that influence policy becomes a major activity of the human resources function in developing general employment as well as recruitment policy. It is also worth repeating at this point that each of the policies listed in Table 3.3 adopted by a board of edu-

---

FOXCROFT CITY SCHOOL SYSTEM

I. Employment Policy and Procedures

It is the policy of the Foxcroft City School System to recruit and maintain the highest caliber of staff possible to fill all positions in the organization structure, and will do so by:

 a. Selecting the best qualified applicant for any position vacancy, based on the *person* and *position* specifications in the *position guide* describing the position to be filled, and without reference to age, sex, race, creed, or national origin.

 b. Filling vacancies by upgrading or promoting from within the system whenever present personnel are qualified.

 c. Encouraging changes in positions whenever they are in the interest of the individual and of the school system.

II. Procedures for Implementing Employment Policy

 a. All system personnel responsible for recruiting, selecting, placing, supervising, promoting, and transferring personnel shall be governed by these requirements.

 b. Notices setting forth the employment policy of the system shall be communicated to applicants, sources of applicants, all system personnel, and included in all communications designed to attract new personnel.

 c. The system will periodically review all opportunities for transfer and promotion to make certain that all members of the system receive equal consideration at all levels.

 d. Responsibility for initiating and maintaining employment policy is delegated to the chief executive officer of the system. The Assistant Superintendent for human resources is responsible for coordinating the administration, implementation, and evaluation of employment policy and procedures.

FIGURE 3.5
Illustration of employment policy and procedures.

cation is usually accompanied by a set of procedures that give explicit directions for policy implementation. A useful tool for implementing employment policies and procedures is a system employment manual that details activities and responsibilities relating to personnel recruitment, selection, and induction. All three parts of a policy (intent, procedure, and responsibility) interact with and are interdependent on each other. Consequently, a key activity of the human resources function is to maintain an audit of personnel policies and procedures to ensure that they are not only adhered to

TABLE 3.3
Policies and procedures of the Foxcroft school system related to the recruitment process.

Policies	Procedures
Nondiscrimination (race, creed, religion, national background, age, gender, physical handicaps, previous arrests, military service, or draft status)	_____
Fairness in promotions, transfer, and separations	_____
Position posting	_____
Seniority principle	_____
Correction of staff imbalances within system	_____
Fairness in recruitment inquiries	_____
Credential requirements	_____
Skill inventories	_____
Special personnel (relatives of board members or staff, veterans, minors, part-time and temporary personnel, working spouses and parents, strikers, and rehires)	_____
Position guides (preparation and adherence to person and position requirements in position guides)	_____
Probationary employment (professional and classified personnel)	_____
Proselyting or pirating (recruitment from other systems)	_____
Outside employment (employment in a second position or job)	_____
Personnel residency (reside within district)	_____
Gifts and favors (related to recruitment of personnel)	_____
Recruitment budget (candidate travel, agency fees, staff travel, printing, advertising, and relocation)	_____
Candidate information (reference checks: [credit, security, character, prior work performance, academic records], interview, application blanks, résumé review and acknowledgment)	_____
Testing (preemployment physical, mental, etc.)	_____
Temporary employment (substitute service)	_____

throughout the system but that they are integrated with systemwide goals and objectives.

Centralized Recruitment, Decentralized Selection. As noted elsewhere, the school system's human resources plan is developed on the basis of information gathered from a variety of sources, including administrators of individual attendance units as well as central office personnel responsible for logistics, instructional personnel, and planning functions. Personnel forecasts will reveal needs that require cooperation among various segments of the system. Need for administrative personnel, for example, may be anticipated at least five years in advance of position vacancies. To provide lead time for induction of competent personnel into these positions, and to ensure their development, coordinated planning is required.

The recruitment process should be considered a centralized operation, usually under the general direction of an assistant superintendent for human resources or an equivalent administrator. During the past few years, the concept of *centralized recruitment and screening and decentralized selection* has gained acceptance as a procedure for giving unit administrators a voice in the selection of the personnel for whose direction they will be responsible. That is, the basic task of recommending recruitment policies and plans to the board of education belongs to the central administration, which includes the chief executive and his/her staff. Execution of recruitment plans and policies is delegated to the individual(s) in the central administration in charge of the human resources function. This sets in motion the recruitment operation, a feature of which is that the central office is responsible for much of the detailed work connected with locating and initially screening all candidates. Candidates who meet initial screening tests are referred to the administrator to whom the position holder reports. *The final decision to reject or accept a given applicant, then, is decentralized.*

Recruitment and System Commitment

If human resources are central to the operation of a school system, if it is true that the odds of identifying a satisfactory candidate through traditional recruitment approaches are below $50/50$, and if everything that goes on in an organization is in some way influenced by its human resources, then recruitment planning becomes absolutely essential to attract and retain individuals whose contributions will aid in moving the system from today's position to a position desired in the future. Moreover, when one considers that faulty recruitment practices result in position-person mismatches and in the likelihood of a person being employed from selection to retirement, as well as the enormous waste of time, talent, and treasure in supervising position misfits, the significance of the recruitment process is inevitable. At the minimum, overall goals, objectives, policies, procedures, and system commitment to proactive recruitment practices should be spelled out in writing, regardless of system size. Figure 3.6 has been included to stress the importance of a school system's official commitment to identifying and attracting the right people for the right positions.

Recruitment and Human Resources Information

It has been noted previously that each functioning part of a viable school system needs a purpose and a process by which an intended goal is achieved.

The Riverpark school system's way of recruiting talent to satisfy its human resources requirements is based on these guidelines:

- Using the time-frame approach suggested in Figure 2.2 to guide recruitment decisions regarding position and person requirements (number, types, location, and technology).

- Linking system policy with public employment policy.

- Defining explicitly, before recruitment, position requirements and responsibilities (performance criteria) the position holder is expected to meet.

- Establishing, before recruitment, person requirements for each position to be filled (education, knowledge, work experience, health, behavioral needs, career interests, and individual skills and knowledge the candidate should have to meet the performance criteria).

- Screening before initial interview for potential candidate pretense (resumes and telephone and reference checks).

- Avoiding legal errors and lawsuits by making recruiters aware of discriminatory pitfalls.

- Analyzing, before recruitment, previous recruitment sources and selection experiences.

- Creating a recruitment action control plan involving internal and external processing of candidates as they take various steps in applying for a position (responsibilities, work units, and recruiters).

- Getting authorization from applicants to make background checks for arrest, conviction, military experience, language barriers, disabilities, and credit.

- Making, when appropriate, a comprehensive screening check of several kinds of records for positions carrying financial responsibility (county and state criminal records, worker's compensation claims, and credit history).

- Coordinating with all work units to interconnect plans for dealing with future flow of talent entering and leaving the system.

FIGURE 3.6
Recruitment committal of the Riverpark school system.

The recruitment process, which is one of the components of the human resources function, requires increasingly a variety of detailed information. The quality of information developed for the function influences the effectiveness of the operation as well as its contribution to system improvement.

Two fundamental factors must be considered in developing recruitment information: the recruitment information base and the recruitment information user. The section that follows deals with both of these factors.

Recruitment Information Base. Several terms relating to recruitment information need to be clarified. *Data* are considered as raw, unevaluated facts or statistics that are readily quantified. *Information* is generally defined as material that has been evaluated, analyzed, and refined, especially for planning purposes. The term *database* or *bank,* frequently referred to in this discussion, is taken to mean the entire system collection of certain data elements. A database element is a component part of the data base. Recruitment data can be either programmed (computerized) or nonprogrammed.

The overall configuration of a recruitment database should be the result of an information needs analysis driven by questions such as the following:

- What recruitment objectives is the database intended to serve?
- What kinds of database elements are needed (system data, core personnel files, government compliance documents, recruitment control information, recruitment communications, user needs)?
- What kinds of data are contained in the database? What kinds of data should be generated?
- In what form is the data needed (programmed, nonprogrammed)?
- Who will be responsible for developing the database (individual, team, committee)?
- Who will be designated as users of the database?
- When will the information be needed (periodically, continuously)?
- Who will oversee management and control of the database?
- What measures will be taken to ensure database accuracy and integrity?
- Who will evaluate the recruitment data for quality, accessibility, utility, adequacy?
- What standards will be established to store, protect, and retrieve recruitment data?

The Two Sides of Recruiting. The act of attracting applicants to fill positions involves considerable communication between the organization and the individual candidate. The individual needs information about the nature of the position, the community, and the system itself and has questions about salary, benefits, working conditions, and reporting relationships. The organization needs information about the candidate regarding such matters as education, work history, family background, health, personality, and economic and social adjustment. Furthermore, the system needs to transmit information about vacancies so that it will come to the attention of prospective candidates. As can be seen from the list that follows, the informational aspect of recruitment is a two-way proposition.

Information the School System Furnishes Candidates	*Information the School System Wants About Candidates*
Position guide	Education
Community data (brochure)	Health
School system data (brochure)	Family responsibility
Physical location of position	Work history
Personnel policies and procedures	Social adjustment
	Personality

Both the candidate and the system need information about each other. For the informational requirements of both parties to be satisfied, plans should be systematized for giving and getting information to facilitate the recruitment process. More specifically, standardized forms are designed to secure information about candidates. Brochures, manuals, fact sheets, and other means of organizing information can be utilized to communicate with candidates about the position and the environment in which it is located. Administering this phase of recruitment means that the human resources director carefully plans communications so that the candidate is fully informed about the position and its relationships; at the same time, he/she takes steps to get whatever information is needed to assess the suitability of the candidate for the position.

THE RECRUITMENT PROCESS

Figure 3.7 illustrates the human resources recruitment process. As the model indicates, the source of action plans and the structure for the recruitment process *are derived from the strategic plan*. In effect, the process model is based on the assumption that decisions have been made through strategic planning as to the number of new positions needed, those not needed, skill requirements for the position openings, and internal reallocation of people and positions. The *operational plan*, which derives from the strategic plan, identifies the action or implementation decisions to be made once the demand for and supply of human resources have been reconciled in the strategic plan.

Recruitment Process Factors

Several aspects of the recruiting process should be introduced at this time. First, many recruiting difficulties are caused by situations or conditions within the school system rather than by those in the external environment. For example:

• Recruitment efforts are past or present rather than future oriented.
• Position descriptions are past and present rather than future oriented.

- Recruitment is not conceived to be a continuous process.
- System is unaware or uncaring about the critical effect employment practices have on its future status.
- Applicants are not matched with strategy requirements.
- Nepotism.
- Inattention or overattention to personnel diversity.
- Failure to deal with the changing composition of the work force.

A second consideration in the conduct of the recruitment process is system status, representation, or image characterized as:

- Small, medium, large
- Expanding, contracting, stabilizing enrollment
- Urban, suburban, rural location
- Proactive or reactive leadership

These factors enter into the manner in which the recruitment process is conceived, organized, staffed, financed, and coordinated. With these considerations in mind, the following discussion examines the process elements listed in Figure 3.7.

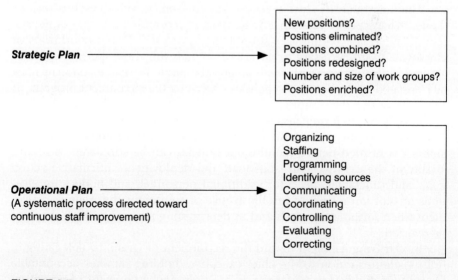

FIGURE 3.7
Model of the recruitment process.

Programming Recruitment Activities. It is generally acknowledged that when a school system attempts to provide qualified personnel in all positions, various administrators from different levels of the system are involved. After human resources plans have been prepared and essential policies developed to carry them out, considerable thought must be given to the task of *organizing* recruitment activities. Once the work of recruitment goes beyond what a single person assigned to the task can do, organization becomes necessary. Recruitment tasks are identified, assigned to different people at various levels of the organization, and coordinated. This section will be devoted to analysis of the responsibilities of key positions in the recruitment process. By examining organization of the recruitment process, the totality of the endeavor can be brought into focus.

The board of education. In matters pertaining to recruitment as well as in other educational matters, functions of the board of education involve policy development and evaluation of results. The hypothesis advanced here is that although recruitment will go on in some fashion in every school system, it will go on better and with more lasting results if the board of education's viewpoint is positive and forward looking. This is not mentioned to repeat the well-known principle that policy-making is the board's function; the broader implication is that unless the board takes the initiative to establish conditions and a climate favorable to administrative action on a sound recruitment program, the chances are good that the best of intentions and plans will subsequently be abandoned.

The board and its chief executive are confronted with questions such as these: "What types of personnel do we need to accomplish the aims of the system?" "What special abilities should they possess?" "What conditions of employment are necessary to attract personnel with these special abilities?" "Where can candidates with these abilities be located?" These concerns must be translated by the board into policies governing the recruitment program. It is important that these issues be resolved well in advance of the time the chief executive begins to formulate specific plans putting policies into operation.

Because of the magnitude and complexity of these problems, extensive analysis is needed before recruitment policies can be stipulated. Size and quality of the existing staff, staff load and deployment, affirmative action goals and timetables, need for additional personnel, and budget implications of staff improvement are illustrative of conditions that require assessment when formulating goals and in determining means by which they can be realized.

By clarifying its intent toward the recruitment program, by delegating in full its administration to the chief executive (holding him/her accountable for results), and by providing means to attain ends, the board of education will have taken major steps to define and to give direction to recruitment plans and procedures as well as to minimize the uncertainty of its intent. The board of education, by virtue of the powers vested in it, is the key agent of the system for interpreting and implementing social values of American democratic society through recruitment policy. The preeminent position that working people are accorded in the United States can be ensured in their place of work only if employers make this condition possible through their personnel policies. This is why the role of the board of education in recruitment policy is of such critical importance. General employment policy established by the board of education is designed to state system intent with respect to policies and procedures such as those listed in Table 3.3. Decision rules provided by employment policy make the task of identification and evaluation of personnel sources more systematic and conducive to ensuring adequate quantities of qualified human resources.

The chief executive.   When we turn our attention to problems involved in recruiting school personnel, we are led quickly to an appreciation of their importance. It is not difficult to realize that the investment made in every position holder is considerable, the success of the system depends on a continuous flow of qualified personnel, future educational leadership is related to present recruitment policies, potential for waste of every kind is enormous if recruitment programs are ineffective, and solutions to *today's* recruitment problems are not unchangingly valid.

It is for these and other reasons that the leadership role of the chief executive in the recruitment program is crucial. The following are representative of his/her many activities in recruitment planning:

* Provides the board with relevant data, counsel, and recommendations for shaping recruitment policies.
* Initiates studies of immediate and long-term personnel needs.
* Develops accurate and realistic staffing specifications by means of position analyses and descriptions.
* Formulates, with the help of the staff and with board approval, qualification standards of professional and noninstructional personnel.
* Focuses plans, staff, and funds on the task of locating candidates capable of meeting qualification standards.
* Explores continually various avenues for bringing the system's personnel needs to the attention of potential candidates.
* Recognizes the importance of sound budgetary procedures through which objectives of the personnel function are realized.
* Makes plans to meet the continuing need for properly qualified professional personnel.
* Cooperates with teacher education institutions by helping them to prepare personnel with the abilities the system seeks.

- Studies developments in personnel supply and demand and their impact on recruitment.
- Plans employment conditions conducive to effective recruitment.
- Employs a variety of communications media to develop understanding of recruitment program objectives.
- Initiates an information system to provide feedback on staffing needs.
- Ensures implementation of public and system employment policies.

How the superintendent of schools carries out responsibility for staffing the administrative unit for effective recruitment depends to a large extent on the administrative organization. If the system is small, this responsibility is generally administered personally by the chief executive; if it is large, it is probable that responsibility will be delegated to an agent or division in the central administrative office. Regardless of system size, a new concept of the role of the chief executive in fulfilling personnel requirements of the school system is emerging. Briefly stated, this notion views human resources administration as a strategic task. It embraces the idea that if schools of modest size and means can afford one assistant to the superintendent for logistics and another for instruction, they should also provide assistance to carry out the human resources function. The argument has force when one considers the importance of people to the operation of the enterprise.

The human resources administrator. We shall assume, for the sake of illustration, that the chief executive has assigned the human resources function, including central responsibility for recruitment, to an assistant superintendent of schools. This staff member is, then, responsible for developing an organization structure within his/her own unit in keeping with the overall system plan of organization.

Central responsibility for overall direction of the recruitment process suggests that numerous activities need to be carefully coordinated. Figure 3.8 illustrates the nature and scope of such activities. Responsibility of several tasks involved in the recruitment process will depend in part on the nature of the organization structure. Regardless of how and to whom the work is allocated, we can identify several features that characterize the organization of almost all successful recruitment efforts:

- Recruitment plans for all personnel are developed and coordinated by the central administration. This phase of the process involves adherence to the human resources plan: deciding what positions are vacant and what standards are to be employed in selecting personnel to fill them. Principals, directors, and other key administrators affected by the recruitment decisions participate in the planning.

Central planning for recruitment of both professional and support personnel.
Coordination of information and decisions on number and types of personnel to be recruited.
Evaluation of recruitment plans for discrepancies between human resources planning assumptions (such as staffing balance and affirmative action) and actual recruitment intent.
Establishment of employment standards.
Development of position guides to clarify employment standards.
Preparation of forms for giving information to prospective candidates about openings in the system and for obtaining needed information about the candidates.
Development of recruitment information system.
Preparation of recruitment activities schedule.
Preparation of recruitment budget.
Orientation of recruiters.
Management of recruitment correspondence.
Systematization of screening procedures.
Advertisement of vacancies in system.
Development of plan to check on the progress of each candidate.
Appraisal of recruitment process.

FIGURE 3.8
Nature and scope of recruitment activities in the Cloudcroft school system.

- Central recruitment planning clarifies and formalizes types of communications that will be initiated between the system and applicants. Standardized forms for getting information from and transmitting information to applicants are developed by the central administration. These include position guides, application blanks, medical forms, questionnaires, brochures, fact sheets, manuals, and related literature.
- The recruitment information system is designed to facilitate and control the candidate flow. That is, this system is completely developed prior to contacting candidates about position openings. Decisions will have been made as to the location at which incoming applications are received, recorded, and acknowledged. In addition, some arrangement is necessary to keep track of each applicant from the period of initial contact until a decision on the application is reached and records to close the case are completed. Computer technology can be utilized extensively in administering the recruitment process, including matching position requirements and applicant characteristics, selection test information, applicant background details, internal search, interview results, and applicant processing progress.

- Scheduling of both annual and day-to-day recruitment activities should also be controlled at a central location, preferably in the office of the human resources administrator. A recruitment calendar is indispensable to the task. The basis of this suggestion is that recruitment is conceived as a year-round effort, despite the fact that there will be times within the school year when recruitment will reach both high and low levels of activity. Questions that illustrate the need for organizing recruitment procedures include "Who will travel on what day to see what applicants?" and "Who will arrange for interviewing candidates who visit the system? On what day and hour?"

- A good recruitment plan will take into consideration ways of processing efficiently the usual volume of correspondence. For every inquiry from an applicant there should be a response. In addition, letters will go to potential candidates who have not applied. For every interested applicant there will be appointments, schedules, forms, records, and related activities that add to the correspondence burden. The real challenge of recruitment correspondence lies in developing ways by which it can be handled accurately and on time. Many good candidates are often lost to organizations because of correspondence problems.

- Recruitment action control (addressed again in the discussion on the processing of individual candidates) is another matter to be carefully organized. *Action control* simply means that once the school system advertises for applicants to fill positions, a scheme is devised to check on the progress of each candidate as he/she takes the various steps in applying. Applicants lose interest, fail to supply certain information and are rejected, fail to appear for interviews, or decline to accept the position when it is offered. Current information on the status of each candidate is essential to the conduct of recruitment.

- School officials recognize that budgeting is an important element in the recruitment process. If recruitment is seriously pursued, it usually calls for expenditures of one kind or another. It may involve, for example, funds for describing existing vacancies and position qualifications; visits to observe candidates in other organizations; consultant services in developing position guides; travel; entertainment; development of standardized forms and printing of brochures; payment of applicant expenses; advertising; and handling of an extensive amount of correspondence. It may well involve relatively large sums if the board of education decides to extend the search to geographic areas beyond the normal supply sources. Staff building is so important to the welfare of any organization that it calls for *systematic planning*. Because the budget is a powerful planning device of the administrative staff, it should be utilized to define recruitment plans and to translate these needs into funds necessary for their support.

It has been said many times that outstanding personnel are not necessarily seeking a change of position. They must be sought out and induced to change their place or position of employment. Clearly, the more intensive and extensive the system recruitment effort, the higher the cost and, it is to be hoped, the greater the expenditure return.

The individual recruiter. Regardless of the manner in which the recruitment effort is organized, it is likely that several persons will be assigned to the important role of making initial contacts and negotiating with applicants. The significance of the individual recruiter to the success of the operation is not always understood or appreciated. Several steps need to be taken by the system with respect to individual recruiters. These include:

- Identifying those persons who will be responsible for contacting and discussing with applicants the vacancies to be filled.
- Making every effort to ensure that the individual recruiter not only has the knowledge and judgment to discuss the position to be filled but also the interpersonal competence and verbal skills essential to the role.
- Clarifying the role of the individual recruiter. (Does the recruiter appraise the candidate's qualifications for the position? To what extent is the recruiter expected to negotiate with the candidate for the position?)
- Deciding on the role the recruiter plays following the initial contact. (Does the recruiter file a report, make an offer, or follow up?)
- Standardizing the role of the individual recruiter so that he/she will follow definite procedures, such as the kinds of information to give to each candidate about the organization and at what point to begin selection activities. (A manual for recruiters can improve the effectiveness of the individual recruiter.)

To sum up, every school system needs to give careful consideration to the selection and special orientation of individual recruiters who make personal contacts with applicants. Moreover, steps should be taken by the organization to structure the role of this agent to the extent that the recruiter is fully aware of what he/she is expected to do, how he/she is expected to perform the role, and the relationships to be maintained in carrying out the various tasks.

In this section, examination of recruitment activities has indicated the diversity of contributions that can be made by the recruitment process to the function. We shall now turn from a discussion of the roles of individuals in the recruitment effort to the development of sources from which prospective personnel may be obtained.

Developing Applicant Sources

We have just examined the manner in which a school system organizes the work that comprises the recruitment process. Specific tasks are to be performed, and there are individuals in the system to whom responsibility for performing the tasks will be delegated to get speedier and more efficient action. The next related step in the sequence of recruitment activities is to identify all known sources from which needed personnel can be found and to divide them into two categories: internal and external.

Internal Personnel Sources. A major objective of personnel recruitment is improved staff quality. Its attainment involves several kinds of analyses of existing staff resources prior to recruitment. The purpose of these analyses is to discuss imbalances in the makeup of the total staff, current potential for filling openings, and number and types of openings available on short- and long-term bases. For example, staff shortages may exist in certain areas, such as the number of out-of-district or out-of-state personnel and the number of ethnically, culturally, and philosophically diverse personnel. There is need for wholesome variation in traits, skills, qualities, points of view, and backgrounds among staff members. The recruitment process should be aimed also at providing balance in the numbers and kinds of staff generalists, specialists, and administrators. This will involve a continuous survey of personnel requirements to assure adequacy and diversity of human resources in the staff as a whole as well as in each operating unit of the system. In brief, the human resources plan and the staff development plan to support it will provide clues to personnel potential within the organization with which to fill some of the position openings.

Intrasystem transfers and promotions. Although it is generally conceded that the system will need to recruit some of its personnel from outside sources (especially for vacancies at the lower level of the structure), it is also considered sound policy to promote and transfer current staff members. It should be clearly understood that there are certain types of positions from which there is not advancement and that there are certain individuals who are satisfied to remain indefinitely in the same position. But the general policy of promotion from within to better and more attractive positions is to be encouraged. Recruiting from the outside should be undertaken when existing personnel cannot meet the necessary requirements.

Personnel transfer may be used effectively under certain circumstances to fill openings in the system. When carried out in accordance with union contracts, transfers can be used to reward personnel who want to change but are not promotable to higher position classifications. Transfer policies should consider the following:

- Balanced representation in work units.
- Opportunities for employees to work at their highest skill level.
- Maximal utilization of all staff skills for the completion of educational goals.
- Fulfilling developing interests of employees.
- Facilitating transfers from teaching to administration.
- Facilitating transfers to positions in more compatible community settings.
- Enabling employees to join more compatible work groups.
- Accommodating personnel to compensate for illness, physical impairment, or diminished physical resources.[6]

The manner in which positions are filled from the inside depends on personnel procedures in the school system. Two methods are generally in operation: selection by the system and position posting. Under the first method, personnel within the system capable of advancing to better positions are identified through the organization's appraisal system. In this approach, information systems are designed to store information, including biographical, skills, and performance data. These can be retrieved instantly when candidates for transfer or promotion are considered. In some instances, personnel will have been singled out and provided with career development experiences before vacancies develop. The internal search, utilizing the information system, should also focus on details relating to the self-behavior maintenance of potential organizational candidates. These data are examined to determine willingness of staff members to accept assignments, tasks, relearning, colleagues, and problems. Also, these data should include such behavioral characteristics as:

- Resistance to modification of teaching goals, materials, and methods.
- Reluctance to be transferred to another working group within the organization.
- Inability to cooperate with other organizations performing the same or similar services.
- Unwillingness to participate in reeducation activities designed to develop new and different skills.
- Rejection of new activities or new tasks.
- Denial of existence of pressing problems.
- Early retirement or resignation following reassignments of duties or work location.[7]

Position posting means that certain types of vacancies are advertised throughout the system, including the position guides that govern the selection process. This approach encourages personnel within the system to take advantage of the opportunity to obtain a better position. Union contracts, especially those relating to support personnel, sometimes contain clauses requiring that the opening be filled on the basis of seniority. One disadvantage of this questionable approach is that qualified personnel are frequently passed over in favor of mediocre staff members with seniority.

Adherence to affirmative action goals (short term, interim, and long term) in the recruitment process, involves consideration of upward mobility procedures. This includes a review of present employment patterns of minority and women personnel, especially for the existence of underutilization. Position progression, transfers, and seniority provisions are elements of the affirmative action plan that enter into the internal search for candidates to fill system openings.

External Personnel Sources.   External personnel sources available to the system are numerous and varied. The extent to which these sources can be cultivated to locate potential recruits depends to a considerable degree on recruitment policy and plans. If the recruitment effort is to succeed, it must produce a pool of applicants well in excess of the number of openings; otherwise, a selection process exists in name only. This implies that a variety of personnel sources should be constantly maintained. Major external sources of supply are illustrated in Table 3.4, some of which pertain to professional personnel and others to support personnel.

Developing Personnel Sources.   If the system is to attract a pool of qualified candidates from the several personnel sources listed, details of developing each source must be worked out. Schools with large numbers of vacancies will utilize different sources and employ techniques different from those preferred by small systems. Those people charged with operating the recruitment program need to anticipate which sources will yield the greatest number of qualified applicants, how much time and money should be invested, and what methods should be employed to induce competent individuals to work in the system. Several of the personnel sources already mentioned will be analyzed in this section to illustrate the nature of decisions to be made and methods to be employed in their development. Every recruitment transaction has a price tag that may exceed the cost some communities are willing or able to afford in time, money, and people. Before any decisions are made about which sources should be used, each needs to be examined in terms of past productivity, cost, speed of return, and present prospects for yielding types of applicants envisioned in the position guides.

Campus and field recruiting.   School systems have occasion to send representatives to college campuses to contact professional personnel, such

TABLE 3.4
Sources for recruiting prospective external candidates for system positions.

	Professional Teaching Positions	Professional Administrative Positions	Support Positions	Professional Technical Positions[a]
Societies, associations	X	X	X	X
Placement bureaus	X	X	X	X
Placement services	X	X	X	X
Unions	X		X	
Walk-ins			X	
Write-ins			X	
Consulting firms		X		X
Advertising	X	X	X	X
Résumés on file	X	X	X	X
Government agencies			X	
Referrals	X	X	X	X
High schools			X	
Vocational schools			X	
Professional technical schools			X	X
Conventions, meetings	X	X	X	X
Phone-in arrangements	X		X	
Solicitation by mail or telephone	X	X		X
Direct solicitation	X	X	X	X
Campus and field recruiting	X			
Minority and women's career centers	X	X	X	X
Temporary-help organizations	X		X	X
Special organizations (women, minorities)	X	X	X	X
Military services	X		X	X

Note: [a]Includes legal, engineering, medical, dental, psychiatric, and security personnel for temporary, part-time, or permanent employment.

as classroom teachers, instructional specialists, and administrators. This effort requires careful planning if it is to be successful. Generally speaking, more recruitment time is essential to develop this source, including candidate contacts and interviews, than almost any on the list.

Field recruiting may be undertaken periodically by the system in need of large numbers of applicants. The gist of this approach is to establish a team of recruiters in a central headquarters, usually in a major urban area where a reservoir of professional personnel exists. Advertising in newspapers or on radio or television programs is initiated before the field trip so that applicants will know of the approaching interviews. The decision to utilize field interviews or other intensive procedures to recruit professional personnel will depend on a number of factors, including cost, availability of applicants, and effectiveness of yield.

Recruitment advertising and literature. Use of advertising to recruit school personnel is generally considered to be an approach with considerable merit, especially with regard to support personnel. But it is fairly evident that extensive advertising can be expensive, and a number of decisions related to its use often require expert counsel. Questions as to the media in which to advertise and frequency of advertising emphasize the point that planning is important. Modern advertising techniques have gone well beyond the help-wanted ad, and the variety of media available for recruitment should not be overlooked. Newspapers, brochures, radio and television, technical journals, and direct-mail advertising can be used with effectiveness to communicate employment needs to wide audiences or selected groups quickly and relatively economically.

Placement and employment agencies. Public, private, and institutional employment agencies are important resources for locating personnel to fill various kinds of openings. If the human resources administrator is to make effective use of the services of employment and placement agencies, it is essential that he/she become familiar with the nature of services rendered by each organization. There are public and private employment agencies that have developed nationwide arrangements to assist in satisfying needs of their clients. In obtaining support personnel—including those in food services, transportation, maintenance, operation, security, and clerical work and those on the secretarial staff—public and private agencies can be helpful. Private agencies are increasingly concerned with employment for professional and technical personnel. It is worth noting, too, that the system can facilitate cooperation with employment agencies through careful preparation of position guides that contain complete information concerning duties, responsibilities, qualifications, and relationships of each position opening so that preliminary screening can be undertaken effectively. Obviously, agencies in possession of such position guides are capable of providing assistance to both the candidate and the system. Candidates can quickly determine whether they have the general qualifications needed and whether the position is of interest to them. The system benefits both from initial screening and from responses usually generated through employment agencies.

Employment of the disadvantaged. For reasons that have deep and enduring cultural roots, there are special groups of people in every society who bear or suffer from some social stigma to the extent that they are at a disadvantage in competing for various types of employment. A profile of special groups with **employment disadvantages** is shown in Figure 3.9. Employment and assimilation of minority or special groups in the field of education create human problems both for the system and for the individual processing one or more special group characteristics (i.e., race, religion, color, age, ancestry, physical handicaps, and gender). Both employment and assimilation factors need special organizational consideration.

In addition to the typical processes applicable to all personnel, there are complex problems involved in employing people from special groups. These problems include ways of increasing employment opportunities of these groups; improving their skills, attitudes, and abilities through continuing education and development; providing upward mobility into positions of status and responsibility; and integrating interests of the individual with the organization and the work of other groups within the system to which they relate. Balancing recruitment efforts so as not to treat any segment of the population unjustly and using criteria for selection, promotion, and separation that do not violate the civil rights of individuals are also complex personnel matters constantly confronting school officials. Moreover, the educational institution as employer has moral, legal, and social responsibilities to be considered in employing members of special groups (included in Figure 3.9), in assimilating them into other groups, and in integrating them into the total system.

The social ideals of the United States embrace equitable treatment of all human beings. Title VII of the Civil Rights Act of 1964 is designed to assure all Americans that employability is not based on race, color, religion, gender, or national origin, but rather on ability and qualifications.[8] Beyond the moral, social, legal, and ethical considerations of employment, discrimination impairs the quality of the human resources planning process because it diminishes the pool of talent from which personnel can be recruited.

Resolution of various sensitive issues involved in the employment of special groups will require more than the unsystematic and crisis-oriented approaches to which many organizations have resorted since the passage of the Civil Rights Act in 1964. What is needed is a human resources planning approach to staffing, such as the one described in Chapter 2. Human

Minority groups: Blacks, American Indians, Japanese, Chinese, Filipinos,
Koreans, Polynesians, Indonesians, Hawaiians, Aleuts, Eskimos, Mexican
Americans, Puerto Ricans, other people with Spanish surnames.
Women
Social-stigma groups: ex-criminals, homosexuals, alcoholics, licentious or
dissolute persons
School dropouts: nongraduates of high school
Under 22 years of age (youth)
45 years of age or older
Handicapped (physical, mental, or emotional)
Unskilled, unemployed, underemployed, undereducated, or underprivileged

FIGURE 3.9
Profile of special groups with employment disadvantages.

resources planning, it will be recalled, focuses on *differential* approaches to
recruitment, selection, placement, development, and utilization of personnel. Further, it is increasingly viewed as linking various personnel processes
into a coherent system whereby position incumbents and potential position
holders can perform effectively; but they are also readied by the system to
assume increasingly greater position responsibilities. Suggestions for relating human resources planning to employment of special groups include:

- *Employment policy*—The wide variety of professional and service positions
  in a school system calls for adoption and adherence to employment policies consistent with the spirit and letter of federal, state, and local
  antidiscrimination laws.

- *Human resources planning*—Projection of the future organization structure
  and staffing needs essential to system viability and effectiveness, as outlined in Chapter 2, will bring into focus both position openings within
  the system as well as recruitment needs from external sources. It is
  through this long-range approach that promotability of individuals from
  special groups can be planned and that the personnel pool from which
  individuals will be recruited can be identified and assessed.

- *Recruitment process*—An effective human resources plan will direct efforts to
  recruit professional and classified personnel in special groups from sources
  in both the public and private sectors that heretofore have been ignored.

- *Selection process*—The selection process (to be examined in detail in Chapter
  4) is planned so that the potential of individuals from special groups can be
  linked to positions and plans for development needs, enabling them to perform effectively therein. One of the functions of the selection process is to

screen out those who are not likely to succeed in the system; but it is also incumbent on that function to search for, identify, and employ personnel from various sources with potential for career development in the system.

• *Development process*—The day has not yet arrived when the majority of school systems in the nation view development of *all* personnel as both a fundamental obligation and an economical approach to more effective staffing. This is especially true of employees who often differ from the norm in motivation, needs, ability, education, and potential. One could argue that development programs need to pay more attention to individuality, meeting individual needs to achieve position effectiveness, and providing feedback mechanisms to and from personnel who need special assistance.

Thus, employment of the disadvantaged is now a matter of social policy, and it behooves all educational institutions to develop longer-range, more systematic plans for its implementation. Although the issues involved in employing the disadvantaged are complex and sensitive, their resolution depends on both system commitment to social ideals and to linking the personnel processes into a coherent design that accepts and is geared to dealing with the challenge of improving opportunities for them.

Coordinating the Applicant Search

Attracting the best applicants available to fill vacancies in the system is a major concern of the function. The recruitment activity moves from the planning stages into goal realization when the individual responsible for recruiting receives authorization to proceed with activities involved in the process. Such authorization entails permission to spend budgeted recruitment funds and to add personnel to the payroll. The authorization also legitimizes the beginning of the applicant search and necessitates what has been referred to earlier as *recruitment action control*. *Action control* refers to activities involved in monitoring the progress of each candidate as he/she takes various steps in applying for a position.

The sections following are concerned with a critical step in the recruiting process: processing the individual who may be a drop-in, write-in, refer-in, invite-in, or go-to-prospect. It is apparent that processing should be systematized prior to the announcement of vacancies. For our purposes, we may categorize the processing system as consisting of both internal and external activities.

Internal Processing. At some point in the recruitment process, there is initial contact between the candidate and the system. The prospective applicant may "drop in" to the central office, make an unsolicited application by letter, be referred by an interested party or agency, or be contacted by a recruiter in the field. Administrative arrangements are established to accommodate these and other recruitment eventualities.

Central office. The nerve center of recruitment activities is a designated office in the central administration with responsibility for processing individual applicants for positions in the system. It is to this office that all solicited and unsolicited applications are referred. The receptionist in this office greets individual candidates and puts them at ease, provides them with information concerning the application process, sees that candidates are interviewed on schedule, and makes sure they complete whatever steps are involved in the total selection process. Another function of the receptionist is to discourage unsolicited applicants who are clearly unqualified. This saves time for those personnel actually conducting the selection process.

The central office staff also handles recruitment correspondence, arranges interview schedules in advance, makes hotel reservations when necessary, completes expense vouchers, schedules luncheons, and arranges visits. Additionally, this staff maintains a central recruitment file so that information about each applicant can be directed to proper locations as the candidate progresses from one phase of recruitment to another.

External Processing. When the recruiter goes into the field, either to contact a known candidate or to locate qualified candidates and encourage them to apply for current vacancies, the plan of action should be determined in advance. The field prospect is given essential information about the vacancy and told of the steps involved in applying. Generally, the individual recruiter is supplied with a kit containing application blanks, brochures, and complete instructions for individuals filing applications. Preliminary interviews are conducted by the recruiter, and on occasion, hiring decisions are made on the spot. In this case, hiring decisions are guided by standards formulated in the central administration. If further interviews are necessary, visits to the system are arranged by the recruiter. The plan described, or one similar to it, may be used to deal with individuals who take the initiative in applying for position openings.

The aim of the recruitment process is to locate qualified individuals and to arrange a contractual agreement between them and the organization. Whether or not this agreement is reached depends to a considerable extent on the manner in which the prospective candidate is treated between the point of initial contact and the completion of the selection process. Careful planning of recruitment procedures can contribute considerably to a favorable image of the organization. If plans are designed to minimize anxieties that usually attend application for employment, to move the candidate as quickly as possible through the procedure, and to develop a feeling of security about the system as a place to work, the chances are good that the time, effort, and money invested will yield anticipated returns.

Recruitment Control and Effectiveness

Two dimensions of recruitment are essential concerns of the human resources function. The first is **recruitment control,** which involves taking stock of how well the school system's recruitment plans are being achieved as well as developing courses of action to correct whatever deficiencies have been identified. The second dimension is **recruitment effectiveness,** which also involves checking recruitment performance against standards, and is the link between strategic aims and the recruitment process. Recruitment control is directed primarily toward an internal analysis of the recruitment process; recruitment effectiveness is directed toward the contribution of the process to the strategic aims of the system for its human resources. Both dimensions are reviewed simultaneously to ascertain progress toward personnel objectives.

If there is any validity to the contention that each component of an organization should be appraised in terms of its operational effectiveness and its contribution to the larger aims of the enterprise, it follows that the recruitment process should be examined continuously. Questions such as the following need to be posed to determine whether recruitment operations are realizing expectations the system holds for them:

- What outcomes are we trying to achieve through the recruitment process?
- To what extent have our recruitment efforts succeeded?
- What is the efficiency of our recruitment sources?
- What is the quality of the recruits we have employed?
- To what extent have recent recruits been promoted? Terminated? Remained after the tenure period?

The foregoing questions give some idea about how the system can set standards for the recruitment of personnel. Wise administration will insist on analyzing the following characteristics of the recruitment program in terms of standards and results.

Careful accounting of recruitment expenditures is essential not only to prepare the budget but also to provide administration with information as to whether or not expenditures are yielding results. In addition to recruitment expenditures allocated to personnel (professional and secretarial), there are operational expenditures: advertising, communications (correspondence, telephone, and faxing), travel and living expenses, medical fees (physical examinations), printing supplies, and equipment. After total recruitment costs have been calculated, unit costs, such as cost per applicant employed, cost per applicant by source, cost by recruiter, cost per contact, and cost per professional versus cost of support employee hired are some of the indicators that may be analyzed to get a clear view of the cost of recruitment.

Some *sources of personnel* are more productive than others. The system is interested in knowing what personnel sources yield the best quality and at what cost. It is quite understandable, for example, that sources of the most satisfactory professionals might not be the nearest teacher education institution. It is also conceivable that advertising might provide more or better contact with secretarial personnel than would an employment agency. The school system is interested also in knowing the cost of utilizing alternative sources of prospective personnel. Presumably, there is a unit cost for each initial contact beyond which investment is not prudent.

In addition to the kinds of unit recruitment costs mentioned, other measures are useful in examining the effectiveness of various recruitment activities. The *ratio of applicants* (both professional and support) *to position offers, ratio of offers to acceptance, reasons for rejections, ratio of applicants to actual interviews,* and *opinions of applicants on the recruitment process* all provide school officials with facts and observations concerning the recruitment operation.

Because the *amount of time that elapses between the applicant's initial contact and the final interview* can be a critical matter to both the candidate and the system, administrators should be interested in narrowing this time span as much as possible. Analysis of records relating to the actual time lapse and its impact on candidate acceptance of a position offer can help to resolve difficulties that often lead to attrition in the number of available candidates.

Results achieved by individual recruiters also bear examination. Cost per recruiter per hire and the number of applicants or interviews per individual recruiter are statistics worth keeping, especially if they reveal highly ineffective performances on the part of certain individuals assigned to this task.

The aim of recruitment controls is to make certain that results of the operation are in keeping with established goals. If this state of affairs is to be realized, collection, analysis, feedback, and utilization of relevant recruitment information are essential.

Table 3.5 has been included to signify the importance of the linkage among the organization, personnel, and recruitment strategies. Evaluation of strategy-recruitment outcomes is useful to (a) extend information about and understanding of issues, problems, obstacles, and opportunities in human resources planning; (b) assess strengths and weaknesses of the existing strategy; (c) identify new conditions in the internal and external environments and their potential impact on the human resources function; and (d) consider the interrelatedness of strategy, recruitment, work to be done, skilled personnel to do the work, environments, and fiscal resources.

REVIEW AND PREVIEW

The theme of this chapter has been that an extensive and aggressive program of recruitment directed toward placing and keeping qualified individuals in every position in the system is essential to organization effectiveness.

TABLE 3.5
Linking human resources strategy to the recruitment process.

Illustrative Linkage Information	Present Condition (Where We Are)	Future Condition (Where We Want to Be)
School system strategy for its human resources		
Recruitment strategy		
Types of positions		
Teaching		
Administrative		
Specialist		
Support		
Number of positions		
Staff recruitment status		
Internal applicants		
External applicants		
Relevant external environmental trends		
Relevant internal environmental trends		
Recruitment budget		

Cyclic activities of the recruitment process include developing recruitment policies and procedures, allocating recruitment activities to individual positions, adopting means to locate and persuade individuals to apply for position vacancies, systematizing internal and external contacts with applicants, and appraising the results of recruitment activities.

Activities in the recruitment process are guided by and coordinated with previously established human resources strategy, personnel development, and selection plans. The human resources plan determines the number of positions to be filled throughout the planning period; the development plan indicates the potential of current personnel to fill certain vacancies; and the selection process focuses on eliminating applicants who do not meet position requirements.

Recruitment is viewed as a centralized operation, usually under the general direction of an assistant superintendent for personnel or an equivalent administrator. To coordinate recruitment planning and operations effectively, consideration should be given to centralizing recruitment and screening and decentralizing selection. When decentralized plans are put into action, however, all phases of recruitment and selection must be tied together by consistent executive action. Chapter 4 examines the process by which the organization differentiates among applicants and selects those most likely to be successful.

REVIEW AND DISCUSSION QUESTIONS

1. Identify and describe briefly the internal and/or external circumstances that will expand or contract the future demand for human resources in a school system of your experience.

2. How should school officials go about determining duties and responsibilities of *every* position on the payroll? Skills needed by *every* person on the payroll?

3. Define the term *demographic trends*. What is the relationship between demographic trends and strategic planning?

4. As a school principal you have been notified of the retirement of one math teacher and one language arts teacher. You are requested to furnish a document to the recruitment committee detailing the position and person specifications that should be considered. Indicate your plan of action including such details as the information for bridging the gap between the positions and the objectives of the school for which you are responsible.

5. What are the relative advantages and disadvantages of internal and external recruiting approaches?

6. Describe how recruitment policy is made in one organization of your knowledge or experience (school system, city council, county government, state government, local housing authority).

7. Which of the following subjects should you pose or refrain from posing in the recruitment search: age, previous experience, sex, race, references, religion, family, marital status, pregnancy, work experience, handicap, military background, arrests, association membership, credit status? Why are some of these items a matter of regulatory concern?

8. If you were directed to check the performance level of a superintendent of schools in another system, which of the following would you choose to interview: newspaper editors, school directors, union leaders, church officials, chamber of commerce president, PTA president, social groups concerned with school affairs? Defend your selection.

9. Develop a one-page response to each of the following statements:

    a. The problem with traditional recruitment and selection methods is that they are past or present oriented.

    b. Recruitment from within is touted as a means to improve morale and develop internal talent. It also tends to strengthen the status quo.

    c. The use of past-oriented job descriptions is even more insidious than the inbreeding and resistance to change that may result from promotion-from-within policies.

10. Describe in a paragraph the relationship between human resources strategy and recruitment.

11. What is the function of legal counsel with regard to recruitment?

12. Should school districts have an affirmative action program whether or not they are government contractors or subcontractors? Whether or not they are large or small employers?

13. Give five examples of traditional recruitment practices that have

been challenged by the courts (e.g., the application form).

14. You are a human resources director. Make a list of actions that you are prohibited from taking when recruiting new staff members.

15. Make a list of effectiveness criteria that should be applied in evaluating the recruitment program.

16. Different studies have produced different results regarding the efficiency of recruitment sources. What steps should a human resources director take in deciding which recruitment sources are most dependable for the school system in which he/she is employed?

17. One facet of contemporary life in the United States is the emergence of powerful forces who seek to influence public policy, especially public education policy. These self-interest groups include people who are black and white, rich and impoverished, native born and alien, old and young, and conservative and liberal. Following are two examples of these forces in the school system's external environment and their intent to influence school personnel decisions have come into prominence through newspaper headlines. (Pair up class members to review and report discussion outcomes relative to the example questions.)

> Example A—Four candidates for the superintendency in an urban school system (in which there were 58 different language groups) appeared before a community forum sponsored by the NAACP. The NAACP, it was reported, "intend[ed] to tell the Board the qualities the new superintendent should have. We would like to influence the char-

acteristics of the person." (Miami Herald, March 4, 1990, 1B.)

Example B—A public demonstration occurred in Selma, Alabama, on the grounds that the white-dominated school board refused to extend the contract of Selma's first black superintendent of schools (Miami Herald, March 5, 1990, 5A.)

Example A questions—(Review the employment criteria cited in Figure 3.4.) Would these criteria be useful in setting forth Board policy regarding recruitment and selection of candidates? How should the Board go about informing the community about employment policy? Would you advise the Board to consider the option of inviting any and all special interest groups, including the teachers' union; political parties; and racial, national, tribal, linguistic, cultural origin, or background groups to sponsor community forums to assess candidate qualities and to provide selection input? Should the Board set forth employment policies and procedures before initiation of the recruitment process?

Example B questions—What criteria should be employed to ascertain whether a school personnel decision is ethnically motivated? Of the 11 personnel processes contained in this text, which would be most likely to yield sources of information to deal with charges that personnel decisions are ethnically motivated? Is it possible for a Board to establish a framework for dealing with contentions that the system's personnel decisions are ethnically motivated (see Figure 3.5.)?

CHAPTER EXERCISE 3.1

Directions: You have been designated as superintendent of schools of the Malaga school district. What questions or concerns would be appropriate for you to raise about the human resources forecast (see Table 3.6) for the strategic plan regarding:

- The internal and external forces that have been taken into consideration in developing the forecast?
- The sources, quantity, and quality of the data from which the forecast was derived?
- The correlation between position openings and enrollments?
- The extent to which staff balance entered into forecast considerations?
- The extent to which changes have been made in designing future positions?
- The link between future position openings and system strategic aims?
- The extent to which the forecast is truly future oriented?
- The number of school attendance units (schools) needed in the future?
- Capabilities of the present staff and future staff requirements?

NOTES

1. Vida G. Scarpello and James Ledvinka, Personnel: Human Resource Management (Boston: PWS-Kent Publishing Company, 1988), 271.

2. Martha M. McCarthy, "Discrimination in Employment," in Joseph A. Beckham and Perry A. Zirkel, Editors, Legal Issues in Public School Employment (Bloomington, IN: Phi Delta Kappa, 1983), 21–22.

3. Scarpello and Ledvinka, 147–48.

4. The Philadelphia Inquirer, June 18, 1989. 5C.

5. The Philadelphia Inquirer, June 13, 1989, 6A. For the reader seeking

TABLE 3.6
Malaga school district human resources forecast 199X–199X.

Submitted by _____		Compiled by _____			Date _____	
Position Code No.	**Position Sector**	**Anticipated Annual Openings in Strategic Plan**				
		Total	**Year 1**	**Year 2**	**Year 3**	**Year 4**	**Year 5**
100	Instruction	15	3	4	3	2	3
200	Administration	6	0	2	2	1	1
300	Supervision	5	0	1	3	0	1
400	Specialists	8	2	0	3	0	3
500	Support	13	6	4	1	1	1
600	Temporary	20	5	4	3	6	2
		67	16	15	15	10	11

more extensive treatment of affirmative action, see William R. Tracey, Human Resources Management and Development Handbook (New York: American Management Association, 1985), 570–574; Henry R. Perritt, Jr., Your Rights in the Workplace (New York: Practicing Law Institute, 1993), 93–110.

6. Claude W. Fawcett, School Personnel Systems (Lexington, MA: Lexington Books, 1979), 49–50.

7. Fawcett, 22.

8. Selection on the basis of skill, ability, and attitude is considered to be a legally accepted procedure.

SUPPLEMENTARY READING

Arthur, Diane. Recruiting, Interviewing, Selecting, and Orienting New Employees. New York: American Management Association, 1986.

Bradley, J. "How to Interview for Information." Training 20, 4 (1983), 59–62.

Camden, Carl; and Bill Wallace. "Job Application Forms: A Hazardous Employment Practice." Personnel Administrator (March, 1983), 31.

Candoli, I. E.; W. G. Hack; and J. R. Ray. School Business Administration. Boston: Allyn and Bacon, 1992.

Foulkes, F. "Organizing and Staffing the Personnel Function." In F. Foulkes, Editor, Strategic Human Resources Management: A Guide for Effective Practice. Englewood Cliffs, NJ: Prentice-Hall Inc., 1986.

Fraser, Jill Andresky. "The Making of a Work Force." Business Month (September 1989), 58–62.

Glinow, Mary Ann Von. "Reward Strategies for Attracting, Evaluating, and Retaining Professionals." Human Resource Management 24, 2 (1985), 191–206.

Hallett, J. "Computers and the HR Professional." Personnel Administrator 31, 7 (1986), 16–20.

Johns, Horace E.; and H. Ronald Moser. "Where has EEO Taken Personnel Policies?" Personnel (September 1989), 63–66.

Powell, Gary N. "Effects of Job Attributes and Recruiting Practices on Applicant Decisions: A Comparison." Personnel Psychology 37 (1984), 721–732.

U.S. Equal Employment Opportunity Commission. Affirmative Action and Equal Employment: A Guidebook for Employees. Vols. 1, 2. Washington, DC: The Commission, 1974.

Wagner, I. D.; and S. M. Sniderman. Budgeting School Dollars. Washington, DC: National School Boards Association, 1984.

Wanous, J. Organizational Entry: Recruiting, Selecting, and Socializing of Newcomers. Reading, MA: Addison-Wesley, 1989.

Zippo, M.; and K. Greenberg. "Reference Checks: Myth and Facts." Personnel 59, 6 (1982), 52–53.

Chapter 4

Selection

CHAPTER OVERVIEW

- Selection: Nature, Scope, and Challenges
- Selection Problem Areas
- The Selection Process

  Preselection

  Selection

  Postselection

CHAPTER OBJECTIVES

- Develop an overview of the nature, scope, and significance of the selection process.
- Stress the importance of acquiring knowledge, techniques, and tools that comprise selection technology.
- Present a model to facilitate the design, implementation, and evaluation of the selection process.
- Identify major influences involved in managing the selection process.
- Acquire a feel for major problems inherent in efforts to locate, employ, develop, and retain personnel capable of contributing to individual, unit, and organizational effectiveness.

CHAPTER TERMS

Adverse impact	Position analysis
Consistency	Position guide
Construct validity	Position requirements
Content validity	Reliability
Criterion	Selection process
Criterion-related validity	Selection technology
Interview	Validity

As the process of securing competent personnel moves from recruitment to the selection phase, a number of formidable problems confront the human resources administration:

- Establishing role requirements.
- Determining kinds of data needed to select competent individuals from the pool of applicants.
- Deciding what devices and procedures are to be employed in gathering the data.
- Securing staff participation in appraising the data and applicants.
- Relating qualifications of applicants to position specifications.
- Screening qualified from unqualified applicants.
- Preparing an eligibility list and selecting suitable candidates for appointment by the board of education.

In brief, one important facet of the human resources function includes designing, initiating, and executing an effective **selection process**.

The intent of this chapter is to examine the purpose, significance, and conceptual foundations of the selection process and to identify situational factors that frequently arise as selection methodology is applied. The chapter begins by describing the nature, scope, and significance of human resources selection, after which selection technology (the steps involved in the selection process) and selection problem areas are explored. The remaining sections of the chapter are devoted to a model for designing and implementing the selection process. Each of the elements in the process model is examined in terms of making the selection process contribute effectively to selection strategies.

SELECTION: NATURE, SCOPE, AND CHALLENGES

By definition selection is a decision-making process in which one individual is chosen over another to fill a position on the basis of how well characteristics of the individual match the requirements of the position.

The primary aim of selection is to fill existing vacancies with personnel who meet established qualifications, appear likely to succeed on the job, will find sufficient position satisfaction to remain in the system, will be effective contributors to unit system goals, and will be sufficiently motivated to achieve a high level of self-development. When the selection process is properly planned, additional benefits are derived. The system is able to exercise an important responsibility on behalf of the community and the profession: elimination of candidates unlikely to succeed. Proper selection helps also to minimize dissipation of time, effort, and funds that must be invested in developing a school staff. Moreover, a rational and uniform basis is provided for personnel selection, which, when consistently applied, provides the applicant, the community, and the school staff with assurance that competency is the key factor determining acceptance or rejection. Thus, the board of education is provided with an instrument of control to maintain and to improve staff quality; and the chief executive, who is ultimately responsible for selection of all personnel, is given a basis for justifying the selections.

Before considering various steps in the selection process, the reader is cautioned against presuming that provision of a model for human resources selection in and of itself will achieve selection strategies. Awareness of certain factors in the internal and external environments and their effects on the selection process is essential so that the school system may be prepared to respond as necessary. In addition to being aware of environmental elements, school officials can help improve selection outcomes by understanding **selection technology** (the knowledge, tools, and practices involved in selection); its complexity, strengths, and limitations; and its impact on other organizational factors.

Figure 4.1 provides a perspective of the interaction of situational factors on the selection process. Among the observations that can be made from analysis of the content of Figure 4.1, the following are noteworthy:

- Virtually every element in human resources selection technology is subject to regulatory controls. Federal, state, and municipal legislation; court decisions; and administrative rulings complicate the choice and application of selection tools, as well as the establishment of employment criteria. The most far-reaching antidiscrimination statute is the Civil Rights Act of 1964 (commonly referred to as Title VII). This and other antidiscrimination laws require objectivity in the selection process. Selection

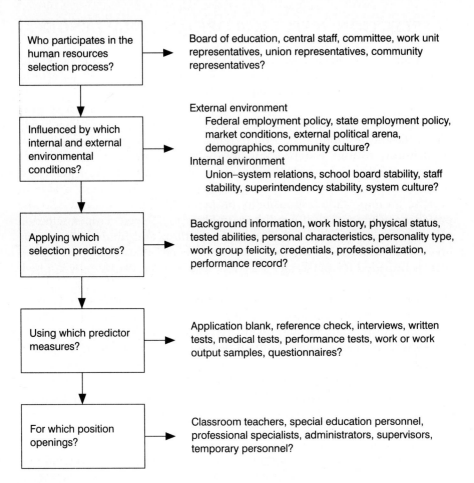

FIGURE 4.1
Illustration of the range of human resources selection factors.

inquiries must have a job-related purpose, and selection information must not be for a discriminatory aim.

- Human resources selection is a process involving measurement and prediction. Despite the strides that have been made in developing selection technology, selection tools such as those identified in Figure 4.2 are still too imprecise to predict with unerring certainty which position candidates are *investment grade, good quality, speculative, or high risk.*

- The impact of public policy on the selection process has not only created greater compliance efforts; greater attention is now being given to the entire selection process. The threat of administrative or court action, the high cost of litigation, and the tarnishing of the organizational image has brought about a host of changes in approaches to human resources selection.

- Forces in the external environment, selection technology, and human resources strategy all affect the manner in which the selection process should be designed for maximum effectiveness.
- The lessons learned in past decades about human resources selection go beyond regulatory compliance. Despite the costs, efforts, time, and probability of error, an effective selection structure (based in part on interpreting and reconciling the multiple influences shown in Figure 4.2) is an organizational imperative.

Despite the fact that few school systems are aware of, have designed, or fully use the selection process potential for improving organizational pro-

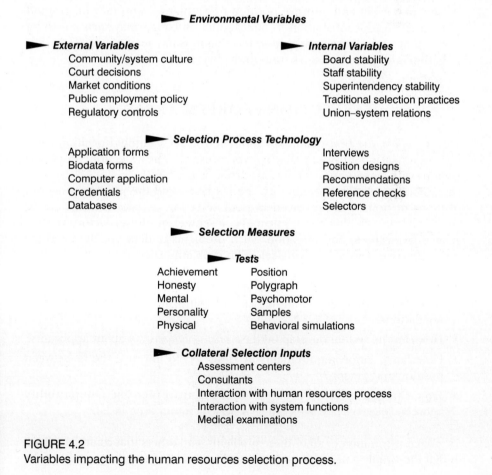

▶ **Environmental Variables**

▶ **External Variables**
Community/system culture
Court decisions
Market conditions
Public employment policy
Regulatory controls

▶ **Internal Variables**
Board stability
Staff stability
Superintendency stability
Traditional selection practices
Union–system relations

▶ **Selection Process Technology**
Application forms
Biodata forms
Computer application
Credentials
Databases

Interviews
Position designs
Recommendations
Reference checks
Selectors

▶ **Selection Measures**

▶ **Tests**
Achievement　　Position
Honesty　　　　Polygraph
Mental　　　　 Psychomotor
Personality　　 Samples
Physical　　　　Behavioral simulations

▶ **Collateral Selection Inputs**
Assessment centers
Consultants
Interaction with human resources process
Interaction with system functions
Medical examinations

FIGURE 4.2
Variables impacting the human resources selection process.

ductivity, a strong case can be made for foregoing traditional selection practices in favor of a formal selection plan, including elements such as those included in Figure 4.3. Some of the benefits of committing the system to sound selection principles and practices are:

- *Cost effectiveness*—The most effective and efficient approach to *school system improvement* is *staff improvement* through better staff selection.
- *Waste reduction*—Adherence to traditional selection practices, such as those mentioned in Figure 4.3, lead to enormous waste of the school system's resources in the form of funds, supervisory time, and diminution of educational outcomes.
- *Post-employment problem minimization*—Selection errors engender behavior problems such as selectees who cannot or will not meet position standards; who require constant supervision; who need extensive appraisal time to correct and improve position performance; who may be granted tenure; whose contribution to educational outcomes may turn out to be less than satisfactory; and whose termination may involve expensive litigation and impact on work unit productivity.

SELECTION PROBLEM AREAS

How to select the best qualified candidate for each unfilled position is an old organization problem that is ever present. The selection process is fraught with possibilities for serious error, results of which can be costly to the school system, the community, the taxpayer, and the pupil population. Millions of dollars are involved in poor selection decisions, which create problems such as alienation, tardiness, absenteeism, unsatisfactory performance, grievances, and litigation. Such problems underscore the need for more effective ways of resolving selection problems, such as:

- How can the system be assured that selection decisions and actions are consistent with selection strategies and conform to applicable laws and regulations?
- How can the system develop better *predictive information* about applicants?
- How can position requirements be designed to improve the fit between position and person?
- How can the system develop information to increase compatibility between selectees and *work situations* in which they are placed?

What is common to all of these problems, and others that could be added, is that they imply a need for greater system commitment to designs that delin-

The Riverpark school system's way of selecting talent to satisfy its human resources requirements is based on the following premises.

We shall:

- Adhere to the system's official human resources policy statements, which provide the basis for an organized approach to decision making regarding employment of individuals who meet established system standards.

- Avoid traditional ways of filling openings (provincialism, informal processes, absence of position posting, political connections, union pressures, system favorites, special interest applicants, pre- and post-application residency requirements, seniority rights, absence of regulatory credentials, kickback practices).

- Restrict collection and application of information to consideration of positions and applicants under consideration.

- Provide selectors with all relevant information and resources essential to identifying talent quality.

- Develop a performance model to assess applicant's ability to meet position and performance standards.

- Comply with regulatory requirements regarding the selection of full-time, part-time, and temporary personnel.

- Define clearly decision points at which applicants move out or move up in the screening period.

- Use a variety of oral and written means to assess the fit between position and person requirements.

- Collect indicator data deemed appropriate to improving the overall quality, retention, and performance of the entire staff.

- Focus time, talent, and resources in the screening process on promising candidates.

- Employ computer technology under certain circumstances to enhance movement of applicants through the selection process.

- Familiarize selectors and selectees with public and system employment purposes, policies, and practices.

- Differentiate position requirements *among position categories* (special education, instruction, administration). *Standardize* position requirements within a position category (administration).

- Require all applicants, whether internal or external, to go through the selection process.

- Establish a talent eligibility pool to maintain a continuous recruitment–selection endeavor to search and induce individuals with the competencies needed in the system's quest to fulfill its mission.

FIGURE 4.3
Selection committal of the Riverpark school system.

eate specific strategies for selection and placement such as the Riverpark school system's approach to talent selection shown in Figure 4.3. This includes programs and procedures for attaining objectives and assigning responsibilities for their implementation. Findings relevant to the selection process are applicable to understanding of and dealing with selection problem areas:

- The selection process is subject to extensive internal and external influences that frequently neutralize organizational efforts to employ personnel on the basis of merit.

- Although modern selection techniques can forecast an applicant's suitability for a position within limits, they cannot eliminate the possibility of selection error.

- Unsatisfactory results in the selection process are frequently due to misapplication or nonapplication of selection techniques. All too often, personnel are chosen on the basis of politics, nepotism, popularity, physiognomy, propinquity, seniority, physical fitness, compromise, hero worship, ethnic background, natural succession, test results, personality traits, and salesmanship.

- The presumption that position guides designed to describe person and position qualifications will guarantee intended results is fallacious. Position guides serve a variety of purposes in the selection process, but the decision to select or reject a candidate is based on human judgment.

- Selection of personnel does not operate independently of the recruitment process. Unless the number of applicants exceeds the number of placements to be made, a selection process becomes unproductive. For every position to be filled, a rule of thumb is that at least ten applicants should be recruited.

- There are constraints that govern the choice of applicants. Legal constraints affect the entire selection process. For example, it was noted earlier that it is illegal to discriminate among applicants on the basis of color, religion, gender, age, or national origin. Moreover, court rulings influence the selection process in such aspects as position specifications, recruiting sources used to attract position applicants, screening and interviewing techniques, and the use of psychological tests.

- The selection process presents a propitious opportunity to correct problems that exist in the organization relating to affirmative action and staff balance. The selection process is the means by which requirements for affirmative action plans can be implemented. The process is also a useful device for correcting staff imbalance in experience, talent, staff adequacy, units lacking expertise in selected areas, and staffing competency.

- Economic constraints also affect the use of tests for selection purposes. The kinds of physical examinations now possible, which often have predictive value in such matters as absenteeism, are expensive, time consuming, and pose questions of cost effectiveness. Economics is also a factor in the use of psychological testing, including tests of abilities, personality, skills, and achievements.

- Changes in the position and in the person occupying the position occur so frequently that performance predictions during the selection process have limited potential. It is a matter of record that technological, occupational, organizational, and administrative changes pose a constant threat to organizational effectiveness and survival. The point is that selection tools for predicting performance cannot be relied on for estimating long-run behavior of personnel. Any personnel choice involves a degree of speculation.

- Constraints are imposed also on the selection process by techniques employed to secure information about applicants and by interpretations made of the information by those responsible for the selection process. Information gathered through **interviews,** tests, reference checks, application blanks, and inventories may be incomplete, erroneous, or misleading. Moreover, different individuals reviewing the same information often differ markedly in their judgments about its meaning and in the importance they attach to different components of information.

What lessons of experience and the foregoing commentary on limitations of the selection process add up to is that, although considerable progress has been made in developing knowledge about selection, the fallibility of the process should be recognized. On the other hand, it is generally acknowledged that many school systems have not made effective use of existing knowledge about human resources selection in making decisions about which people will be accepted or rejected for employment.

It is to this topic that we will devote the remainder of this chapter (beginning with the first step in the model of the selection process as outlined in Figure 4.4), with a focus on ways by which the limitations of selection techniques referred to earlier can be minimized.

THE SELECTION PROCESS

Whether a school system is small or large, a considerable amount of systemwide and unit planning is necessary if the thrust of the selection process is to achieve congruency between people and positions. The care with which the process is designed and implemented depends to a considerable extent on the importance school officials attach to attracting and retaining competent personnel for employment in the system. It is not difficult to make a case for thorough selection procedures, regardless of system size. The expenditure of time, money, and

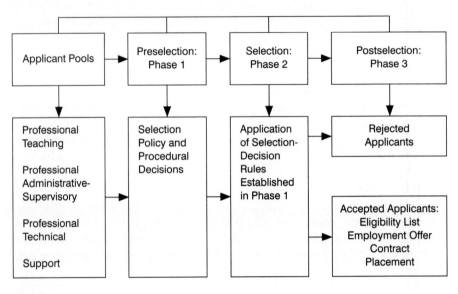

FIGURE 4.4
Model of the human resources selection process.

effort is wasted when people selected for positions fail to meet organizational expectations. Furthermore, the impact of poor teaching on children is so serious that the selection process in education is a matter of critical concern.

Figure 4.4 enables the reader to visualize the selection process as a whole. The model illustrates the sequential nature of the activities and serves as an outline for discussing each of the steps involved. As the process shown in Figure 4.4 becomes institutionalized, benefits that it generates are significant. Adherence to a model saves time, money, and human energy. It enhances the system's ability to forecast more readily a candidate's suitability for a position, minimizes internal and external influences on candidate selection, facilitates the decision-making process, provides the system with a plan to meet legal requirements of public employment policy, and creates means for improving the linkage among other personnel processes, such as human resources planning, recruitment, and induction.

Although the selection process should be varied to meet special problems, needs, and characteristics of every system, there are numerous preselection decisions that are universally applicable. As indicated in the selection process model in Figure 4.4, the first step toward effective personnel selection is the design of a set of personnel selection plans, the heart of which is employment policy.

Policy and related plans to be developed during the preselection phase of the selection process, an illustration of which appears in Figure 2.3, will be the subject of the section that follows.

Preselection

Examination of the preselection phase (Phase 1) of the process model shown in Figure 4.4 indicates there are two major tasks: (a) development of selection policies and (b) formulation of procedures for implementing policy. The crux of the preselection phase of the selection process is that a decision system in the form of system policies and procedures (see Figure 4.6), developed prior to initiation of the actual selection process, helps to focus organizational effort on selection objectives. Key policy and procedural elements will be examined next.

Development of Selection Policy. The basis for developing a unified system of plans for selecting personnel originates with the board of education. Board policy, in the form of a written statement, indicates to the community, school staff, and all who apply for employment in the system the intent of the board regarding selection, and it serves as a guide in the selection process. The purpose of policy is to set forth the board's commitment as to personnel selection and to establish guidelines within which administrators responsible for the selection process will operate. It is more than likely, in view of the composite character of the process, that several statements concerning selection policy will be combined to convey the board's intent. More specifically, one approach to the development of selection policy is to link *general human resources policy* and *selection policy*. For example, *general personnel policy*, illustrated in Figure 2.4, contains several policy statements that can serve as guidelines in the selection process, including board intent regarding merit selection, employment discrimination, career development (promotion from within), fair treatment of personnel, utilization of member abilities, opportunities for advancement, and safeguards against arbitrary treatment. In addition, policies negotiated with the union regarding any aspect of personnel selection (i.e., promotion from within) as well as public employment policy are merged into a single document for regulating selection activities. Figure 4.5 illustrates an employment policy statement focusing on personnel selection.

Preselection Procedural Decisions. There are numerous preselection decisions necessary to implement selection policy. The nature and scope of these decisions are exemplified in the procedural framework diagrammed in Figure 4.5. To ensure that each phase of the selection process will be properly managed requires specific attention both to elements of each of the procedural areas shown in Figure 4.5 as well as to shaping plans for resolving problems arising from variations in the types of positions to be filled within the system. The strength of the model is that it focuses on the need for preselection decisions and gives explicit attention to each of the necessary selection components. In addition, the model emphasizes establishment of reasonable selection criteria *prior* to choice.

It is the policy of the Goodville school system when filling vacancies to:

- Choose the person best qualified for the position, with a view toward suitability for further advancement.

- Adhere to federal, state, and local regulations regarding equal employment opportunity.

- Establish procedures whereby race, color, religion, age, sex, national origin, or membership in any lawful organization shall not be a consideration in (a) employment, promotion, or transfer; (b) recruitment or recruitment advertising; (c) rates of pay or other forms of compensation; (d) selection for training; and (e) demotion or termination.

- Employ, promote, and develop personnel on the basis of sex or age where these factors are essential to the position performance.

- Employ women on a basis equal to that of men without restriction as to type of work, except as to limitations imposed by physical ability.

- Permit employment of persons related by blood or marriage to any member of the Board of Education on consent of two-thirds of the Board membership.

- Fill vacancies by upgrading or promoting from within whenever present staff members are qualified.

FIGURE 4.5
An employment policy statement.

The weaknesses of the model are: (a) decisions needed in each category are complex and difficult to establish with finality because of insufficiency of knowledge relating to various performance predictors and (b) extensive variation in the size and other characteristics of educational organizations keeps the model from being a universal approach to the selection process. Each of the decision areas listed in Figure 4.6 will be reviewed in the following discussion.

Selection Laws—Regulations. When a school district engages in the process of choosing from a list of applicants the person to fill a position opening, environmental circumstances affect that choice. These circumstances include organizational culture, the applicant pool, the union, and public employment policy. Of these influences, the latter is one that has a growing impact on selection decisions in both public and private employment sectors. Because of public employment policy expressed through legal controls as well as social expectations toward fair employment procedures, the twilight of arbitrary decision making about hiring and promotion is at hand. Few selection decisions can be made without regard for some law, regulation, order, or court decision. Moreover, rare is the selection process that is flawless. Consequently, every organization is continuously confronted with designing a selection process that does not produce biases and that focuses on the rights of both the candidate and the organization. The candidate has the right to be judged fairly on the basis of reasonable position require-ments; the employer has both the right and obligation to seek and employ the candidate best qualified for the position. Consequently, one of the salient tasks in designing a selection system is adoption of a proactive stance through a strategy that will reduce the likelihood of employment discrimi-nation and ensure equal employment opportunities for applicants and cur-rent personnel. Minimization of selection problems related to legal compli-ance can be achieved if:

- A policy statement is issued to guide selection decision making (see Fig-ure 4.5).
- An affirmative action plan is developed to correct system imbalances (see Chapter 3).
- System audits are conducted to assess work units for balance in role, color, age, gender, religion, and national origin.
- Selection mechanisms are reviewed to eliminate potential legal pitfalls. These include position models, application blanks, tests, and interviews (see the discussion that follows).
- An executive in the central administration is directed to develop and oversee a legal compliance program.
- Staff personnel involved in planning and implementing the selection deci-sion have a working knowledge of major EEO legislation (see Table 3.2).[1]

Selection Decision: Components. Another of the preselection proce-dural decisions listed in the decision framework shown in Figure 4.7 is

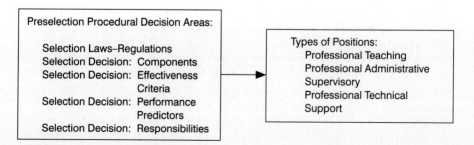

FIGURE 4.6
A framework for developing preselection procedural decisions.

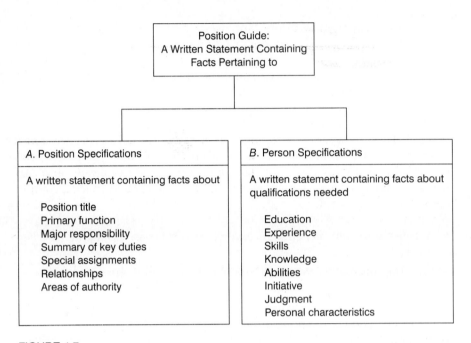

FIGURE 4.7
Elements of a position guide.

establishment of *position* and *person* requirements. These two components form the backbone of the selection process when viewed from either a legal or an operational standpoint. The tool employed to establish position and person requirements is referred to here as a **position guide** or model.

Position requirements. **Position analysis** and specification is based on the assumption that until there are clearly delineated requirements for each position, selection of personnel is difficult to conduct in systematic fashion. If the selection process is to focus on employment of people who can perform effectively in a position, then the requirements of that position need to be prescribed in advance. Moreover, judgments about whether an individual performs effectively in a position should be based on the degree to which his/her position behavior conforms to position requirements. Elements of a position guide are outlined in Figure 4.7 and illustrated in Figure 4.8. The position guide is a tool for *formalizing* the position and person requirements governing the selection of personnel in a school system. It is designed prior to seeking available applicants to facilitate matching of person and position requirements. Position guides direct attention to school purposes. What the school intends to achieve will affect the kinds of personnel selected. Because diversity of purpose calls for specialization, the orga-

---

FAWN GROVE SCHOOL SYSTEM POSITION GUIDE
Part A: Position Requirements

Position Title
Principal, Fawn Grove Elementary School

Purpose of Position
To advocate, develop, execute, and assess the results of plans designed to facilitate the growth and development of pupil personnel assigned to this attendance unit.

Principal Responsibilities

- Formulate, define, clarify, and interpret to pupils, staff, and community the objectives of this attendance unit within the context of organizational purposes.
- Define unit objectives and subunit goals within the framework of systemwide purposes.
- Advocate, develop, execute, and assess the results of the learning experiences in the curriculum of this school.
- Advocate, develop, execute, and assess the results of instructional theories designed to facilitate the growth and development of pupil personnel assigned to this attendance unit.
- Provide effective supervision of human and nonhuman resources allocated to this attendance unit.
- Assess the results of all central and unit plans for facilitating the growth and development of pupil personnel assigned to this attendance unit.
- Advocate, develop, and assess the results of human resources plans for this attendance unit.
- Provide for effective coordination of unit plans with those of other system units and those of the central administration.

Principal Organizational Relationships

- Is under the general direction of the assistant superintendent for instruction.
- Directs the work of all subordinates assigned to this attendance unit.
- Integrates the activities of this unit with those of other units within the system.
- Consults with the assistant superintendent for instruction, advice, and assistance and renders advice and support to him/her.

Areas of Authority	*Authority*
• Supervision of attendance unit personnel.	Full
• Recommendation of new unit plans or modification of existing unit plans.	Full

---

FIGURE 4.8
A position guide for an administrative position.

145

- Execution of previously established plans.   Full
- Appraisal of unit personnel.   Full
- Selection of personnel.   Partial
- Compensation of personnel.   None
- Control of unit funds and facilities.   Partial

Some Factors Considered When Performance Is Judged (Performance Indicators)

- The extent to which this attendance unit facilitates the growth and development of all children assigned to this attendance unit.
- The quality of instruction provided in this attendance unit.
- The diversity and richness of educational opportunities provided to children in the attendance unit.
- The nature, extent, and quality of individualized instruction provided in this unit.
- The leadership qualities demonstrated in planning, organizing, leading, and controlling the activities related to this attendance unit.
- The nature, quality, timeliness, and quality of supervision rendered to subordinates assigned to this unit.
- The extent to which coordination is effected with other organizational units.
- The extent to which this organization attracts and retains personnel needed to make it function effectively.

Part B: Position-Holder Qualifications

Preparation, Experience, and Skills

- Doctorate degree or equivalent, including ability to meet certification requirements for position.
- Demonstrated ability to exercise the responsibilities allocated to unit.
- Demonstrated ability to apply conceptual, human, and technical skills to position of this type.
- Demonstrated ability to motivate subordinates to cooperate voluntarily in attaining unit and organization aims.
- Demonstrated ability to understand the implications of social, political, educational, and economic changes and the significance they hold for the attendance unit, and to initiate and direct appropriate change within the attendance unit based on broad societal changes.

FIGURE 4.8, *continued*

nization needs to define those teaching and support functions for which personnel are recruited. System purposes need to be translated into position specifications so that, on the one hand, the individual responsible for staff selection knows what to look for, and on the other hand, the applicant knows what the school system is seeking.

The use of position guides will help strengthen efforts to resist pressures to employ unqualified personnel. Their use also makes it possible to administer the selection process objectively and openly. Position guides provide applicants and personnel agencies with a clearer understanding of school personnel requirements and qualifications. Placement, compensation, development, and union relationships are additional facets of the human resources function in which position guides are utilized. In the final analysis, any device that helps to define aims and to relate those aims to position specifications is worthy of attention.

The position guide, as illustrated in Figure 4.7, enables the system to provide one of two major elements included in the information system for personnel selection. The first of these, *information about the position,* includes responsibilities, relationships, position standards, special features, and behavioral characteristics needed by the position holder to perform effectively (Part A). The second element, *information about the applicant,* is needed to determine how well the *candidate's* qualifications match the *position requirement* (Part B).

Position guides specify minimum requirements of the position and personal qualifications needed for appointment to the position. Part A of Figure 4.8 is designed to illustrate the manner in which *position requirements* are described, including the following components: position title, purpose, major responsibilities, area of authority, organizational relationships, and performance indicators.

Examination of Table 4.1 indicates there is no simple solution to the thorny problem of developing position requirements in a school or in any other type of organization. Different positions have quite different characteristics, and it is erroneous to assume that a position guide for one particular situation will fit all others within that category.

Unresolved questions involved in preparing position guides for teaching and administrative positions are among the most difficult and persistent organizational problems, yet considerable progress has been made in utilizing this tool for resolution of numerous personnel problems. The following observations can be made about position guides:

- The concept of developing position guides for teachers is not without controversy. There are those who argue that all teaching positions are alike, and therefore development of different position guides for similar positions is a waste of organizational time and effort. Arguments have centered also on the assumption that the role prescriptions place undue limitations on the

TABLE 4.1
Performance activities for positions in the Goodville school system.

Types of Positions	Illustrative Performance Activities
Administrative and supervisory Superintendent Assistant superintendent: business, human resources, instruction Directors, department heads, deans, principals, assistants, assistants to . . .	Strategic and tactical planning, organizing, leading, controlling, representing, communicating, and directing attainment of objectives
Instructional Teachers, instructional specialists, and paraprofessionals	Planning for teaching, motivating pupils, developing classroom climate, managing the classroom, interacting with pupils, and rendering personal services to pupils
Classified (supporting) Secretarial, clerical, maintenance, operation, food service, transportation, and security	Routine, semiroutine, standardized, and supporting activities involving sensorimotor, manipulative, and achievement skills
Technical Architectural, computer, dental, legal, medical, psychological, psychiatric, and security services	Special professional technical skills, such as designing, diagnosing, advising, conceptualizing, and prescribing

individual in performing the role. Although these criticisms have some validity, they are not so telling as to warrant elimination of position guides.

- Position design in education is undergoing considerable change and the need is for improving rather than dispensing with the specification of position requirements. Although the search goes on for more definitive ways of specifying teacher behavior, the practicing administrator must proceed on the basis of existing information relative to position requirements. He/she cannot wait for tomorrow's developments and still avoid internal conflict and stress about what roles people are to perform in the system.

- Preparation of position guides is a task undertaken in light of established goals of the system, objectives assigned to attendance units, and positions established within each unit. Methods of gathering information about position requirements include examination of existing position guides, observations of the performance of the position holder, interviews with the position holder, descriptions of the position by the incumbent, and design of position models for testing assumptions about actual requirements (see Figure 4.9).

- The minimum requirement of a position guide is *clarity*. All administrative components in the school system and all individuals occupying a position within that component need to know what they are expected to do to perform their roles successfully, to whom they report, and where to go for whatever is needed—information, funds, facilities, supplies, or equipment—to perform according to expectations. In addition to understanding individual role requirements, position holders need to know the relationship between what they do and what the school system is intent on doing. In brief, the position guide is a useful tool for bringing about a closer understanding of the manner in which individual position objectives are linked to system goals.

- Preparation of guides for positions other than those related to instruction should include analysis of precise duties to be performed as well as other relevant factors, such as special features of the position, level of responsibility and authority, structural relationships of the position, conditions of employment, nature of supervision received, extent of initiative required, and the physical environment involved (especially for certain types of support positions).

- Design of every position in the school system provides an opportunity for designers to focus on results rather than skills, competencies, or activities involved in attaining results.

Directions: Information is compiled by the *applicant assessment team* for probing the following questions:

- In order for the applicant to be successful in this teaching position, what strengths are needed? Academic? Teaching? Classroom control? Pupil evaluation? Influence on work group?

- Compatibility strengths? Team membership? Existing personnel? Community? System?

- Does the position have characteristics that dictate uncommon performance requirements?

- Are the strengths needed unique to this position? To the work group? To the school system?

Information relevant to the questions above is developed through the system's selection technology and utilized along with other assessments to determine position fitness.

FIGURE 4.9
An applicant-position strength probe.

- Federal guidelines adopted by the EEOC require an organization's job specifications to meet two basic standards: they must be realistic and they must be directly job related. Extensive or unnecessarily high educational requirements, artificially high prior experience requirements, insistence that persons hired for positions have the capacity for early promotion, and physical requirements or appearance and dress standards unrelated to successful job performance are among the most flagrant illegal violations in this context.[2]

- Reference has been made previously to the fact that virtually all subprocesses of the human resources function are closely scrutinized for compliance with federal and state regulatory controls designed to counteract discrimination in employment. The seminal reference work on public selection policy is the 1978 Uniform Guidelines on Employee Selection Procedures. These guidelines contain three important concepts with which school officials in charge of the personnel selection process should be familiar:

> **Adverse impact**—Human resources policies and procedures that have an adverse impact on employment opportunities on any race, either sex, or any ethnic group.
>
> **Validity**—The degree to which measures obtained by a selection procedure are related to performance measures on the job. To what extent do teacher competency tests measure teacher performance? **Content validity** refers to the extent to which a selection technique is representative of the skills, knowledge, or abilities essential to job performance (e.g., Are items in National Teacher Examinations representative of elements that will actually be performed on the job?). **Construct validity** refers to the extent to which a trait measure of performance measures performance on the job (e.g., Is the score on an intelligence test relevant to a mathematics teacher's performance?). **Criterion** is the standard by which performance is judged. **Criterion-related validity** is the extent to which selection procedure is statistically related to one or more measures of job performance (e.g., scores on a teacher examination are correlated with supervisory ratings of a teacher's actual performance).
>
> **Reliability**—Reliability refers to the degree of **consistency** of results obtained by application of a selection technique.[3]

In addition to these guidelines, the EEOC has established provisions relating to age, religious and national-origin discrimination, and sexual harassment.[4] Personnel selection is influenced also by child labor, licensure, privacy, and lie detector laws.[5]

In view of these considerations, it should be apparent that development of position requirements is challenging as well as complex, especially as it pertains to identifying tasks that comprise a position, the order of their accomplishment, and their relative importance. The ensuing section examines the other side of the selection coin, that is, information needed about the applicant to determine how closely she/he meets position requirements.

Person requirements. From information obtained through *position analysis* and *position specification,* it is possible to develop a *person analysis* and *person specification*. Table 4.2 contains a framework for illustrating the nature and scope of the person requirements for four categories of positions in the Blue Mountain school system. Elements listed in Table 4.2 are described variously in the literature, including competencies, terminal behavior objectives, outcome models, behavioral characteristics, performance criteria, and personnel effectiveness criteria. The essence of the content in Table 4.2 is that the school system's plan for defining the person requirements includes three components: personal characteristics, tasks to be performed, and task outcomes. For example, a product criterion for a support position would be a requirement that a typist must be able to type 50 words per minute. A process criterion for a teacher would be the ability to plan teaching-learning situations in accordance with accepted principles of learning. The key criterion for a professional technical position, such as an architect, is that of product or outcome.

The rationale for developing person requirements, such as those outlined in Table 4.2, is that once the information from the person requirements has been generated it is possible to complete the position guides as well as the most useful procedures for identifying applicants who possess the desired qualification(s).

Position and person specifications have always been an important aspect of personnel selection, but this function is even more important today because of EEO legislation. The system must be able to demonstrate that the relationship between position requirements and person requirements does not result in discriminatory selection practices. It is for good reasons, then, that organizations take seriously the task of articulating person and position requirements in the form of position guides or models. In sum, EEO and improvement of the quality of employment decisions would not be possible without them.[6]

Selection Decision: Effectiveness Criteria. After the position and performance requirements have been formalized into a position guide or model, the next task is to obtain or develop measures to be used as performance or success predictors. Tests, interviews, reference checks, and preparation and experience requirements are referred to collectively as *predictors*. One of the practical steps in making a decision about what performance criteria are to be measured and what predictors will be used to judge individual differences in position applicants on relevant variables is to define what the organization

TABLE 4.2
Framework for illustrating person requirements criteria for positions in the Blue Mountain school system.

| | Types of Positions | | | |
Personnel Selection Criteria (Performer Requirements)	Professional Teaching	Professional Administrative—Supervisory	Support	Professional—Technical
Personal characteristics				
General health, work motivation, oral and written expression, initiative, emotional stability, and mental ability	X	X	X	
Process criteria				
The tasks that must be performed	X	X		
Product criteria				
The outcomes of the process	X	X	X	
Combination of traits, process, or product	X	X	X	X

means by performance criteria for each of the position categories. As illustrated in Table 4.2, positions vary widely in their demands and functions. Consequently, effectiveness criteria will differ among position categories.

Establishing employment standards.   Once the selection criteria have been established, decisions must be made about which performance predictors will be used and what employment standards will be specified. Table 4.3 contains information about the kinds of personnel characteristics usually considered in selecting school personnel, as well as the tools employed to secure information related to each of these behavioral components. One of the difficult problems in personnel selection is determining which behavioral characteristics listed in Table 4.3, and which combinations of them, are valid predictors of position performance. More specifically, the system needs to know which personal characteristics are the best predictors for effective performance in specific positions.

Examination of selection criteria illustrated in Table 4.3 suggests that employment standards (criteria levels) must be defined more completely and specifically when included in the performance effectiveness predictors. A selection standard is a degree or level of excellence required for employment. A college degree, for example, may be specified as one of the selection standards for a teaching position. Various forms of employment standards are:

* *Level of education*—Should an applicant for a teaching position be required to have a master's degree? Is a doctorate degree required for the superintendency?
* *Level of intelligence*—What degree of mental ability should be required of a chemistry teacher? Nurse? Secretary? Custodian?
* *Level of preparation*—Is or should a license or certificate be required for the position?
* *Level of experience*—Will position-related experience be required for employment?
* *Level of specialized skills*—What should be the level of performance for teachers, relative to lesson design?
* *Level of personal characteristics*—What should be the quality of interpersonal skills for a receptionist?
* *Quality of background*—What should be the quality of medical history, noneducational work history, educational history, and/or work history (absenteeism, dismissal, promotions, and academic achievement)?

Although employment qualifications specified in success predictors are vital, they are often subjectively determined. Because of legal guidelines for fair employment practices, criteria *levels* should be carefully specified. Schneier sug-

TABLE 4.3
Selection criteria and performance predictors.

Performance Effectiveness Predictors

Selection Criteria	Application Blank	Preliminary Interview	Diagnostic Interview	Performance References	Medical Examination	Paper-Pencil Tests	Placement Agency	Performance Assessment	Biographical Inventory	Transcript
Candidate background information	X	X		X			X		X	X
Personal characteristics:										
Aptitudes		X	X	X		X		X		X
Role commitment		X							X	
Value system			X						X	
Emotional stability			X		X			X	X	
Physical stamina					X	X	X			
Attitudes, interests, and needs	X	X	X							
Ability to perform key duties	X	X		X	X			X		X
Position-related preparation and experience	X			X			X	X		X

154

gests that criteria for experience and education levels should be included only if they have been shown in the past to discriminate between successful and unsuccessful performers. It is better, he advises, to state knowledge requirements than degrees held. The applicant's background can then be analyzed and, coupled with other selection information, used to assess whether appropriate knowledge is possessed.[7] As will be stressed in the following section, a single selection technique or criterion should not be relied on exclusively. Rather, the employment decision should be based on a combination of techniques to maximize the probability of achieving the desired match between position and person.

Selection Decision: Performance Predictors.   Once selection requirements have been established, it is time for the next step: to hypothesize which measures will best differentiate applicant differences on relevant selection criteria. As mentioned previously, these measures are called *predictors*. One approach to selection of predictors is to utilize methods available at the time of employment; another is to develop appropriate methodologies for determining whether or not a given predictor is actually operating effectively, that is, whether it is actually predicting behavior it should be predicting.[8] The former approach is the topic of discussion in this section.

Figure 4.10 illustrates various issues involved in choosing performance predictors in the preselection phase of the selection process. Examination of Figure 4.10 elicits the following observations:

- The selection decision process encompasses a series of hurdles. During each stage of the process, predictors are employed to measure applicant abilities to meet selection standards.

- The number of hurdles and types of selection measures employed vary widely among school systems. Generally speaking, the more important the position in the organizational hierarchy, the more extensive the selection process.

- The list of predictors shown in Figure 4.10 is incomplete. The number employed varies, depending on system size, sophistication of the selectors, cost, time, consumption, and importance of the selection process in the eyes of the system.

- None of the predictors listed in Figure 4.10 is infallible. The combination of techniques that empirical information indicates best matches persons and positions is the approach toward which selection efforts should be directed.

- Each hurdle has a purpose, that is, to secure selected information. Methods should be designed to gather relevant information about the candidate as he/she progresses from one step to another.

The remainder of this section will focus on the traditional or standard predictors identified in Figure 4.10.

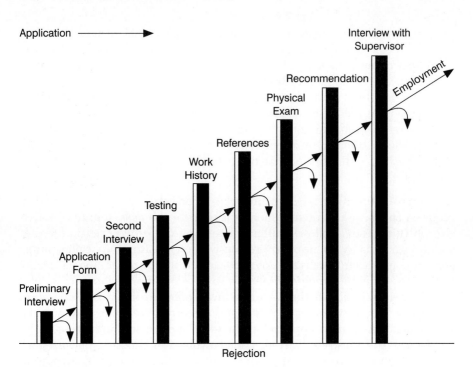

FIGURE 4.10
Successive hurdles in the selection decision process.

Source: Dale Yoder and Paul Staudohar, Personnel Management and Industrial Relations, 7e, © 1982, p. 176. Reprinted by permission of Prentice-Hall Inc., Englewood Cliffs, New Jersey.

Preliminary screening interview. The preliminary screening interview represents the initial contact between employer and candidate for employment. It's purpose is (a) to determine whether the applicant understands key requirements of the position, (b) to ascertain whether the applicant possesses minimal position qualifications, and (c) to judge whether the applicant—on the basis of (a) and (b)—warrants further consideration. In some organizations, the applicant is required to complete the application blank, which is then employed in the screening interview to secure information from the candidate relative to certain critical qualifications. In brief, the initial screening interview provides an opportunity for the selector and the applicant to exchange meaningful information about the position requirements and reasons for the candidate's interest in the position.

The EEOC has issued a publication noting that application forms and preemployment interviews have traditionally been instruments for eliminating, at an early state, "unsuited" or "unqualified" persons from consideration for employment. They have often been used, according to the report, in such a way as to restrict or deny employment opportunities for women and members of minority groups. The EEOC advises that in devising or reviewing application forms or in seeking information from job applicants, employers should ask themselves:

- Will the answer to this question, if used in making a selection, have a disparate effect in screening out minorities or members of one gender (i.e., disqualify a significantly larger percentage of members of one particular group than other groups)?
- Is this information really needed to judge an applicant's competence or qualifications for the job in question?

In this connection, it is worth reporting suggestions by Miner and Miner on the interview:

- Do not leave the first screening of applicants to a receptionist or secretary who is too likely to say or do something that the prospective employee can interpret as discrimination.
- Personnel department interviewers must be knowledgeable about job vacancies, and they must limit questions to job-related items. A standard set of questions is suggested for each position.
- A written report should be filed following each interview and should summarize what the interviewers told the applicant.
- Questions asked by the final decision maker should also focus on requirements in the job description. If this indicates that "social skills" are significant, the hiring officer and personnel department should agree on the level of social skills needed.[9]

According to Byham, questions regarding the following items should not be posed in an interview:

- Age if applicant is over 40; in Massachusetts, if the applicant is under 18 or over 65.
- Race
- National origin (New Jersey law prohibits questions regarding citizenship).
- Religion
- Marital status
- Dependents
- Child-care problems
- Housing (i.e., own home, rent, live with parents?)
- Arrest records
- Health status
- Type of discharge from military

- Willingness to work on Saturday (or Sunday), unless inability to assign the person to such work would cause chaotic personnel problems.
- Any information from minority or female applicants not routinely requested of white or male applicants.

Federal law prohibits not only direct questions but also questions that might imply the above information.[10]

In summary, a preliminary screening interview is an indispensable tool in the selection process, but it should be designed and applied in accordance with objectives such as those outlined. Thus, decision rules for the initial interview, when established and communicated by the system prior to initiation of the selection process, may help to prevent violation of antidiscrimination laws and to screen out candidates clearly unqualified.

Application blank biodata. Collection of biographical information on position applicants is absolutely essential to the conduct of the selection process. Methods of collecting biographical information include the application blank, weighted application blank, biographical inventory, and future biography.

The primary function of the application blank is to obtain information (in the applicant's own handwriting), to establish his/her identity, and to make tentative inferences about that applicant's suitability for employment in the specific position for which he/she is being considered. If the candidate is hired, the application document becomes a component of the system's personnel file.

It is probably true that there are superfluous items on the majority of application blanks. The validity of each item, the completeness of information elicited for the interviewer, and its effectiveness in transmitting needed information to members of the selection team are criteria to be considered if every item in the selection blank is to be of worth in the selection process. Ideally, the items in the application form should be valid predictors of success or failure in position performance. It goes without saying that the application blank should be designed so that the interviewer need not secure and record factual data that can be obtained by the applicant's completing the form.

In designing the application blank, consideration should be given to whether specific forms should be prepared for each category of applicants listed in Table 4.1. It should be noted that items included in the form should be designed to secure information that will help to match person and position and to help predict success or failure in the position. The weighted application blank, for example, is designed to assign different values to answers applicants give to various questions, the rationale being that some items predict success better than others. The difference between a weighted and an unweighted application blank is that, in the case of the former, the value or significance of the items of information furnished by the applicant is known.

Another option to be considered in designing the application blank is the possibility of using two forms: (a) a *short* or *preliminary application form,* used for initial screening, to make tentative judgments as to whether the candidate has employment qualifications that merit further analysis; and (b) a *full application blank* for those who appear to have employment characteristics that merit extended consideration.

An emerging issue in the design of application blanks is the inclusion of items designed to elicit from the applicant either personal information, authorization to verify information, or agreement to certain conditions if employed. Such statements may include authorization to verify information, consent to undergo physical or other examinations, a liability release for those supplying information, agreement to a probationary appointment, conditions relating to misinformation, declarations as to previous arrests or subversive activities, and certification of the truth of the application information.

Instead of limiting the employment application to its traditional purpose of a factual summation, this selection device can be designed to secure attitudinal information, which can be explored during the interview. The applicant's perceptions regarding the role under consideration, reasons for wanting the position, feelings about the position, and views on the terms of employment are illustrative of information that will help to round out the overall understanding of evaluators.

Landy and Trumbo indicate that the application blank has three purposes: (a) to determine whether the candidate meets minimum hiring requirements, (b) to serve as a supplement to and preparation for the interview, and (c) to obtain biographical data and work-history information that may be used actuarially to predict some assessable aspect of job proficiency. These three purposes, the authors suggest, represent criteria for deciding what items should be included in the application blank, such as:

- Is the item necessary for identifying the applicant?
- Is it necessary for screening out those who are ineligible under the company's basic hiring policies?
- Does it help to decide whether the candidate is qualified?
- Is it based on analysis of the job or jobs for which the applicant will be selected?
- Has it been pretested on the company's employees and found to correlate with success?
- Will the information be used? How?
- Is the application form the proper place for the item?
- Will answers provide information not obtained in another step in the selection procedure, for example, through interviews, tests, or medical examinations?

- Is the information needed for selection at all, or should it be obtained at induction or even later?
- Is it probable that the applicant's replies will be reliable?
- Does the question conform to any applicable federal or state legislation?[11]

With regard to the weighted application blank, it has been reported that its development for a position takes about 100 hours; so it makes sense to develop such application blanks only for positions with many jobholders.[12] If the organization is willing to devote talent, time, and money to development of the weighted application blank, it can be as useful a predictive device as some psychological tests. Further, it has been noted that it can be graded or scored as objectively as a test, thus eliminating any personal bias in the selection procedure.[13]

Two other biodata formats are the *biographical inventory* and *future autobiography*. The biographical inventory extends the nature and scope of information on the applicant's life history by focusing on background experiences that correlate with success on the job. Questions are stated in multiple-choice answer form and cover a wide range of behavioral characteristics.[14] In the future autobiography, applicants write about what they expect or hope to be doing at some time in the future.[15]

Use of application blanks in the selection process involves awareness of three potential problems: (a) incompliancy with EEOC regulations (some items may be viewed as discriminatory), (b) the possibility of falsification or distortion of application information, and (c) the potential for misuse of application information by assessment team members. There is considerable evidence at hand indicating that applicants are not averse to falsification or distortion about previous work experience and biographical questions. One study indicated that 76 of 221 applicants claimed to have experience performing a nonexistent task. It is reported that this kind of falsification may cost the life insurance industry $30 million or more a year, through investment in people who were hired but later failed on the job.[16] Other studies note distortion of application information relative to reasons for leaving previous positions, previous salary earned, and duration of previous employment.[17] Misuse of application blanks refers to biases on the part of those involved in the selection process who restrict the choice of application items to support selection preferences.

Second interview. The interview remains one of the most important selection tools for securing information and impressions about applicants. Despite its limitations, the interview can yield data and observations about candidates that other methods are incapable of providing. In no other selection device is it possible to secure information not provided in transcripts and application forms, observe interpersonal skills and responses, test thought processes, and judge values and aspirations. The following is a summary of important considerations to be observed in planning interview procedures:

- The number and length of interviews with a candidate increase with the importance of the position to be filled. A *preliminary* interview, mainly for screening purposes, is standard in most selection processes. Its chief purpose is to eliminate from consideration candidates who, for a variety of reasons, are clearly unqualified. The *decentralized* interview takes place between the candidate and the official under whose jurisdiction the candidate will serve. This type of interview is diagnostic and in depth, aimed at determining closeness of fit between person and position specifications. *Team* interviews involve several persons who interview a candidate simultaneously. The *group* interview is that in which a single interviewer discusses position openings with several candidates. Each type of interview is designed to minimize the amount of time devoted to interviews. The *final* selection interview is generally devoted to clarification of conditions of employment. Various types of interviews can be used to give information to and get information from applicants.

- Interviews are also categorized as being either *structured* or *unstructured*. The patterned or structured interview utilizes a standard list of questions prepared in advance and from which the interviewer does not deviate. A structured list of questions prepared for each position category and responses to the questions are recorded on the same form. The unstructured interview may or may not be based on a list of predetermined questions. The difference between the unstructured and structured interview lies in the freedom the former method allows the interviewer in eliciting information from different types of applicants. Research findings indicate that structured interviews result in greater reliability when several interviewers are involved and follow a guide than when interviews are conducted without a guide.

- The interview is the best point in the selection process for the interviewer to integrate information from all sources about the applicant. In addition, the interviewer can assess personal characteristics of the candidate that cannot be gleaned as well from other sources. These include personal appearance, mannerisms, attitudes, interests, avocations, family structure, and other relevant considerations.

- The team approach to the selection interview generally yields better results than those derived from interviews conducted by one person.[18]

- Criticisms of the interview as a selection device include the questionable validity of employment interviews, untrained interviewers, variability of interview content, question variability, uneven interpretation, premature decisions, negative approach, halo effect, interviewer bias, failure of interviewer to listen, and interviewer tendency to focus on negative information. Webster's list of nine research findings illustrates the complexity of interviewing:

> Interviewers usually reach decisions within a few minutes.
>
> Unfavorable information almost always carries more weight than favorable data.
>
> The effect of unfavorable information about an applicant depends on when it is perceived and when the judge records impressions.
>
> Once a judge is committed to accept an applicant, additional information increases confidence in all decisions but does not improve its quality.
>
> Nonverbal as well as verbal interactions influence decisions.
>
> Training and experience have minimal effects on the quality of judgment.
>
> Training may reduce interview error, but there is no evidence that the reduction of error improves judgment.
>
> If several really promising or very unpromising applicants have been evaluated in succession, one who is "average" will be under- or overrated.
>
> Interviewers develop a stereotype of the good applicant and seek to match applicant to stereotype.[19]

- The selection interview has three major purposes: (a) securing sufficient information from the candidate that, when integrated with other information, will enhance the possibility of making the correct choice from among the candidates; (b) providing the candidate with the information needed to accept or reject the position if offered; and (c) creating a favorable impression about the organization and the environment in which the work will be performed.

- Despite limitations of the selection interview, the indispensability of this tool in the selection process should be recognized. It is the principal means by which the system links identity of the individual with the application blank, and it is also an important means for bringing into focus human aspects of employment. Both parties are able to communicate face to face, exchange information and views, and identify both applicant and system needs. The interview is a way of personalizing what has been described as a most impersonal process.

- Perhaps the most important decision to be made in the preselection phase of the selection process is whether the goal of the interview should be a broad-based or global assessment of the individual, or a consideration of only a few traits presumed to be related to success on the job.[20]

In view of the fact that the structured interview provides a firmer base and has the potential for higher predictive validity than the unstructured interview, greater attention is being given to its employment. Because the second interview is the most time-consuming and important step in the selection process and because it is designed to differentiate among those applicants who have survived previous hurdles, attention to improving its effectiveness as a predictor is warranted. By way of illustration, a school system may develop the structured interview by selecting information categories that need to be probed, such as personal qualities, academic achievement, position-related experience, interpersonal competence, and career orientation. Data that have been previously tested by hiring officials are then included in the structured interview format, such as:

- *Personal qualities*—To what extent do you possess the personal qualities needed to perform the position tasks effectively (meeting obligations, enthusiasm, attitude toward constructive criticism, and willingness to meet with pupils and parents outside the instructional day)?

- *Academic preparation*—Give your personal appraisal of your academic preparation in relation to the position tasks outlined in the position guide (development of classroom climate, planning for teaching, and managing the classroom).

- *Position-related experience*—Describe prior work experience you believe to be indicative of your ability to perform the key role requirements (development of classroom climate, planning for teaching, and managing the classroom).

- *Career orientation*—What are your immediate career goals? How persistent are you in attempting to achieve work requirements? Explain activities in which you have engaged to improve your teaching skills.

On completion of the interview, a final summary is made of observations and impressions indicating the interviewer's evaluation of the applicant. The summary is essential for a variety of reasons, including recording information needed to compare candidate assessments as well as for use in the event of discrimination complaints.

Personnel testing. Numerous tests can be used in the selection of personnel, including intelligence, aptitude, interest, achievement, and personality tests. Their primary use is to predict the ability of applicants to perform effectively in relation to a given position. Whether or not tests should be used in the selection process is a question that cannot be answered categorically. They are useful under certain circumstances. However, because of the costs, specialized personnel needed, variations in predictive validity and reliability, applicant acceptance of test requirements, charges of discrimination when tests are required, possibilities of litigation, and union as well as other pressures to eliminate testing, the addition of tests to the selection process becomes a matter for careful deliberation. Because there is not general agreement about the value of tests for generating useful information about applicants, school systems that use them need to be aware of administrative, technical, social, legal, and ethical problems involved. Information derived from tests alone should not be used to make the hiring decisions; when test data are used in combination with data from other sources, a more intelligent decision will probably result. Mounting criticism of the use of tests in the selection of personnel, especially the use of psychological tests for personality assessment and prediction of position performance, focuses on the applicant's right to privacy versus society's right to information, neither of which can be resolved readily.

Standardized teacher examinations are used on occasion as one of the devices by which to secure information to judge professional qualifications of the candidate. Results of examinations such as these, together with analysis of the candidate's academic transcript, have been used with or in place of classroom observation to arrive at an estimate of the candidate's professional qualifications (see Figure 4.11).

Guidelines developed by the Educational Testing Service (ETS) for NTE tests indicate that information gained from NTE tests is significant but limited. The information is significant because it is substantially related to future professional performance and limited in the sense that the knowledge and skills tested do not include many elements important to professional performance, such as dedication, motivation, and caring.[21]

The new generation of teacher assessments planned by ETS serve the basic licensing functions of NTE, utilizing a variety of different methods and content. The new assessments focus on evaluating teaching skills directly.

ETS has developed three publications that outline the format about the 1992 Praxis Series.[21] These publications outline the general makeup of the Praxis Series, describe the underlying concepts that guided its development, and set forth the guidelines for its use. The Praxis Series offers measures of academic skills, subject knowledge, and classroom performance. The publications are:

• 21st Century Teacher Assessments
• Guiding Conceptions and Assessment Principles for the Praxis Series: Professional Assessment for Beginning Teachers
• Guidelines for Proper Use of the Praxis Series: Professional Assessment for Beginning Teachers

Selection

Steps examined in the selection process (Phase 2 in Figure 4.4) thus far have emphasized systematization of information gathering and information pro-

Pittsburgh Public Schools

Application Procedures for Professional Positions

State law requires that professionals place on an eligibility list in their *certification area* to be considered for employment in the Pittsburgh Public Schools. In addition to placing on the eligibility list, **you must have Pennsylvania certification or be able to present evidence that you will have certification by your date of hire.** An Act 34, Act 33, and a Medical Clearance are also required for hiring.

Requirements	Maximum points
1. **Tests (Tests c & d listed below are given to applicants on the day of the Panel Interview.)**	
a. NTE Communication Skills and Professional Knowledge Tests. (School Nurses, Dental Hygienists, and Vocational Education applicants are not required to take these two tests. Nurses and Hygienists must submit a copy of their state license. Vocational Education applicants must submit a copy of their Occupational Competency Certificate.)	5
b. NTE Specialty Area Test. (School Nurses, School Social Workers, Dental Hygienists, and Vocational Education areas do not have a Specialty Area Test. Vocational Education applicants will be scheduled for a Pittsburgh Area Test that is conducted at the Pittsburgh Board of Education Administration Building at no cost. You should notify the Office of Human Resources when you wish to be scheduled. If you are interested in placing on two or more lists, the NTE Specialty must be taken in each of those subject areas.)	10
c. Classroom Management Test. This test is given to all applicants except Social Workers, School Nurses, Dental Hygienists, and School Psychologists.	5
d. Content Area Tests are administered in respective certification areas. Professional applicants are required to take the test in the area that you wish to be assigned. However, if you are interested in placing on two or more lists, the content area test in each of those subject areas is required.	10
2. **Credential Evaluation**	30
Evaluation of credentials includes the application, transcript(s), handwritten letter, professional references, and/or placement file from college.	
3. **Panel Interview**	40
Conducted by a committee of the Pittsburgh Public Schools Staff. These standardized interviews are designed to evaluate applicants for placement on the list and should not be confused with a recruitment interview or a final interview.	

Applicants must meet the minimum required score for each of the three criteria listed above in order to place on an eligibility list.

FIGURE 4.11

Selection criteria employed in the Pittsburgh, Pennsylvania, public schools.

Source: Pittsburgh Public Schools, Pittsburgh, PA.

cessing that leads to a decision to hire a particular individual for a given position. The next step in the selection process focuses on the question of how good is the match. Stated another way, To what extent do the qualifications of this individual meet the requirements for the position under consideration?

Consequently, investigation of references and background of those who survive the initial screening process is essential. The more important the position in the organization, the more exhaustive the investigation should be.

Appraising the Data and the Applicants.   Seldom is the information furnished by a referrer to be taken at face value. This is especially true of written statements. Whether obtained by telephone, mail, or direct contact, information should be checked to determine its accuracy and to ensure its adequacy.

Three types of applicant measures that are selectively employed before a hiring decision is made in cases where needed information is difficult to acquire through traditional channels are:

- *Preemployment physical examinations—The American Disabilities Act,* effective in 1993, precludes the use of physical examinations prior to a conditional offer being made to the applicant.
- *Drug testing*—Drug testing has become a part of the selection process in some institutions, one form of which is a requirement that all applicants must pass a urinalysis test for marijuana and cocaine.
- *Behavioral simulation exercises*—A manual or computerized exercise that simulates or imitates position specifications. This measure involves responses to position problems, work situations, and analyses of types of tasks to be performed. In-basket techniques and analyses exercises are illustrative.

Each of these methods of acquiring information about the applicant offers strengths and weaknesses. Factors to be considered are cost, application limits, quality and availability of professional specialists, risks of information disclosure, applicant disagreement with conclusions, charges of discrimination if the candidate is not hired, and a provision in the *Americans with Disabilities Act* that makes the qualified person with disabilities a protected class under the equal employment opportunity laws.[22]

Reference and background checks are essential because there is ample evidence of information misrepresentation in application blanks, personal references, and biographical data. Cases of salary history inflation, work record fabrication, credential distortion, academic degree embellishment, criminal background concealment, falsification of performance appraisal records, and concealment of actual reasons for desire to change place of employment are not uncommon. Personal references provided by the applicant (friends, colleagues, and relatives) are not considered reliable sources for reference checking. Employment references, on the other hand, are suitable because the reference check is focused on employment history. Other reference checking sources include those provided by current or previous employers or sources known to or secured by the reference checker.[23]

Personal and academic references are less useful than those provided by employers, but do provide helpful information, especially when specific questions concerning the candidate are asked. Of considerable import in the reference and background investigation is the presence or absence of conflicting information. When information does conflict, that is a signal to investigate other sources to determine whether differences in opinions, judgments, or records of events are truly meaningful to the employment decision. Many school systems systematize the reference check by preparing a reference check form to make certain that the specific information needed is covered in the investigation, including appraisal of position performance, strong and weak points, reason for leaving, compensation history, absenteeism, and willingness of the former employer to rehire or give a position recommendation.

Rejection or acceptance of a position applicant is a prediction based on information collected using various selection tools and techniques. Table 4.4 illustrates one strategy for assessing characteristics of a candidate. The underlying ideal is to place a numerical value on information from each of the several information sources as it relates to various position requirements. One of the implications of Table 4.4 is that before data can be utilized by persons charged with responsibility for selecting school personnel, they must be evaluated and organized to facilitate analysis. Data relating to impact of applicant on the behavioral characteristics of pupils are worthy of special attention because they are readily quantified and related to instructional goals and objectives.

One important task in dealing with applicant data is to summarize them so that they are meaningful to selectors. Raw scores from tests can be converted into percentile ranks or standard scores so as to be comparable with normative information. Graphic profiles may also be used to portray the results of evaluation. Whenever possible, information should be expressed in quantitative terms. When descriptive data cannot be quantified readily, judgments of responsible individuals will have to be relied on to order the rankings. By treating data from application blanks, interview guide sheets, reference and background check forms, tests, and other sources so that they can be capsulized into a profile of the diverse dimensions of a candidate, the task of relating characteristics of applicants to specifications in the position guides can be accomplished more effectively.

Figure 4.12 illustrates a summary assessment form employed to summarize judgments of candidates for the principalship. The model, it should be noted, is limited to skill requirements for the position. The format can be extended to include other requirements, such as personal characteristics and knowledge. Figure 4.12 contains criteria employed in an urban school system to judge applicants for professional positions.

TABLE 4.4
Position-person compatibility profile employed in the selection process.

| Sources of Information about Applicant | Position Requirements—Rate Applicant Information as Follows: 1 = Marginal, 2 = Acceptable, 3 = Desirable | | |
	A Ability to Perform Key Duties	B Personal Qualifications	C Position-Related Preparation and Experience
Application blank	1	3	3
Interviews			
Preliminary		3	2
Diagnostic		1	3
Biographical inventory		1	3
References	3	2	3
Academic transcripts			
High school			2
College			3
Graduate school			3
Tests			
Medical			
Paper-pencil			
Teaching performance	3	3	3
Performance assessment	3	3	2
Placement agency data	2	2	3
Total for applicant	12	18	30
Standard for position	10	16	22
Difference	+2	+2	+8

Note: Column A = Ability to perform key duties: (a) planning for teaching, (b) developing classroom climate, and (c) managing the classroom.
Column B = Personal qualifications: (a) aptitudes, (b) role commitment, (c) interests, (d) physical requirements, and (e) social requirements.
Column C = Position-related preparation and experience.

An important task confronting selectors is to find meaning in the many bits and pieces of information gathered for each applicant. When all the information about a candidate is juxtaposed with the requirements of the position and those of the school system, the selector must compare the two sets of information and then predict whether the applicant will perform according to expectations. However, out of the considerable pool of infor-

Name of Applicant _____ Date _____ Assessor(s) _____

Key Skill Requirements for Principalship	Performance Level Indicators	Assessment Summary		
		Weight of Requirements	Assessment of Applicant	Weighted Assessment
Instructional leadership	Promoted to present position on basis of assertive instructional leadership role.	10	9	90
Participation in staff selection	Relies heavily on central staff recommendation.	9	5	45
Provision of support to teaching staff	Not as assertive as desired in enforcing discipline.	9	6	54
Staff development	Staff development programs not closely tied to instructional program.	10	5	50
Classroom observation	Judged to spend considerable time in observing teaching–learning activities.	9	8	72
Implementation of systemwide purposes, policies, and programs	Understands system mission and focuses activities of school attendance unit on linking individual unit and systemwide plans.	10	8	80
				(Total) 391

FIGURE 4.12

Assessment summary form for principalship applicants (with previous principalship experience) at Green Mountain school district.

mation, it is important to consider what facts, information, impressions, and incidents are predictive of performance.

Behavioral consistencies and inconsistencies, if they can be identified and documented, provide certain clues. Similarly, the critical-incident technique, or variations of it, can be used to probe for further information or to verify impressions about candidate potential. The critical incident is a significant incident, event, or happening in the life of an individual that indicates highly effective or ineffective behavior. Incidents are examined in terms of whether responses to problems encountered in previous positions are predictive of success or failure in the position for which application has been made. The selector's role in evaluating critical incidents is to draw inferences from facts and predict whether the applicant will perform satisfactorily. One danger in the use of this method is that certain incidents may be overemphasized or underemphasized or that improper inferences may be drawn. A means designed to minimize judgmental errors about the meaning of information is to involve all members of the selection team analyzing the significance of applicant information in relation to the position under consideration.

In making the decision about a candidate for a given position, it should be noted that data may contain clues, as is evident in these questions:

- Does the applicant show a good record of achievement?
- Has the applicant held responsible positions?
- Are there sudden shifts in careers?
- Are the cultural values of the applicant and the system compatible?
- Is the applicant a transient?
- Does the résumé clearly indicate whether the candidate is currently employed?
- Does the title fully describe the applicant's role?
- Is the résumé clear about education?
- Does the candidate suffer from a self-improvement syndrome?
- Does the candidate give a true picture of his/her marital history?
- What salary does he/she command?
- Is the résumé canned?
- Why does the applicant want the job?

The selection decision, it should be noted, is influenced to a considerable extent by the assumptions selectors hold. These include assumptions about achieving perfection in matching persons and positions, possibilities of people and positions changing after the selection process has been completed, and the validity and reliability of the initial information gathered about a member of the system being considered for a change in position.

Selection Decision: Responsibilities.   As illustrated in Table 4.5, organization of the selection process entails a series of decisions as to which activities can best be carried out by positions in the central administration and which by those in school attendance units. The intent of Table 4.5 is to illustrate the need for planning the selection process and for allocating responsibilities to achieve both efficiency and effectiveness. It would seem to be clear from examination of problems involved in personnel selection that continuity of and results deriving from the selection process are best achieved through organized effort, including preparation of plans in advance of the actual task of matching people and positions.

Postselection

After candidates for a position have been evaluated, individual decisions must be made regarding each applicant in the postselection phase (Phase 3 in Figure 4.4) of the selection process. The decision will rest on what is known about the applicant and on judgments about how effectively he/she will perform under known and unknown conditions. Decisions also need to be made about the terms of employment that should be established. There are several possibilities at this point in the selection process, that is, the system may decide to employ or reject the candidate or the candidate may decide to accept or reject the offer.

In various school systems, one employment technique is to place those individuals judged to be qualified for a position on an eligibility list. Although the definition of an eligibility list probably varies somewhat among school districts, it is generally taken to mean that those persons responsible for selecting personnel have designated as suitable for employment applicants who have met established qualifications. The eligibility list adheres to the merit principle and provides a list of applicants, in rank order, eligible for appointment as vacancies occur.

Before personnel nominations are made from the eligibility list, it is customary to require evidence from each candidate that certification or license regulations specified by law as being essential to the performance of a particular position have been met. Teachers, lawyers, engineers, administrators, nurses, and doctors are usually required to have certificates to perform their functions. This stage of the selection process would appear to be an appropriate time for the system to make certain that certification requirements have been satisfied.

As noted earlier, ability to sustain the integrity of the personnel program depends on a number of conditions, one of which is the separation of policy formulation and execution. In the selection process, the chief executive should have the exclusive responsibility for making all recommendations for appointment to positions or jobs in the system. Final approval or

TABLE 4.5
Distribution of responsibilities involved in the personnel selection process.

Selection Activities	Responsible Agent							
	Superintendent	Assistant Superintendent	Personnel Director	Principal	Assistant Principal	Supervisor	Department Head	Other
Development of selection policy								
Organization and administration of selection process								
Budgeting for selection process								
Provision of clerical and secretarial support								
Employment of consultant services								
Conduct of training sessions for personnel selection								
Development of position guides								
Formulation of selection criteria								
Development and administration of forms and records to facilitate selection process								

Selection Activities	Responsible Agent							
	Superintendent	Assistant Superintendent	Personnel Director	Principal	Assistant Principal	Supervisor	Department Head	Other
Gathering applicant information								
Checking applicant information								
Processing applicant information								
Evaluation of applications								
Selection of personnel								
Notification of unsuccessful applicants								
Employment of personnel								
Assignment of personnel								
Evaluation of results of selection process								
Updating and improving selection plans								

rejection of recommendations made by the chief executive is a responsibility of the board of education.

One of the difficulties in the selection process is that posed by the time factor. Many desirable candidates are lost to competing systems because of the time lag between the initial interview and official election by the board of education. Every effort should be made to keep to a minimum the time involved in selecting a candidate; it is especially important that there be no delay in notifying candidates of official appointment.

In the selection process, it is not unusual for situations to develop in which applicants considered do not meet current position requirements. A range of alternatives (which can be explored in this connection before a decision is made to offer employment or to place an individual on the eligibility list) includes these possibilities: (a) delay filling the position, (b) renew the search, (c) provide specific developmental experiences for persons considered to be good risks but who need to improve skills to fill position expectations, (d) fill the position temporarily, and (e) employ the applicant, but for a different opening.

Contracts. A contractual agreement is essential before hiring is completed. By definition, a contract is an agreement between two or more people to do or not to do certain things. A teaching contract, for example, is an agreement between the board of education and the teacher that specifies the nature of the personal services the board intends to purchase in exchange for a specified sum of money. The general elements of a contract include (a) mutual assent (i.e., offer and acceptance), (b) consideration, (c) legally competent parties, (d) subject matter not prohibited by law, and (e) agreement in the form required by law.

Terms of Employment. It may be useful at this point to review the relationship of contracts for school personnel to the total selection process. The contract should be viewed as a personnel tool of considerable value in furthering the career-service concept: controlling the quality of personnel who enter the school system and the profession, contributing to the security of staff members who render satisfactory service, and clarifying terms of employment and conditions of service. Thus, the employment agreement between the individual and the organization may be conceived as a control device, one use of which is to withhold permanent tenure from probationary personnel who have proved unsatisfactory. This practice is emphasized because it has proved to be much more effective and realistic than the difficult process of dismissing unsatisfactory teachers who have gained tenure.

Before the selection process is completed, the applicant and the organization must come to an agreement on the terms of employment. This is a crucial stage of selection because it is the time when complete understanding should be reached between the two parties as to conditions of employment. Misunderstandings frequently occur about salaries, duties, authority, office or work space, secretarial assistance, collateral benefits, overtime, and extra pay for extra work. Employment agreements made by telephone should be confirmed in writing. This practice has considerable merit, regardless of the means by which agreements are made. The position guide is helpful, for example, in defining position expectations, but written contracts can help to elaborate on and specify in clear and understandable language the key terms of employment. Many people become disgruntled and develop negative attitudes toward the organization when promises made during the selection period are not fulfilled after the position has been accepted. Therefore, it is good practice, during the final stages of selection, to use a checklist containing the terms of employment. This checklist should be designed to ensure that the prospective employee knows the exact nature of the position and its responsibilities, moonlighting policy, compensation structure and its relationship to the applicant's paycheck, terms of the probationary period, collateral benefits, terms of any union or associational contracts in force, and provisions unique to a given position, such as status or status symbols.

REVIEW AND PREVIEW

Every organization recognizes the inevitability of personnel turnover and of vacancies created by new positions and promotions. This chapter has examined the process by which positions and people are matched to fulfill the human resources requirements of the system. The basic idea behind the selection process is to organize activities in such a way that information about applicants can be compared to position requirements. The process may be simple or elaborate, depending on the size of the school system, the number of vacancies, and the board's recruitment policy.

Generally speaking, most selection processes include the following steps: reception, central screening interview, completion and review of application blanks, completion of tests required by the system, decentralized interview, background investigation, nomination, and appointment.

A well-organized selection process governs all actions necessary to achieve its mission and indicates who should do what and when. Attention to some of the important details in selection is of considerable importance both to the candidate and the organization. The manner in which applicants are treated during the selection process has a good deal to do with the way they perceive the system and interpret the perceptions of others.

Because the selection process determines which personnel will enter the system, the central administration must give careful attention to the design and operation of the process. In doing so, it must free itself of certain illusions, including the belief that a good selection process will eliminate personnel selection errors, selection of people is an exact science, and position guides and selection ratings are infallible techniques for matching people and positions.

In Chapter 5, the personnel induction process is treated as another stage in the human resources management life cycle to facilitate development and career path planning of individuals new to the system or new to another position in the system.

REVIEW AND DISCUSSION QUESTIONS

1. Cite five court decisions relevant to the selection of school personnel.

2. Identify four major problems in reference checking.

3. Explain how position analysis (commonly referred to as job analysis) is related to recruitment, selection, appraisal, development, and compensation.

4. Define and distinguish among differences in the following terms: validity, reliability, criterion, criterion-related validity, and content validity.

5. How does one judge the validity and reliability of an application blank? A teaching aptitude test?

6. Why do so few school systems attempt to validate their selection techniques?

7. Make a list of items you would consider questionable when developing an application blank (items that may violate public employment policy).

8. Why is it necessary to consider personnel selection instruments in terms of validity and reliability?

9. *Interview exercise*—The instructor will provide members of the class with materials essential for conducting an actual interview (position description, completed application blank, school system, work site, and related employment data). One four-person group will conduct a structured interview that has been developed by another four-person group. One class member will act as the interviewee, and a third four-person group will critique the exercise.

10. According to a report in the Miami Herald (February 20, 1990), IA, 192 of 1,506 Dade County public school bus drivers (13 percent) have been arrested on felony charges (burglary, drugs, sex crimes, and assault). Nine have been convicted (including two for murder). What are the implications of these data in regard to:

   • The selection process?
   • Employment of support personnel who have contact with children?
   • Criminal history checks?
   • The information system?

CHAPTER EXERCISE 4.1

Directions: You are a member of the Board of Education of a school system. Would you vote for or against each of the following practices governing the selection of human resources?

• Employing relatives of members of the Board.
• Requiring candidates to reside in the school district in pre- and post-application.

- A suggestion by a school board member that votes on every candidate should be "equal and fair rather than equal and stupid."
- Employment by trial.
- Position previews for all applicants.
- Preemployment medical testing.
- Reference checking by telephone.
- Résumé checking for all applicants.
- Board members interviewing all applicants.
- Board members making all employment decisions.
- Employing applicants with disabilities.
- Probationary period before benefit eligibility.
- Union participation in selection decisions.
- Retaining application forms of unsuccessful candidates.
- Testing applicants for physical or mental stress.
- Requiring applicants to "sell themselves."
- Stipulating that some positions are for men, others for women.
- Requiring all candidates to agree in writing to adhere to system dress code.
- Disclosing criminal convictions.
- Using a consumer (credit) report in evaluating a candidate for employment.
- Requiring disclosure of arrest records.
- Requesting detailed information on marital, housing, religion, family, and child care matters.
- Requiring comprehensive information on medical condition.
- Using a professional psychologist to evaluate prospective employees.
- Retaining legal counsel regarding the selection process and all preemployment decisions.
- Permitting community political party currently in power to nominate all support personnel.
- Refusing to hire extremely overweight applicants because obesity is an unacceptable health risk.
- Adjusting test scores to account for an applicant's race.

NOTES

1. The following list of publications devoted to affirmative action and EEO includes magazines and updated loose leaf services arranged alphabetically by topic: Mary F. Cook, Editor, The Human Resources Yearbook, 1993 / 1994 Edition (Englewood Cliffs, NJ: Prentice-Hall Inc., 1993), 18.22; Bureau of National Affairs, Affirmative Action Compliance Manual (Washington, DC: Pub:Monthly); Affirmative Action Register (St. Louis, MO: Pub:Monthly); Commercial Clearing House, Inc., EEOC Compliance Manual (Chicago, IL: Pub:Periodically); Bureau of National Affairs, EEOC Compliance Manual (Washington, DC: Pub:Periodic updates); Commerce Clearing House, Inc., Employment Practices Guide (Chicago, IL: Pub:Bi-Weekly); Maxwell Macmillan, Equal Employment Opportunity Compliance Manual (Englewood Cliffs, NJ: Pub:Monthly); Bureau of National Affairs, Fair Employment Practices (Washington, DC: Pub:Bi-Weekly; Bureau of National Affairs, Index to Government Regulations (Washington, DC: Pub:Monthly); Bureau of Business Practices, Legal Insights for Managers (Waterford, CT: Pub:Monthly).

2. Erwin S. Stanton, Successful Personnel Recruiting and Selection Within EEO/Affirmative Action Guidelines (New York: American Management Associations; 1977); see also Commercial Clearing House Inc., EEO Compliance Manual (Chicago, IL: Pub:Periodically).

3. Federal Register 43, 166 (8.25.78), 38290–92.

4. Fair Employment Practices Manual (Washington, DC: Bureau of National Affairs, updated edition).

5. Vida G. Scarpello and James Ledvinka, Personnel/Human Resources Management (Boston, MA: PWS-Kent, 1988), 293–94.

6. EEOC, Pre-Employment Inquiries and Equal Employment Opportunity Law (Washington, DC: Equal Employment Opportunity Commission, Office of Public Affairs, 1983), 1.

7. Craig Eric Schneier, "Content Validity: The Necessity for a Behavioral Job Description," Personnel Administrator (February, 1976).

8. A. K. Korman, Industrial and Organizational Psychology (Englewood Cliffs, NJ: Prentice-Hall Inc., 1971), 178–204.

9. M. G. Miner and J. B. Miner, Employee Selection within the Law (Washington, DC: Bureau of National Affairs, 1978); see also Richard S. Lowell and Jay A. DeLoach, "Equal Employment Opportunities: Are You Overlooking the Application Blank?" Personnel 59, 4 (July-August 1982), 49–55; and Jerome Siegel, Personnel Testing Under EEO (New York: American Management Association, 1980).

10. William C. Byham, "Screening and Selection," in William R. Tracey, Editor, Human Resources Management & Development Handbook (New York: American Management Association, 1985), 573.

11. Frank J. Landy and Don A. Trumbo, Psychology of Work Behavior, Revised Edition (Homewood, IL: Dorsey Press, 1980), 220.

12. William F. Glueck, Personnel: A Diagnostic Approach, Revised Edition (Dallas, TX: Business Publications, 1978), 202.

13. Duane P. Schulz, Psychology and Industry Today, Third Edition (New York: Macmillan Publishing), 94.

14. Schulz, 94–96.

15. See Schulz for detailed description of future autobiography.

16. Malcom Ritter, "Trying to Reduce Lying by Applicants for Jobs," Philadelphia Inquirer (September 5, 1989), D13.

17. Scarpello and Ledvinka, 331.

18. See Dale S. Beach, Personnel: The Management of People at Work, Fourth Edition (New York: Macmillan Publishing, 1975), Chapter 10.

19. Edward C. Webster, The Employment Interview (Schomberg, Ontario, Canada: S.I.P. Publications, 1982), 13–14.

20. Landy and Trumbo, 219.

21. Educational Testing Service, P.O. Box 6108, Princeton, NJ.

22. For the reader interested in additional treatment of human resources testing and its regulatory boundaries, see Mary F. Cook, The Human Resources Yearbook: 1993 / 1994 Edition (Englewood Cliffs, NJ: 1993); Henry H. Perritt Jr., Your Rights in the Workplace (New York: Practicing Law Institute, 1993); University of Nebraska Press, Mental Measurements Yearbook (Lin-

coln, NE); University of Nebraska Press, Tests in Print (Lincoln, NE); William B. Werther and Keith Davis, Human Resources and Personnel Development (New York: McGraw-Hill Inc., 1993).

23. See Robert P. Vecchio, "The Problem of Phony Resumes: How to Spot a Ringer among the Applicants," Personnel 61, 2 (March-April, 1984).

SUPPLEMENTARY READING

Arvey, Richard; and James Campion. "The Employment Interview: A Summary and Review of Recent Research." Personnel Psychology 35 (Summer 1982), 305.

Blocklyn, Paul. "Preemployment Testing." Personnel (February 1988), 66—68.

Boe, Erling E.; and Dorothy M. Gilford. Teacher Supply, Demand and Quality: Policy Issues, Models, and Data Bases. (Washington: National Academy Press, 1992).

Broussard, Richard D. "Credential Distortions: Personnel Practitioners Give Their Views." Personnel Administrator (June 1986), 129.

Castetter, William B. "Administering the School System's Human Resources Function." National Forum of Educational Administration and Supervision Journal (1993), 3–17.

Collyer, Rosemary M. "Preemployment Medical Testing: An Overview." Legal Report (Summer 1989), 1–8.

Haberman, Martin. Recruiting and Selecting Teachers for Urban Schools. New York: ERIC Clearinghouse on Urban Education, 1987.

Herman, Susan J. Hiring Right: A Practical Guide. Thousand Oaks, CA: Sage Publishing Inc., 1993.

Lotito, Michael J. "The Employee Polygraph Protection Act: Striking a Balance Between Employer and Employee Rights." Legal Report (Winter 1988), 1–8.

Panaro, Gerard P. "Minimize the Danger of Giving References." Personnel Journal (August, 1988), 93–96.

Rice, J. D. "Privacy Legislation: Its Effect on Pre-Employment Reference Checking." Personnel Administrator (February 1978), 46–51.

Rothwell, William J. Effective Succession Planning. New York: American Management Association, 1994.

Sewell, Carol. "Pre-Employment Investigations: The Key to Security in Hiring." Personnel Journal (May 1981), 376–379.

Chapter 5

Induction

CHAPTER OVERVIEW

CHAPTER OBJECTIVES

- Stress the importance of the induction process to inductee socialization.
- Present a working model of the induction process.
- Focus on ways to help inductees achieve the highest level of performance in the shortest period of time.
- Identify adjustments essential for inductees to perform effectively.
- Link the induction process to individual career planning.

CHAPTER TERMS

Career Planning   Norms

Induction   Organizational culture

Induction process   Socialization

Educational institutions are created and maintained to achieve purposes and objectives. Attainment of desired results in any organization depends on the behavior of the people it employs. The purpose of this chapter is to explore means by which the induction process can be designed to enhance the development of desirable performance-related behavior of individuals as they are initiated into new assignments. The discussion will begin with an examination of the concept of induction as it relates to human performance. After discussing the behavioral foundations of induction, we will present a model of the induction process, examining in detail the sequence of induction activities designed to achieve long-range induction strategy.

INDUCTION AND HUMAN PERFORMANCE

Induction may be defined as a systematic organizational effort to assist personnel to adjust readily and effectively to new assignments so that they can contribute maximally to work of the system while realizing personnel and position satisfaction. This definition of induction, it should be noted, goes beyond the conventional view that induction is concerned only with personnel new to an assignment, such as someone new to the system or someone within the system taking over a new assignment because of forced or voluntary transfer or reassignment. It includes personnel assuming new assignments after returning from a leave of absence, those reassigned because of system or unit reorganization, or those assuming new roles because of a reduction in the work force (see Figure 5.1).

A school system can recruit, select, assign, reassign, and transfer personnel, but until these individuals become fully adjusted to the work they must perform, the environment in which it is performed, and colleagues with whom it is performed, they cannot be expected to give their best effort to attaining goals of the institution. Initiation of an effective **induction process** is one way the organization can contribute to assimilation of personnel as well as to their personal development, security, and need satisfaction. Probably at no other time during the employment cycle does the newly appointed or newly assigned staff member need more consideration, guidance, and understanding than between the day of the new assignment and the time when one becomes a self-motivated, self-directed, fully effective member of the enterprise.

One of the emotional needs of every employed individual is an organizational environment in which one can find a reasonable degree of security and satisfaction. The school employee beginning in the new position is no exception. This inductee is apprehensive of many things, such as the community, co-workers, or ability to succeed. The newcomer is generally unaware of "the way we do things here." This individual is ordinarily uninformed about school objectives, specific duties and responsibilities, school and community traditions and taboos, and personal and position standards to which members are expected to adhere. Voluntary resignations in school systems are known to occur during the probation period. One of the causes to which this problem has been attributed is the absence of well-planned induction practices. The variety of adjustments newly assigned staff members need to make before they are totally assimilated into the organization is extensive and important enough to warrant administrative efforts to assist them through well-planned induction programs. It is clear, for example,

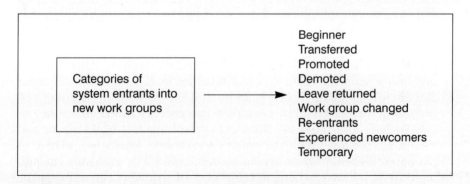

FIGURE 5.1
Entrants and re-entrants included in the induction program.

that the number of first-year teachers who leave the profession is higher than it ought to be, and the loss is higher than the profession ought to sustain. It is also true that personnel turnover represents an economic loss to the system. Investment in recruiting, selecting, inducting, and supervising new personnel is dissipated when they leave the system voluntarily. One of the aims of the induction process is to minimize this drain on the system's financial and human resources.

To say that educational systems have not been or are not now concerned with the problems of the inductee would be a misstatement; many excellent programs are in operation. However, it is probably fair to say that for some systems, approaches to induction have not been developed through systematic planning. Induction will take place for personnel, regardless of system action or intent. Because induction plays so vital a role in attainment of system, unit, and individual goals, it is essential that the process be properly designed and controlled.

Due in part to various studies and literature relating to organizational entry, the subject of induction has taken on a new and more crucial importance for reasons including:

- People change their behaviors when they become members of groups.[1]
- Research suggests that formal induction programs tend to be superior to unplanned activities.[2]
- The induction period is of prime importance to both the organization and the inductee, representing a time in which the **socialization** process enables the newcomer to learn about the organization's culture, norms, and standards of behavior. The organization, through the induction process, is able to initiate programs designed to enhance the quality of the social system within the institution.
- Entry problems, such as a lack of supervisory induction skills, inappropriate first assignment, absence of feedback regarding early performance, and lack of relevant information needed by inductees, can be minimized with carefully designed programs.[3]
- Various induction studies have identified numerous types of induction problems of newcomers, including the need for respect, liking, belonging, and a sense of competence; difficulties in classroom management and discipline; unknown expectations; and the necessity of planning and preparing for teaching. Five everyday professional problems for beginners include difficulties in affiliation, control, parent relationships, and time management.[4] With the emergence of state legislation relative to basing certification on classroom success,[5] as well as problems encountered by first-year teachers, development of strategies for utilizing the induction process to enhance teacher professional competence becomes an important aspect of the human resources function.

BEHAVIOR AND THE INDUCTION PROCESS

Strategy behind the induction process is twofold: (a) the short-range tactic is to facilitate adjustment of the individual to the new role, and (b) the long-range strategy is to utilize the process to initiate what is referred to as *shaping* or *selected reinforcement of performances* that approach some socially acceptable standard.[6]

Luthans and Kreitner, in explaining the shaping process, note that at the time of joining an organization, an individual possesses a behavior repertoire that can be classified into four general categories: desirable performance-related behavior, potentially disruptive performance-related behavior, behavior unrelated to performance, and performance behavior deficiencies.[7]

One aspect of the relationship between these behavioral categories and the induction process is presented in Figure 5.2, which divides personnel performance into two zones: unacceptable and acceptable. This design format assumes that the induction process is the time during which and the means by which the organization initiates the shaping process through which positive control is exercised to encourage and enhance development of those performances conducive to individual, unit, and organizational goals. During the induction process the system gathers information about newcomers relative to position-related behavior, seeks to positively reinforce those behaviors that are acceptable, gathers information on performance deficiencies, develops through a management-by-objectives approach a series of performance targets to correct performance deficiencies, and through day-by-day supervision helps the individual to achieve organizational socialization. Although the concept of shaping is employed in other human resources processes (and will be discussed subsequently in this and other chapters), the point of the concept illustrated in Figure 5.2 is that the induction process is the starting point in the employment cycle for performance analysis and improvement. It is, in essence, the process by which the system's technology is applied to measure, analyze, understand, predict, and guide performance-related behavior; strengthen and increase performances that are goal oriented; and minimize, suppress, and eliminate those categories of behavior that are disruptive and nonsupportive.

The terms *induction, placement, organizational entry, assignment,* and *orientation*—often used synonymously in the literature dealing with personnel administration—mean the process by which personnel newly appointed to

Unacceptable Behavior Zone	Acceptable Behavior Zone

FIGURE 5.2
Performance-related behavior zones.

positions are assisted in meeting their need for security, belonging, status, information, and direction in both the position and the organizational environment. The process is conceived as beginning in the recruitment stage and ending when the inductee has made the necessary personal, position, organizational, and social adaptations that enable one to function fully and effectively as a member of the school staff. It involves more than plans for making new personnel feel at ease in an unfamiliar environment; the induction processes, in its broadest sense, is an extension of the recruitment and selection process (in which administrative efforts are designed to match person and position). A corollary objective of the process is to enable the person to achieve position satisfaction. In addition, the process should help to fully utilize satisfactions and abilities of the person for attaining goals of the educational program.

NATURE AND SCOPE OF THE INDUCTION PROCESS

Figure 5.3 represents a conceptualization of the induction process. Examination of this figure will show that the steps envisioned in the process include activities normally associated with any administrative endeavor: planning, organizing, leading, and controlling. An additional observation should be made about Figure 5.3, that is, the induction process represents another of the components or subsystems of the human resources function; it is linked to other subsystems within and outside of the personnel sector, and it is woven into the total configuration of the system.

Although we encounter the various steps outlined in Figure 5.3 in more detail in the discussion that follows, these questions have been framed to illustrate the kinds of decisions that confront administrators as they plan for assimilating personnel into the system:

- What does the *system* expect to achieve through the induction process? What should happen to the *institution* as a result of the induction process? The *inductee*?

- What types of activities are needed to achieve expectations of the induction process? How will induction activities be allocated into organiza-

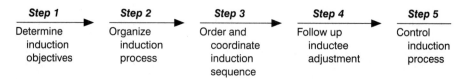

FIGURE 5.3
Model of the induction process.

tional assignments? How will separate assignments be integrated so that purposeful action will result?

- Which induction activities will be assigned to the central administration of the system? To attendance units?

- How should induction activities be phased? What actions should be taken prior to appointment? Before the employee has reported for work? Before work begins? During the probationary period? Who does what during each of the phases of the induction cycle?

- What controls should be exercised to make the induction process conform to plan? What kinds of appraisals are necessary to determine the effectiveness of the process?

We can get at the heart of most induction problems by focusing on these questions. The following sections consider in detail how a school system puts to use, in actual practice, concepts suggested in the questions and in the outline shown in Figure 5.2.

GOALS OF THE INDUCTION PROCESS

What does the school system expect the induction process to accomplish? This question focuses on one of the primary elements of planning—deciding what should be achieved (Step 1 of Figure 5.3.). The purpose of the process is to facilitate adjustment of new personnel to the work environment in which they render service to the system. This statement will have little significance for people who plan the process or for those responsible for its implementation unless it is translated into more specific objectives (the first step in the induction process). An elaboration of objectives of the process follows, beginning with an illustration of the several objectives listed in Figure 5.4, which have been gleaned from research studies, human resources manuals, and current literature relative to the induction process.[8]

Knowledge about the induction process indicates that (a) turnover tends to occur primarily during the early period of employment; (b) turnover often engenders hostility and resistance within the system, particularly if a replacement in a position of authority represents the force of change; (c) change within a social system generally tends to be viewed unfavorably, particularly where membership change affects group stability and relationships; (d) haphazard induction procedures can precipitate anxiety, discouragement, disillusionment, or defensive behavior; (e) security, belonging, esteem, and information problems of inductees can be minimized during the induction period; and (f) frustrations develop when newly appointed personnel discover inconsistencies between realities of organizational life and their expectations and values at the time of employment. Objectives of the process, then, need to be

- Assist members to appreciate the values, abilities, expected behaviors, and social knowledge essential to undertaking a system role and contributing to its mission.
- Provide inductees with complete and uniform information about the school system's mission, organization, structure, functions, policies, and work requirements.
- Develop loyal, effective, and productive workers.
- Reduce the likelihood of rule violation, discharges, resignations, and grievances.
- Address performance problems before they occur.
- Minimize the gap between employment expectancy and reality.
- Ease the transition from one institutional or work environment to another.
- Promote professional and personal well-being of inductees.
- Satisfy regulatory mandates.
- Develop a basic knowledge of the need for positive adjustment to external, internal, position, cultural, social, and personal aspects of system membership.
- Place inductees in positions so as to balance school system needs with individual competencies and aspirations.
- Reduce inductee anxiety.
- Reduce cost and supervisory time.

FIGURE 5.4
Induction objectives.

focused on minimizing difficulties that a change in membership poses both for existing personnel and individuals about to enter the system.

An important aim in the induction process is to provide information not fully covered during the recruitment and selection processes. For example, the individual recruiter may not have been capable of explaining to the recruit all the ramifications involved in a given position assignment. The administrator to whom a newcomer is assigned will need to take care of whatever remains to be done for the latter to make full adjustment to system life.

The process should enable every inductee, from caretaker to chief executive, to be fully informed about the community; duties, relationships, and responsibilities of the position; characteristics of the system (purpose, policies, procedures, personnel, customs, and history); and the building unit to which the inductee will be assigned. One of the major expectations of induction is that newly appointed personnel will be furnished with whatever information is necessary to facilitate their adjustment.

Position satisfaction and growth in ability of new personnel to be self-directing are legitimate and practical ends of induction. The process should contribute to position satisfaction and increasing the ability of the inductee to perform at a level of efficiency that lessens the need for supervision. This involves a carefully designed and controlled series of activities planned by the system to analyze and improve human performance by (a) identifying the present performance level of the individual newly assigned to a position, (b) clarifying acceptable and unacceptable levels of performance, (c) measuring personnel-related behavior, (d) identifying potential performance improvement areas, (e) establishing performance targets, (f) measuring change in performance, and (g) recycling performance targets.

Interests of the system regarding the newcomer extend beyond immediate activities involved in the induction process. For every newly employed individual, a positive attitude toward the system should be developed, one that will endure throughout a career period. This is an ultimate system objective. Other organization interests relate to having the individual remain in the system and become an effective operant in the assigned position, work independently, engage in self-development, and exceed role expectations through innovative and spontaneous behavior. These are long-term system objectives for which foundations can be laid during the induction process.

At the core of the induction process is a formal commitment of the board of education regarding induction policies and practices. One example of this official stance, which serves as a keystone for the Riverpark school system's induction policies and practices, is presented in Figure 5.5. This statement represents a formal declaration of the system's guiding principles:

- It provides a vision for realizing short- and long-term induction objectives.
- It communicates official board of education induction intent.
- It embodies a formalized proactive induction planning design, as well as an open forum for employee participation in developing policies and practices that affect their lives and their world of work.

ORGANIZATION OF THE INDUCTION PROCESS

Organization of the induction process (Step 2 of Figure 5.3) consists of dividing and grouping induction activities homogeneously and establishing relationships among individuals responsible for performing various functions connected with induction objectives. This section deals first with variables that influence implementation of the induction process, then with problems of induction around which activities are organized, specifically with the matter of who does what in initiating, maintaining, and controlling the process.

To create a stimulating environment for the investiture of inductees (initial hires, internal transfers, promotees, demotees, and temporaries) the Riverpark school system gives primacy to these courses of action:

- Envision inductee placement in the context of future system positions and human resources strategy.
- Embody state-of-the-art practices in the induction process.
- Establish lines of authority and responsibility for the conduct of the induction process.
- Ensure maintenance of ethical standards and integrity in the conduct of the induction process.
- Deal ethically and professionally with problems posed by special groups (disabled, inexperienced, underprivileged).
- Emphasize variation in work assignments such as team concept, work unit culture, and individual responsibility.
- Give consideration, when there is a diversity of positions available, by comparing an individual's aptitudes, abilities, interests, and temperament with requirements of various openings to determine inductee suitability.
- Design the induction process to enhance the ability of inductees to proceed from "newly appointed" to productive team members without loss or interval of time.
- Form cooperative and interdependent relationships in the system's social, work, and community environments.
- Shape the induction process through policies, programs, purposes, and procedures conducive to performance expectations, position expectations, and retentive power.
- Contribute to assimilation, socialization, security, personal development, and need satisfaction of position entrants.
- Gear the induction process to create a bonding among the three induction phases (preappointment, interim period, and probationary service).
- Update the human resources manual to provide for current information needs of appointees and members of the induction team.
- Utilize, during each of the induction stages, selected induction approaches for systemwide, departmental, work unit, and position application.

FIGURE 5.5
Form and structure of the Riverpark school system induction process.

In the spirit of current educational reform and restructuring, various types of induction programs are being installed and implemented. There are different induction approaches in place throughout the United States, depending on location, size, budgetary constraints, regulatory mandates, leadership, and proactive and reactive stances to institutional change.

One way to characterize contemporary induction activity is in terms of five types of programs, such as:

- University-school system collaboration
- Consortium programs for area school systems
- Districtwide programs
- School-based programs
- Admixture of various program components

One of the basic properties of any induction program is the form of co-worker support or assistance provided the inductee for adjustment purposes during and after induction preliminaries. Multiple plans are employed in school systems to assist the individual to change from a state of dependence on others to a state of relative independence as a mature staff member possessed with a personal set of behavioral determiners. This assistance includes various forms of supporting resources, designated in the literature by labels such as peer coaching, buddy system, master teacher support, mentor-protégé, and clinical teacher-support. Presumably, the types of staff assistance provided inductees are focused on enhancing the stages of member development, depending upon the individual's personality and willingness to adjust and adapt to the internal and external aspects of the workplace.

Variables Influencing Induction Planning

Building on the definition of the induction process discussed in the initial section of this chapter, we can now provide a framework that incorporates key induction variables and a foundation for examining their administrative implications.

Figure 5.6 illustrates the need for administrators to consider four important elements:

- *Scope of the induction process*—Includes all personnel employed by the system.
- *Variation in personnel adjustments*—Adjustments personnel need to make are both internal and external.
- *Adjustment needs*—Vary among individuals and assignments.
- *Variation in induction approaches*—Reassignment, transfer, and promotion require approaches different from those for initial assignments.

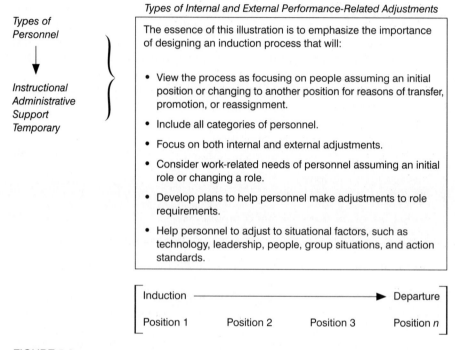

FIGURE 5.6
Variables influencing implementation of the induction process.

The definition of induction also implies that the core of the sequential induction process goes beyond the welcoming ritual. Induction should be viewed as the initial phase of a new assignment in which performance effectiveness is diagnosed, using such criteria as personal, position, interpersonal adjustment, and goal achievement. For newcomers, induction is a probationary period in which performance effectiveness is carefully diagnosed, a time during which positive behavior is reinforced and performance deficiencies viewed as the bases for development programs. For roles involving promotions, transfers, and reassignments, performance effectiveness is considered to be multidimensional, which suggests that these types of induction problems have many aspects of performance effectiveness that must be assessed and then utilized to improve performance behavior.

Induction Problems

Growing interest in induction problems of school personnel is reflected in the increasing amount of literature devoted to the subject. During the last several decades, various investigations have noted the absence of systematic induction programs, the paucity of systematic efforts to evaluate personnel orientation programs, and discrepancies between actual program designs for personnel newly assigned to positions and the real needs of such personnel. The point is frequently made that the concept of planning for induction of new personnel is neither widely understood nor accepted and that its applications are not widely practiced. Problems experienced by personnel newly appointed to school positions, as revealed in the literature dealing with the subject, include:

- Problems in becoming acquainted with the *community* and making adjustments in it.
- Problems involved in becoming knowledgeable about the *system* and its aims, policies, programs, procedures, controls, resources, customs, values, personnel, and history.
- Problems in becoming acquainted with the *position*. For teachers, this would include curricula, courses of study, pupil personnel, parents, pupil services, and learning resources. For support personnel, physical location of the position, reporting relationship, tools, supplies and equipment, and nature and expectations of the assignment are matters of concern.
- Problems in *performing* the assignment.
- Problems in getting to know *personnel* in the system.
- Problems of a *personal* nature, such as locating suitable living accommodations and finding banking, shopping, health, and transportation facilities.
- Problems in separating two aspects of induction: assistance and assessment. At a propitious point beyond the supporting and nurturing phase of induction, some form of evaluation of the individual's position performance, including strengths and limitations, is essential for a variety of reasons, including staff development, compensation, tenure, promotion, career development and self-assurance. Research indicates that inductees welcome "beneficial feedback" from clinical support teachers so long as these "friendly critics" are not in a formative evaluation role.

Many of the difficulties of first-year teachers, such as those mentioned, have been attributed to faulty programs of induction. The discussion that follows is designed to elaborate on the nature of such induction problems.

Community Adjustment

It is an article of faith among educators that the community is an important conditioner of educational quality. Moreover, research on effectiveness in schooling and teaching indicates the importance of the community in school improvement. The more effective schools:

. . . enlist the community in the service of education. They scoop up community resources and they involve community members in educational roles—as aides, tutors, and as providers of educational resources through businesses, museums, and other settings.[9]

Effective schools have been found to have more parent and community contact than less-effective schools, and effective schools usually have more positive parent-initiated contacts than do less-effective schools.[10] An interesting paradox, however, is that studies of teacher induction consistently point out that means employed to inform prospective or newly appointed teachers about the community or to help them make adjustments therein generally are less than satisfactory. As a matter of fact, the incidence of difficulties experienced by teachers in securing information about the community and in making adjustments to it is serious enough to reinforce the contention that administratively much more can and should be done to help inductees become fully acquainted with the community structure and characteristics. If the relationship of the community to the school is as strategic as it is purported to be, then it would appear that the system should develop plans to help the school staff, especially newly appointed members, in understanding the community and its effect on the school.

Inductees, whether new teachers, new administrators, or new members of the support staff moving into the community, need a variety of specific kinds of information not only for making adjustments in the community but also for helping them to fulfill their roles. Information on such matters as community geography, economy, housing, government, religious agencies, educational resources, law enforcement agencies, public safety, health conditions, medical resources, recreation facilities, child care, family welfare agencies, and community planning resources is needed by beginners to help them adjust to new surroundings.

The school has an important responsibility to raise the level of public understanding of education. It shares also in the responsibility for community improvement. What the school staff contributes to these ends depends to a large extent on staff understanding of the community. The induction process provides the administration with favorable opportunities for helping newcomers to become adjusted to the community, acquainting them with avenues therein through which they can achieve personal objectives, and demonstrating how community resources can be employed to contribute to the betterment of the school system.

Position Adjustment

Indications are that newly appointed personnel experience difficulties in understanding their assignments, and many of these problems are related to lack of a clear and workable conception of the school's mission and its goals. These difficulties also indicate lack of knowledge about using special services provided for children by the system. It is manifest that the position the new employee is to assume be of paramount importance in determining what his/her information needs will be. The value of position guides in helping the new employee become acquainted with his/her assignment and its relationships should be noted at this point. Position guides should not only prevent applicants from accepting positions for which they are unqualified, they should also provide information to those responsible for the selection of personnel so that the task of matching candidates and positions can be performed more effectively. The inductee's immediate supervisor, with the aid of position guides, should be able to describe to a newly assigned employee the purposes and organizational expectations of the position and should be able to appraise the employee's performance on the basis of duties, responsibilities, and relationships specified in the position guide.

After the selection process is completed, the person new to the position is assigned to a work unit within the organization. Presumably, the system will have given consideration in advance of the placement decision to questions such as:

- How well does the individual fit the leadership style of the work unit?
- How well will the individual fit into the unit work environment?
- Will the newcomer be accepted by the work group?
- Will the assignment positively or negatively affect the types of staff balance (operating unit, competency, racial-ethnic-gender, staff category, program, load, utilization, and staff size) referred to in Chapter 2?

The cost of improper placement can be high. Widespread dissatisfaction may occur in the work unit when overqualified or underqualified personnel become part of the group. Similarly, serious consequences develop when newcomers are perceived by the work group as sources of disruption and restriction. Special problems arise also for the newly employed whose expectations, values, and goals are inconsistent with the realities of organizational life or for the individual whose assignment is viewed by the work group as being made on bases other than merit. Unless the selection and placement decisions are sound, effective organizational socialization for misplaced individuals is not likely to occur.

The selection process frequently overlooks these important placement elements: leadership and followership styles of the applicant, style of the persons the applicant will report to, styles of those who will report to him/her (if the position is administrative), and the structure of the job situation.[11] In the discussion of the selection process, it was emphasized that *information* is the key to making judgments about placement of an individual in a position. This includes learning as much as possible about the applicant and the specific position in which he/she will be working, so that a careful judgment can be made as to compatibility. Placing an ineffective individual in any position or a competent person in the wrong position often leads to years of administrative grief, low individual productivity, and interference with system goal attainment.

Organizational Culture Adjustment

Every organization faces the problem of informing members of its purposes, policies, and procedures. Newly appointed staff members want to know, for example, what the total operation is and how they fit into it. They need to know not only essential components of the system but also how the parts interact, contributing to the success (goal attainment) of the whole—in other words, the **organizational culture**. The system is largely responsible for seeing that personnel receive this information.

A survey of newly hired personnel indicated that of experiences related to organizational socialization, the following were mentioned most often:

- Formal on-site orientation
- Off-site residential training
- Information from other employees
- Friendly relationship with a senior executive
- Mentor relationship with a senior executive
- Information from an immediate supervisor
- Information from secretaries and support staff
- Daily interactions with peers
- Social and recreational activities with co-workers
- Business travel with co-workers[12]

An important part of the individual's adjustment to the system is awareness of specific expectations of the role. Customs associated with the role, rules that affect position performance, and the degree of autonomy permissible in fulfilling the role are kinds of information needed by individuals to enable them to fit easily and promptly into the work pattern relating to their positions.

Inductees often encounter difficulties in the socialization process that takes place between the individual and the organization. Schools may have unique belief systems that conflict with those held by new members of the staff. Opinions of individual teachers on academic freedom, teaching of controversial issues, the role of the teacher as a citizen, selection of reading matter, student behavior and appearance, and student discipline may differ considerably from the system's official values and objectives. To a certain extent, every system seeks to assimilate new personnel by orienting them to its unique values, traditions, customs, beliefs, and goals. Whether staff members will accept or reject the institution's value system, in whole or in part, is not assured. But awareness of values prevailing in the organization is essential if the inductee is to adjust effectively during the period when he/she is being considered for permanent membership in the institution.

A four-stage framework developed by Wanous to explain the socialization process includes the following developments:

- Newcomer learns the reality of the work environment.
- Newcomer identifies **norms** of co-workers and the boss.
- Newcomer makes accommodations between conflicts at the work setting and at home.
- Newcomer accepts organizational norms and realizes the organization is satisfied with his/her behavior.[13]

Every school system has a culture, that is, a set of interrelated values and priorities, norms and expectations, ideas and ideals. Norms, according to Smithers, serve a variety of useful functions, such as (a) establishing standards and shared expectations that provide a range of acceptable behavior for group members, (b) providing guidelines for unsocialized individuals to fit into the ongoing group, and (c) establishing standards for behavior that facilitate interaction between members and are a means of identifying with one's peers.[14]

Cultural shaping and reinforcement are important aspects of the induction process. During and beyond organizational entry, the system develops and implements plans for cultural transmission and acquisition by helping inductees to understand the organization's expectations for its members as well as the various means by which its desired culture is communicated. By way of example, the position guide specifies person and position requirements. A code of ethics may stress system moral and ethical standards, conflicts of interests, confidential information, and compliance with rules and regulations. Policies indicate system intent toward its human resources. The human resources handbook and union contract articulate selected roles and relationships for personnel. Expected and actual levels of performance are communicated through the appraisal system. The informal organization as well as direct and indirect behavioral influences exercised by the organization are additional means by which culture is transmitted and reinforced. Thus, the induction process represents a timely opportunity to translate system philosophy into cultural reality by describing and interpreting for persons new to a position those roles, relationships, and behaviors necessary for individual, unit, and organizational effectiveness.[15]

Personal Adjustment

For those inductees new to the community, personal problems encountered outside the actual school assignment merit attention at this point. These are problems experienced by any person who relocates: locating suitable living accommodations; arranging transportation; finding educational, religious, cultural, banking, and recreational facilities; and numerous other details that must be attended to in the process of adjusting to the new environment. The ease with which the individual is able to cope with these problems is of concern to the administration because complete adjustment to the new role is not likely to be effected until anxieties involved in getting established are relieved.

It would be unrealistic to assume that the institution could or should help individuals solve all of the many problems they will encounter in the process of being inducted into the system; many personal difficulties and conflicts must be resolved by the inductee. But the school can help by a planned program of induction that will minimize the kinds of dilemmas newly appointed personnel are likely to face. This program, the nature of which will be discussed subsequently, is necessary to improve personnel performance by aiding in the emotional adjustment every new person confronts. Such a program can also contribute to improvement of performance by providing assistance to enable personnel to become increasingly secure in their environment and progressively independent of administrative counsel and direction. A major goal of the program is individual self-direction.

Because the work of the system is carried on by and through people, the matter of developing effective interpersonal relations becomes especially important to the individual new to the system. This means that to be successful in satisfying their needs, newcomers must understand the behavior of people with whom they work, both as individuals and as members of groups. It means also that they must acquire skills to enable them to work effectively with individuals and groups. They must learn, for example, which members are most influential in informal groups, attitudes of colleagues toward the organization, and the nature of social groups with which they will be involved. They must understand also that pressures to conform to group standards can be anticipated from these groups. On this point Sherif suggests that individuals cannot remain independent of their membership groups; membership in a group will be a major influence in one's development.[16]

The function of the induction process in this regard is to facilitate integration of individuals with work and social groups in which they are likely to participate. A good deal of what the individual learns about the community, culture and subcultures of the system, formal and informal groups within the system, power structures, and position expectations will be from other individuals and groups. Consequently, the extent to which new employees satisfy their needs, achieve high productivity, and identify with the system is to a considerable degree dependent on system efforts to promote communication bonds between staff members and new personnel.

ORDERING AND COORDINATING THE INDUCTION SEQUENCE

The third step in the induction process presented in Figure 5.3 involves linkage of phases, agents, and activities, referred to here as the *individual induction sequence*. This step is conceptualized in Figure 5.7 to illustrate the sequence of induction activities continually in operation in the system. The success of this step in the process requires a conviction on the part of the board of education and school staff that these induction activities are important and often mean the difference between success or failure in retaining competent personnel. The board and staff must be convinced that

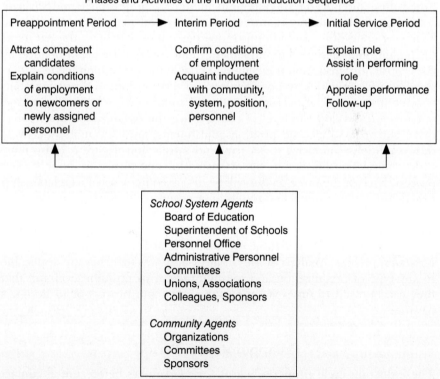

FIGURE 5.7
Linkage of phases, agents, and activities of the individual induction sequence.

the induction process is a continuing planning responsibility. Planning decisions include those relating to kinds of activities to be initiated to achieve results desired, time sequence of activities, and definition of responsibilities for carrying out specific plans.

The scope of activities in the induction cycle will be determined by a number of factors, including past experience in personnel replacements, anticipated need for new staff members, nature of the community, and size of the school staff. Induction problems vary from one system to another. The type of program developed for a given institution will be the result of balanced judgment arrived at by giving due consideration to factors such as those mentioned.

The induction process properly begins during recruitment and generally terminates on completion of the probationary period. During this time span, different types of induction activities are needed to serve specific purposes. The three phases of the induction cycle are the *preappointment period, interim period,* and *initial position occupancy period.* In each of these phases of induction, different types of activities are initiated by various agents and groups from within and outside the system, including lay, professional, and advisory committees; community organizations; unions and personnel associations; boards of education; and administrative personnel. Whatever the nature of the organization designed to implement induction activities, coordination by the central administration is essential to enable the new appointee to understand clearly the duties, responsibilities, and relationships of the assignment; become acquainted, if necessary, with the community, school system, and school staff; develop the level of competence the organization anticipates; make personal, social, and position adjustments; and deal more effectively with conditions conducive to security and satisfaction. Figure 5.7 also illustrates the relationship among agents, activities, and phases of the induction process. Each of the three phases will be discussed in terms of its relationship to activities to be initiated and results anticipated.

Figure 5.8 has relevance at this point in the discussion of personnel induction. Induction guidelines presented in Figure 5.8 are based on a research study, and they became one system's rationale for the design of its induction process. Analysis of the findings indicates that they are applicable to any type of organization and to any function or position level and that they can be used to improve an existing induction process or to design a new one.

Preappointment Period

The induction cycle properly begins for newcomers before initial contact between the institution and the applicant. Whenever a vacancy is anticipated and the system announces its intention to fill the position, a position guide containing person and position specifications should be prepared to

1. *Early impressions are lasting.* The most lasting impressions about an organization are formed early, within the first 60–90 days. These impressions, if poor, lead people to look around for other jobs—maybe not right away, but sometime during the first three years. It's critical to reinforce that "I made the right choice."

2. *The pre-arrival period is part of orientation.* The time between the acceptance of the job offer and the first day of employment should be used to maintain contact with the new person; help with housing, information about the community, and so forth; and have everything ready on the job for the new person's arrival.

3. *Day One is crucial.* New people remember their first day of employment for years, so it must be well managed.

4. *New people have an interest in the total organization.* New employees *are* interested in, and need, a sense of the total company; its objectives, policies, values, and plans are where they and their own organization fit in. And they need this early on; it's just as important to them as the more apparent need for information about their own job, department, and so on.

5. *Teach the basics first.* People become productive sooner if we give them time at the outset to learn the basics—to establish a foundation. People need to know the hows, wheres, and whys of getting things done before starting their regular assignments. The old process of throwing people right into the job to learn by their mistakes won't work any more—if it ever did.

6. *Give the new person major responsibility for his or her own orientation.* Adults learn best if they have a responsibility for their own orientation. They do this best by a process known as guided self-learning—learning by doing, but under direction.

FIGURE 5.8
Guidelines for planning the induction process.

give direction to those responsible for recruitment and selection; to make clear to the applicant the qualifications, duties, and responsibilities of the position; and to enable placement agencies and recruiters to locate candidates who can meet position requirements. Clarification of position requirements is suggested as a first step in the induction cycle because neither the interests of the system nor those of the applicant will be served if there is ambiguity about the role to be played or if the nature and qualifications of the role are misrepresented. In addition to providing position guides, it is the practice of some systems to prepare brochures for applicants to acquaint them with characteristics of the community and the system.

7. *Time the giving of information to fit the new employee's needs.* New people need to know certain things at certain times. Try to provide the information just before the person needs to use it.

8. *Avoid information overload.* Related to timing is the question of overload. It's important to consider how much a person can absorb at one time. "A little bit at a time" is a good rule.

9. *Understand that community, social, and family adjustment is a critical factor.* Orientation systems can—and should—address the needs of the new person (and his or her family) to become part of the new work group and the new community. Studies confirm, over and over, that people will leave the job if they or their families don't make a good adjustment to the community and their co-workers. In fact, some studies show that the views of the spouse are the single most important factor in a married person's decision to stay with, or leave, an organization.

10. *Remember that it's the individual that counts.* Focus on orienting each person, not just a group. Designers of orientation systems need to build an orientation process—not a "program"—so that solid orientation occurs with each person and is not dependent on group orientation.

11. *Make the supervisor the key.* The basic responsibility for orienting new people lies with the supervisor. Others are important, but the ultimate responsibility is the supervisor's. The long-term success of the new person depends to a great extent on how well the supervisor carries out this responsibility.

12. *Emphasize solid orientation as a "must" for productivity improvement.* Orientation must be viewed as an essential part of the employment process, like the interview or a medical exam, and is the first step in the training process. In short, recognize orientation as a *vital part of the total management system*—the foundation of any productivity effort.

FIGURE 5.8, *continued*

The initial interview between recruiter and applicant provides an opportunity to furnish the latter with a variety of information likely to be needed in making a decision to accept or reject the position. Moreover, during the interview the individual is able to clarify with the interviewer questions about the position or to secure information on a range of relevant matters.

There are a number of advantages in having the interview in the system. A system-based interview enables the candidate to meet with administrative officials and school personnel and to visit the community. If this procedure is followed and efforts are made to furnish pertinent information needed by the candidate, a major step will have been taken to satisfy the primary goal of the first phase of the individual induction sequence; that is, fully informing the applicant about the position, the conditions of employment, and the school and community environments in which the work is performed.

Interim Induction Period

The realities of formal appointment to a position pose problems for both the individual and the institution, problems different from those confronting either party prior to this juncture. The plan of assistance to inductees, from the time of appointment until the first day on the job, will differ somewhat among the various personnel categories. Induction activities for teachers, for example, should not be the same as those designed for secretarial or custodial personnel. Illustrated in the following list are some of the preliminary steps planned and initiated by the human resources office to assist a teacher assigned to the Stevens School in making various types of adjustments:

- Letters of welcome are sent by the board of education, superintendent of schools, and local teachers' association.
- An experienced teacher is assigned to serve as a sponsor to the new teacher.
- A brochure is prepared for teacher sponsors that explains the aims of the induction program and the responsibilities of sponsors.
- A preliminary conference is held between sponsors and the principal.
- A conference between the principal and the new appointee is held to discuss the teaching assignment. The principal avoids the tendency to assign to the new teacher a heavy teaching load, students with behavior problems, or unusual duties that make it difficult for the beginner to achieve a measure of success in the first year. The practice of making assignments, whenever possible, on the basis of teacher preference, and reducing the work load of the inexperienced teacher during the first year is commendable.
- Copies of the school handbook as well as selected inventory of living quarters are furnished to the beginning teacher.
- Conditions of employment are confirmed. The organization makes certain that the newcomer understands salary, collateral benefits, extra pay, merit, and other facets of the compensation structure.

These activities highlight the importance of the individual induction sequence. It is sound planning to initiate the sequence prior to the time the individual assumes his/her responsibilities. Elimination of some of the problems of newly appointed personnel before the first work day facilitates an earlier realization of their full service potential.

The induction checklist is an effective tool to assist heads of work units in a school system, such as principals, directors, supervisors, and division administrators, in making induction activities effective. Different lists are prepared for various personnel categories, the intent of which is to systematize induction activities undertaken by administrators for persons newly assigned to their jurisdiction. Such lists are used so that all the activities in the individual induction sequence will be given attention.

Before a new teacher actually meets his/her class for the first time, he/she may also be exposed to induction activities such as those in the following discussion.

Preopening Conference. The preopening conference technique, which may assume a variety of forms, is almost universally employed in school systems. It provides opportunities to acquaint new personnel with members of the school staff and with plans and procedures established to operate the educational program. Some conferences involve the entire school staff, some are restricted to the building staff, and some are designed specifically for new personnel.

The building principal is responsible for helping the inductee to adjust readily to his/her teaching assignment. Assistance may include interpreting plans for the coming year, including those for appraising teacher performance and evaluating pupil progress; acquainting the inductee with physical facilities, teaching resources, records, and pupil and teacher services; and explaining general school policies and office routines.

Because the work of the school and that of the individual teacher are inevitably related to the life of the community, and because school personnel are, in fact, members of the community by virtue of their function, an investment of time and effort in assuring the new member's acceptance into the life of the community is important. Group conferences with parents of children assigned to this teacher, receptions by the board of education, and other social activities will help to facilitate the newcomer's transition into the new environment.

It is not suggested that the induction activities listed are exhaustive or that a given sequence of activities will suffice in all situations. The wide range of induction problems with which different institutions are confronted rules out from this discussion a prescribed program. Each system can best achieve goals of the induction process by developing and assessing techniques and activities most effective for particular situations and conditions.

Figures 5.9 and 5.10 lend specificity to the foregoing suggestions. These forms illustrate a three-part induction plan for the time prior to the newcomer's actually assuming his/her role. The following is the substance of the plan:

- Sessions 1 and 2 are *central administration* responsibilities. The intent is to explain the organization and administration of systemwide personnel policies and procedures applicable to new members.
- Session 3 is position and unit oriented. The intent is to acquaint individuals with the roles for which they will be responsible and to introduce them to the colleagues with whom they will work. Responsibility for this session is delegated to the administrator of the unit in which the position is located.

Foxcroft School System

Form 100

Induction Checklist for New Personnel
(To Be Processed by Central Administration)

Directions—Form 100 has been designed to facilitate the induction of new staff members to the Foxcroft School System. The content of the three-phase induction program is outlined below, the intent of which is to provide newcomers with an information perspective so that they may readily become informed system members.

Name of new staff member _____ Starting date _____

Unit and position location _____ _____

Session 1: Human Resources Policies and Procedures

    Date _____ Time _____ Place _____ Responsibility _____

    a. System mission and administrative structure _____ Policies _____

    b. Compensation

       Salary _____ Collateral benefits _____ Extra pay _____

    c. Performance appraisal _____ Probationary period _____

    d. Development _____

    e. Personnel inventory _____

    f. Leaves of absence _____ Holidays _____ Vacations _____

    g. Personnel services _____

    h. Community relationships _____

    i. Code of ethics _____

Session 2: Human Resources Policies and Procedures

    Date _____ Time _____ Place _____ Responsibility _____

    a. Review and questions on Session 1 _____

    b. Union relations _____

    c. Tenure _____ Retirement _____ Social security _____

    d. Academic freedom and responsibility _____

    e. Payroll: Deductions __ Issuance __ Adjustments __ Responsibility __

    f. Transfers _____ Promotions _____

    g. Grievance procedures _____

All items checked have been discussed with inductee _____

Central administration representative _____ Date _____

Returned to personnel office for individual personnel file _____

Reviewed _____ Filed _____ by personnel office

Signature of inductee _____

FIGURE 5.9
The three-phase induction plan of the Foxcroft school system (sessions 1 and 2).

```
┌─────────────────────────────────────────────────────────────────────┐
│                    Foxcroft School System                            │
│                                                     Form 200          │
│              Position Orientation Checklist for New Personnel         │
│                  (To Be Completed by Unit Administrators)             │
│                                                                       │
│   Directions—This checklist has been designed as a part of the       │
│     induction pro-                                                    │
│     gram of the Foxcroft School System. Its primary intent is to      │
│     acquaint new                                                      │
│     staff members with the position to which they have been assigned  │
│     and the                                                           │
│     performance requirements that the roles involve. This step of the │
│     induction                                                         │
│     process is one of several planned to enable the individual to     │
│     adjust quickly                                                    │
│     to the position, the school, the system, and the community.       │
│     Directions for                                                    │
│     processing the checklist are included below.                      │
│                                                                       │
│   Name of inductee _____                    │
│                                                          Discussion   │
│         Session 3: Position and Building Orientation     Completed    │
│                                                                       │
│   1.  Welcome and introduction to Foxcroft School System.   _____  │
│                                                                       │
│   2.  Describe unit organization, objectives, functions, and rela-    │
│       tionships to system at large.                         _____  │
│                                                                       │
│   3.  Provide copy of position guide to inductee and explain          │
│       contents.                                             _____  │
│                                                                       │
│   4.  Explain the relationship the position inductee will hold to     │
│       unit and system objectives.                           _____  │
│                                                                       │
│   5.  Explain position performance standards for continuance          │
│       of employment.                                        _____  │
│                                                                       │
│   6.  Explain performance appraisal process and its relation-         │
│       ship to continuance of employment and promotion.      _____  │
│                                                                       │
│   7.  Explain conditions of employment in unit, including:  _____  │
│                                                                       │
│       Hours of work              Provisions for lunch                 │
│       Lunch hours                Parking                              │
│       Building facilities        Transportation                      │
│       Supplies and equipment     Services                            │
│       Behavior                   Other                               │
│                                                                       │
│   8.  Introduce to colleagues within unit and to other contact        │
│       personnel.                                                      │
│                                                                       │
│   Date _____                                                 │
│                                                                       │
│   Signature of inductee _____          │
│                                                                       │
│   Signature of unit administrator _____          │
│                                                                       │
│   Returned to personnel office for individual personnel file  _____  │
│                                                                       │
│   Reviewed _____ Filed _____ by personnel office    _____  │
│                                                                       │
└─────────────────────────────────────────────────────────────────────┘
```

FIGURE 5.10
The three-phase induction plan of the Foxcroft school system (session 3).

- Copies of forms are furnished to inductees to acquaint them with the nature and scope of the conditions of employment, constraints that govern, and opportunities that will become available in role performance.
- The inductee and administrator responsible for conducting the session sign the forms, which become a component of the new staff members' files.
- Instructional devices available for orientation sessions are virtually limitless, ranging from programmed instruction materials to filmstrips, slides, films, tapes, cassettes, records, charts, transparencies, flip charts, videotapes, brochures, booklets, and mimeographed materials.

This discussion has focused on the classroom teacher, but it should be noted that special types of orientation plans for new personnel in other categories are commonplace. They range from those designed for top-level executives to those for personnel to be employed in classified positions. Existence of a wide range of orientation plans indicates that there are possibilities for specialized instruction programs to meet requirements of different system positions. The new superintendent of schools or the new assistant superintendent for instruction will be vitally concerned about the goal structure and functions and levels of responsibilities, whereas the individual employed in a classified position will need considerable counseling and coaching in matters not directly related to system direction and control.

FOLLOW-UP OF INDUCTEE ADJUSTMENT

Initial Occupancy

Responsibility for new personnel does not terminate with the opening of school. Dimensions of the induction concept range from recruitment to tenure. Recruitment can improve the quality of applicants. The selection process attempts to match person to position. But until one has had an opportunity to demonstrate ability under actual conditions and the school organization has had an opportunity to appraise the suitability of the newcomer for the position, the appointment cannot be considered final. It is for this reason that a probationary period for all personnel new to the system is becoming increasingly a matter of institutional policy.

It is a fact that no inductee comes to the position ready to perform the new assignment flawlessly. It is also a fact that the best selection process is fallible. Administration cannot ignore its responsibility for planning and administering a follow-up program (Step 4 in Figure 5.3). Whatever the nature of the new appointee's assignment, follow-up visits and interviews by the unit head are essential, especially during the first few weeks of employment. Timing of such assistance is important because the inductee may have trouble in understanding the assignment or encounter difficulty in performing it.

A well-developed induction process specifies such matters as the number, frequency, nature, and phasing of follow-up interviews. In addition, follow-up reports are submitted by the operating head to the central administration, which appraises such characteristics as quality of performance, difficulties encountered, and other factors deemed important to position effectiveness.

Appraisal during the probationary period, as a phase of the total appraisal process, is designed not only to assist the competent but to spot the potentially incompetent, marginal, or undesirable probationer. Those individuals not able to perform satisfactorily in one position may be reassigned, given more personal supervision, or provided with intensified training opportunities to overcome deficiencies. Prompt rehabilitation or elimination of appointees clearly unsuitable for roles to which they have been assigned will save money, time, and effort for the system. Damages suffered by children constantly exposed to poor teaching are incalculable.

Figures 5.11 and 5.12 have been included to illustrate a feedback mechanism that may be employed during the period of initial occupancy to indicate to inductees that the system has a continuing interest in their welfare, their adjustment to the assigned position, and their contribution to the organization. Figure 5.11 is a self-appraisal form for the inductee; it is designed to provide feedback to the unit administration on position problems and on progress toward effective role performance. Figure 5.12 is a form for reporting by the unit administrator, to both the central administration and the inductee, observations of performing progress during the initial period of position occupancy. The information provided through its use forms the basis for counseling and coaching discussions during follow-up sessions between inductee and unit head. In addition, the information becomes a component of both the inductee's personnel file as well as the personnel inventory.

CONTROLLING THE INDUCTION PROCESS

Follow-up of new personnel by the system is essential for a variety of reasons. Investment in recruiting, selecting, and inducting new personnel is considerable. The loss suffered by the system when the inductee's service is terminated or when the individual separates himself/herself from the organization voluntarily cannot be ignored. Because the system also has responsibilities during the probationary period, an appraisal of the *induction process* is essential.

In theory, recruitment, selection, and induction processes should result in attraction and retention of the number, kinds, and quality of personnel needed by the system. Periodic appraisal of actual results (Step 5 of Figure

Position Design
Do you have a clear understanding of the expectations your immediate supervisor has for you in your present position?
Do you have a clear understanding of the goals of the work unit to which you are assigned?
Does your immediate supervisor give you specific help in improving your position performance?
Do you feel you are well-placed in your present assignment?

Performance Appraisal
Does your immediate supervisor give you the necessary information to enable you to know how you are getting on with your role?
How worthwhile was your last performance appraisal in helping you to improve your performance?
Summarize the overall strengths and weaknesses you have demonstrated in performing your present assignment.

Development
How much assistance have you been given by your supervisor in planning your career development?
How do you feel about the progress you have made thus far in performing your role?
How confident are you that your career aspirations can be met by remaining in this organization?
Do you feel you have potential beyond your present assignment?
How have you demonstrated this potential?

Communication
Do you receive sufficient information to perform your role effectively?
Do you receive sufficient information to understand the relationships among your role, the unit to which you are assigned, and the mission of the school system?
Is your supervisor well-informed about your requirements for performing the role effectively?

Role Satisfaction
How do you feel about the kind of work you are doing in your present position?
Are there significant observations that you think should be noted about the dimensions of your position that affect your performance and should be brought to the attention of your unit, such as unit objectives, position design, organization structure, supervisory process, and results achieved?
How effectively do you feel you have met the responsibilities of your position?

Signature of inductee _____ Date _____

FIGURE 5.11
Self-appraisal form for inductees.

Adjustment Progress and Problems	Analysis by Unit Administrator	Analysis by Inductee
What progress has been made by the inductee during the review period in making the following adjustments: a. Community adjustment? b. Position adjustment? c. System adjustment? d. Individual and group adjustment? e. Personal adjustment?		
What are the obstacles to achieving adjustment expectations in the areas listed above?		
What comments should be made on the results achieved for each of the adjustments listed above?		
In what areas has the inductee made the most progress in adjustment? The least progress?		
Do the adjustment expectations need to be revised?		
What are the plans and priorities for achieving adjustment expectations?		

Name of inductee _____ Organization unit _____ Position _____

Signature of inductee _____

Signature of unit administrator _____

Date of review _____ Next review period _____

FIGURE 5.12
Form for performance review of new personnel by the unit administrator.

5.3) derived from these three processes should minimize turnover costs stemming from faulty recruitment, selection, and placement. Such appraisal will provide information on personnel need satisfaction; position compatibility; attitude of the operating head toward effectiveness of the employment transaction; and validity of recruitment, selection, and induction processes. If and when these processes do not lead to the desired results, corrective action can be taken.

Appraisal should be focused on such matters as determining whether personnel perform effectively, to what extent the organization accepts or rejects applicants, how well appraisals made of candidates and predictions of performance prior to selection agree with subsequent experience, what the system's success is with probationers, whether exit interviews or other data reveal anything about strengths or weaknesses of the selection process, and what the evidence is with regard to sufficiency of each of the several tools used in the selection of personnel. The ultimate purpose of making an intensive analysis of the recruitment, selection, and induction process is to determine how well the system is succeeding in attracting and holding a competent staff. The evaluation should reveal what adjustments must be made to realize organizational expectations.

Figure 5.13 presents a hypothetical illustration of correlation analysis, one of various methods employed to evaluate personnel decisions. This technique is designed as an aid in illuminating the effectiveness of personnel decisions, to judge the extent to which objectives of the selection process are being realized, and to determine what modifications may be necessary to improve selection decisions. The method of rank difference illustrated in Figure 5.13 is designed to determine the degree and direction of the relationship between personnel ratings of teachers prior to employment and their performance ratings after one year of service. Correlation analysis shows the magnitude and direction of the association between selection decisions and performance ratings. Although association may or may not indicate a cause-and-effect relation, it does point the way to investigate the status of this system's selection model and ways to enhance its effectiveness.

The model presented in Figure 5.13 is designed to stress the proposition that the recruitment-selection-induction cycle occurs over time and must be constantly scrutinized to develop more reliable ways of identifying applicants who will realize position requirements. Starting with the view that all selection procedures should be investigated to determine their predictive accuracy or validity, the system probes to what extent application blanks, interviews, tests, and references predict which applicants will be the more effective performers. To illustrate, newly appointed teachers are evaluated at the end of the first year on how well they have met position expectations. Evaluation ratings are then correlated statistically with ratings on individual selection predictors (interviews and tests) to determine the strength of the relationship. If, for example, those teachers who scored high on the interview also scored high on performance evaluation and those who scored low on the interview did so on the evaluation, there is an indication that the interview is discriminating between potentially effective and ineffective performers.

Although it is true that much time, money, and talent is invested in the recruitment-selection-induction aspects of the human resources function, it is also true that person-position mismatches are considerably more costly, time-consuming, and counterproductive.

Teacher	Selection Rating	Performance Rating	Selection Rank	Performance Rank	Difference between Ranks (D)	Difference Squared (D²)
A	76	87	9	4	5	25
B	93	78	4	5	1	1
C	63	61	12	10	2	4
D	98	95	2	1	1	1
E	100	89	1	2	1	1
F	86	55	6	12	6	36
G	89	74	5	6	1	1
H	96	71	3	7	4	16
I	66	88	11	3	8	64
J	75	70	10	8	2	4
K	78	65	8	9	1	1
L	81	60	7	11	4	16
						170

$$N = 12 \qquad rho = 1 - \frac{6\sum D^2}{N(N^2 - 1)} = 1 - \frac{6 \times 170}{12 \times (143)} = 0.41$$

Commentary—As noted above, the correlation between selection and performance ratings using the rank-difference method of correlation (rho) is 0.41, a weak positive correlation. As an exploratory device, correlation analysis points the way to additional probing: Is the association genuine or spurious? Should teacher C have been appointed? Why are the selection ratings not better predictors of performance? How reliable are the performance ratings? The selection ratings? What can be done to improve the selection ratings so that greater reliance can be placed upon their predictive value?

FIGURE 5.13

Illustration of outcome analysis of personnel selection decisions by the rank-difference (rho) method of correlation.

INDUCTION AND HUMAN RESOURCES STRATEGY

Throughout this text the various functions of a school system (presented in Figure 1.2) as well as the subprocesses (shown in Figure 2.1) have been implicitly viewed as interdependent. For instance, recruitment, selection, appraisal, and development are considered to be intertwined. Because this interdependence of personnel processes exists, it should be taken into account in shaping human resources strategy. Thus viewed, induction, as one of the processes of the personnel function, has considerable potential for achieving the idealized aims for system members, especially the right to be informed, coached, mentored, and assisted in various ways to achieve goals.

The induction process is focused on entry-level hires, the initial work state in the careers of most system personnel. This chapter has stressed the view that an effective induction process serves a number of purposes, including socialization; reduction of personnel anxieties, turnover, and supervisory time; helping individuals to understand themselves; and helping the system to understand those employees who are newly hired. The forced reshaping of education in the United States, however, has caused more and more school systems to reconsider and reshape the induction process in ways that will put into place a career development perspective that will enable members to realize their full potential, achieve personal and position satisfaction, and contribute to enhancement of system effectiveness.

Career Modeling

When considering a change from traditional induction stereotypes to those that embrace **career planning,** it is beneficial to use a model or entity that takes into account the most important aspects of the process and their relationships to each other.

The conceptual career planning model for teaching personnel at the entry level, outlined in the following discussion, includes three phases: Phase I—individual career planning; Phase II—human resources (system) planning; and Phase III—career development planning. This approach assumes that entry level is the time period between first employment and tenure. The model provides a guide for redesigning personal growth programs, identifying individuals' key competencies and system development needs, and developing human resources strategies that help individuals to perceive their present and potential strengths as they move through the career cycle. Figure 5.14 has been included to define terms generally associated with teacher career planning.

Phase I—Individual Career Planning. As defined in Figure 5.14, individual career planning is the personal process of establishing career

Career. (a). An ongoing sequence of work-related activities; (b) a field for or pursuit of progressive achievement over the span of one's work life.

Career anchor. A preferred career path based on an individual's abilities, motives, goals, attitudes, organizational security, creativity, and competence.

Career cycle. Stages or periods through which a person's career takes shape.

Career development. The process of obtaining the necessary experience, skills, motivation, and attitudes for career progression. Includes counseling, staff development, career information systems, career pathing, performance appraisal, position enrichment, and position previews.

Career goals. Personalized immediate, intermediate, and long-term objectives toward which an individual's strategic aims are directed.

Career information. Programs designed to make available information about position openings and qualifications needed to fill them. Includes opportunities for career dialogues between personnel and counselors, assistance in reviewing career goals, and procedures by which members may apply for these opportunities.

Career instruction. A process employed to inform personnel about career paths through workshops, seminars, group study, and self-study activities.

Career ladder. A promotion path involving a hierarchy of specialized assignments. Teaching, for example, becomes the career anchor, while opportunities are provided to engage in other teaching-related activities such as being a master teacher, mentor, consultant, and director of induction or special instructional projects. Career ladder teachers are sometimes referred to as stage I, II, or III career ladder teachers.

FIGURE 5.14
Terms commonly employed in career planning and development.

goals and approaches by which they can be attained. Career planning, it should be emphasized, is primarily an individual responsibility.

The process of individual career planning involves system members making assessments and then initiating plans to acquire:

- *Self-knowledge*—Knowledge or understanding of one's own character, education, experience, capabilities, motivations, career orientation, special talents, work-preferences, career anchor, strengths, and weaknesses.

- *Position knowledge*—Knowledge or understanding of career opportunities within the school system, career paths (functional, horizontal, and geographic), position requirements, position openings, potential assignments, reassignment, transfer, and promotion policies.

Career lattice. A network of positions that permits individuals to move across job families. Establishes the movement of members among grade levels, departments, divisions, and programs.

Career life stages. Early adulthood, mature adult, midlife, and old age. Often compared with career stages such as establishment, advancement, maintenance, and withdrawal.

Career management. Choices an individual makes in deciding which occupational opportunities will enhance attainment of career objectives.

Career path. A sequence of specific positions that enables members to match aspirations with system needs and opportunities.

Career planning. The process of establishing individual career goals and the manner in which they can be achieved.

Career stages. Phases individuals pass through during their careers, such as prework, establishment, advancement, maintenance, and retirement.

Career strategy. Consideration by system members of their vocational strengths and weaknesses, opportunities for advancement, skills needed, and means of giving long-term direction to their careers.

Career strengths and weaknesses. Analysis of individual competitive advantages and disadvantages in developing a career strategy. Includes education, experiences, abilities, aptitudes, special talents, career inventory, and sponsorship.

Career transition. Change in positions along a career path.

- *Career development knowledge*—Knowledge or understanding of the system's commitment, policies, and procedures positioned to assist individuals in self-analysis so they can determine career opportunities and choices, career objectives, and performance improvement plans.

Within the context of an enriched induction period, the school system can put to effective use various personnel processes (recruitment, selection, placement, appraisal, counseling) to not only meet its staffing needs but also to design programs that encourage individual career planning activities and make challenging initial assignments possible. Induction is a time during which individuals should have opportunities and encouragement to understand their potential and to shape short- and long-term aspirations accordingly.

Phase II—Human Resources Planning. Human resources planning refers to the school system's management role in creating, supporting, and encouraging career perspectives for its people. In brief, it is the system's responsibility to make the human resources function and the subprocesses more effective conduits through which an organizational climate is nurtured to enhance individual career planning. Unless there exists in the system a set of values that places a premium on activities designed to achieve desired individual performance and increase the value of the organization's human resources, there is little chance that individual career planning will result in positive outcomes.

Organizational strategies to make the entry-level stage a period when career development begins to take shape include consideration of three variables: the *individual, positions,* and the *organizational climate.* Courses of action to link these components include:

- Establishing policies, programs, and procedures on which to base operational activities involved in career planning.
- Providing orientation, counseling, and mentoring services to assist persons with problems relating to entry-level adjustment, self-evaluation, and career planning considerations.
- Designing appraisal systems that provide performance feedback linked to career planning.
- Initiating a plan for analyzing and specifying job requirements, from which essential information can be gleaned for describing position content and characteristics of persons who might perform the roles successfully.
- Shaping challenging first jobs and enriched assignments.
- Making career planning workshops, seminars, career path information, job previews, and psychological and aptitude test services available to newcomers.
- Establishing programs and practices to integrate career development with present and future staffing needs.

System involvement in career planning is currently necessary and will become even more so as changes develop in the kinds of skills that are needed to cope with social and technological changes; as organizational environments (internal and external) evolve; and as ways are sought to adjust to the shortage of available skills and the variety of personnel demands stemming from reform-driven forces.

Phase III—Career Development Planning. Phase III of the career planning model acknowledges that contemporary school systems are facing the demands of a changing culture and will continue to do so. This phase of the model is viewed as a shared or joint responsibility between the individual and the organization in which a comprehensive career development program is fostered to meet career growth aspects of a diverse teaching corps.

Questions that should be asked and answered in career development planning include the following:

- Is there a performance appraisal process in place designed to encourage career growth and upward movement? Does the process stress the importance of performance diagnosis? Behavioral objectives? Does the performance appraisal model fit the system's human resources strategies?
- To what extent is the supervisory staff committed to the conviction that entry-level personnel need assistance and encouragement in position performance and career planning? That the sink-or-swim induction model is a strategy whose time is departing?
- Which of the following endeavors are in place to assist newcomers in planning individualized performance improvement actions and career movements: formal and informal counseling, career information, position posting, talent profiles, skills inventories, position previews, role exploration, and position rotation?
- Are there mentoring programs for guiding, developing, and assisting individuals in their quest for establishment in the system, self-actualization, performance effectiveness, peer acceptance, and career mobility?

Although the foregoing discussion has centered on individualized plans for new hires, personnel development is also accountable for new tasks for present personnel and for those employees preparing for new positions. These latter aspects of personnel development are treated in Chapter 6 in terms of plans featuring elements such as types of learning needed to achieve individual and group objectives, environments for optimum learning, cost-effective programming, and delivery systems compatible with staff development needs.

REVIEW AND PREVIEW

In this chapter, analysis of induction problems suggests that initiation of an effective induction process is one way that the system can contribute to assimilation of new members as well as to their personal development, security, and need satisfaction. A school system can recruit and select personnel, but until newly appointed members become fully cognizant of and adjusted to the work to be performed, the environment in which they will function, and the colleagues with whom they will be associated, they cannot be expected to contribute efficiently and effectively to the realization of organizational expectations. In short, an induction process is needed to assist newly appointed personnel to resolve community, system, position, and development process whereby the system creates plans to enhance position knowledge, skills, and behavior of its members in human and personal problems with which they are confronted. Use of this process indicates recognition of and an attempt to do something about the fact that human maladjustment is expensive, detrimental to the satisfaction of individual and organizational expectations, and harmful to the socializing and personalizing processes that take place between the individual and the system. Also inherent in the process is the assumption that the main determinant of motivation is the attraction the posi-tion holds for the individual and induction activities that are designed to enhance potentialities for motivated action that will result in more effective role performance.

Chapter 6 is concerned with the ways conducive to realization of individual, unit, and system goals.

REVIEW AND DISCUSSION QUESTIONS

1. Define organizational culture and explain its importance in relation to the induction process.

2. Form two groups of five members each (Groups A and B). Each group member is to describe the culture of an organization (e.g., school, church, local community, government, hospital, commercial corporation, or political entity). Each group will identify and report to the entire class the shared values, beliefs, cultural reinforcement, and group behavioral patterns that influence individual behavior; and then the class will debate whether the culture is positive or negative.

3. Define socialization and its importance in the induction process.

4. Give your response to this statement: "Socialization begins with the selection process—applicants should be rigorously screened in order to discourage those who may not fit into the culture."

5. How should a school system go about the task of communicating its culture to inductees? Outline your plan.

6. List the strategic aims of socialization.

7. Describe the major steps you would take to increase the likelihood that an induction process will lead to desired and permanent changes in behavior.

8. What should school systems do about deviant inductees—unsocialized individuals who reject group norms and behave independently (e.g., eating lunch alone, violating dress code, and disregarding performance culture)? Should they be punished, ostracized, closely supervised, terminated, or given some amount of tolerance?

9. What aspects of contemporary induction programs appear to be most neglected? For what reasons?

10. To what extent should school systems develop induction programs for support personnel? Temporary personnel? What should be the form and content of such programs?

11. Complete the following exercise:

Column A	*Column B*
List what you consider to be early career problems for teachers.	List your proposals to counteract early employment problems listed in Column A.
1.	
2.	
3.	1.
	2.
	3.

12. What would you consider to be your visionary career plan? What work experiences have you had that would contribute to your ideal career plan? What types of satisfactions do you anticipate from a career plan? What obstacles do you envision in achieving a career plan? What course of action should you fashion in order to achieve your career goals?

13. Give your response to the following statement: "The induction process is the least suitable state of employment to consider career planning."

14. Examine the following statements regarding organizational culture and indicate the extent to which you are in agreement or disagreement with each:

    • "A school system's culture is reflected in the pattern of signals the administration sends to its personnel, indicating how they are expected to behave."
    • "The culture of a school system can be positive or negative."

    • "The leadership style of a school principal tends to define the culture of the school."
    • "The organizational culture of some school systems rewards ineffective performance."

15. There are those who aver that a well-designed and implemented recruitment and selection program eliminates the need for an induction program. Refute or defend this assumption.

16. What unique induction considerations might arise in a rural school? Suburban schools? Large city school?

17. Should a teachers' union participate in the induction process? If so, define the role.

18. Develop a one-page description of the components of a plan to evaluate the effectiveness of a school induction process in a suburban school system.

CHAPTER EXERCISE 5.1

Directions: Indicate which of the induction program components (listed in Table 5.1) you would designate as being appropriate for matching inductee needs and program content. The code at the base of the chart identifies each of the component choices.

NOTES

1. Robert D. Smithers, The Psychology of Work and Human Performance (New York: Harper and Row, 1988), 361.

2. Wendell L. French, The Personnel Management Process, Sixth Edition (Boston: Houghten Mifflin Company, 1987), 297.

3. Ibid.

4. T. Bienenstok and W. R. Sayres, Problems in Job Satisfaction among

TABLE 5.1
Induction program chart.

Type of Inductee	Program Components												Total
	1	2	3	4	5	6	7	8	9	10	11	12	
A. Beginner	—	—	—	—	—	—	—	—	—	—	—	—	—
B. Transferred	—	—	—	—	—	—	—	—	—	—	—	—	—
C. Promoted	—	—	—	—	—	—	—	—	—	—	—	—	—
D. Demoted	—	—	—	—	—	—	—	—	—	—	—	—	—
E. Leave Returnee	—	—	—	—	—	—	—	—	—	—	—	—	—
F. Work Group Changed	—	—	—	—	—	—	—	—	—	—	—	—	—
G. Experienced Newcomer	—	—	—	—	—	—	—	—	—	—	—	—	—
H. Temporary	—	—	—	—	—	—	—	—	—	—	—	—	—

Code

1 = Formal approach	7 = On-the-job approach
2 = Informal approach	8 = Off-the-job approach
3 = Personal development	9 = Mentor support
4 = Linkage with university	10 = Coaching and counseling
5 = Refresher approach	11 = Anticipatory experiences
6 = Career emphasis	12 = Placement review

Junior High School Teachers (Albany, NY: New York State Education Department, n.d.); B. Dell Felder, Loye Y. Hollis, Martha K. Piper, and Robert W. Houston, Problems and Perspectives of Beginning Teachers: A Follow-Up Study (Houston, TX: University of Houston Central Campus, 1980); Frances F. Fuller and Oliver H. Brown, "Becoming a Teacher," Teacher Education, 74th Yearbook of the National Society for the Study of Education (Chicago: NSSE, 1975); Nathalie Gehrke and Kaoru Yamamoto, "A Grounded Theory Study of the Role Personalization of Beginning Secondary Teachers," Paper presented at the annual meeting of the American Educational Research Association, Toronto, Canada, March 1978; Robert W. Houston and B. Dell Felder, "Break Horses, Not Teachers," Phi Delta Kappan 64, 7 (March 1982), 457–60; Joseph Liguna, What happens to the Attitudes of Beginning Teachers? (Danville, IL: Interstate Printers & Publishers Inc., 1970); Dan C. Lortie, Schoolteacher (Chicago: University of Chicago Press, 1975); Janet M. Newberry, "The Barrier between Beginning and Experienced Teachers," Journal of Educational Administration (May 1978); Kevin Ryan et al., Biting the Apple: Accounts of First-Year Teachers (New York: Longman Inc., 1980); John P. Cotter, "Managing the Joining-Up Process," Personnel 49 (July–August 1972), 46–56; Donald C. Feldman, "A Socialization Process that Helps New Recruits Succeed," Personnel 57 (March–April 1980), 11–23; and Donald R. Cruikshank, "Five Areas of Teacher Concern," Phi Delta Kappan 64, 7 (March 1982), 460.

5. See Houston and Felder, 460; also Chris Pipho, "State Line: Education Reform Highlights 1984 Legislative Action," Phi Delta Kappan 65, 9 (May 1984), 589.

6. Fred Luthans and Robert Kreitner, Organizational Behavior Modification (Glenview, IL: Scott, Foresman & Co., 1975), 97.

7. Ibid.

8. See Educational Research Service Inc., Orientation Programs for New Teachers (Arlington, VA: Educational Research Service, 1977); D. M. Brooks, Editor, Teacher Induction: A New Beginning (Reston, VA: Association of Teacher Educators, 1987); S. Feinman-Nemser, S. J. Odell, and D. Lawrence, "Induction Programs and the Professionalization of Teachers: Two Views," Colloquy I(2) (1988), 11–19; G. Hall and S. Loucks, "Teacher Concerns as a Basis for Facilitating and Personalizing Staff Development, Teachers College Record 80, 1 (1978), 36–53; L. Huling-Austin, S. Odell, P. Ishler, R. Kay, and R. Edelfelt, Assisting the Beginning Teacher (Reston, VA: Association of Teacher Educators, 1989); L. Huling Austin and S. C. Murphy, Assessing the Impact of Teacher Induction Programs (Manhattan, KS: National Staff Development Council, 1990); S. J. Odell, "Stages of Concern of Beginning Teachers in a Collaborative Internship Induction Program," Paper presented at the annual meeting of the Association of Teacher Educators (Houston, TX, 1987); P. O. Paisley, The Development Effects of a Staff Development Program for Beginning Teachers, Unpublished Doctoral Dissertation (Raleigh: North Carolina State University, 1987); Lois M. Thies-Sprinthall and Edwin R. Gerler, Jr., "Support Groups for Novice Teachers," The Journal of the National Staff Development Council 11, 4 (Fall, 1990), 18–22.

9. Bruce R. Joyce, Richard H. Hersh, and Michael McKibbin, The Structure of School Improvement (New York: Longman Inc., 1983), 113.

10. W. Brookover et al., "Elementary School Social Climate and School Achievement," American Educational Research Journal 15, 2 (1978), 301–18.

11. For a detailed discussion of the interaction of leadership and followership styles in the placement aspects of induction, see Daniel A. Tagliere, People, Power, and Organization (New York: American Management Association, 1973).

12. M. L. Louis, B. Z. Posner, and G. N. Powell, "The Availability and Helpfulness of Socialization Practices," Personnel Psychology 36 (1983), 857–66.

13. J. P. Wanous, Organizational Entry (Reading, MA: Addison-Wesley, 1980).

14. Smithers, 368–69.

15. Useful information on organizational culture is contained in Michael Albert and Murray Silverman, "Making Management Philosophy a Cultural Reality, Part II: Design Human Resources Programs Accordingly," Personnel 61, 2 (March–April 1984), 28–35; Edwin L. Baker, "Managing Organizational Culture," Management Review 69, 7 (July 1980), 8–17; and Fred Luthans, Richard M. Hodgetts, and Kenneth R. Thompson, Social Issues in Business, Fourth Edition (New York: Macmillan Publishing, 1984), Chapter 4.

16. M. Sherif, Group Conflict and Cooperation: Their Social Psychol- ogy (London: Routledge and Kegan Paul, 1966).

SUPPLEMENTARY READING

Arends, R. I. "Beginning Teachers as Learners." Journal of Educational Research 7, 4 (1983), 236–42.

Bradley, Leo; and Stephen P. Gordon. "Comparing the Ideal to the Real in State-Mandated Teacher Induction Programs." Journal of Staff Development 15, 3 (Summer 1994), 44–50.

Brooks, D. M. Teacher Induction: A New Beginning. Reston, VA: Association of Teacher Education, 1987.

Driscoll, A.; et al. "Designing a Mentor Program for Beginning Teachers." Journal of Staff Development 6, 2 (October 1985).

Egbert, Richard T. The Employee Handbook. Englewood Cliffs, NJ: Prentice-Hall Inc., 1990.

Evan, William M. "Peer Group Interaction and Organizational Socialization: A Study of Employee Turnover." American Sociological Review 28 (1963), 436–40.

Griffin, G. A. "Crossing the Bridge: The First Years of Teaching." National Commission on Excellence in Teacher Education (1984), 250–92.

Haines, R. C.; and K. F. Mitchell. "Teacher Career Development in Charlotte-Mecklenburg." Educational Leadership 433 (November 1985), 11–13.

Hartzell, G. "Induction of Experienced Assistant Principals." NASSP Bulletin 75, 533 (1991), 75–84.

Heckman, Paul. "Understanding School Culture." In John I. Goodlad, Editor, The Ecology of School Renewal: 86th NSSE Yearbook, Part 1. Chicago: National Society for the Study of Education, University of Chicago Press, 1987.

Hoffman, G.; and S. Link. "Beginning Teacher's Perceptions of Mentors." Journal of Teacher Education 37, 1 (January-February 1986), 22–25.

Jacoby, David. "Rewards Make the Mentor." Personnel 66, 12 (December 1989), 10–14.

Josefowitz, Natasha; and Herman Gordon. How to Get a Good Start in Your New Job. Reading, MA: Addison-Wesley, 1988.

Lasley, T. J., Editor. "Teacher Induction." Journal of Teacher Education (Special Issue) 37, 1 (1989).

Mardenfeld, S. "The Best Way to Get a New Employee Up to Speed." Working Woman 4 (November 1989), 34.

Moran, Sheila W. "Schools and the Beginning Teacher." Phi Delta Kappan 72, 3 (November 1990), 210–14.

National Staff Development Council. The Journal of Staff Development 11, 4 (Fall 1990), 2–50. This issue contains a wealth of information on teacher induction, including these articles: Stephanie A. Hirsh, "New Teacher Induction: An Interview with Leslie Huling Austin"; Ardra L. Cole, "Helping Teachers Become 'Real': Opportunities in Teacher Induction"; Sandra J. Odell, "A Collaborative Approach to Teacher Induction That Works"; Louis M. Thies-Sprinthall and Edwin R. Gerler, Jr., "Support

Groups for Novice Teachers"; Stephanie A. Hirsh, "Designing Induction Programs with the Beginning Teacher in Mind"; Gary N. Hartzell, "Induction of Experienced Teachers into a New School Site"; Joellen P. Killion, "The Benefits of an Induction Program for Experienced Teachers"; Victoria L. Bernhardt and Geraldine M. Flaherty, "Assisting New Teachers in Isolated, Rural School Districts"; Mary M. Harris and Michelle P. Collay, "Teacher Induction in Rural Schools"; and Harriet P. Feldlaufer, Joan M. Hoffman, and Larry Schaefer, "Support Teachers in the Connecticut Induction Program."

Newcombe, E., Editor. Perspectives on Teacher Induction: A Review of the Literature and Promising Program Models. Baltimore, MD: Maryland State Department of Education, 1987.

Reinhartz. Teacher Induction. Washington, DC: National Education Association, 1989.

Shuman, Baird R. Classroom Encounters, Problems, Case Studies, Solutions. Washington, DC: National Education Association, 1989.

Sikula, J., Editor. "Teacher Induction." Action in Teacher Education (Special Issue) 8, 4 (1987).

Steffy, B. Career Stages of Classroom Teachers. Lancaster, PA: Technomic Publishing Company, 1989.

Veenam, V. S. "Perceived Problems of Beginning Teachers." Review of Educational Research 54, 2 (1984), 143–178.

Yeager, Neal. Career Map: Deciding What You Want, Getting It, and Keeping It. New York: John Wiley and Sons, 1988.

Chapter 6

Development

CHAPTER OVERVIEW

- Staff Development by Design
- Staff Development Problems: Deterrents and Determinants
  Deterrents
  Determinants
- Staff Development Domain
- Staff Development Process
  Phase 1: Diagnosing Development Needs
  Phase 2: Design of Development Plans
  Phase 3: Implementing Development Programs
  Phase 4: Evaluating the Staff Development Program

CHAPTER OBJECTIVES

- Develop an awareness of the importance and extensive implications that staff development has for achieving system strategies for its human resources.
- Consider internal and external conditions that influence staff development programs.
- Illuminate key elements in the staff development process.
- Stress the importance of organizational development policies and procedures that enhance attainment of individual, unit, and system aims.

CHAPTER TERMS

Career stages

Development design cues

Development process

In-service education

Staff development

Staff development needs

The central idea underlying the discussion that follows is that human resources administration is a continuing function, one that must be carried on day in and day out, year in and year out, if the school system is to perform its role effectively. More specifically, the human resources function does not halt its activities when vacancies have been filled—it must concern itself with the destiny, productivity, and need satisfaction of people after they are employed. This involves activities relating to staff development, health, tenure, leaves of absence, substitute service, employee associations, grievances, and retirement. The emphasis in this chapter is on the administrative process by which plans for development of human resources are conceived, implemented, and controlled. A framework is presented in the form of a model to guide the discussion on the process by which plans for *organizational, group,* and *individual development* are planned, implemented, and evaluated.

STAFF DEVELOPMENT BY DESIGN

It is the thesis of this chapter that the school system that embraces the concept of continual staff development is one that provides itself with important strategic advantages. Key features of an organizational culture based on a continuous improvement philosophy include:

- Continuously challenging how current staff development programs are performed, with the goal of improving individual, unit, and system performance.
- Highlighting ineffective and inefficient development activities as candidates for *improvement* or *elimination*.
- Designing and shaping development programs to attain strategic human resources goals and objectives.
- Defining staff development objectives in a manner that shapes the formation of the development process.
- Linking subprocesses of the human resources functions, such as information, recruitment, selection, induction, and performance appraisal to the staff development process.

- Viewing staff development as an important vehicle for *career development* plans.
- Considering the strategic importance of *changes in the internal and external environments* (judicious integration of advanced technologies into development programs, changes in community and pupil population, changes in the regulatory environment, and discrepancies between present and optimal states of performance outcomes). How, for example, do internal and external changes influence future development needs, programs, and management responsibilities for development?
- Establishing a planning culture that anticipates rather than reacts to development needs.
- Basing staff development programs on the assumption that the needs of the individual school system (avoiding the temptation to imitate other development programs) are paramount and critical to any development endeavor. In the words of Joyce, Hersh, and McKibbin: "District, county, regional, and federal initiatives will also be effective only as local school sites are able to receive and adapt them to *their particular conditions*. Hence, our belief in the development of an organization—local administrators, teachers, and community members who examine the health of their schools continuously, select targets for improvement, and draw on knowledge about school improvement to implement desired change."[1]
- Upgrading investment in staff development in those areas that are deemed to have the *greatest impact on performance improvement*.
- Creating a master plan that identifies high impact development activities, and identifying anticipated outcomes and costs necessary to achieve optimal results.

STAFF DEVELOPMENT PROBLEMS: DETERRENTS AND DETERMINANTS

Deterrents

Amid nationwide concern about declining educational standards, literacy, numeracy, and preparation for further academic training, staff development as one of the processes of the human resources function has not escaped criticism regarding its programs and practices. If we define staff development problems as deviations from expected performance, or from criteria for judging staff development contributions to educational outcomes, it is clear that new approaches are needed to correct such negative deviations and deterrents to individual, group, and system effectiveness. Figure 6.1 is illustrative of the kinds of negative deviations from expectations that confront contemporary staff development change agents.

- Allocating staff development resources without knowing what, if anything, has been derived from the expenditure.
- Spurning the concept of staff development as a tool for leveraging human resources strategy.
- Viewing staff development as an end in itself rather than as a means to an end.
- Initiating unguided and unorganized staff development programs.
- Disregarding the need for professionalization of internal change agents.
- Giving individual development precedence instead of linking individual, group, and system development.
- Taking for granted that there is a close fit between programs and individual and group needs.
- Failing to apply recruiting, selection, and induction strategies to find, attract, and retain the right candidates.
- Minimizing the importance of validating job-relatedness of staff development programs.
- Offering tuition reimbursement programs without linkage to position requirements.
- Disregarding needs assessment when granting funds for self-nomination development plans.
- Assuming that correcting staff development problems will solve major organizational problems.
- Lacking models to analyze whether programs produce changes; whether they were desired ones; and whether changes in performance met targeted need.
- Viewing staff development conventions as vacation time, as rest and recreation, as a position perquisite, as a hiatus in position demands.
- Failing to aim the staff development process at specific behavioral objectives in advance of program initiation.
- Emphasizing program activities rather than facilitation of learning and resultant behaviors.
- Extending benefit provisions of system–union negotiated contracts without serious review of objectives, costs, outcomes, or linkage to aims of strategic human resources planning.
- Precluding greater centralized control over the cost effectiveness of staff development programs.

FIGURE 6.1
Illustration of contemporary staff development problems.

Examination of the illustrated list of contemporary staff development problems appearing in Figure 6.1 brings into focus questions such as the following:

- Do school systems have adequate professional expertise to design and operate staff development programs?
- Do school systems know how to spend staff development money?
- To what extent do subordinates participate in staff development designing and decision making?
- To what extent do social and political change hinder or enhance program development?
- Is behavior modification a concept interwoven into the fabric of staff development programs?
- Do change agents focus continuously on isolating weaknesses in staff development plans in order to fine-tune them to an acceptable level of effectiveness?
- Are the intended program outcomes expressed in behavioral terms?

Although it is true that problems identified in Figure 6.1 have been the subject of historical research in the quest for resolution, efforts in recent years to prepare for and manage school system change have illuminated the importance of *staff development* within the context of *organizational development*. Current literature and practice indicate an activism in public education that is forcing revisions in the anatomy of staff development regarding what will be learned, how and at what cost, who is eligible and why, where and when will programs take place, components of program content, and who will be in charge.

Political action in the late 1970s resulted in the creation of federally-supported teacher centers as a means of upgrading staff development programs.[2] In the 1980s state legislators and administrators of local school districts saw staff development as a key aspect of school improvement efforts.[3] A 1990 report advocated expanding the staff development process so as to conceive educational organizations as wholes.[4]

Determinants

One of the current staff development trends is to view staff developers as organization development specialists, which places in-service education in a broader perspective.[5] Another current staff development determinant that promises to condition the outcome of development objectives is a systems approach linking the human resources function, of which staff development

---

- Each individual is a part of a whole—every individual action has consequences for the system as a whole.
- To change the outcomes of an organization, one must change the system—not just its parts.
- Organizations must focus on the root causes of problems and long-term goals and consequences, not the symptoms.
- Effective change occurs by understanding the system and its behaviors, and working with the flow of the system, not against it.

  Effective staff development for a systems approach includes:
- Training in the concepts, values, and specific tools of systems thinking.
- Ongoing processes that involve all segments of the organization in a dialogue so that there is collective rather than individual staff development.
- A focus on the application of the beliefs and tools of the system in the context of day-to-day workings of schools and the school system.
- Questioning and examining underlying assumptions and beliefs.

FIGURE 6.2
Key principles of systems thinking.

Source: Gelareh Asayesh, "Using Systems Thinking to Change Systems," Journal of Staff Development 14, 4 (Fall 1993), 8–140.

is one of its processes, to comprehensive plans for institutional improvement. This approach is exemplified in Figure 6.2, which stresses a thoughtful way of approaching deviations from institutional expectations. Systems thinking is a tool for dealing with divergent organization problems that are difficult to resolve by the temporary application of isolated practices. One of the benefits of applying systems theory is that it enables planners to consider both internal and external dimensions of organizational behavior. School systems, for example, acquire substantial resources from external sources, are regulated externally, must satisfy a host of external interests, and are subject to various forces over which they have no control. Thus, systems theory embraces the view that organizational effectiveness depends on the ability to adapt to the demands of the external environment and to shape the culture of its internal environment.

The staff development compact shown in Figure 6.3 represents a planning tool that can be employed to condition staff development outcomes. The compact is an agreement or covenant between the system and its human resources to envision, design, direct, and deliver staff development programs that contribute to overall improvement of the organization.

The Riverpark school system's way of continually nurturing the growth and development of its human resources is exemplified in the design of its staff development process. Provisions include:

- Designating financial resources for approved development programs as an integral part of the annual and long-term budgetary processes.
- Including arrangements for all persons on the system payroll, as well as board members, in development programs aimed at increasing their performance competence.
- Providing developmental opportunities to carry out present and future responsibilities effectively.
- Planning staff development programs on the basis of a constantly evolving technology to accommodate nearly all individual learning needs of students and staff members.
- Arranging for members to initiate reviews of their performance and qualifications for new or vacant positions as they arise.
- Designing development programs and projects to promote personal growth, professional development, problem solving, remedial action, upward mobility, and position security.
- Requiring programmers and change agents to submit formats for budgetary approval, including components such as program purposes to be served, content, setting, and resources.
- Structuring the staff development process to include diagnostic, design, operations, and evaluation stages.
- Aiming staff development program evaluation at assessing effectiveness of provisions for individual, group, and system needs; adequacy of operational mechanisms; quality of progress monitoring; and extent of feedback on outcome attainments, existing problems, needed controls, and corrective measures to be initiated.
- Putting emphasis primarily on organizational and group change and secondarily on individual changes.
- Employing system intervention regarding changes in policy, structure, staffing, programming, and responsibility where appropriate.
- Providing ethics training to selected system members to resolve ethical dilemmas that become omnipresent in every organization culture. This includes making staff development decisions, judgments, and actions that meet standards of proper conduct specified in the system's code of ethics.[*]

[*] See Chapter 1 for viewpoints on ethics in the workplace.

FIGURE 6.3
Compact of the Riverpark school system's staff development process.

STAFF DEVELOPMENT DOMAIN

Staff development is preeminent among those processes designed by the system to attract, retain, and improve the quality and quantity of staff members needed to solve its problems and to achieve its goals. The process of staff development is vitally linked to human resources planning because, as it will be recalled, a sound human resources plan calls for:

- Improving the performance in their present positions of all incumbent position holders.
- Developing key skills of selected personnel so as to fill anticipated vacancies.
- Promoting the self-development of all personnel in order to enhance their influence as individuals and to facilitate need satisfaction.
- Provide a basis for identifying and developing successors in each employee group—from executives to support personnel—across the school system.

Provision of systematic means for the continuous development of skills, knowledge, problem-solving abilities, and attitudes of system personnel has been a cardinal tenet of professional occupations for centuries. Although staff development in the field of education has existed in some form for many years, there are different perceptions of what the term **staff development** means. It is referred to variously as **in-service education,** staff development, training, professional development, continuing education, and *advanced degree work*. One view of the differences between in-service education and staff development is expressed as follows:

> Conceptually, staff development is not something the school does to the teacher but something the teacher does for himself or herself. While staff development is basically growth-oriented, in-service education assumes a deficiency in the teacher and presupposes a set of appropriate ideas, skills, and methods which need developing. Staff development does not assume a deficiency in the teacher, but rather assumes a need for people at work to grow and develop on the job.[6]

The nature of in-service education has been defined to mean:

> . . . any planned program of learning opportunities afforded staff members . . . for purposes of improving the performance of an individual in already assigned positions.[7]

The definition of staff development, as considered here, includes both informal and formal approaches to the improvement of human resources effectiveness. As illustrated in Figure 6.4, staff development embraces both short- and long-range activities; each has different objectives, involves dif-

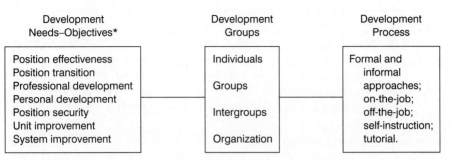

Development Needs–Objectives*	Development Groups	Development Process
Position effectiveness Position transition Professional development Personal development Position security Unit improvement System improvement	Individuals Groups Intergroups Organization	Formal and informal approaches; on-the-job; off-the-job; self-instruction; tutorial.

* A need is defined as a discrepancy between an actual and desired state. Objectives are the counterpart of needs and are employed to translate problems into programs.

FIGURE 6.4
A typology of personnel development.

ferent levels of personnel, and addresses itself to a variety of ways for conceptualizing and organizing the staff improvement function. In effect, staff development is the process of staff improvement through approaches that emphasize self-realization, self-growth, and self-development. Development includes those activities aimed at improvement and growth of abilities, attitudes, skills, and knowledge of system members.

Examination of Figure 6.4 indicates that the concept of staff development embraces the view that various kinds of situations continually arise in every work organization that call for some form of individual or group development. The following examples are illustrative:

- Individual development:

  > *Teacher*—Joseph Morton, a chemistry teacher, has not kept abreast of current knowledge, theories, developments, and teaching technology in the field of chemistry.
  >
  > *Administrator*—Mary Degnas, principal of the Ford Elementary School, is not functioning as an instructional leader and does not feel comfortable representing that role.
  >
  > *Support person*—The board of education has directed the superintendent of schools to develop a plan that will make the capabilities of modern office technologies available to all office-based personnel.

- Group development:

  > Reading, mathematics, and science achievement levels in the Beverly Hills Elementary School are less than satisfactory.

- System development:

  Findings of studies reported by the state department of education and a regional accrediting association to the board of education indicate the accreditation of the school system will be withheld until extensive changes as recommended in the reports are made.

- Board member development:

  Harry Jones, board president, has told school board members they need instruction on the difference between policy making and policy implementation.

To resolve specific complex problems of individual and organizational needs such as those listed above, various approaches are needed to modify behavior patterns of individuals and groups so that organizational effectiveness may be maximized. Examples of positive assumptions intended to give direction to the underlying belief structure and operational activities of a comprehensive staff development effort include:

- The concept of interrelationships among system, unit, and individual goals has implications for the design and implementation of development programs.
- Development includes all school personnel on the payroll. Although emphasis on the professional staff is quite proper, application of the discussion that follows is to total staff development.
- Development entails satisfying two kinds of expectations: the contribution of the individual to the school system and the material and emotional rewards anticipated by the individual in return.
- Development involves all activities designed to increase an individual's ability to perform assignments effectively, whatever the role and whatever the level of performance.
- Development is focused on two kinds of activities: (a) those specifically planned and administered by the school system (formal approaches) and (b) those initiated by personnel (informal approaches).
- Development is concerned with values, norms, and behavior of individuals and groups.
- Development is designed to serve the following purposes: personal growth, professional development, problem solving, remedial action, motivation, upward mobility, and member security.

- Development programs initiated by the system are aimed at educating individuals above and beyond the immediate technical requirements of positions.
- Development programs sanction activities related to resolution of immediately practical and position-oriented needs as well as to longer-range purposes focused on full development of the individual.
- Development encourages career-long staff development for all personnel as an organizational necessity.
- Development activity has been, for the most part, judgmentally rather then experimentally evaluated.
- School systems have not fully capitalized on existing knowledge and theory regarding staff development.
- Staff development programs have been subjected to an array of fads and fashions that have not been based on components of a sound process development model (such as human resources objectives) or carefully designed, administered, and tested experiences.
- Staff development represents a powerful tool for effecting individual, unit, and system change.

Improvement of human performance calls for a variety of approaches to modify behavior patterns of individuals and groups so that organizational effectiveness may be maximized. A framework by which efforts are systematized to deal with the host of development problems that arise continually in school systems, whether individual or group in nature, is referred to as a *process model*. The section that follows presents a comprehensive development process and model consisting of sequential and interrelated phases.

STAFF DEVELOPMENT PROCESS

A process model to examine ways in which a school system plans, implements, and evaluates its personnel development plans is outlined in Figure 6.5. The **development process** is similar to other personnel processes examined in preceding chapters. There are several observations to be made about the process outlined in Figure 6.5. The elements included are considered as an outline of integrated tasks to develop an understanding of the total process and the intermediate points. Each phase is interdependent on the other; each has subordinate elements. The development process model provides a means for creating long-term improvement strategy, facilitating issue and action identification, monitoring progress, and forming feedback on personal and organizational outcomes. Each of the major elements in Figure 6.5 is examined next.

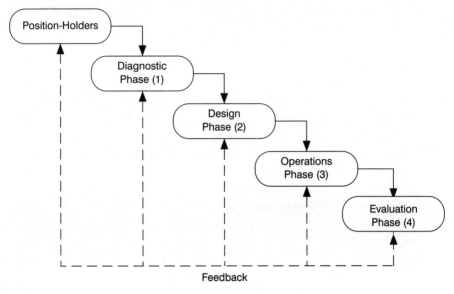

FIGURE 6.5
Model of the personnel development process.

Phase 1: Diagnosing Development Needs

The conceptual model presented in Figure 6.5 contains four phases or steps, beginning with diagnosis of **staff development needs**. Needs are determined by analysis of three levels: individuals, groups, and the system. *Individual needs,* as indicated in Figure 6.5, include matters relating to position effectiveness, position transition, personal and professional development, and position security. *Group needs* can be illustrated by conditions that indicate the need for site-based faculty development programs designed to ensure that students who speak little English are not barred from any program because of their language barrier. *Organizational needs* are those involving the total system, such as the creation of opportunities for women and minorities, systemwide improvement of office technology, or adherence to state legislation governing minimum pupil competency requirements.

Table 6.1 contains a list of hypothetical development problems in a school system around which the discussion later in this chapter (on designing realistic and workable plans of action for developing personnel) is centered. As indicated, there are several considerations involved in planning personnel development programs. The first is the *total development needs of the organization;* the second is the needed improvements in the specific *knowledge and skills of individual incumbents;* and the third is the *potential* of the incum-

TABLE 6.1
Interrelatedness of personnel processes in planning staff development programs.

Problems in Personnel Performance, Procedures, or Systems	Sources of Needs Information									
	Personnel Records	Personnel Inventory	Performance Appraisal	Recruitment Process	Selection Process	Development Process	Compensation Process	Master Plans	Budgets	Survey Reports
Professional obsolescence of personnel	X	X	X					X		X
Curricula obsolescence								X		X
Personnel shortages and surpluses	X	X		X		X	X		X	
Individual performance problems			X							
Technological changes affecting positions								X		X
Social changes affecting positions										X
Changes in position requirements		X	X	X		X	X	X		X
Ineffective departmental performance			X					X		X
Problems in vertical mobility of personnel		X	X							
Problems in horizontal mobility of personnel	X	X	X							
Problems in personnel motivation						X				X
Problems in information system										X
Problems in organizational communication										X

bents for growth and development. Another consideration is the needed improvement of *group and intergroup performance*. The hypothetical situation posed in Table 6.1 assumes that every organization will have discrepancies in performance, procedures, and systems. Sources of data shown in Table 6.1 are interrelated. Data gathered in the performance appraisal process, for example, can be applied to the development process. An important aspect of the concept illustrated in Table 6.1 is that output from one personnel process or procedure can provide input for another process or procedure. Information gained in the recruitment, selection, and appraisal process is important input to the development process. Many school districts occasionally find it necessary to employ inexperienced personnel or discover that they have employed individuals not fully qualified to perform assigned roles. The need for development programs for personnel in these categories is apparent if they are to become reasonably effective in their work.

Table 6.2 supplements the information shown in Table 6.1 by identifying major development factors and the considerations they pose in designing a development program. The reader's attention is directed to sources of needs information other than those listed in Table 6.1, which can be employed to address questions such as those identified in Table 6.2. These sources include interviews, questionnaires, consultation, individual and group discussions, instructional test results, discussions with position holders and work groups, surveys, records, reports, and audits.

Thus, development needs surface at varying levels, with differing degrees of impact. They are considered to reflect a gap between an existing and a desired condition, whether the gap is viewed as a deficiency or part of the organization's culture that stresses continual growth and development for all system members.

Prior to translating needs into program designs, it is important to point out that several salient planning considerations need to be examined. For example, Is there evidence on which there is a consensus among decision makers that a general need exists? How important is the need in terms of system development priorities and resources? Is the need one that can or should be resolved through system action? What are the probabilities that satisfaction of the need will be cost-effective?

A second consideration is achieving a consensus on whether a need should become a component of the system's development program. Although need identification is an *analytic* process, need satisfaction is a *political process*, meaning that for a need to achieve program status requires that persons, powers, and parties be clearly aligned.[8]

The essence of this discussion points to the premise that ongoing diagnoses of system development are an essential management task to identify which needs are vitally important to individual, group, and organizational effectiveness, as opposed to those that are faddish, fashionable, and clearly unnecessary.

TABLE 6.2
Summary of major factors to be considered in assessment of staff development needs.

Development Factors	Current and Future Development Concerns
External environment	What is the present impact of the regulatory environment on staff development programs? What should the system anticipate regarding future regulatory requirements?
School system	Do current indices show that staff development programs are reducing discrepancies between expectations and outcomes?
Position holder	Does the individual understand the position require-ments? Is he/she able to perform the requirements? Is the performance level satisfactory? Can it be improved?
Position	Are there work standards for the position? Are the work standards in compliance with regulatory controls? Are the work standards obsolete? Has present technology changed the performance requirements?
Position–person match	To what extent is there compatibility between the position standards and the skills, abilities, and attitudes of the position holder?
Position context	Are there organizational climatic barriers influencing indi-vidual or group performance?
Work group	Have performance discrepancies been identified in work groups (e.g., administrative, instructional, specialist, and support groups)?

Phase 2: Design of Development Plans

Development needs may surface at various levels (organization, unit, or individual), at different times, and for various reasons. Personnel shortages may occur, legislation may be passed requiring new programs, or informa-tion may be compiled that indicates certain types of teaching skill deficien-cies. Consequently, every development need is likely to be subjected to some form of priority analysis to determine whether it should be included as a component of the comprehensive staff development plan currently in oper-ation. Preparation of staff development design or plan includes a document featuring the following minimum essentials:

- A statement of reasons for undertaking the training (the problem or the need).
- A description of the specific goal(s) and objectives selected as outcomes.
- A detailing of the participants to be served and how or why they (groups or individuals) are related to goals and objectives.

- A plan for identifying and developing successors for critically important positions.
- A calendar of major events showing their relationship to objectives and participants.
- A designation of the responsible person or group assigned to each major event.
- A list of resource requirements for each major event and one for overall coordination.
- A description of the procedures for evaluating the plan providing timely feedback on the operation.
- A schedule and list of procedures for monitoring the total operation.[9]

There are additional criteria for reviewing a staff development plan that could be added to this list. These criteria include importance to the system mission, unit goals, and total development program; importance to management priorities; measurability of outcomes; alternative means of achieving outcomes; time period needed; cost to satisfy need; and importance to the future of the system, individual school, or individual staff member.

A variety of factors are involved in shaping the design of a staff development program. Among these **development design cues** are system size, state legislation, court decisions, bargaining contracts, school board policy, research investigations, and emerging practices. Employment of system policy, research findings, and emerging practices to improve staff development designs will be the subject of the discussion that follows.

Design Cues from System Policy. It is important for the board of education to indicate publicly what it wants to happen regarding the development of personnel and what it is willing to support financially. This declaration of intentions is presented as written policy, as in the following example:

> *It is the policy of the Cloudcroft school system to provide its personnel with opportunities to become more effective in performing their current or future work assignments through increased knowledge, education, training, and experience. Moreover, it is our policy to help each individual progress in the service of the system. When vacancies occur, incumbent personnel are entitled to first consideration. It is our intent to provide an appropriate development program for every individual in our employ, regardless of his/her work assignment.*

Policies in writing provide the administrator and his/her staff with authorization needed to establish overall plans for personnel development. A policy statement is needed to formalize and crystallize system intent toward staff development and to create a climate in which realistic plans can be developed to meet organizational needs. A declaration, such as the illustration preceding, provides the administrative team with far-ranging opportunities to create a comprehensive design for development of the system's human resources.

Planning Cues From Research.   Findings from investigations of staff development practices warrant consideration in the planning, implementation, and evaluation stages of personnel development programs. Information about effective contemporary staff development practices for teachers has been reported by Sparks and Loucks-Horsley.[10] Their review has been organized around five staff development models, which are capsulized in Table 6.3. These models are viewed in the field as having solid foundations in research and/or practice and are in operation to a considerable extent in the nation's schools.

The gist of what Sparks and Loucks-Horsley have reported is that staff development is most successful in organizations where:

• Staff members have a common, coherent set of goals and objectives that they have helped to formulate, reflecting high expectations of themselves and their students.

• Administrators exercise strong leadership by promoting a "norm of collegiality," minimizing status differences between themselves and their staff members, promoting informal communication, and reducing their own need to use formal controls to achieve coordination.

• Administrators place a high priority on staff development and continuous improvement.

• Administrators and teachers employ a variety of formal and informal processes for monitoring progress toward goals, using them to identify obstacles to such progress and ways of overcoming these obstacles, rather than to make summary judgments regarding the "competencies" of particular staff members.

• Knowledge, expertise, and resources, including time, are drawn on appropriately, yet liberally, to initiate and support the pursuit of staff development goals.[11]

Sparks and Loucks-Horsley have also taken note of the importance of organizational supports necessary for effective staff development. Various studies confirm the necessity of:

• Schools possessing norms that support collegiality and experimentation.

• District and building administrators who work with staff to clarify goals and expectations, and actively commit to and support teachers' efforts to change their practice.

TABLE 6.3
Five Models of staff development for teachers.

Types of Staff Development Models	Model Assumptions
Individually guided staff development	Individuals can best judge their own learning needs and are capable of self-directed and self-initiated learning. Individuals will be most motivated when they select their own learning goals based on their personal assessment of their needs.
Observation/assessment	Observation and assessment of instruction provide the teacher with data that can be reflected on and analyzed for the purpose of improving student learning. Reflection by an individual on his/her own practices can be enhanced by another's observation.
Involvement in a development/ improvement process	Adults learn most effectively when they have a need to know or a problem to solve. Teacher acquires important knowledge or skills through involvement of school improvement or curriculum development processes.
Training	There are behaviors and techniques worthy of replication by teachers in the classroom. Teachers can change their behaviors and learn to replicate behaviors in their classrooms that were not previously in their repertoires.
Inquiry	The most effective avenue for professional development is cooperative study by teachers themselves into problems and issues arising from attempts to make their practice consistent with their educational values. The approach aims to give greater control over what is to count as valid educational knowledge to teachers.

Source: Dennis Sparks and Susan Loucks-Horsley, "Five Models of Staff Development for Teachers," Journal of Staff Development 10, 4 (Fall 1989), 40–57.

- Efforts strongly focused on changes in curricular, instructional, and classroom management practices with improved student learning as the goal.
- Adequate, appropriate staff development experiences with follow-up assistance that continues long enough for new behaviors to be incorporated into ongoing practices.[12]

Despite the progress that has been made in designing staff development programs in the past decade, much remains to be learned about the research base essential to improving teaching and learning. According to Sparks and Loucks-Horsley, areas that need analysis are related to:

- Which models are most effective for which outcomes with which teachers?
- What is the impact on student learning of the four nontraining models?
- What impact will blending the models described in Table 6.3 have in comprehensive development programs?
- Which staff development programs are most or least cost-effective?
- What is the relationship between staff development programs and teacher professionalism:[13]

Much of what has been learned and what remains to be learned about staff development brings into perspective the realization that teacher improvement, with its link to recruitment, selection, induction, and appraisal, becomes a critical component in the current pursuit to improve school instructional programs, practices, and learning outcomes.

Another summary of staff development findings by Joyce et al. indicates:

- Relatively few teachers have experienced workshop or course training powerful enough to implant new teaching skills and strategies into their repertoires, although many do get useful ideas.

- Teachers report that the informal contact they have with other teachers is their major growth-producing activity, with respect to the improvement of their teaching.

- Teacher growth activities can be categorized by three domains: (a) the formal system of staff development, (b) the informal system of interchange with the school and the school district, and (c) personal activities in their private lives. Few people maintain the same growth state across all three domains.

- There is enormous variation in the extent to which individual teachers pull potentially growth-producing experiences from their environment and exploit formal and informal learning experiences.

- Collaborative governance appeared to produce a more vigorous and integrative type of in-service experience, one that was hands on, job embedded, and course related.[14]

The value of these findings is that they are explicitly developmental, representing a spirit of inquiry and continuing commitment to validating existing approaches to staff development. In addition, the information indicates some important factors to be considered in designing a staff development program, notably those elements in the technical system (positions) and the nature of the technical system that a development plan must accommodate.

Planning Cues From Value Trends. Figure 6.6 contains a list of trends derived from current literature on staff development. The emerging value trends cited in Figure 6.6 provide cues for the design of staff development programs in that they explicitly bring into focus these considerations:

- Position technology changes over time.
- Staff development concepts change over time.
- Practices employed in establishing staff development programs can become outmoded and unworkable as internal and external organizational conditions and situations change.
- Social and organizational changes have been so rapid and extensive in the latter stages of the twentieth century that modern organizations have found it necessary to experiment with a variety of approaches to improve their human resources in order to achieve both organizational and individual goals.

Cues From Career Stages.   Increasing attention is being devoted in the literature and in the work world to the relationship between **career stages** and staff development. Table 6.4 contains descriptions of career stages from three sources. The intent of each is to stress that staff development occurs over time, goes through several stages, cuts across a wide range of development issues, and includes changing tasks and personal needs.

The main implications that emerge from research and practice regarding inclusion of career stages in the design of development programs are:

- When career development becomes an organizational policy commitment, it signifies system willingness to provide continuing improvement opportunities for personnel. These include career goals, career counseling, and career pathing; information about position openings; and various forms of development programs, some of which address special needs such as problems relating to outplacement, retirement and preretirement, inductees, and choices confronting midcareer staff members and those who have developed physical disabilities.
- Administrative responsibility for career development is both a central function and a matter for individual work groups. These responsibilities include leading the way, developing policy, providing financial and opportunity initiatives, and influencing units that lag behind to pursue advances pioneered by other work groups.
- Opportunities for enhancing career development exist among many lines. Decision making should include those to develop programs most suited to specific work group needs.
- Considering that the pool of skilled help is tightening, organizations throughout the nation are broadening their roles regarding staff develop-

Away from.	Toward. . . . . .
Top-down approach	Bottom-up approach
Narrow approach to staff development	Comprehensive approach to staff development
Isolated projects	Interactive and interdependent programs
Control	Empowerment
Off-the-shelf projects	Customized programs
System-initiated changes	System and staff initiated changes
Inattention to school culture	Collaboration to change school culture
Centralized plans	Site-based plans
Solving problems for staff members	Building staff capacity to solve own problems
Individual emphasis	Individual and team emphasis
Preparation and experience emphasis	Performance emphasis
Indifference to development outcomes	Emphasis on staff development outcomes
Development of teaching staff	Development of all classes of personnel
Sole emphasis on self-fulfillment	Individual, unit, and system goals
Development as an event	Development as a continuous process
Sporadic and disorganized programs	Systematic strategies and well-defined objectives
Limited financial support	Local, state, and federal support
Focus on remediation	Focus on remediation and growth
Administrative initiative	Administration–individual initiatives
Formal approaches	Formal and informal approaches
Programs preplanned	Staff participates in planning
Reliance on external agents/ agencies	Inside or outside support as appropriate
Assuming positive program impact	Evaluating actual impact
Intuition and prior experience	Theoretical exploration
Role development	Role and career development
Random-based planning	Systems-based planning
System evaluation	System and self-evaluation
Uncoordinated, ad hoc, and fragmented projects	Staff development models
Limited use of electronic technology	Emerging emphasis on use of electronic technology
Limited methods and types of delivery	Unlimited methods and types of delivery
Lack of application of systems thinking	Using systems thinking to change systems

FIGURE 6.6
Value trends in staff development.

TABLE 6.4
Three descriptions of career stages.

1. Early stage	2. Pre-work stage	3. Establishment stage
Tenured stage	Initial work stage	(early adulthood)
Retirement stage	Stable work stage	Advancement stage
All stages[a]	Retirement stage[b]	(mature adulthood)
		Maintenance stage
		(midlife)
		Withdrawal (old age)[c]

Sources: [a]University of Pennsylvania, Almanac Supplement (February 28, 1989), IX-XII. [b]John M. Ivancevich and William F. Glueck, Foundations of Personnel/Human Resource Management, Third Edition, (Plano, TX: Business Publications Inc., 1983), 523. [c]L. Baird and K. Kram, "Career Dynamics: Managing the Superior-Subordinate Relationship," Organizational Dynamics 11 (1983), 209–16.

ment and retention. (This is especially true in the cases of women and minorities.)

- Included among emerging issues relating to the design of career development programs are: What are the system's ambitions for the career stages of its human resources? Does the system have sufficient mechanisms in place to support career development? In an era of increased competition for personnel, what career plans are best calculated to retain and improve current and future staff members?

- Are there particular kinds of development incentives, such as sabbaticals, tuition grants, research accounts, and flexible teaching loads, that have the potential for enhancing the pursuit of careers within the system?

- Have proactive steps been initiated to ensure for the future availability of talent needs for all levels of the system?

Cues From the External Environment. As school systems consider development projects, criteria for their adoption represent an implicit strategy. The strategic plan should provide guidance to help make development strategy consistent with human resources strategy. One of the important reasons for carefully examining present strategy is to determine whether continuation of what the system has been doing developmentally is *justifiable in the years ahead*. In today's society there are at least three influences at work that must be considered when answering the question of whether today's developmental techniques are adequate for tomorrow's staff development problems: (a) expanding educational technology, (b) workforce supply and demand, and (c) external educational initiatives.

The age in which contemporary education takes place is an external environment development that has not yet been fully maximized for teaching and learning purposes. School systems have yet to ensure that available technology is being used to best advantage for the organization, its employees, and its student body.

Modern technology has made rapid strides in increasing the amount and kinds of teaching and learning resources available to educational institutions. Among these are broadcast and closed-circuit television; calculators; audio- and videotapes; videodiscs; data storage and retrieval systems; word processors; and computers used as textbooks, workbooks, and other forms of teaching and learning.

Staff development is related to external technological developments in that currently there is a lack of knowledge, skills, and abilities for incorporating and combining available technology into existing instructional programs, and for preparing pupils to make optimal use of this extensive array of modern learning resources.

In short, school systems need to give more than token recognition to external technological developments that have application for improving teaching and learning. Critical areas of technological deficiencies can be identified and highlighted in staff development designs to strengthen the school's potential for improving its effectiveness with technological devices.

Boards of education and their executives who consider staff development as an ongoing process rather than a periodic event are bound to take note of an emerging reality for human resources planning—the dramatic shift taking place in the work force of this country, which affects every employer in America—that is, the labor force's growth is slowing and its diversity is increasing. There is the emerging and widely recognized problem that recruiting and retaining knowledgeable personnel has become a difficulty of serious proportions. The U.S. Department of Labor predicts that only 15 percent of new entrants into the labor force between 1987 and the year 2000 will be native white males, compared with 47 percent who were in that category in 1987. Nearly one-third of all new entrants will be from minority groups.[15] Among the broad initiatives that should be considered as school systems prepare to cope with these changes of the modern work force are identifying and maximizing the talents of personnel within the system capable of making teaching and learning more effective, emphasizing ongoing development programs for all members at all levels, creating a culture that attracts the kind of talent essential to achieve system goals, and designing compensation programs that encourage and reward contributions to teaching and learning.

Virtually everybody agrees that the nation's economic future hinges on major improvements in education at all levels, and that the nation's schools are "disturbingly deficient." With such a perspective there is every reason to assume that (a) there will be extended initiatives and new stances in the external environment to improve schooling, and (b) staff development will take on added significance to deal with those deficiencies that have been repeatedly reported in recent years in national reports on elementary and secondary education.

By way of illustration, efforts are currently under way in the external environment to restructure and enrich vocational education; reshape programs to teach disadvantaged children; enlarge the scope of early childhood education; and boost federal aid to education at all levels to help overcome glaring deficiencies in the way Americans, particularly the poor, are educated. Federal and state efforts are under way to mold vocational education into a critical component in training the nation's future work force. School systems will be directed to integrate basic academic skills into vocational courses with emphasis on current and emerging high technology.

The instructional skills to implement these and other anticipated external initiatives will depend to a considerable extent on the leadership responsible for development strategies. Staff development should be considered one of the critical tools for creating the reservoir of talent within each school system. Through this process the capability exists for equipping staff members with the knowledge, skills, attitudes, and performance behavior essential to attain instructional goals.

Program Format Design.   Every staff development program must be created, organized, planned, and directed within the context of what might be referred to as the comprehensive or macrodevelopment plan. The macroplan may be viewed as a group of microplans or subplans that represent a systemwide operational design for the development of its human resources. Microplans are developed by means of a program format, a description of which follows. If, for example, the system decides to initiate a program for school principals to increase their effectiveness in classroom observation, details are specified in a *program format*, which consists of *program content, methods, setting, participation,* and *resources.*

Program formats.   *Format,* as the term is used here, refers to the way in which program elements, such as development needs and groups, are translated into program specifics. Format components include program methodology, content setting, resources, and explication. Figure 6.7, incorporating a framework for designing personnel development program formats, identifies five major elements: *content, methods, setting, participation,* and *resources.* Each of the elements will be discussed in the following sections, the intent of which is to tie together the discussion of program formats so that the reader can gain a perspective of the variables involved and their interconnections.

Program content.   Block 1 in Figure 6.7 indicates that there are two types of learning to be considered in designing a program format: (a) theories, concepts, and principles, and (b) learning their application. The two types of learning are not mutually exclusive and do not have to be sepa-

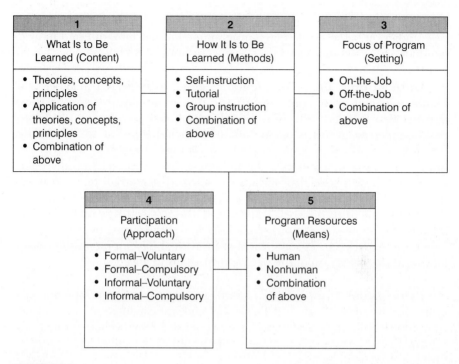

FIGURE 6.7
Framework for designing personnel development program formats.

rated. The key task of program designers is to decide which of the elements is involved in achieving the program objective and how either element can best be learned by personnel in the development program. Major methods employed in personnel development programs to assist system members in learning position requirements and how to perform them more effectively are the focus of the following discussion.

Program methods. Block 2 in Figure 6.7 identifies four methods of learning: (a) self-instruction, (b) tutorial, (c) group instruction, and (d) a combination of these methods. The choice of method(s) to be used in a particular program format will depend on a number of factors, such as the objectives of the program, number of personnel involved, cost per participant, availability of personnel to conduct the program, availability of learning aids, and learning ability of group members. Research indicates that all methods are effective, some more so than others. Effectiveness will depend on learning conditions, including what is to be learned. Especially important, according to research, is relevance of a particular method of attaining a particular organizational goal. Methods to be employed are extensive, including lectures, lecture discussions, demonstrations, projects, sensitivity training, conferences, case studies, in-baskets, role plays, programmed instruction, directed individual study, clinic sessions, task forces, and workshops.

Locus of program. The program setting, as indicated in Block 3 of Figure 6.7, can be on the job, off the job, or a combination of these approaches. Probably the most widely employed setting for personnel development programs is on the job. This includes personnel orientation through the induction process, position rotation, coaching, mentor programs, internships, assistantships, committee-directed projects at the system or unit level, and special programs for selected personnel (e.g., first-year teachers). They may take place at the system level, in the unit location, or in the actual teaching or work station. Off the job settings or forms may include the university campus, conferences, field projects, or evening and extension courses. Or, in some cases of individual development, the setting may be at the discretion of the person or persons involved.

Participation. Approaches to staff participation in development programs are listed in Block 4 of Figure 6.7 and are classified as voluntary or compulsory. Voluntary and compulsory programs may be both formal and informal in approach, depending on the program objective. Examples featuring each type include:

- *Formal-voluntary*—System conducts problem-centered seminar for new teachers. Attendance voluntary.
- *Informal-voluntary*—Teachers awarded budgetary allowance for personal and professional development.
- *Formal-compulsory*—System conducts seminar on force-field analysis for supervisory personnel.
- *Informal-compulsory*—System establishes deadline for personnel to meet certification requirements. Individuals are free to choose approaches to meet requirements.

Examination of these examples leads to several observations about approaches to personnel participation, one of which is that uniformity in the design of development programs is neither feasible nor desirable. A second inference is that program format planning calls for considerable flexibility in meeting development needs. Moreover, the extent, flexibility, and detailed planning involved in deciding on programs and formats require careful and constant coordination.

Resources. Resources for development programs include instructors, facilities, funds, time, materials, and organization. One of the key questions usually involved in preparing a program format is, Where can we find the most competent instructor? To resolve this question, the search may lead to colleges or universities, regional education agencies, commercial enterprises, private consultants, and personnel within the system. Resources in the form of funds and facilities are usually limited; as a result, some organizations share instructors, facilities, and materials.

Another kind of resource problem is that of finding time to free personnel for development purposes. Solutions to this problem require that the organization subsidize the time of personnel in the form of paid leaves of absence, time off with pay, or time off during the school day without extra pay. Also helpful are other patterns of staff deployment, such as team teaching aides and student tutors. Because time is an essential factor in any approach to development and redevelopment, size of the school staff should be such as to enable individuals to devote a portion of their time to personal and professional growth.

Lack of funding has been a major deterrent to improvement of continuing professional development programs. In this connection, progress in improving development programs depends on the creation of legal, conceptual, design, and support frameworks for the preparation of educational personnel, and that these are reflected in the laws, regulations, policies, and practices of the state legislature, the state education agency, school administrators, higher education agencies, and teacher education organizations. Such frameworks can be developed at the state level to undergird operational programs. Sanctions for this approach, it has been observed, must be gained through the political arena.[16]

Another of the resource elements in a development program is administration. Each program format, if it is to achieve its ends, involves an administrative process that includes planning, organizing, directing, coordinating, and controlling. This calls for a combination of data, power, competence, and participation, which is provided by both the system and its parts. In effect, a program format is one component in a total operational process that encompasses systemwide effort to achieve significant instructional objectives. Each program format that is effective and efficient requires competent management that focuses on arrangements as to personnel, place, funds, facilities, schedules, correspondence, records, and responsibilities.

Explication. Specifics of each program format for staff development need to be summarized and disseminated for review, formalization, and implementation. A framework linking program formats to development objectives is shown in Figure 6.8. The central idea underlying Figure 6.8 is that each individual development program, prior to implementation, should be reviewed for links between program format and objectives. By analyzing the elements contained in Figure 6.8, planners are able to visualize whether varying development objectives have been translated into

Form D-10

DEVELOPMENT PROGRAM PLANNING FORMAT

1. Title of program: _____

2. Program purpose:

   ___ Personal development ___ Professional development

   ___ Position effectiveness   ___ Position transition ___ Position security

   ___ School unit improvement ___ School system improvement

3. Specific program objective:

   ___ Dissemination of knowledge ___ Developing skills

   ___ Acquisition of knowledge   ___ Creating organizational climate

   ___ Interpersonal skills   ___ Changing attitudes

   ___ Problem-solving skills   ___ General development of personnel

4. Organized for: ___ Administrative and Supervisory Personnel

                      ___ Instructional Personnel   ___ Support Personnel

5. System level: ___ Elementary ___ Intermediate ___ Other

6. Level of learning: ___ Simple   ___ Complex   ___ Highly complex

7. Content: Theories, concepts, and principles: application of theories and concepts

8. Program scope: ___ Systemwide   ___ Building   ___ Individual

9. Duration: _____ to _____

10. Number of participants: _____

11. Funds allocated: ___ Amount   Source of funds: ___ Internal ___ External

12. Program/methods: ___ Self-instruction ___ Tutorial ___ Group instruction

13. Program setting: ___ On the job   ___ Off the job

14. Participation: ___ Voluntary   ___ Compulsory

15. Linked to performance appraisal: ___ Yes   ___ No

16. Program resources needed:

   ___ Funds   ___ Facilities   ___ Materials   ___ Personnel

   ___ Management   ___ Information

17. Program leadership: _____

18. Program evaluation responsibility: _____

19. Evaluation criteria: ___ Participant reaction   ___ Learning behavior

                          ___ Results

20. Outcome intent: In what way will system, unit, or individual change as a result of the program?

FIGURE 6.8
Development program planning format for the Cloudcroft school system.

increasingly specific operational levels and whether the program format is capable of achieving the ends in view. The format analysis should reveal existing gaps and revisions needed prior to implementation of plans.

A major reason for devoting attention to program format design is that it represents a tool for guiding implementation of a staff development plan from abstract concepts into operational realities. For example, the preceding discussion on program format design was initiated by illustrating a program objective: to increase the effectiveness of school principals in classroom observation. The program format design (as illustrated in Figure 6.8) is, then, employed to give greater specificity to this general objective. The subobjectives may include any or a combination of knowledge, skill, attitude, position behavior, and group outcome objectives relating to classroom observation by school principals. After specific goals and related major objectives are identified, other details of the program can be structured, as shown in Figures 6.7 and 6.8.

Phase 3: Implementing Development Programs

Reexamination of the model of the staff development process outlined in Figure 6.5 indicates that completion of Phase 2 (program design) leads to Phase 3 (implementation of development activities). Phase 3 occurs when the design of the program is shaped into an operational structure and when the planning decisions are put into effect. It is a time when Phases 1 and 2 are meshed to link individual, unit, and organizational development, because individual development programs are inseparable from broader programs of organizational change and improvement. Basically, development activities are a means of attaining organizational goals and desired results. Organizational and individual development are viewed as being mutually supportive—neither can be fully effective in the absence of the other. Well-designed development programs for enhancing conceptual, technical, and interpersonal skills will fail if the organizational climate is not conducive to improved behavior. As are all projects and activities within a school system, development programs are monitored, reviewed, and evaluated in terms of the extent to which intended objectives are achieved.

A *development program,* as the term is used here, is an organized set of activities, unified by a comprehensive plan, to achieve specific objectives in accordance with established policies and budgetary allocations. It involves determination of specifics as to how each will be carried out in units of the school system, selection of purposeful activities, time span for each of the several programs, personnel involved, how the money will be spent, physical facilities required, appraisal procedures, and structures needed in each unit to put the program into effect.

Criteria offered by Bishop for the implementation phase of individual staff development programs include:

- Administration and broad policy support must be evident.
- The rationale and objectives must be clear.
- Professional staff members must know how to participate and relate to the program.
- There must be adequacy, quality, and coordination in the materials to be used.
- Relevance and realism for professionals (as well as for learners) is necessary.
- A reasonable plan for achievement of desired objectives is essential.
- Leadership and role responsibilities (performance expectations) for all staff members should be defined.
- Communication flow and feedback must be a part of the process and program.
- Support and modification must be observable in all components of the system.[17]

The focus of development planning, it will be noted, is on the operating unit (line, staff, or support unit). This means that even though certain development programs will be initiated at the top level of the system, much of the responsibility for planning and implementing specific programs will rest with unit heads, such as principals, department heads, supervisors, directors, and coordinators. This hypothesis is in keeping with the thought that each unit should understand its organizational role, both ideal and actual, and perceive clearly the development that must take place in personnel so as to advance from the latter to the former condition. Theoretically, much of the evidence of the need for staff development will come from unit heads, and much of the change in behavior of individuals will be the result of the quality of the relationship between supervisor and subordinate. Conferences that summarize the subordinate's performance and make plans for his/her growth are at the heart of the process.

It is an article of faith among executives that behavior patterns of personnel can be modified in directions desired by the system through effective programs of development. Two corollaries to this are that (a) the line, staff, and support units in a school system have prime responsibility for advocating and implementing development programs; and (b) heads of units are major determinants of program effectiveness.

If we hold to the assumption that the unit head is the key figure in modifying the behavior of his/her subordinates in desired directions, then it follows that the system must give considerable thought to development of all administrators in the system who direct the work of other adults. It is the unit head (e.g., the principal) who inducts personnel into the system, conducts their follow-up interviews, determines their strengths and weaknesses, learns to understand their feelings and problems, conveys to them the need for and importance of development, sets mutually agreed upon development goals, checks progress toward achievement of goals, serves as teacher and coach, and recognizes work well done.

In addition, the unit head advises the central administration on development policies and programs and makes certain that necessary activities are being implemented and programs are being carried out effectively. The implication here is that the system must conduct a development program for its administrators, one aimed at increasing their understanding of the process of staff development, including the way needs are identified, how development plans for individuals and units are prepared, how learning theories are linked to development purposes, and how the success of the development effort is appraised.

Phase 4: Evaluating the Staff Development Program

The development process, as introduced in Figure 6.5, includes Phase 4 (evaluation) as a culminating step, because activities related thereto involve expenditure of considerable human effort and physical resources of the system. The board of education, its agents, and the community in general expect a fair return on resources invested in this activity. Two kinds of questions usually raised regarding operation of any organizational activity relate to *administrative* and *technical rationality*. The first kind of question seeks information on the extent to which *administrative know-how* is applied to the development process; that is, the manner in which it is planned, organized, directed, and controlled. The second question seeks information on the *degree of effectiveness* with which available technical knowledge is applied to the process. For example, the school system may want to know whether the best theories of learning are being used to modify the behavior of personnel in the program and whether ways of determining development needs are valid.

Additionally, a final and much more difficult question is whether the development program is really helping the organization to realize its daily, annual, and long-term goals. Determining what measurable gains have been made by what people in what activities is a skill most organizations have not yet mastered. As the quest for improved ways to appraise results of development goes on, the system can appraise the development program as to its impact on achievement of behavioral objectives by personnel, responses of unit heads to results accomplished, and the contribution of the program to system effectiveness.

Development efforts have been criticized frequently because they do not focus on significant individual or organizational needs, they attack the wrong problems, or they attempt to solve the correct problems with inappropriate instructional techniques. Two additional shortcomings of development programs should be noted: (a) in some school systems, evaluation does not take place at all, and (b) evaluation frequently occurs to planners as an afterthought.

A plan of evaluation should be developed *concurrently with the definition of behavior change, selection of content, and design of instructional methodology.* The plan should include gathering data on whether the problem on which the development project is focused has been resolved and whether the learning transaction brought about results intended in position performance. If the development problem is not resolved, modifications in development approaches to lead to the desired improvements are in order.

It is worth reinforcing the point that program content (what to teach) and program methods (how it should be taught) represent decisions critical to the design and evaluation of staff development programs. The learning process by which new behaviors (skills, knowledge, abilities, and attitudes) are acquired involves practicing those behaviors to the end that they result in relatively enduring change.

There are various theories or sets of ideas about the way in which learning takes place. Three learning theories mentioned frequently in the literature are behavioral (learning through trial and error), social (learning from others), and cognitive or Gestalt (learning is affected by a variety of factors).[18] Implications of learning theories for personnel development include identification of key behaviors to be acquired, enlisting learner cooperation, demonstrating to the learner the nature and importance of the behavior, providing practice opportunities, reinforcing correct behavior, giving feedback, and recognizing and rewarding permanency of desired change.

Types of questions used to evaluate whether or not intended objectives of a development project have been achieved include:

- *Participant impact*—What has the project done to change the behavior of the participant?
- *Position impact*—Did the participant's performance improve in the position setting?
- *Organizational impact*—In what ways and to what extent do the development efforts contribute to attainment of organizational goals?

Examination of these questions brings into focus the need for carefully specifying objectives of a development program and related criteria by which they will be measured. If objectives are not clear, difficulties in selecting or devising appropriate measuring techniques or in judging whether the intended results were achieved are foreseeable. For example, a system is considering whether to grant X number of dollars of tuition money for each teacher completing X hours of graduate credit. It is obvious that cost effectiveness of this program will be difficult to evaluate until it is known what specific results are anticipated by governing officials. Thus, a graduate course that costs $1,000 per teacher but contains no stipulation as to specific development objectives may be assumed to be high in cost (dollar outlay) and low in effectiveness (contribution to objectives of a specific effort per dollar expended).

Key Evaluation Considerations. Every school system is confronted at varying times with decisions relating to selection, adoption, support, value, continuation, and remediation of staff development programs. Rational decisions can be made with greater conviction if there is some basis for determining whether improvement programs have been or will be effective and efficient. Questions relating to what extent changes have occurred in the knowledge, skills, attitudes, position behavior, and organizational impact are omnipresent. In addition, inquiry-minded persons want to know whether changes in the variables listed can be attributed to the staff development program.

If the evaluation phase is omitted from the staff development process (Phase 4 of Figure 6.5), there is lack of feedback to correct program defects, little useful information to enhance decision making, and no sound foundation for improving the total development effort. There are many constraints

TABLE 6.5
Major considerations in the evaluation of staff development programs.

Factors	Illustrative Questions
Purposes of evaluation	What is to be evaluated? (Program objectives? Methods? Program? People? Processes? Products?)
Principles of evaluation	Will the evaluation be based on principles? (Systematic? Objectivity? Relevance? Verification of results? Quantification? Feasibility? Specificity? Cost effectiveness?)
Types of evaluation	Evaluation of a specific program? Specific technique? Total program effort? (Formative? Summative?)
Criteria	Reaction criteria? Learning criteria? Behavioral criteria? Results criteria? Combinations of above?
Criterion measures	What criterion measures will be employed? (Observational techniques? Tests? Ratings? System performance records? Interviews?)
Evaluation data	How will the data be recorded? Analyzed? Interpreted? Valued?
Outcomes	What type of outcomes will be evaluated? (Professional competency? Learner gain? Program improvement? Training validity? Performance validity? Intraorganizational validity? Interorganizational validity?

involved and many obstacles to surmount in the evaluation of staff development programs. Additionally, there are varying viewpoints regarding the necessity for, approaches to, effects of, and values derived from evaluation. Nevertheless, collective opinion supports the proposition that improvement of staff development without evaluation is most unlikely. Moreover, there is considerable agreement that awareness of important factors in the evaluation phase of the staff development process makes it possible to avoid useless evaluations and enhances the possibility of deriving information that will be helpful in giving direction to staff development planning. It is in this connection that key considerations involved in evaluation of staff development programs are outlined in Table 6.5.

Analysis of the content in Table 6.5 brings into consideration these observations:

- The evaluation process is complex, extensive, and requires sophisticated competencies to initiate, implement, and coordinate all of its facets.

- The evaluation phase of the staff development process requires knowledge, skills, attitudes, and position behaviors that represent content for a staff development program to improve the system's evaluation capabilities.

- Purposes of evaluation constitute, so to speak, the engine that pulls the evaluation train. Evaluation methods, criteria, criterion measures, and collection and refinement of data derive from evaluation purposes.

We may summarize this section on the evaluation phase of staff development by suggesting that nurturing an organization's human resources is a primary leadership responsibility. Inherent in this obligation is organizational investment of considerable time, money, and talent to the resolution of major evaluation problems. These problems—either by design or default—have been seriously neglected and will become even more critical in light of social change, technological developments, and erosion of the public view of the quality and effectiveness of the country's schools.

REVIEW AND PREVIEW

This chapter advanced the proposition that the school system that embraces the policy of continual development is one that provides itself with important strategic advantages. Key features of this thesis include:

- School improvement through personnel development is best accom-

plished within school attendance units and school systems. Duplication of "best" or traditional practices is a less-than-satisfactory approach to generating effective staff development programs.

- The staff development process includes identifying of needs, establishing program objectives, creating plans to achieve objectives (including methods of instructional delivery), and evaluating program outcomes.

- Staff development includes individual, group, system, and board member development.
- Major factors to be considered in assessment of personnel needs are the external and internal environments, school system, positions, position holders, position-person matches, position context, and work groups.
- Cues for designing programs can be derived from system policy, research and practice, value trends, career stages, and the external environment.

- Formal development program design consists of program content, methods, setting, participation, and resources.
- Criteria for evaluating staff development programs include the participant, position, work group, and organizational impact.

In chapter 7 the appraisal process will be treated as one that is closely intertwined with the staff development process, and one from which meaningful information can be derived to help decision makers resolve questions relating to the selection, implementation, and evaluation of both development methods and the entire development effort.

REVIEW AND DISCUSSION QUESTIONS

1. Would you defend or refute each of the following statements?

   - A school system's culture is set by the board of education.
   - Culture is the prevailing attitudes and values that characterize its employees.
   - A school system's culture is set by its union culture.
   - When personnel do not perform up to par, it is because they do not know what par is.
   - The most popular development technique in school systems is coaching by superiors.
   - The primary purpose of team building is to help a work group solve major school system problems.
   - Learning cannot be observed; only its results can be measured.
   - The primary criterion for developing a staff development program is trainee preferences and capabilities.

   - Needs assessment reveals shortcomings that can be traced directly to the human resources function.
   - Each position in a career path should be specified in terms of educational credentials, age, and work experience.
   - Recruitment, selection, and orientation processes may minimize or eliminate altogether the need for staff development.
   - No school system endeavor has so completely eluded scrutiny as the myriad activities that now comprise staff development.
   - Current evidence suggests that group processes improve through team building development programs.
   - Experienced teachers as prospective mentors generally have effective training and coaching abilities to develop successful mentoring relationships.

- Change must be introduced incrementally because you can never go back to the way things were before the change.
- Staff turnover data are good indicators of the effectiveness of staff development programs.
- The most important outcome a staff member wants from a job is advancement opportunity.
- Self-development is a paper strategy that rarely reaches the point of reality.
- The evidence at hand suggests that attendance at staff development conventions, university courses, and lectures produces measurable payoffs.
- It is considered to be well nigh impossible to assess outcomes on the basis of objectives.
- Restructuring and staff development programs are identical in purposes.

2. Why is knowledge of how people learn important in designing development programs?

3. Three theories of learning (behavioral, social, and cognitive) are considered important in designing development programs. What are the implications of each for deciding how and what to teach?

4. List ten reasons why staff development is crucial to individual, group, and system effectiveness.

5. What are the implications of career planning for staff development? For administrative personnel? Supervisory personnel? Support personnel?

6. What is the organizational motivation for linking career planning to staff development?

7. Do individuals have a responsibility for managing their own careers?

8. Develop a model for determining development needs of a school sys-tem with an enrollment of 10,000 pupils.

9. Critique this statement: "There is no hard evidence to support the contention that sabbaticals improve performance effectiveness."

10. What are some of the problems encountered in evaluating the effectiveness of staff development programs?

11. For the system in which you are employed, complete the following staff development inquiry. To what extent have staff development programs been initiated in the past five years? For administrative personnel? Supervisory personnel? Teaching personnel? Support personnel?

12. Which of the development programs listed in question 11 have been evaluated in terms of systemwide outcomes? Participant outcomes? Instructional outcomes? Administrative outcomes?

13. As you view the staff development needs of your institution, what currently are the most crucial development needs at the management level? Supervisory level? Teaching level? Support level?

14. A report in the *Dallas Morning News* noted that the Texas State Textbook Committee recommended that Texas become the first state in the nation to adopt a videodisc curriculum. This program would clear the way for Texas public school districts to begin using educational videodiscs in place of textbooks in elementary science classes.[19] Answer the following questions: If this proposal is formalized, what are the implications for staff development in making the change from traditional methods of teaching science to a videodisc curriculum? For teacher recruitment and selection?

For the personnel appraisal process? For supervisory services? For the relationship of this learning strategy to other forms of instructional technology? Do this and other contemporary curriculum developments imply any link between staff development and organizational change?

CHAPTER EXERCISE 6.1

Directions: Review the staff development models in Table 6.3 and study the format in Table 6.6. Then, respond to the following:

- Study the matrix in Table 6.6 and indicate, in your judgment, which staff development models (vertical columns) are most suitable for meeting the variable staff development needs (horizontal columns).
- Study the matrix in Table 6.6 relative to staff development models. Which staff development models in the table are appropriate for meeting staff development needs in order to implement the type of videodisc curriculum proposed by the Texas State Textbook Committee? Write out the rationale underlying your decision.
- How would you advise your superiors concerning steps to implement any one of the five models in Table 6.6? Justify your answer.
- What are the major steps in implementing the training model? The inquiry model?

CHAPTER EXERCISE 6.2

Directions: Examine Tables 6.7, 6.8, and 6.9. The data, the results of a survey, provide a profile on staff development and staff developers in North America. After examining the data, respond to these questions:

- Do the data in Tables 6.7, 6.8, and 6.9 represent current practice *norms* (averages) or *standards* to be adopted by school systems?
- What do the standard deviation figures mean in Tables 6.8 and 6.9?
- What is the meaning of organization development as presented in Table 6.9?
- To what do you attribute the minimal use of computer technology as reported in Table 6.7?
- In what respect do your views on staff development differ from the views presented in Tables 6.7, 6.8, and 6.9?
- To what extent does the staff development profile presented in Tables 6.7, 6.8, and 6.9 differ from profiles in school systems of your acquaintance?
- Give your opinion of the following two statements: (a) higher education is not meeting the needs of staff developers, and (b) formal course work is the least likely source for continuing education in staff development.
- Does the profile (Tables 6.7, 6.8, and 6.9) reflect the diversity of school systems in North America? Cultural, geographic, student, suburban, urban, rural, community, and faculty diversity?

TABLE 6.6
Staff development matrix linking staff development needs to staff development models.

	Staff Development Models (Types of Personnel)				
	Individually Guided Staff Development	Observation/ Assessment	Involvement in Development/ Improvement Process	Training	Inquiry
Teaching Personnel					
Beginning					
Experienced					
Marginal performer					
Meets position requirements					
Exceeds position requirements					
Administrative–Supervisory Personnel					
Beginning					
Experienced					
Marginal performer					
Meets position requirements					
Exceeds position requirements					
Support Personnel					
Marginal performer					
Meets position requirements					
Exceeds position requirements					
Board of Education					
Beginning					
Continuing education					

Note: See Table 6.3 for details of staff development models.

TABLE 6.7
Instructional methods and
types of delivery.

Workshops	85.8%
Meetings	61.9%
Cooperative Learning	60.2%
Videotapes	59.0%
Seminars	54.4%
Lectures	46.2%
One-on-one Instruction	23.8%
Laboratory Learning (Human Interaction, etc.)	21.2%
Games and/or Simulation	18.5%
Role Plays	16.6%
Case Studies	13.2%
Computerized Instruction (Videodiscs, etc.)	10.5%
Films	10.2%
Audiotapes	9.6%
Slides	7.9%
Self-testing Instruments	6.1%
Visualization/Visioning	6.0%
Video Teleconferencing	5.9%
Teleconferencing	3.8%
Non-computerized Self Study (Distance Education, etc.)	3.2%
Computer Conferencing	1.5%

Source: Neil Davidson, Jim Henkelman, and Helen Stasinowski, "Findings From and NSDC Status Survey of Staff Development and Staff Developers," Journal of Staff Development 14, 4 (Fall 1993), 58–64.

NOTES

1. Bruce R. Joyce, Richard H. Hersh, and Michael McKibbin, The Structure of School Improvement (New York: Longman Inc., 1988), 8.

2. Joseph R. DeLuca, "The Evolution of Staff Development for Teachers," Journal of Staff Development 12, 3 (Summer, 1991), 45.

3. Ibid.

4. Ibid.

5. J. P. Killion and C. R. Harrison, "An Organizational Development Approach to Change," Journal of Staff Development 11, 1, (1990), 22–25.

6. Thomas J. Sergiovanni and Robert J. Starratt, Supervision: Human Perspectives (New York: McGraw-Hill Book Company, 1979), 290–291.

7. Ben M. Harris, Improving Staff Performance through In-Service Education (Boston: Allyn and Bacon, 1980), 21.

8. Leslie J. Bishop, Staff Development and Instructional Improvement

(Boston: Allyn and Bacon, 1976), 34.

9. Harris, 108–109.

10. Dennis Sparks and Susan Loucks-Horsley, "Five Models of Staff Development for Teachers," Journal of Staff Development 10, 4 (Fall, 1989), 40–57.

11. Ibid 52.

12. Ibid 54.

13. Ibid 55.

14. Joyce et al., 163.

15. Thomas R. Horton, "The Workforce of the Year 2000," Management Review 78 (August, 1989), 5.

16. Roy A. Edelfelt and Margo Johnson, Editors, Rethinking In-service Education (Washington: National Education Association, 1978), 295–302.

17. Bishop, 121–122.

18. These learning theories are detailed in Vida G. Scarpello and James Ledvinka, Personnel/Human Resource Management (Boston: PWS-Kent Publishing Company, 1988), Chapter 16.

19. Dallas Morning News, August 22, 1990, 23.

SUPPLEMENTARY READING

Andreson, Kathleen, M.; and Omar Durant. "Training Managers of Classified Personnel." Journal of Staff Development 12, 1 (Winter 1991), 56–60.

TABLE 6.8
Views of an ideal staff development program in terms of external and internal consultants.

View	Mean*	Standard Deviation
1. Staff development programs should make use of both external and internal expertise.	1.2	0.4
2. Staff development programs should be planned and overseen by an advisory committee with representation of, and accountability to, all affected groups and individuals in the organization.	1.5	0.7
3. Staff development programs should make use of internal consultants only.	3.6	0.6
4. Staff development programs should make use of external consultants only.	3.8	0.5

*(1 strongly agree, 4 strongly disagree)

Source: Neil Davidson, Jim Henkelman, and Helen Stasinowski, "Findings From and NSDC Status Survey of Staff Development and Staff Developers," Journal of Staff Development 14, 4 (Fall 1993), 58–64.

TABLE 6.9
Views of individual/organization development.

View	Mean*	Standard Deviation
1. Individuals and the organization should be developed concurrently.	1.4	0.6
2. Organizations/schools are realizing more and more the value of their human resources.	1.9	0.7
3. Organizations/schools value curriculum development over human resource development.	2.5	0.9
4. Development of the whole organization should take precedence over individual development.	2.8	0.9
5. Individual development should take precedence over the development of the organization.	3.1	0.7

*(1 strongly agree, 4 strongly disagree)

Source: Neil Davidson, Jim Henkelman, and Helen Stasinowski, "Findings From and NSDC Status Survey of Staff Development and Staff Developers," Journal of Staff Development 14, 4 (Fall 1993), 58–64.

Berry, Barnett; and Rick Ginsberg. "Creating Lead Teachers: From Policy to Implementation." Phi Delta Kappan 71, 8 (April 1990), 616–62.

Bird, Tom; and Judith W. Little. From Teacher to Leader: Training and Support for Instructional Leadership by Teachers. San Francisco: Far West Research Laboratory for Educational Research and Development, 1985.

Brown, Brenda. "Designing Staff/Curriculum Content for Cultural Diversity: The Staff Developer's Role." Journal of Staff Development 13, 2 (Spring 1992), 16–22.

Burke, Peter J.; Judith C. Christensen; and Ralph Fessler. Teacher Career Stages: Implications for Staff Development. Bloomington, IN: Phi Delta Kappa, 1984.

Caldwell, S., Editor. Staff Development: A Handbook of Effective Practices. Oxford, OH: National Staff Development Council, 1989.

Christensen, Judith C.; John H. McDonnel; and Jay R. Price. Personalizing Staff Development: The Career Lattice Model. Bloomington, IN: Phi Delta Kappa, 1988.

DeMoulin, D. F. "Staff Development and Teacher Effectiveness: Administrative Concerns." Focus (1988), 8+.

DeMoulin, Donald F.; and John W. Guyton. "An Analysis of Career Development to Enhance Individualized Staff Development." National Forum of Educational Administration and Supervision Journal 7, 3 (1990-91), 301+

Fitch, Margaret E.; and O. W. Kopp. Staff Development: A Practical Guide for the Practitioner. Springfield, IL: C.C. Thomas, 1990.

Gilley, Jerry W.; and Steven A. Eggland. Principles of Human Resource Development. Reading, MA: Addison-Wesley, 1989.

Gross, James A. Teachers on Trial: Values, Standards, and Equity in Judging Conduct and Competency. Ithaca, NY: ILR Press, 1988.

Houston, W. Robert, Editor. Handbook of Research on Teacher Education. New York: Macmillan Publishing, 1990.

Jandura, Ronald M.; and Peter J. Burke. Differentiated Career Opportunities for Teachers. Bloomington, IN: Phi Delta Kappa, 1989.

Joyce, Bruce; and B. Showers. Student Achievement through Staff Development. New York: Longman Inc., 1988.

Katzenmeyer, Marilyn H.; and George A. Reid, Jr. "Compelling Views of Staff Development for the 1990s." Journal of Staff Development 12, 3 (Summer 1991), 30–34.

Lambert, Linda. "Staff Development Redesigned." Phi Delta Kappan 69, 9 (May 1988), 665–69.

Lee, J. F.; and K. W. Pruitt. "Staff Development: An Individualized Staff Development Model." Record (1983), 51–54.

McKay, Ian. Thirty-Five Checklists for Human Resource Development. Brookfield, VT: Gower Publishing Company Ltd., 1989.

Mecklenburger, James A. "What the Ostrich Sees: Technology and the Mission of American Education." Phi Delta Kappan 70, 1 (September 1988), 18–20.

Miller, Leslie M.; William A. Thompson; and Robert E. Rousch. "Mentorships and Perceived Educational Payoff." Phi Delta Kappan 69, 9 (February 1989), 465–68.

National Staff Development Council. "Nine Perspectives on the Future of Staff Development." Journal of Staff Development 12, 1 (Winter 1991), 2–12.

Neubert, Gloria A. Improving Teaching Through Coaching. Bloomington, IN: Phi Delta Kappan, 1988.

Owen, Jim Mirman. "Three Roles of Staff Development in Restructuring Schools." Journal of Staff Development 12, 3 (Summer 1991), 10–16.

Perelman, Lewis J. Technology and Transformation of Schools. Alexandria, VA: National School Boards Association, 1987.

Quinn, Michael J. "Staff Development: A Process of Growth." The Education Digest LV 7 (March 1990), 43–47.

Showers, B.; B. Joyce; and B. Bennett. "Synthesis of Research on Staff Development." Educational Leadership 45, 3 (1987), 77–87.

Sousa, David A. "Ten Questions for Rating Your Staff Development Program." Journal of Staff Development 13, 2 (1992), 34–38.

Thompson, Jay C.: and Van E. Cooley. "National Study of Outstanding Staff Development Programs." Educational Horizons 86, 1 (1986), 94.

Wood, Fred H.; and Sarah D. Caldwell. "Planning and Training to Implement Site-Based Management." Journal of Staff Development 12, 3 (Summer 1991), 25–30.

Wood, F.; S. Thompson; and F. Russell. "Designing Effective Staff Programs." In B. Dillon-Peterson, Editor, Staff

Development/Organizational Development. Alexandria, VA: Association for Supervision and Curriculum Development, 1981.

Wood, Fred H.; and Steven R. Thompson. "Assumptions About Staff Development Based on Research and Best Practice." National Staff Development Council 14, 4 (Fall 1993), 58–63.

Chapter 7

Performance Appraisal

CHAPTER OVERVIEW

- The Context of Performance Appraisal
- Traditional Appraisal Systems
  Impediments to Performance Appraisal
- Purposes of Performance Appraisal
  Contemporary Modifying Forces
- Design of the Performance Appraisal System
  Behavioral Assumptions and Performance Appraisal
- The Performance Appraisal Process
  Model Assumptions
  Phase 1: Appraisee—Appraiser Planning Conference
  Phase 2: Setting Performance Targets
  Phase 3: Performance Analysis
  Phase 4: Performance Progress Review
  Phase 5: Performance Rediagnosis and Recycle
  Phases 6 to 9: Summative Performance Decision—Remediation
- Performance Appraisal: Ethical Aspects

CHAPTER OBJECTIVES

- Understand what performance appraisal is expected to accomplish.
- Describe the organizational context of performance appraisal.
- Identify the purposes of performance appraisal.
- Develop a model of the performance appraisal process.
  Discuss the ethical aspects of performance appraisal.
- Emphasize the employment litigation factor in performance appraisal.
- Describe the interaction of performance appraisal and the human resources function.

CHAPTER TERMS

Administrative rationality

Appraisal ethics

Formative appraisal

Goal-setting model

Performance appraisal

Performance culture

Performance effectiveness

Performance standards

Performance targets

Summative appraisal

Technical rationality

The overall intent of this chapter is to draw together several streams of thought indicating that performance appraisal (a) is focused on improving individual, group, and organizational effectiveness, (b) is successful to the extent that a multitude of variables are productively coordinated, (c) is not based on a universal approach considered to be successful in all situations and circumstances, (d) should be approached from a descriptive rather than prescriptive point of view, and (e) is becoming more result and scientifically oriented.

THE CONTEXT OF PERFORMANCE APPRAISAL

Performance appraisal may be defined as a process of arriving at judgments about an individual's past or present performance against the background of his/her work environment and about his/her future potential for an organization. The appraisal process is an activity designed to assist personnel to achieve individual and group as well as organizational benefits.

It has long been an accepted proposition that appraisal of human performance is an activity essential to the well-being of society. Performance appraisal is commonplace in everyday living: a professional baseball player's ability is judged by his batting average; a quarterback's skill is evaluated by the number of his pass completions; salespersons are paid on the basis of the number of products or services they sell; and so on. During their lifetimes, few people escape having their vocational performance judged. Seldom do people question the need for appraising individual performance; the real problem is to develop and improve valid and reliable appraisal procedures and to create greater understanding of the purposes and limitations of performance appraisal so that results derived from its application will not be misused.

Growth of formal organizations and recognition of their critical importance to a complex society have brought about the need for formal and systematic approaches to performance appraisal. In the first several decades of the twentieth century, criticism of casual, haphazard, unsystematic, highly personalized, and esoteric plans for judging the worth of individuals to organizations brought about a wide variety of efforts to reform performance appraisal plans. These included federal and state civil service legislation governing the *rating* of personnel, such as the Federal Civil Service Classification Act of 1923, the Taft-Hartley Labor Act of 1947, the Fair Labor Standards Act of 1963, the Civil Rights Act of 1964, and later Equal Employment Opportunity legislation during the 1970s[1] (see Table 3.2). Between 1962 and the advent of the 1990s, several significant events and advances combined to influence every one of the human resources functions shown in Figure 1.2, including performance appraisal. These events and advances include:

- The Civil Rights Act of 1962
- Computer technology
- Court decisions affecting workers and the workplace.
- Legal and political activism in the teaching profession.
- Education reform movements in the 1980s and 1990s.

Numerous assertions during the educational era, from congressional committees, politicians, media, think tanks, federal and state education agencies, and educators, about the shortcomings of and proposed remedies for education in the United States have led to the appraisal process becoming an organizational cynosure (a center of attention or interest). Examples from the preceding sources, as well as from court cases and judicial decisions, include:

- Condemnation of the negative stance of teacher unions.
- Teacher personnel reporting negative feelings about the nature and ambiguity of performance reviews.

- Mishandling of personnel terminations.
- Inability of personnel administrators to deal promptly with the causes of expensive and variable financial and educational costs engendered by personnel litigation.
- Absence of meaningful policies regarding emerging issues such as comparable worth, termination at will, and position analysis practices.
- Reluctance to link rewards to performance.
- Failure to link position profiles to educational program objectives.
- Unwillingness to rid the system of its incompetents.
- Lack of progress in moving the performance base away from teacher traits and teaching activities and toward learning outcomes.
- Public opinion polls favoring teacher pay based on performance.
- System inertia in creating an organizational **performance culture**.

The breadth and depth of developments relating to performance appraisal in the twentieth century have contributed to these and other performance improvement directions:

- Changes in the way performance appraisal is viewed and administered.
- Greater sensitivity on the part of school officials regarding the treatment of its human resources.
- Increasing demands for *equity* and *ethics* from appraisers.
- Vulnerability of those charged with making personnel decisions.
- Growing awareness of the need to modernize the traditional performance appraisal process.

TRADITIONAL APPRAISAL SYSTEMS

The quest in the last half-century for ways of eliminating favoritism, seniority, and inequitable treatment in compensation plans led to a multitude of rating programs within and outside of government organizations. These plans are referred to as *traditional approaches*[2] to performance appraisal. Traditional plans, for the most part, were psychometrically oriented and consisted of appraisals of personality traits or preconceived characteristics deemed essential to the role an individual performed in the organization.

Traditional or conventional appraisal systems embrace a wide variety of approaches, including ranking, person-to-person comparison, grading, graphic scales, checklists, forced-choice methods, and critical incident techniques. In the field of education, a host of traditional techniques have been and still are employed to appraise the professional performance of school personnel. These include self-rating as well as ratings by pupils, school administrators, supervisors, colleagues, special committees, outside professionals, and lay citizens. Some plans base appraisal on the character of instruction, personal characteristics, cumulative personnel record information, changes in pupil behavior, classroom social climate, and written responses (questionnaires and examinations).

Weaknesses in traditional appraisal systems, after nearly a half-century of experience, appear to be legion. Criticisms include:

- Appraisals are focused on an individual's personality rather than what he/she is expected to do or results he/she has achieved.
- Most administrators are not qualified to assess the personality of an individual.
- Appraisal tools lack validity.
- Raters display biases.
- Ratings and raters are subject to organizational influence.
- The appraisal system does not apply to all personnel.
- Results of appraisal are not utilized to assist individual development.
- Appraisees are fragmented into personality parts, which, when added together, do not reflect the whole person.
- Appraisal devices do not provide administrators with effective counseling tools.
- Most plans do not establish organizational expectations for individuals occupying specific positions.
- Appraisals are arbitrary or unjust when used for discipline, salary increases, promotion, or dismissal.
- Personnel do not understand criteria on which their performance is appraised.
- Performance is not evaluated in terms of its contribution to enterprise goals.
- Traditional appraisal procedures hamper effective communication between appraiser and appraisee. Heavy reliance by appraiser on *feeling* instead of *fact* generates defensive behavior on part of appraisee.
- Appraisal methodology does not provide an environment conducive to change in individual behavior.
- Appraisal methodology does not encourage satisfaction of higher-level needs of individuals, such as self-expression, creativity, and individualism.
- Performance appraisal models are not complementary to appraisal purposes.

Most traditional performance appraisal plans in the first half of the twentieth century were devoted to *nonadministrative* personnel. Their primary purpose seems to have been to link the organizational value of an individual's performance to the size of the paycheck. Review of the history of performance appraisal within and outside of school systems leads to the following observations:[3]

- For the better part of a century, organizations have been experimenting with performance appraisal of various types. From this experience, about the only consensus that has developed is that performance appraisal is not a matter of choice, but rather an essential and continuing activity in the life of an enterprise. The methodology employed to conduct the performance appraisal, however, remains a matter about which diverse viewpoints prevail.
- Increasingly, performance appraisal is being considered as a means of *personnel development*. Performance appraisal is not something done *to* personnel; it is something done *for* personnel.
- Many appraisal systems have been ineffective because of a low level systematization. Failure to link appraisal procedures to organizational purposes, to unit objectives, and to position goals has created considerable personnel dissatisfaction with the results of performance appraisal.
- The fact of organization is as old as man; the theory of organization is modern. The practice of formal appraisal of personnel performance as well as the theory on which it is based is contemporary. In the second half of this century, a resurgence of interest in performance appraisal has become apparent, especially in developing total appraisal systems that include *all personnel* in an enterprise so as to integrate objectives of individuals with those of the organization and its long-term goals. Some of the forces behind this resurging interest are discussed later in this chapter.
- Accountability, cost-benefit, and quality-assurance concepts have filtered down from federal and state to the local level, forcing school officials to reconsider the purposes, design, and methods of implementing appraisal systems.

There is general agreement that performance appraisal is a school system's most neuralgic problem, yet remains the key to achieving a satisfactory level of individual, group, and organizational performance. Of the eleven *processes* identified in Figure 1.2, performance appraisal is probably the most difficult of those within the *human resources function* to design, implement, monitor, and evaluate effectively.

Impediments to Performance Appraisal

It has been recorded countless times that effective, dynamic performance appraisal is the exception and not the rule in educational institutions. Some of the key reasons why progress in improving performance appraisal systems is less than satisfactory include:

- *Administrative irrationality*—**Administrative rationality** refers to making use of the best possible methods of guiding organizations. Examples of administrative irrationality include adherence to obsolescent concepts such as: performance appraisal is unnecessary; performance is not tied to results; performance is not linked to behavior; performance appraisal means rating; administrators should not be involved in performance appraisal; performance appraisal never involves confrontation; performance has little to do with individual, group, and system objectives; and teaching does not lend itself to adequate measurement of performance.

- *Technical irrationality*—**Technical rationality** refers to judicious use of the extensive array of techniques, operations, materials, the growing fund of knowledge, and know-how that can be applied to the conduct of a performance appraisal system. As noted throughout this chapter, the list of instances is a long one wherein absence or abuse of available technology can impede progress in the development of effective appraisal systems.

- *State legislation*—State-generated performance appraisal systems based on the use of a numerical system to *rate* personnel performance.

- *Administrative board of education*—School board participation in the formal and informal evaluation of school employees, rather than to restrict its role to policy making.

- *Administrative-supervision dichotomy*—The point of view that there is a clear line of demarcation between administration and supervision.

- *Environmental impediments*—Influences of unions, courts, the regulatory environment, boards of education, political organizations, community groups, and power groups that impede effective operation of appraisal systems.

PURPOSES OF PERFORMANCE APPRAISAL

It is generally agreed that both formal and informal appraisal systems exist in every organization. The informal system is one by which judgments are made about **performance effectiveness** of personnel without benefit of systematization of such judgments. As viewed herein, a formal evaluation system is one established by an educational institution, endorsed by the governing board, and operated systematically to determine the extent to which appraisal system objectives have been achieved. The purposes for which a performance appraisal system exists represent another of the critical choices to be made in designing an appraisal system. Anyone who has examined the literature relating to the purposes of an appraisal system or who has analyzed objectives established by school systems for their appraisal systems has to be struck by the array of views that prevail on this critical design element (see Figure 7.1).

A useful framework for considering the purposes of performance appraisal systems is that proposed by Borich. His framework indicates that the objectives served by appraisal data fall into three broad categories: *diagnostic, formative,* and *summative*. The diagnostic decisions are made in the *preoperational* stages of performance appraisal and are applied to diagnostic decisions *prior* to employment, such as selection, placement, and development. Formative objectives related to decisions during initial and intermediate stages of employment are aimed at personnel development. Summative purposes of appraisal systems are those that focus on decisions to implement personnel actions, such as compensation, tenure, dismissal, promotion, and reemployment.[4]

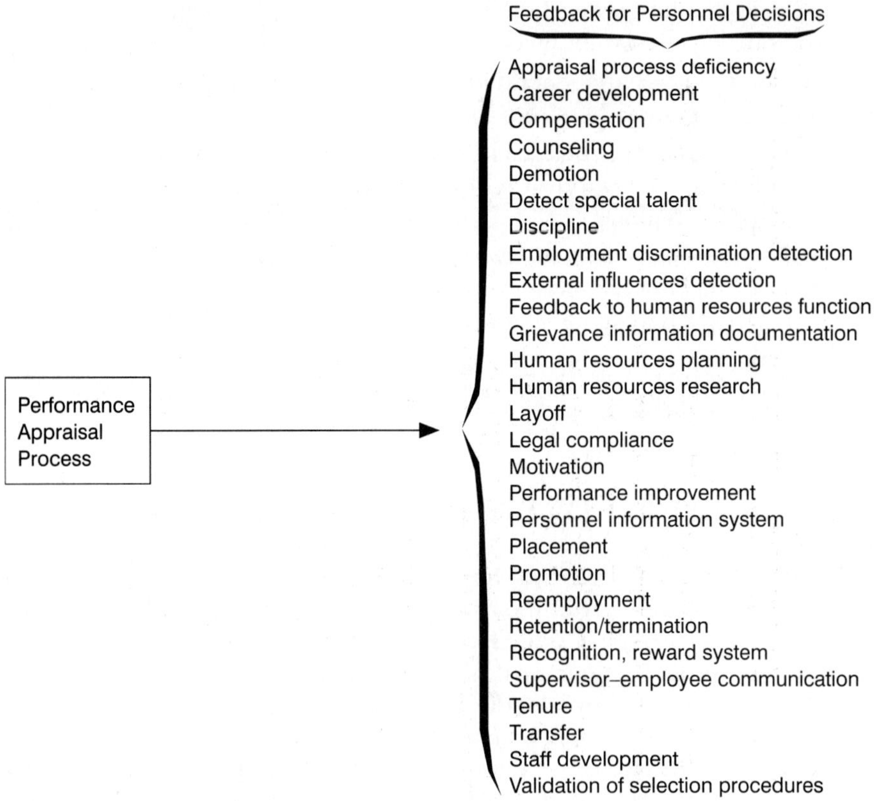

Feedback for Personnel Decisions

Performance Appraisal Process →

Appraisal process deficiency
Career development
Compensation
Counseling
Demotion
Detect special talent
Discipline
Employment discrimination detection
External influences detection
Feedback to human resources function
Grievance information documentation
Human resources planning
Human resources research
Layoff
Legal compliance
Motivation
Performance improvement
Personnel information system
Placement
Promotion
Reemployment
Retention/termination
Recognition, reward system
Supervisor–employee communication
Tenure
Transfer
Staff development
Validation of selection procedures

FIGURE 7.1
Uses of performance appraisal in the human resources function.

Most of the purposes of evaluation can be grouped into the five following categories: (a) determine personnel employment status, (b) implement personnel actions, (c) improve individual performance, (d) achieve organizational goals, and (e) translate the authority system into controls that regulate performance. In summary, performance appraisal systems have multiple uses. Properly designed, they produce benefits for the individual, work group, and total system. Reference will be made subsequently to the application of diagnostic, formative, and summative purposes of evaluation and their significance to the human resources function.

Contemporary Modifying Forces

Figure 7.2 portrays some of the pressures currently bringing about modifications in the traditional performance appraisal system for school personnel. *Organizational changes*, for example, have brought about an awareness of the inadequacy of appraisal plans divorced from personnel need satisfaction as well as from organization purposes. *Social changes* have convinced many organizational personnel that there is substantial discrepancy between what appraisal systems are and what they ought to be. To many, the traditional appraisal system is dehumanizing—an organizational barrier to self-realization and to the development of a career in which the experiences one realizes on the job are meaningful and satisfying. *Economic changes* have increased salaries to a level more nearly in keeping with the responsibilities with which these positions are charged. With improving compensation have come demands from the electorate for school personnel to perform effectively in its behalf. *Client reaction* to school systems has been heard across the nation, expressed by the term *accountability*. Although the word *accountability* means different things to different people, one of its implications is that schools today are not functioning effectively in terms of their major purposes. Clients are demanding better schools, and school officials are seeking better appraisal systems to assist them in motivating personnel to consistently higher levels of performance.

Personnel reaction to traditional performance appraisal systems is strong in its contention that a host of administrative barbarities have been perpetrated on them in the name of appraisal. The catalogue of alleged dysfunctions is a long one, ranging from organizational failure to identify its expectations for members to a total disregard for the application of appraisal results to the improvement of personnel performance. *Theorist reaction* to the traditional appraisal system has been responsible for a variety of ideas from the behavioral scientists, resulting in a de-emphasis on quantitative approaches to appraising subordinate behaviors. Educational systems planning, management by objectives, competency-based teacher education, behavioral objectives, performance contracting, mutual goal setting, counseling, progress review, integration of individual and organizational goals,

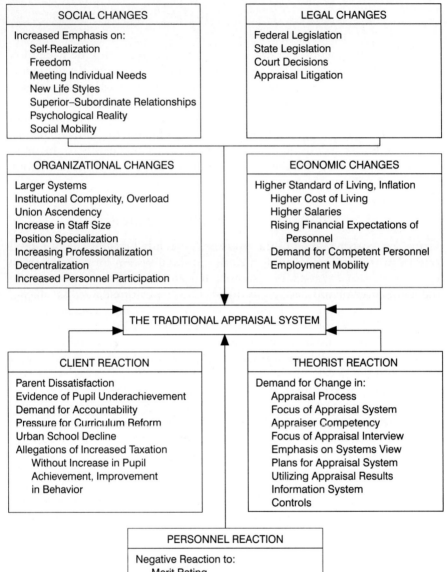

FIGURE 7.2
Interacting forces impinging on the traditional personnel performance appraisal system.

and need satisfaction of staff members are but a few of the contributions of theorists to performance appraisal to which modern organizations are heir.

Legal changes have helped to fashion considerable modification in performance appraisal systems. These include Title VII of the Civil Rights Act of 1964, state legislation governing teacher evaluation, court decisions, and an increasing amount of litigation challenging current performance appraisal systems. A variety of employment decisions, including transfer, promotion, compensation, layoffs, and development programs, fall within the legal purview of performance appraisal.

The preceding discussion dealt with problem areas of the performance appraisal process, as well as the renewed interest that has developed in recent years in both its design and management. Attention of reform efforts on performance appraisal derives from several factors, including the need to improve the performance of school system human resources, the central role performance appraisal plays in organizational development, widespread dissatisfaction with traditional appraisal models, appraisal-related litigation, and expanding efforts in the literature and in practice to utilize the human resources function to move educational institutions to a higher level of effectiveness.

The purpose of the following section is to portray a configuration of the parts that make up the appraisal process. This framework begins with a consideration of design elements that comprise the centerpiece of the appraisal system. First, the design elements and the environment in which they will function are identified. Then, they are assimilated into a performance appraisal goal-focused model that includes a series of five interrelated and interdependent stages.

DESIGN OF THE PERFORMANCE APPRAISAL SYSTEM

In the review of performance appraisal earlier in this chapter, it was noted that the concept of performance appraisal seems to be universally accepted as an essential and continuing activity in the life of an enterprise. The choices a school system has relative to performance appraisal lie in the system design. A framework for considering decision elements that comprise the appraisal system design is presented in Table 7.1. These choices, as listed in Table 7.1, include the following: (a) the basic assumptions about human behavior that will be followed in designing the system, (b) purposes for which the system is designed, (c) nature and scope of the appraisal process, and (d) ethical values to be adhered to in operating the performance appraisal system. These decisions are made prior to the act of appraisal to enhance the system's validity. Design elements listed in Table 7.1 are discussed in the following text in terms of their relationship to overall design of the appraisal system.

TABLE 7.1
Framework for designing the performance appraisal process.

Design Elements	Design Particulars	Personnel Categories				
		A	B	C	D	E
Appraisal purposes?	Diagnostic? Formative? Summative? Combination?					
Design roles?	Board? Central administration? Unit administrator? Appraiser(s)? Appraisees?					
Appraisal policy?	Assumptions or beliefs on which appraisal system will be planned, organized, administered, and controlled?					
Who is appraised?	Professionals? Support? Temporary?					
What is appraised?	Quality of services rendered? Quality of services received? Personal characteristics? Some combination of the three?					
Who appraises?	Supervisors, appraisal teams, peers, consultants, parents, board, students, self-appraisal?					
Methods of appraisal?	Process analysis, product analysis, trait analysis, or some combination? Frequency of appraisal? Feedback? Performance reviews?					

Design Elements	Design Particulars	Personnel Categories				
		A	B	C	D	E
Ethics of appraisal?	Ethical boundaries? Information representativeness, sufficiency, relevancy, use and restrictions?					
Appeal procedure?	Formalized? Communicated to all appraisers and appraisees?					
Appraiser qualifications?	Training? Planning involvement? Review of effectiveness?					
Personnel decisions?	Who is involved? Organization of decision-making process? Formal? Informal? Who makes personnel decisions?					
Personnel information system?	Manual? Computerized? Storage? Retrieval? Access? Uses? Responsibilities?					
Legal services?	Availability? Arrangements?					
Appraisal process evaluation?	Who evaluates process effectiveness? Evaluation criteria? Timing? Uses?					

Note: A = professional administrative personnel; B = professional instructional personnel; C = professional support personnel; D = noncertified personnel; E = temporary personnel.

Behavioral Assumptions and Performance Appraisal

One of the first tasks an organization faces in designing an appraisal system is that of determining assumptions on which it will be planned, administered, and controlled. In effect, to develop a set of premises about an appraisal system is to set forth the organization's beliefs or convictions concerning appraisal of personnel. These premises form a basis for *achieving integration of individual and organizational interests*. The basic mission of educational systems is to deliver effective services to clients to satisfy both the needs of the individual and those of society. Personnel employed in educational systems have certain expectations of the organization. Expectations include a given amount of pay for a given amount of work, participation in organizational decisions affecting work conditions, machinery for adjustment of grievances, strong leadership, opportunity for self-realization, position and personal security, the right to be heard, fair treatment, and application of up-to-date administrative practices.

Organizational expectations of personnel include members' acceptance of the hierarchy of authority, of the concept of appraiser-appraisee relationships, and of the authority system, including rules, regulations, procedures, controls, and rituals. Acceptance of these expectations by members is considered essential by the organization if it is to accomplish its mission. Frequently, the expectations of the individual and those of the organization conflict.

The performance appraisal system, with its humanistic potential, is a forceful mechanism for achieving an integration of the interests of both parties. The concepts it embraces, including mutual goal setting, flexibility in position performance, occupational mobility, self-development, and work creativity are conducive to development of personal attachment of the individual to the organization and to securing voluntary cooperation in achieving position goals as well as the long-range mission of the system.

Advancing the self-development of personnel is one of several aims of the performance appraisal system. Development refers to activities undertaken by both the individual and the organization to improve personnel performance from initial employment to retirement. It is aimed at satisfying two kinds of expectations: the contribution required of the individual by the school system and the material and emotional rewards anticipated in return by the individual.

Within the past several decades, a profound conceptual shift has taken place with regard to the function of an appraisal system. The trend toward *management by results* has shifted the focus of the system from its traditional role of determining the size of a person's paycheck to facilitating his/her on-the-job performance. This change in values and outlook of organizations regarding the central concern of the appraisal system should not be interpreted to mean that performance appraisal and compensation are unrelated. Rather, this new development involves a deliberate attempt to stretch the potentialities of the appraisal system beyond compensation concerns and to improve the affinity of the individual and the organization in their quest to satisfy mutual expectations.

The quality of the appraiser–appraisee relationship influences to a considerable extent the effectiveness of the performance appraisal process. The basic act of performance appraisal occurs between two people. Although information about the performance of an appraisee may be derived from several sources, the act of performance appraisal is a continuing experience between appraiser and appraisee. The experience is intensely personal and emotional. In it, two people are attempting to establish an individual–organizational fit. They need to develop and maintain an emotional climate in which (a) what the appraisee wants to accomplish for himself/herself and for his/her position can be identified and (b) what the appraiser wants to realize for himself/herself for his/her position and for the organization can be identified.

Clearly, it is the quality of the relationship between appraiser and appraisee that makes an organization run. Without a relationship that is emotionally attractive and psychologically and occupationally gratifying, the support plans we described earlier as essential to the performance appraisal system are of little avail.

It is clear that there is an increasing awareness of the necessity for change in performance appraisal systems. Present-day members of educational institutions, with all their intelligence, education, and organizational know-how, will not tolerate a performance appraisal system that inhibits personal freedom, self-development, creativity, and organizational democracy. The organization, on the other hand, if it is to become more effective in the twentieth century, must make adaptations that will enable personnel to join with it to realize the ends for which it has been established. These reflections lead to a more detailed consideration of the components underlying a performance appraisal system, discussed in the following text.

Purposes of Appraisal. As suggested earlier, the three basic overall purposes of appraisal are *formative, summative,* and *diagnostic.* These three purposes, it was noted, are central to every aspect of the human resources function, are utilized in a range of personnel decisions, and have extensive implications for both appraisers and appraisees. Consequently, one of the imperative tasks in designing the appraisal system is to specify purpose intent and to direct coordinated actions that are in accord with this commitment.

What Is Appraised? What will be appraised is a decision equally important as that governing purposes of the appraisal system. It is within the context of this decision that the system must determine what is meant by *personnel effectiveness.* As indicated in Table 7.2, a matrix for deciding what personnel effectiveness means in an organization includes the following alternatives:

- Personnel effectiveness is a set of personal characteristics.
- Personnel effectiveness is a process.
- Personnel effectiveness is a product.
- Personnel effectiveness is any combination of (a), (b), or (c).

The foregoing framework can be used as a decision model to determine and to convey to administrative, instructional, and support personnel what will be appraised and how data will be gathered. In effect, once the decision is made about what will be appraised, many of the supporting decisions relating to the appraisal process can be brought into focus. These factors on which an individual is evaluated are called *performance criteria*. Four characteristics of effective criteria, as suggested by Patricia Smith, are:

- *Relevant*—Valid and reliable measures of the characteristics being evaluated.
- *Unbiased*—Based on the characteristic, not the person.
- *Significant*—Directly related to enterprise goals.
- *Practical*—Measurable and efficient for the enterprise in question.[5]

Evidence on performance criteria, according to Glueck, is clear that single performance measures are ineffective because success is multifaceted. Most studies indicate that multiple criteria are necessary to measure performance completely.[6]

Table 7.2 highlights choices involved in the selection of appraisal criteria and key factors that affect the choices. The essence of Table 7.2 is that in selecting appraisal criteria, purposes to be served by the appraisal; personnel to whom the appraisal criteria will be applied; and the extent to which the criteria meet tests of relevance, objectivity, significance, and practicality need to be taken into consideration. The closer the criteria are related to performance outcomes, the more likely will be the effectiveness of evaluation.

Who Is Appraised?   The discussion of appraisal criteria just presented indicates the need to consider *various categories of personnel* in a school system for whom criteria are designed. The text that follows looks at the relationship between what is appraised and who is appraised. Out of the evolutionary development of the human resources function in work organizations has evolved the modern view that *performance appraisal should be applied to all system members* under employment contracts. This view is rooted in current systems approaches to the management of organizations; it holds that (a) every position in the organization structure is linked to results deemed essential to system stability and viability and (b) the organization is responsible, through performance appraisal, for enhancing behavior of position holders that is productive and for minimizing random and uncoordinated behavior that is counterproductive.

TABLE 7.2
Illustration of decision matrix for choosing personnel appraisal criteria.

Column 1 Appraisal Criteria (Teaching)	Column 2 Personnel Categories	Column 3 Characteristics of Criteria	Column 4 Purposes of Appraisal (Formative, Summative)
Personal characteristics criteria Health, appearance, loyalty, work motivation, cooperation, and interpersonal relations. ***Process criteria*** In-class behavior: teacher presentation, questions, feedback, teaching style, effective style, and individualization. Out-of-class behavior: noninstructional responsibilities. ***Product criteria*** Student accomplishments, as measured by tests, projects, and observation of student behavior. A set of predetermined performance targets or growth levels to be accomplished. Products could mean either pupil outcomes or individual staff member outcomes. ***Multiple criteria*** A combination of traits, product, or process. The criteria may be weighted, unweighted, or combined into a single measure of effectiveness.	By personnel *categories* is meant the support, administrative, and instructional personnel to whom the appraisal criteria are applicable. Different criteria may apply to different personnel categories.	The choices in this column are concerned with *relevance, objectivity, significance,* and *practicality* of the appraisal criteria in Column 1. Questions such as these should be raised: How useful are the criteria in summative evaluations? In formative evaluations? What about the ease of use by appraisers? What about the ease of understanding by appraisees? Are the appraisals needed across a space of time? Will the criteria measure all dimensions of performance that should be assessed?	This column is designed to point out that there are relationships among Columns 1, 2, 3, and 4. This is to say that the appraisal criteria will differ, depending on the purposes of evaluation as well as the categories of personnel in Column 2 to whom the criteria will apply. If the main purpose is summative, such as a promotion, multiple criteria may be applied. If the major purpose is formative, the emphasis may be more on the side of *product* than *process*.

In total, specific techniques chosen to appraise performance effectiveness should vary with the type of work performed in a given position. It is worth repeating at this point that position guides contain standards of performance of what the system expects of personnel assigned to each position. One of the elements in performance appraisal is comparison of standards for performance effectiveness with actual performance. To state this point in another way, the definition of performance effectiveness for a custodian will be different from that for a mathematics teacher. Hence, the way in which one appraises the former will differ from the approach employed to evaluate the latter. The task attributes in each of the three levels of position categories (administrative, instructional, and support) vary in terms of responsibility, knowledge and skill, autonomy, interactions, and range of work-related activities.

Who Appraises?   Another of the decisions in designing the appraisal system involves who actually should make the appraisal. Table 7.3 has been included to portray the interconnection among three types of variables involved in making this decision: purposes of appraisal, sources (appraisers), and appraisees. Determining the appropriate agent to make the appraisal, as illustrated in Table 7.3, depends on the purposes of the appraisal. A diagnostic appraisal, which occurs prior to employment when purposes are primarily personnel actions relating to recruitment, selection, and placement, usually involves internal rather than external appraisals. Formative appraisals, on the other hand, which focus on personnel improvement and occur during immediate and intermediate stages of employment, may appropriately involve both internal and external personnel. Peer evaluation and self-evaluation have been introduced in some organizations to minimize problems of stress and perceived threat. Research findings indicate that:

- Peer evaluation and self-evaluation work best in formative appraisals, under conditions of high interpersonal trust, highly specialized skills, and high visibility among peers.
- External appraisal personnel are useful on occasions, especially where specialists are needed to assess performance effectiveness of executives.
- Committees are employed infrequently but have the advantage of reviewing personnel performance when appraisal judgments are questioned, or of offsetting biases that may exist on the part of an appraiser.
- The immediate superior is responsible most frequently for preparing summative appraisals. Occasionally, external personnel are involved in this type of personnel action.
- Although the research is limited, reports of evaluations of appraisers by appraisees have indicated positive results.[7]

TABLE 7.3
Appraisees, appraisers, and appraisal purposes.

Appraisers	←Purposes of Appraisal→		
	Diagnostic	Formative	Summative
Internal			
Self		A I S	
Students		I	
Peers	A I S	A I S	
Appraisal group or committee	A I S	A I S	A I S
Supervisor	A I	A I S	A I S
External			
Consultants	A I	A I S	A I
Parents		A I	
System-related groups		A I	
Union representatives		I	I S

Note: Appraisees: A = Administrative-supervisory personnel; I = Instruction personnel; S = Support personnel.

What research findings and actual observations on the source of appraisals add up to is that a combination of agents is likely to be involved in appraisal systems, depending on intent of appraisal and on the level or category of personnel being appraised.

Methods of Appraisal. We have now arrived at the point in our analysis of factors to be considered in designing an appraisal system where we need to discuss appraisal methodology. Once the system has decided what performance effectiveness will be for each of the personnel categories (Table 7.4), information must be gathered by means of appraisal devices to assess those position-related personnel characteristics, processes, products, or combinations of these elements that are a function of the definition of personnel effectiveness.

As illustrated in Table 7.4, the constant search for new and better methods to appraise personnel performance has led to development of a variety of appraisal systems and techniques. By and large, these methods cluster around three basic classes of methods: (a) those designed to measure personal characteristics, (b) those focusing on the process by which the individual performs his/her assigned role, and (c) those that are product oriented or results oriented.

Another important observation that can be made of information on appraisal methodology contained in Table 7.4 is that there is an extensive set of appraisal tools available to serve diagnostic, formative, and summative purposes of appraisal. Research and practice indicate that there are limitations to any single instrument, any single observation system, or any single criterion for assessing performance effectiveness. Different methods are applicable to different purposes and to different kinds of positions. On the other hand, some approaches to assessing performance are better, not in an absolute sense, but in a relative sense of their being more appropriate to a given set of circumstances. There are problems, situations, and conditions in every organization that may limit or enhance use and effectiveness of certain appraisal methods.

A third observation relating to appraisal techniques listed in Table 7.4 is that familiarity of system decision makers with the variety of appraisal techniques available will help to equip them with a repertory of approaches to be applied to personnel categories in various levels of organization structure.[8] There are a variety of appraisal alternatives to serve different purposes and different personnel. Performance evaluation systems as generally practiced today in educational institutions are regarded as less than satisfactory, and testing and developing of existing and newer appraisal techniques is essential to both the system and its members. The solution lies not in eliminating performance appraisal altogether and replacing it with a seniority system for compensation, furloughs, promotions, and transfers; rather, it lies in making effective use of knowledge now available and in continuous experimenting with techniques that promise to yield positive results.

The purpose of the section that follows is to propose a model process for appraising the performance of school personnel. It will (a) examine the several phases of the process; (b) note some of the organizational and human obstacles to be encountered in establishing the process; and (c) examine the sequential, interrelated steps in process implementation. Undergirding the treatment of the design and operation of the performance appraisal process is the reminder that there is no ideal performance appraisal. Its shape is determined by various factors, including (a) whether the process is to be *developmental, remedial,* or *maintenance* in purpose; and (b) the extent to which collective external and internal conditions contribute to the formation, operation, and maintenance of its desired mode of existence.

THE PERFORMANCE APPRAISAL PROCESS

A model for performance appraisal of system personnel is illustrated in Figure 7.3. The model portrays a process consisting of two types of appraisals: formative and summative. The **formative appraisal** structure is based on the premise that (a) each system member will strive for performance effectiveness; and (b) the formative appraisal is standard or routine for all system personnel, the design of which is to assist individuals to achieve and exceed performance levels that have been established for all positions in the form of position guides. The **summative appraisal** structure is fashioned around two major tasks: (a) those relating to individuals whose performance has

TABLE 7.41
Appraisal connections: purposes—personnel—methods.

Appraisal Methods	Appraisal Purposes		
	Diagnostic: Recruitment Selection Placement	*Formative:* Development	*Summative:* Compensation Promotion Transfer Reassignment Furlough Dismissal
Instructional personnel			
Graphic rating scales	X		
Teacher performance tests	X		
Observation systems		X	X
Student outcomes (standardized tests, pupil gains)		X	
Performance objectives (MBO)[a]		X	X
Behaviorally anchored rating scales		X	X
Essay (narrative reports)	X	X	X
Critical incidents (description of position behavior)		X	X
Checklists	X	X	
Models of teaching		X	
Ranking systems	X		
Interview evaluation	X		
Paired comparison systems (rank order)	X		
Forced distribution techniques (predetermined distribution)	X		

been judged to be less than satisfactory in routine formal appraisals and (b) those relating to performance enhancement or to situations or conditions unrelated to ineffectiveness, such as layoffs or a reduction in force.

Before discussing the dual aspects of the performance appraisal model portrayed in Figure 7.3, the underlying assumptions on which the total model is based need to be explained.

TABLE 7.4, *continued*

Appraisal Methods	Diagnostic: Recruitment Selection Placement	Formative: Development	Summative: Compensation Promotion Transfer Reassignment Furlough Dismissal
Appraisal Purposes			
Administrative personnel			
Performance objectives (MBO)		X	X
Graphic rating scales	X		
Essay (narrative reports)		X	X
Assessment center technique	X		
Critical incidents		X	
Interview evaluation	X		
Performance tests (in-basket technique)	X		
Support personnel			
Rating scales	X		
Performance objectives (MBO)		X	X
Performance tests	X		
Essay technique	X	X	X
Critical incidents		X	X
Ranking	X		
Interview evaluation	X		
Observations systems		X	X

Note: [a]MBO = management by objectives.

This table is illustrative; its intent is to stress the point that appraisal techniques should be linked to appraisal purposes. The *X* indicates the *conventional* use of appraisal techniques listed.

Model Assumptions

Model assumptions include:

- The appraisal process proposed in Figure 7.3 is an extension of the design of the performance appraisal system outlined in Table 7.1. It assumes that preoperational decisions identified in Table 7.1 have been concretized.

- The model shown in Figure 7.3 is designed for both *formative* and *summative* appraisals. This implies that one of the primary purposes of the model is to enhance personnel development. The information derived from application of formative appraisals, however, is employed in summative appraisals as well as in the evaluation of progress toward unit goals and the broader system mission. The assumption is that compensation, promotion, dismissal, and transfer reviews are separate from formative appraisals. *Compensation appraisals* are treated in Chapter 11; *terminal appraisals* in Chapter 9.

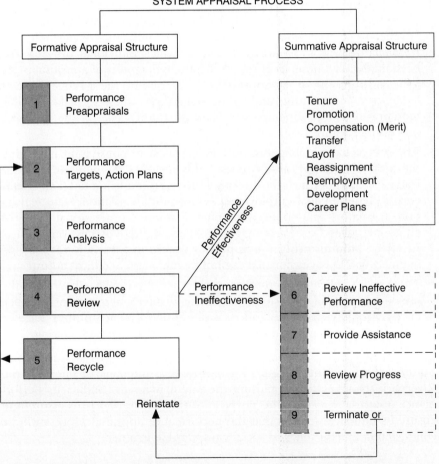

FIGURE 7.3
Performance appraisal goal-focused model.

- The model may be employed to appraise personnel in any of the major groups of system positions.
- The thrust of the model is away from *rating systems* and toward measurable intended outcomes.
- A key assumption underlying the model is that performance effectiveness is considered to be attainment of individual, unit, and system *outcomes*.
- The basic appraisal criterion of the model is a set of predetermined performance targets or growth levels to be accomplished by the appraisee. In effect, the model is a component of an MBO or MAR (management by objectives and results system) that features (a) a collaborative agreement between appraiser and appraisee that defines in advance results to be achieved for a particular period; (b) the establishment of action plans in advance to achieve intended results; (c) the conducting of periodic performance reviews to assess the extent to which individual progress has been made in attainment of results; (d) the rediagnosis of appraisal problems and recycling of the appraisal process; and (e) the arrangement for feedback to system units and to the system as a whole to make possible modifications and refinements of plans for future cycles of the appraisal process (see Figure 7.4).
- The system has an obligation to conduct itself responsibly in managing the performance appraisal process. This includes the general legalistic framework within which the appraisal process is implemented (i.e., adherence to federal equal employment opportunity legislation, state legislation, regulatory guidelines, and court decisions), professional codes of ethics, negotiated contracts, system policies, and due process procedures. In effect, administering the appraisal system in a socially responsible manner includes behavior that exemplifies an eminent ethical posture.
- The system's obligation to conduct itself responsibly can be enhanced by the use of four planning vehicles: a) statement of intent, b) statement of policy, c) responsibility structure, and d) position-performance profile. Each of these parts of the appraisal system are considered in the text following.

Statement of Intent.   Figure 7.4 illustrates a statement of intent by the Riverpark school system regarding the way it plans to conduct its performance appraisal process. The purpose of the declaration is to assure and ensure its human resources that the performance appraisal process will be conducted in an ethically and socially responsible manner.

Statement of Policy.   Initiation and maintenance of a performance appraisal system require a variety of plans in addition to systemwide purposes. One of the principal plans to guide organizations in carrying out broad purposes is policy, an illustration of which is provided in Figure 7.5.

The Riverpark school system's way of appraising the performance of its human resources is to inculcate the following plan of action in conducting the performance appraisal process. The system is dedicated to:

- Designing and implementing policies, directives, and decisions regarding the performance appraisal process to maximize the interests of the organization and its closely intertwined human resources.

- Maintaining a systematic performance appraisal process that includes: a) periodic review of personnel performance; b) assessing the extent to which performance meets performance standards; c) communicating performance outcomes; d) getting agreement on position holder strengths and performance needs; e) preparing a plan of action to enhance strengths and shore up weaknesses; f) focusing the appraisal process on performance improvement to enable appraisees to realize their full potential.

- Funding staff development plans for those who conduct performance appraisals in order to emphasize ethical conduct, performance criteria, and the competencies that appraisers need to develop.

- Documenting fully and thoroughly appraisal information for use in human resources decisions affecting individuals, groups, and the organization.

- Linking individual performance to group and system productivity.

- Establishing an appeal mechanism to deal with appraisee rejection of appraisal interview information, mistrust of appraiser, and errors in appraiser judgment.

- Ongoing review of the performance appraisal process to correct flaws identified through process evaluation. Includes directing planning efforts to focus on the question, How can we improve our appraisal process so that it results in positive personnel performance, outcomes of which will raise the level of individual, group, and organizational productivity?

FIGURE 7.4
Statement of intent for administering Riverpark school system's performance appraisal process.

With the policy statement reflecting the position and intent of the school system concerning its appraisal process, the chief executive and staff are in a position to further plans and organize action for their implementation. The observation can also be made that, although policy does not answer all questions about the appraisal system, it does clarify for system members the organization's views on why performance appraisal is necessary, to whom it applies, and the general manner in which it will be carried out.

Position-Performance Profile. Throughout the discussion in this section on types of plans needed to support a performance appraisal system, it

It is the policy of the Fawn Grove school district to appraise the performance of all personnel in its employ in order to help each individual improve effectiveness, to determine appropriate salary action, and to estimate individual potential. Every effort will be made by the school system to communicate to position holders the general goals of the system, the specific objectives of the position, the plans that have been made to support them as they perform their roles, the standards of performance the system has established, the criteria it will employ in assessing performance, the information it will gather to make the appraisal, and the steps it will take to improve individual effectiveness on the basis of the appraisal. It is the intent of the Board of Education, in the process of performance appraisal, to treat all personnel as individuals with the respect, dignity, and consideration owed one individual from another in a free society.

FIGURE 7.5
A performance appraisal policy.

has been noted that determination of purposes precedes all other organizational activities. Once purposes of the organization have been established, its structure is planned by allocating to units the work to be done. Within each unit the number, nature, and scope of individual positions are decided. Design of individual positions, of course, has a close relationship to the performance appraisal system.

Design of any and every position in the school system is of critical importance because it determines the kind of competence required, qualifications necessary to perform the role, and compensation required as well as the individual development program essential for the incumbent if he/she is to fulfill position expectations. But more significantly, position design indicates to both appraiser and appraisee expectations the organization holds for the position; and those in turn establish, to a considerable extent, the basis on which the incumbent's performance will be judged. To say it another way, position design determines results the organization expects the holder to achieve; it also provides the basis on which the appraiser determines the extent to which results have been achieved. In the final analysis, it is the gap between expectations and performance that determines the program of self-development decided on by appraiser and appraisee.

Responsibility Structure. Figure 7.6 illustrates the manner in which performance appraisal responsibilities can be structured. Structuring of performance appraisal responsibilities involves assignment of duties to school officials, granting of permission to take actions, and creation of obligations on the part of appraisees and appraisers. Inasmuch as the days of nonac-

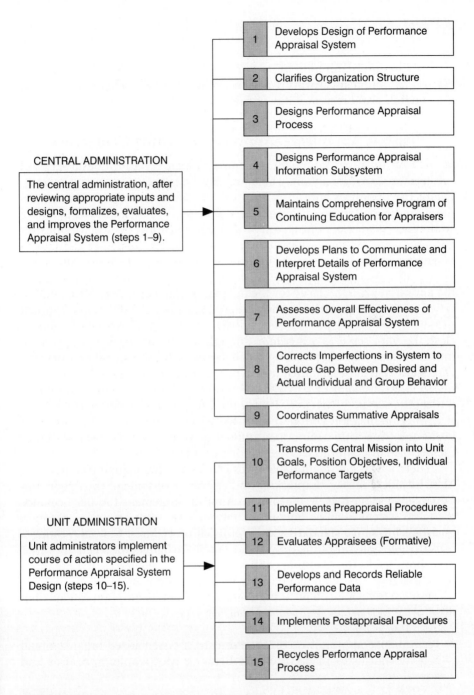

CENTRAL ADMINISTRATION

The central administration, after reviewing appropriate inputs and designs, formalizes, evaluates, and improves the Performance Appraisal System (steps 1–9).

1. Develops Design of Performance Appraisal System
2. Clarifies Organization Structure
3. Designs Performance Appraisal Process
4. Designs Performance Appraisal Information Subsystem
5. Maintains Comprehensive Program of Continuing Education for Appraisers
6. Develops Plans to Communicate and Interpret Details of Performance Appraisal System
7. Assesses Overall Effectiveness of Performance Appraisal System
8. Corrects Imperfections in System to Reduce Gap Between Desired and Actual Individual and Group Behavior
9. Coordinates Summative Appraisals

UNIT ADMINISTRATION

Unit administrators implement course of action specified in the Performance Appraisal System Design (steps 10–15).

10. Transforms Central Mission into Unit Goals, Position Objectives, Individual Performance Targets
11. Implements Preappraisal Procedures
12. Evaluates Appraisees (Formative)
13. Develops and Records Reliable Performance Data
14. Implements Postappraisal Procedures
15. Recycles Performance Appraisal Process

FIGURE 7.6
Focus of responsibilities in the performance appraisal system.

countability in organization appear to be numbered, steps 1 through 15 in Figure 7.6 suggest appraisal activities that can be delegated and the accountability and responsibility of the participants.

Phase 1: Appraisee—Appraiser Planning Conference

Phase 1 of the appraisal model presented in Figure 7.3 includes a series of substeps or activities, among which are those designed to acquaint or reacquaint the appraiser and appraisee with the nature, scope, intent, procedures, and expectations of the appraisal process. The preappraisal planning conference is an essential channel of communication by which appraiser and appraisee exchange information to bring about change in the latter's behavior. Generally speaking, it is designed to perform these functions: enable appraiser and appraisee to inform and to become informed about the appraisal process, clarify for the appraisee what expectations the organization has for the position he/she occupies, elucidate the difference between present and desired position behaviors, establish performance targets to close the gap, serve as a medium through which appraiser and appraisee influence each other in planning for the appraisal process, and link the psychological system of the individual to the organizational structure.

In effect, a major task in Phase 1 of the performance appraisal process is a communications function. It is in the preappraisal planning conference that the organization communicates to the position holder the design of his/her position within the organizational structure, and the relationship of the performance appraisal system to that position.

There are several identifiable steps involved in the planning conference. They include a review of appraiser and appraisee of some of the major support plans established by the organization to implement the performance appraisal system, such as organizational purposes, unit objectives, position goals, **performance standards,** and appraisal procedures. Communicating a considerable amount of the information to be exchanged between appraiser and appraisee in the planning conference can be facilitated by the organization through preparation of a performance appraisal manual.

It is useful at this point to highlight important assumptions about what takes place in a *preappraisal planning conference:*

- Performance appraisal is considered to be a systematized organizational activity that takes place primarily between two people: appraiser and appraisee.

- One of the purposes of a planning conference is to discuss the organization's view of the position and the manner in which it expects the work to be performed.

- The first and focal point of the planning conference should be the improvement of performance in the position now held by the appraisee.

- An equally important assumption about the planning conference is that it focuses on development and self-realization of the appraisee.

- The preappraisal planning conference should help to orient the position holder to the behavior or performance desired in the position and inform the position holder as to the manner in which the organization will assist him/her in achieving the desired level of behavior and how it will measure his/her performance. In addition, the session should be directed toward dissecting the nature of the position and work behavior necessary to perform the role effectively as well as toward discovering difficulties perceived by the incumbent in performing according to plan.

- There are *four major position concepts* associated with the performance appraisal process that are reviewed by appraiser and appraisee in Phase 1. These concepts include *performance effectiveness, performance effectiveness areas, position performance standards,* and *position performance targets.* These concepts are outlined in Table 7.5.

Although we shall consider *appraisee self-evaluation* as an important element in Phase 4 (appraisal review), it is important to note at this point that self-evaluation by the position holder is also a significant aspect of Phase 1. It is generally agreed that self-evaluation by the incumbent *precedes* the appraiser's evaluation. This way, the appraiser has been given perceptions and other information to be reviewed, and the sequence of events helps to minimize chances of the appraisee being squelched or perceptions of his/her performance being colored by those of the appraiser.

As we move from *preappraisal into the actual appraisal phases* of the model process outlined in Figure 7.3, the concern will be with two key ingredients of performance appraisal: (a) the collaborative setting of performance targets and (b) the behavior of appraisers in their efforts to improve the performance of their units and their subordinates. One of the hard lessons organizations have been learning about the appraisal process is that its success depends to a considerable extent on changes appraisers effect in their own behavior.

Phase 2: Setting Performance Targets

The intent of the previous section was to demonstrate that when the appraiser understands what the appraisee's performance behavior means and what the performance needs of the individual are in relation to position performance, the next phases of the performance appraisal process shown in Figure 7.3 can be implemented. These phases include performance target setting, measurement of behavior change and performance improvement, and a program of individual development based on the outcome of the appraisal review.

TABLE 7.5
Major position concepts involved in appraising and documenting performance of school personnel.

Performance Effectiveness	Performance Effectiveness Areas	Position Performance Standards	Position Performance Targets
Performance effectiveness is the extent to which an individual administrator achieves the general and specific objectives of the position to which he/she is assigned. Effectiveness is construed as results actually achieved rather than what activities the position holder engages in to achieve the results.	Key functional areas associated with a position constitute performance effectiveness areas.	Position standards are statements of conditions that will exist when the responsibilities assigned to the position are being carried out effectively. Standards are desired end results the individual is being paid to accomplish; they specify the conditions that exist when the role is being performed satisfactorily.	Position performance targets are specific statements agreed on by appraiser and appraisee that indicate what is to be accomplished to meet a specific position objective. Position performance targets are time bounded, measurable, and focus on what a position holder should achieve (results) rather than on the means by which it is to be accomplished.

Let us consider the first of the activities in Phase 2, setting performance targets. As discussed previously, appraiser and appraisee are not concerned with just any targets. Moreover, the point was made previously that targets are set collaboratively. Neither the appraiser nor the appraisee can set targets effectively without advice and counsel of the other. Criteria by which performance targets can be judged are contained in these questions: Do the performance targets have priorities? Are they limited in number? Are they doable? Have time limits been set? Are they measurable? Are they specific? Are they understandable?

Several additional points about setting performance targets should be noted, including types of performance targets to be set, target derivation, the target-setting process, and the mechanics of target documentation. The following text discusses what specific aspects of these elements should be considered in setting targets.

Types of Performance Targets. There are two major types of **performance targets** involved in performance appraisal when the primary purpose is individual development: *position targets* and *behavioral targets*. A position target is an outcome to be achieved in one of the key results areas established for the position. The intent of a position target is to convert by means of specific and operational terms a functional activity of a position into desired outcomes or results. The principal of a middle school, for example, has for one of his/her key results or effectiveness areas the management of pupil information. The conversion of this performance effectiveness area into performance targets might be accomplished as follows:

- Increase by year end the amount and quality of feedback regarding the actual performance of teachers in the school.
- Improve ability to assist each teacher this year to write performance objectives clearly and specifically.
- Improve by the beginning of the school year the efficiency and systematic maintenance of necessary and desirable individual pupil records.
- Provide by the beginning of the school year for the maintenance and use of special-purpose short-term records.
- Initiate by the beginning of the school year a plan for managing the confidentiality of student records.

A behavioral target, on the other hand, refers to the behavior needed by the individual to achieve position targets. The improvement, acquisition, or modification of human, technical, or conceptual skills and the work habits needed to achieve position goals indicate the general nature of behavioral targets. They represent individual behavior needed to make it possible to achieve the performance target. Learning about and acquiring skills in a summer seminar to initiate a teacher self-evaluation plan through use of audiotaping and videotaping procedures, completing within two weeks a self-diagnostic instrument that appraises leadership performance by using 12 situational exercises, getting to work on time, controlling one's temper in negotiations with a union representative, and improving one's skill in oral and written communication are indicators of behavioral targets that may be needed to achieve given position targets.

Target Derivation.   Performance targets will be derived *initially* from a variety of sources, such as observations of appraiser and appraisee about common problems in the key results areas that need attention; indicators from surveys, audits, assessments, and student evaluations of teachers; classroom interaction analyses; and complaints about less-than-satisfactory aspects of position performance. *After* the performance appraisal plan has been initiated, the performance targets will emerge (Phase 3 and 4) from appraisee self-evaluation and from analyses of the appraisee's performance by the appraiser during periodic performance reviews throughout the incumbent's term in the position.

Target-Setting Process.   The point was made earlier that, in setting performance targets, neither appraiser nor appraisee is able to or should act independently. Targets must fit into and link with desired results of the position and with other positions within the unit as well as with system goals and unit objectives. There are both internal and external constraints that need to be considered. Union contracts governing conditions of work, leadership style of the appraiser's superior, and personality and length of service of the appraisee as well as contemporary pressures for system, unit, and individual change are forces with which the appraiser must contend in the target-setting process.

Target Documentation.   The performance target-setting process is brought to full circle by means of a written record of events occurring in Phase 2 of the appraisal process model shown in Figure 7.3. Essential features of a form for recording performance targets and the results achieved are illustrated in Figure 7.7, which includes a written record of specific targets the appraisee will work toward and serves as a primary source of documentation. Moreover, this form can be used as a document for developing an action plan and for reviewing the extent to which performance targets have been achieved. The items to be documented include effectiveness areas, objectives, priorities, appraisal methods, performance results, and signatories of the form.

Appraiser Style.   Probably the most fundamental responsibility of a unit administrator, such as a principal, is to ensure that system goals, unit objec-

1. *Appraisee*
   Title of position _____
   Position location_____ Central administration _____ Attendance unit_____
   Reports to (give position to which this position reports) _____
   Nature of
       responsibility: Line ___ Staff ___ Professional experience
   No. of professional staff   Years of professional exp. 19__ to 19__
       reporting to position _____
   No. of supportive staff   Years of teaching exp.   19__ to 19__
       reporting to position _____
   Incumbent_____ Age _____   Years of administrative exp. 19__ to 19__

   Education   Previous administrative positions
   B.A. from _____ Year _____   _____ 19__ to 19__
   M.A. from _____ Year _____   _____ 19__ to 19__
   Doctorate from _____ Year _____   _____ 19__ to 19__

2. *Appraiser*
   Title of position _____   Position location_____
   Name of incumbent _____   Dates of quarterly reviews _____

3. *Position*
   If position is in central administration, indicate with which of the following major organization functions is chiefly concerned:

   Ed. program ___ Logistics____ Personnel ____ External relations____ Planning___

   If position is at attendance unit (building) level, indicate the following:
   Pupil-teacher ratio _____   Faculty experience _____
   Pupil-professional staff ratio ____   % non-English speaking pupils_____
   Client composition _____   Types of special programs (nonsystemwide)
   Pupil mobility_____   _____
   Socioeconomic level _____   _____
   Faculty preparation_____   _____

FIGURE 7.7

Administrative position review form from the Camelot school system (items 1-3: position record sheet; items 4-8: performance target record form).

tives, and individual performance targets possess a logically integrated network. Coordination of contributions of individuals to the interlocking goals involves the concept of chain of command. This concept embraces the idea that by holding every position holder responsible to some appraiser, the chain of command operates to test everyone's performance against the expectations of the appraiser. Consequently, the manner or style in which the appraiser coordinates efforts of appraisees has considerable impact on effective individual, unit, and system performance. A dimensional model of appraiser behavior by Letton, Buzzotta, Sherberg, and Karraker describes leadership styles as follows:

4.	Common position dimensions	With which of the following common position dimensions is the performance target primarily associated? Systems dimension _____ Leadership dimension ____ Human resources dimension _____
5.	Performance target	a. What specific performance condition needs to be improved to achieve the performance target? Priority no. __ b. Is this performance target focused on: Routine objective _____Problem-solving objective __ Innovative objective_____
6.	Appraisal method	How will the appraiser judge when the performance target has been reached? By what means?
7.	Performance target action plan (What is the plan of action? What steps are to be taken to achieve the performance target?)	(see table below)
8.	Performance results	To what extent was the performance target (not the program of activities) actually achieved? Appraiser _____ Appraisee _____ Date_____

For item 7:

Performance target activity serial number	Performance target activity	Planned date of completion	Date actually completed
1.0	What does		
1.1	appraisee do to		
1.2	move from the		
1.3	present condition		
1.4	to the future		
1.5	condition (target)?		
1.6	What specific steps must be taken and in what order?		

FIGURE 7.7, *continued*

- Appraiser behaviors can be grouped according to these characteristics: (a) *dominance* is the exercise of control, taking charge; (b) *submission* is following the lead of others, going along; (c) *hostility* is a lack of regard for others and a cautious, skeptical approach to them; and (d) *warmth* is regard for others and a basic trust in them.
- The four basic patterns of behavior described in the quadrants in Figure 7.8 include: (a) Q1 behavior (dominant-hostile), (b) Q2 behavior (submissive-hostile), (c) Q3 behavior (submissive-warm), and (d) Q4 behavior (dominant-warm).
- Appraisers display all four patterns of behavior at various times. A superior's most repetitive behavior is his/her primary strategy.[9]

Dominance

Quadrant 1

Basic attitude—People work best when they're somewhat scared. If you want results, make your people feel insecure, build on their fears, and keep them moving.

Control—Very tight. Exerts close supervision.

Involvement–Discourages ideas from subordinates. Convinced that they rarely have any worthwhile suggestions.

Decisions–Makes decisions alone. Expects subordinates to carry them out without questioning.

Conflict—Suppresses dissent. Insists on own position and views.

Quadrant 4

Basic attitude—People work best when they see how their work can help them achieve their own goals. They're most likely to get good results when they're actively and intelligently involved in their jobs.

Control—When possible, exerts control by generating understanding of, and commitment to, job goals.

Involvement—Encourages independent thinking; believes subordinates can be a source of innovation and improvement.

Decisions—Bases decisions, when possible and advisable, on candid exchange of views and subordinates.

Conflict—Faces up to conflict, and seeks its reasons before resolving it.

Hostility ———————————————————————— **Warmth**

Quadrant 2

Basic attitude—People are lackadaisical about work. Not much can be done to motivate them; they'll work when they want to.

Control—Keeps people in line by reminding them of what *his/her* boss expects ("The boss upstairs won't like it if you. . . . ").

Involvement—Minimal. Doesn't seek out or encourage suggestions from subordinates.

Decisions—Waits to see what the boss wants, then makes decision on that basis.

Conflict—Ignores dissent, hoping it will go away in time.

Quadrant 3

Basic attitude—People work best in a cheerful, harmonious environment. If you want results, make sure your subordinates are happy.

Control—Expects hard, loyal work to follow automatically if people have good personal relationships with the boss.

Involvement—Encourages suggestions. Tries to follow through on popular ones and avoids those that are unpopular.

Decisions—Tries to make decisions that subordinates will accept readily and be happy with.

Conflict—Settles disagreements by compromise and appeasement.

Submission

Mode	Predicted Outcome
Q1 Style (dominant–hostile)	Average outcome
Q2 Style (submissive–hostile)	Mediocre outcome
Q3 Style (submissive–warm)	Mediocre outcome
Q4 Style (dominant–warm)	Consistently high outcome

FIGURE 7.8
Dimensional model of appraiser behavior.

Source: Robert E. Letton, V. R. Buzzotta, Manuel Sherberg, and Dean L. Karraker, Effective Motivation Through Performance Appraisal, © 1977, John Wiley and Sons, Inc.

Phase 3: Performance Analysis

If we return to the model shown in Figure 7.3, we note that Phase 3, which we are about to consider, is the very heart of the process. It calls for a *self-appraisal* by the appraisee of the extent to which he/she is achieving the goals of his/her position. In addition, the appraiser makes an independent judgment of the results achieved by subordinates in relation to performance targets that have been established jointly. As will be illustrated later, results of both appraisals are recorded separately because both inputs are essential to the appraisal process.

Appraisee Makes Self-Appraisal and Records Problems and Progress. One of the essential activities in Phase 3 (performance analysis) is self-appraisal by the incumbent of his/her administrative performance. To a considerable extent, the appraisee goes through the same analytical process as the appraiser does to determine the degree to which he/she is meeting requirements of the position. A few of the multiple approaches used by teachers in self-evaluation to probe their performance effectiveness include teacher performance as perceived by students, student knowledge of instructional goals and objectives, parent attitudes toward pupil outcomes, and analysis of time spent with individual students and groups.

Figure 7.9 lists kinds of questions the appraisee asks about his/her performance. The self-appraisal process has at least three purposes: (a) to assist the subordinate to analyze his/her present performance; (b) to provide information for a progress review conference with the appraiser; and (c) to help the incumbent identify strengths, weaknesses, and potential as well as to help make plans for improving performance.

Appraiser Observes Performance of Appraisee. Let us now look in detail at the problem of how the appraiser goes about basing a performance evaluation on the dimensions previously noted in Figure 7.3. It will help to make the point that the appraiser must appraise the performance of the appraisee from two standpoints:

* Are the goals of the position being achieved? Here we are talking about the long-range goals of the position, especially in terms of those goals established by the organization in the position guide. The appraiser is constantly interested in determining the extent to which the appraisee performs in terms of the way the performance standards indicate the work should be performed.
* To what extent are the short-term goals or performance targets being achieved? The relationship between performance targets and long-range results examined by the appraiser in performance appraisal is illustrated in Figure 7.10. The performance targets are relatively short term,

1. Summarize the overall strengths that you have demonstrated in performing your present assignment.

2. Do you feel that you are well placed in your present assignment? If not, please explain.

3. In what areas of your present assignment or in the way you perform your present assignment do you think you can improve your performance?

4. Do you feel that you have potential beyond your present assignment? How have you demonstrated this potential? What can you suggest as your next assignment?

5. Are there significant facts that you think should be noted about the dimensions of your position that affect your performance and that you think should be brought to the attention of your superior, such as:

   Unit objectives
   Position design
   Human, technical, and conceptual skills
   Social setting
   Situational factors
   Results achieved

6. How effectively do you feel you have met the responsibilities of your position?

   Signature of appraisee _____ Date _____

FIGURE 7.9
A self-appraisal form.

decided on jointly by appraiser and appraisee in order to give day-by-day direction to the latter. Performance targets suggest priority actions to be taken by the appraisee as well as the skills, habits, and attitudes needed to improve total position performance.

It is worth reiterating here that appraisal techniques employed should be linked to appraisal purposes and positions. Some approaches serve one purpose better than others; some are more appropriate for one position than for others. If the primary purpose of appraisal is the evaluation of a new classroom teacher, the **goal-setting model** may be a more appropriate approach than rating. If the primary purpose is to decide on teacher tenure, a combination of techniques may be used.

Appraiser Records Observations. For a variety of reasons, the appraiser needs to record observations concerning the performance of staff

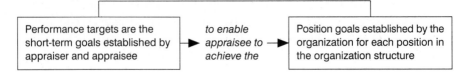

FIGURE 7.10.
Relationship of performance targets to position goals.

members. These reasons include recording of information for the follow-up conference with the appraiser, for performance analysis, for the action program to be developed, and *for the performance history of the individual*. Essential features of forms for recording observations on the performance of an individual occupying an *administrative position* are as described in Figure 7.7.

Phase 4: Performance Progress Review

Once performance appraisals are completed by the appraiser and appraisee, the next step in the appraisal process as shown in Figure 7.3 is the performance *progress review conference,* sometimes referred to as the *postappraisal interview*.

One of the purposes of the progress review conference is an exchange of information between the appraiser and appraisee about the latter's performance. The information is exchanged between both parties. The appraiser prepares for the conference by reviewing carefully the results of completed appraisals. Likewise, the appraisee, who receives a copy of the report, reviews it in preparation for the discussion.

A second purpose of the progress review conference is to clarify viewpoints about the appraisee's performance. Differing perceptions of the position goals, responsibilities, authority, and relationships can be identified, examined, and clarified. The appraisee's feelings toward achieving performance targets can be studied. Obstacles to individual progress, whether they be individual or organizational, are topics open for discussion.

Emphasis on the self-development of the appraisee is a third purpose of progress review conference. As noted earlier, performance appraisal is designed not only to accomplish organizational ends, but also to help the individual attain personal objectives, one of which ought to be performance improvement. It is at this stage of the conference that the appraiser attempts to counsel or coach the appraisee on the resolution of problems affecting performance.

Figure 7.11 illustrates a means by which the appraiser can compare judgments with those of the appraisee on the latter's performance. The information in this form provides the basis for the *progress review conference* and the *individual development program*.

Individual Development Program.   Another aspect of Phase 4 in the appraisal process is the joint development of an action program for the appraisee based on the progress review conference. The essence of the individual development program may be summarized as follows:

- The performance appraisal reports should indicate to both appraiser and appraisee how well the latter has done in reaching previously established targets.
- On the basis of the progress review conference (which should make clear both results achieved and results to be achieved), appraiser and appraisee come to a common understanding on what performance targets should be reestablished for the next review period.

Name of appraisee _____   Organization unit _____

Position _____

1. What progress does the *appraiser* think the *appraisee* made during the review period in closing the gap between actual and desired performance?

   What progress does the *appraisee* think he/she has made in closing the gap between actual and desired performance?

2. In what areas does the *appraiser* think the *appraisee* can improve?

   In what respects does the *appraisee* think he/she can improve?

3. Since the last appraisal, in what ways does the *appraiser* think the performance of the *appraisee* has improved?

   Since the last appraisal, in what ways does the *appraisee* think his/her performance has improved?

4. What specifically does the *appraiser* plan to do to improve the performance of the *appraisee*?

   What are the *appraisee's* plans for helping himself/herself?

5. What follow-up action will be taken by the *appraiser* on the basis of this review?

   What appears to be the general reaction of the *appraisee* to (a) the performance appraisal and (b) the ways by which performance can be improved?

Signature of appraiser _____

Date of review _____

FIGURE 7.11
Performance progress review form.

- During the period set for the individual development program, considerable responsibility is placed on the appraiser for guiding and motivating the behavior of the appraisee in terms of performance targets.

Figure 7.12 presents parts of a questionnaire used in organizations to evaluate appraisee perceptions of a performance appraisal interview. The instrument enables collection of data on particular characteristics that are of interest (i.e., equity, accuracy, and clarity). The seven-point scales measure a person's perceptions of the degree to which performance appraisal interviews possess a given characteristic.[10] Other applications of the instrument include feedback for the appraiser, system evaluation of the performance appraisal process, documentation of appraisee assessment of appraisal process, and for the individual performance profile in the system data base.

The Performance Decision Screen. Examination of Figure 7.3 indicates that on completion of the formative performance review (Phase 4), a performance decision screen is established to serve three purposes: (a) identify and place in the summative appraisal process those individuals who have not achieved performance standards, (b) recycle the formative appraisal process (Phase 5) for those who have performed satisfactorily, and (c) invoke the summative appraisal process for making decisions relative to effective performance when conditions arise (tenure, promotion, etc.) such as those listed in Figure 7.3 (summative structure). The summative decision structure will be analyzed in a subsequent section of this chapter.[11,12]

Phase 5: Performance Rediagnosis and Recycle

As shown previously in Figure 7.3, Phase 5 of the performance appraisal model is the time for rediagnosis of performance results and recycling of the appraisal process. This phase of the process is designed to check results of the individual development program and to establish new or modified performance targets for the ensuing review period. In effect, the appraisal process is being recycled. As performance standards are reached in any of the dimensions under consideration, the process is redirected toward other areas of performance where improvement is needed. Quite obvious is that the intent of rediagnosis is to establish continuity and stability in the development program of the individual. Concrete plans should emerge for extending the program in areas where it has been good. Kindall and Gatza make several interesting points with regard to checking results:

- Here is a key point in the understanding of this appraisal program: hitting the target is not the measure of success. It is to be expected that

Directions: Circle the number that best describes your opinion of the most recent appraisal interview.

		Very False					Very True	
1.	The appraisal interview covered my entire job.	1	2	3	4	5	6	7
2.	The discussion of my performance during the appraisal interview was covered equitably.	1	2	3	4	5	6	7
3.	The appraisal interview was accurately conducted.	1	2	3	4	5	6	7
4.	I didn't have to ask for any clarification.	1	2	3	4	5	6	7
5.	The interview was fair in every respect.	1	2	3	4	5	6	7
6.	The interview really raised my anxiety level.	1	2	3	4	5	6	7
7.	The interview's purpose was simply not clear to me.	1	2	3	4	5	6	7
8.	The appraisal interview really made me think about working smarter on the job.	1	2	3	4	5	6	7
9.	The interview was encouraging to me personally.	1	2	3	4	5	6	7
10.	I dreaded the actual interview itself.	1	2	3	4	5	6	7
11.	The boss was totally aboveboard in all phases of the interview.	1	2	3	4	5	6	7
12.	The interview gave me some direction and purpose.	1	2	3	4	5	6	7
13.	The interview really pinpointed areas for improvement.	1	2	3	4	5	6	7
14.	The interview was disorganized and frustrating.	1	2	3	4	5	6	7
15.	I disliked the interview because the intent was not clear.	1	2	3	4	5	6	7
16.	The appraisal interviewer (boss) was not well trained.	1	2	3	4	5	6	7
17.	The interview has been my guide for correcting weaknesses.	1	2	3	4	5	6	7
18.	I understood the meaning of each performance area better after the interview.	1	2	3	4	5	6	7
19.	The interview time was too rushed.	1	2	3	4	5	6	7
20.	I received no advanced notice about the interview.	1	2	3	4	5	6	7
21.	The interview analyzed my performance fairly.	1	2	3	4	5	6	7
22.	I was often upset because the interview data were not accurate.	1	2	3	4	5	6	7
23.	My record as it was introduced in the interview contained no errors.	1	2	3	4	5	6	7

FIGURE 7.12
Appraisal interview questionnaire.

Source: John M. Ivancevich and Michael T. Matteson, Organizational Behavior and Management, Third Edition (Homewood, IL: Richard D. Irwin, Inc. 1993), 69–70.

some targets will be surpassed, some never even approached. The person who sets meager targets and always hits them is certainly of no greater value to the company than the person who sets unreachable targets, falls short consistently, yet in doing so makes substantial improvements on his past work.

If one's "score" in hitting the bull's-eye is not the important thing, what is? Simply this: the results achieved by the total process of establishing targets, striving to attain them, and analyzing what intervenes between planned and actual performance. When a judgment must be made, the individual is evaluated on his ability to set targets as well as his ability to attain them.

- In checking results, we feel the superior should do all he can to emphasize success—to build on successful accomplishment, the superior should help the subordinate. This help takes many forms: coaching, training, work assignments, allowing the subordinate to substitute for the superior, and so on.

- There is nothing in the recommended appraisal procedure that suggests that a superior should abdicate his managerial responsibility. Suppose that after coaching, training, and other help, a subordinate fails to set and reach targets deemed realistic by his superior. At this point the boss should act, even though it might mean demotion, transfer, or release of the subordinate.[13]

Another aspect of Phase 5 worthy of consideration is that in addition to rediagnosis of individual development, the unit administrator also includes in the periodic review the progress being made by the unit toward its objectives and system goals. Rediagnosis and recycling of unit objectives and performance are designed to induce intralevel coordination of plans and results of plans.

Summative Appraisal Process. The goal-focused model of the performance appraisal process outlined in Figure 7.3 is designed around five assumptions:

- All system personnel are obliged to undergo performance appraisals within each academic year.

- The system is comprised of a dual structure: formative and summative. The formative structure emphasizes personnel development and excludes the use of summative decisions so long as satisfactory progress is made toward meeting performance requirements.

- On completion of the formative review (Phase 4), personnel who cannot or will not perform satisfactorily are placed in the summative appraisal process (Phases 6 to 9).

- The summative process is also utilized for making summative personnel decisions relating to *effective* performance, most of which are developmental in nature.

- A standing performance review panel is formed by the chief executive to coordinate all summative reviews and decisions.

Phases 6 to 9: Summative Performance Decision—Remediation

When any system member fails to meet performance standards (Phase 4), this individual is placed in what may be referred to as a performance deficiency mode (Phases 6 to 9 of Figure 7.3). This arrangement is designed to determine whether the causes of ineffective performance are remedial. These phases are involved:

- *Phase 6*—Conference between the individual and the performance review panel to (a) review reasons for placing the individual in the deficiency mode, (b) indicate the performance behaviors needing correction, (c) identify the improvement plan to be initiated, (d) establish the form of and time frame for reviewing performance, and (e) communicate to the individual the positive or negative outcome that will emerge from the summative progress review.

- *Phase 7*—Individual receives various forms of developmental and counseling assistance. This may include developmental interviews, modeling, and guided and individualized experiences; restructuring the position or the work environment (mismatches); and selected types of counseling (instructional, evaluative, disciplinary, problem solving, or developmental).

- *Phase 8*—Performance review panel gathers and reviews documented information from unit head (or other sources) to determine whether the individual has shown sufficient progress to be removed from the deficiency mode and returned to the formative appraisal plan or whether progress is so lacking that employment should be terminated.

- *Phase 9*—System member is notified of panel's summative decision. If the decision is positive, unit head and member confer regarding the setting of new performance targets. If decision is negative and employment is to be terminated, the panel proceeds with termination procedures, with the assurance that individual contractual terms, legal obligations, due process, union contractual provisions, and professional ethics have been observed.[14]

Summative Performance Decision: Rewards.   The summative appraisal structure shown in Figure 7.3, as one aspect of the system appraisal process, is designed to deal with decisions for enhancing performance effectiveness by means of a reward structure. Elements of the structure, as shown in Figure 7.3, include tenure, promotion, merit pay, transfer to position openings, layoff, reemployment, reassignment for developmental purposes, special forms of development plans, and generation of career plans for deserving personnel. Summative decisions regarding performance enhancement become the responsibility of the performance review panel and are based on information derived from formative appraisals.

Performance enhancement through a summative appraisal approach minimizes some of the long-standing criticisms of performance appraisal, such as elimination of a single system for both formative and summative decisions, placing the focus on self-evaluation and development, and removing the appraiser from the position of sole authority.

Summative Decision: Layoff and Reemployment. Cyclical movements in the nation's economy as well as other factors have prompted some school systems to downsize their school staffs. The model shown in Figure 7.3 indicates that personnel layoffs are summative decisions, and thus, become the responsibility of the performance review panel. The tasks involved in layoff decisions include resolving such issues as the basis for layoff, method of notification, an appeals procedure, reemployment rights, and counseling and outplacement services.

The usual approach to reduction in force is referred to as LIFO: last in, first out. This procedure is contained in many union-system contracts and represents a sound first step to dealing with the stress of organizational contraction. The LIFO concept, however, has certain critical limitations that create considerable human and organizational difficulties when applied without due consideration for its potential negative effects on both personnel and the organization.

Although LIFO is an acceptable first-order strategy, its simplistic application can be mischievous or even disastrous, according to Ketchum. He suggests a set of caveats, including the following:

- The arguments for LIFO, which ignore considerations of performance and promise, invariably tend to be sociological and psychological rather than economic in essence.
- Closing down a new operation (computer technology) just because it is new and before it has had a chance to prove itself is the corporate equivalent of infanticide.
- Any analysis that takes LIFO as the principal spring of action will inevitably select out a disproportionate number of the very groups (minorities and females) that affirmative action has been at pains to advance.
- Cutting out marginal units instead of wounding units across the board may be a more selective use of LIFO strategy.[15]

All of the foregoing considerations are important for an organization faced with the prospect of making summative layoff decisions regarding personnel whose performance is judged to be effective. Careful planning, taking into consideration factors such as those noted, is essential for layoff decisions that minimize the negative impact on individuals and the system.

PERFORMANCE APPRAISAL: ETHICAL ASPECTS

Every appraisal system needs a set of values to guide the conduct of appraisers who make judgments about the appraisees whom they supervise and whose judgments may affect either positively or negatively short- and long-run interests and destinies of their subordinates. Ethical values referred to are established and reinforced at the central level of the system and set forth standards of behavior expected of those responsible for appraising personnel. The most desirable form of administrative morality prevails in the appraisal process when there are system considerations and a climate conducive to human dignity, status, career growth, equitable compensation, competent leadership, and maximum use of human potential. Individuals who are appraised should have assurances such as:

- *Preparation*—Appraisers are properly prepared to engage in the appraisal process.
- *Confidentiality*—Appraisers exercise confidentiality in control and use of information pertaining to the appraising relationship between appraiser and appraisee.
- *Communication*—Appraisers communicate to appraisees position expectations and how they will be evaluated.
- *Objectivity*—Appraisers utilize objective means to secure accurate, relevant, representative, and complete information about the appraisee's performance.
- *Reports*—Appraisers record and report a reliable picture of the appraisee's performance.
- *Feedback*—Appraisers provide appropriate feedback so that appraisees know the current status of their performance and measures involved in its improvement.
- *Participation*—Appraisees are able to engage in dialogue with appraisers about the performance evaluations.
- *Access*—Appraisees have access to appraisal judgments.
- *Constraint*—Appraisers restrict judgments to general and specific responsibilities of the appraisee's position.
- *Security*—Appraisees will have position security based on effective performance.
- *Appeals*—Appraisees have a line of appeal regarding negative judgments of their performance.
- *Due Process*—Appraisees have access to due process procedures.

• *Equity*—Appraisees will be treated equitably in appraisal judgments relating to compensation, promotion, transfer, demotion, furlough, and dismissal.[16]

In brief, the central administration establishes the system's moral tone and ethical expectations for appraisers and consistently enforces behavioral standards relevant to performance appraisal. Consistent application of **appraisal ethics** can be the best insurance an individual can have that security interests will be protected as an integral part of the appraisal process.

REVIEW AND PREVIEW

The essence of this chapter consists of these particulars:

• The performance appraisal process in public school systems is not working well as presently structured.
• A performance appraisal model is a useful planning vehicle for designing and redesigning performance appraisal systems.
• A comprehensive appraisal system is based on three key purposes: diagnostic, formative, and summative.
• The appraisal process encompasses all personnel under contract to the system.
• There are at least eight types of decisions needed to make an appraisal system fully operational: appraisal assumption, appraisal purpose, what is appraised, who is appraised, who

appraises, method of appraisal, ethics of appraisal, and the responsibility structure.

Part II addressed personnel processes regarding recruitment, selection induction, development, and appraisal. Part III addresses justice, continuity, and information processes. The first of these chapters, employment justice, considers ways in which school systems fashion appropriate measures to protect the employment rights of its human resources through a justice system framework. This practice includes concern-complaint procedures, grievances, tenure, and academic freedom as well as finding workable, intelligent solutions to the full range of critical contemporary issues stemming from working conditions and employee-employer relations.

REVIEW AND DISCUSSION QUESTIONS

1. Using the list of personnel decisions from Figure 7.1, examine the manner in which these decisions are made in a selected school system. How is the decision system organized? Which school officials are involved? To what extent?

2. Give your response to these statements derived from the literature on performance appraisal:

• The most significant trend in teacher evaluation in recent years has been the heavy emphasis on the use of research on teaching for appraisal criteria.

- The summative portion of the evaluation process should be conducted very early in the cycle so that the activities undertaken during the remainder of the cycle can be clearly formative.
- Much that is right and much that is wrong in current organizations can be explained in terms of the evaluation process.
- Measure excellent people on a different scale; expect more from them; when they deliver, be prepared to offer commensurate rewards.
- A mediocre appraisal program designed by system members is better than an ideal program designed by management.

3. Why is there so much criticism of performance rating scales?

4. Develop a directive to school principals on how to conduct an appraisal interview.

5. Make a list of ten things to do and ten things to avoid in appraising performance.

6. Why is timely performance feedback important? List five criteria that should be established for performance feedback.

7. Develop a procedure to minimize a school system's vulnerability to litigation generated by the appraisal process.

8. Give your definition of these appraisal terms: leniency, strictness, bias, halo effect, and central tendency.

9. What are some organizational determinants of performance? Individual determinants?

10. The literature describes two types of performance measures: (a) non-judgmental (e.g., the number of words a secretary can type per minute) and (b) judgmental (e.g., a person's skill in teaching slow learners.) What are some issues related to each type of measure?

11. Read the following and compare the findings with your experience in or knowledge about performance appraisal in the public sector. A performance appraisal survey including more than 3,500 participants in the private sector indicated that:

- Managers tolerate poor performance too long.
- Supervisors do a poor job of solving "people problems."
- Supervisors fail to give performance feedback regularly.
- Supervisors tolerate below-par employee performance.
- Responsible employees are tired of picking up the slack.

12. If you were to choose an evaluation technique to be applied to your position, which would you select? Why? Under what circumstances is each of the following kinds of appraisal appropriate in the appraisal process: appraisal by supervisor, peers, self-appraisal, group or committee, parents, and pupils?

13. Should individual pupil characteristics be considered in judging teacher effectiveness?

CHAPTER EXERCISE 7.1

Directions: Form the class into five groups to examine the content of Table 7.6. Use the matrix as a device to interview a superintendent of schools and his/her staff regarding the documentation of performance appraisal of personnel in his/her system.

Group A—Focus the interview on the uses, sources, and techniques of performance appraisal documentation for teaching personnel.

Group B—Do the same for administrative and supervisory personnel.

Group C—Do the same for support personnel.

Group D—Do the same for temporary personnel.

Group E—Focus the interview on the quantity of documentation, quality of documentation, contradictions in documentation, and the effectiveness of existing documentation.

CHAPTER EXERCISE 7.2

Directions: Reexamine the contents of the appraisal interview questionnaire (Figure 7.12). Which of the following applications of Figure 7.12 should be included as potential components of the performance appraisal process:

A. *System Application*

- Discriminatory actions
- Evaluation of appraisal process (clarity, effectiveness, corrections needed)
- Legal pitfalls
- Employee handbook
- Central information system database
- Ensure employment rights
- Privacy of personnel files
- Difficult employee problems

B. *Appraiser Application*

- Self-assessment

- Employee appraisal records
- Position clarification
- Performance improvement
- Feedback to appraiser
- Performance control
- Conflicting perceptions of performance appraisal

C. *Appraisee Application*

- Self-assessment
- Position clarification
- Performance clarification
- Employee motivation
- Feedback to appraisee
- Conflicting perceptions of performance appraisal
- Appraisee-appraiser use of information for appraisee self-development
- Improving appraisee—appraiser relationship

NOTES

1. See Dena B. Schneir, "The Impact of EEO Legislation on Performance Appraisal," Personnel 55, 4 (July-August 1978), 24–35.

TABLE 7.6
Uses, sources, and techniques of personnel performance documentation in a school district.

	Documentation Sources		
	Appraiser	Appraisee	Third Parties
Uses and techniques of appraisal documentation			
Appraisal of performance			
Development (maintaining and improving performance)			
Communication (feedback)			
Information			
Compensation			
Discipline			
Tenure			
Promotion			
Demotion			
Grievances			
Termination			
Litigation			
Substantiation			
Verification			
Documentation techniques			
Files, notes, and calendar			
Notebooks, journals, and tapes			
Summaries, reports, and films			
Warning letters			
Memos			
Manuals			
Policies			
Critiques			
Transcripts and minutes			
Commendations and awards			
Performance outcomes			
Track records			
Termination letters			

2. Terminology to describe traditional appraisal plans includes *merit rating, efficiency rating,* and *employee rating.*

3. Information relative to the history of personnel evaluation in the twentieth century is contained in William B. Castetter, The Personnel Function in Educational Administration, Fifth Edition (New York: Macmillan Publishing, 1992), 256.

4. Gary D. Borich, The Appraisal of Teaching: Concepts and Process (Reading, MA: Addison-Wesley Publishing Company, 1978), Chapter 10.

5. Patricia Smith, "Behaviors, Results, and Organizational Effectiveness," in Marvin Dunnette, Editor, Handbook of Industrial and Organizational Psychology (Chicago: Rand McNally & Company, 1976).

6. William F. Glueck, Personnel: A Diagnostic Approach, Revised Edition (Dallas, TX: Business Publications Inc., 1978), 299.

7. Ibid. 298.

8. Descriptions of various techniques listed in Table 7.4 are contained in Richard A. Fear, The Evaluation Interview (New York: McGraw-Hill Book Company, 1984); Wendell French, Personnel Management Process, Sixth Edition (Boston: Houghton Mifflin Company, 1978); John M. Ivancevich and William F. Glueck, Foundations of Personnel/Human Resource Management, Third Edition (Plano, TX: Business Publications, Inc., 1986); and Robert L. Mathis and John Jackson, Human Resources Management, Fifth Edition (St. Paul, MN: West Publishing Company, 1988).

9. Robert E. Letton, V. R. Buzzotta, Manual Sherberg, and Dean L. Karraker, Effective Motivation Through Performance Appraisal (New York: John Wiley and Sons, Inc., 1977), 29.

10. John M. Ivancevich and Michael T. Matteson, Organizational Behavior and Management, Third Edition (Homewood, IL: Richard D. Irwin, Inc., 1993), 69–70.

11. For descriptions of other formative-summative appraisal models, see Larry W. Barber and Karen Klein, "Merit Pay and Teacher Evaluation," Phi Delta Kappan 65, 4 (December 1983), 247—251; and Ben M. Harris, "Teacher Evaluation: Why Not Make It Work?" National Forum of Educational Administration and Supervision 1, 3 (1984-85), 7–12.

12. Useful information on teacher self-evaluation is contained in Edward F. DeRoche, An Administrative Guide for Evaluating Programs and Personnel (Boston: Allyn and Bacon, 1981); and Jason Millman, Editor, Handbook of Teacher Evaluation (Beverly Hills, CA: Sage Publications, Inc., 1981).

13. Reprinted by permission of Harvard Business Review. An excerpt from "Positive Program for Performance Appraisal" by Alva F. Kindall and James Gatza, 41 (November/December 1963). © 1963 by the President and Fellows of Harvard College; All rights reserved. Developmental and counseling assistance is treated extensively in Edward Roseman, Confronting Nonpromotability (New York: American Management Associations, 1977).

14. For insights into the legal aspects of personnel termination, see William H. Holley and Hubert S. Feild, "Will Your Performance Appraisal System Hold Up in Court?" Personnel 57, 1 (January-February 1982), 59–65; Emily A. Joiner, "Erosion of the Employment-at-Will Doctrine" Personnel 61, 5 (September-October 1984), 12–19; Garry L. Lubben, Duane E. Thompson, and Charles R. Klasson, "Performance Appraisal: The Legal Implications of Title VII" Personnel 57, 3 (May-June 1980), 11–21; Gary G. Whitney, "When the News is Bad: Leveling with Employees" Personnel 60, 1 (January-February 1983), 37–45; and Stuart A. Youngblood and Gary Tidwell, "Termination at Will: Some

Changes in the Wind" Personnel 58, 3 (May-June 1991) 14–25.

15. Robert Ketchum, "Retrenchment: The Uses and Misuses of LIFO in Downsizing an Organization" Personnel 59, 6 (November-December 1982), 25–31; see also Robert Fuller, Cassandra Jordan, and Robert Anderson, "Retrenchment: Lay-Off Procedures in a Nonprofit Organization" Personnel 59, 6 (November-December 1982), 14–25. Reprinted by permission of publisher, © 1982.

American Management Association, New York. All rights reserved.

16. These items are based on a discussion of appraisal ethics. Reprinted by permission of publisher from What to Do About Performance Appraisal, Revised Edition, by Marion S. Kellogg, © 1975 AMACOM, a division of American Management Associations, New York. All rights reserved, Chapter 2.

SUPPLEMENTARY READING

Bridges, E. The Incompetent Teacher: The Challenge and the Response. Philadelphia: Taylor and Francis, 1988.

Cook, Mary F., Editor. The Human Resources Yearbook, 1993/1994 Edition. Englewood Cliffs, NJ: Prentice-Hall Inc., 1993.

Educational Leadership. "Progress in Evaluating Teaching." Educational Leadership 44, 7 (April), entire issue.

Harris, B. Developmental Teacher Evaluation. Rockleigh, NJ: Allyn and Bacon, 1986.

Jenkins, George H. Data Processing: Policies and Procedures Manual. Englewood Cliffs, NJ: Prentice-Hall Inc., 1994.

Klein, Theodore J. "Performance Reviews that Rate an A." Personnel 67, 5 (May 1990), 38–41.

Langlois, D. E.; and M. Colarusso. "Improving Teacher Evaluation." The Education Digest 54 (November 1988), 13–15.

Milman, J., Editor. Handbook of Teacher Evaluation. Beverly Hills, CA: Sage, 1981.

Mohrman, Allan M., Jr.; Susan M. Resnick-West; and Edward E. Lawler III. Designing Performance Appraisal Systems and Organizational Realities. San Francisco: Jossey-Bass, 1989.

Phi Delta Kappa. Teacher Evaluation: The Formative Process. Bloomington, IN: Phi Delta Kappa, 1985.

Plachy, Roger J.; and Sandra J. Plachy. Performance Management. New York: American Management Associations, 1988.

Popham, W. James. Educational Evaluation. Third Edition. Rockleigh, NJ: Allyn and Bacon, 1992.

Popham, W. James. "The Merits of Measurements-Driven Instruction." Phi Delta Kappan 68, 9 (May 1987), 679–83.

Schuler, Randall S.; and Vandra L. Huber. Personnel and Human Resources Management. Fifth Edition. Saint Paul, MN: West Publishing Co., 1993.

Schuler, Randall S.; and James Walker, Editors. Managing Human Resources in the Information Age. Washington: Bureau of National Affairs, 1991.

Szilagi, Andrew, Jr. Management and Performance. Glenview, IL: Scott Foresman, 1988.

Thomas, M. Donald. Performance Evaluation of Educational Personnel. Bloomington, IN: Phi Delta Kappa, 1979.

Werther, William B., Jr. Human Resources and Personnel Management. New York: McGraw Hill Inc., 1993.

Wittrock, M. C., Editor. Handbook of Research on Teaching. Third Edition. New York: MacMillan Publishing, 1986.

PART III

Human Resources Processes: Justice, Continuity, and Information Technology

Chapter 8
Employment Justice

Chapter 9
Employment Continuity

Chapter 10
Information Technology and the Human Resources Function

Part III consists of three chapters designed to:

- Analyze the human resources justice process and ways by which it can be designed to enhance arrangements needed to reach positive solutions regarding internal and external problems generic to organizational life.
- Illuminate policies, procedures, and practices conducive to resolving human resources problems connected with continuity of employment.
- Bring into focus the evolution of information technology and its potential as an organizational resource: how it can be used to help system members to inform or be informed, influence or be influenced, and direct or be directed.

Chapter 8

Employment Justice

CHAPTER OVERVIEW

CHAPTER OBJECTIVES

- Examine provisions for establishing a framework within which the day-to-day system and personnel relationship are conducted.
- Identify arrangements that help to ensure due process for members who believe the system has treated them unfairly.
- Explore the concepts of academic freedom and tenure, their interdependence, and the conditions under which these privileges are established.

CHAPTER TERMS

Academic freedom

Controversial issues

Due Process

Employment security

Grievance

Grievance procedure

Justice system

Legally protected rights

Ombuds practitioner

Tenure

The concept of personnel justice, as discussed here, may be introduced by the observation that in the course of making a living, people are exposed to many kinds of employment insecurities. The threat of losing one's position, status, power, and relative freedom of action or speech has always existed in all types of organizations. To counteract threats to work security, workers have invented and struggled ceaselessly to put into operation a variety of protective arrangements. The scope of modern provisions for lessening work-related anxieties of individuals employed in the field of education can be illustrated by examining protections accorded the classroom teacher; constitutional protection of the First and Fourteenth Amendments, continuing employment (tenure), postemployment financial provisions (retirement benefits), protection from arbitrary treatment (grievance procedure); position and financial safeguards in the event of illness or temporary disability; and the support of unions or teacher associations to maintain and extend ways of continuing member security within the school system. Indeed, human craving for security in the latter part of the twentieth century has become so intense that for many its attainment appears to be an end rather than a means to peace of mind. Preoccupation with position protection in recent years has been brought into focus by emerging developments in legislation, judicial and administrative decisions, collective bargaining agreements, and arbitration awards. Although absolute protection against economic hazards and organizational tyranny is impossible, the school system is obligated to make arrangements to protect its personnel from threats that affect both their productivity and self-realization.

It has been noted that the decade from 1965 to 1975 produced the greatest advances in the area of individual public rights since the birth of the nation; at the same time, it produced the greatest threat to the economic security of public employees. Three reasons have been advanced for this ironic development:

- The severe economic turndown forced employers to take a more rigorous approach to existing personnel practices within budgetary limitations. Thus, position retention by system personnel has taken over customary demands for economic improvements.

- Inefficient personnel practices have been exposed; and public and management demands for productivity, accountability, merit pay, and subcontracting have been renewed.

- Federal and state policies have been established that require removal of employment discrimination barriers and establishment of affirmative action programs that seek to change the composition of both public and private sector work forces.[1]

Another aspect of position security for teachers emerged from United States Supreme Court landmark decisions in the Roth[2] and Sindermann[3] cases. These rulings, handed down on June 29, 1972, have had positive effects on teacher rights and due process. The court reaffirmed the First Amendment rights of teachers to free speech and association. At the same time it held that nontenured teachers are not automatically entitled to due process on dismissal or renewal of contract unless they can show that the actions of the employer deprived them of "liberty" or "property" interest. Thus, the U.S. Constitution was incorporated into the employment contractual relationship of teachers and the public educational institutions that employ them.

CONTEMPORARY DEVELOPMENTS

New and unprecedented developments are taking place in both the public and private sectors to protect and enhance personnel employment rights. These include government legislation (i.e., EEO laws); union contracts that underscore a bilateral approach to personnel security matters; court decisions that have affirmed civil rights of system members in such areas as privacy, freedom of inquiry, freedom of conscience, and due process; legal challenges to the doctrine that management has the right to discharge employees arbitrarily; and the evolving concept that employment is a right to which there must be a process with respect to removal.

More specific insights into some of the areas in which employees have **legally protected rights** have been summarized by Levesque as follows:

1. To collective representation of their employment interests by affiliation with a recognized labor union or employee organization; or to represent their own interest before their employer.

2. To file claims (discrimination, wage and hour, worker's compensation, safety) with administrative compliance agencies to have a complaint or alleged employer wrongdoing adjusted without coercion, harassment, retaliation, or recrimination by the employer.

3. To have their employer treat personal information about them with the utmost confidentiality.

4. To not be the victim of arbitrary or capricious decisions that affect their employment or life in an adverse fashion.

5. To receive fair and reasonable treatment in their employment relationship with their employer.

6. To not be required to violate laws, public policy, or perform any illegal, unethical, or otherwise harmful obligations in their employer's interest.

7. To be treated with the same dignity and respect that would reasonably be afforded to any human being.[4]

Figure 8.1 brings into context the expansion of legally protected employee rights and the application of principles of corrective justice as noted in the preceding list. Examination of Figure 8.1 provides a perspective on one of the most important dimensions of the human resources function, corrective justice. Although the problems identified in Figure 8.1 relating to system treatment for present and future personnel are appearing at a critical period in the history of American education, it seems that their resolution has an important impact on personnel motivation, attitude, and performance outcomes. One of the most vital contributions that the human resources function can make to organizational well-being is the advisory service regarding potential legal challenges to decisions issuing from the personnel-related matters listed in Figure 8.1.

Although school organizations need personnel practices that eliminate discrimination and other forms of unfair treatment in the workplace, most are presently restricted because of a variety of factors, including underrating the role of the human resources function; school system size and resources; failure to effectively integrate the personnel-legal relationship; ignorance of or indifference to the economic, legal, and human implications inherent in personnel rights violations; and weak personnel professional practice. *Few school systems are large or affluent enough to afford full-time legal or personnel specialists.* Consequently, principals, department heads, supervisors, and other administrative officials must become fully involved in the processes of the human resources function, especially as they relate to

Types of Grievance Issues	
Academic freedom	Medical examinations
Addictive behavior	Misconduct
Age discrimination	Obesity
AIDS policy	Overtime
Appraisal, performance	Personal lifestyle
Behavioral standards	Political activism
Civil rights	Polygraph examination
Collective bargaining	Position specifications
Compensation inequities	Pregnancy
Defamation	Privacy rights
Disability Act	Problem personnel
Discharge	Record keeping
Discrimination	Reference checks
Documentation	Safety (health)
Due process	Sexual harassment
Employment-at-will	Slander
Gender discrimination	Speech, freedom of
Handbook, employee	System rights
Information disclosure	Tenure
Interviewing practices	Time off
Layoff	Workers' compensation
Management improprieties	Workplace romance

FIGURE 8.1
Types of grievance issues about which corrective justice has been invoked.

employee rights. There are several lessons to be learned from the host of contemporary challenges to personnel decisions, the high cost of flouting employee rights, and the refusal to accept the emerging legal climate in which school administration must be practiced. Foremost among them are:

- The need for a comprehensive unifying concept of personnel rights that will replace the narrow traditional approaches that rely on reactivity rather than proactivity in thought and action, which tilt toward adjudication as opposed to passive problem resolutions.
- The design and description of explicit, workable, and multifaceted strategies to achieve sustainable personnel safeguards. In addition to enhancing personnel security, the long-term outcome of the approaches should be minimization of expensive litigation, absenteeism, work disruption, loss of personnel commitment and loyalty, and chronic dissatisfaction with employment conditions.

• Generating a system culture that insists on prompt resolution of inevitable day-to-day conflicts, disputes, and contractual differences; providing system members with guarantees against arbitrary and capricious supervisory decisions; and encouraging the location, reporting, analysis, and treatment of security problem sources.

One design tool in the human resources justice system is illustrated in Figure 8.2. The intent of the illustration is to convey Riverpark school system's commitment to provide an orderly method for addressing and resolving employee grievances. The Riverpark embracement of a formal justice system focuses on aims such as: (a) providing an outlet for employee concerns, complaints, and grievances with a systematic approach to problem resolution; (b) reducing the likelihood of a legal claim; (c) taking informal action in advance of a formal grievance invocation; (d) communicating to system personnel its pledge to abide by its own policies and rules; and (e) abiding by the terms of an employment contract.

The human resources justice problems and issues listed in the following are those of which the Riverpark school system is fully conscious and morally committed to address through its justice process in a manner that is right and proper. Our way of achieving balance among conflicting interests is through dispassionate application of justice fundamentals to which we are pledged to adhere. Our framework of the justice process entails:

• Conducting an annual review of all member complaints, grievances, and charges of discrimination to ascertain sources from which they originate and for remedial action when this step is in order.

• Communicating to staff members and position applicants the system's stance on fair treatment for its human resources.

• Adhering to all regulatory requirements regarding discrimination.

• Consulting with legal counsel concerning legal ramifications of provisions in the justice process and its operation.

• Providing programs for administrators and supervisors regarding the justice process and the manner in which it is implemented.

• Establishing informal justice machinery such as appointment of an ombudsman to resolve problems before further action is invoked.

• Encouraging position holders to report actions or events considered to be in violation of system justice standards, such as infringement of the system's code of ethics.

FIGURE 8.2
Contours of the justice process of the Riverpark school system.

EMPLOYMENT SECURITY

Many initiatives to protect personnel from managerial abuses are rooted in the desire for employment tenure. Although the concept of **employment security** is a sound one and should become a fundamental component of personnel policy, when considered from an organizational viewpoint, there are several considerations regarding the concept and its implementation that should be noted. First, school systems want employment security to contribute to several objectives, among which are the inducement of quali-fied people to seek membership, develop creative solutions to position problems, contribute to attainment of objectives, and adhere to and enhance performance culture. Second, employment security and position security are not identical in meaning. The system cannot guarantee that certain positions will not be abolished; merged with other positions; or modified to meet changing economic, contractual, technological, and effi-ciency requirements. Employment security policy is based on the view that the system intends to make full employment available for position holders on the condition that they will be flexible and adaptable in order to accom-modate changes that are inevitable in every position and structure. Third, employment security carries with it a *quid pro quo*. The system has certain behavioral expectations of its members, among which are loyalty, commit-ment, self-initiation of improvement in position performance, and accep-tance and application of the most effective instructional technologies avail-able. However, the history of union contracts indicates that employment security does not lead automatically to commitment to such expectations. In sum, employment security depends on the contributions individuals make to ensure its existence.

In the section that follows, a framework is presented to enable the reader to recognize salient elements involved in the justice process and to make one's understanding of its complexities more concrete. This area of the human resources function, it is worth noting, is one in which the need for reform is compelling and one that poses challenges and presents oppor-tunities for enhancing both individual and organizational aims.

JUSTICE SYSTEM FRAMEWORK

The diagram in Figure 8.3 represents a framework for viewing a human resources **justice system**. The structure is offered as a nucleus for identifying and defining elements involved in the justice process. Important points to note are (a) the structure contains four elements that encompass virtually all aspects of position rights of system members; (b) when grouped together, the elements form the basis for an organizational justice system; (c) the structure includes both formal and informal grievances; (d) the thrust of a justice system is proac-

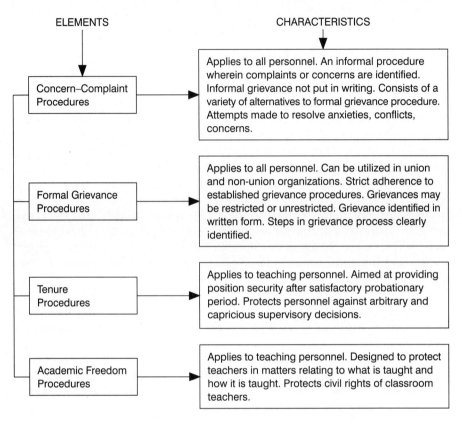

FIGURE 8.3
Human resources justice structure.

tive, meaning that organizational culture focuses on identifying root causes of concerns and conflicts and resolving differences before they become formal grievances; (e) complaints or concerns extrinsic to a contractual agreement are treated as though they are within the boundaries of contractual grievances; (f) the justice system encompasses all system members, although tenure and academic freedom matters involve professional personnel; and (g) concepts underlying the justice system, as well as their execution, represent a means by which to achieve personnel treatment that is right and just to all.

NATURE OF CONCERNS, COMPLAINTS, AND CONFLICTS

Regardless of how well union contracts, personnel policies, codes of ethics, and personnel handbooks are written and understood by the system and its membership, complaints, concerns, and grievances will arise. The idea behind the structure depicted in Figure 8.3 is that organizational planning is basic to resolution of both trivial and serious disagreements that arise between individuals, groups, or the organization and the individual group. These differences between and among individuals, groups, and the organization, are sometimes referred to as *conflicts of interest.*

In Figure 8.3 there is an arbitrary division between complaints and grievances. A complaint, in the broadest sense of the term, is a concern, dissatisfaction, or conflict that is outside the area of a negotiated grievance procedure. A member of the secretarial staff may be concerned about or dissatisfied with work overload, which in his/her particular situation is not covered in the union contract. A **grievance,** on the other hand, as viewed in Figure 8.3, is a specified formal dissatisfaction expressed through an identified procedure (see Figure 8.4). A teacher who has been denied a leave to attend a family funeral (a denial that is in violation of the union contract) may be considered to have a grievance. Thus, a grievance in the narrow view is what the bargaining agreement construes it to be.

IDENTIFICATION OF COMPLAINTS AND GRIEVANCES

One of the important developments occurring in personnel security management, as indicated in Table 8.1, is the increase in the number of channels for identifying and dealing with complaints. The content presented in Table 8.1 relates the functions of a complaint system to each of the structures or procedures for dealing with personnel concerns. Some of the structures involve all functions; others have limited roles. Several of the more important channels for upward communication of personnel complaints are reviewed later.

Perhaps the most important element shown in any complaint system is the traditional **grievance procedure,** shown in Figure 8.4 as a multistep appeal system. Because of its importance in discovering and resolving serious conflicts of interest, more attention will be given to this element in the following section. Grievance administration comprises the greatest amount of activity in bargaining relationships and requires an understanding of how the procedure operates, channels for minimizing formal grievances, and complexities associated with their settlement.

In Table 8.1 various options are presented for identifying and settling disputes *before* they reach the formal grievance stage. One of these is *direct observation* by means of the *supervisory process* or through the *performance appraisal system.* Either approach provides the alert supervisor with clues to unusual or undesirable personnel behavior (such as chronic dissidence, protests, and emotional incidents) or information that brings to the surface perceived violations of an individual's rights. The **ombuds practitioner**

TABLE 8.1
Internal-informal complaint review structure of a school system.

Informal Situational Review: Levels and Options	Complainant Review Options (A)	Complainant Advisory Counseling Options (B)	Informal Investigation Conciliation Mediation Adjudication Actions (C)	Feedback to Executive Review Board (D)
1 Supervisor	•			•
1 Human resources representative	•	•		•
1 Informal organization	•	•		•
1 Ombudsman	•	•		•
1 Performance appraiser(s)	•	•		•
1 Union	•	•		•
2 Office above supervisor	•	•		•
3 Peer review panel	•	•		•
4 Panel resolution committee			•	•
5 System executive review board	•		•	•

Note: Counseling with complainant may be on a confidential basis.

(ombudsman or ombudswoman) is a person designated by the organization to receive and investigate concerns, complaints, disputes, frustrations, and feelings of unfair treatment or system injustices. Benefits that can accrue to the system from this approach are numerous, in many cases including eliminating the need for filing a formal grievance, enabling system members to talk freely and confidentially about complaints and feelings of unfairness, identifying and bringing to the surface problems that are incipient in nature, and discovering inadequate personnel policies and procedures.

Other informal approaches to complaint handling include the *question* or *gripe box,* in which individual concerns are expressed anonymously. The *informal organization* or personnel network is a channel utilized on occasion to bring matters of concern to the attention of system officials. The *exit interview* has been utilized for complaint identification, especially when a member resigns because of failure to satisfactorily resolve a conflict of interest.

In addition to the structures mentioned for identifying real or alleged injustices, complaints, and trouble spots, the organization's *information system* should not be overlooked. A comprehensive information system will have records of formal grievances filed, ombuds reports, performance appraisal reviews, absenteeism and lateness, litigation against the system, resignations, transfers, union concerns about inequities or injustices, dismissals, and external complaints about system personnel policies and procedures. This information, when viewed in the aggregate, may reveal weak links in the organizational chain of components designed to prevent personnel injustice and inequity.

INFORMAL COMPLAINT RESOLUTION

There are at least three alternatives to position holders for resolving conflicts, complaints, inequities, or dissatisfaction arising out of the employment relationship, including (a) informal resolution, (b) grievance machinery, and (c) statutory alternatives to filing a grievance. Table 8.1 shows that informal resolution of complaints is a most essential element of organizational justice, and one which, when conducted properly, is generally beneficial to all concerned. Examination of Table 8.1 indicates various approaches to conflict resolution, uses of which are situational depending upon the circumstances surrounding the complaint. In addition to alternative mechanisms for the complainant to pursue, there are opportunities to counsel with individuals or groups to solve an employment problem in the beginning steps of a complaint-grievance procedure. Complaints invoked may be due to various causes such as real or perceived pay inequity, personality clashes, discrimination, rejection of performance appraisal reports, or inattention by supervisors to violation of system employment practices and policies.

Equally important to the system is that most complaint problems are or can be resolved through informal communication endeavors. One of the key factors in complaint resolution is the skill and knowledge applied to problem resolution by those designees indicated in Table 8.1 charged with this responsibility. Although the use of complaint procedures will vary considerably among school districts, the benefits of informal resolution are too attractive to ignore. They include improvement of working relationships, minimization or avoidance of legal costs and personnel time loss, and those direct and indirect factors that accountants consider, such as the number of steps involved in resolving the problem, lost productivity, personnel involved, resolution time required, and salaries of those involved. Moreover, when the human stress and potential negative publicity factors are taken into consideration, the full cost of informal resolution appears to have considerable advantages over the formal grievance route.

GRIEVANCE MACHINERY AND HUMAN RESOURCES JUSTICE

Although grievance resolution will be discussed in Chapter 13 in connection with contract administration, the subject is treated in this chapter as it relates to general provisions all systems need to enhance personnel security, regardless of stipulations in the negotiated contract for grievance arbitration.

The dictionary defines a *grievance* as a just or supposed ground of complaint. Every school system probably has its share of each. Whether a grievance is real or imagined, automatic means for redressing dissatisfactions are not yet available in every educational institution. Unless there are established procedures for recognizing and initiating action to deal with grievances, suppressed complaints may lead to poor morale and antiorganization behavior. Grievance procedures are usually contained in comprehensive agreements between boards of education and personnel representatives. Some states have teacher tenure laws that include provisions for appeal of school board decisions regarding the contract status of a permanent or tenured teacher.[5] Review of state education collective bargaining laws by the Education Commission of the States indicates grievances are frequently defined in state laws as complaints, by either party, related to application or interpretation of a bargained agreement. Provisions in most state laws, according to the report, (a) grant public employees the right to discuss and file grievance complaints as individuals, not necessarily represented by the employee bargaining unit, and (b) allow for the inclusion of procedures, in bargained agreements, for the resolution of grievance complaints. A significant number of state laws require grievance procedures to be negotiated. Because a number of the state laws list "failure to comply with the terms of the bargained agreement" as an unfair practice, procedures for resolution of griev-ance complaints and unfair practices charges may be the same.[5]

Causes of grievances are many, ranging from misunderstandings to neglect of human problems. The pattern of grievance in educational institu-tions differs somewhat from those in the private sector. School personnel generally have greater job security than nonpublic employees. The nature of employment is different, as are the compensation structure, job classifica-tion system, objectives of the enterprise, and employer–employee relation-ship. Hence, grievance problems are different in educational institutions, but they do exist. Procedures for handling grievances in school systems vary widely. During the first half of the twentieth century, few school systems established formal grievance machinery of any kind for the examination and solution of personnel complaints; most difficulties were handled by an open-door policy of the chief administrator. Unionization of public school employees, especially in the latter years of the 1960s, has done much to stimulate incorporation of formal grievance procedures as an integral part of the collective bargaining process.

Purposes of the Grievance System

Generally speaking, a grievance is considered as an expression of disagree-ment or dissatisfaction about conditions of employment that is brought to the attention of management. Grievance process is an organizational justice system for resolving such disagreements, disputes, or conflicts. Grievance machinery serves various purposes; probably its most vital role is as a chan-nel of communication for system personnel. Security of personnel is enhanced when they know there is a system of justice through which they can appeal discontent or dissatisfaction should the need arise. Moreover, the employee is assured there will be no retaliation for taking an appeal through successive steps in the grievance process if this should be necessary. Several authorities insist that the psychological effect resulting from avail-ability of grievance machinery to organizational personnel is more impor-tant than the degree to which it is utilized. When sincere administrative efforts are made to deal with personnel problems, the number of cases that run the line of appeal is likely to be reduced. This approach entails a will-ingness of administration to encourage personnel to identify sources of dis-satisfaction and to enlist their judgment in remedying unsatisfactory condi-tions. Staff involvement in development of appropriate procedures appears to be indispensable for dealing positively with grievances.

An equally important purpose of grievance machinery is to enable the system to identify potential sources of conflict between the individual and the organization. By examining the nature and incidence of grievances, an alert administration can focus attention on correcting conditions that portend conflict. If the grievance procedure brings to light problems, needs, and expectations of personnel not being met satisfactorily, the planning process can be employed to make necessary adjustments. The grievance system serves also as a check on arbitrary administrative action. The individual administrator is less likely to misuse authority when such behavior is subject to careful scrutiny at every level to which an appeal is carried.

The grievance procedure is an important facet of the collective bargaining process. It serves several purposes, such as providing a means whereby both parties can secure a measure of justice in administration of the agreement, clarifying terms of the contract, and identifying elements in the contract that need revision or clarification at contract renewal time. The procedure serves also as an effective channel of communication from personnel to management.

The Grievance Procedure

The anatomy of most grievance machinery is fairly simple and consists of a prescribed series of steps or line of appeals, beginning with presentation of the problem to the immediate supervisor. If the system member finds no redress at one level, he/she may take the case to consecutively higher officials in order of authority, for example, to the principal, superintendent, board of education, and finally the state education agency. There is usually a committee that acts in an advisory capacity and as a liaison between the aggrieved and the administration representative.

Figure 8.4 illustrates a grievance procedure showing (a) successive steps involved, (b) bilateral representation, (c) line of appeal, and (d) arbitration as a final step if actions in previous steps fail to resolve the grievance.

The number of grievance cases is lessened when administrators at the operating level closest to the employee are able to identify sources of discontent. Sensing an incipient problem and dealing with it promptly, tactfully, and informally often forestalls the need for complicated grievance procedures.

Foremost among conditions necessary for dealing with staff discontent, complaints, misunderstandings, or dissatisfactions are the following:

- A policy declaration by the board of education that clearly indicates its intent toward expression and consideration of grievances (see Figure 8.5).

- Administrative procedures for implementing grievance policy. These include preparation of a personnel guide or handbook indicating what constitutes a grievance, how the grievance is presented, to whom it is presented initially, steps in the line of appeal with the routine to be followed in each step, and the time limits within which each phase of the grievance process should be completed.

- Constant assessment of conditions of employment so as to locate and deal with personnel problems.

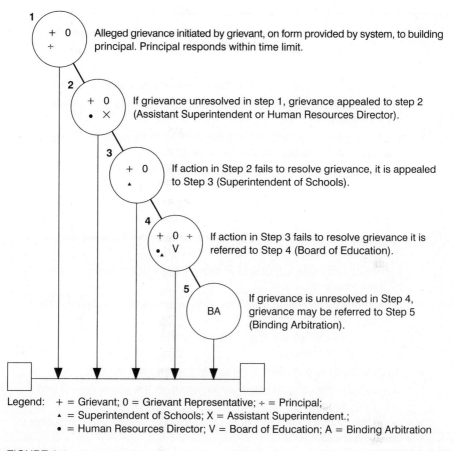

Legend: + = Grievant; 0 = Grievant Representative; ÷ = Principal;
          ▲ = Superintendent of Schools; X = Assistant Superintendent.;
          • = Human Resources Director; V = Board of Education; A = Binding Arbitration

FIGURE 8.4
A grievance procedure.

The policy-procedural checklist shown in Figure 8.5 is intended to illustrate types of elements utilized to maintain an orderly method for addressing employment complaints and grievances.

Several approaches can be employed to reduce the number of personnel grievances. These include improvement of the total personnel process, of conditions of employment, of leadership styles of administrative personnel directly responsible for implementing collective bargaining contracts, and of the manner in which any grievance within the system is processed.

In summary, systematization of grievance handling can help the system to minimize discontent and dissatisfaction and thus enhance personnel cooperation. Careful attention to individual grievances improves the chances that conflict will be dealt with in a positive manner and result in individual

- Has the school system established a formal policy for addressing employment complaints and grievances?
- Is there a union agreement establishing grievance machinery?
- Does the policy encourage consideration of any and all grievances?
- Do the policy and procedures provide ways of ensuring a receptive hearing for the grievant?
- What provisions are made for independent assessment of an issue not resolved to the satisfaction of either party?
- Is there a provision in the policy for discussing situations not covered in the agreement?
- Do system members in the resolution levels (Figure 8.2) have the knowledge and skills to interpret and apply resolution policies and procedures?
- Have criteria been established to determine whether the complaint or grievance is factual?
- Have criteria been established for determining whether there is a basis for the complaint?
- What procedures exist to deal with solution of potential problems before they become real problems?
- What procedures are established for presenting complaints or grievances to the system?
- Are time limits specified for filing a grievance at each level?
- Is the informal resolution stage written into both the system policy and union agreement?
- Does the system have checkpoints for reviewing answers to complaints and grievances?
- Are the system's policies and procedures for filing and handling grievances conveyed to all members on the payroll?
- What steps are taken to provide the grievant with assistance in presenting the claim in required form?
- What steps have been taken procedurally to ensure a receptive hearing for the grievant?
- Has the formal grievance process been reviewed independently for inclusion of norms and tests designed to meet courtroom standards?

FIGURE 8.5
Policy and procedural checklist for reviewing the grievance machinery of a school system.

adjustment. Success in this effort will contribute to the ability of the individual school unit and the system to carry out plans.

TENURE

Tenure, in the broadest sense, embodies a system designed to provide educators with continuing employment during efficient service and establishes an orderly procedure to be followed before services are terminated. Salient features of the tenure system include:

- Completion of a specified probationary period, construed to mean a temporary appointment during which time the individual is carefully supervised and appraised in terms of ability to render efficient service to the school organization.
- Automatic tenure status at the end of the probationary period to personnel who meet performance standards.
- An orderly procedure for dismissal of personnel. This includes provision for notifying the individual that his/her services are unsatisfactory as well as reasonable opportunity to show improvement before notification of intent to dismiss is given.
- Notification of intent to terminate services of the individual in the event that desired improvement in performance has not been attained. Written notice of intent to dismiss details specific reasons for the contemplated action.
- A hearing before local school authorities that provides an opportunity for the affected staff member to defend himself/herself against the charges.
- The right to appeal an adverse decision to higher educational authorities and to the courts.

The meaning and operation of tenure laws are not always understood by some persons within the professional ranks or by many laypersons. Perhaps this misunderstanding has given rise to the relatively high incidence of tenure litigation as well as to refusal of certain states to enact ironclad statewide tenure legislation.

The following discussion considers the legal nature of tenure. In general, tenure is construed to be a privilege granted by the state rather than an obligation the state owes to the educator. The latter has no inherent right to permanent employment merely because he/she has complied with state certification requirements or served a probationary period during which satisfactory service has been rendered in the eyes of the employer. It is generally held by the courts that a tenure statute is not in the nature of a contract between the state and the teachers affected by it, that an act of the legislature is only an expression of current legislative policy, and that the acts of one legislature do not necessarily bind future legislatures unless the intent to do so is clear.[6]

The phrase *permanent employment* is frequently the cause of many misinterpretations of tenure legislation. Customary practice is to grant permanent tenure after an individual has served a probationary period. Permanent tenure, however, does not necessarily mean the local board of education has no authority to make changes affecting persons who have gained tenure status. It does not mean, for example, that the board, so long as its actions are not arbitrary and capricious, cannot transfer a teacher from one school to another. Tenure of employment and tenure of assignment are not necessarily synonymous. Nor does it mean that tenured teachers cannot be reassigned to different tenure positions. If the board decides to reduce the size of the staff because of declining enrollments, existence of tenure legislation does not prevent the board from taking such action. In brief, it is generally not the intent of tenure laws to prevent boards of education from making necessary changes involving tenured personnel. Permanent employment does not mean an absolute absence of change in conditions of employment. If this were so, administrators would be powerless to cope with the day-to-day personnel problems with which they are confronted.

Among objectives most frequently cited for establishing tenure for professional educators are:

- Security of employment during satisfactory service.
- Protection of personnel against unwarranted dismissal.
- Academic freedom in the classroom.
- Permanent employment for best-qualified personnel.
- Staff stability and position satisfaction.
- Freedom outside the classroom commensurate with that of any other citizen.
- Liberty to encourage student freedom of inquiry and expression.

State activity in tenure legislation is generally defended on the basis of social benefit. The state seeks to improve the school system through the instrumentality of tenure, which is designed in part to protect the people and their children from incompetent teaching. The state's purpose in protecting the teacher against arbitrary acts inspired by political, personal, or capricious motives is to grant freedom required to render effective professional service. Tenure legislation is not intended by the state to establish an occupational haven for the unqualified.

Thus, tenure is designed to protect not only the interest of personnel but also the state, the system, and its clients. Few matters in school administration are more in need of attention than seeing to it that tenure laws serve the social interest. Every system having the authority to grant tenure can contribute by engaging in more effective deliberation before granting tenure. Tenure laws of most states can be materially improved. In some instances, for example, the law provides only token personnel protection.

Opportunities at the local level to improve tenure by other than legislative means are considerable; to this end, efforts of personnel administration can be properly directed. Selective elimination of probationary personnel; clarification of policies on transfer, reassignment and promotion; definition of seniority rank in the event of staff reduction; development of procedures to cope with reduction in status or compensation; determination of means by which probationary teachers are dismissed; clarification of board policies on tenure; and related measures will help to provide desired staff competence and security requisite to effective performance.

The Tenure Process

Treatment of tenure legislation in the preceding sections was brief and selective, intended to show the interrelationship between tenure problems and human resource administration. The following discussion examines the tenure process more fully to illustrate its role in contributing to goals of school administration.

Although it is clearly not in the interest of taxpayers, children and youth, or the system to allow marginal performers to gain continuing employment status, it is in the interests of society to prevent loss or dismissal of competent personnel. The tenure process must be considered as one means by which both ends can be served. Discussions of various aspects of the process, including the probationary period, the tenure privilege, termination of service, and the right of appeal, follow. Suggestions offered are intended to be illustrative rather than prescriptive.

The Probationary Period

Continuing appointments to the school staff represent long-term commitments in administrative judgment, public trust, and budget appropriations. In view of these commitments, the probationary period is considered here because of its strategic importance in determining tenure.

There are at least three purposes to be served during the probationary period. One has to do with assessment of the individual, that is, his/her competency and potential, compatibility as a member of the working team, and ability to serve future staff needs of the organization. Another purpose is validation of the original selection and placement. The probationary period provides an opportunity over an extended period of time to determine the degree to which the original choice and placement have conformed to expectations. Finally, and most important, the probationary period provides an opportunity for selective elimination, permitting the organization to employ on a permanent basis only those who have attained the excellence required for such appointments.

Several major questions relating to the probationary period should be considered, for procedural reasons, by boards of education:

- Are *experienced* teachers new to the system required to serve a probationary period? If so, what should be the length of the probationary period?
- Should notice of unsatisfactory work be given during the probationary period? If so, how frequently?
- Should professional growth requirements be established for probationary teachers? If so, what should be the nature and scope of the requirements?
- Should teachers be allowed to serve more than one probationary period?
- Should substitute service count toward fulfillment of the probationary period?
- What procedure should be followed when dismissal of probationary teachers is contemplated?

Answers to these and other questions pertaining to teachers who have not yet been granted tenure are set forth in laws of some states. In other states, the laws are completely silent. Regardless of the presence or absence of specific legislation, many problems can be avoided if the local board of education takes positive steps to clarify procedures in effect during the probationary period. When policies and procedures are reduced to written form (policy and personnel handbooks) in order to provide greater understanding by those affected, solution of probation problems is facilitated.

Measures to be taken by the organization during the probationary period to ensure a capable and stable teaching corps include:

- Consistent attention of the administration to induction and development of the probationer.
- Provision of funds for continuing staff development programs.
- Consistent appraisal of and counseling with probationary personnel by the administrative head of each attendance unit, aided by the supervisor, department head, and key teachers assigned to this role..
- Continuity in the selection process, including early dismissal of those decidedly inferior or barely acceptable; administrative decisions relating to marginal probationers are among the most important decisions relating to tenure.

It is recognized by educators that factors that can interfere with or prevent development of a capable staff are numerous and vexing. For example, some administrators ignore qualitative aspects of staffing, with the consequence that the unfit are permitted to gain tenure status. Moreover, as the proportion of ineffective staff members increases, the ability of the district to recruit and retain superior personnel tends to decrease. The waste of time, money, administrative effort, and educational opportunities incurred through admission of unsatisfactory personnel to the profession is incalculable. Opportunities to minimize such errors of judgment are available in the recruitment, selection, appraisal, and development processes.

The Tenure Privilege

Acceptable practice in implementing tenure consists of assurance of continuing employment after successful fulfillment of the probationary period, termination of employment only for defensible cause, and limitations on the dismissal procedure. In return for the tenure privilege, all tenured personnel are expected to assume certain obligations, such as adherence to the code of ethics for the teaching profession and fulfillment of a psychological contract. The notion of a psychological contract has implications such as the following:

- The individual has a variety of expectations of the organization and the organization has a variety of expectations of the individual.

- These expectations include how much work is to be performed for how much pay and the pattern of rights, privileges, and obligations between the individual and the organization.

- The organization enforces its view of the contract through authority. The individual enforces his/her view of the contract through upward influence, whether as a free agent or as a member of the union.

- These elements are not written into any formal agreement between the individual and the organization, yet they operate powerfully as determinants of behavior.[7]

The reciprocal character of tenure assumes that the local board of education will protect employment security of personnel during efficient service. It assumes also that personnel will fulfill obligations attending the service for which they are employed.

Some of the tenure problems that create difficulty eventuate in dismissal proceedings; others may involve transfer and reassignment, reduction in salary, demotion, and abolition of positions because of enrollment, curriculum, or financial exigencies. Although the right of administrators to transfer and reassign personnel is generally recognized by the courts, demotions under some tenure laws violate the tenure agreement. It can be argued cogently that administration has the obligation to accord all personnel to be demoted in status or salary the right to be notified, given a written statement of reasons for the action, and afforded a fair hearing.

Termination of Service

From time to time, school districts will have reason to dismiss tenured personnel. In many cases dismissal is not so much a reflection on the individual as it is on the recruitment, selection, placement, and appraisal processes. As almost everyone knows, there are personnel whose immoral, intemperate, or insubordinate behavior leaves the administration no choice but dismissal. Legal channels exist for accomplishing this purpose. But the individual whose regressive inefficiency becomes the cause for dismissal proceedings is another problem, especially if the incidence of such cases is excessive. Although the reasons why competent persons gradually become incompetent have not been clearly isolated, there are grounds for assuming that some of the responsibility lies with the institution. Some staff members stagnate because of lack of opportunity; some become inefficient because of excessive teaching loads; some fail because of lack of proper supervision; some become embittered as a result of a lack of adequate grievance procedures; and some do not succeed in spite of their willingness. The point of concern here is that the organization must not fail in its effort to provide optimum climate and conditions of employment conducive to success. Until the organization does its utmost to match the person and the position and to create conditions requisite to success, dismissal is unjust. Termination of service should be regarded as a last resort, to be used only when all other remedies have failed.

Figure 8.6 illustrates a model for personnel-retention resolution. If Option 1 is chosen as the solution, it involves at last three suboptions; if Option 2 is selected, several possibilities are available by which the decision can be imple-

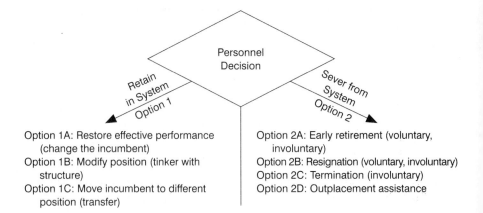

FIGURE 8.6
Model for personnel retention-termination resolution.

mented. Of the three possible courses of action that can be taken if a decision is made to retain the incumbent, certainly the possibility of restoring an individual to a satisfactory level of performance cannot be overlooked.

Notice of the decision to separate a tenured teacher from the system should follow accepted legal procedure and, in addition, should provide ample time for the affected teacher to search for another position. Causes and procedures for dismissing a tenured teacher are generally set forth in the statutes, although there is considerable variation in statutory language and interpretations possible under various state tenure laws. In most tenure laws, notice of intent to dismiss must be given within a specified time limit prior to dismissal. Similarly, it is usually held that if the teacher intends to withdraw from service, school authorities will be given notice in ample time to secure a replacement. State laws typically require a notice of 30 to 60 days.

A fair hearing, preceded by written notice of intent to dismiss (including a statement of charges against the accused), are among essentials of an acceptable tenure law. Those in charge of the hearing should provide opportunity for the accused teacher to be heard in his/her own defense, permit the accused to have counsel and to present witnesses, and prepare a stenographic record of the hearing to be available in case of appeal.

In the event that results of the hearing are not in favor of the accused and the dismissal action stands, the statutes generally provide opportunity for appeals through administrative recourse to the state superintendent or state board of education as well as ultimate legal recourse through the courts. In the Roth and Sindermann cases referred to previously, it has been noted that if a primary or dominant reason for *not* renewing a teacher's contract is based on a real claim that falls within the ambit of the First Amendment free speech clause of the U.S. Constitution, a hearing is required by the **due process** clause of the Fourteenth Amendment.

Reasons for Dismissal.   Although the discussion here is focused on ineffective performance as the reason for termination of an individual's employment, there are other bases, as outlined earlier in the text. Legislation governing employment in the public schools usually prescribes reasons for which an employee may be dismissed. A systematic termination plan goes beyond statutory prescriptions for dismissal and clearly defines in the organization or personnel manual the reasons for and the procedures by which a dismissal action is carried out. The reasons for putting the termination plan in writing are numerous, including a uniform approach to applying the same criteria to all personnel; a system document that is explained to each newly appointed staff member; a formal plan, which is essential in the event of litigation; and a means by which the system clarifies for all concerned what is meant by ineffective performance, how it is determined, and steps that are taken to prevent its occurrence.

Dismissal Procedure. The formidable array of constraints against severance of personnel makes development of and adherence to a systematic dismissal procedure an organizational obligation of high priority. Guidelines are outlined here and in Figure 8.7 to bring into focus the significance of the dismissal procedure to both the individual and to the system. Examination of the model shown in Figure 8.7 indicates that it is based on these considerations:

- Implicit in every contract of service is the assumption that the individual performer will carry out contractual obligations.

- Implicit in every contract is the assumption that the system will assist the individual through supervision, facilities, and related means to perform his/her obligations.

- The system has a right and a responsibility to require that the individual effectively perform the services agreed to in the contract.

- The system has the right and responsibility to conduct its operations with maximum efficiency and effectiveness. In the event that individuals do not perform according to expectations, the system has the responsibility to maintain and to adhere to an orderly and equitable arrangement for personnel separation.

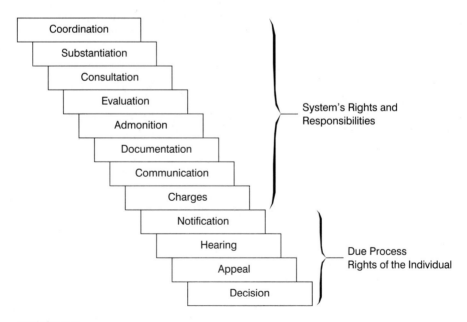

FIGURE 8.7
Model of the dismissal procedure.

• Protection of the rights of the individual through contractual, legal, and quasi-legal arrangements as well as through evolving social values has come to occupy a central position in any consideration of termination of the service agreement.

• The system has the obligation to accord the individual due process in any action initiated to terminate services. Due process, as viewed by the United States Supreme Court in the landmark case of *Goldberg* v. *Kelly,* includes the following elements: (a) timely and adequate notice detailing the reason for the proposed termination, (b) effective opportunity to defend oneself by confronting adverse witnesses, (c) opportunity to cross-examine witnesses, (d) adequate notice before the hearing, (e) opportunity to be heard, and (f) assurance that the decision makers' conclusions will be based only on evidence presented during the hearing and that they will be impartial (*Goldberg* v. *Kelly,* 397 U.S. 254).

Symptoms of Tenure Malfunction

As a trend toward collective behavior of personnel gathers impetus, so do the demands for elimination of state tenure laws. Two studies of teacher tenure in Pennsylvania, one covering the period 1940–70 and another reviewing the years 1971–76, indicate that the number of teachers who have been dismissed for all the reasons permissible is considerably below normal personnel standards.[8] The second study (1971–76) notes that between 1971 and 1976 there were 505 public school districts employing an average of 113,146 teachers, K through 12, in Pennsylvania. The 11 teacher dismissal cases owing to incompetence appealed to the Secretary of Education during the five-year period actually represent only .000097 percent of the total teaching staff. Dividing this percentage by five gives a yearly figure for teacher incompetence cases of .000019 percent of the teachers in Pennsylvania. On an annual basis, the probability of a teacher's being charged with incompetence was one in a half million.[9]

Numerous criticisms have been made of tenure laws. These include the harmful effect of the incompetent tenured teacher on the growth and development of pupils, the negative impact of the incompetent tenured teacher on total staff effectiveness, and impediments to system mission achievement created by tenure malfunction. The assault on tenure has been linked to the accountability movement, based on the hypothesis that tenure and accountability are incompatible. Critics of the tenure concept view tenure as the "fool's fortress," irrevocable retention, leading to more complacency, having no contemporary relevance, and having no counterpart in other professions.[10]

The protections many teachers are now enjoying—*contractual protection* as well as *legislative protection*—appear to be in for increasing attack and probable modification. The American Association of School Administrators, noting popular as well as professional disillusionment with the consequences of teacher tenure, has advocated alternative measures to deal with tenure-related problems.[11]

Federal retirement laws may provide the final incentive to consider elimination of tenure. The unintended effect of the legislation is that lifting the retirement age will cause legislatures, school boards, and college and university governing boards to rethink their tenure policies. As courts in recent years have accorded all teachers the full protection of the First Amendment, one of the major reasons for the existence of tenure has been removed.[12]

Tenure Law Developments. Data regarding tenure law status (1994) compiled by the Education Commission of the States indicates that:

- Forty-two states have teacher tenure or continuing contract laws.
- Six states have no tenure provisions.
- There are different rules for different cities with first-class designations.
- Some states provide continuing contracts only; no tenure provisions.
- Some states provide no tenure but establish continuing contracts after successful completion of a probationary contract.
- Four states have repealed tenure laws, including Colorado, Massachusetts, New Mexico, and Oklahoma.
- The tenure repeal provision of the Massachusetts Education Reform Act of 1993 has been described as a balance between the overriding interest of students not to be subjected to incompetent teachers and the significant interests of teachers in fundamental fairness.[13]

From the data available it is becoming clear that gradual modifications are taking place in state tenure laws. Whether in the form of tenure repeal, tightening of due process requirements, and changes in other aspects of tenure privileges, steps are being taken to remove barriers to removing those individuals who cannot or will not meet performance standards.

Before conducting the last rites for the tenure system, with all of the abuses to which it has been subjected in the twentieth century, this observation is worth making: although there is widespread discontent with tenure systems, part of the dissatisfaction arises from the assumption that tenure protects incompetents. The existence of incompetents in any organization, however, cannot be blamed totally on legislative provisions designed to protect position security of teachers *as well as the school system.* Available evidence indicates that inaction of school boards and administrators in dismissal and supervisory efforts deserves substantial blame.[14] Tenure systems do not prevent school systems from designing effective appraisal and personnel development processes. They do not prevent the administration from taking action against incompetents. Both tenure laws and contemporary court cases reinforce the concept that teacher tenure establishes employment security within a framework of due process.

Unions, courts, governments, and school systems have gone to considerable lengths in the twentieth century to provide for personnel security, which is one of the basic psychological needs of humankind. Tenure for educators, protection under civil service for many classes of noncertified personnel, contracts with seniority provisions, due process, and grievance systems are illustrative. Complete security for any individual, however, is an illusion. Fluctuations in the economic system, school closings and consolidations, individual health, and performance obsolescence all affect security. Without extensive opportunity for individual self-development and without better processes for staff liberation through motivation, security will become more of an illusion.

ACADEMIC FREEDOM AND EMPLOYMENT SECURITY

Free minds for free humans is in the tradition of the liberal democratic ideal. Accordingly, freedom of thought and expression are crucial concerns of education in a democracy and of the human resources function responsible for its attainment. If children and youth are to be free to learn, the teacher must be free to teach. By protecting one freedom, the system seeks to ensure the other. Although data are not available to indicate the full extent of problems relating to **academic freedom** in educational institutions, there is considerable evidence that threats to the intellectual, political, and personal freedom of the teaching community do exist.

A Working Definition

The concept of academic freedom means different things to different people. To some it means absence of restraint on scholarship; to others it means the right to present conflicting and unpopular points of view in the classroom. Some would place certain limitations on academic freedom; others would not. Some maintain that academic freedom is a matter that concerns only university faculties; others hold that it refers to the liberty to inquire, to discuss, and to interpret any aspect of culture at all levels of instruction. Some believe it refers solely to teacher freedom. Increasingly, it is argued that student freedom is equally involved. Krug has suggested, for example, that the definition of intellectual freedom has two parts: (a) the right to believe what one wants on any subject and to express one's beliefs orally or graphically, publicly or privately, as one deems appropriate and (b) total and complete freedom of access to all information and ideas regardless of the medium of communication used.[15] A statement by the American Civil Liberties Union on academic freedom reads as follows:

> Academic freedom and responsibility are here defined as the liberty and obligation to study, to investigate, to present and interpret, and to discuss facts and ideas concerning all branches and fields of learning. No limitations are implied other than those required by generally accepted standards of responsible scholarship. The right within and without institutions of learning to be free from any arbitrary limitations of investigations, expression, and discussion should be inviolate.[16]

The preceding statements on academic freedom are buttressed by a decision of the U.S. Supreme Court, noted in Figure 8.8.

The concept of both academic freedom and tenure are constantly undergoing redefinition. Both are interdependent and inseparable. Recent writings and court decisions, according to one report, "reflect oppositions to the excesses of absolute freedom and abandoned responsibility and provide a groundwork for narrowing the current broad definition of academic freedom."[17]

In the following discussion, *academic freedom* refers to the extent to which professional personnel are able to exercise intellectual independence and encourage it in the classroom. As such it is not to be considered a special kind of privilege for the educator but a condition essential to free inquiry for the student and the teacher, which is basic to freedom of learning. *Tenure* is construed to mean the right to protection against arbitrary or capricious reasons. Conditions of tenure do not carry with it the right to unbridled behavior within or outside the classroom. Tenure does not translate into sinecure or unlimited security.

The U.S. Supreme Court on academic freedom

Our Nation is deeply committed to safeguarding academic freedom, which is of transcendent value to all of us and not merely to the teachers concerned. That freedom is therefore a special concern of the First Amendment, which does not tolerate laws that cast a pall of orthodoxy over the classroom. "The vigilant protection of constitutional freedoms is nowhere more vital than in the community of American schools" . . . The classroom is peculiarly the "marketplace of ideas." The Nation's future depends upon leaders trained through wide exposure to that robust exchange of ideas which discovers truth "out of a multitude of tongues, [rather] than through any kind of authoritative selection."

Keyishian v. Board of Regents, 385 U.S. 589 at 603 (1967)

FIGURE 8.8
U.S. Supreme Court decision on academic freedom.

Forms of Restraints and Pressures

It is no secret that there are many individuals and communities who take issue with concepts of intellectual freedom expressed in the preceding paragraphs. Efforts to ban ideas, limit information, remove textbooks, and censor libraries and school curricula are commonplace.

Examination of restraints and pressures imposed on students, teachers, and administrators provides a wide range of illustrations. These include:

- Elimination from classroom or library certain textbooks or resource materials unacceptable to a particular segment of society (the annual total of book banning cases remains constant—approximately 300 cases—according to the American Library Association's office for intellectual freedom).[18]

- Pressures to punish personnel for nonconforming statements concerning sex, race, ethnic cultures, nudity, pornography, drugs, and literary works deemed offensive.

- Restrictions on teaching of allegedly **controversial issues,** such as nuclear war, welfare rights, communism, socialism, fascism, the right of organized labor to bargain collectively, sex education, building a new social order, poverty, AIDS, abortion, air and water pollution, integration, gay rights, evolution, and discrimination.

- The 1989 banning by a Mobile, Alabama, judge of 36 textbooks from the state's public schools on the grounds that the books promoted "the religion of secular humanism."

- Restrictions on teacher participation in political activities.

- Requirement that all educators in institutions receiving state aid take a special loyalty oath.

- Restrictions on the purchase of conspicuously controversial teaching materials.

- Books by authors considered homosexual.

- Restrictions prohibiting educators from holding public office.

- Dismissal of teachers who take the Fifth Amendment.

- Legislation forbidding a certain subject to be taught.

- Denial of permission for student organizations to invite guest speakers who are "controversial."

- Restrictions on wearing apparel of students and teachers.

- Denial of the right of teachers to join education associations or unions.

- Elimination of experimental curricula, methods, or textbook series on the grounds that they are "progressive," "liberal," "ultraliberal," or otherwise conflicting with established views.

- Restrictions on the expression of political, economic, or religious views of teachers.
- Works by "un-American" authors.
- Demands for removal of programs that violate constitutionally protected rights of privacy.

The concern about these and other forms of restraint on academic and personal freedom of public school personnel is that safeguards are needed in school systems to ensure conditions conducive to effective conduct of the teaching-learning process. However, difficulties in achieving these safeguards are formidable. There are boards of education who see no point in establishing policies on academic and personal freedom. Others have come to believe that limitations on these freedoms are both desirable and necessary.

An example of the latter point of view, which was advanced in policy form but not adopted by a local school district in Pennsylvania, is shown in Figure 8.9. There are those, however, who take issue with attempts to stifle censorship:

> . . . that the public school curriculum is sacrosanct and that protests against it are inherently illicit.

> We could contemplate these issues more clearly, and discuss them more civilly if we could set aside the notion of censorship in the public schools.

> For too long, opportunistic charges of censorship have, like censorship itself, squelched democratic deliberation.[19]

The following sections are devoted to examination of the kinds of constructive action that can be taken by boards of education, administrators, communities, and teachers to ensure freedom of thought and information.

Human Rights and Administrative Responsibility

Local control of certain aspects of public education has lost ground in the wake of recent legislation and judicial decisions. In a changing social order where the issue of human rights is ever in the forefront, rights of school personnel have not gone unnoticed. Court decisions favor strict adherence to safeguarding civil rights of teachers and other school personnel. There are indications that administrative authoritarianism and paternalism have been dealt the coup de grace by courts and legislatures, and that the movement to implement the theory and practice of human rights will move forward, especially in educational institutions, which are supposed to be one of the important guarantors of human freedom. It is worth noting that a U.S. District Court ruling on a case involving academic freedom includes the fol-

---

Proposed school board policy

The proposed Octorara school board policy would prohibit the following.

- psychological and psychiatric treatment that is designed to affect behavioral, emotional or attitudinal characteristics;

- nonacademic personality tests;

- values clarification, including use of moral dilemmas, discussion of religious or moral standards, role playing or open-ended discussion of moral issues, including life/death decision exercises;

- sensitivity training, group encounter sessions, self evaluation, magic circle techniques or any strategy designed for self disclosure;

- discussing sexual deviancy, i.e., sexual behavior other than in the context of family values and reproduction;

- hypnotic techniques, imagery, centering, suggestology and guided fantasy techniques;

- witchcraft and the occult, including horoscopes and zodiac signs;

- death education, including abortion, euthanasia, suicide and use of violence;

- political affiliations and beliefs of student or family;

- questionnaires on personal life, views and family;

- personal diaries;

- and critical appraisals of other individuals with whom the students have close family relationships.

FIGURE 8.9
Illustration of a proposed school board policy viewed by a teachers' union as curriculum restriction and censorship.
Source: Pennsylvania State Education Association, VOICE XXIV 10 (September 1993), 4.

lowing salient points: (a) academic freedom is a constitutional right; (b) that right is a variable depending on the level of the education involved and decisions made by the board regarding the nature of the presentation of the educational program; and (c) through a collective bargaining agreement the constitutional right of academic freedom may be bargained away.[20]

Responsibilities of the Board

To an appreciable extent, establishment and maintenance of academic and personal freedom of school personnel depend on board of education leadership. This state of affairs is in keeping with the doctrine of organizational accountability, which is construed to mean the responsibility of authorities in an organization for the actions of personnel under their direction. If development and maintenance of intellectual independence in the school system are to be encouraged, the board of education must take certain steps to see that these conditions are established.

What steps can be taken by the board of education to encourage and protect the freedom essential to growth of the democratic ideal? Although the board can do many things, its first obligation is to understand clearly the purposes of education in a democratic society, for the events that take place in a classroom (the discussion, the methods, and the materials employed) must be appraised in terms of purpose.

Another step the board can take is to make clear the conduct it expects the staff to maintain within and outside the academic environment. Some of the problems that need to be resolved in doing so are suggested by the following questions: How does the board expect the staff to deal with controversial issues? Does the board feel responsible for institutionalizing the basic moral and intellectual commitments inherent in a democracy? Does the board perceive development of curriculum as a professional task? If the board is committed to this principle, does it resist pressures to eliminate certain textbooks? Does it resist attempts to change those parts of the curriculum not approved by the professional staff? Does the board support the principle that a teacher outside the classroom has no less freedom than any other citizen? Does it support freedom to express one's convictions on political, economic, and religious subjects? These and other issues call for policies by the board of education that will safeguard personnel in their responsibilities as teachers and citizens.

In brief, the board and the community have an important responsibility for establishing the climate within which academic freedom can flourish. Although a precise formula for doing this has not yet been written, much can be accomplished if the board is alert to its responsibilities for maintaining intellectual freedom.

These responsibilities include willingness to objectively examine all criticisms of the school and its staff, avoid hasty action to satisfy pressure groups, establish machinery for dealing with charges or attacks against school personnel, and develop policies consonant with freedom of expression. Figure 8.10 illustrates policy and procedures employed in one school system to deal with one facet of academic freedom.

Responsibilities of the Administrator

The administrator has the difficult and delicate responsibility for maintaining academic and personal freedom of the school staff. The task is to give

Policy Statement

Training for effective citizenship is accepted as one of the major purposes of the Atlanta Public Schools. The instructional program developed to achieve this purpose properly places great emphasis on teaching about our American heritage, the rights and privileges we enjoy as citizens, and the citizenship responsibilities that must be assumed in maintaining our American ways of life. In training for effective citizenship, it is frequently necessary for students to study issues that are controversial. In considering such issues it shall be the purpose of the Atlanta Public Schools to recognize the student's right:

- To study any controversial issue that has political, economic, or social significance and concerning which, at the appropriate level, he/she should begin to have an opinion.
- To have free access to all relevant information, including the materials that circulate freely in the community.
- To study under competent instruction in an atmosphere of freedom from bias and prejudice.
- To form and express opinions on controversial issues without thereby jeopardizing relationships with teacher or the school.

Procedures to Implement Policy

- Good teaching of subjects involving controversial issues requires particular skill and so far as possible only teachers of superior training and experience will be assigned subjects in which a large body of material deals with such issues.
- The approach of the teacher to controversial topics must be impartial and objective.
- Teachers should use the following criteria for determining the appropriateness of certain issues for consideration as a part of the curriculum:
  a. The treatment of the issue in question must be within the range, knowledge, maturity, and competence of the students.
  b. There should be unbiased and objective study materials and other learning aids available from which a reasonable amount of data pertaining to all aspects of the issue can be obtained.

FIGURE 8.10
Policy statement and procedures governing the teaching of controversial issues in the Atlanta, Georgia, public schools.

c. The consideration of the issue should require only as much time as is needed for satisfactory study by the class, but sufficient time should be provided to cover the issue adequately.

d. The issue should be current, significant, real, and important to the students and teacher. Significant issues are those that in general concern considerable numbers of people, and are related to basic principles or at the moment are under consideration by the public, press, and [electronic media].

- In discussing controversial issues, the teacher should keep in mind that the classroom is a forum and not a committee for producing resolutions or dogmatic pronouncements. The class should feel no responsibility for reaching an agreement.

- It is the teacher's responsibility to bring out the facts concerning controversial questions. The teacher has the right to express his/her opinions, but in doing so it is important that the students understand that it is the teacher's own opinion and is not to be accepted by them as an authoritative answer.

- The principal bears a major responsibility for the administration and supervision of the curriculum, including the selection of materials and methods of instruction. The principal must be continuously aware of what is being taught in his/her school.

- A teacher who is in doubt concerning the advisability of discussing certain issues in the classroom should confer with his/her principal as to the appropriateness of doing so. If the principal and the teacher are unable to agree, the issue should be referred to the Assistant Superintendent for Instruction or through him/her to the Superintendent.

- It is recognized that citizens of the community have a right to protest to the school administration when convinced that unfair and prejudiced presentations are being made by any teacher. In considering such protests, the Board of Education shall provide for a hearing in accordance with American principles of justice if in its judgment such a procedure is required. Teachers of subjects involving controversial issues are assured of the Board's support, if it is found that such teachers have been subjected to unfair criticism or partisan pressures from individuals or groups.

FIGURE 8.10, *continued*

Source: Adapted from Atlanta Public Schools, Atlanta, Georgia.

support, meaning, and direction to principles of academic and personal freedom. This means, among other things, that the administrator:

- Understands and studies our civilization, its cultural heritage, values, and ideals; without this understanding, ability to provide democratic leadership is limited.
- Seeks diversity in employment of personnel, inasmuch as beliefs and attitudes of the teaching staff determine the extent to which free exercise of the intellect is achieved in the classroom.
- Exercises authority delegated to him/her as the system's educational leader to establish educational objectives, curricula, and methods that encourage development of intellectual independence.
- Clarifies for teachers their rights and responsibilities regarding academic freedom.
- Seeks adoption of policies that emphasize the professional prerogatives of teaching in the selection and utilization of instructional materials as well as the right and responsibility of the school board and administrators to establish and protect curriculum standards.
- Resists attempts to limit or destroy intellectual freedom.
- Ensures that there is broad representation of pupils, parents, and staff in development and implementation of plans for academic freedom.
- Exercises leadership in promulgation of a written document or code governing teacher rights in and outside the classroom.
- Initiates programs to acquaint all personnel, parents, and pupils with the nature and intent of provisions for ensuring human rights.
- Interprets fully and clearly to the board, community, and school staff the role of academic freedom in ensuring the intellectual vitality of the school system.
- Proposes for adoption by the board of education written policies and procedures for the selection and review of instructional materials utilized in the educational program.
- Initiates a set of procedures for dealing with complaints, criticisms, and challenges relating to instructional materials.
- Establishes a plan for keeping staff and citizens informed about the manner in which teaching and related materials are selected, the process by which challenges are dealt with, and the convening of public hearings to air viewpoints on the system's approach to the protection of freedom of thought and intellectual development.[21]

Because of the long-standing though challenging tradition that regards the teacher as a nonpolitical, no-issue citizen—one whose task should be confined to understanding and maintaining the status quo—the role of the administrator in seeking solutions to problems relating to intellectual freedom is both difficult and challenging. Moreover, because of the rapidity with which social changes have occurred in America and in the world, an increased share of the responsibility for encouraging development of free minds has been placed on leadership. The task requires an intellectual climate conducive to adaptive behavior and strong defenses against restraints and attacks on the freedom of teaching and learning.

Responsibilities of the Teacher

Two kinds of responsibility should be stressed in connection with the teacher and academic freedom. One pertains to the teacher's obligation to conduct the teaching-learning process in keeping with principles on which academic freedom rests. There is little point in establishing elaborate academic safeguards if the spirit of inquiry is not encouraged by the school staff. If controversial issues are ignored, if varying points of view are not tolerated, if the right to dissent is forbidden, if the teacher is careful not to bring up controversial topics, and if he/she evades an opinion solicited by students, where does this leave us? In certain respects, it leaves us with students who have little understanding of scientific inquiry or with citizens who are unable to make intelligent decisions because their education was conducted in an atmosphere in which the spirit of free inquiry was not encouraged.

This leads us to the difficult question of the levels at which such educational experiences are appropriate. As one author has pointed out:

> Until the learner has reached some stage of responsible maturity, not only must conduct be restrained to a larger extent than later, but the learning process must be affirmatively conditioned to secure the transmission to the newcomer of the prevailing cultural heritage. It is a delicate matter, as every parent and professional educator knows, to transmit the wisdom of the past and of the present consistently with freedom for the learner and with the attitude of devotion to basic beliefs, accompanied by tentativeness of view, that in our culture, must somehow be communicated. Yet, clearly, at an early age in the learner's course, the more certain knowledge and the relatively prevalent attitudes must be conveyed. Gradually criticism and questioning accompanied by methods of evaluation and of arriving at independent conclusions can be developed until the stage of complete freedom, testing all knowledge and all values without destroying them, is reached.[22]

This viewpoint reflects the essence of a 1989 Supreme Court decision confirming the right of schools to exercise ultimate editorial judgment over the content of school publications. In reality, adults have always exercised review and restraint over youth. The issue, it is argued, is not whether restraint should be exercised, but at what age this authority should be relinquished. Age distinctions and age-specific requirements are an essential part of our legal system in the forms of ordinances, statutes, and the U.S. Constitution. Thus, design of developmental processes whereby determination of the manner in which intellectual independence is established is one of the staff's most challenging professional responsibilities and opportunities.

Finally, there is another kind of teacher responsibility related to academic freedom: the self-discipline inextricably related to such freedom. It is the obligation to maintain those standards of personal and professional integrity in keeping with the noble purpose the teacher serves. The standards of teaching, learning, and scholarship to which he/she adheres must be conducive to attaining the aims of the educational system. This is, in essence, academic freedom's justification.

REVIEW AND PREVIEW

Various arrangements have evolved in the twentieth century to protect school personnel from internal and external threats to employment security. The scope of modern provisions for lessening work-related anxieties in educational institutions includes tenure, employment contracts, grievance procedures, due process, academic freedom, and policies for protection against arbitrary and capricious treatment.

This chapter has identified types of personnel treatment that call for redress through a corrective justice system (Figure 8.1), presented a personnel justice structure (Figure 8.3), outlined a grievance procedure for dealing with formal and informal personnel complaints (Figure 8.4), and included decision models for considering personnel retention or termination (Figures 8.6 and 8.7).

The concepts of academic freedom and tenure, it was noted, are constantly undergoing redefinition because of abuses, unionization, litigation, and conditions in the external environment.

Academic freedom and tenure are considered to be interdependent. The conditions under which each is granted entail both privileges and responsibilities that do not translate into sinecure or unlimited security. Each is viewed as essential to system aims through positive and prudent nurturing by the board of education, administrators, and teachers (Table 8.1).

In Chapter 9 we shall examine the process of personnel continuity, which includes those activities of the human resources function involved in keeping the organization continually and effectively staffed.

REVIEW AND DISCUSSION QUESTIONS

1. *Each class member:* Reexamine the content of Figure 8.1, which is indicative of personnel areas that have the potential for invoking corrective justice. Identify one of the listed elements that has occurred in an educational institution with which you are familiar. What action

was taken by officials to resolve the problem? Was the problem resolved formally or informally? What was the composition of the group involved in resolving the matter?

2. *Instructor:* Collate the information derived from the preceding exercise, and review for the class any central tendency or variation in the events reported by class members.

3. What is the difference between academic freedom and tenure? Can you cite instances in your state of textbook banning, unjust dismissal of personnel, or litigation relative to academic freedom?

4. What kind of behavior does one anticipate from a faculty member who perceives himself/herself to be victimized by organizational injustice?

5. Develop an outline of your ideas of what fairness and justice should encompass in an organizational setting.

6. Develop a procedure for handling complaints of unfair treatment through informal arrangements.

7. List the steps a principal, department head, or supervisor should take to first recognize the development of personnel dissatisfactions and then attempt to resolve them at the point of origin.

8. The right of personnel to object and to be heard without recrimination are two facets of what is referred to as *due process*. Due process systems are found in the military, civil service, labor organizations, and institutions of higher learning. What are their strengths and weaknesses? What is the relationship of due process to improved personnel performance? To personnel employment security?

9. In October 1988, the Chicago School Board enacted an Education Reform Law, which vested certain authority with local community councils comprising parents, teachers, and principals at each school. Among the councils' powers was renewal or termination of principals' contracts (principals could not vote on their own contracts).[23]

   • What are the implications of this arrangement for due process for administrative personnel?
   • Are there legal implications regarding board delegation of authority?
   • Is the council structure (six of eleven council members are parents) conducive to conflict? To system synergy? To position satisfaction? To position security? To personnel justice?
   • Should parents serve in an advisory rather than a decision-making capacity?
   • Should personnel termination authority be lodged with those not elected to office and those not generally acquainted with personnel appraisal concepts and criteria?
   • What are the implications of board-council disagreement on personnel retention or terminations?

10. On November 30, 1990, the Illinois Supreme Court ruled unconstitutional that part of the Education Reform Law empowering councils to decide on personnel contracts. However, the court ruled that another provision of the act eliminating tenure for principals was *constitutional*.

   • What are the staffing implications (recruitment, selection, continuity, collective bargaining for administrators, development, and appraisal) of this legal development? For "site-based management" as it relates to the principalship?

- Does it follow that the way to curtail school dropouts and poor test scores is to neutralize the role of principalship, its administrative status, and position security?

11. Using the format in Table 8.2, review the policies of a selected school system designed to cope with complaints arising over the content of curriculum and library materials, modes of teaching controversial issues, and the age at which children are exposed to such issues. Establish criteria for evaluating the merits of each type of complaint and then determine the extent to which policies of the selected school are in accord with the evaluative criteria.

12. Directions: Read the following descriptions of two justice system-related cases involving two basketball coaches, each from a different school, and then write a brief summary in response to the questions that follow:

> *Coach A Details:* After-game obscenity-laced outburst; threat-ened opposing coach. Three previous violations of generally accepted standards of conduct. No formal system of progressive disciplinary procedure. Community outraged about management action. *Management action:* one game suspension.

> *Coach B Details:* Coach B claimed racism as reason for not being promoted to head coach. Not interviewed for position. Position opening not posted. Coach B filed racism complaint with State Human Relations Commission. Coach B preferred to use *statutory alternative* to the *system contractual grievance machinery. Management action:* notified Coach B that services as assistant coach were no longer required.

- Was the management action in each case appropriate?
- Did either case go through the classic problem-solving stages?
- Would an informal resolution process be appropriate in each case?
- Was Coach B entitled to due process?
- Should Coach B have employed the contractual grievance

TABLE 8.2

Complaints About . . .	Evaluative Criteria	Current Policy
Curriculum materials	_____	_____
Library materials	_____	_____
What *is* taught	_____	_____
How it is taught	_____	_____
When it is taught	_____	_____
What *should* be taught	_____	_____
By whom it is taught	_____	_____

machinery to which he was entitled rather than the statutory alternative?

- In your view, how should each case have been handled?
- Should formal standards of conduct be applied in each case?
- In the case of Coach A, should *progressive discipline procedure* have

been employed? (A: *verbal warning;* B: *written warning;* C: *suspension;* D: *termination*.)

- In Coach B's situation, should the position opening have been posted?

CHAPTER EXERCISE 8.1

Directions: This exercise is designed to identify your assumptions about justice systems in educational institutions. Do not justify your response on what newspapers, textbooks, professors, or colleagues consider to be the right answer. Determine whether you strongly disagree, disagree, agree, or strongly agree with each of the following statements:

- Management rights clauses in a union contract should reserve system right to make decisions vital to its effectiveness.
- Senior employees should be given preferential treatment in transfers, job assignments, promotions, layoffs, vacation scheduling, and compensation.
- The primary cause of any grievance is due to a grievant's political aspirations.
- Of all of the commonly known methods of communicating complaint-grievance procedures, the most appropriate is through union communication machinery.
- Justice systems in school organizations, as viewed by school employees, do not adhere to civilized procedures for resolving workplace problems.
- Justice systems in public schools have had little effect on ridding systems of personnel whose behavior is considered inimical to school interests.
- Modern school system grievance machinery eliminates the possibility of employee termination-at-will.

- Employee standards of conduct have been generally effective in minimizing employee misconduct.
- Listing of employee standards of conduct treats employees as children and not as professionals.
- Primary responsibility for communicating standards of conduct belongs to the central administration.
- A standards of conduct framework should include all of these provisions: counseling, verbal and written warnings, transfer, and suspension.
- Sexual misconduct between teachers and students can best be controlled by the system's standards of conduct.
- School systems should place selective restraints on the academic freedom of classroom teachers.
- The school system has no right to restrict the academic freedom of classroom teachers.
- Most school systems have policies and procedures that spell out the degree to which the academic freedom of classroom teachers is restricted.

NOTES

1. June Weisberger, Recent Developments in Job Security: Layoffs and Discipline in the Public Sector (Ithaca: New York State School of Industrial and Labor Relations, 1976), 13.

2. 408 U.S. 564 (1972).

3. 408 U.S. 593 (1972).

4. Joseph Levesque, The Human Resource Problem Solver's Handbook (New York: McGraw Hill Inc., 1991), I.5.208.

5. Education Commission of the States, Cuebook: State Education Collective Bargaining Laws, Report F 78–79 (Denver, CO: Education Commission of the States, 1980), 7.

6. Theoretical, legal, and political aspects of tenure are covered in Myron Lieberman, "Tenure: A New High-Priority Issue"; William R. Hazard, "Tenure Laws in Theory and Practice"; Frank W. Masters, "Teacher Job Security under Collective Bargaining Contracts"; and Theodore H. Lang, "Teacher Tenure as a Management Problem," all Phi Delta Kappan 56, 7 (March 1975); Donald Keck, "Tenure: Who Needs It?" Phi Delta Kappan 54, 2 (October 1972), 124; and J. Leo Freiwald, "Tenure: Another Sacred Cow About to Bite the Dust," Phi Delta Kappan 61, 1 (September 1979), 50.

7. Edgar H. Schein, Organizational Psychology, Third Edition (Englewood Cliffs, NJ: Prentice-Hall Inc., 1980), 22, © 1980, reprinted by permission of Prentice-Hall Inc.; and American Association of School Administrators, Administrator's Bill of Rights (Arlington, VA: American Association of School Administrators, 1975).

8. Pennsylvania School Boards Association, "Tenure Must Go," Informative Legislative Service 10, 10 (March 10, 1972), 8–9.

9. Harry J. Finlayson, "Incompetence and Teacher Dismissal," Phi Delta Kappan 61, 1 (September 1979), 69; see also Fenwick W. English, "Merit Pay: Reflections on Education's Lemon Tree," Educational Leadership 41, 4 (December 1983–January 1984), 72–80.

10. William E. Eaton, "The Many Myths of Teacher Tenure," Changing Education 5, 4 (Winter–Spring 1974), 26–27; see also Betty E. Sinowitz, "What About Teacher Tenure?" Today's Education 62, 4 (April 1973), 40–42.

11. American Association of School Administrators, Teacher Tenure Ain't the Problem (Arlington, VA: American Association of School Administrators, 1972).

12. Thomas J. Flygare, "Mandatory Retirement Is Fading Fast; Will Tenure Be Next?" Phi Delta Kappan 59, 10 (June 1978), 711–12.

13. Education Commission of the States, "Teacher Tenure/Continuing Contract Laws," Clearing House Notes, as amended, 1994 (Denver, CO: The Commission.)

14. Hazard, 454. See also F. L. Hipp, "Tenure for School Teachers?" New York University Education Quarterly 9, 4 (Summer 1978), 26–27; J. O. O'Toole, "Tenure: A Conscientious Objection," Change (June–July, 1971), 24–41; Linda Wilkins Rickman, "The Teacher Tenure Controversy," Education Digest 47, 6 (February 1982),

30–32; and "Suppose We Lost Tenure," Educational Leadership 35, 3 (December 1977), 183–86.

15. Judith F. Krug, "Growing Pains: Intellectual Freedom and the Child," English Journal 61, 6 (September 1972), 805–13.

16. American Civil Liberties Union, Academic Freedom, Academic Responsibility, and Academic Due Process in Institutions of Higher Learning (New York: American Civil Liberties Union, 1966), 6. For other definitions and discussions of academic freedom, see Richard M. Blankenburg, "Does Academic Freedom Apply to Public School Teachers?" Educational Forum 35, 2 (January 1971), 153–56; Lawrence Kassam, "The Serpent in the Garden," Phi Delta Kappan 54, 5 (December 1972), 261–65; Alan H. Levine, "Impressionable Minds, Forbidden Subjects: A Case in Point," School Library Journal 98 (February 1973), 595–601; L. B. Woods, Censorship Involving Educational Institutions in the United States, 1965–1975 (Austin: Doctoral Dissertation, University of Texas, 1977); and L. B. Woods, "Is Academic Freedom Dead in the Public Schools," Phi Delta Kappan 61, 2 (October 1979), 104–6.

17. Allan Tucker and Robert B. Mautz, "Academic Freedom, Tenure, and Incompetence," Educational Record (Spring 1982), 22–25.

18. "The Growing War: Pro- and Anti-Censorship Forces Use Schools as Battlegrounds," Phi Delta Kappan 61, 10 (June 1980), 722.

19. Stephen Bates, "How Cries of 'Censorship' Stifle the Schools Debate," The Wall Street Journal Vol. LLXXII, No. 122 (December 22, 1993).

20. *Cary* v. *Board of Education* of the Adams-Arapahoe School, School District 28J, Civil Action No. 76M-200 (1977).

21. See Michelle Marder Kamhl, "Censorship vs. Selection—Choosing Books for Schools," American Education 18, 3 (March 1982), 11–15; also Stephanie Abraham Hirsch and Frank R. Kemerer, "Academic Freedom in the Classroom," Educational Leadership 39, 5 (February 1982), 375–78; and Jack Taylor and Arthur Steller, "Curriculum Development and Censorship," Ohio Media Spectrum 3383, 4 (Fall-Winter 1981), 27–30.

22. Ralph F. Fuchs, "Intellectual Freedom and the Educational Process," American Association of University Professors Bulletin 42, 3 (Autumn 1956), 471–72.

23. Miami Herald, March 2, 1990, 4B.

SUPPLEMENTARY READING

Business and Legal Reports, Inc. How to Recognize and Prevent Sexual Harassment in the Workplace. Madison, CT: Business and Legal Reports, Inc., 1992.

Donelson, Ken. "Six Statements/Questions from the Censor." Phi Delta Kappan 69, 3 (November 1983), 208–14.

French, Wendell L. "Organizational Justice." In Personnel Management Process, Sixth Edition. Boston: Houghton Mifflin Company, 1985, Chapter 4.

Gest, Ted. "The Textbook Tug of War Heats Up." U.S. News and World Report, November 17, 1986, 29.

Goldstein, William. Controversial Issues in Our Schools. Bloomington, IN: Phi Delta Kappa, 1980.

———Controversial Issues in Schools: Dealing with the Inevitable. Bloomington, IN: Phi Delta Kappa, 1989.

Gordon, Leonard J. "Complaints and Grievances." In William R. Tracey, Editor, Human Resources Management and Development Handbook. New York: American Management Associations, 1985, Chapter 50.

Hubbartt, William S. Personnel Policy Handbook. New York: McGraw-Hill Inc., 1993.

Jackson, Gordon. Labor and Employment Law Desk Book. Englewood Cliffs, NJ: Prentice-Hall Inc., 1993.

Jenkinson, Edward B. "The New Age of Schoolbook Protest." Phi Delta Kappan 70, 1 (September 1988), 66.

Lang, Theodore H. "Teacher Tenure as a Management Problem." Phi Delta Kappan 56, 7 (March 1975), 459–62.

LoBoco, Mary Ellen. "Nonunion Grievances Procedures." Personnel (January 1985), 61–64.

Lovell, Ned B. Grievance Arbitration in Education. Bloomington, IN: Phi Delta Kappa Educational Foundation, 1985.

Masters, Frank W. "Teacher Job Security under Collective Bargaining Contracts." Phi Delta Kappan 45, 7 (March 1975), 455–58.

Perritt, Henry H., Jr. Your Rights in the Workplace. New York: Practicing Law Institute, 1993.

Seely, Robert S. "Corporate Due Process." HR Magazine (Alexandria, VA: Society for Human Resources Management, 1992).

Stahlschmidt, Agnes. "A Workable Strategy for Dealing with Censorship." Phi Delta Kappan 64, 2 (October 1982), 99–101.

Waterman, Cecily A. "Update Handbooks to Avoid Risk." HR Magazine (Alexandria, VA: Society for Human Resources Management, 1992).

Werther, William B., Jr. "Reducing Grievances Through Effective Contract Administration." Labor Law Journal (April 1974), 211–216.

Wishnietsky, Dan H., Editor. Sexual Harassment in the Educational Environment. Bloomington, IN: Phi Delta Kappa, 1992.

Chapter 9

Employment Continuity

CHAPTER OVERVIEW

The Human Resources Function and Retirement Planning
• Death

CHAPTER OBJECTIVES

• Present an organizational vista—a comprehensive awareness of a series of management tasks related to personnel maintenance.
• Acquaint the reader with the day-to-day changes in positions that occur owing to time-off practices, promotions, absences and lateness, transfers, layoffs, retirement, and death.
• Identify approaches to and problems involved in moving personnel from one position to another as well as removing them from the system altogether.
• Stress the legal ramifications associated with management decisions relating to continuity of personnel service as well as the potential for costly court litigation.

CHAPTER TERMS

Absenteeism	Family and Medical Leave Act
Americans With Disabilities Act	National Health Care Insurance Proposals
Career passage	Pregnancy Disability Act
Continuity process	Reduction in force
Demotion	Temporary personnel
Disability	Transfer

We have examined various processes of the human resources function essential to attracting competent people into the system, including human resources planning, compensation, recruitment, selection, and induction. In addition, we have looked at ways of helping personnel to develop abilities and to integrate individual and group interests with those of the organization. In brief, these processes seek to transform inexperienced outsiders into qualified insiders.

In this chapter, we will look at organizational provisions designed to retain personnel and foster continuity in personnel service. We will focus on detailed plans for improving continuity of service as well as on the process by which such plans are designed, implemented, and controlled. In so doing, we will see what organizations can do to maintain health and occupational mobility of members, provide for their well-being, arrange for their separation from the system, and have replacements available when, for any of a multitude of reasons, they are unable to perform their work.

Even in institutions where the system's concepts are subscribed to and implemented, things do not always run smoothly. Sustained effort must be made to keep any organization operating effectively on a day-to-day basis. Human beings have a way of interfering with plans, violating rules, and behaving in other ways inimical to the interests of the organization. So long as individuals fill positions in organizations, there will be problems. Some will become physically or mentally ill, others obsolescent. Some will need to be absent from work. Some will have work-connected accidents. Some will be affected by the physical conditions of employment, such as the amount of light, heat, ventilation, or noise, as well as sanitation conditions and safety hazards. Some will have stresses connected with work, home, or interpersonal relationships that will require counseling. Some may become unproductive if they do not have leaves of absence for self-renewal. Some will be dismissed, promoted, or reassigned. Some will be separated because of external conditions over which they or the system have no control.

The system must deal with these personnel problems primarily because they affect two of its strategic goals: stability and development. The system needs healthy, productive people continuously on the job who are physically and mentally able to contribute maximally to the work of the enterprise and who maintain a favorable attitude toward their roles and the environment in which they function.

The nature and scope of provisions for maintaining continuity of personnel service are determined by the system. It decides to what extent provisions should be made for enhancing continuity of service, what types of programs are needed, and how they will be organized and administered. We will next examine the process by which plans for continuing employment are designed and implemented.

THE EMPLOYMENT CONTINUITY PROCESS

Keeping the system continually staffed with competent personnel involves consideration of and action on problems related to leaves of absence, substitute service, health, safety, promotion, reassignment, separation, resignation, termination, and retirement. The employment **continuity process** by which the foregoing problems are dealt with varies from but has much in common with arrangements for making and carrying out other organizational decisions. Operations relating to some phases of personnel service recur frequently; leaves of absences, health, substitute service, and safety are aspects of personnel administration that confront administrators daily. One important use of the process outlined in Figure 9.1 is to help planners isolate the recurring elements of these problems and to standardize the manner in which they are treated. If, for example, a relative of one of the system's teachers dies, the procedures employed in handling requests by teachers for such leaves of absence to attend funerals should be routinized well in advance of such events.

It is not suggested that the activities listed in Figure 9.1 occur sequentially; rather, the intent of the process outlined is to show that if the system is to be staffed properly and continuously, a course of action must be projected. In this case, it consists of making a series of decisions about continuity of service, including (a) what the plans are expected to achieve, (b) types of plans needed to realize expectations, (c) who will be responsible for what phases of the program, (d) the specifics of each type of program, and (e) how results of the process will be determined. In sum, plans are developed for each of the subprocesses listed in Figure 9.1. This includes selecting activities to implement each subprocess, having the human and physical resources available when and where they are needed, and linking these plans to other plans and subplans relating to personnel administration.

Personnel Continuity Process

Analysis of activities involved in the personnel continuity process outlined in Figure 9.1 indicates that there are two clusters of activities. One group is concerned with the health, safety, and mobility of continuing personnel; the second is focused on members who are voluntarily or involuntarily leaving

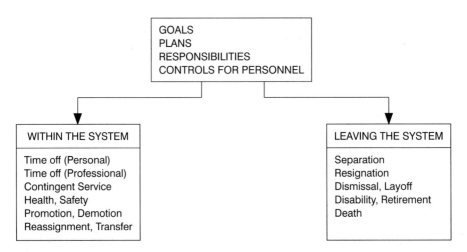

FIGURE 9.1
Framework of the employment continuity process.

the system. Expectations or results that the system intends to achieve from plans for service continuity are both long- and short-range and include:

- Improve ability of the system to perform its function.
- Improve the system's physical, psychological, and organizational environment.
- Prevent and control occupational stress.
- Control personnel costs.
- Provide position security for personnel.
- Control avoidable absenteeism and lateness.
- Furnish financial protection against risks such as illness and accidents.
- Reduce personnel turnover.
- Facilitate change within the system.
- Improve individual and system effectiveness.
- Prevent accidents.
- Maintain position and system performance standards.
- Comply with statutory requirements.
- Provide opportunity for personnel self-development and self-renewal.
- Establish program limits.
- Attend to preretirement problems of personnel adjustment.

Once the goals for maintaining continuity of personnel service have been set forth, implementation by school officials follows. Early in the planning stages, at least two types of action are necessary. One of these is preparation of a series of policy statements to guide members in designing and implementing specific programs. The other is a set of specific plans needed to carry out policy intent, such as the manner in which personnel continuity programs will be organized and administered, as well as controls essential to resolution of personnel problems associated with their health and safety, internal mobility, and employment termination. Thus, we find the Riverpark school system defining its policies as illustrated in Figure 9.2.

The employment continuity policy contained in Figure 9.2 illustrates an approach to reducing desired outcomes through the continuity process. The policy intent is to (a) exercise continuous direction, guiding influence action and control over planning and implementing the process; (b) influence action and conduct of system members regarding employment continuity; and (c) serve as a precedent or guiding principle for the growth of the work force and its organizational entity. The following supporting statements are employed to interpret and translate the Riverpark school system's continuity policy into more specific operational plans and procedures.

It is the policy of the Riverpark school system to:

- Provide continuity of personnel employment insofar as this is economically feasible.
- Control reduction in force on the basis of performance, ability, and length of service. When these factors are approximately equal, length of service with the system will govern.
- Grant leaves of absence for acceptable reasons.
- Provide assistance to individual staff members in maintaining and improving physical and mental health.
- Provide an attractive and efficient environment by maintaining good physical working conditions.
- Install every practical safety device, take every measure to prevent accidents, guard against mechanical failure, and provide adequate equipment for accident and fire prevention.
- Make available adequate substitutes for absentees.
- Fill vacancies by upgrading or promotion from within whenever present employees are qualified.
- Encourage reassignment when it is in the interest of the individual and the system.
- Protect personnel against unfair separation from the system.
- Assist personnel to plan for retirement.

FIGURE 9.2
Illustration of employment continuity policy.

- *Policy*—Policies apply systemwide and establish a referral basis for managerial thinking and action about employment continuity problems. The policy manual is a key tool employed to communicate existing policies, coordinate human resources actions, and provide for consistency in dealing with continuity matters.
- *Process*—The mechanism through which the continuity process operates includes these steps: adoption, design, implementation, monitoring, evaluation of outcomes, and adjustment through corrective measures. The policy manual and employee handbook define operational aspects.
- *Prior Review*—Prior review of continuity actions includes legal counsel review of decisions likely to have negative consequences, full documentation of decision-related actions, and assurance that due process is accorded members affected by any contemplated proceedings.
- *Continuity Regulation*—Administration of the continuity process is governed by a set of official regulations. Specific statements in the policy

manual, human resources handbook, and system newsletter update and explain current provisions and why they are put into effect.

TIME-RELATED BENEFITS

Of the two clusters of personnel activities shown in Figure 9.1, one focuses generally on personnel health and development and the other on personnel separation. In the following text we will consider activities in the first cluster and their relationship to continuity of personnel service. First we will examine time-off provisions in the context of the continuity process.

As indicated in Figure 9.1, time off may be categorized as (a) personal or (b) professional. Time-off policies express the system's attitude toward permitting personnel to take time off from work without severing the employment relationship and the extent to which the individual will be paid for time lost. Table 9.1 lists types of absences grouped under personal and professional time off.

Personnel time off may be defined as time away from employment by permission, with or without compensation, for a stated period of time without severing the employment relationship. Regardless of system size, time-off policies and procedures are essential, as may be seen from the many reasons listed in Table 9.1. Increasingly, school systems throughout the nation are initiating or improving provisions governing personnel time off.

Although a time-off plan serves many purposes, its primary focus is on the satisfaction of individual needs. In safeguarding personnel mental and physical well-being, maintaining employment security, and fostering professional growth and morale, these benefits are not considered to be gratuitous or a generous gesture of the board of education. The investment is made on the assumption that it will provide conditions of employment conducive to personnel productivity and work satisfaction. Time off with pay consumes a significant amount of the total costs of collateral benefits, and the trend is toward expansion in both number and kind.

Characteristics of Time-Off Provisions

It is customary, and frequently mandatory, to establish provisions governing absence of personnel because of illness and other reasons. *Illness plans* can be classified as either limited or unlimited. The limited plan, frequently, established by statute, generally contains provisions governing:

- Extent of compensation for time lost.
- Number of days allowed each year for authorized absences.
- Accumulation of sick days from year to year, including total number of days that can be accumulated.

TABLE 9.1
Types of personal and professional time-off provisions.[a]

Personal Time Off	Professional Time Off
Illness	Exchange teaching
Maternity, paternity	Research
Family and bereavement	Serving professional organizations
Marriage	Professional improvement
Voting	Grievances and negotiations
Civic duty	Conferences
Jury and trial witness duty	Receiving degrees
Military duty	
Social services	
Religious holidays	

Note: [a]Authorization of time-off provisions may derive from *statutes, negotiated contracts,* or *board of education policy.* Such provisions are generally considered to be intrinsic forms of pay that extend coverage of the benefit program.

- Number of days for which authorized absence is granted with full or part salary.
- Verification of illness.
- Board regulations extending period of absence with pay in excess of statutory provisions.
- Waiver of sick-leave provisions in the event absence is the result of injury when personnel are engaged in remunerative work unrelated to school duties.

Some states have statutory regulations that determine the amount of sick leave on the basis of length of service, some specify how many days of sick leave are mandatory at full pay, and others leave this matter to board discretion.

Extended absences because of physical disability are governed by provisions for salary continuation or health and accident insurance policies. Allowances are designed to pay less than regular salary as an incentive for personnel to return to work.

The unlimited sick-leave plan, in effect in relatively few school districts, places no limit on the number of days personnel may be absent because of illness. This type of leave may provide for full or part pay or for a combination in which full pay is granted for a limited number of days, after which time part pay is granted without time limitations.

Organizational experience with sick-leave programs provides little support for the assumption that such programs increase job satisfaction or member motivation. Experience indicates also that (a) the potential for abuse of the sick-leave privilege is extant in any organization; (b) illness has a significant impact on instructional continuity; (c) the cost of sick leave and other benefits has risen so dramatically in recent years that school systems are struggling to prevent imbalance among salaries, wages, benefits, and nonsalary performance incentives; (d) changing social attitudes and public school economics are placing greater emphasis on maintaining *wellness* and rewarding good health than on extended illness provisions; and (e) the concept of a sick-leave bank plan provides an alternative to traditional sick-leave practices. This approach includes development of a pool of sick-leave days by system members in order to protect those physically unable to perform their duties for an extended period of time. Alternative means of stressing the wellness concept are included in comprehensive health maintenance programs, a discussion of which is provided later in this chapter.

Leaves of absence for purposes *other than illness* are less often prescribed by statute. These include leaves for professional development, professional service, civic duties, and personal matters. Death in the family, professional study, exchange teaching, maternity, paternity, and attendance at educational meetings account for a majority of leaves granted for reasons other than illness. By and large, these provisions for time off are usually the subject of union-system negotiations.

Guidelines for Administering Time-Off Programs

A comprehensive personnel time-off program, which increasingly appears to be an organizational necessity as well as a national tendency, calls for resolution of many varied issues, including:

- Reasons for which a school district should grant personnel time off.
- Limits on the amount of personal or nonillness time off.
- Conditions that will attach to each type of absence, type of application required, salary on return to service, service required after return from leave, assignment on return to service, termination of absence, and notice of intention to return to service.
- Plans for minimizing abuse of the time-off privilege.
- Arrangements necessary for safeguarding the education of pupils.
- Priorities of the time-off program (nonmandatory features) being set forth in the negotiated contract.
- Plans for keeping personnel informed of current practices and recent changes.
- Records and reports needed to administer time-off programs effectively.

Although it is inappropriate to suggest here what the authorized time-off program for an individual system should be, certain suggestions can be made as a guide to planning. Analysis of the system's experience with time-off provisions over a period of years is a useful starting point. One of the purposes of such an audit would be to determine the nature and scope of time-off requests, frequency of occurrence, budgetary requirements, priorities, privileges subject to abuse, and suitability of existing administrative controls. The leave-of-absence planning grid, shown in Figure 9.3, is a convenient technique for union-system reviewing and planning a leave program. If we consider the 90 cells shown in Figure 9.3, we can gain a perspective of planning decisions required by a time-related benefits plan that includes all personnel on the system payroll. In addition, the grid can be used to identify priorities, estimate financial support required, and review the need for addition or elimination of components from the program.

Personnel absence is the subject of statutory law and is frequently litigated in the courts, especially legal rights relative to sabbatical leave. The matter of mandatory maternity leaves, for example, has received consideration in government and in the courts. In precedent-setting decrees, courts and federal and state authorities have branded compulsory maternity leaves either unconstitutional or illegal.[1] Increasingly, disabilities or illnesses caused or contributed to by pregnancy, miscarriage, abortion, childbirth, and recovery therefrom, must be treated like any other **disability** or illness by the employing school system. Personnel disabled because of pregnancy or childbirth are entitled to the same leaves of absence, sick-leaves, and job rights as any other temporarily disabled personnel.

The unpaid leave of absence, although infrequently employed, is a provision needed for dealing with personnel situations that arise occasionally. Most school systems, either through policy or contractual agreement, permit unpaid leaves of absence for a variety of reasons, including graduate study, child care, teacher burnout, pursuit of other interests or other forms of employment, health restoration, and political or social action. (Leaves for political or social action are gradually being incorporated into general personnel policy).

Regulatory Influence on Leaves of Absence

Leaves of absence are influenced in various ways by the regulatory environment. Federal, state, and local lawmakers pass laws that empower these agencies to take various forms of regulatory action; and the court oversees this process by resolving disputes among the school system and its employees. The following federal regulatory provisions illustrate the direct and indirect impact of leave-related provisions.

- *Pregnancy Disability Act of 1978* (PDA)—Amends Title VII of the Civil Rights Act of 1964. Prohibits discrimination on the basis of pregnancy, childbirth, or related medical conditions.[2]

Time-Off Provisions	Application Procedures	Eligibility Requirements	Conditions of Absence	Termination Procedures	Compensation
Personal Illness					
Maternity					
Paternity					
Family					
Bereavement					
Marriage, divorce					
Voting					
Civic duty					
Jury, trial witness duty					
Social service					
Religious holidays					
Professional Exchange teaching					
Research					
Professional service					
Professional improvement					
Grievances, negotiations					
Travel					
Receive degrees					

FIGURE 9.3
A planning framework for time-related benefits in union or nonunion systems.

- *Americans With Disabilities Act* of 1990 (ADA)—Designed to change the attitudes of employers and to give people with disabilities an equal chance in the workplace.[3]
- *Family and Medical Leave Act* of 1993—Guarantees employees up to 12 weeks a year off, unpaid, for births, adoptions, or the care of sick children, spouses, or parents.
- *National Health Care Insurance Proposals*—Implosion of the movement for health care reform in the United States involves the issue of legislated reform of the health care system as opposed to health care market innovations. Whether legislated reform or market forces or some combination of these elements create a realigned health care system, many health care issues will become sticking points in the teacher union-system contract negotiations. These issues include cost-containment, a choice between managed care and paying out-of-pocket for indemnity coverage, health care dollars spent on administrative expenses, and cost sharing between employer and employee. (See Appendix B for congressional initiatives in 1994 on national health insurance.)

Examination of these governmental mandates indicates that the United States has been witness in recent years to an unrelenting succession of legislation affecting the human resources function in a variety of ways (See Figure 3.2 for other human resources-related regulations). These comprehensive pieces of legislation have created the foundation for change and conflict in employee and employer relationships and the need for reconsideration of ways of adhering to statutory requirements regarding employee health, leave conditions, and fair treatment for persons with disabilities.

School systems are not out of the range of the regulatory environment concerning human resources legislation. In one way or another, school systems as well as other organizations are on the brink of a radical shakeup in the way they provide and manage leave provisions, health care, and disability statutes, each of which is linked directly and indirectly to the human resources function and its various processes.

Leave-Related Employment Issues

Each of the legislative pieces mentioned previously involves certain leave-related employment issues that require various kinds of administrative action in the form of policies and procedures for their implementation. What should be done, for example, about:

- Controlling employee malingering?
- Preventing discrimination against young women because they will be the most likely to take leave?

- Dealing with the problem of returnees who have become disabled?
- Minimizing leaves of absence in a school year to curtail interruption of system operations?
- Minimizing abuse of leave time (e.g., use of time off for vacations)?
- Resolving leave problems of those who intend to quit but demand benefit retention?
- Paying for temporary replacements while providing benefits for those on leave?
- Helping administrators to understand the legal implications of faulty leave-related decisions?

A good place to begin for those in charge of the human resources function is to design, implement, and communicate an action plan aimed at putting the legal requirements into effect. This step involves spelling out what is referred to as *the conditions of leave,* the subject of the text following.

Conditions of Leave

Figure 9.3 indicates that five components are associated with time-related benefits. The key component, from an administrative standpoint, is definition of the conditions of leave. Aims of the conditions of a leave structure are to (a) communicate system leave policies and procedures, (b) avoid litigation, (c) minimize misunderstandings and complaints, and (d) control leave-related costs engendered by inflation and mismanagement.

Although the matrix shown in Figure 9.3 entails considerable attention to development of policies and procedures that govern each type of absence, it is an appropriate way to deal with questions, disputes, conflict, employee concerns, and potential legal liabilities.[4] The array of leave-related elements shown in Figure 9.3 requires a comprehensive, coordinated, and integrated leave structure that contains controls for resolving problems inherent in management of leaves of absence. This includes such actions as:

- Using a task force to review and reconsider existing leave policies and procedures for each type of leave, such as those identified in Figure 9.3.
- Including in the conditions of leaves those defined by regulatory agencies.
- Updating and communicating policies and procedures in the human resources handbook regarding leave provisions.
- Defining eligibility for employee benefits while employees take leave of absence.
- Specifying employment rights governing acceptance of employment while on leave.

- Training administrative personnel in the leave of absence process and how it is administered.

The previous discussion addressed the *supply side* of leaves-of-absence—arrangements the school system provides for its employees when personal and professional need arises for such uncertainties as illness, maternity, bereavement, mental and physical stress, and jury duty. Because of the rising cost of leave provisions, as well as the increasing demand for such benefits, there is mounting evidence that both public and private employers are initiating moves to control the *demand side* of the health care equation. Thus, health system promotion initiatives, designed to improve the overall health of its human resources, as well as to engender positive effects on health care costs, are the subject of the section that follows.

HEALTH MAINTENANCE PROGRAMS

School systems in contemporary society are confronted with resolution of a variety of issues related to the health and safety of personnel, such as:

- Selecting applicants significantly free of health problems.
- Maintaining and improving the health of the entire school staff.
- Making professional advice available to unit leaders to assist them in dealing with performers ineffective because of health or emotional problems, prolonged illness, absenteeism and substance abuse, stress, and infectious diseases.
- Identifying and removing health hazards.
- Planning for health-related emergencies.
- Maintaining confidentiality of medical records.
- Initiating plans for emergency treatment.
- Promoting good health (e.g., by way of blood banks, food services, and exercise programs).
- Developing plans for special health problems (e.g., alcoholism, drug abuse, absenteeism, contagious diseases, maternity, body odors, smoking abstention, stress management, cancer detection, hypertension screening, and diet/weight control).
- Hiring, placement, and health maintenance of people with disabilities.
- Providing a clean and aesthetically appealing work environment.
- Addressing the health education of personnel from foreign countries where health is neglected and health services are not readily available.
- Preventing exposure to hazardous materials.

• Providing adequate health insurance (dealing effectively with such issues as rising costs, adequate coverage, selecting from coverage options available, handling the conflicting and shifting health-care needs of personnel).

A desirable feature of any plan for maintaining continuity of personnel service is a comprehensive physical and mental *health maintenance program*. This is a responsibility every educational institution must assume, if for no other reason than the welfare of the school child. The purpose of the health program for school personnel is to maintain an optimum environment for children; reduce personnel absence; secure maximum personnel performance; and place personnel in positions compatible with their physical, mental, and emotional qualifications. Basic elements of a health program for school personnel include:

• A selection process designed to eliminate from employment those applicants chronically subject to health problems.

• Placement of handicapped personnel in positions suitable to their performance level.

• A counseling program designed to assist unit administrators in dealing with personnel who have mental or physical problems that interfere seriously with their day-to-day performance.

• Periodic examinations to ensure physical and emotional fitness of personnel.

• Arrangement to care for personnel involved in accidents or medical emergencies.

• Provisions for evaluating physical fitness of personnel employed for or transferred to work entailing physical stress, such as transportation or gymnastics, and of personnel returning to work after extended absence owing to illness or injury.

Employer Involvement in Employee Health Maintenance

There has never been serious challenge to the proposition that one of the school system's fundamental responsibilities is to put into place and maintain plans for a healthy work force. Contemporary employer initiatives to encourage wellness and to promote healthy life styles have led to various forms of health-related incentives and disincentives. Underlying greater system involvement in health care maintenance is the general intent to realize improved employee health and system medical cost containment. Examples of both health incentives and disincentives are summarized in the sections that follow.

Health-Related Incentives. Health-related incentives represent one approach to encourage employees to improve and maintain physical fitness.

These incentives include on-and-off site classes, workshops, newsletters, educational and training materials, health risk appraisals and assessments, and preventive care accounts.[5]

Health-Related Disincentives.   Disincentive plans are designed to link employee health to medical plan coverage. Data from the *Human Resources Yearbook, 1993/1994 Edition* indicate that certain types of health insurance plans provide less favorable coverage for health risk individuals in the form of higher insurance contributions and higher deductibles. Risk factors include tobacco use, obesity, seat belt use, physical status, cholesterol, chemical dependency, and alcohol abuse.[6]

Despite present provisions in current health maintenance programs, the uncertainty surrounding enactment of a National Health Care Plan leads to the likelihood that modification of traditional health care models for public and private employees is considerable. So varied are the possibilities for reformation of health care in the United States that one of the likely outcomes will be a design in which federal, state, and local interests will be served, including some form of incentives and disincentives as noted.

EMPLOYEE ASSISTANCE PROGRAMS

Special kinds of personnel health problems noted previously that have emerged in the latter half of the twentieth century have become so widespread that many organizations, including school systems, have taken steps through various approaches to develop what is generally referred to as *employee assistance programs* (EAPs). Underlying the need for such support systems is the fact that more employees than ever before are showing signs of performance dysfunction. Sources of deterioration in work performance stem from both internal and external environmental factors, such as changes in work load or work relationships, discrimination, marital adjustment, stressful superior-subordinate conditions, and various forms of substance abuse.

Organizational consequences flowing from disruptions to an employee's mental or physical functions are numerous and far-reaching. These include personal disorganization, **absenteeism,** tardiness, increased costs for health insurance, grievance filing, litigation, and most importantly, erosion of the relationship of the school system to personnel well-being.

There are three important reasons underlying the formation of personnel support systems: (a) humanitarian considerations basic to assisting members to deal with problems affecting performance expectations, (b) cost containment, and (c) maintenance of performance continuity and strengthening of the link between individual and system effectiveness.

With health insurance premiums rising at nearly twice the rate of inflation, medical costs 5 to 10 percent of the payroll, benefits ranging from 30

to 40 percent, and all of these numbers moving upward annually, controlling health-related costs has become a key factor in collective bargaining, in
efforts to reduce insurance claims, and in increasing the system's ability to
arrange a viable support system for its members.

Regardless of system size, member behavior problems of various kinds are
inevitable and warrant carefully designed plans essential to meeting objectives
of the human resources function. Employee assistance programs include these
options: (a) *wellness* programs, which stress preventive health maintenance; (b)
programs focusing on personnel behavior problems that stem from *work
assignments* or *work relationships;* (c) programs designed to treat *personal problems*
that affect member performance; and (d) any combination of these options.

The kinds and extent of programs offered depend on a variety of factors, including program objectives, system size and resources, problem
prevalence, and organizational recognition of problem existence and commitment to its resolution. In general, there is a positive relationship
between system size and program breadth: the larger the system, the
greater the likelihood that the program services will be more extensive.

In order to properly design, implement, and monitor an employee
assistance program, certain issues must be addressed. These issues are
brought into focus through questions such as:

- To what extent have personnel problems been identified that warrant initiation of a support program (e.g., absenteeism, tardiness, gambling,
  stressful work-related conditions, personal problems affecting individual
  performance, and substance abuse)?
- Of the four options regarding employee assistance programs described previously, which is most suitable as a planning strategy? This issue involves
  enlisting employee participation in decisions concerning courses of action
  designed to maintain their well-being as well as that of the system.

Some of the factors considered important to the success of health-
related programs include:

- *Policy*—A policy statement forms the bedrock on which to establish both
  wellness and assistance programs. Policy is intended to make clear program objectives; board of education commitment; the scope, nature, and
  extent of assistance eligibility (e.g., salaried, nonsalaried, or contingent
  personnel); and internal and or external provisions for referral, counseling, and treatment stipulations.
- *Procedures*—Programs that center on dysfunctional behavior require
  established procedures. These include such steps as problem identification, referral (system or self), diagnosis, treatment, and follow-up.
- *Sponsorship*—Costs of assistance programs remain a disturbing issue; and
  the extent to which expenses should be borne by the employer, union,

individual, or a combination of these must be considered. Because expenditures for all forms of benefits are reaching new heights and more personnel seek or are urged to seek various forms of treatment, cost considerations enter into policy and program decisions. System trends in health maintenance costs and forecasts of health risks are among the kinds of information that should become part of the system's personnel data base.

* *Education*—Educating all supervisory personnel and position holders about procedures for dealing with both wellness and assistance programs is deemed an integral component for program implementation purposes. Program objectives, procedures, confidentiality of information, and forms of treatment and care are examples of program elements about which personnel need to be informed and educated.

* *Flexibility*—Due to the size range of school systems in the United States, both wellness and assistance programs must be modelled to fit experiences, conditions, trends, and needs of individual systems and individuals within the systems. Need identification is diagnosed through such sources as insurance claims, medical records, surveys, performance appraisal information, and budgetary indicators.

In sum, examination of the contemporary social scene, changing member expectations, and stressful conditions in both internal and external environments lead to the realization that wellness and assistance programs are no longer only theoretical issues. The school system's concern in this regard is how to position the organization and the human resources function so that whatever health maintenance strategies are adopted, they will result in closing performance gaps at individual, group, and organization levels.

TEMPORARY PERSONNEL

Temporary personnel, referred to also as *substitute, part-time,* or *contingent employees,* are defined in general terms by the U.S. government as those employees working fewer than 35 hours a week. Part-time employees in school systems may be categorized as those who (a) are regularly employed on a part-time basis (e.g., cafeteria, transportation, and communications personnel, and those who regularly render legal, engineering, architectural, or medical services); (b) are temporarily employed for short periods of time (e.g., clerical, substitute, and consultant services personnel); (c) are phasing out their careers by making the transition from full-time to part-time to retirement; and (d) share a full-time position on a part-time basis (e.g., traffic, security, and teaching aides personnel).

Because of unprecedented changes taking place in all work organizations, the human resources function has been forced to reconsider strategies for recruiting, selecting, orienting, developing, appraising, and compensating persons employed less than full time. Until recent years, temporary school system personnel consisted of "substitute teachers." Rapid changes in the internal and external environments are having a decided impact on planning approaches involving temporary employment. For example, generous paid-leave plans create the need for part-time replacements due to absenteeism, jury duty, graduate education, conferences, maternity and paternity leaves, and long-term disabilities. Revolutionary developments in office technology, including the use of personal computers, electronic mail, and fax machines, have forced many school systems to seek replacements for clerical personnel from temporary service agencies or outside contractors. Shortages in personnel qualified to teach mathematics, computer applications, and the range of science subjects have led to modification of some state certification provisions, which makes part-time employment of skilled professionals possible. Pressures to cut personnel costs have led to outside contracting for services related to custodial work, food service, transportation, seasonal work, and unanticipated job openings calling for immediate personnel for limited periods. Looking beneath the contemporary employment scene, a more complex picture emerges. The number of positions in school systems requiring skilled personnel will continue to grow faster than the labor pool. Predicted decreases in the percentage of qualified people in the future work force and anticipated dips in the U.S. functional literacy rate are additional factors that enter into the necessity of recruiting, retaining, and maximizing the performance of the temporary work force.

With fundamental changes taking place in contemporary work organizations, the concept and practice of employing temporary personnel are accepted as essential components for meeting personnel needs. Experiences concerning the use of part-time personnel demonstrate that there are both blessings and burdens involved in their employment. Blessings include reduced personnel costs, lower turnover, job satisfaction, reduced on-the-job stress, fewer problems of absenteeism, and opportunities for temporary personnel to advance to full-time employment. Burdens include lack of loyalty, costly supervisory time, uncertainty of need occurrence, exclusion from collective bargaining agreements, few or nonexistent benefits, less than satisfactory compensation, failure to accept or to become assimilated in the organizational culture, and increases in student disciplinary cases that attend the use of substitute teachers.

We can better understand how to manage a contingent work force by studying its relationship to the human resources function. The basis of the previous briefing on temporary personnel is to show that the school system that (a) approaches the task with awareness of its emerging importance, (b) treats it as an ongoing process rather than a periodic event, and (c) stresses the concept of continual improvement is enjoying strategic and psychological advantages. Contemporary organizational experience indicates that management of temporary personnel can be improved through:

- Development of a framework, as illustrated in the following example, for classifying types of temporary personnel and for allocating administrative responsibilities.

Classification of Temporary Personnel	Employment Status	
Professional instructional	Regular (part time)	Short term
Professional noninstructional	Regular (part time)	Short term
Support instructional	Regular (part time)	Short term
Support noninstructional	Regular (part time)	Short term

- Formulation of a specific plan to be followed in administering the part-time program (including absence procedures for full-time personnel) and the application of all personnel processes as they apply to replacements or substitutes.
- Written specifications for employment of part-time personnel.
- Development of plans to improve position satisfaction and assimilation of substitute teachers into the system.
- A permanent, specialized corps of replacements to meet minimum system needs, to be composed of competent personnel, selected and trained to deal with special problems of substitution (a salary incentive is suggested because of the exacting nature of the assignment).
- A second group of temporary personnel to be employed seasonally when the demand for replacements cannot be filled by the permanent corps; this group to be recruited and selected on the basis of criteria for personnel able to perform in this capacity.
- Clear definition of responsibilities for carrying out details of the replacement plan, including development, assignment, and full utilization of the permanent corps as well as recruitment, selection, orientation, supervision, and appraisal of temporary personnel.
- Experimentation with alternatives for replacing absent teachers either in addition to or in place of substitute teachers, such as the use of professional and career persons from the school community, incentive plans for teachers to save on substitute costs by advance preparation for absences, a planned enrichment program of events to act as a replacement for teachers, use of high school honor students, and greater use of educational television and films.[7]
- Preparation of a handbook for temporary employees routinizing procedures to be followed and helping to clarify and minimize problems usually encountered when regular personnel are absent.

- Advance planning in each building unit by the principal and regular staff regarding preparation and maintenance of plans to be used by temporary personnel (this point is important because continuity of instruction can be enhanced by clear directions).

- Continuous appraisal of the replacement plan (records of the daily, monthly, and yearly absence rates are necessary to improve various aspects of this service, such as the predictable need for temporary personnel and effects of whatever plan is employed on the quality of instruction).

- Differential pay scales for short- and long-term substitutes and for substitutes with different educational backgrounds.

- Use of computer technology to facilitate the search for and to select the best possible teacher for the assignment at hand.

The need for temporary help is not confined to professional instructional personnel; there are occasions when professional noninstructional personnel are needed to render legal, medical, architectural, engineering, and other forms of advisory or consultative services. Temporaries are needed occasionally to supplement the regular support force during work peaks, to temporarily fill a position that has been vacated while a study is made to determine whether the position should be continued, or to tentatively occupy a position being developed until such time as the position description is formally developed and written.

For a school system to effectively manage the temporary personnel sector, all aspects of designing, directing, and controlling it should be integrated into a master plan. This requires that the human resources function is upgraded so that (a) all of the processes of the function contribute to program strategies, (b) all forms of temporary work are identified and creative ways found to attract a qualified work force, (c) alternatives are examined to determine which approaches to part-time employment will have the greatest impact on performance expectations, and (d) uncertainty is reduced regarding the manner in which every aspect of the operation will be carried out.

The increase in the use of temporary personnel in all types of organizations is undeniable. Their employment has proven to be a cost-effective method for filling positions through temporary, part-time, contract, and consulting assistance. Temporary help agencies, it should be noted, are capable of responding quickly to school system personnel needs, especially for support positions.

ABSENTEEISM AND LATENESS

Absenteeism and lateness are directly related to steady-state staffing plans. There are various kinds of absences (such as arranged, excused, occasional, and chronic), but the focus of this discussion is on the habitual absentee, the individual who chronically stays away from work for reasons not beyond his/her control. Lateness may be defined as arriving for work after the designated starting time.

Reasons for absenteeism and lateness are almost as varied and fanciful as excuses given in court for traffic violations. The impact of these two conditions on the operation of the system, however, can be significant. The teacher, secretary, custodian, bus driver, or cafeteria worker absent or late impairs the work of the school and interferes with the daily routine of other staff members. The cost to the system is poor instruction, work delay, frustration, and high work imbalance, even when absentees are not paid. It is essential to reduce to a minimum avoidable absence and lateness rates in the school system. One viewpoint considers absenteeism to be a cultural problem. To deal with it, a cultural solution is needed, one that involves changing the norms of the organization that are traceable to leadership, environment, and group expectations. Table 9.2 lists norms that influence people to work or stay at home. Examination of the information contained in Table 9.2 indicates that many of the processes involved in personnel administration are related to the absenteeism culture.

In the previous discussion, the point was made that provision for personnel time off with pay is a requisite of contemporary organizational life. Negative outcomes of this privilege are the extent to which the leave privilege has been abused as well as skyrocketing costs of absenteeism in both

TABLE 9.2
Factors that enhance or inhibit the absenteeism culture.

Norms That Influence People to Work or Stay at Home, Thus Helping to Create the Absenteeism Culture	To Change an Absenteeism Culture Requires . . .
Leadership commitment	Involvement of employees at all levels
Leadership modeling	Results orientation
Recognition and compensation systems	Sound data
Organizational policies and procedures	A positive focus
Policy interpretation and implementation	A systematic approach
Recruitment and selection	Follow-through
Orientation and training	
Performance appraisal	
Health factors	
Job satisfaction	
Relationship of attendance to specific events	

Source: Reprinted, by permission of publisher, from Personnel, Jan/Feb 1990 © 1990. American Management Association, New York. All rights reserved.

public and private sectors. Documentation of absenteeism in public education has created both an awareness of the problem as well as a variety of suggestions for its remediation.

Influences on Personnel Attendance

Although much has been written about the problem of absenteeism and numerous ideas have been offered to resolve the dilemma, more analyses need to be made of the root causes of the absenteeism culture, how various facets of the culture interact, and how problem resolution can be linked to its major causes. Figure 9.4 presents a model based on the premise that the desire to come to work is influenced largely by two factors: *job satisfaction* and *pressure to attend*.

Redesign Features

It is clear from a review of the literature that an absenteeism culture exacts significant organizational, psychological, social, and pupil learning costs. The problem goes beyond position dissatisfaction and the view that liberal benefit provisions permit system members to attend work whenever they choose to do so. There are basic societal, individual, and organizational forces that underlie and, indeed, contribute to high rates of absenteeism. Major innovative efforts are needed to deal with such contributing factors as weak or indefinite administrative approaches to the problem, social tolerance of absenteeism, abuse of leave benefits, low work motivation, immaturity, a stress-prone society, alcoholism and drug abuse, and lenient supervision. Redesign efforts tend to avoid piecemeal approaches and rely more heavily on a coordinated or systems approach to achieve a lasting impact on the broad aim of improving individual and organizational effectiveness.

Systemic and comprehensive design efforts to improve individual productivity and reduce absenteeism include the following:

• Diagnosis

> Continuous study of facts concerning lateness and absence in the system. Useful in this connection are lateness and absence rates by system and by building unit as well as reasons, time patterns for absence and lateness, age and gender of absentees, and conditions that may be a source of malingering behavior.
>
> Concentration by unit heads on discovering real causes of absence and lateness. The source of the difficulty is often with the individual; but working conditions, position incompatibility, and leadership style

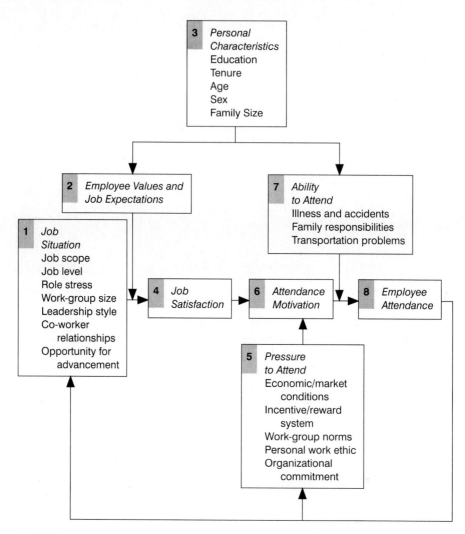

FIGURE 9.4
Major influences on personnel attendance.

Source: Reprinted, by permission of publisher, from Personnel, Nov/Dec 1980 © 1980. American Management Association, New York. All rights reserved.

often contribute to negative personnel behavior. Staying away from work is considered to be a common defense mechanism to avoid unrewarding work or position-related problems.

Involvement of a medical team in the absence control program, including medical treatment of and consultation with chronic offenders.

Review of prior absence record of new applicants.

Review of system activities that generate absences (faculty meetings, position stress, appraisal system, physical facilities and working conditions, in-service programs, and student assembly programs).

Consideration of relationship of plans for dealing with teacher absences in the development of new facilities.

• Communication

Incorporation of rules in the personnel handbook governing absence and lateness. This includes the requirement that each employee report lateness or absence on forms especially devised for control purposes.

Communication to all personnel of absence, lateness, and enforcement procedures.

Development and communication of individual, unit, and organizational absence profiles.

Review of absence-reporting system during orientation period.

• Proactive provisions

Creation of attendance-oriented culture.

Advancement of proactive sick leave policies.

Payment for unused sick leave.

Creation of sick leave banks.

Provisions for physical examinations, exercise programs, and counseling programs.

• Control

Review of collective bargaining agreements to control unnecessary teacher absence.

Review of state school laws to ensure that payments for sick leave are legal and permissible.

Use of progressive discipline, including counseling of absence- and lateness-prone personnel, followed by warnings and dismissal when such behavior continues to be chronic.

Treatment of unexcused absences and lateness as unpaid leave.

Centralization in the personnel office of records and reports relating to absenteeism and lateness.

Curtailment of absenteeism abuse through less favorable coverage, higher insurance contributions, and higher deductibles.

The preceding outline contains a variety of redesign approaches to reduce absenteeism. School officials have a twin responsibility in this regard: revision of the many organizational elements related to absenteeism into an internally consistent whole and enhancement of the work environment and the personal work ethic so as to improve the quality of work life for all system members. Potential contributions of positive absentee policies and absence-control programs to school system continuity are numerous, including greater continuity in teaching and learning, lower turnover, lower benefit costs, more career-oriented personnel, and improved personnel performance.

PROMOTION, TRANSFER, AND DEMOTION OF PERSONNEL

The model of the employment continuity process outlined in Figure 9.1 indicates that maintenance of staffing steadiness includes provisions for dealing with personnel mobility problems, including *promotion, transfer,* and *demotion*. Each of these areas will be examined subsequently.

Promotion

Promotion is generally taken to mean an advance in status or position. Frequently, it implies a change in duties, responsibility, and compensation. It belongs to the cluster of administrative problems relating to movement of personnel into and out of the organization—recruitment, selection, placement, transfer, and separation. Promotion is a significant aspect of personnel administration. The system is dependent on availability of qualified replacements at all structural levels. Opportunity for promotion is related to recruitment and retention of personnel. It is also necessary so as to maximize realization of the desires and interests of personnel.

Major issues involved in personnel promotion are (a) seniority or position fitness, (b) internal or external promotion, (c) formal or informal promotion, (d) past performance or future position potential, (e) promotion criteria, and (f) negative effects. Forming a school system promotion policy also involves consideration of the following:

- Because of the small size of most school systems in the United States, as well as the limited availability of positions to which members can be promoted, the potential for advancement through career paths is extremely limited.
- Until contemporary models of career development replace traditional practices, the likelihood of individuals progressing through predictable and satisfying career stages is not encouraging.

- Competition for administrative positions, with their higher compensation, has resulted in a loss of excellent classroom teachers.

- Development or career ladders for classroom teachers are often centered on preparing for administrative positions rather than improving teaching performance or the educational program.

- Extensive encouragement of classroom personnel to prepare for administrative positions has a detrimental effect on maintenance of a superior teaching staff.

Throughout this text, the importance of designing and implementing a proactive human resources strategy has been stressed. One aspect of this strategy is getting the right people into the right positions. Promotion policy should be shaped to advance individuals who have the abilities, skills, attitudes, and commitment to enhance strategy. Under this arrangement, promotions are bestowed on those who not only meet but exceed performance standards. Promotion criteria help to identify people whose strengths are needed to achieve position and system aims and to place such individuals where their strengths can be fully exercised.

Promotion policy should be readied for a departure from practices that place less emphasis on performance strengths and are tilted toward political, union, special interest, minority, ethnic, and seniority considerations. If the thrust of organization culture is performance-based, the promotion decision issues (seniority, internal-external, formal-informal, and negative effects) can be dealt with more decisively.

Once the practice of fostering promotion strengths is established, administrative specifics are needed for its operation. These may be expressed in several ways. One step is to analyze those positions to which applicants will be promoted in terms of strengths needed to fulfill position expectations. A second step is to develop profiles of persons within the system who have the potential for success in performing effectively in those positions. This is followed by the process of matching positions and profiles, aided by data derived from the personnel information system and related channels. Part of the assessment involves analysis of applicant-group compatibility. By excluding such factors as loyalty, friendship, consistent agreement with official viewpoints, exhibitionism, and favoritism from promotion practices, those who have not been promoted have little basis for grievances, court suits, and charges of discrimination. Through a carefully planned career development program, officials can identify persons with promotable capabilities within the system, provide opportunities in which such capabilities can be assessed, and establish a talent bank from which to fill vacancies as they occur. Such a program tends to minimize the issues mentioned above because it complements human resources strategy, which aims at preparing personnel for position advancement when the opportunity arises.

Transfer

Transfer, promotion, and dismissal of personnel are closely linked to one aspect of human resources planning, that is, the need to shift position holders within the system to staff vacancies, place personnel in positions in keeping with their interests and abilities, and correct staffing errors. The term *transfer,* as used here, refers to movement of personnel from one position, office, department, or school to another. The movement is generally horizontal and may or may not involve increased responsibilities or compensation. Transfer should not be confused with *reassignment,* which means a change in assignment within the same office, department, division, or school. In general, transfers are initiated either by the administrative staff (involuntary) or by organization personnel (voluntary) and affect both professional and support employees.

Transfer of personnel is an important aspect of school administration, one that deserves more attention from a policy standpoint than it is usually accorded. Some understanding of the extent of the transfer problem can be gained from Table 9.3. This table makes it evident that every school system

TABLE 9.3
Reasons for personnel transfer.

Transfers Initiated by the Administration (Involuntary)	Transfers Initiated by Personnel (Voluntary)
Overstaffing in certain units	Desire to work in a new school
Enrollment increase or decrease	Personal friction
Changes in the organization of instruction	Physical reasons
Unsatisfactory service	Blind alley jobs
Technological advances in maintenance and operation affecting work load of support personnel	Monotony and stagnation
Deterioration in personal relationships	Desire to work in schools that are not in low-income areas and that are not obsolescent
Planned experience for future administrative service	Desire for advancement in status or compensation
Efforts to identify future administrative talent	Desire to work closer to home
Gender, racial, talent, and experience balance	Contract rights to more favorable working conditions (seniority)
More appropriate placement	
Needs of system	
Closing and opening of facilities	
Court decisions	
Staffing a new program	

should give attention to establishment of personnel transfer policies and procedures. The central consideration should be the welfare of school children. A plan that places senior members of the faculty in the "favored" schools and inexperienced teachers in the "difficult" schools does not meet this criterion.

Although it is not the purpose of this discussion to prescribe what type of transfer plan should be established in a given district, certain important decisions need to be made in developing a course of action. These relate to questions such as the following:

- What forms of employee transfer are officially recognized in the system's transfer policy (employer initiated, employee initiated, work unit initiated, temporary, indefinite, permanent)?
- What are the conditions of transfer (seniority, promotion, demotion, compensation)?
- What criteria shall apply in evaluating employee transfer requests?
- What contractual considerations are involved in employee transfer?
- What system policies and procedures govern transfer relative to position openings?
- What arrangements exist to consider personal reasons of employees who request or refuse transfer?[8]
- For what reasons will transfers be made? It is advisable to establish a minimum length of service that personnel must render in a general assignment before a transfer can be effective. Underlying reasons for establishing control of the transfer process are to enable the administration to appraise the performance of the individual, determine suitability of the original placement, and avoid interruptions in the instructional program.
- What are the circumstances or conditions for which transfer requests will be considered? Conditions under which transfers will be granted should be clearly defined. The plan should set forth circumstances under which the administration may initiate transfer as well as when personnel may do so.

It is important for these conditions to be publicized in the personnel manual or through other media to minimize misunderstandings. Under the typical collective bargaining agreement, the initial assignment of personnel is the responsibility of the central administration, subject to constraints imposed by the location of vacancies after voluntary internal transfers have been accommodated. Once initial assignment has been made, involuntary transfer of personnel is limited under many existing agreements. For example, a teacher may be reassigned satisfactorily in one situation but not in another. Without widespread understanding among administrators of aims of the transfer plan, its chances for success are minimal.

Transfers should be encouraged whenever they are in the interest of the individual and the system. Transfer is a valuable administrative device for improving staff development and flexibility. It should be construed as a means of putting into practice the concept that administration has a continuing responsibility for matching persons and jobs.

Continuous appraisal of transfer policies and procedures should make it possible to improve the operation. It should help administration to secure information on the scope of the transfer problem, the effect of transfers, improvement of service, and those aspects of the transfer plan that are effective as well as ineffective. Appraisal of personnel performance is fundamental to the success of the transfer plan, for the information it yields is essential in making judgments and decisions about transfer problems.

Many transfer problems revolve around what is referred to as the *dislocated individual,* one who has become a marginal performer because the position outgrows the person or because of other reasons, such as aging and senility, professional obsolescence, low work motivation, and rejection by peers. Several options are available to the system in dealing with the dislocated individual. These options include carefully planned trading between organizational sub-units, retraining, demotion, transfer, and dismissal. If the decision is made to retain the individual in the organization, it is essential that whatever approach is adopted should be conducted with the objective that the individual must attain and maintain a prescribed level of performance. A plan not aggressively pursued will not alleviate problems generated by dislocated personnel.

Demotion

Demotion has been defined as a form of transfer or reassignment involving a decrease in salary, status, responsibility, privilege, and opportunity. Some demotions are beyond the control of the individual, especially in the case of staff reductions. Others are undertaken by the system for a variety of reasons, such as overqualification for the position, marginal performance, disciplinary action, or to correct an error in initial placement. Forms of demotion include lowered job status with the same or lowered salary; same status with lower compensation; being bypassed in seniority for promotion; moving the person to a less desirable job; keeping the same formal status, but with a decreased span of control; being excluded from a general salary increase; insertion of positions above the person in the hierarchy; moving to a staff position; elimination of a position and reassignment; and transfer out of direct line for promotion.

From the standpoint of the system, one of the most important aspects of demotion is that appropriate procedures for such action are established and adhered to scrupulously. Due process violations in demoting personnel are numerous, and they occur because of failure to observe individual rights guaranteed under the First, Fifth, Sixth, and Fourteenth Amendments to the U.S. Constitution. In addition, use of legal counsel prior to action on personnel demotion is advisable, because ignorance of the law is not an accepted excuse for violating it.

Behavioral aspects of demotion are also important considerations when such action is contemplated. To many individuals, work is the most important element in their lives. To be subjected to a demotion is to most persons a rejection, a crushing blow, one that is likely to generate the severest kind of antiorganizational behavior. For the long-service employee or for those who have performed faithfully and effectively over time, demotion may not be the appropriate action if certain responsibilities to which such individuals are assigned can be shifted temporarily to other positions. Other alternatives include transfer to a less demanding position without loss of pay or status, or incentive provisions for early retirement. Such solutions are preferable when they can be arranged without due interference with system operations and without creating role inequities that may lead to conflict.

As noted in previous chapters concerning conditions of leave, performance effectiveness, and various forms of employee benefit provisions, a precise definition of control terms that make clear the framework governing demotion is imperative from legal, moral, ethical, employee, and employer standpoints. The main reasons for demotion are considered to be *ineffectiveness* or *inefficiency*, although others have been invoked including conflicts regarding employee behavior and performance standards, behavior reflecting poorly on the institution, individual-organizational ideological differences, employee-system differences about management conduct, layoff, and position elimination.

Whatever the reasons for demotion, the decision should be based on a clear definition of what kinds of behavioral or system circumstances may lead to demotion. Given these definitions, the system is then in a stronger position to effect appropriate demotion prerogatives. In any event, an act of demotion rightfully deserves system attention to determine the underlying causal conditions and to what extent, if any, there are weaknesses in the policies and procedures that have been established to prevent such management actions as demotion.

Resolution of demotion-related situations may include these actions: (a) informing the employee of intent to demote; (b) providing options, where feasible, such as transfer to a position of lower status, responsibility, and salary readjustment; (c) endeavoring to negotiate a settlement acceptable to both parties; (d) formalizing and informing the individual of the reasons for demotion; (e) notifying concerned parties of the official starting date; and (f) prescribing new position responsibilities.[9]

SEPARATION

School systems are comprised of people working together to achieve a common goal. People create a viable organization, breathe life and purpose into its structure, and give it color, depth, and vibrance. Personnel processes discussed throughout this text are means by which a steady state in the number, quality, and motivation of personnel is achieved. As illustrated in Figure 9.5, one of the subprocesses of the personnel function is designed to effect a high degree of staffing continuity, which requires attention to problems of people who enter the system, those who remain, and those who, for various reasons, are separated.

With appropriate cautions for jurisdictional variations, certain generalizations seem to emerge concerning legal aspects of RIF:

1. RIF is primarily a matter of state statutes; thus, the specific legislative provision should not be neglected in ascertaining legal developments nationally.

2. Statutory RIF reasons vary within a predictable pattern, ranging from enrollment decline to a catchall "good cause" category.

3. Where a RIF reason is statutorily specified, it should be strictly followed and factually supported.

4. Courts tend to defer the evidence and decisions of local school boards unless the plaintiff-teacher can show the proffered reason to be a subterfuge for an impermissible basis (e.g., race discrimination or union activity).

5. A minority of statutes specify criteria with respect to the order for RIF. Where such criteria are specified, seniority and tenure status predominate; merit is given a relatively limited role.

6. Where statutes are silent or ambiguous about the order of release, courts tend liberally to read in an inverse seniority standard, to be more restrictive about inferring a tenure priority, and to allow but not generally require other criteria, such as merit.

7. Bumping rights provided by these criteria are limited by the court-construed contours of legal qualification, realignment of duty, and affirmative action. Legal qualification generally is interpreted to mean certification, realignment duty is typically limited, and affirmative action tends to take priority over traditional RIF criteria.

8. Courts have tended not to interpret statutory and constitutional procedural due process protections expansively in relation to RIF plaintiffs.

9. Recall rights are legislated and litigated less than release rights, with roughly although not exactly parallel results.

FIGURE 9.5

Generalizations concerning legal aspects of reduction in force.

Source: Joseph A. Beckham and Perry A. Zirkel, Editors, Legal Issues in Public School Employment (Bloomington, IN: Phi Delta Kappa, 1983), 189.

To provide the reader with a perspective on personnel separation, it is useful to consider separation as either no-fault or individual fault. Thus, the discussion that follows is devoted to the termination of personnel employment for reasons beyond the control of the individual (no-fault). Permanent separation from the payroll, usually referred to as discharge, is generally the result of some behavioral inadequacy of or offense by the individual (individual fault). This aspect of personnel separation is examined in detail in Chapter 7. The intent of the discussion that follows is to bring to bear on the topic insights, practices, and problems to be considered if personnel separation is to be performed humanely, effectively, and purposefully.

Resignation

One of the most common forms of personnel separation is *resignation,* an action initiated by the individual rather than by the system. Some resignations are frequently beyond control of the system for a variety of reasons, such as opportunities for higher compensation, illness, promotions, relocation, and maternity. Certain resignations, however, are controllable, especially those associated with poor supervisory practices and unsatisfactory working conditions. Whatever the reasons for resignations, the impact on the system is sizable in recruitment, development, and replacement costs as well as in interruptions in the teaching-learning process. Consequently, resignations from the system call for some form of analysis. This analysis is usually referred to as *turnover analysis* (the patterns of movement of the work force into and out of the system). Turnover rate in school systems can be calculated as the ratio of separations to total work force x 100 for a given period. Calculating turnover on the basis of accessions rather than separations focuses attention on costs. The formula would be:

$$TR \ (turnover) = [A \ (accessions) \div F \ (total \ work \ force)] \times 100$$

Related approaches include:

- Exit interviews (questionnaires to terminees six months after departure).
- Statistical analysis (total attrition rates as well as rates by age, unit, and position).
- Comparison of terminees by categories (such as "those we hate to see go and will miss," "those we will not miss," and "all others").
- Analysis of those areas where there is little turnover.

Every separation from the system should involve some sort of procedure carefully adhered to for numerous reasons. In the case of resignations, the procedure involves (a) notification by the individual staff member of the intent to resign; (b) documentation (in the form of a letter) by the school system that the resignation is voluntary; (c) notification of persons in the system who need to know about the resignation; (d) processing of paperwork related to resignation; (e) the exit interview, results of which are analyzed by the system to determine the extent to which the causes are controllable, and what action, if any, is in order; and (f) careful record keeping for a variety of reasons, including legal challenges and unemployment compensation. There is, according to Gellerman, a positive side to turnover. He suggests that it gives the organization an opportunity to bring in new talent, minimizes the number of employees whose salaries rise beyond the midpoint of their range, and is a practical solution to the problem of dull or dead-end jobs that cannot be made more attractive. The system can discourage turnover, Gellerman notes, primarily by making it financially or psychologically disadvantageous for the employee to leave.[10] There are studies to enhance the Gellerman premise. For example, a research study on turnover by Kesner and Dalton draws attention to the fact that research on the consequences of turnover has often been one-sided. Their data indicate that there are turnover benefits and that further research may indicate that it *might not be cost-effective* to reduce the incidence of responsible levels of voluntary turnover.[11]

Reduction in Force

In the last quarter of the twentieth century, a number of factors impacting on educational institutions in the United States have reduced the number of persons employed by these organizations. These factors involved in **reduction in force** include declining enrollments, declining revenues, increasing costs, societal concerns about the total costs of government services, reduction of educational programs and services, and conflict over which government services should receive which priorities.

Personnel layoffs are a major management problem, especially because of the impact of such action on the security of the individual position holder. Weisberger, after reviewing the body of recent court, administrative agency, and arbitral decisions regarding layoffs and job abolition, concluded that in the absence of specific and express restrictions on the public employer's basic right to determine layoffs or to abolish positions, public employees challenging these decisions have little chance of success. Public financial exigencies rarely have to be justified. Where claims are made by public employees that required procedures for layoffs or job abolition have not been complied with and these facts are not basically in dispute, the chances for success by public employees are high.[12] Beckham and Zirkel's review of educational *legislation* and *litigation* relating to reduction in force (RIF), which is capsulized in Figure 9.5, brings into focus the impact of RIF on school personnel, the widening concern, increasing interest, and continuing litigation in this evolving and complex personnel matter.[13]

Legal, administrative, educational, and human implications of RIF actions are such that school systems need to give considerable attention to the systemwide planning involved in reduction in force programs. Table 9.4 illustrates the kinds of decisions that are involved in designing RIF *policies* and *procedures*. Examination of the policy and procedural elements listed in Table 9.4 gives the reader an indication of the nature and extent of problems generated by RIF actions and to which boards of education need to respond.

One comprehensive study of work force reductions indicates that the process consists of three phases:

TABLE 9.4
Policy and procedural elements to be considered in developing RIF programs.

Policy Elements
Conditions under which RIF is initiated
Forestalling and minimizing layoffs
Due process to be followed
Individual rights protected
Adherence to federal and state laws and union contracts
Seniority (sole factor, primary factor, secondary factor, or equal with other factors)
Notifying and consulting provision
Work sharing
Staff and program needs of system
Equity of results for pupils and teachers
Quality of programs and services protected
Fair basis of reduction (same ratio of minority-majority employees and male-female employees)

Procedural Elements
Personnel groupings and subgroupings (bases for RIF)
Service computation date
Bumping and retreating rights
Vacancies
Notification
Appeal procedure
Status during layoffs
Reinstatement procedure
Rights after reinstatement
Termination
Employment of new personnel
Future changes in policies and procedures (board and individual rights)

- *Recognition period*—The organization confronts the need to reduce its work force.
- *Actual downsizing*—The organization reviews or establishes severance policies and procedures.
- *Forward motion*—The roles of remaining employees are restructured, often with broader roles for key players.[14]

School systems may respond mechanically or creatively to resolution of problems related to RIF. Experience indicates that if appropriate decisions are made, layoffs can be effected with compassion and competence. Coping effectively with problems of personnel layoffs while improving employee relations in general are desirable objectives of personnel administration. Attainment of these ends includes plans that will meet the following criteria satisfactorily:

- Specify in advance, through policies and procedures, the manner in which RIF programs will be put in operation.
- Adhere strictly to legal and board requirements, rulings, and union contracts relating to reduction in force procedures (proper reasons, order of release, and order of restoration).
- View RIF as one of several approaches to dealing with the economics of operating an educational system. Alternative approaches include greater attention to long-range planning, which would indicate in advance changing economic, social, political, and cultural conditions that will impact on the operation of the organization.
- Assume that efficiency and effectiveness are paramount system objectives and operate the system accordingly. This involves initiating and maintaining human resources planning as an essential process of personnel administration.
- Adhere to the psychological contract between the individual and the organization.
- Consult with personnel prior to layoffs.
- Provide a variety of forms of assistance (outplacement services being foremost).
- Disclose fully the conditions that generated RIF actions.

Even though school systems often decide unilaterally what criteria will be employed in the layoff of unorganized personnel, a systematic approach for dealing with layoff problems is an organizational necessity. The procedure should be designed to resolve layoff issues equitably and efficiently, regardless of the presence or absence of a union. This is to say that for personnel who may be affected by a layoff, the system needs to decide in advance and communicate to personnel conditions that will govern layoff (the essence of which is outlined in Table 9.4).

Disability

Physical disability of personnel over a protracted period of time is another kind of separation problem relating to personnel continuity. Major problems connected with physical disability include (a) deciding whether an individual is physically incapable of fulfilling the assignment because of illness or injury, (b) establishing the amount of time a disabled individual is to be kept on the payroll, (c) timing of replacement, and (d) provisions for lessening the financial impact of physical disability. Again, system guidelines need to be established and communicated in advance to all personnel on the payroll so that indecision and inequity will not hold sway when disability problems arise.

When personnel suffer disabilities, handicaps, and long illnesses, numerous questions arise that should be referred to qualified professional medical personnel. Medical problems, ranging from heart disease and cancer to full and partial physical immobility, raise questions about whether an individual should return to work and under what conditions. In other cases, malingering may be suspected. Consequently, the system's responsibility in matters of incapacity involves gathering available evidence, consulting with medical personnel, and assessing prospects for return and level of performance anticipated. Most disability problems are extremely sensitive, especially as to the manner in which the affected individual perceives treatment and sympathy accorded by the system. Terminal illnesses and permanent physical immobility are matters deserving careful attention, especially with regard to the timing of replacements. Collateral benefits are of financial assistance in disability cases. In addition, insurance plans for long-term disability are now at hand and are becoming a standard feature of collateral benefit plans.

The American With Disabilities Act of 1990 (ADA) was referred to earlier in this chapter in connection with leaves of absence. The range of provisions in the ADA is extensive and should be taken into consideration in administration of the human resources function. Provisions include:

- *Planning process*—Definitions, policies, and procedures for accommodating persons with disabilities.
- *Recruitment*—Discrimination in hiring.
- *Selection*—Types of tests applied, that is, preemployment medical examinations.
- *Induction*—Position placement.
- *Development*—Shaping programs to meet disability needs.

- *Appraisal*—Position standards.
- *Justice*—Complaint procedures, equal opportunity, fair treatment.
- *Continuity*—Performance effectiveness, leave provisions, transfer.
- *Information*—Legal compliance records, accommodation documentation.
- *Compensation*—Equal pay.
- *Bargaining*—Contract adherence.

In addition to the ADA there are other protective provisions in most state laws, Title VII of the Civil Rights Act, and the Rehabilitation Act of 1973. The implications for organizational accommodation of the legal employment rights of the disabled is extensive, and as noted above, require inclusion in the several processes of the human resources function.[15]

CAREER PASSAGE: RETIREMENT AND BEYOND

Retirement may be viewed as a process in passing from one life stage into another or a withdrawal from one's position or active working life. Within the past decade interest has heightened in the significance of retirement education as a human resource issue. Retirement planning comes within the purview of the human resources function as one of the four stages of personal and career development: *establishment, advancement, maintenance,* and *retirement* (see Table 6.5). Retirement planning is also concerned about a fifth stage, referred to herein as postretirement living. Special needs of individuals nearing the retirement age brings into consideration retirement education programs to assist employees to make the transition from work life to after-work living. This is the theme of the text following.

The Human Resources Function and Retirement Planning

Institutional retirement programs of the 1990s and beyond are different from those of the 1960s. The winds of change relative to one's retirement have been propelled by oncoming generation retirees concerned about how to deal with problems associated with retirement. These problems include health maintenance, financial security, what to do with retirement time, early or mandated retirement, taxation of the elderly, medical reform, where to live comfortably and securely, stability of the state retirement system, benefit adequacy, and the extent to which retired persons will be affected by political, social, and economic uncertainties.

The retirement planning framework presented in Figure 9.6 includes six components:

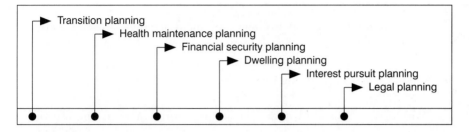

FIGURE 9.6
Illustration of retirement program planning components.

- *Transition Planning*—Covers the retirement landscape, the information needed and where to get it, regulatory requirements, state retirement system options, retirement starting time, and responses to the host of questions involved in retirement planning.
- *Health Maintenance*—Stresses health maintenance and life styles entailed in resolving problems related to nutrition, stress, exercise, and abstention from health disincentives such as alcohol, drugs, obesity, and tobacco.
- *Financial Planning*—Major emphasis is on what a desirable lifestyle will cost and the financial resources needed to achieve expectations.
- *Dwelling Arrangements*—Examines dwelling options: where to live in the future and with whom (alone, retirement community, present arrangement); examines options and information needed to make proper choices.
- *Interest Pursuits*—Presents options for making decisions about part- or full-time employment, avocation pursuits, and volunteer activities.
- *Legal Affairs*—Discusses ordinary wills, living wills, trusts, estates, power of attorney, and events related to mental or physical incapacity.

The preceding components entail various assumptions. These assumptions include:

- The retirement planning program will be based on joint planning initiatives between the system and system participants.
- The system's prime responsibilities include motivation of participants to plan for and take action in the preretirement stage to develop a desirable and achievable program for after-work living.
- The individual is responsible for the kinds of decisions implicit in each of the components. The system renders assistance in providing information, planning options, and pitfalls to avoid.
- Program content includes time-related segments, each of which is spread over a time span well in advance of retirement start-up.

- Present retirement policies, laws, and assumptions are not cast in stone. Federal, state, local, and school system retirement arrangements are subject to change, depending on political, economic, social, and global circumstances.
- Participants will be responsible for professional consultation needed in certain aspects of planning (legal, medical, and health).

With *early retirement* programs becoming more common, the individual school system has several important responsibilities. One is to establish policies and practices to assist its members in preparing for satisfying and secure retirement. Another is to link retirement planning to staff improvement. A third responsibility is to develop an understanding of possible legal implications and permissible activities as they relate to personnel retirement decisions. A fourth obligation is to take initiatives, along with teacher associations and unions, to achieve the types of improvements needed in state retirement systems (as noted in AARP, Wall Street Journal studies).[16]

School systems are steadily increasing policies and practices to assist those individuals in the preretirement stage to make the transition to retirement and postretirement. Retirement assistance preparation programs can be described as including three forms: *preretirement preparation, flexible or phased retirement,* and *postretirement assistance.*

Preretirement programs are considered to be inexpensive benefits to provide information and counseling on problems and opportunities of a variety of matters of interest to potential retirees, as well as to gather information for future staffing purposes.

Flexible or phased retirement refers to opportunities for personnel nearing retirement to reduce their work load through part-time positions, leaves of absence, and reduced work days, work weeks, or work years.

Organizational retirement planning includes development of flexible ways of moving out of the system people who, for a variety of reasons, are no longer capable of performing effectively or whose services are no longer needed. Consequently, the system is interested in career-change programs for its personnel from two standpoints: (a) developing better methods of helping staff members make the adjustment from a working to a nonworking or part-time employment status and (b) developing approaches that will motivate people to separate themselves from the system both for their own welfare and for the good of the system. Decision making concerning early retirement often involves consideration of the question, Is early retirement favorable or unfavorable to the organization? To the individual?

Personnel retirement preferences vary. There are those who elect to retire early, those who opt to remain until the traditional specified age of 65, and those who choose to work until the age of 70. This discretionary state of affairs, coupled with contemporary retirement legislation, has been attended by various kinds of legal issues.

Mandatory Retirement Legislation.   On April 6, 1978, President Carter signed the Age Discrimination in Employment Act Amendments of 1978. The original Age Discrimination in Employment Act of 1967 was designed to promote employment of older persons based on ability rather than age, prohibit arbitrary age discrimination in employment, and help employers and workers find ways of meeting problems arising from the assumed curtailment of worker ability and efficiency by advancement of chronological age. The 1978 amendments to the law make three significant changes: (a) they expand coverage to workers in private industry and state and local government so as to provide continued protection after they reach 65 and before they attain 70 years of age; (b) they generally eliminate mandatory retirement in the federal sector; and (c) they *invalidate provisions in pension plans and retirement systems covering both private and public employment that mandate involuntary retirement during the protected age*.

Some of the pros and cons of extending the mandatory age limit from 65 to 70 include the following:

- Increased life expectancy.
- Age discrimination.
- Inflation.
- Lessening strain on the Social Security system.
- Public backing.
- Impact of retirement legislation (such as the Age Discrimination in Employment Act—ADEA).
- Neutralizing mandatory retirement laws.
- Rising employee health care costs.
- Significant losses of real talent.
- Pressure to improve performance appraisal process.
- Harsh treatment of marginal personnel who are above the age of 60.

The effect of the 1978 amendments is certain to add retirement to the growing list of challenges to personnel administration, such as equal employment opportunity, tenure, safety, performance appraisal, dismissal, and collateral benefits. One of the impacts of extending the protected retirement age that can be expected is in the area of tenure, where legislated position security may change to negotiated position security. Another factor is the continuing effort at the congressional level to pass federal legislation providing bargaining rights for state and local public employees. Observers now predict, as a result of these and related developments, increased efforts to abolish tenure and to eliminate mandatory retirement for teachers and professors at any age.

The 1978 amendments governing mandatory retirement also affect approaches to performance appraisal. What to do about the marginal performer wishing to retain employment between the ages of 65 and 70 is illustrative. Appraisals of such personnel, when confronted with legal challenge, must be able to withstand the test of ageism (age discrimination).

Thus, it is to be anticipated that transitive consequences of mandatory age legislation for school governance will be extensive, including the need for new approaches to induce personnel to leave the system voluntarily before the retirement age, reexamination and revision of troublesome provisions in collective bargaining contracts, and improvement in the design of performance appraisal systems.[17]

DEATH

Death of a member of the school system involves the following minimum responsibilities for the human resources function: (a) reporting responsibility, (b) representation responsibility, (c) fiscal responsibility, and (d) replacement responsibility. It is generally the responsibility of the administrator in charge of the function to notify relevant persons and organizations of termination in the case of the death of a staff member. These parties include the retirement system, the Social Security agency, the union organization, the unit administrative personnel to whom the deceased was assigned, and the unit within the system responsible for personnel payroll and benefits. The reporting responsibility also involves preparation of information, usually in the form of a memorandum to the school staff that includes whatever details are appropriate.

Contact with the deceased employee's next of kin or estate is an essential personnel activity. The assignment is usually delegated to a staff member who will represent the school system in providing whatever information, communications, or services are needed to expedite details relating to benefits, monies due, and incidental matters.

Various fiscal problems arise in connection with the termination of any staff member, including salary monies due, retirement, and benefits. Although all financial procedures relating to termination are usually established in advance, legal questions may arise in connection with fiscal payments, especially when no beneficiary has been designated by the deceased.

Replacement of persons separated from the system, for whatever reason, must be viewed as an aspect of the human resources planning process and subjected to system guidelines for dealing with positions as they become vacant. Open positions need to be scrutinized carefully from various perspectives. Initially, analysis of the position is needed to determine whether replacement is absolutely necessary or whether duties can be performed effectively by combining them with those of another position. If the decision is made to retain the position, the usual recruitment and selection processes will be invoked. If the position is administrative in nature, some unusual procedures may be employed. It has been said, for example, that the only time the central administration has a clear opportunity to make changes or innovations needed in a unit of the system is when the unit head is separated from the organization. Although this assumption is open to question, it is true that vacancy in a leadership position does make it possible for the system to identify the future direction it expects the unit to take and to select leadership capable of initiating and maintaining a course of action to achieve organizational expectations.

REVIEW AND PREVIEW

This chapter has dealt with organizational provisions designed to retain personnel and foster continuity in personnel service. Analysis of the personnel continuity process indicates there are two clusters of activities: one is concerned with the health and mobility of continuing personnel; the second is focused on members voluntarily or involuntarily leaving the system.

As outlined in this chapter, the process for maintaining continuity of personnel service stresses the need for a projected course of action based on a series of decisions relating to what plans for personnel continuity are expected to achieve; types of plans needed to realize expectations; and program organization, administration, and control. Expectations or results that the system derives from plans for service continuity are both long- and short-range and include improvement of the system's ability to perform its mission; improvement of individual effectiveness; and improvement of system physical, psychological, and organizational environments. Models have been included to examine the employment continuity process, continuity policy, time-related benefits, absenteeism and lateness, reduction in force, and retirement. Other continuity aspects treated include employee assistance programs, health maintenance, temporary personnel, promotion, transfer, demotion, disability, and death.

Development of an informative system, based on accurate recording, refinements, storage, retrieval, and utilization of relevant internal and external events, is the subject of Chapter 10.

REVIEW AND DISCUSSION QUESTIONS

1. List five policy points that should govern the employment and supervision of temporary (contingent) support and professional employees.

2. Prepare a response to the notion that "from the point of view of motivation, promotion should be based on competence rather than

on seniority" (or, "on seniority rather than competence").

3. Develop a proposal to be used in requesting the resignation of a system member. Include legal, ethical, moral, internal, and external considerations.

4. Assume you are a superintendent of schools. One of your employees, a marginal performer, has reached the age of 65. She informs you that she plans to remain on the job until age 70. Explain your approach in resolving this matter to the extent that both parties agree on an amicable solution.

5. Assume you are a principal of a secondary school and have reports that one of your teachers is an alcoholic. Explain your approach in addressing this problem.

6. What are the legal and safety issues involved in managing employees with AIDS related conditions?

7. To what extent are the following performance matters covered by performance management policies in school systems in which you are working or have worked: (a) attendance (e.g., tardiness, leave abuse, or emergencies), (b) health, (c) on-the-job-conduct, (d) quality of performance, and (e) criminal acts.

8. List five work stressors that make unusual demands on your ability to perform position and organizational expectations (e.g., stimuli or forces—such as supervisory practices, union pressures, or colleague behavior—exerting physical, mental, or emotional strain on your ability to perform effectively.

9. What should the school system do about system personnel who are potential health risks (for example, from smoking, alcohol and drug abuse, obesity, high cholesterol, high blood pressure, certain life styles)?

10. The Age Discrimination in Employment Act (ADEA) enacted in 1979 is intended to protect employees after they reach 65 and before they attain 70 years of age from arbitrary and age-biased discrimination in recruitment, promotions, training, compensation, discipline, and termination. What policies and procedures should be established to deal with age-related discrimination problems?

11. Evaluate a continuity-related policy in a school district or other organization of your choice. Specifically, to what extent are these provisions extant: (a) leave purpose, (b) leave policy, (c) leave procedures, and (d) leave controls?

CHAPTER EXERCISE 9.1

This exercise is designed for classroom discussion purposes.
Directions: Keep in mind a school system in which you are or have been employed and consider each of the following employment continuity related factors. Do you consider each factor a major problem, a minor problem, no problem, or are you unsure?

A. Human Resources Continuity Problems

    Time off, personal

    Time off, professional

    Temporary personnel service

    School violence

    Promotion

       Demotion

       Reassignment

       Transfer

       Layoff

       Employee disability

       Employee separation

       Retirement planning

B. Employee Health Maintenance

       Alcohol

       Drugs

       Tobacco

       Absenteeism

       Obesity

       Employee lifestyle

C. Employment Stress Factors (stimuli or forces exerting physical, mental, or emotional strain on your ability to perform your work effectively)

       Work station conditions

       Building conditions

Co-workers

System leadership style

Board of education effectiveness

Position expectations, personal

Career development, personal

Union leadership

Community support

Intergroup behavior and conflict

Work group behavior

Cultural diversity

Communication

System policies and procedures

Compensation

Availability of resources

Information technology

Quality of work life

System support to reduce stressors

Behavior of problem personnel

NOTES

1. "Goodbye, Mandatory Maternity Leaves," Nation's Schools 90 (October 1972), 10–14; and "Pregnant School Girls and Pregnant Teachers: The Policy Problem School Districts Can No Longer Sidestep," American School Board Journal 160, 3 (March, 1973), 23–31.

2. For an elaboration of the Pregnancy Disability Act of 1978 and other federal regulations referred to in this chapter, see Mary F. Cook, Editor, The Human Resources Yearbook, 1993/1994 Edition (Englewood Cliffs, NJ: Prentice-Hall Inc., 1993), 12.10.

3. Cook, 1.9, 6.10, 6.21, 9.2, 12.10.

4. For an extended treatment of leaves of absence, see William S. Hubbartt,

Personnel Policy Handbook (New York: McGraw-Hill Inc., 1993), Chapter 9.

5. For further details regarding health incentives, see Cook, Chapters 6, 12, 17.

6. Ibid. Chapters 6, 12, 17.

7. Linda E. Kelly and James R. Gaddy, "Substitute Program Redesign," Clearing House 51 (March 1978), 35–38.

8. See Hubbartt for illustrations of transfer policies, procedures, and checklist.

9. See William R. Tracey, Editor, Human Resources Management and Development Handbook (New

York: American Management Association, 1985). Demotion and separation are examined in terms of procedures and record keeping requirements.

10. Saul W. Gellerman, "In Praise of Those Who Leave," Conference Board Record 11, 3 (March 1974), 35–38.

11. Idalene F. Kesner and Dan Z. Dalton, "Turnover Benefits: The Other Side of the 'Costs' Coin," Personnel 59, 5 (September–October 1982), 69–76.

12. June Weisberger, Recent Developments in Job Security: Layoffs and Discipline in the Public Sector (Ithaca, NY: New York School of Industrial and Labor Relations, 1976), 424.

13. Joseph Beckham and Perry A. Zirkel, Editors, Legal Issues in Public School Employment (Bloomington, IN: Phi Delta Kappa, 1983), 189.

14. American Management Association, Responsible Reductions in Force (New York: American Management Association, 1987), 11.

15. For further information on federal laws, see U.S. Equal Employment Opportunity Commission, A Technical Assistance Manual on the Employment Provisions (Title I) of the Americans With Disabilities Act (Washington: The Commission, January 1992).

16. Two studies on state school retirement systems are: National Retired Teachers Association, Fifty State Teachers' Retirement Systems: A Comparative Analysis (Washington: The Association, 1987); and Ellen E. Schultz, "Teachers are Judges on Retirement Plans," The Wall Street Journal, February 10, 1994, C15.

17. Hubbartt and Tracey provide important information on human resources retirement practices.

SUPPLEMENTARY READING

Applebaum, Stephen H.; and Barbara T. Shapiro. "The ABC's of EAPs." Personnel 66, 7 (July 1989), 39.

Bahls, Jane Esther. "Getting Full-Time Work from Part-Time Employees." Management Review 79, 2 (February 1990), 50–52.

Bradley, John. "Developing and Implementing a Policy on AIDS." Management Review 79, 2 (February 1990), 64.

Green, R. W. Carmell; and P. Gray. 1992 State by State Guide to Human Resources Law. New York: Panel Publishers, 1992.

Hoffman, Jeffrey. "Sweetening Early Retirement Programs." Personnel 67, 3 (March 1990), 18–20.

Hudock, Arthur W. "Preretirement Counseling: A View from the Other Side." Personnel 66, 9 (February 1989), 36.

Ivancevich, John M.; and William F. Glueck. Foundations of Personnel/Human Resources Management. Third Edition. Plano, TX: Business Publications Inc., 1986.

Jesseph, Stephen A. "Employee Termination, 2: Some Do's and Don'ts." Personnel 66, 2 (February 1989), 36.

Levesque, Joseph D. Manual of Personnel Policies, Procedures, and Operations. Englewood Cliffs, NJ: Prentice-Hall Inc., 1986.

Lewis, William; and Nancy H. Malloy. How to Choose and Use Temporary Services. New York: American Management Association, 1990.

Metropolitan Life Insurance Company. The Metropolitan Life Survey of the American Teacher 1993: Violence in America's Public Schools. New York: Metropolitan Life Insurance Company, 1994.

Milner, Guy W. "Professional 'Temps' in Today's Workforce." Personnel 56, 10 (October 1989), 26.

Nobile, Robert J. "The Laws of Severance Pay." Personnel 67, 11 (November 1990), 15.

Olmstedt, Barney; and Suzanne Smith. Creating a Flexible Workplace: How to Select and Manage Alternative Work Options. New York: American Management Association, 1989.

Roth, Robert A. "Emergency Certificates, Misassignment of Teachers, and Other 'Dirty Little Secrets.'" Phi Delta Kappan (June 1986), 725–27.

Rothman, Miriam M. "Employee Termination: A Four-Step Procedure." Personnel 66, 2 (February 1989), 36.

Sharffe, William G. "Layoff Is a Dirty Word." Phi Delta Kappan 65, 1 (September 1983), 60–61

Chapter 10

Information Technology and the Human Resources Function

CHAPTER OVERVIEW

CHAPTER OBJECTIVES

- Demonstrate the potential of the human resources information system to enhance and extend the organizational capabilities of the human resources function.
- Provide a model of the human resources information structure.
- Utilize an information process model to depict design details of a human resources information system.
- Give special emphasis to the role of leadership in designing, implementing, and controlling the human resources information system.

CHAPTER TERMS

Archives

Data

Data base

Data processing

Information policy

Information process

Information system

Privacy laws

Records

Records center

Technology

HUMAN RESOURCES INFORMATION IN PERSPECTIVE

Chapter 9 described the process of employment continuity: the purposes, policies, programs, and procedures relating to members who enter, remain, and leave the system. This chapter places special focus on information technology and the human resources function: the purposes, scope, technology, user demand, process, and the manner in which the information revolution is propelling change in the conceptualization, redesign, and implementation of the human resources information system.

Technology

As indicated in Chapter 1, **technology** refers to the totality of means employed in the human resources function to achieve its aims as well as the broader mission of the school system. Included in information technology are member skills, knowledge, tools, mechanisms, techniques, and know-how to carry out the function's objectives. In assuming a broad definition of technology—namely the application of organized knowledge to the information process, as well as every form of recorded information, electronic and nonelectronic, programmed and nonprogrammed, computer hardware and software, *supported* and *supporting* activities, and information specialists—the meaning of information technology becomes more apparent.

Technology has both internal and external aspects. Technological advancements produced by the external environment, such as computer technology, models for developing instructional systems, research findings, and information processing, illustrate the importance of technology as a force that affects a school system and its operation. One of the many reasons why school systems need to be continuously concerned about information technology is that prevailing knowledge, techniques, tools, and processes help to *extend individual, group,* and *system capabilities* to perform tasks more efficiently and effectively.

Records. **Records** are considered to be any form of recorded information. The information may be recorded on paper, microfilm, audiotapes, computer generated, or other medium. Records are fundamentally a means of recording facts or events in order to solve human resources problems. They represent vital activities relative to the human resources function and create essential information material. A **records center** is defined as a storage area for *inactive records,* which can be located on site or off site. A *file* is a device (for example, a folder, case, or cabinet) where papers or publications (records) are arranged or classified in convenient order for storage, retrieval, reference, or preservation purposes.[1] An **archive** is a place where public records or historical documents are preserved. Labelled folders in a metal or wooden filing cabinet located in school attendance units has for many school systems embodied the concept of an information system.

Data, Data Base, and Data Processing

Data are considered to be factual information (as measurements or statistics) capable of being converted into information. A **data base** is a collection of organized data (as employee personal data) especially for mass retrieval, usually computer arranged for rapid expansion, updating, or retrieval. **Data processing** involves the conversion of raw data to machine readable form and its subsequent processing and refinement into information.

Information and the Information System

Information is knowledge consisting of facts that have been analyzed in the context of school system management. An **information system** is a plan designed to acquire, refine, organize, store, maintain, retrieve, and communicate data in a valid and accurate form. Material from the human resources information system is used as a basis for discussing, reasoning, calculating, forecasting, and resolving problems related to the human resources function.

In the following sections, the connection among information, the human resources function, and the information revolution is given special focus.

Information and the Human Resources Function

Information is intimately and indelibly bound up with planning, organizing, directing, and controlling a school system. It plays a critical role not only in maintaining the daily life of an organization but also in providing for its survival and growth.

The school system can be viewed as an organized combination of elements, including mission, input, process, structure, and control, designed to form a unitary whole. Systems are also composed of subsystems (individual schools) and homogeneous functions (planning, curricula, logistics, human resources, and external relations). Each subsystem needs information unique to itself, but there is information common to all subsystems, some of which is needed between or among certain subsystems. Figure 10.1 illustrates the concept of unification of subsystems within an organization through information. Five major functions of a school system, shown in Figure 10.1, are linked to each other and to the system as a whole by means of an integrated information system.

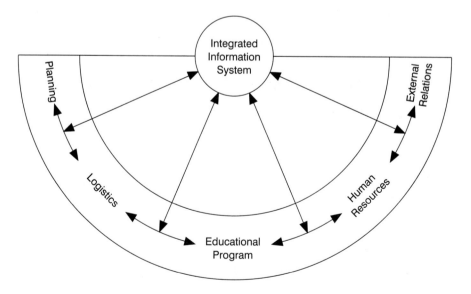

FIGURE 10.1
Human resources subsystem interactions with other organization subsystems.

The concept of information integration, as shown in Figure 10.1, may be illustrated by reference to the human resources function and such subfunctions as human resources planning, recruitment, selection, compensation, and appraisal. Recruitment, selection, and induction activities cannot be performed effectively without information pertaining to personnel planning. Hence, there is an *interdependence* of personnel activities within the human resources function. The need for *integration* among the major functions shown in Figure 10.1 becomes readily apparent when, for example, newly appointed personnel are put on the system payroll. In this case the human resources and logistics functions are linked through information provided by one function to another.

A school system, like other organizations, is comprised of purposes, people, plans, tasks, technology, and a structure for fitting its parts together. The ability of the system to function depends on the *bonding* of these elements. Each element has an impact on other elements and, thus, on the whole. Interaction of the various parts to achieve broad system purposes is effected through an integrated *information system*. Information makes it possible to link individualized but coordinated action plans for positions, sections, departments, units, and schools into the overall mission of the system.

THE INFORMATION REVOLUTION AND THE HUMAN RESOURCES FUNCTION

Four criteria for evaluating the effectiveness of information systems include the quality of (a) records creation, (b) records storage, (c) records retrieval and analysis, and (d) information generation. Contemporary school systems are not lacking in record creation but are known to be seriously deficient in the application of information to records management that is both cost effective and state of the art.

For those school systems in which records are created and maintained manually, the paperwork necessary to satisfy record keeping requirements seems needlessly tedious and time consuming. To those who have to generate records, paperwork seems to serve no purpose but to fill up new file drawers or computer tapes. Poor records management leads to records that are either forgotten or inaccessible when human resources problems arise suddenly, such as responses to a state or federal regulatory inquiry, personnel litigation, collective negotiations information, salary and wage disputes, disciplinary or termination cases, grievances, and planning information. In brief, many school systems are deficient in record storage and maintenance, as well as in retrieval and analysis. Rarely do they meet the criterion of *information generation*. There is considerable credibility in the point of view that gathering and storing data does not result in information or in making system officials cognizant of conditions in the human resources function.

Reasons for Information Deficiencies

There are many reasons why records in school systems enter the purgatory of the file drawer and cost the system dearly in time, treasure, talent, and paper. Among the more prominent are (a) the cost of producing and delivering information, (b) failure to integrate electronic technology into the information system, (c) inability or unwillingness to comprehend the organizational significance of the shift from manual to electronic record keeping, and (d) inability or unwillingness to accept the enabling effects of a comprehensive design for improving the human resources function through the use of emerging information technology. The attitude that the traditional model of the human resources information process should remain intact, with minor changes, represents a form of blindness to technological reality and its organizational potential.

HUMAN RESOURCES INFORMATION AND THE COMPUTER

It has been said that information technology is the most fundamental revolutionary force in modern times. The list of changes being propelled by electronic technology has been striking. In the corporate world, for example, the advent of the facsimile machine has made Western Union obsolescent in the field of overseas communication. Illustrative of change in the public domain is the fact that preparation of a ranked salary analysis manually takes about one-half day; the process by electronic means takes about five minutes. Tracking, accumulating, and summarizing employee attendance saves hours of manual labor. Applicant tracking, payroll preparation, position control, individual employment files, and résumé scanning can be added to the repertoire of human resources activities for which information can be compiled from various records, analyzed, and presented in a standard format.

While the debate in education over school reform, outcome-based education, and site-based decision making goes on, emerging and enhanced technologies and technological opportunities are revolutionizing the world. More extensive application of technology to school district information systems and human resources subsystems can be designed to play an essential part of the information revolution, which is bidding to change information creation from a paper to a paperless endeavor.

Computer Availability and Application

For a human resources information system to be effective and efficient, it must be capable of providing the kind of information required by those who use it in personnel practice. It should be designed to make available to all authorized personnel the essential quality and quantity of information when, where, and in what form it is needed. Computer availability helps the human resources function to fashion the kind of information it requires to provide the capability to capture and process current data for meaningful analysis in the personal decision-making process.

In order to determine the manner and extent to which a computer should be linked to an information system, several factors must be considered. Among the more significant factors are (a) the kinds of information needed to operate the human resources function effectively, (b) the strengths and limitations of a computer to provide desired information, (c) what the role of a computer will be in the information system, (d) the people who will create the data designs and make the key decisions about their processing, and (e) the procedures and processes to be employed to optimize computer applications.

One of the critical antecedents in developing computer inputs is to consider which questions are to be answered by the outputs. For example, in which processes and to what extent will the computer be applied to speed up the availability of data and the analytical capability of those in charge of the human resources function (recruitment, selection, collective bargaining, compensation, and/or planning)? What important personnel information can the computer provide in each of these areas that is not otherwise readily attainable? Is the computer role to be limited to payroll, accounting, and personal information components? Will the computer be employed in forecasting enrollments, staff size, personnel budgets, and/or selection interviewing? How can the human resources function take full advantage of computer capabilities in such components as skills inventory, career interests, performance appraisal, and the analysis of historical interview responses to validate and predict potential for tenure, absenteeism, and promotion?[2] The information outputs, based on questions such as these, will influence the kinds of computer hardware and software to be purchased, who will do the programming, and who will be the data users.

The strengths and limitations of computer application in the human resources function are factors that should be taken into consideration. Computers are readily adaptable to provide selected types of information, save time, and relieve programmers of considerable effort in data processing. A computer can be viewed as a way to extend the human mind, enable it to identify personnel problem indicators, and take a wider view of data in decision making. For example, up-to-date information makes it possible to take corrective action, initiate investigative action, or take steps to resolve identified difficulties before they magnify. In effect, the capabilities of today's computer are numerous and far-reaching, insofar as they enable the system to gather, process, and apply information that in years past was too expensive, too labor intensive, and in many respects beyond the power of existing information systems to obtain.

The *limitations* of computers should be considered in developing or expanding their use in the human resources function. Most importantly, the concept of an information system, as will be noted subsequently, *embraces more than computer application*. Moreover, usefulness of a computer depends on what program designers apply to its capabilities in the form of intelligence, vision, imagination, and creativity. The computer will not suffice to generate special kinds of information, nor to respond to certain on-the-job situations, such as those involving information in face-to-face exchanges, counseling, and establishing performance objectives. In brief, the computer is assuredly an important tool in the performance of the human resources function. However, this exceedingly valuable instrument cannot define personnel system information needs, nor can it make those personnel decisions that are a never-ending organizational responsibility.

HUMAN RESOURCES INFORMATION: PURPOSE AND SCOPE

As noted earlier, and as a prelude to the discussion that follows, *information* is defined as data that have been refined for use in maintaining and improving organizational, unit, and individual effectiveness; and an *information system* is a systematic plan designed to acquire, refine, organize, store, maintain, protect, retrieve, and utilize data to satisfy organizational needs.

Human resources information can be employed to serve significant purposes, regardless of school system size, location, complexity, structure, or leadership styles. Cogent reasons for the development and implementation of the best personnel information system that can be devised are given in the following sections.

Organizational Effectiveness. Organizational effectiveness refers to the degree to which system, group, and individual aims or intended effects are accomplished. Prudently applied, information can make a considerable contribution to optimizing the quality of those educational outcomes the system seeks, sparking the motivation of members involved in the educational process, and satisfying the various constituencies to which the system responds, such as pupils, staff, parents, the community, the government, and employers.

Decision Making. School system leadership involves making a variety of personnel decisions, ranging from recruitment to retirement. Information is needed to select appropriate choices of action from among various feasible alternatives, and helps to identify problems, determine objectives, and make decisions on how they are to be reached, how personnel resources are to be allocated, and who is to be recruited, hired, fired, transferred, rewarded, promoted, and demoted. Moreover, proper use of information in the decision-making process allows decision makers to identify priorities and allocate resources that will provide the highest return to the institution.

Human Resources Function. The centerpiece of this text consists of 11 personnel processes. From the standpoint of an information system, they are considered to be a set of units or modules. Each module, such as appraisal and compensation, has its own information input forms, as well as unique data elements, processes, and outputs essential to its designated activities. Among its many uses in implementing the function, information acquired through its several processes can be linked or combined between and among processes, as well as joined with other administrative functions such as planning, logistics, and the educational program.

Employment Communication. The embryo of a personnel information system is not formed on a computer chip. It is established at the more fundamental and personal level of employment communication—the giving and receiving of information between teacher and principal, and superintendent and associate superintendents, or even plumber and maintenance supervisor. It includes intercommunication of detailed information about the requirements of a position, ways in which they are to be met, resources involved, how well the role is currently being carried out, and feedback from position holders about problems encountered or ideas relating to task improvement. Information channels are not established on a computer printout; the proper role of personnel communication is to facilitate position performance through timely, two-way exchanges between those who do the work and those responsible for its supervision.

Legal Requirements. Congressional intervention in the field of employment has touched and continues to touch every aspect of the personnel function in both public and private sectors. This development is reshaping personnel practice, making it imperative for every organization to understand and respond to the regulatory environment, establish plans for compliance with laws governing equal opportunity, and create an information system to deal with those areas from which most lawsuits arise—recruitment and selection, compensation, termination, affirmative action, and antidiscrimination.

The kinds of information needed to respond to regulatory agency requests for information as well as to deal with charges of unfair employment practices include (a) understanding and acquainting administrative personnel with the details of laws governing personnel practice; (b) developing information to anticipate, prevent, and deal with critical issues as well as legal problems and changes that may arise; and (c) shaping the personnel information system so that vital records are created and preserved to defend the system against charges of personnel law violations.

Thus, acquisition, processing, storage, and retrieval of information relating to the regulatory environment has to be viewed as an integral part of a human resources information system.

Human Resources Function Control. Any organizational component as important as the human resources function requires determination of whether the function objectives are being met. This aspect of human resources management is referred to as *control* and involves (a) use of *information* to evaluate personnel processes, both separately and within the function; (b) assessment of progress toward organizational objectives; (c) feedback on the extent to which there are deviations between activities and intended outcomes, as well as their outcomes; and (d) initiation of corrective measures.

Success of human resources function control depends on the quality of measures employed to gather information in order to form a feedback system that provides data that, when refined and interpreted, make it possible to determine courses of action needed to improve the level of function performance. Control mechanisms, for example, should yield reliable information about areas such as turnover, legal compliance, union-system relations, personnel complaints and grievances, recruitment-selection and selection-retention ratios, performance outcomes, transfers, and compensation inequities.

Without a systematic approach to securing information through evaluation of the personnel processes, it is likely that important personnel decisions will be made on the basis of intuition, ignorance, biases, whims, and hunches.

Quality of Organizational Life. Human resources information is being increasingly applied to assess and improve the quality of organizational life. The motivating force for concern about and ways to improve the quality of work life is job satisfaction. Dissatisfaction with working conditions, the desire of personnel to have more control over their careers, the way in which work must be performed, and feedback on how well the job is being done has generated efforts to secure more and better information about how satisfied people are with their work, working conditions, and the context within which work takes place. As more position holders ask questions about why conditions in the school system are the way they are, and as personnel resistance to change grows, the greater will be the need for personnel information systems to improve methods of gathering information about working conditions and their impacts on why some members behave in the interests of the system and others do not.

Job satisfaction, it has been reported, has not been directly linked to performance but has been shown to be a factor in turnover, absenteeism, sabotage, and a person's mental and physical health. These factors indirectly affect a person's and an organization's effectiveness.[3] Sources of information relative to conditions of organizational life include union-system negotiations, contract administration, staff meetings, interviews, team problem solving, reports of state departments of education and regional accrediting associations, exit interviews, job satisfaction survey feedback, grievances and complaints, and programs of a participative nature that encourage mutual system-member involvement.

DEMAND FOR HUMAN RESOURCES INFORMATION

Information needed to conduct the human resources function can be thought of as a component of the total information system of the organization. It consists of a planned network of *forms, files, reports, records,* and *documents.* The nature and variety of information needed to conduct the human resources function can be inferred from the outline of information needs shown in Figure 10.2. More specifically, there is an insatiable demand from within and outside of the system for an extensive array of human resources information to (a) conduct day-to-day operations, (b) resolve short- and long-term personnel problems, (c) comply with external demands, (d) satisfy system needs for research and planning data, and (e) plan for and implement collective bargaining agreements.

As school administrative units become larger and more complex, demand for more and varied types of information increases. The necessity for creating, collecting, processing, storing, retrieving, disseminating, and integrating data to aid in the administration of an organization is hardly a matter for debate. It is becoming increasingly clear that sole dependence on the time-honored manual system of data processing is no longer appropriate to keep a modern educational institution abreast of informational requirements. As more school administrative units become large enough to offer comprehensive educational programs, it is inevitable that improved data processing methods will be employed to integrate information for major areas of the school system—*instruction, funds, facilities,* and *personnel.* There is, however, evidence to suggest that school district use of computer technology in administering the personnel function has not reached full fruition.[4]

The substance of what has been discussed in the foregoing text is that operation of a modern school system, with all the organizational, legal, political, governmental, and social ramifications entailed, has caused the volume of essential records and reports to soar. To cope with problems of record keeping and to make effective use of records that are collected and stored, a new approach to records management is in order. This need can be met in part through application of technological improvements to the

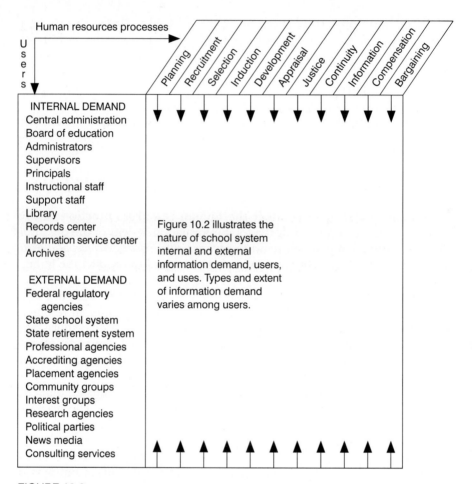

FIGURE 10.2
School system information demand, users, uses, and human resources processes.

information system. Innovation can and should be geared not only to improvement of the human resources function in general, but also to the welfare of each individual employed in the system. Considerable advances have been made in the use of electronic data processing equipment to facilitate collection of data and dissemination of information for decision making. These systems make possible storage and retrieval of highly detailed and organized personnel data that is useful in administering the human resources function. Although it is true that many personnel decisions cannot be programmed, it is reasonable to assume that personnel decision making can be improved by data that are better organized, more accurate, more complete, and more rapidly reported.

ARCHITECTURE OF THE HUMAN RESOURCES INFORMATION SYSTEM

It is inconceivable that any school system could operate effectively, even for a short period of time, without acquiring and disseminating information about human resources—those who enter, remain in, and leave the organization. Every school system is constantly confronted with information-communication problems centering on such matters as keeping abreast of the quantity and quality of information needed, making information accessible to users when they need it, and furnishing information to position holders that will contribute to their achieving the position objectives for which they are employed.

Figure 10.3 portrays the nature of human resources information structure, including sources of personnel information; information modules; and criteria that should govern acquisition, analysis, synthesis, storage, retrieval, dissemination, integration, and communication of information.

Figure 10.3 indicates that there are three sources through which personnel information can be acquired: *oral, written,* and *graphic*. Oral information, for example, includes various kinds of personnel interviews, such as recruitment, appraisal, and exit interviews. Telephone reference checks, observations of the performance of a teacher in the classroom, a personnel counsel-

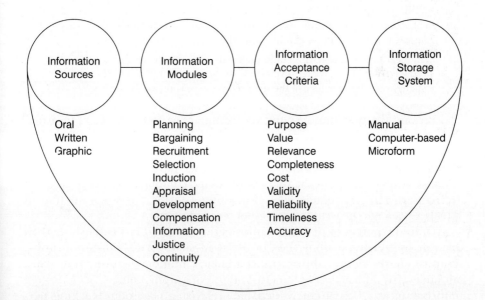

FIGURE 10.3
Model of the human resources information structure.

ing session, conversations among administrators about personnel, and board discussion on personnel policy illustrate the nature and variety of oral sources of personnel information. Meltzer points out that much valuable personnel information is irretrievably lost because the potential for this kind of information is frequently overlooked. He notes that the advantages of recording oral communications for information retrieval are manifold:

- A permanent record of precisely what was said is available.
- The permanent record may be filed and retrieved at any time for reference, review, or analysis.
- The record reproduces not only exactly what was said but also how and under what circumstances.
- Misunderstandings are minimized, because usually they can be resolved immediately by the parties involved.
- Others not present at the time of the conversation or conference can be correctly informed of what was said and in what tone of voice.
- If a request for information is involved, both the request and the reply can be recorded.
- More complete information can be given because of the relative ease with which matters can be explained orally compared with the laborious task of writing them down.
- The timelessness of oral communication can be combined with the benefits of written communication.
- Because oral communication is instantaneous and spontaneous, its honesty or lack of honesty can be gauged by listening to the replay.
- Rehearing the exact conversation not only reminds the listener of the words spoken, but often evokes the emotion of the time as well. This is extremely beneficial when analysis of the material is the purpose of the review.[5]

Beyond the medium of sound recording are written sources of information that comprise the major portion of the human resources data base in a school system. Basic to written sources of personnel information are such elements as personnel handbooks, personnel policy manuals, bulletins, memos, annual and periodic reports, circulars, computer printouts, and the well-known (and extremely useful) personnel forms, the accumulation of which represents the written personnel record system.

Graphic sources of personnel information are used less extensively than oral or written types, but they do exist in such forms as photographs, graphs, charts, tables, slides, transparencies, motion pictures, filmstrips, and televised information. On occasion, use of graphic sources of personnel information can be extremely valuable. Televising classroom teaching performances has proved, for example, to be useful in appraisal and development of classroom teachers.

THE HUMAN RESOURCES INFORMATION PROCESS

Figure 10.4 is designed as a general model with which to analyze the human resources **information process**. The model is representative of relationships in the process and will be used to examine these associations.

The design as outlined in Figure 10.4 consists of five phases: (a) diagnosis, (b) preparation, (c) implementation, (d) evaluation, and (e) feedback. Each of the phases will be examined in the following discussion in terms of the total personnel information process, elements comprising the process, interrelationships among the elements, and integration of the information system to the total personnel function and to the entire system. The design can be viewed as an organizational mechanism through which efforts are made to achieve a desired state relative to personnel information.

Diagnosis

The first phase of the information process outlined in Figure 10.4 is *diagnosis,* meaning the fact-finding or data-collection activities designed to assess the extent to which the present information system is providing essential data to achieve the goals of the human resources function. Diagnostic efforts will be focused around questions relating to what information is now collected and utilized; capability of the system to retrieve information easily and economically; level of information accuracy and sophistication needed; relationship of the information system to the size, structure, goals, organiza-

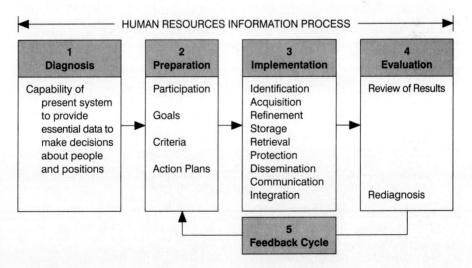

FIGURE 10.4
Model of the human resources information process.

tion style, nature of work, and composition of the work groups; and quantity and quality of information needed at the operating and planning levels. The diagnostic phase of the information process should focus on these kinds of decisions: Is the general system acceptable? Is the system operating as it should? Should the current system be revised? Is a new system needed? Should processing be centralized or decentralized?

Figure 10.5 illustrates some of the questions involved in diagnosing which aspects of the human resources information system are in need of improvement, as does the more detailed examination of the information process, which is the theme of the text that follows.

Preparation (Goals and Criteria)

Figure 10.4 indicates that *preparation* is the second major activity in the information process. This phase is concerned with translating diagnoses garnered thorough Phase 1 (diagnosis) into decisions leading to a series of action plans to improve the personnel information system. Central to the preparation phase is a set of goals for the human resources information system along lines such as the following:

- Improvement and enhancement of the information system for collecting routine data, computerizing these transactions wherever possible.
- Elimination of information duplication.
- Elimination of useless information.
- Standardization, wherever possible, of methods for gathering information.
- Justification of information from the standpoints of efficiency and effectiveness.
- Improvement in availability, accuracy, flexibility, consistency, accessibility, and utility of information.
- Systematization of collection of nonroutine data.
- Involvement in the design of the information system of key people who will actually use both routine and nonroutine types of data.
- Development of criteria that will govern identification, acquisition, refinement, storage, protection, retrieval, dissemination, communication, and integration of information (see Figure 10.4).
- Organization and administration of the human resources information system in an effective and efficient manner. (The information system should be part of a master plan to use funds, facilities, people, technology, and machines to achieve system objectives. This means appointment of knowledgeable personnel with authority to manage the information system, update the plan annually, and focus on specific objectives for hardware, software, personnel, budgets, space, and applications.)

- How adequate are the records in the information system regarding human problems in such areas as recruitment, selection, induction, appraisal, development, justice, compensation, continuity, and union relations?

- To what extent is information accessible regarding grievances, transfers, discharge, discrimination, communications, rewarding, discipline, tenure, promotions, resignations, level of technical competency, medical visits, strikes, alienation, job satisfaction, work stressors?

- Does the information system indicate which of the human resources problems are position-related? Nonposition-related (personal)?

Nonhuman Information Inadequacies

- *Technology Information Inadequacies*—Which of the following factors are considered to be obstacles to achieving desirable information system standards: money, materials, facilities, personnel, and equipment?

- *Record-keeping inadequacies*—To what extent are the following record-keeping facilities adequate: records creation, processing, automation, retention and disposal, security, legal requirements, records management, forms management, records center, and archives?

Organization Information Inadequacies

- How effective are school system provisions regarding the design, implementation, maintenance, and evaluation of the human resources information system? Regarding interfacing with other system functions?

- To what extent does the system utilize tools of human resources research to gather information about the effectiveness of the information system? (Questionnaires, interviews, audits, reports, statistics, critical incidents, comparative studies, historical analysis, and individual and work unit responses to information communication.)

Organizational Impact of Information System Inadequacies

- What is the organizational impact of the information inadequacies on the well-being of the human resources function?

Organizational Implications for Action Planning

- What actions should the system take to remove inadequacies in the human resources information system?

FIGURE 10.5
Probing for inadequacies and issues in and answers for the human resources information system.

In addition to these guidelines, a set of conventions or protocols governing the shaping of an information system through **information policy** is shown in Figure 10.6.

Preparation (Information Modules)

Implementation plans of the information process referred to in Phase 2 of Figure 10.4 are aimed at developing means for collecting and managing personnel information from each of the modules shown in Figure 10.3. In the discussion that follows, each will be construed as a personnel information module. The context will focus on the nature and significance of information in each of the functional modules and its pertinence to resolution of personnel problems. In analyzing the information needs of each, it should be noted that information may be viewed as either programmed or nonprogrammed. In other words, certain data can be computerized (as illustrated in Table 10.1), but other information, that of a conceptual, hypothetical, judgmental nature, is not readily amenable to computer programming. Both types of information will be discussed shortly in relation to the processes listed in Figure 10.4.

Human Resources Planning Process. The human resources planning process (discussed in Chapter 2) includes such key activities as developing planning assumptions, projecting structure and human resources requirements, preparing a human resources inventory, forecasting changes in the present work force, and developing a human resources plan. These activities focus on estimating the difference between the current staff and its estimated future size, and on deciding which alternatives are most appropriate to meet the human resources requirements. Essential to the effective performance of these two activities is an information system for classifying and locating personnel within the school organization. As shown in Table 10.2, there are at least eight main bodies of data that comprise the information base for human resources planning. Examination of the base for human resources planning outlined in Table 10.2 makes it apparent that (a) the breadth and depth of input data required are more extensive than those in the other personnel processes, (b) items of information are capable of being stored and retrieved in a computer-based information system, and (c) the data can be designed to serve a variety of human resources purposes, including identification of needed educational and developmental experiences, determination of recruitment needs, planning of individual careers, forecast of internal personnel movements and turnover, projection of the organizational structure, and preparation of personnel reports.

Recruitment Process. Even in those schools having an effectively managed human resources function, occasions will arise that require recruitment of personnel from the outside to fill certain positions within the organiza-

It is the policy of the Riverpark school system to maintain an information system to facilitate the creation, refinement, reporting, utilization, storage, retrieval, and protection of recorded information. Key components include:

- *Purpose.* Establish a course of action to guide and determine present and future decisions concerning all aspects of the human resources information system. Improve individual, unit, and system effectiveness, decision making, and information processing efficiency. Establish paper-based and computer-based records to satisfy both internal and external information requirements.

- *Scope.* Create a uniform filing plan within the central information system to locate and retrieve any record readily, whether the file is centralized or decentralized. Institute guidelines governing the scope and boundaries of administrative decisions pertaining to the collection, storage, retrieval, retention, access, distribution, and disposition of human resources information.

- *Responsibility.* Set forth human resources information guidelines for administrative responsibilities in the central administration, attendance units, and support units relative to the scope of information described above. Place overall operational responsibility in one office, with a systemwide purview, to oversee the progress of human resources information through the several stages of its life cycle (*active, inactive,* and *archival*). A records center and or an information service center become the responsibility of the position (supervisor of records). Prepare a system records manual to communicate to employees the manner in which the information system operates at both the central and work unit levels (individual schools, departments, and offices). System members, as part of the information network, are instructed in standard uniform filing procedures.

- *Access.* Identify which classes of information are restricted, how access to restricted categories is granted, who has the authority to grant access or release which categories of information, and what controls will govern photocopying or other means of recorded reproduction.

- *Budget.* Include funding in the annual budget to maintain and improve the effectiveness of the information system.

- *Individual employee file.* The individual employee data base consists of three files (*basic file, evaluative file,* and *supervisory file*).

    Basic file: Objective material and no third-party evaluation or personal opinions. Employment profile, payroll, work data, etc., (see Table 10.1).
    Evaluative file: Performance data regarding employment retention tenure, probationary review, and position effectiveness. Destroyed within five years after decisions.
    Supervisory file: Confidential property of supervisor. Destroyed after supervisor's death, termination, or retirement.

- *Regulatory.* Adhere to regulatory provisions governing employee records and privacy safeguards.

FIGURE 10.6
Information policies, practices, and technology of the Riverpark school system.

TABLE 10.1
Illustration of programmed and nonprogrammed personnel information.

Programmed Information		Nonprogrammed Information
Payroll	Résumé	Personnel policies and procedures
Benefits	Certification	Performance appraisals
Attendance	Positions	Personnel motivation
Retirement	Master files	Personnel actions
Grievances	Tax reports	Organizational actions
Skills inventory	Turnover	Organizational structure
Personnel budget	Leaves	Personnel planning premises
	Compensation profile	Strategies and supporting plans
	Personnel statistics	

tion. The recruitment process, when properly managed, forecasts personnel needs and skills well in advance of the time they are needed, and initiates those activities that result in the right people being available at the right time and in the right numbers. If the information system is properly designed, it will make available such items of data as (a) positions to be filled and (b) position characteristics, including title, location, salary range, classification, responsibilities, key duties, organizational relationships, level of education and experience needed, and additional information about special characteristics of the position. Such information is often included in the personnel requisition form. The position guide contains information on both person and position specifications. As explained in the discussion of the recruitment process (Chapter 3), two kinds of information are essential: (a) full information about the position for which personnel will be recruited and (b) full information about each applicant for the position. Other types of information utilized in managing the recruitment process include effectiveness of recruitment sources and methods, budget allocations, cost/benefit analyses, tracking and control of applications, description of candidate pool, and time span required to fill a position. To obtain analyses such as these, some of the data will need to be transformed through the use of mathematical and statistical techniques.

Selection Process.   The selection process (Chapter 4) is perhaps the most vital of all of the personnel processes, because it is the key activity wherein decisions are made about which personnel will fill positions that become vacant. This process involves a position-matching plan designed to link available personnel with the position requirements. If a computer-based information system is employed, information on personnel is stored that describes certain characteristics of every member of the system. When the personnel search is conducted, the computer matches information on personnel and position requirements. Whether the personnel search is made manually or mechanically, the information system should provide accurate summaries of qualified candidates in sufficient detail to facilitate matching persons and positions and enhance the use of personnel within the system through promotion and transfer. Selection interviews, for example, are usually structured around information relating to the candidate's work history, education and training, early home background, present social adjustment, mental ability, motivation, and maturity. For those applicants selected for employment in the system, the foregoing information becomes an important part of the permanent files. Other uses of applicant information include identification of good and poor selection practices, relationships between performance predictors and after-employment performance, development programs based on shortcomings revealed in the selection process, follow-up studies on interview ratings and actual performance, and evaluation of the total selection process and the personnel involved in its operation.

Induction Process. The reader will recall from Chapter 5 that the primary goal of the induction process is to assist the staff member in adjusting quickly and harmoniously to a productive relationship with the school sys-

TABLE 10.2
An information base for human resources planning.

Bodies of Data	Information Components
Personal	Age, gender, race, citizenship, military status, handicaps, Social Security number, marital status, and dependents
Payroll	Date of hire, classification, salary range, benefits, last year's total earnings, next salary review date, retirement number, and date of last increase
Education	Educational level, major and minor fields of study, standing, honors, specialties
Experience	Previous employment, length, type, time, and level of experience
Skills	Data about each staff member's skills, abilities, work preference, and achievements
Appraisal and promotions	Performance appraisal record, advancement potential, and promotions
Deployment of personnel (by positions)	Number and type of positions in school system by unit and present position holders
Internal mobility of personnel	Accessions, promotions, transfers, demotions, retirement, death, resignation, leaves, and dismissal

tem. A variety of information is needed to facilitate the best possible adjustment to the community, system, position, and system personnel. Consideration should be given to the importance of information on the leadership style of the unit administrator who will supervise the new staff member, followership style of the new staff member, and the position situation in assuring appropriate placement of personnel. Those elements are crucial to personnel selection and placement.

During the induction process, the new staff member not only provides the system with facts about himself/herself but also receives a great deal of information in return, including system literature, an employee manual, compensation and benefit schedules, position guides, and written statements of system expectations. Personnel files for inductees, reactions of inductees to the induction program, and personal induction checklists are illustrative of information aspects of the program. If the informational aspects of the induction process are carefully designed, they should provide the newcomer with information needed to adjust to the position role and to the system's internal and external environment.

Appraisal Process. Appraisal of human resources (Chapter 7) should be directed toward achieving meaningful personal, position, unit, and system goals. A comprehensive performance appraisal program involves tools used in a variety of procedures and contexts, including observation, self-analysis, personality measurements, performance testing, and interface appraisals. Information derived from application of these tools requires considerable skill. Figure 10.7 illustrates an outline of an information structure designed to maintain and improve the performance appraisal process for school personnel. Some of the information listed in Figure 10.7 will be part of the appraisee's permanent file; other information will be prepared by the system in the form of organizational purposes, unit objectives, and position guides.

Examination of Figure 10.7 indicates also that a wide variety of information is needed by the appraiser on every subordinate for whom he/she is responsible. One of the assumptions on which the appraisal process is based is that helping individuals to improve their performance involves collecting, processing, storing, retrieving, and utilizing various personnel data.

As illustrated in Figure 10.7, information on the results of the performance appraisal process is derived largely from records and reports relating to the preappraisal planning conference, the actual performance appraisal, and the individual development record. (Illustrations of these have been included in Chapter 7.) Kinds of information the organization needs to assess results of the performance appraisal process may be stated in question form:

• Is there evidence to indicate that the appraiser has made progress in achieving position expectations?

Sources of Appraisee Information	Appraisee Central Personnel File	Preappraisal Planning Conference Record	Performance Appraisal Record	Individual Development Record
Nature of Information	Interests Work History Education Health Personal-Social Characteristics Home/Family Background Aptitudes	Organizational Purposes Unit Objectives Position Guide Performance Targets	Appraisals by Appraiser and Appraisee on Differences Between Planning and Actual Performance Results Achieved	Individual Plan for Self-improvement, Assignments, Development Experiences, Progress Review, Results Achieved, Related New Goals
Uses of Information	Position Career Guidance	Clarify Organization Purposes, Unit Objectives, Position Goals, Position Responsibilities, Performance Standards, Appraisal Procedures	Identify Progress, Problems, Obstacles, Strengths, Weaknesses; Development Programs for Individuals, Units, System	Coaching, Counseling Determine Potential Follow-up
Appraisal Information Restricted to Files of	Central Personnel Appraiser	Appraiser Appraisee	Central Personnel Appraiser Appraisee	Central Personnel Appraiser Appraisee

FIGURE 10.7

Information structure to maintain and improve the performance appraisal process.

- What is the potential of the individual for other assignments in the system?
- Are the performance measures employed valid?
- To what extent is the appraisal process contributing to the identification of marginal performers? High achievers? Promotion potential? Personnel to be reassigned or given special assignments? Availability of personnel for critical positions?
- Are the support plans for the appraisal system effective?

Information as to whether performance is proceeding according to plan has various operational implications, especially with respect to the human resources function. The links between information on the results of individual performance and activities of the human resources function, such as human resources planning, compensation, recruitment, selection, appraisal, and development, are self-evident.

Those in charge not only need to know whether the performance appraisal process is actually helping to improve the performance of individual employees but also need to have information about effects of the process on the organization. The following questions indicate that concern:

- Is the performance appraisal process helping individual units within the system as well as the system itself to achieve expectations established for each?
- Does each of the components in the performance appraisal system (people, processes, and plans) contribute to realization of system goals?

These questions, it should be noted, are concerned with information that focuses on results of the appraisal system as a whole. This approach is macroscopic in that it views performance appraisal at large as a subsystem of the total human resources function. Results of performance appraisal, difficult as they are to determine, are essential to decisions that need to be made relative to maintaining and improving the performance appraisal plan if it does not do what it has been designed to do. If the plan is not helping to improve performance, if it is not contributing to the larger aims of the organization, remedial action is in order to make happen what the organization wants to happen.

Development Process.   Improving the performance of people (Chapter 6) is a never-ending process. Because the focus of the organization is on performance for both the individual position holder and the entire staff, establishment and attainment of high performance standards are requirements of high priority. Central to improving achievement of the individual or group is *feedback information* on performance. If a teacher is to initiate and to exercise control over his/her self-improvement, that teacher must have continuous information to compare his/her performance against position standards and to take appropriate corrective action. Hence, motivation of members of an organization involves use of feedback information. Carefully controlled studies have shown that a number of characteristics must be present for feedback to be useful to the position holder. The information feedback is useful when (a) it is precise, (b) it is timely, (c) the individual has the ability to correct his/her performance, (d) the source of feedback is appropriate, (e) the individual has the incentive to improve, and (f) the feedback is objective. The real value of feedback information is that it provides the individual position holder with timely, relevant information that focuses on his/her role and enables the position holder to measure and guide his/her own improvement.

Information relating to development of personnel is also focused on opportunities for people in the system to enhance their career plans. The continuing skills inventory, for example, can be matched against the system's need for replacements and improved skills. The personnel mobility patterns provide information relative to development needs of the system as it pertains to individuals who should be transferred, promoted, given extended education, or provided with opportunities for experiences beyond their current assignment. Computer technology may be employed to list teachers due for certificate renewal, maintain records of participation in staff development activities, track career movement patterns, and predict potential skill shortages and training needs. Information is basic to planning of both promotion paths and career movements, especially in those positions within the administrative structure. In sum, if development is focused on people, then people must be furnished with information to enable them to measure, plan, and control their career movements.

Compensation Process. Information on the compensation the system provides for staff members is needed for a multitude of purposes. In addition to information from traditional payroll, accounting, auditing, and reporting records, there are requests for information from unions and from federal, state, and local government agencies.

Administration of compensation involves planning, implementation, and control activities. Each of these functions involves internal (system) personnel and external (union, government, or society) relationships. Each requires an information base to plan annual and long-range budgets, to ensure internal and external equity in compensating personnel, and to administer individual pay actions to implement promotion, transfer, recognition, termination, and reorganization of duties. As noted in Chapter 12, the compensation process aims for rationality of design as well as fairness of execution. Without adequate information, excellence in planning, deciding, administering, and explaining compensation plans and procedures will be impossible to attain. A report of school district use of computer technology indicates that information relating to salaries and contracts is being increasingly processed with the aid of computers. Moreover, computer technology is applied more frequently to the compensation module than to any of the other modules in the personnel information system.[6]

Bargaining Process. The observation is made in Chapter 13 that the collective bargaining process involves three basic activities: (a) planning, (b) negotiations, and (c) administration. Each phase of the process requires a wide variety of information, much of which is not computer based. Union preparations for negotiations, for example, include contract analysis, review of grievances and arbitration decisions, contract comparison with other negotiated agreements, collection of information on economic and noneconomic issues to be considered, and advice from union membership on demands to be submitted. Preparation for bargaining by the system includes recording experiences in working with the agreement; analyzing grievance and arbitration records; reviewing other contracts; analyzing economic and noneconomic information on local, regional, and national trends in contractual elements; and examining contract violations.

Because a factual basis is an essential requirement for effective collective bargaining, a systematic approach is basic to collection and communication of negotiations data. Such data include a history of the current contract; demands of both parties; annual budgets; wage, salary, and cost benefit projections; minutes of negotiation sessions; comprehensive information on salaries, wages, and benefits in relation to salary levels of position classification; economic surveys; proposals and counterproposals; and external data on the local and national cost-of-living index.

Factual information is also needed if and when a third party becomes involved in the bargaining process. Although the knowledgeability and skill of mediators is important to conflict resolution, availability of up-to-date, precise, and relevant information is equally critical. If public negotiations are to be based on the assumption that government service, whatever its nature, must continue to be performed without interruption, a continuous flow of information will be required to satisfy union, system, and public interest.

There is growing awareness on the part of school systems that preparation for negotiations requires both programmed and nonprogrammed information. The following items give some indication of the extent of the task: negotiations, legal framework, costing out changes in contract terms, sources for developing bargaining items (mandatory and nonmandatory), history of contractual relationship, current situation, system contractual objectives, complaints and grievance history, and problems arising out of day-to-day contract administration.

Justice Process. If democratic principles are to have real meaning for members of the system, steps must be taken to secure and promote them through policies, plans, procedures, and processes employed to achieve institutional goals (Chapter 8). If the belief is held that the needs, rights, and interests of system participants should be respected, promoted, and protected, then the development and communication of information relating to personnel rights and responsibilities is an exceedingly important human resources function. Three types of communication about personnel security are indispensable: (a) translation of system goals into clearly stated written policies, plans, and procedures relating to fair treatment, participation, adjustment of grievances, position and personal security, and academic freedom; (b) transmission of this information to system members, both in the central administration and attendance units; and (c) feedback of information on the extent to which the goals relating to personnel security are being achieved and require modification to achieve system expectations. This information is sharply focused on enhancement of the individual personality—the system's highest value.

In addition to generating system records on complaints, grievances, tenure status of personnel, and complaints about the teaching of or materials relating to controversial issues, the documentation function becomes a major security information matter. The organization must assume that litigation will arise concerning personnel security. This means that security information must be documented, stored, and capable of being readily retrieved in the event or threat of litigation.

Continuity Process.   The process of employment continuity (Chapter 9) involves numerous and varied activities. People are recruited, selected, inducted, placed, appraised, compensated, developed, promoted, transferred, demoted, separated, and retired. Without adequate coordination to keep positions staffed with people who have the skills, knowledge, experience, and other qualifications required to perform their duties effectively, a great deal of time, money, and effort can be wasted on unnecessary, inappropriate, or ineffective activities. If one of the goals of the system is to have the right number of people in the right positions at the right time, along with the right conceptual, interpersonal, and technical skills, key elements in attainment of this goal should be the quality and quantity of information needed to make the process effective. Some of the information needed in the continuity process, it should be noted, overlaps with information employed in other processes, including recruitment, selection, induction, appraisal, and development. The focus of the information should be on finding better ways to (a) fill specific positions with people who have matching skills to perform the roles effectively; (b) encourage growth and development of all personnel on the payroll; (c) separate from the system those individuals who cannot or will not perform effectively; (d) minimize personnel turnover by designing positions that enable the holder to experience a sense of satisfaction and achievement; and (e) keep the system staffed with a continuing supply of competent, imaginative, and well-qualified personnel.

If the continuity process is to operate effectively, those in charge must have pertinent information to identify *variances between actual and desired* continuity conditions. Most critical in this regard is information generated from records of absenteeism, substitute services, health and safety of personnel, promotions, demotions, transfers, reassignments, dismissals, reductions in force, disabilities, retirements, and death of system members.

Implementation

Once the school system has defined objectives of the personnel information system, determined what kind of information is needed, reviewed information sources and acceptance criteria as outlined in Figure 10.3, and allocated responsibilities for administering various activities related to the system, the next phase (implementation) of the personnel information process can be initiated. This phase, as outlined in Figure 10.8, consists of nine key

FIGURE 10.8
Key activities related to implementation of the personnel information process.

activities: identification, acquisition, refinement, storage, retrieval, protection, dissemination, communication, and integration. In the following discussion, each of the key activities will be examined in terms of its relationship to the personnel information process.

Identification of Information. The initial activity in the personnel information process, as depicted in Figure 10.8, is identification of information. Its primary focus is on implementing decisions by the central administration governing what information is needed to achieve the goals of the system; purposes for which the information is needed; who will use the information; and what means shall be employed to gather, store, retrieve, and communicate it most effectively and efficiently. Consequently, the initial act in the information process calls for a conceptualization by the central administration of the kind of personnel information system it plans to operate to influence personnel behavior in ways conducive to goal attainment. This perspective is outlined in Figure 10.9, which construes the purposes of all information to be mission oriented. Administration, as viewed in Figure 10.9, links information to action of various kinds. Some of the information will indicate what has happened (past), some will be focused on what is happening (present), and some will be needed to plan what ought to happen in the system (future). All will be oriented toward influencing behavior of people to satisfy both individual and system needs.

Acquisition of Information. Acquisition of information, as noted in the personnel information process shown in Figure 10.8, follows plans for its identification and is defined by objectives of the system as well as the user's needs, including those of administrators, staff, board, clients, and public. Acquisition of information includes identification, selection, development, and purchase of source material. Source material, as noted previously, encompasses many forms of oral, written, and graphic information. Acquisition of personnel information encompasses a network of forms, records, files, and reports. A *form* may be defined as a standardized method of recording data, as illustrated by a personnel application form. *Records* are the accumulation and organization of information regarded as of more than temporary significance. A personnel *file* (folder, case, or cabinet) is a collection of related information arranged in order for preservation or reference. Three kinds of personnel files are illustrative. The *basic* file contains objective material and no third-party evaluations or opinions. A *confidential* appraisal file contains supervisory reports, appraisals, and psychological and test assessments by third parties. The *career* file contains information regarding positions or assignment information within or outside of the organization, including career anchor, career ladder, and special talents, skills, and abilities. File control criteria points include purposes a file is to serve, file location and jurisdiction, access criteria, and disposal conditions.

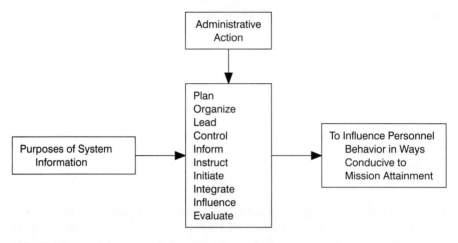

FIGURE 10.9
Goal-oriented purposes of information in educational administration.

Finally, *reports* utilize records to communicate information. Other sources of personnel information include letters, profiles, studies, external and internal personnel data, and documents of various types.

As suggested in Figure 10.3, acquisition of information should be governed by criteria, such as *purpose, value, relevance, completeness, cost, validity, reliability, timeliness,* and *accuracy.* Timeliness, or the currency of data, is an important criterion in determining whether information should be acquired. A personnel roster is of little use to the payroll department if it is not kept current. Information files on recruitable talent, promotable personnel, and position holders who have reached performance plateaus are useless if they have not been updated. Use of information on collateral benefits for administrative personnel in collective bargaining will be determined, for example, by its timeliness and by the aforementioned criteria. Up-to-date information is expensive to maintain. Although always desirable, it must be judged in terms of the cost/benefit concept. Certain kinds of information cost more money than other kinds of information to obtain, and their worth must be judged in terms of benefit to the system.

Refinement.   Most data acquired by the system need to be refined, some to a greater and some to a lesser degree, before they are stored for usage. Refinement includes checking data for accuracy. Information on paychecks, retirement contributions, and certification of personnel, for example, must be precise. Complete and accurate information concerning the skill of every staff member is essential to conduct the human resources planning process effectively. On the other hand, any collected data should include only those items the system really needs, inasmuch as the collecting and storing of information is relatively expensive. Other forms of data refinement include editing all forms of information entering the system, eliminating redundant information or overlapping information-gathering efforts, and incorporating error checks into the information system in order to call attention to missing or erroneous data. In effect, the purpose of refining information is to ensure that it meets acceptance criteria mentioned earlier. Refinement is conceived as a kind of screen to separate useful from useless information, to code and prepare acceptable information for entrance into the information system, to ensure that the information is valid and reliable, and to bring together one form of data with another that, when combined, will create new information and perhaps new perspectives that were not possible before the information elements were related.

The concept of information refinement includes many and varied activities aimed at acquiring and storing data in forms that enhance the work of the system. Refinement may include editing information inputs (such as payroll verification), combining quarterly performance appraisal reports for a performance profile, employing statistical techniques for meaningful summary descriptions of raw data, and drawing inferences from personnel data under conditions characterized by uncertainty. Refinement of information helps to make complex system phenomena more understandable and in some cases enables the system to achieve a new level of understanding about its human problems.

Storage. After information has been acquired and refined, arrangements must be made to store it for future use. As shown in Figure 10.4, information can be stored in manual, computer-based, or microform systems. Manual storage systems include direct files, inverted files, optical coincidence cards, edge-notched cards, and punched cards. Microform storage systems include a roll film, microfilm jackets, aperture cards, microfiche, and opaque microcards. A computer-based storage system is one that processes data by electronic machines quickly, accurately, and automatically. Data processed by a computer are stored on memory devices, such as magnetic tapes, and must be programmed—that is, the computer must be instructed as to what operations are to be performed and in what sequence.

The decision as to which system or combination of systems will be used to store personnel information will depend on a variety of factors, including size of staff, uses to be made of the information, availability of fiscal resources, and whether there are competent staff personnel to design and operate the system. Because the primary function of a personnel information system is to provide information when it is needed, where it is needed, and in the form in which it is needed, the storage system should be designed to enhance this objective.

Generally speaking, manual and microfilm storage systems are used to record historical information; and a mechanized system should deal with current information. Information on the current status of personnel may best be stored in a mechanized system; the history of performance of each individual can be recorded in all three systems. The point to consider is that mechanized storage of certain kinds of information, such as the historical performance profile of an individual staff member, may be prohibitive from a cost standpoint.

Retrieval. Information retrieval, one of the activities in the implementation of the personnel information process outlined in Figure 10.4, refers to methods and procedures for recovering specific information from stored data. It goes without saying that information users should be able to retrieve stored information readily and in the form needed. Such is not always the case. Information stored manually, for example, is sometimes irretrievable because procedures employed in storing it were faulty. Information not properly classified, indexed, and coded will create problems when retrieval queries are posed. Consequently, one of the requirements for operating an effective information storage-retrieval system is training staff personnel in procedures for classifying, indexing, and coding all incoming material.

Retrieval begins with a *search strategy* designed to locate information to solve problems posed by the user. This search strategy includes evaluation of stored information to determine its relevance to such problems. The search is also conducted with consideration for breadth and depth of information needed. The significance of the foregoing observation is that there are various constraints affecting the search for personnel information, including time, funds, and personnel. Because information is truly the substance that holds an organization together and keeps it viable, design of the storage-retrieval system and training personnel to operate it efficiently and effectively are matters of importance to the administrative team.

Protection. Any organization that includes data about individuals in its personnel information system must concern itself with **privacy laws.** There are two federal laws that should be noted: the Freedom of Information Act of 1966 (Public Law 89-487; codified in 1967 by Public Law 90-23), amended in 1974; and the Privacy Act of 1974 (Public Law 93-579). The Freedom of Information Act requires government agencies to make available certain records that are requested. The Privacy Act is designed to resolve problems relating to disclosure, recording, inspection, and challenges to information about individuals in federal agency files.

The impact of the Privacy Act differs for various kinds of organizations, but its thrust is such that every organization needs to be knowledgeable about legal ramifications of personnel information and their implications for administering the information system. What records may be disclosed, by whom, for what purposes; how disclosures are to be recorded; controls on individual inspection of records; and processing of disagreements about individual file information are among the problems involved in the protection of information.

Dissemination.   Dissemination is defined as distribution of information (especially from a gathering or storage point, such as an information center) to individuals within and agencies outside of the system. Certain kinds of personnel information will be stored in each of the attendance units. Most will be stored in various offices of the central administration, especially those data vital to the operation of the human resources function. Some of the more important of these data are:

Personnel records	Position code
Personnel forms	Education of personnel
Payroll registers	Entrance-exit dates
Retirement plans	Appraisal reviews
Personnel rosters	Staffing policies and strategies
Personnel inventory	Personnel budget
Income tax computations	Personnel forecast
Salary schedules	Absenteeism
Worker's compensation	Turnover
Wage rates	Recruitment files
Leaves of absence	Selection data
Vacation eligibility	Personnel development
Insurance coverage	Collective bargaining
Hospital contract numbers	Tenure
Position classification	Separations

Communication.   Observers of information systems are generally on record that there is a difference between information and communication. Peter F. Drucker has observed, for example, that "communication and information are different and indeed largely opposite—yet interdependent."[7] The subordinate may receive a periodic report on the appraisal of his/her performance, but if there is an absence of communication, the information may have no meaning for him/her whatsoever. This is true especially if there has been no prior communication between the subordinate and supervisor about the system's expectations for the position and its occupant, how the incumbent views the role, problems in performing it, and how it ought to be performed.

It has been noted that personnel performance and organizational communication are closely related. The individual's understanding of what the organization expects him/her to accomplish and how to accomplish it, how the organization plans to achieve its aims, and whether it considers his/her work satisfactory all depend on efficiency of the communication network.

It is generally agreed that within an organization there are many instances of failure to communicate, and these result in unsatisfactory individual performance, misunderstandings, resignations, lack of concern for systemwide goals, and general decline in coordinated behavior. In one sense, communication is an organization's peripheral nervous system; without it, organizational behavior is haphazard.

Integration.   The point was made earlier that information performs a linking function among individuals, groups, and the organization. This concept is portrayed in Figure 10.10, the intent of which is to stress these points:

- One of the continuing and critical management tasks is to make effective personnel decisions.
- Personnel decisions cover the spectrum of system activities (plans, funds, facilities, people, and structure) as well as internal and external environments.
- The key to personnel problem solving and decision making is a human resources information system.
- The need for a unified information system has been accentuated by an increase in the number and types of human problems in organizations as well as the need for more and quicker decisions by which they can be resolved.
- One of the results of an integrated information system should be the extent to which the organization, the units, and individuals therein are able to perform more effectively and efficiently because they are furnished with the quality and quantity of data essential to decision making and problem solving.

In sum, contemporary change in modern organizations is such that human resources decisions make mandatory an integrated information system that will enhance decision-making and problem-solving capabilities.

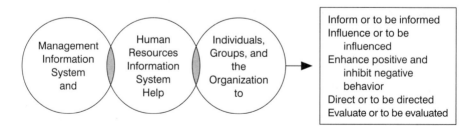

FIGURE 10.10
Linkage between information and management of human resources.

Evaluation and Feedback

The human resources information process outlined in Figure 10.4 includes *evaluation* and *feedback* as activities essential to its operation and improvement. Every organization needs to know how well the system as a whole and each of its parts are achieving assigned objectives. This is done through control procedures by which events that have taken place are compared to those desired. If deviations from plans are discovered, corrective action is taken. So it is with the personnel information system. The organization wants to know, for example, whether:

- The present system is effective.
- Parts of it need to be preserved or modified.
- The system is providing information to operate the human resources function effectively and efficiently.
- The system is capable of recording and reporting events daily, as they occur.
- Information security tests meet criteria emphasized in the Privacy Act (see Table 3.2)
- The information module interfaces properly with the total organization information system.

Securing answers to these concerns involves various types of diagnoses, including determination of what the major problems in the information system are, forces causing the problems, nature and timing of changes needed to resolve the problems, goals to be brought about by the change, and how goal attainment will be measured. Through evaluation and feedback, needed improvements in the information system can be brought about so as to facilitate organizational decisions regarding personnel processes, policies, and the organization structure; provide higher quality of information to individuals and operating components; and generate improved knowledge and understanding of the function.

REVIEW AND PREVIEW

A school system includes various interrelated components working in conjunction with each other to achieve the overall mission. *Information,* as one of these components, is considered to be the indispensable resource, the adhesive force by which the several parts are combined and strengthened to bring about desired organizational effects. This chapter stressed the following information-related points:

- An information system is a systematic plan designed to acquire, refine, organize, store, maintain, protect, retrieve, and utilize data to satisfy school system needs.

- Five major functions of a school system (planning, educational program, logistics, human resources, and external relations) are linked to each other and to the system as a whole by means of an integrated information system.
- The human resources function, as one of the modules of a total information system, consists of a planned network of forms, files, reports, records, and documents.
- In order to determine the manner and extent to which the computer should be linked to a personnel information system, factors that bear analysis include the kinds of information needed to effectively contribute to personnel practice, the strengths and limitations of computers to provide essential information, the role of computers in the personnel information system, the people who will create the data designs and make the key decisions about their processing, and the procedures and processes needed to optimize computer applications.
- The personnel information process, as modeled in this chapter, consists of five phases: diagnosis, preparation, implementation, evaluation, and feedback.
- Policy points or protocols for bringing about order, method, and uniformity in the personnel information system include policy purpose, scope, responsibility, access, and active-inactive records.

Chapter 11 discusses processes and methods school systems are currently using, as well as those they ought to use, to create equitable pay systems that have the qualities to attract, retain, and motivate employees to achieve personal and performance satisfaction.

REVIEW AND DISCUSSION QUESTIONS

1. Give reasons why you agree or disagree with the following assertions:
   - "Small schools (enrollment under 500) do not need an information system."
   - "Most school systems, large or small, are not organized to take full advantage of modern computer technology."
   - "Computer technology is too sophisticated for most school systems to include in their information systems."
   - "If school systems employ computers, there will be a dramatic improvement in the quality of decision making."
   - "A file is not a place to put things, it is a place to find things."
2. How can a personnel information system be fashioned to respond to questions such as: Why am I not being paid fairly? What happened to my promotion bid? Why wasn't I hired? Why don't I get any help from my principal with on-the-job problems? Should I plan to file a grievance regarding my latest performance appraisal report? Why is teacher absenteeism so persistent in this school district?

3. Discuss what information is needed to properly support or rebut this criticism: "Our teachers are not rewarded for improving outcomes, but for following routines."

4. Assume a school system purchased or designed a software tracking information module aimed at computerizing the following: personnel *attendance records* for individuals, units, and the school district;

absence averages; daily absences by department and reason; comparison of current and past year absence data instead of previous year totals; a ranked absence list; and benefits accruing to system members on a yearly basis for illness, vacation, and personal time. Indicate how the results should be utilized.

5. It has been estimated that in most school systems less than 1 percent of essential or desirable personnel information is available in electronic form. Suggest underlying reasons for this condition, and estimate what percentage of personnel information created in a school system each year should be available in electronic form to optimize resolution of current and emerging personnel problems. (See Table 10.1 for types of personnel information that can be processed electronically.)

6. What type of feedback did you receive from your appraiser regarding your position performance review? Did the review pinpoint areas for improvement? Give some direction and purpose? On what information was the review based?

7. Explain the link between recruitment data and personnel selection.

8. Respond to each of the following assertions pertaining to personnel information:

- "Information needs created by new technology in the area of electronic information create supplemental needs that require supplemental resources."
- "New information and new technologies do not replace old information and old technologies."
- "Management of information itself—its planning, acquisition, storage, dissemination, and disposal—emerges as critical to achieving the ends of the system."
- "A school system must plan and manage information resources just as it must plan and manage its funds, facilities, and personnel."

9. It has been reported that the federal government has approximately 150 different accounting systems. What kinds of information problems can be created by this sort of information fragmentation?

10. Consider this statement: Powerful school officials exist because they have access to important information, allocate required resources, and make crucial decisions. In the organization you work for, which officials have decision-making power because they have access to or control important information?

CHAPTER EXERCISE 10.1

Directions: Consider a school system or other organization that you work or have worked for. Describe the human resources information system in terms of the provisions in the list that follows. Determine whether you would rate each provision as nonexistent, less than satisfactory, satis- factory, or very satisfactory. The instructor will divide the class into two critique groups to review the responses provided by group members. Each group will present to the entire class its critique of the responses. The entire class will critique the exercise review, focusing on these questions: To what extent are there differences in the responses of each group? The extent to which provisions of the organizations under consideration meet the standards of a human resources information system? Are high scores indicative of highly bureaucratic, tight control measures? Are low scores indicative of informal, adaptive controls exercised to meet information situations as they arise? Do very low scores indicate unawareness of the importance of a well-designed information system? Are you in favor of tight or loose control of school system information? Should any controls governing information exist?

Exercise Evaluation:

- This school system has clearly defined and communicated to its employees the retention of human resource records required by law, as well as the protection of personnel records.
- The system keeps complete records documenting personnel decisions.
- Effective forms management is achieved through continual review and systematic analysis of forms at a central point within the system. This review includes design, coordination, standardization, simplification, elimination, technology, and cost containment of all system *forms*.

- The system has employed an information procedural manual regarding the information process as it concerns its human resources.
- Every member of the system is aware of what records and related information go into the personnel files.
- Computerized personnel records are considered to be state of the art.
- Every work unit official has been instructed in procedures governing the human resources information system.
- In this school system every member has been informed of the steps taken to protect confidentiality of paper and computerized records.
- Member requests to see personnel files are granted and inspected in the presence of a designated school official.
- The school system has established a human resources information center to service day-to-day information needs of internal and external users.
- Employees are not permitted access to other employee personnel records.
- The information system contains modules (recruitment, compensation, justice) for each of the eleven processes in the human resources function.
- The school system maintains a records center and archives as elements of a contemporary information system.

NOTES

1. For an elaboration of purposes, principles, practices, and technology of records management, useful sources include: Jesse L. Clark, The Encyclopedia of Records Retention (New York: The Records Management Group, 1990); Susan Z. Diamond, Preparing Administrative Manuals (New York: AMACOM, 1991); Susan Z. Diamond, Records Management, Second Edition (New York: AMACOM, 1991); Directory of Information Management Software for Libraries, Information Centers, Record Centers (Studio City, CA: Pacific Information, Inc., Latest Edition); How to File and Find It (Lincolnshire, IL: Quill Corporation, 1989); Donald S. Skupsky, Recordkeeping Requirements (Den-

ver, CO: Records Clearinghouse, 1990).

2. Computerized information systems are discussed in Gary D. Dessler, Personnel Management, Fourth Edition (Englewood Cliffs, NJ: Prentice-Hall Inc., 1988), 261–62; John M. Ivancevich and William F. Glueck, Foundations of Personnel/Human Resource Management, Third Edition (Plano, TX: Business Publications Inc., 1986), 210–11; and Vida G. Scarpello and James Ledvinka, Personnel/Human Resource Management (Boston: PWS-Kent, 1988), 234–35; 238; 717–18.

3. R. Dennis Middlemist and Michael A. Hitt, Organizational Behavior (St. Paul, MN: West Publishing Company, 1988), 172.

4. Educational Research Service Inc., School District Use of Computer Technology (Arlington, VA: Educational Research Service Inc., 1982), 53–61.

5. Morton F. Meltzer, The Information Imperative (New York: American Management Associations, 1971), 32–33.

6. Educational Research Services Inc., 53.

7. Peter F. Drucker, Management: Tasks, Practices, Responsibilities (New York: Harper and Row, 1974), 483.

SUPPLEMENTARY READING

Alphabetic Filing Rules. Prairie Village, KS: ARMA International, Latest Edition.

Bureau of National Affairs. Human Resources Information System. Washington, DC: Bureau of National Affairs, 1989.

Connors, Eugene; and Thomas Valesky. Using Microcomputers in School Administration. Bloomington, IN: Phi Delta Kappa, 1986.

Fedders, John M.; and Lauryn Guttenplan. "Document Retention and Destruction: Practical, Legal, and Ethical Considerations." The Notre Dame Lawyer (October 1990).

Freed, Melvyn N.; Robert Hess; and Joseph M. Ryan. The Educators Desk Reference. New York: Macmillan Publishing Company, 1990.

Guideline for a Vital Records Program. Prairie Village, KS: ARMA International, Latest Edition.

Guideline to Records Center Operation. Prairie Village, KS: ARMA International, Latest Edition.

Guide to Record Retention Requirements in the Code of Federal Regulations. Washington, DC: U.S. Government Printing Office, Latest Edition.

Mandel, S. I. Computers and Data Processing Today. St. Paul, MN: West Publishing Company, 1986.

Marshall, J.; and S. D. Caldwell. "Information Management and Evaluation in Staff Development." Journal of Staff Development 3, 1 (1989), 84–101.

Meltzer, Morton F. Information: The Ultimate Management Resource: How to Find, Use, and Manage It. New York: American Management Association, 1981.

Meyer, Gary J. Automating Personnel Operations: The Manager's Guide to

Computerization. Madison, CT: Business Legal Reports, 1984.

Palmer, R. P.; and H. Varnet. How to Manage Information: A Systems Approach. Phoenix, AZ: The Oryx Press, 1990.

Tinsley, Dillard B. "Future Flash: Computers Facilitate Human Resources Function." Personnel 67, 2 (February 1990), 32–36.

Walker, Alfred J. Handbook of Human Resource Information Systems. New York: McGraw Hill Inc., 1992.

Zand, Dale E. Information, Organization, and Power. New York: McGraw-Hill, 1981.

PART IV

Human Resources Processes: Compensation and Bargaining

Chapter 11
Compensation: Fundamental Concepts

Chapter 12
Compensation of Administrative Personnel

Chapter 13
Collective Bargaining: Planning, Negotiating, and Contract Administration

Part IV places special emphasis on two human resources processes: compensation and collective bargaining. Compensation is a process that deals with all forms of remuneration, whether direct or indirect in form. The collective bargaining process (Chapter 13), in which compensation is a major consideration, entails negotiations between school system and employee representatives in order to reach a contractual agreement concerning the range of working conditions.

- Chapter 11 develops a foundation for resolving compensation problems, with special focus on strategies by which employee remuneration becomes the engine that propels the system's strategic objectives. Particular attention is given to redesigning traditional compensation models into types that are performance driven.
- Chapter 12 develops a model for compensating members of the administrative staff.
- Chapter 13 puts into context the planning potential of the bargaining process for achieving human resources goals.

Chapter 11

Compensation: Fundamental Concepts

CHAPTER OVERVIEW

- Human Resources Compensation: Perennial Challenge

  The Purpose Perspective
  The Exchange Perspective
  The Environmental Perspective
  The Education Reform Perspective
  The Total Compensation Perspective
  The Compensation System Redesign Perspective

- Compensation Process
- Compensation Strategy

  Strategy Planning And Policy

- Compensation Policy
- Compensation Structure
- Economic Value of Positions
- Economic Value of Position Holder

  Designing the Pay Structure

- Compensation Administration
- Compensation Control And Adjustment

CHAPTER OBJECTIVES

- Develop an understanding of current compensation practices and problems.
- Provide a model or blueprint for designing the compensation process.
- Analyze the compensable factors that comprise the pay structure.
- Identify external and internal factors that influence pay policies and levels.
- Describe approaches to developing the economic worth of positions and position holders.
- Stress the importance of assessing compensation process outcomes and the criteria by which they are reviewed.

CHAPTER TERMS

Base pay	Nonsalary benefits
Benefits	Pay structure
Compensation policy	Performance (merit) pay
Compensation structure	Position structure
Differentiated pay	Psychic income
Incentive compensation	Salary
Market-sensitive pay	Wages
Noneconomic benefits	

HUMAN RESOURCES COMPENSATION: PERENNIAL CHALLENGE

For the better part of the twentieth century, school personnel and their representatives, practitioners, protagonists and antagonists, academicians, reformers, school boards, special interests groups, and the media have propounded the matter of fair and adequate compensation for school system employees. Individuals as well as concerned parties have offered for consideration their convictions about the merits and demerits of the single salary schedule, benefits, merit pay, comparable worth, pay for performance, pay equity, pay levels, pay structure, pay form, rewards, incentives, and union influence on compensation. Yet the problems involved in concepts for and execution of a compensation plan so that the school system and its human resources achieve mutual goals remain perennially unsettled.

For those who have observed the ebb and flow of compensation cycles, it is idle to expect that the vexing problems just noted, which have long stymied authorities and experts, are about to be resolved. They appear to be too deep for quick resolution in order to satisfy both the school system and those who render its services.

The intent of this chapter is to view human resources compensation as unfinished business. It seeks to draw organizational sustenance from past and contemporary compensation patterns, practices, and programs so that better remuneration designs can be developed for dealing with short- and long-range compensation eventualities.

The focus of the text that follows is designed to provide a perspective on compensation decision making, the goal of which is to resolve, in an effective and efficient manner, pay problems that affect the interests of the school community, the system, and its members. This perspective includes the central strands that form the compensation process, leading the reader through the subprocesses by which the economic worth of positions and persons is determined, as well as the environmental influences that are brought to bear on compensation determination.

The Purpose Perspective

One of the central tasks of educational administration is to allocate funds, facilities, personnel, and information in such a way that the difference in educational achievement between entering and leaving students is maximized. To that end, the general purpose of the compensation process is to allocate resources for salaries, wages, benefits, and rewards in a manner that will attract and retain a competent school staff.

A compensation system properly conceived and administered can make an important contribution to attainment of specific objectives of the organization as well as to individual satisfaction of its members. Goals to which the formal organization can gear its compensation planning include:

- Attracting and retaining competent career personnel.
- Motivating personnel to optimum performance.
- Creating incentives to growth in individual competence.
- Getting maximum return in service for the economic investment made in the compensation plan.
- Developing confidence of personnel in the intent of the organization to build equity and objectivity into the compensation plan.
- Making the plan internally consistent and externally competitive.
- Relating compensation levels to importance and difficulty of positions.
- Making salaries commensurate with the kinds of personnel the organization requires.

- Establishing a compensation structure conducive to giving economic, social, and psychological satisfaction to personnel.
- Minimizing union and individual grievances.
- Exercising careful control over salaries, a budgetary item that generally encompasses four-fifths of the expenditure plan.
- Developing plans to ensure continuity of funds needed for an effective salary, wage, and benefits program.
- Minimizing personnel turnover.

This list of aims, it should be noted, pertains to all personnel in the employ of the organization. Although goals such as these are not difficult to state, establishing procedures by which they are attained is a more formidable task.

Analysis of these aims brings into focus complexities involved in designing the compensation process needed to achieve them. In a formal organization, a satisfactory compensation plan is the basic element by which human resources requirements are satisfied. Without an effective compensation plan, all other system plans, programs, and processes lose their force.

The Exchange Perspective

A useful way of viewing employment is in terms of an exchange between the individual and the organization in which each gets something in return for giving something. According to Belcher, compensation represents a transaction between the individual and the organization that involves an employment contract. The transaction may be viewed from each of the following perspectives:

- *Economic transaction*—Payment for employee services is an economic transaction in which the purchaser attempts to obtain the greatest quantity and the highest quality for his/her money; the worker sells his/her services to obtain income and holds out for the highest price he/she can command.
- *Psychological transaction*—Employment represents a psychological contract between humans and the organization in which the individual exchanges certain types of desired behavior for pay and other sources of job satisfaction.
- *Sociological transaction*—Compensation represents a sociological transaction because organizations are associations of persons, and employment is an important relationship to both individuals and organizations.
- *Political transaction*—Compensation represents a political transaction involving the use of power and influence.
- *Ethical transaction*—Compensation represents an ethical transaction in terms of fairness to both parties.[1]

The foregoing perspective on employment as an exchange transaction leads to the generalization that the belief system that prevails in any organization with respect to compensation must take into consideration a variety of interrelated factors. As illustrated in Figure 11.1, elements that determine the amount of money going into an individual's paycheck are not exclusively pecuniary. Employment exchanges between individuals and organizations are perceived differently by both parties. One of the major problems in compensation planning is to reach agreements between parties by reconciling the nature of the input-output relationship.

The Environmental Perspective

Compensation programs are subject to external and internal influences. The fact that they are constantly affected by the aggregate of surrounding circumstances to which they are subjected indicates that school systems must develop a capability to respond to changing environments. The following overview of the relationship between compensation components and their linkage to human resources planning begins by noting that achievement of a school system's pay objectives is dependent upon a thorough understanding of the external and internal environments in which the remuneration process is imbedded. As portrayed in Figure 11.2, the surrounding environment in which the compensation process occurs includes a variety of forces, factors, and conditions that influence compensation outcomes. The primary mechanism through which the system responds to environmental forces that affect compensation decisions is referred to as organizational strategy. In essence, how well educational administration brings the system into an acceptable equilibrium with its environment enhances compensation and organizational well-being.

The system agrees to 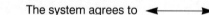 The individual agrees to

The system agrees to	The individual agrees to
• Equitable compensation	• Join
• Rights and privileges	• Stay
• Position security	• Exceed role expectations
• Assist in improvement	• Work independently
• Proper placement	• Self-improvement
• Fair treatment	• Cooperate
• Opportunity for advancement	• Adhere to system expectations

---

FIGURE 11.1
Conceptualization of the exchange theory of compensation.

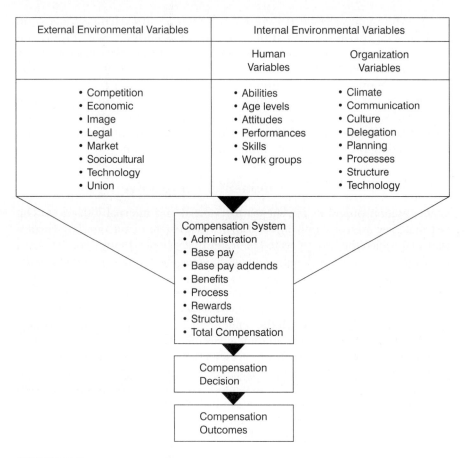

External Environmental Variables	Internal Environmental Variables	
	Human Variables	Organization Variables
• Competition • Economic • Image • Legal • Market • Sociocultural • Technology • Union	• Abilities • Age levels • Attitudes • Performances • Skills • Work groups	• Climate • Communication • Culture • Delegation • Planning • Processes • Structure • Technology

Compensation System
• Administration
• Base pay
• Base pay addends
• Benefits
• Process
• Rewards
• Structure
• Total Compensation

Compensation Decision

Compensation Outcomes

FIGURE 11.2
Illustration of compensation variables that influence compensation outcomes.

The External Environment. The view that the contemporary status of school employees has been brought about to a considerable extent by external rather than internal forces deserves particular attention. External forces (Figure 11.2) include legal, political, technological, economic, and social factors, the cumulative effect of which plays a large part in determining the characteristics of a school compensation system. Much of the compensation component of a school budget is funded by state, local, and federal governments. Political action affects pay levels, retirement provisions, benefit programs, pay for time not worked, and various other politically sensitive elements that intertwine with public school finance. Moreover, school systems have virtually no control over the amount of economic resources for their support, public attitude toward union demands, community commitment to schooling, taxpayer resistance to school support, prevailing salaries and wages, and cycles governing the standards and cost of living. For example, as of July 1, 1972, the protection of the Equal Pay Act of 1963 [Public Law 88-38, 77 Stat. 56, 29 U.S.C.A., S206 (d)] as administered by the U.S. Department of Labor, Employment Standards Administration, was extended and made applicable to certain employees otherwise exempt, including administrative and other professional personnel in the public schools.[2] Salient provisions of the act and amendments as they relate to school personnel include the following:

- The Fair Labor Standards Act, as amended, is a federal statute of general application, which established minimum wage, overtime pay, child labor, and equal pay requirements affecting employment of all public school personnel.

- The validity of a claim based on an alleged violation of the Equal Pay Act is determined on the basis of the following four elements: (a) equal skill, (b) equal effort, (c) equal responsibility, and (d) equal conditions.

- Exceptions are provided in the Equal Pay Act where it can be shown that the wage differential is based on a seniority or merit system, a system measuring earnings by quantity or quality of production, or on any other factor not related to gender.

The point is also worth making that governments and their agencies impact on public education in many ways and from multiple directions. Those employed in a school system have a canopy of protection by combined levels of government in the form of legislation regulating pay, jobs, tenure, health, justice, retirement, and employee representation.

Internal Environment.   For those involved in defining, designing, redesigning, and implementing compensation systems, it is important to recognize that these responsibilities entail dealing not only with forces in the external environment but also with those that are internal to the school system (Figure 11.2). More precisely, internal variables may be thought of as consisting of two clusters: human and organizational. Examination of the variables shown in Figure 11.2 suggests that these elements are frequently changing and require direction and coordination so as to align the organization with the larger environment of which it is a part.

Thus, the compensation system serves as one of the most important processes of the human resources function for integrating human and organization variables with their surrounding environments. Problems stemming from both human and organizational characteristics require strategic decisions to shape present and future responses to environmental developments and potential opportunities that may lie therein.

Planning Implications.   Because the internal and external environments possess strong potential for directly influencing conditions of work in educational institutions, and especially their pay programs, they deserve the practitioner's close and abiding attention. Minimizing a compensation system's weaknesses while enhancing its strengths depends upon three types of administrative action:

- *Anticipatory action*—Organizational sensing or perceiving emerging external and internal developments that influence compensation planning (health care, layoffs, forthcoming regulatory requirements, economic downturns, and legislative actions affecting curriculum and instruction).
- *Opportunistic action*—Sensing and capitalizing on external and internal developments that are compensation sensitive (unanticipated federal and state financial windfalls, improved economic conditions, and employee acceptance of cost benefit sharing).
- *Modeling action*—Gathering data indicating important compensation problems (base salary, base salary addends, benefits, and rewards) and developing strategies for responding to conditions in the environments that influence attainment of compensation objectives.

A compensation model is designed to highlight areas of needed change, identify factors that influence problem areas, and shape responses such as policies, programs, and processes. The administrative actions alluded to help to stimulate the solutions to problems and to heighten awareness of the need of thoughtful strategic approaches to present and emerging issues.

The Education Reform Perspective

An article on redirecting education reform states that:

> . . . the education reform movement of the 1980s and 1990s has produced disappointing results. *Policy makers* who have labored on federal, state, and local reform initiatives blame the results on the reluctance or incompetence of practitioners. *Everyone* wants to blame the delivery system that fragments the social, medical, psychological, nutritional, and educational resources and services provided for children.[3]

As will be noted subsequently, the compensation system is an element in this delivery system.

Because of a variety of contemporary developments, including education reform movements, compensation legislation, teacher unionization, competition for qualified personnel, and the fluctuating image of teaching and its rewards, various efforts to reform traditional models of teacher compensation have developed. To illustrate reasons for calls for modifying current pay systems, characteristics of traditional models of teacher compensation, which have been in vogue for the better part of the twentieth century, are capsulized in Figure 11.3. The education community has long resisted efforts to modify traditional compensation models, particularly those efforts to link compensation to performance and to changing preparation and experience, two stalwart elements of what is referred to as the single salary schedule.

Figure 11.4 contains indicators of the direction of compensation remodeling being advanced in various quarters. Compensation aspects that have been advanced as necessary change ingredients, it will be noted, represent adjustment to external changes, pressures for pay equity, low supply and high demand for selected skills, and planning efforts to develop comprehensive models aimed at transforming school systems for effectiveness in a changing society.

The Total Compensation Perspective

It has been noted previously that administration of a compensation program involves more than determination of payment to an individual for services

---

Traditional Models Maximize Support for . . .

Single-salary schedules (equivalent salaries for equivalent preparation and experience).

Uniformity of all instructional positions (all positions are equal in importance and responsibility).

Automatic pay progression through salary range.

Equal pay for unequal performance.

Teaching experience as a determinant of pay increases, without regard to performance.

Teacher preparation as a determinant of pay increases, without regard to performance or type of preparation.

Uniform distribution of rewards to all personnel.

Traditional Models Minimize Support for . . .

Differentiated salary schedules.

Importance of the pay-performance relationship.

Importance of position descriptions and their application to compensation.

Acceptance of the necessity for performance appraisal to determine compensation.

Differentiated salaries for team-teaching responsibilities.

FIGURE 11.3
Characteristics of traditional models of teacher compensation.

Focus of Change in Compensation Planning	
Away from . . .	**Toward . . .**
Compensation based on piecemeal additions and deletions	Compensation based on a comprehensive model, including all personnel on payroll
Compensation policy shaped by professional negotiators	Compensation based on strategic design, concerned with organization goals for its human resources
Compensation designed for current staff	Compensation includes current staff but is designed to support future system plans
Benefits package excludes options	Benefits package includes options
Position emphasis	Performance emphasis
Market-insensitive salaries	Market-sensitive salaries
Single-salary schedule	Variable compensation plan
Equal pay for unequal performance	Performance rewarded through various options
Unequal pay for comparable positions	Equal pay for comparable positions
Cost-saving pay plans	Cost-effective pay plans
Pay secrecy	Pay openness
Base pay addends limited to merit	Merit concept embraces a variety of addends
Reward system limited	Comprehensive reward plan
Equal pay for all	Disparate compensation to reward specified behavior
Event-prone compensation practices (what others pay)	Compensation designed to meet organizational needs
Rewards limited to monetary considerations	Nonmonetary factors included in reward structure
Performance appraisal emphasis on process and input	Performance appraisal emphasis is on outcomes
Union-driven compensation	Strategy-driven compensation
Rewards based on performance appraisal	Rewards based on specific individual and group outcomes
No balance between salary and benefits	Link between salary and benefits
Unsystematic position classification	Systematic position classification

FIGURE 11.4

Direction of compensation remodeling.

Source: William B. Castetter, "Designing and Administering Teacher Compensation," National Forum of Educational Administration and Supervision Journal 6, 3 (1989–90), 40.

rendered to the system. Development of an orderly process of determining compensation and its payment includes consideration of compensation policy, as well as development of principles and procedures to implement policy. Compensation planning is concerned with all personnel at every position or job level in the system and with all phases of personnel compensation, including salaries, wages, collateral benefits, nonsalary payments, and noneconomic provisions. Obviously, total compensation planning is concerned with policies, structures, levels, methods of payment, position analysis and comparison, and appraisal of personnel performance. It encompasses psychological, sociological, philosophical, political, and economic issues. It is the responsibility of the administration to design and administer the compensation process with a minimum of dissatisfaction to individual staff members, the system, and taxpayers. In doing so, consideration must be given to external factors that affect compensation, such as economic conditions, national crises, federal and state legislation, and other current developments and trends that govern the ability of the system to attract and retain essential human resources.

Before we undertake analysis of the compensation process, definition of several words and phrases used in this chapter is in order. The term **wages** refers to compensation paid for services to personnel who generally have no guarantee of employment throughout the year. For the most part, wages are paid to hourly rated personnel. **Salary,** on the other hand, is a term used to describe compensation for work of professional, supervisory, and clerical personnel whose contracts usually stipulate weekly, monthly, or annual compensation. *Collateral benefits* are direct or indirect forms of compensation, and generally apply to all personnel; they do not require additional services to be performed beyond those called for under the basic compensation structure. **Nonsalary payments** include extra payments to professional personnel for extra work, overtime hourly wages to support personnel, and merit or incentive payment of any kind. **Noneconomic benefits** are sometimes referred to as **psychic income**. They include a variety of satisfactions in addition to financial rewards, such as recognition, position security, latitude for initiative, appreciation, status symbols, privileges, authority and power, information, proper and pleasant physical facilities in which to work, absence of close supervision, and position compatibility. The **compensation structure** refers to the interrelated provisions governing salaries, nonsalary payment, wages, collateral benefits, and noneconomic benefits of school personnel. Structures create differentials in compensation within, between, and among positions and position levels, and may be viewed as a hierarchy within which wage and salary levels for the system are established. **Base pay** refers to entry-level pay for any position in the organization structure. **Performance (merit) pay** means extra compensation in addition to regular salary or wages. **Differential pay** is salary or wages that vary according to the value or importance of a position. **Market-sensitive pay** refers to salary or wages based on supply and demand for personnel for a given position.

Figure 11.5 illustrates an application of the total compensation concept, that is, the aggregate of compensation forms and their relationship to each other. The total compensation package described in Figure 11.5 consists of four forms: base salary, base salary addends, **benefits,** and special forms of remuneration (perquisites and emotional dividends). The manner in which this entire package is designed to achieve compensation objectives such as personnel attraction, retention, and motivation is of considerable significance to the organization and its human resources. It should take into consideration such variables as proportion among the four forms just mentioned, cost, school taxes, ease of administration, how it is communicated to and perceived by recipients, and its competitive power. Above all, dissemination about the program redesign should emphasize its strategic purposes, its relationship to objectives of the human resources function, and actions taken to eliminate errors of omission and commission in the existing compensation plan.

Forms of Compensation in the Riverpark School System

A. Direct Financial Income (cash received)

    (1) Base salary or wages (entry level)
    (2) Salary addends (automatic increases, overtime pay, pay for performance, special assignments, etc.)
    (3) Total direct financial income = A1 + A2

B. Indirect Income

    (1) Benefits (health, retirement, employee assistance program, career development, nonworking time, etc.)
    (2) Perquisites (position-related grants, equipment, recognition, extra space, clerical assistance, parking, cafeteria, and emotional dividends)
    (3) Total indirect income = B1 + B2

C. Total Compensation = A3 + B3

ILLUSTRATION: Teacher X (199X–199X fiscal year)

    Entry level salary = $25,000; base salary addends (pay for performance)

    = $2500; direct income = $27,500; benefits = 40% of entry level salary
    = $10,000. Total benefit income = $10,000. Perquisites (tuition stipend)
    = $950.00; reading experiment grant = $2,200. Total perquisites
    = $3,150. Total indirect income = $13,150. Total compensation for Teacher X
    = $27,500 + $10,000 + $3,150 + $40,650.

FIGURE 11.5
Illustration of the total compensation concept.

The Compensation System Redesign Perspective

According to the *Statistical Abstract of the United States*,[4] there are approximately 15,000 school districts in the United States. Among these public institutions there is considerable variance in such factors as geographic location and boundaries, size and diversity of pupil population, quality and quantity of the work force, resources, community and school system cultures, organizational climate, unionization, political circumstances, affirmative leadership, and breadth and depth of educational opportunity. The point of noting these individual, environmental, and organizational characteristics is that they contribute directly and indirectly to the fabric of a compensation system.

Every school system has some model of compensation for its human resources, whether it be considered formal or informal in context. For the most part, compensation systems are considered generational, traditional, or conventional, representing past or antiquated practices that are not formalized, are reactive rather than proactive, and are technically rather than strategically oriented.

For illustrative purposes we shall assume that most school system pay plans can be improved by some ongoing modification and that the gap can be narrowed between compensation realism and idealism. Further assumptions are that (a) compensation is an important element to any work force and (b) compensation can and should be employed to generate the kinds of individual and group behavior needed to realize what are regarded as predetermined educational objectives. These assumptions form the thrust of the following discussion on compensation refinement planning.

Refining the Compensation System.   Because of the dynamics of environmental change, compensation planning is subject to continuous adjustment to maintain its balance. The planning activities as portrayed in Figure 11.6 provide a framework for making major or minor adjustments in compensation to guide the transition from an existing to a desired condition.

The first step in the renewal process, as indicated in Figure 11.6, is a review and definition of compensation system objectives. To put the objective factor into proper perspective, planners need to decide what outcomes should be generated by the operation of the compensation system. Specific compensation outcomes such as the following are illustrative:

- Equitable compensation structure.
- Effective and efficient compensation administration.
- Satisfied and productive workforce.
- Enhanced performance culture.
- Reduction in strikes, turnover, lateness, absenteeism, disloyalty, and hostility toward performance expectations.

Phase	Action
A	Review and revise compensation objectives as needed.
B	Assess current compensation condition.
C	Identify gap between objectives and current system condition.
D	Analyze objective constraints.
E	Project desired state of compensation system.
F	Generate alternative approaches to desired state.
G	Select appropriate objectives strategy.
H	Implement compensation system improvement plan.
I	Monitor compensation program course of action.
J	Modify course of action and reexamine objectives.

FIGURE 11.6
Examples of actions employed in refining the compensation system.

Inasmuch as a compensation system is considered to be a mechanism for committing resources to create future benefits or advantages for both the school system and its human resources, the consideration of yield expectation should be at the forefront of planning agenda concerned with investment decisions that are fiscally and strategically prudent.

Examination of the various phases and actions involved in the compensation review (Figure 11.6) indicates the need for gathering information of various kinds in order to identify current system conditions, constraints, alternate approaches to pay plan modification, and appropriate goal-focused strategies. Tables 11.1 and 11.2 illustrate ways of developing information about present program strengths and shortcomings, as well as influential internal and external factors that affect plans for projecting courses of action leading to a desired compensation condition.

By defining and redesigning the compensation structure following the examples in Figure 11.6, various possibilities emerge, such as the formation of major strategies, programs, process coordination, and types of criteria needed for continuous evaluation of pay plans, actions, and outcomes. Although the compensation system review and related advancement activities previously suggested may not fully realize advancement toward planning expectation, the internal aftereffects likely to accrue from this management endeavor ordinarily pay out in more than tokens.

COMPENSATION PROCESS

As illustrated in Figure 11.7, the compensation process conceptualized in this chapter consists of six subprocesses:

- Linking organizational strategy and compensation process.
- Designing compensation structure.
- Determining economic value of positions.
- Determining economic worth of position holders.
- Establishing administrative procedures.
- Adjusting the compensation process to changing needs and events, and to improve effectiveness and efficiency.

For clarity and analysis, each of these six subprocesses is discussed as though it were a clearly identifiable step in an orderly sequence of activities. In the real world, however, the compensation process is not as orderly as illustrated in Figure 11.7. The analysis contained in this chapter is designed to familiarize the reader with the principal forces, factors, and conditions to

TABLE 11.1
Guide for assessing compensation components of the Riverpark school system.

Directions: On a scale of 1 to 5 rate (x) the present status or condition of the school system compensation components.

Compensation system components	1	2	3	4	5
Base salary minimum and maximum	—	—	—	—	—
Base salary addends	—	—	—	—	—
Benefits	—	—	—	—	—
Special forms of remuneration	—	—	—	—	—
Single salary schedule for teachers	—	—	—	—	—
Compensation structure	—	—	—	—	—
Pay system	—	—	—	—	—
Pay structure	—	—	—	—	—
Pay levels	—	—	—	—	—
Pay forms	—	—	—	—	—
Pay compression	—	—	—	—	—
Organization structure	—	—	—	—	—
Compensation planning	—	—	—	—	—
Compensation controls	—	—	—	—	—
Performance-pay linkage	—	—	—	—	—
Human resources advisory involvement	—	—	—	—	—
General increases	—	—	—	—	—
Pay ranges	—	—	—	—	—
Compensation communication	—	—	—	—	—
Compensation information system	—	—	—	—	—
Salary grade overlapping	—	—	—	—	—
Compensation progression (merit, seniority)	—	—	—	—	—

TABLE 11.2
Guide for assessing environmental influences on the compensation system of the Riverpark school system.

Directions: On a scale of 0 to 5 indicate the extent to which each of the internal and external factors will influence within the next three years the compensation factors listed below.

Compensation Influences Internal and External	Base Salary 0 1 2 3 4 5	Base Salary Addends 0 1 2 3 4 5	Benefits 0 1 2 3 4 5	Nonfinancial Items 0 1 2 3 4 5	Total Compensation 0 1 2 3 4 5	Numerical Total 0 1 2 3 4 5
School enrollment increase						
School enrollment decrease						
State financial aid						
Federal financial aid						
Community financial support						
Reform movements						
Unionization						
Retrenchment conditions						
Layoffs						
Demand for human resources						
Supply of human resources						
Compensation structure						
Economic recession						
Regulatory environment						
System leadership						
Compensation administration						
Social change						
Technological developments						
Political developments						

be reckoned with and reconciled in compensating personnel. It is well to bear in mind that each of the subprocesses identified in Figure 11.7 contains problems concerning salaries and wages, and resolution of these problems affects the caliber of the compensation system. So interdependent are various facets of the compensation process that proper solution of problems relevant to each cannot be left to chance or treated in isolation.

Most of the problems in compensation plans are dealt with through three types of decisions: the *level of system compensation,* the *system compensation structure,* and *compensation of individual members of the system.* Elements of these three key decisions are summarized in Table 11.3. In addition, these decisions (*X, Y,* and *Z*) will be used as referents in the discussion of the compensation process that follows. As will be noted at various points in the text, Decision *X* is related to compensation policy; Decision *Y* involves development of a compensation structure that determines pay relationships among different system positions; and Decision *Z* determines amounts of pay

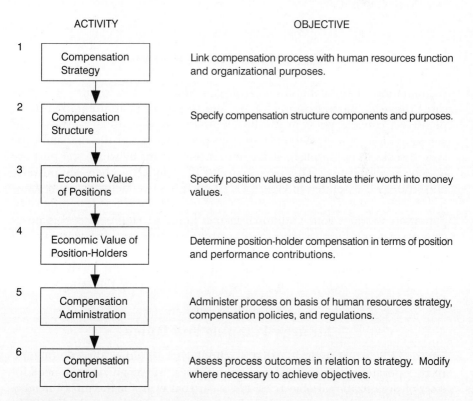

FIGURE 11.7
Model of the compensation process.

TABLE 11.3
Three essential decisions in the compensation process.

Decisions X, Y, and Z	Key Element
X What shall be the system's *level* of compensation for system personnel?	Compared to personnel working in *other* systems?
Y *How much* compensation should be awarded to system personnel who have *different* positions?	Within the *same* system?
Z What differences should there be in compensation for personnel?	Within the *same* system in *similar* positions?

received by individuals performing the same work. At various points in the following discussion, analysis will be made to illustrate factors that affect Decisions *X, Y,* and *Z.*

COMPENSATION STRATEGY

Examination of the compensation process illustrated in Figure 11.7 indicates that the starting point for designing school system compensation plans is a consideration of the link between organizational purpose and compensation strategy. Organization purpose focuses on the outcomes the system seeks to accomplish; strategies are the means by which the purpose is to be accomplished. This perspective of the connection between purpose and strategy is extended in Figure 11.8, which is a five-factor diagram showing that the system mission (purpose) provides the basis for designing compensation strategy. Four additional factors noted in Figure 11.8—organizational strategy, human resources strategy, compensation strategy, and compensation policy—are related considerations essential to developing plans for mission implementation. The significance and interactions of these factors in compensation planning are treated in the following text.

Strategy Planning and Policy

Figure 11.8 is a recognition that a school system, either directly or indirectly, operates within a framework of purposes. In recognizing the need for a set of organizational objectives, it is clear that even for the most unelaborate of school districts, formation of a cluster of objectives may be helpful in transforming them into an operational framework.

The broad intent of Figure 11.8 is to stress the view that even though the general mission of a school system is central to its creation and existence, other organizational objectives must come into play. Thus, the elements of Figure 11.8 provide a guide to some strategic propositions.

Mission.   System mission is the starting point in designing compensation strategy so as to serve the overall system purpose more effectively. Absence of a linkage between system mission and the compensation structure creates a hollow circle in the compensation program. The school system mission, as noted in Chapter 1, should be based on responses to questions such as the following:

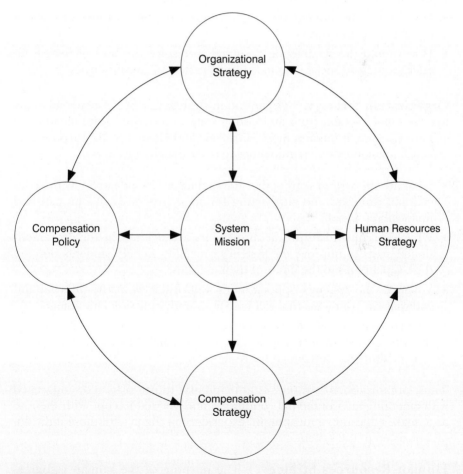

FIGURE 11.8
Link between system mission and organizational strategies.

- Taking into account the purposes for which the school district has been created, and the statutory and collateral expectations it is required to meet, what should be its future dimensions and boundaries?

- Using Goodlad's classic overview of the functions that school systems should perform for society (academic, vocational, social/civic/cultural, and personal),[5] in what regard should the school system be shaped to meet these goals?

- What current programs and services should be emphasized? De-emphasized?

- Will the changes we make match the social and economic demands of the nation?

- How should the strategy be shaped to meet the new realities with which the nation is confronted?

- How should the strategy be designed to resolve the host of increasing educational and social demands from a variety of constituencies?

Organization Strategy. Organization strategy is a set of plans for moving the school system from an existing state to a desired state in order to achieve the system mission more effectively and efficiently. Its purpose is to establish mission-oriented guidelines to resolve such questions as:

- What are the system's strengths and weaknesses in such areas as the educational program and supporting services, structure, and human and financial resources?

- What current and future arrangements are needed in the aforementioned areas to improve the system's capability to help students develop their capabilities to the limits of their abilities?

- What are the system's opportunities and obstacles in the internal and external environments that will help and hinder mission attainment?

- In what areas are our intended outcomes less than satisfactory? What systemwide plans are necessary to give visibility to and create an organizational culture for outcome improvement?

Thus, organizational strategy is anticipatory, future oriented, concerned with emerging environmental conditions, and devised to cope with them so as to make education a meaningful experience in the lives of those individuals entrusted to the system.

Human Resources Strategy. The purpose of the human resources strategy is to prescribe what actions the school system should take in order to (a) facilitate organizational strategy and (b) generate the quantity and quality of human resources essential to meet the educational needs of a changing environment. Strategy gives general direction to resolving the substantive content of human resources issues, such as:

- The number and kinds of existing and new positions (administrative, instructional, instructional specialist, and support) necessary to achieve the system mission needed to achieve organizational strategic objectives.
- Skills, abilities, and attitudes needed to fill the proposed position structure.
- Staff development and career development for those entering and those remaining in the system.
- Nature of educational and supportive technology to be introduced throughout the system, and types of personnel and training needed to make the technology outcome effective.
- Transfer, advancement, termination, and retirement decisions.
- Staff balance within work groups to improve productivity.
- Union-system negotiation to effect operational changes.

This complex web of human resources elements, when integrated into a strategic planning framework, provides the basis for guiding the many administrative judgments involved in strategy formulation and implementation.

Compensation Strategy.   Compensation strategy may be viewed as a set of interrelated decisions focused on allocating fiscal resources to move the system from its current compensation status to conditions that will contribute more effectively to organizational strategy. This includes plans that direct attention and resources to the system's present and emerging pay problems, such as direct and indirect compensation, incentives, benefits, market conditions, performance-dependent pay, marginal performance, and rewarding outstanding contributions to educational outcomes.

The questions that follow are indicative of strategic concerns fundamental to keeping compensation reform on track and to formulating approaches in which student learning, classroom teaching, and compensation are integrated more effectively:

- What should be the major aims of teacher compensation?
- What compensation components should be included in the compensation structure?
- What arrangements are necessary to make the classroom-compensation axis the locus of teaching and learning effectiveness?
- Of the numerous kinds of teacher performance incentives, which are the most appropriate for tailoring an incentive program to a school system?
- Which incentives are affordable? Appraisable? Feasible?

- What should the relative resource allocations be to a teacher incentive plan and its various components?
- How should links be established between incentives and instructional needs?
- What performance criteria should govern determination of base pay, monetary incentives, and nonmonetary incentives?
- What policies should govern the teacher incentive plan?
- What administrative processes, procedures, and rules are essential to implementing incentive compensation?

The following discussion will address these concerns in more detail.

COMPENSATION POLICY

As illustrated in Figure 11.9, one of the elements of the mission plan for guiding lower-level compensation decisions is **compensation policy**. This is to say that the governing body of the organization should stipulate in writing its intent with respect to compensation of all personnel. Such a statement indicates, in general terms, the position of the highest authority in the organization on personnel compensation. To illustrate the importance of a statement expressing compensation policy, consider the illustration in Figure 11.9.

Examination of the policy statement on compensation in Figure 11.9 indicates that it sets forth the intent of the organization with respect to treatment of personnel in matters pertaining to salaries and wages. In addition, it can serve as a general guide to development of procedures for implementing the compensation plan. It is true that a policy cannot possibly be so precise that it tells officials exactly what decisions to make on numerous problems that develop in connection with compensation, but this is not its purpose. Policy is a general guide to the aims of the organization—a tool for making actions consistent and for systematizing the manner in which the organization as a whole deals with problems.

Compensation policy indicates the system's intent with reference to compensation obligations and responsibilities. Several guides can be identified for implementing compensation policy. The following guides are intended to make clear how derivative plans *are linked to general policy* and how indispensable policy is to effective compensation planning (Decisions X, Y, and Z refer to information found in Table 11.3):

- The compensation structure should be designed to include personnel working in every capacity, regardless of income level or position responsibility (see Decision X).
- Position guides should be prepared for all positions, professional or support (see Decision Z).

Riverpark School System's *Compensation Process*

Standards formulated by the Riverpark School System to give ideal form as well as to influence planning, implementing, monitoring, evaluating, and adjusting its compensation process include the following:

- Compensate all personnel equitably in proportion to the effectiveness with which they perform the services for which they are employed.
- Establish a compensation structure internally consistent and externally competitive.
- Include in the structure personnel working in each category (administrative, instructional, support, part-time, temporary) regardless of income level or responsibility.
- Provide these forms of remuneration in exchange for services rendered: base pay addends, benefits, perquisites.
- Use a variety of plans (purposes, policies, programs, procedures, and process) to link compensation to individual, unit, and system goals.
- Recognize and reward exceptional attainment.
- Establish a standing compensation review panel as a collaborative structure to review compensation practices that have monetary implications, such as the adequacy of the total compensation package; market-sensitive pay; tenure; promotions; transfers; benefit cost-shifting; legal, economic, and political aspects of pay decisions; pay inequities; and all matters of pay discrimination.
- Maintain an open pay system to communicate to all concerned the economic value of positions; furnish annually to position holders a summary of what total compensation amounts to in the form of base pay, increments, incentives, or rewards. Summary includes system contribution and that of the individual to the paycheck.
- Provide balance among compensable factors (base pay, addends, benefits, and incentives or rewards).
- Comply with regulatory standards and union contracts.
- Contribute to attainment of individual, group, and system objectives, and to the social, economic, and psychological satisfaction of personnel.

FIGURE 11.9
A compensation policy.

- Income levels for all positions should be competitive, in keeping with duties and responsibilities of the position, and sufficiently high to attract and retain the caliber of personnel capable of performing the service for which they have been employed (see Decision X).
- Satisfactory service should be the primary criterion for advancement in income (see Decision Z).
- Differentiated pay and market-sensitive pay should be employed to overcome limitations of the single salary schedule and merit pay (see Decision Z).
- Performance pay should be used selectively, especially in the compensation of administrative and support personnel (see Decision Z).
- Quality of service should be rewarded (see Decision Z).
- Collateral benefits should be an inherent feature of the compensation structure (see Decision X).
- Noneconomic benefits (psychic income, recognition, and emotional remuneration) in a variety of forms should be conceived as an integral part of the compensation structure (see Decision X).
- The compensation structure should be designed to address, in a positive way, the motivation of personnel at all levels to perform effectively, and to enable them to achieve their aspirations in a framework of equity, achievement, and administrative and technical rationality (see Decision Y).
- The compensation structure should be so planned that it will gain personnel and public acceptance (see Decision Y).

COMPENSATION STRUCTURE

Once a compensation policy has been established that is consistent with the district mission, a decision framework is needed to translate the policy into operational reality. The diagram shown in Figure 11.10 indicates that there are three interrelated components involved in shaping the design of a *compensation structure*. The first component relates to position structure, the second to position holders, and the third to the pay structure. The variable factors involved in these components are such that a holistic approach to remuneration appears to be essential if strategic compensation aspects are to be achieved. The details of such an approach are discussed in the sections that follow.

ECONOMIC VALUE OF POSITIONS

Before a sound compensation structure can be developed, economic value of positions established, and judgments made about the economic worth of position holders, information relating to the following questions must be gathered:

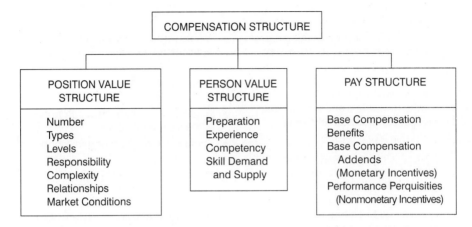

FIGURE 11.10
Three types of decisions involved in designing a compensation structure.

- How many positions have been established in the school system?
- What is the function of each position?
- What elements in the position distinguish it from other positions?
- What position clusters exist within the organizational hierarchy?
- What is the relative importance of the several position clusters within the organizational structure?
- What is the relative importance of positions within the clusters?

Examination of these questions indicates that the problem of developing a **position structure** as the basis for compensation involves *determining relative values through some form of position appraisal.*

To place a value on any position, a description of what is involved in the performance is essential. Skills needed to perform the work associated with the position, duties of the position holder, and amount of responsibility inherent in the position are factors usually taken into consideration in making judgments about its relative value in the position hierarchy.

Figure 11.11 illustrates *instructional position structure*. It is designed to establish responsibility levels that form the basis for the position structure shown in the figure. Responsibilities range from maintenance of existing program standards (Level 1), through program and professional development (Level 2), to attracting and retaining instructional personnel who are in short supply (Level 3). Note that *this structure departs from the traditional teacher compensation model,* which is based on the untenable assumption that all instructional positions are identical in responsibility and skill requirements. Moreover, contemporary modifications in the breadth and depth of

Responsibility Level	Placement Criteria of Position Candidate
Level 1: Foundation Program[a,b,c] Instructional positions in this program are intended to carry forward the instructional mission of the school district. The program also provides a base in which to erect incentives toward innovative and model strategies for instructional refinement.	• Meets regulatory controls (citizenship, certification, health, and residence). • Meets school district entrance requirements. • Eligible for retention in accordance with tenure regulations. • Carries out position requirements.
Level 2: Developmental Program[a,b,c] Instructional positions in this program level are intended to supplement those in the foundation program so as to encourage program innovation and development, and provide a climate with incentives for professional advancement.	• Leads in devising, testing, and establishing pilot programs or innovative methods. • Assists in improving and perfecting existing program(s). • Helps system to identify and remedy instructional shortcomings. • Instrumental in improving status and instructional effectiveness of colleagues. • Participates in trial of alternative instructional strategies.
Level 3: Magnet Program[b,c] Instructional positions at this program level are intended to meet the needs of the school district to attract and retain instructional personnel who are in short supply, establish model instructional standards for selected positions, and motivate the highest achievement of system enrollees and instructional personnel.	• Meets criteria for Levels 1 and 2. • Meets standards established by search committee. • Represents type, level, and/or class of instructional positions in short supply (see definitions below). • Chooses to teach in organizational climate, focusing on instructional effectiveness. Attracts similarly qualified personnel to system.

Notes: [a] By definition, the magnet program will consist of a relatively small number of teaching positions. Incumbents at other levels who qualify for placement are automatically included at the applicable compensation level.

[b] Monetary compensation is determined by ratio to base compensation and addends established for Level 3 (see Table 11.5).

[c] Designated percentages of instructional and noninstructional time are set aside for professional, position, and program development. This will require corresponding adjustments in staffing ratios used for projecting the budget.

FIGURE 11.11
An instructional position structure.

educational programs suggest that a diversity of instructional positions will be needed to meet reform-driven existing and emerging developments.

Assume that the relative position values in a school system have been decided according to some type of position evaluation procedure and that this procedure has been employed to establish a *position hierarchy* such as the one illustrated for instructional personnel in Figure 11.11. This means that those positions involving greater responsibility and difficulty will be valued more highly and will receive more compensation than those of less difficulty and responsibility. The administrative personnel position cluster, for example, will be valued relatively higher than the support personnel cluster. Within the administrative personnel cluster, the position of school superintendent will be valued more highly than the position of elementary school principal.

ECONOMIC VALUE OF POSITION HOLDER

The next step in the compensation process, according to Table 11.3, is determining the economic worth of individuals who hold positions in the system. This step, it has been noted, takes place after the relative worth of positions within the several personnel clusters has been established. Involved in determining compensation policy and levels are factors cited previously, including salary and wage legislation, prevailing pay plans in both the profession and the geographic area, standard and cost of living, ability to pay, supply and demand, and collective bargaining. There is considerable evidence to support the conclusion that of all the factors affecting compensation policy, competitive area or regional compensation is considered to be most influential.[6]

Once basic compensation levels have been established for each of the clusters of personnel groups in a school system (classroom teachers, specialists, and administrators)[7] several decisions must be made, including:

- Positions to be allocated to each of the established personnel salary clusters.
- Size and number of pay intervals in each salary plan.[8]
- Differentials among the several salary cluster plans.
- Actual dollar amounts to be assigned to pay intervals within each plan.
- Criteria for moving through the salary range.
- Adjustments for individuals whose compensation is not in keeping with the design of the pay plan.

Individual Pay Actions. After the position hierarchy has been established, position values are converted into monetary values, whereby a specific rate or salary is established for each position. Frequently, a salary or wage range is established with a minimum and maximum figure for each position classification. After the salary or wage ranges are decided on, the specific salary within each range must be determined. Various methods are employed to determine how the individual will progress from the lowest to the highest point in the salary or wage schedule. Factors used to determine pay progression vary, depending on position classification. Teachers, for example, usually progress through the salary range on the basis of two factors: *preparation* and *experience*. For support personnel, seniority and characteristics assumed to be associated with satisfactory performance are often used to determine salary increases.

Methods used to administer the salary increase program include automatic, across-the-board, cost-of-living, merit, and combination increases. In some school districts, there are procedures stipulating that an individual cannot be denied an automatic increase more than once. The implication of such a stipulation is that marginal performers should be separated from the organization. To a considerable extent, then, the initial salary or wage of each position is determined by position; subsequent increases are based on a combination of factors. Placing a dollar value on a position is impersonal, for it takes into consideration the worth of the position to the system. Determining the individual pay of a position holder, however, involves decisions as to whether differentials will be established for individuals holding positions of similar value. Differences in individuals' total compensation may be due to automatic differences in salary within the ranges or to discretionary performance-pay increases.

Designing the Pay Structure

Pay structure is a term used to describe an integrated framework of all remuneration elements that provides an equivalent for personnel services. As indicated in Figure 11.10, pay structure is the third component of the compensation structure and includes *base compensation, base compensation addends (monetary incentives), benefits,* and *performance perquisites* (nonmonetary incentives). This network is employed as a mechanism to define specific pay components in order to transform compensation strategy into operational reality. The pay structure provides a perspective of the totality of components entering into the transaction that exchanges monetary and nonmonetary rewards for personnel services.

Tables 11.4 and 11.5 illustrate in greater detail the nature of a pay structure. Table 11.4 displays those elements *currently employed* in a teacher compensation structure, as well as pertinent objectives, advantages, disadvantages, and emerging refinements pertaining to each category. Table 11.5 outlines a structure designed to accommodate *various types of pay strategies.*

Base Pay.　Base pay refers to a fixed sum of money paid to a staff member periodically and incrementally in exchange for rendering specified ser-

TABLE 11.4
Framework of teacher compensation components.

Compensation Component	Objectives	Possible Advantages	Possible Disadvantages	Emerging Refinement
Base compensation	Attract, retain, motivate, and satisfy members Establish standard for salary administration Develop equitable and competitive structure Provide foundation for compensation package design	Create structure for planning and administering total compensation package Understandable Efficient to administer Capable of reshaping Smoother income flow than incentive plan Internal equity easier to monitor	Not performance-dependent Equal pay for unequal performance All positions considered identical Not structured to deal with market sensitivity	Base pay linked to performance Preparation and experience shifted to incentive component; automatic feature eliminated Base pay maintained above geographical average Position differentiation is part of base pay design
Base compensation addends (monetary incentives)	Elicit specified behaviors from individuals and groups to enhance attainment of individual, unit, and system objectives Reward excellence	Performance-dependent Complement base pay Provide variety of incentive options Linked to instruction delivery and outcome	Require differentiated performance appraisal bases Not appropriate for all organization cultures Difficult to design differentiated addends for dissimilar work units Not feasible where salaries are not externally competitive, internally competitive, or internally equitable Differentiated awards conducive to dissatisfaction	Pay structure includes a variety of incentive plans Performance-dependent Incentives linked to desired outcomes Rewards applicable to individuals and groups

Compensation Component	Objectives	Possible Advantages	Possible Disadvantages	Emerging Refinement
Collateral benefits	Enhance quality of work life Advance economic, social, and physical security of personnel Fulfill societal obligation Motivate personnel	Favorable tax status Cost savings through group purchasing Enhance personnel security	Benefit costs difficult to control Not performance-dependent Current plans overly rigid Not congruent with two-career households Benefit demands insatiable	Change from uniform to choice of variable benefit program Benefit extension and costs being capped Portions of funds for benefits shifted to base and base addends Tighter controls over benefit program abuses
Performance perquisites (nonmonetary incentives)	Create opportunity for psychic income Create high-status performance value Lure, motivate, and retain personnel Enhance lasting quality of performance Encourage feeling of effectiveness Improve working conditions	Performance-dependent Reinforce personnel involvement Permit teacher to create his/her own performance designs Minimize barriers to effective classroom teaching	Assessment of outcomes difficult Not appealing or effective in motivating all teachers Standards for eligibility and appraisal require administrative sophistication Initial implementation difficult	Extend exploration of ways to link personnel improvement with satisfaction of inner needs Greater teacher involvement in designing own objectives Provide variety of ways in program design to improve working conditions

TABLE 11.5
Illustration of model for planning teacher compensation.

Compensation Model Components	Model Options						
	1	2	3	4	5	6	7
I. Base salary compensation	+	+	o	+	+	o	+
II. Incentive compensation (monetary)							
A. Preparation increment	+	+	+	o	+	o	o
B. Experience increment	+	+	+	o	+	o	o
C. Teacher performance	+	+	+	o	+	o	o
1. Extraordinary classroom performance							
a. Faculty performance							
(1) School site service	+	+	+	+	o	+	o
(2) System service	+	+	+	+	o	+	o
(3) Extrasystem service	+	+	+	+	o	+	o
b. Professional performance							
(1) School site service	+	+	+	+	o	+	o
(2) System service	+	+	+	+	o	+	o
(3) Extrasystem service	+	+	+	+	o	+	o
D. Teacher improvement							
1. Intraschool plan	+	+	+	+	o	+	o
2. Extraschool plan	+	+	+	+	o	+	o
III. Incentive compensation (nonmonetary)							
A. Intrinsic							
1. Task completion	+	+	+	+	o	+	o
2. Achievement	+	+	+	+	o	+	o
3. Autonomy	+	+	+	+	o	+	o
4. Personal growth recognition	+	+	+	+	o	+	o
B. Extrinsic							
1. Extra responsibility	+	+	+	+	o	+	o
2. Promotion	+	+	+	+	o	+	o
3. Position perquisites	+	+	+	+	o	+	o
4. Facilitative service (position assistance)	+	+	+	+	o	+	o
IV. Collateral benefits							
A. Uniform	+	o	+	+	o	+	o
B. Variable	o	+	+	o	+	+	+

Notes: This grid analysis, which outlines seven model options, indicates that consideration may be given to a number of model compensation options. Market-sensitive pay is established initially in the base salary range. Recipients of market-sensitive pay must earn incentive compensation. Incentive compensation can be applied to both individuals and groups. Variable compensation models, such as those outlined above, are designed to elicit specified behavior (individual or group) that will contribute to system effectiveness.

+ Indicates inclusion of component; o indicates omission of component vices. Base pay is structured by establishing a money span that covers a minimum and maximum in order to define the pay range. It is considered to be the structural foundation around which the number, kinds, and amounts of other compensable items are integrated.

Examination of Table 11.4 indicates that base pay has both strengths and weaknesses. In the public sector, the base consists of what is referred to as the *single salary schedule*. Critics have long decried the assumptions underlying this arrangement, especially that (a) all teaching positions are identical, (b) equal pay is given for unequal performance, and (c) there are automatic increments in base pay regardless of the quality of performance. Few would advocate elimination of base pay from the compensation structure, but those who favor modification of an obsolescent model are legion. Consequently, the urging of reformers to enhance the base format with incentive supplements should be given serious consideration. Issues that need to be examined with regard to altering and enhancing the base pay component are listed in Table 11.6.

Incentive Compensation.   The purpose of **incentive compensation** is to pay for specified types of performance. It may be monetary or nonmonetary in form, either of which is designed to reward outstanding contributions by staff members. The incentive addend to base pay is favored as a conditional rather than a permanent reward, renewable during continuity of performance excellence. Nonmonetary compensation represents an indirect reward in forms other than pay addends or increments. Its general intent is to recognize and promote professional growth and personal fulfillment. Figure 11.12 illustrates various forms of incentives that can be included in the base pay addend, the major purpose of which is to reward teachers directly or indirectly for performance excellence. Two noteworthy

TABLE 11.6
Base pay deliberations.

- Should reward for preparation and experience be shifted from the base pay to the incentive component?
- Should position complexity be considered in establishing the base salary?
- Should market sensitivity regarding certain positions be factored into the base pay component?
- Should incentive pay be linked proportionally to base pay?
- What role should regional salaries play in determining the base salary for individual school districts?
- What performance appraisal criteria should be employed to differentiate between base pay and incentive rewards?

I. For teacher performance

    A. Extraordinary classroom performance

        1. Instructional delivery (focus is on major teaching functions: instructional strategies, time management, student behavior, instructional presentation, instructional monitoring, and feedback)

        2. Instructional outcomes (pupil achievement)

    B. Extraordinary extraclassroom performance

        1. Faculty performance

            a. School site service (e.g., as staff development instructor, school-based project leader, extra duty assignment, lead teacher, department head, or program coordinator)

            b. System service (e.g., as teacher monitor, peer observer, staff development instructor, part-time or joint appointment, extra duty assignment, special assistant, or teacher assistance project leader)

            c. Extrasystem service (e.g., as collaborative project leader, community educational project leader, or PTA project leader)

        2. Professional performance

            a. School site service (e.g., as research project leader, experiment project leader, or model development planner)

            b. System service (e.g., as research project leader, experiment leader, special assignment, or project consultant)

            c. Extrasystem service (e.g., for publication: textbooks and articles; teaching professional courses; or professional consultation)

II. For teacher improvement (professional development)

    A. Intraschool plan (innovative curriculum project; innovative teaching project; extension of position requirements or exceptions; or extraordinary professional development through conferences, clinics, seminars, in-service activities, or special projects)

    B. Extraschool plan (graduate-level coursework, advanced degree attainment, recertification, retraining, or multiple approaches to professional improvements in addition to those cited above)

FIGURE 11.12
Forms of teacher incentive compensation.

features of the incentive format shown in Figure 11.12 are (a) that incentives are multidimensional and (b) that incentives are linked to performance by assessing behaviors that lead to expected outcomes, by assessing actual outcomes, and by a combination of these means.

All three approaches can be used to assess teacher performance. The incentive forms included in Figure 11.12 provide a perspective of the multiple options around which to fashion incentive compensation, as well as the radius of planning considerations that need to be addressed.[9]

Collateral Benefits.   Collateral benefits, as noted in Table 11.4, may be categorized as either uniform or variable. Uniform benefits are those without dissimilarity in application (all personnel are covered by the same benefits). In a variable benefits program, each member receives that amount of money the system allocates for benefit purposes and may then spend that amount for benefits individually desired. A collateral or fringe benefit is a form of direct or indirect compensation, in addition to the base salary, that does not require additional services to be performed beyond those required by the contractual agreement.

The central assumption underlying such pay-free awards is enhancement of position and personal satisfaction of system members. Benefits are assumed to create a nourishing environment for personal development and to engender psychic income associated with excellence in position performance. This component extends compensation beyond base pay and incentives. It is intended to be dollar-free, and to focus on a variety of protective arrangements in addition to monetary components.

Criticism is mounting and changes are being initiated in the design and administration of the benefit component. The following points are illustrative:

- Benefit demands are insatiable.
- Benefit costs in many instances approximate half of all personnel costs.
- Benefits are not performance-dependent.
- Benefits are not congruent in two-career households.
- Benefits, like seniority addends, are not designed to motivate high performance.
- Research suggests that there is little reason to assume that benefits have a positive impact on performance.

Exploding expenditures for organizational health care benefits (20 to 30 percent a year) and the increasing demand for and cost of most other personnel benefits have:

- Brought about greater interest in cafeteria-style benefit plans (plans whereby a school system allocates a lump sum for benefits and allows personnel to choose the types of benefits that they each prefer) as one means of controlling personnel benefit costs.

- Forced school systems to implement various benefit cost-containment controls.
- Brought about efforts to reverse current trends in benefits, in that they are creating an imbalance in the total compensation structure.
- Stimulated calls for reexamination of the role as well as the value of benefit plans in improving personnel performance.

Consequently, design of teacher compensation plans should involve careful evaluation of existing or proposed benefits in terms of their impact on base salary, incentive compensation, and teacher performance.[10]

Computation of Individual Compensation. Table 11.7 presents a model to illustrate a method for linking and making operational components of the pay structure, as outlined in Table 11.5. This approach makes it possible to compute compensation budgetary requirements as well as individual pay packages. Table 11.7 also summarizes what has been discussed up to this point about compensation components. The model calls for *assumptions* regarding the base salary range, number of compensation levels, length of work year, minimum employment requirements, base salary addends, incentives, and benefits.

One final point should be made concerning the model illustrated in Table 11.7, that is, the *assumptions* are for illustrative purposes. As illustrated in Table 11.5, a school system has a variety of options for designing compensation components and the assumptions for making them operational. The choice of components and assumptions will depend on external and internal conditions that influence the choice of those elements deemed to elicit specified behaviors (individual and group) to enhance system effectiveness.[11]

COMPENSATION ADMINISTRATION

As every administrator knows, the best ideas and plans can be of little practical value to the system until they are put into action. However well designed a compensation plan is, it must be adopted formally by the board of education and incorporated into the annual or preferably the long-term budget. Even when these steps are completed, the plan is by no means self-administering.

Changes occur daily in every organization. People enter and leave the system. Positions are added and eliminated. Salary expenditures become excessive unless controlled. Promotions and dismissals are not uncommon. Entire compensation structures or parts thereof become outmoded. As indicated in Step 5 of Figure 11.7 administration of the compensation plan is a cyclic operation, to be dealt with anew with the preparation of each budget.

TABLE 11.7
Summary computations of individual teacher compensation requirements.

Part I.   Assumptions Underlying Compensation Computations

A. Base salary range = ($22,000–$28,119). Based on prevailing market conditions.
Base salary (BS) + Across-the-board (ATB) if any + Preparation addend (P) remain part of the salary. Extended service addends (ESA) and monetary and nonsalary addends are rearmed each year. If performance does not justify addends, salary is frozen at (BS + ATB + P) during the next budget year. Model precludes reduction of (BS + ATB + P). When base salaries at responsibility levels are increased across the board (ATB) they should be multiplied by the responsibility index. If not, the ratios used will be diminished.

B. Number of compensation levels = 3. (For rationale, see Figure 11.11 and column 2, Part III, Table 11.7).

C. Work year = ten months (union-system contract).

D. Minimum employment requirement = Bachelor's degree + State certification.

E. Monetary addends (required):

    1. Preparation addend = 40 percent of base salary (MS = 20 percent; Doctorate = 40 percent).
Academic course work, formally approved for instructional purposes, represents incentive addend for teacher improvement (see Figure 11.12).

    2. Extended service addend (ESA) = 0–80 percent (4 percent per annum).

F. Monetary incentives (optional) 0–40 percent (not to exceed 50 percent of base salary).

G. Nonsalary incentives = 0–20 percent (see Figure 11.12 for list of incentives).

H. Collateral benefits = flexible benefit plan. Each teacher selects desired benefits from approved list (not to exceed $6,010) (based on 25 percent of base salary average. See Part III for computation).

Part II.   Formula: Base salary + Required monetary addends + Monetary incentives + Nonsalary incentives + Collateral benefits = Budgetary support required for each teaching position.

- The dollar values shown in columns 7 and 8 (Part III) represent indirect payments. For example, collateral benefits and nonsalary incentives (research account, tuition, replacement cost for released time, and funds for reading project) are teacher costs, but are not included in the paycheck.

- The flexibility of this model provides for adjustment of all compensable components to accommodate changing internal and external organizational circumstances.

Part III. Computation of Individual Budgetary Compensation Requirement

1	2	3	4	5	6	7	8	9
Position Holder	Compensation Level	Base Salary	Preparation Addend (required)	Extended Service (ESA) (required)	Performance Incentives Monetary (optional)	Performance Incentives Nonsalary (optional)	Collateral Benefits (required)	Individual Dollar Value Total
Teacher grade 5	1	$22,000	—	3(.04) = $2,640	—	—	$6,010	$30,650
Teacher—math middle school	1	22,000	MS = $4,400	4(.04) = 3,520	(.08) = $1,760	(.05 × BS) = $1,100	6,010	38,790
Teacher—kindergarten	1	22,000	MS = 4,400	5(.04) = 4,400	(.05) = 1,100	(.08 × BS) = 1,760	6,010	39,670
Teacher—computer technology	2	24,039	MS = 4,808	2(.04) = 1,923	—	(.05 × BS) = 1,202	6,010	37,982
Teacher—chemistry senior high school chairperson, team leader	3	28,119	MS = 5,624	2(.04) = 2,250	(.10) = 2,812	(.05 × BS) = 1,406	6,010	46,221
Teacher—physics senior high school	3	28,119	Ph.D. = 11,248	—	(.05) = 1,406	—	6,010	46,783
Teacher—middle school sociology	1	22,000	—	8(.04) = 7,040	(.16) = 3,520	—	6,010	38,570

Note: Column derivation:
Column 2: See Figure 11.11 for rationale of compensation levels.
Column 3: See Part I-A for base salary range.
Column 4: Column 3 × .20 = MS; Column 3 × .40 = Doctorate (see I-E).
Column 5: Column 3 × years of experience × .04 (see Part I-E 2).
Column 6: Optional percentage × Column 3 (See Part I-F).
Column 7: Optional percentage × Column 3 (See Part I-G).
Column 8: (See Part I-H).
Column 9: Total (Columns 3 + 4 + 5 + 6 + 7 + 8).

Testing the Compensation Plan. The discussion up to this point contains certain propositions for developing a total compensation structure, all or part of which may or may not be useful in establishing a pay plan in a given school system. One way to test the advisability of implementing a new plan is to forecast, to the extent possible, the results it will produce. Will it be superior to the existing plan? What will be the cost of implementing the plan over a period of years? Will it remove or minimize existing inequities? Will it appeal to the personnel for whom it is intended? These and other questions need to be posed to elicit information that will be presented to governing officials for their consideration.

Each school organization must decide what kind of compensation structure it is able to implement and maintain. Working through various structural designs illustrated in this chapter and using the same or a different set of assumptions will help planners to decide whether the consequences produced by the plans are preferable to those yielded by the one in operation. The core of the approach discussed throughout this chapter is about ways to establish a systematic and rational method for determining the relative value of positions in the system, for establishing position guides to facilitate securing competent personnel to occupy the positions, and for arranging salaries and wages so that they are equitable within and between structural levels as well as externally competitive with those of other systems. These are among the tests that any salary plan proposed to the governing body should meet.

Adoption of the Plan. Earlier in the discussion it was noted that a compensation policy should be formally adopted by the board to guide organization thinking and action with respect to compensation problems. In addition, it is suggested that the board formally approve a salary plan prepared by the chief executive and staff to implement the policy statement. This amounts to extensive preparation and submission of details of the plan, including items previously discussed, such as:

- Explanation of the total compensation structure proposed for the school system, an outline of which is shown in Figure 11.10.
- Preparation of an organizational manual that includes an organizational chart showing the hierarchy of positions and levels of responsibility; and preparation of position guides listing principal duties and relationships as well as preparation, experience, skills, and length of work year required.
- Definition of elements to be included in determining placement on the compensation scale and salary progression within position levels.

Reasons for formal adoption of the plan are numerous. Acceptance by the board not only gives it official status but also makes it an important document in developing annual and long-term budgets. Moreover, it furnishes evidence of good faith on the part of the board and a sense of security to the personnel to whom it applies.

Explaining the Compensation Plan to Personnel.   It has been said that every compensation plan should aim for both *excellence of design* and *excellence of execution*. The execution phase of the compensation process should include systematic communication of information to personnel about the compensation structure as well as the way in which it is administered. Personnel need to know, for example, how the economic worth of various positions is determined, what the nature of the pay differentials is and how they operate, intent of compensation policies, when an individual is paid, the structure of a paycheck, how errors in pay are adjusted, how objectivity is maintained, and what collateral benefits are included in the compensation plan. It is not uncommon for personnel information about the compensation structure to be at considerable variance from system information. Without an effective system of communicating compensation information to personnel, rumors, suspicion, and mistrust are inevitable. Data on pay-system preferences and their correlates support previous findings on different types of data: open systems have greater motivational qualities than secret systems. The success of financial incentives depends on communication of purpose and linking of the incentive system to this purpose. Much of the research on communication and compensation systems indicates that open systems minimize personnel misunderstanding and mistrust commonly associated with closed information practices.

Open salary information is one of the areas of pay administration in which significant improvements have been made. Research indicates that secrecy tends to cause people to overestimate the pay of individuals at the same organizational level and that the greater their overestimation, the greater their dissatisfaction. Thus, pay secrecy may do more to cause pay dissatisfaction than to reduce it.[12]

Administering Individual Pay Problems.   Certain technical aspects of compensation administration relating to individual pay actions should also be noted. These include establishing and maintaining procedures governing:

- Placement of new personnel in appropriate salary or wage range.
- Promotional increases (person moved to higher-level position).
- Demotion (person moved to lower-level position).
- Downgrading (changing value of position within its cluster).
- Upgrading (person placed in higher level).
- Reevaluation increases (compensation adjustment because of changes in position or position holder).

- Inequity increases (compensation adjustment for purpose of achieving equity).
- Pay increases (bases, frequency).
- Promotion between grades.
- Equity of pay plans among personnel group.
- Special conditions—individual receives more than maximum of pay range in which position is classified; individual remuneration is below minimum of position level; remuneration exceeds maximum of pay level; and pay increases are not justified on the basis of established procedures.

Updating the Compensation Plan.   Another important aspect of compensation administration is keeping the plan abreast of changes in (a) the position, (b) relative worth of the position, and (c) value of the individual in the position. In effect, the compensation information system should be designed to yield information about changes in the status or the occupant of the position (promotion, demotion, and so on), in external competitiveness, and in its equitable or inequitable characteristics.

Union and Government Controls.   Compensation administration implies proper implementation of any collective bargaining agreement or adherence to any government control relating to payment of personnel. Whatever items of agreement have been reached as they affect money and conditions of work, they must be adhered to scrupulously. In fact, the system must anticipate that every facet of the collective bargaining agreement will be closely monitored by union stewards. Thus, it is apparent that there is need for machinery to implement collective bargaining agreements, to assess their impact on the system, and to plan for translating agreements into tools for improving personnel effectiveness.

In general, the foregoing problems indicate the necessity for a well-conceived plan of administration for resolving individual pay problems relating to contractual agreements, legislation, overpayment, underpayment, inequities, overtime, extra pay for extra work, and promotions and demotions from one pay grade or one pay plan to another, all of which cannot be resolved by establishment of an overall structure. *Excellence of execution,* then, is a phase of the compensation process aimed at utilizing the financial factor in achieving organizational objectives and in satisfying personnel needs.

Figure 11.13 contains an incomplete but illustrative list of compensation matters to which consistent attention must be devoted. The compensation problems shown in Figure 11.13, and their complexity, should be considered in terms of bringing the system into acceptable equilibrium with environmental elements such as government, position holders, differentiated system pay groups, unions, and the total organization. From this perspective, it

- *Goals.* Attracting, retaining, and motivating school personnel. Linking compensation goals with human resources strategy and system mission.
- *Fairness.* Providing fair remuneration for services rendered, fair pay relative to higher and lower jobs, pay competitive with regional school systems, equal pay for comparable worth, and reasonable and consistent pay decisions.
- *Management tools.* Using policies, plans, programs, strategies, practices, budget audits, reviews, forecasts, standards, performance reviews, and short- and long-term plans to administer compensation system.
- *Paychecks.* Reducing administrative compensation costs per paycheck through direct deposits.
- *Regulatory compliance.* Ensuring compensation decisions and actions are in conformity with applicable laws and regulations.
- *Grievances.* Complaints, conflicts, and questions. Developing resolutions to questions, grievances, complaints, and concerns in a prompt, even, fair, and consistent manner.
- *Information.* Applying computer-based technology to facilitate management of the compensation system.
- *Information.* Employing a variety of communication strategies to explain, inform, and provide explanations to personnel about the compensation system, which they need to know.
- *Benefits.* Bringing burgeoning benefit costs to balance with other components of compensation system. Stretching health dollars without sacrificing program quality. Controlling mental health and substance abuse costs. Evaluating the manner in which amounts are allocated to base salary, base salary addends, benefits, and special forms of remuneration so that there is no imbalance among the various forms of compensation.
- *Projection.* Comparing the compensation system's present position with a desired position. Translating needs into compensation objectives. Envisioning compensation requirements needed to meet future human resource objectives such as attracting personnel needed to staff projected types of positions, to retain those who meet performance standards, and to provide motivational mechanisms to enhance their self and career development.
- *Integration.* Integrating the compensation process with other personnel processes such as recruiting, orientation, and staff maintenance.

FIGURE 11.13
Illustration of types of activities involved in compensation administration.

becomes clear that the serious art of solving substantive problems through pay administration requires managerial competence with practical knowledge of affairs entailed in exchanging remuneration for services rendered.

COMPENSATION CONTROL AND ADJUSTMENT

With the organization structure drawn up, people assigned to positions, and the compensation plan in operation, there will be the inevitable questions, How is the plan working? Is it producing the results anticipated? The facet of the compensation process by which the organization assesses the extent to which performance conforms to plan is referred to as *control* (Figure 11.7). Control, as noted previously, is one of the major activities of administration, consisting of three steps: (a) setting standards, (b) checking on deviations between standards and performance, and (c) taking corrective action.

In assessing the extent to which the actual operation of the compensation plan conforms to standards, goals suggested earlier may well be used as standards. Briefly stated, the success of the plan can be judged by the extent to which it attracts competent personnel, the extent to which it motivates individuals to cooperate voluntarily in achieving goals of the system, the effectiveness with which external and internal equity are achieved under existing legal constraints and collective bargaining agreements, and whether economic investment results in improved conditions for teaching and learning. Figure 11.14 contains a list of questions that can be employed in reviewing compensation outcomes.

Control Points.   Because ramifications of any compensation system are so extensive, checks are required to determine how well compensation plans are reinforcing other plans in contributing to organizational purposes. For example, compensation practices play a key role in determining long-range and operating plans for (a) recruitment and selection of personnel, (b) appraisal and improvement of performance, (c) design of the organizational structure, and (d) budgeting of expenditures. The following discussion is devoted to consideration of these strategic points.

The first strategic point considered here is the selection of personnel prior to assignment to positions. Every organization, regardless of the nature of its compensation system, should design a selection plan to carefully screen all applicants for system positions. With the help of position guides, qualifications of applicants can be checked against position requirements to determine how well they are fitted to perform the function and to estimate the potential they have for advancement. It is at this point that determination should be made as to whether base salaries at each level of the compensation structure are adequate to attract qualified personnel. One

In reviewing the compensation program, what impressions are gathered about:

- *Design*—Are all compensation components intertwined and focused on program objectives?

- *Structure*—Are these components (base pay, benefits, and incentives) imbalanced? Does existing core support enhance teaching excellence? Are there particular kinds of existing or needed incentives that enhance faculty improvement (research or project accounts, sabbaticals, or flexible teaching loads)?

- *Board of education*—Does the system have ambitions to recruit outstanding faculty over the next five years? How well does the system currently support its faculty?

- *Administration*—Is the organization structure arranged so that a central body exercises strong leadership to carry out compensation policies? Does the administration seek to create, maintain, and improve performance culture?

- *Appraisal process*—Does it rid the system of incompetence and reward competence?

- *Development*—Do current personnel policies and programs foster faculty improvement?

- *Organizational avoidance*—Are there indicators of low base pay, absence of or tendencies to underfund incentives, rigid benefit provisions, high rates of absenteeism, inability to recognize or to dismiss incompetents, rewarding fellow incompetents, absence of timetables or priorities for accomplishing compensation objectives, or lack of personnel accountability?

- *Organizational readiness*—Is the condition of the union-system relationship such that changes in both the compensation structure and the attendant appraisal process would not be conducive to desired results?

FIGURE 11.14
A compensation looking glass.

Source: William B. Castetter, "Designing and Administering Teacher Compensation," National Forum of Educational Administration and Supervision Journal 6, 3 (1989–90), 40.

test of adequacy is how closely compensation at each level conforms to regional norms. The question to be asked is, How much would it cost to replace a position incumbent with a person with the desired qualifications?

The second strategic control point considered here is the performance appraisal of each individual after assignment to the position. Results of the performance appraisal, aside from yielding information necessary to making judgments about salary increases, should contribute to plans for individual development of staff members and to determining whether each should be retained in the position, transferred to another position, promoted, or dismissed. Here the test of effectiveness of the compensation plan is whether it provides for systematic appraisal of personnel performance.

The third strategic point for consideration is the organizational structure. This area is constantly in need of review and, occasionally, revision. As positions are added, eliminated, or modified, these changes should be reflected in the organizational structure and ultimately in the compensation index and the incumbent's salary. The criterion for this test of the compensation structure is its congruency with the organizational structure. It should be self-evident that a sound organizational structure is indispensable both to the integrity of the compensation plan and the workability of the appraisal process.

The final point for consideration, control of expenditures for the compensation plan, is an essential requirement. One check on the compensation plan is information relating to its impact on the annual and long-term budgets, such as anticipated salary changes by adoption of the compensation plan, annual cost, and impact of the plan on the tax structure.

In a very real sense, then, controlling the compensation plan is as vital to its success as the design of the structure on which it rests. Information yielded by checking the foregoing points as well as others not mentioned can be collected, analyzed, and presented to the board periodically so that the final step in the control processes—corrective action—can be taken to make certain that the goals of the plan are constantly being realized.

REVIEW AND PREVIEW

In this chapter, we have been examining the compensation process and its relationship to the human resources function. Although satisfying monetary needs of members of the school system is not the whole substance of administration, absence of a sound compensation plan creates human problems that defy easy resolution. Because the size of the paycheck is related to satisfaction of both economic and noneconomic needs, the process by which remuneration in a school system is determined is of crucial significance to its ability to implement an effective human resources plan.

The compensation process conceptualized in this chapter consists of various subprocesses, including developing compensation policies, negotiating with unions, establishing the position structure, determining economic value of positions and economic worth of position holders, making provisions in the compensation structure for administrative and support personnel, formalizing the compensation plan, and keeping the plan current.

There are a number of interrelated factors that affect the amount of an individual's paycheck. These factors include compensation legislation, prevailing salaries, collective bargaining, supply and demand, ability to pay, standard and cost of living, and collateral considerations. Although all these factors enter into compensation levels established in an organization, one factor or combination of factors may be more important at a given time than others, depending on circumstances.

Employment may be viewed as an exchange transaction between the individual and the organization in which each gets something in return for giving something. The employment exchanges between the individual and the system are perceived differently by both parties.

One of the major problems in compensation planning is to reach agreements between parties by reconciling the nature of the input-output relationship.

Having now introduced a compensation model depicting major designs elements, concepts, and a point of view, we turn in Chapter 12 to the question of how organizations can make use of that model to improve compensation planning for administrative personnel.

REVIEW AND DISCUSSION QUESTIONS

1. Explain why the following aspects of pay structures have not been widely introduced in school systems: incentive rewards, flexible benefit plans, performance-dependent remuneration, and market-sensitive salaries.

2. Two criticisms directed at many salary programs are that they are inequitable and that the income does not compare favorably with other school systems or other professions. Do these criticisms have any basis in fact?

3. Develop the elements of a pay structure that would provide the kinds of rewards that are important to you.

4. Is there any truth to the assertion that pay based on merit rating is but one of many kinds of incentive options? Do incentives have to be based on a *performance appraisal rating*?

5. How do unions influence pay practices directly? Indirectly? How do boards of education influence compensation practices?

6. In what ways are the compensation practices of public school systems influenced by state governments? The federal government?

7. Many states have passed comparable worth legislation for the public sector (ensuring that women and minorities receive payment commensurate with the value of their jobs). Does compensation discrimination exist in female-dominated occupations (clerical, teaching, nursing)? Have teacher unions pursued the comparable worth issue in negotiations? To what extent?

8. Compare and contrast three different types of incentive plans.

9. Why is the cost of contemporary benefit plans being subjected to stricter controls?

10. Develop a set of guidelines for improving incentive plans.

11. Examine the hypothetical salary schedule (Table 11.8) for teachers in a suburban school district. Respond to each of these questions:
    - What are the strengths and weaknesses of the salary schedule?
    - Do you agree with the experience factor as a measure of performance effectiveness?
    - Does the schedule provide an achievement opportunity structure (incentives)?

TABLE 11.8

Experience[a]	1996–97	1999–2000
0	$30,056	$44,700
1	30,709	45,700
2	31,361	46,700
3	32,363	47,700
4	33,363	48,700
5	34,363	49,700
6	34,363	50,600
7	35,364	51,600
8	35,364	52,700
9,10	36,364	53,700
11	37,364	54,700
12	38,364	54,700
13	38,364	55,700
14	39,364	55,700
15	40,364	56,700
16	40,364	60,700
17	42,056	60,700
18	46,056	64,700
19+	50,056	64,700

Note: [a] Years of teaching experience.

- Does the schedule address criticisms of the single-salary schedule generated by the education reform movement?
- Does the pay scale in the pact violate the federal Age Discrimination Employment Act of 1967? (94 percent of the teaching staff are 45 years of age or older.)
- Will the average pay raise over five years benefit more-experienced or less-experienced teachers?

- If collateral benefits in this school system amount to 35 percent of total salaries for teachers, what would be the compensation costs for a teacher in 1999 with 16 years of experience? (Assume all benefits are uniform for all teachers.)

CHAPTER EXERCISE 11.1

Directions: This exercise is designed to be an extra-class activity in which each class member works through sections A, B, C, and D.[13] The instructor will then (a) review each section and (b) entertain comments from class members. The objective of the exercise is to increase member understanding of the importance and relationship of benefits to total compensation, as well as to create an awareness of the problems involved in benefit administration.

A. Examine the structure and value of collateral benefits of a representative Goodville school system teacher (Table 11.9) and answer the following questions:

  • Are the benefits of the Goodville teacher representative of those generally provided by competing systems?

  • Is the *range* of benefits adequate, inadequate, or generally satisfactory?

  • Should the benefits structure permit employee choices to meet personal situations (e.g., life stages or both family parents employed)?

  • Should the rank order of benefits as shown in Table 11.9 be altered? In what form?

  • How do you interpret the number 126.75 (total compensation)?

  • If you were the Goodville teacher in Table 11.9, would you prefer increasing benefits costs and decreasing salary costs, decreasing benefit costs and increasing salary costs, or maintaining the ratio indicated.

B. Examine the budgeted expenditures for salaries and collateral benefits of the Goodville school district (Table 11.10) and answer the following questions:

  • The highest expenditure costs for benefits in the Goodville school system are for administrative personnel, and the lowest for other programs and student activities. What explanation(s) can you offer for the differentials?

  • How high should the total benefit percentage for all budgeted functions be permitted to rise before an imbalance is created among other budget functions?

  • The spread among benefit budgeted functions ranges from 28.1 to 30.4 percent. Should some budgeted categories be sharply

TABLE 11.9
Structure and value of collateral benefits of a representative Goodville school system teacher.

Compensation Component	Dollar Value	Benefit as % of Base Salary	Rank Order
Base salary	$44,888.00	100.00	—
Benefits			
Medical insurance	4,565.64	10.17	1
Dental insurance	729.36	1.62	5
Workers' compensation	329.60	0.73	6
Group life insurance	14.13	0.03	7
Retirement	3,344.15	7.45	2
FICA	1,716.96	3.83	3
Employee assistance program	9.00	0.02	8
Tuition, leaves, awards, grants	1,300.00	2.90	4
Total Benefits	12,008.84	26.75	—
Total Compensation	56,896.84	126.75	—

TABLE 11.10
Budgeted expenditures for salaries and collateral benefits, Goodville school district, 19XX–19XX.

Budgeted Function	Salaries	Benefits	Benefits as % of Salaries	Positions Included
Instruction				
Regular Programs	$11,997,534	$3,517,324	29.3	Classroom teachers, Asst. for Curriculum and Instruction, Supervisors, Instructional Support Staff.
Special Education	988,167	282,015	28.5	Classroom teachers, prorated portion of Director, Support Staff.
Other Programs	181,601	51,120	28.1	Summer School, Homebound Instruction, Reimbursed Programs.
Support Services				
Pupil Personnel	936,730	278,885	29.8	Director Educational Support Programs, Guidance, Psychological Services, Social Work Services, Student Accounting/Census Sec.
Instructional Staff	481,866	137,843	28.6	Audio-Visual, Library, Staff Development.
Administration	1,405,238	426,555	30.4	Superintendent, Principals, Personnel Office, Legal, Tax Collection, Board Functions.
Pupil Health	275,851	79,152	28.7	Health Services Professionals, Assistants, Clerk.
Business	357,952	106,423	29.7	Business Manager, Director of Accounting, Clerks.
Operation/Maintenance	1,468,349	418,036	28.5	Director, Supervisor, Skilled Service Employees, Custodians.
Student Transportation	1,280,445	364,890	28.5	Director, Dispatcher, Mechanics, Drivers, Trainer, Clerk.
Student Activities	431,550	121,481	28.1	Staff for Associated Programs.
Community Services	34,315	9,660	28.2	Staff for Associated Programs.
Total, All Functions	19,839,598	5,793,384	29.2	

increased? Sharply decreased? Remain the same?

C. Examine the Goodville school system annual employee compensation-benefit-cost statement (Figure 11.15) and answer the following questions:

• What assumptions can be made about the intentions of the Goodville school system Board

---

Name of Employee _____ Hired _____ 09.1.19XX

Preparation: M.A. + 15 semester credits   Assignment _____

Work Unit _____

	Cost to System	Cost to State	Cost to You	Total Cost
Base Salary	$ ___	$ ___	$ ___	$ ___
Benefits Provided				
• Dental Insurance	___	___	___	___
• Workers' Compensation	___	___	___	___
• Group Life Insurance	___	___	___	___
• Retirement	___	___	___	___
• FICA	___	___	___	___
• Employee Assistance Prog.	___	___	___	___
• Tuition, Leave, Awards, Grants	___	___	___	___
• Total Benefits	___	___	___	___
• Total Compensation	___	___	___	___

Notes:
• State contribution rates: Social Security (FICA) @ .03575; Employee Retirement @ .0995.
• System contribution rates: Social Security (FICA) @ .0375; Employee Retirement @ .0995; Workers' Compensation @ .0052; Negotiated premium payments; Hospitalization (contract); Dental (contract); Life Insurance (contract).
• In addition to the benefit provisions listed above:
   All personnel have benefit provision for sick leave, extended sick leave, leave for bereavement, personal, and special needs; tuition reimbursement; unemployment compensation.
   Twelve-month personnel qualify for vacation and holiday pay.
   Hospitalization definitions include: H-W = Husband-Wife; IND = Individual; FAM = Family; INC-C = Individual-Child; IND-CN = Individual Children.

FIGURE 11.15
Goodville school system annual employee compensation-benefit-cost statement, 19XX–19XX.

of Education to issue annual employee total compensation statements?

- What purposes do the data serve regarding (a) the school system, (b) the recipient, and (c) the computer analyst?
- To what extent can the information be computerized?
- What do you consider to be the ideal future state of any school system benefit program?
- Do you agree with current thinking that benefits do not contribute measurably toward improving employee satisfaction, motivation, or performance improvement?

D. For a school system or other organization for which you work or have worked, develop information indicating whether computerization is employed in processing the following aspects of compensation administration (rate the degree of computerization for each item on a scale from 1 to 4):

- Changes in cash flow account
- Check writing
- Compensation data organizing and retrieving
- Data manipulation
- Financial record keeping
- Individual salary history
- Known and projected human resources
- Payroll preparation
- Position documentation
- Position evaluation
- Salary and system budgeting
- Salary budgeting and planning
- Spread sheet analysis
- Union-system negotiations data
- Word processing

NOTES

1. David W. Belcher and Thomas J. Atchison, Compensation Administration (Englewood Cliffs, NJ: Prentice-Hall Inc., 1974), 2e, © 1987, pp. 3–8. Adapted by permission of Prentice-Hall Inc.

2. Section 13(a) of the Fair Labor Standards Act of 1938, as amended by Public Law 92-318, the Education Amendments of 1972, 82 Stat. 235, 86 Stat. 375, approved June 23, 1972 and effective July 1, 1972.

3. David L. Clark and Terry A. Astuto, "Redirecting Reform: A Challenge to Popular Assumptions About Teachers and Students," Phi Delta Kappan 75, 7 (March 1994), 512–521.

4. U.S. Department of Commerce, Statistical Abstract of the United States, 114th Edition (Washington, DC, 1994), 295.

5. John I. Goodlad, A Place Called School: Prospects for the Future (New York: McGraw Hill, 1984).

6. See Allan N. Nash and Stephen J. Carroll, Jr., The Management of Compensation (Monterey, CA: Brooks/Cole Publishing Co., 1975) 61.

7. An alternative to the position-cluster idea is the single-salary schedule, which includes all personnel in the system from custodian to superintendent of schools. Under this plan, all positions on the payroll are ranked in order of importance or responsibility.

8. In pay structures for support personnel, rate width and overlap are elements usually given consideration in designing pay intervals.

9. For a detailed analysis of incentive compensation, see National School Boards Association, Rewarding Excellence: Teacher Compensation and Incentive Plans (Alexandria, VA: National School Boards Association, 1987).

10. Benefits are treated extensively in Jerry Rosenbloom, The Handbook of Employee Benefits (Homewood, IL: Dow-Jones/Irwin, 1988).

11. The model illustrated in Table 11.7 is developed on the basis of assumptions identified in Part I of Table 11.7.

12. Edward E. Lawler III, "New Approaches to Pay: Innovations That Work," Personnel 53, 5 (September-October, 1976), 12–13.

13. The data in Table 11.9, Table 11.10, and Figure 11.15 were derived from William B. Castetter, Richard S. Heisler, and Bruce W. Kowalski, "Personnel Benefits: Changes in the Wind," National Forum of Educational Administration and Supervision Journal 9, 33 (1992–93), 4–28.

SUPPLEMENTARY READING

Association for Supervision and Curriculum Development. Developing Teacher Incentive Programs. Alexandria, VA: Association for Supervision and Curriculum Development, 1987.

Berry, Barnett; and Rick Ginsberg. "Creating Lead Teaches: From Policy to Implementation." Phi Delta Kappa 71, 8 (April 1990), 616–22.

Bruno, J. E. "An Alternative to the Fixed Step Salary Schedule." Educational Administration Quarterly 6, 1 (1970).

Cook, Mary F., Editor. The Human Resources Yearbook: 1993/1994 Edition. Englewood Cliffs, NJ: Prentice-Hall Inc., 1993, Chapters 5, 6.

Cresap, McCormick, and Paget. Teacher Incentives: A Tool for Effective Management. Washington, DC: Authors.

Giblin, Edward J.; Geoffrey A. Wiegman; and Frank Sanfillippo. "Bringing Pay Up to Date." Personnel 67, 11 (November 1990), 17–18.

Haddad, Samir A. "Compensation Benefits." In William R. Tracey, Editor, Human Resources Management and Development Handbook. New York: American Management Associations, 1985, 638–660.

Henderson, Richard A. Compensation Management. Reston, VA: Reston, 1986.

Iseri, Billy A.; and Robert Cangemi. "Flexible Benefits: A Growing Option." Personnel 67, 3 (March 1990), 30–34.

Lawler, Edward A. III. Strategic Pay. San Francisco, Jossey-Bass, 1990.

Masterson, Joe. "Benefit Plans That Cut Costs and Increase Satisfaction." Management Review 79, 4 (April 1990), 22–34.

Plachy, Roger J. Building a Fair Pay Program: A Step-by-Step Guide. American Management Association, 1986.

Rock, Milton L.; and Lance A. Berger, Editors. The Compensation Handbook: A State-of-the-Art Guide to Compensation Strategy and Design, Third Edition. New York: McGraw Hill Inc., 1991.

Shanker, Albert. "The End of the Traditional Model of Schooling and a Proposal for Using Incentives to Restructure Our Public Schools." Phi Delta Kappan 71, 5 (January 1990).

Taylor, Raymond G. "Linear Programming and Alternative Models for Merit Pay Distribution." National Forum of Applied Educational Research Journal 2, 1 (1988), 18–24.

Taylor, Raymond G.; and William Reid. "Forecasting the Salaries of Professional Personnel: An Application of Markov Analysis to School Finance." Journal of Educational Finance 12, 3 (1987).

Wallace, Marc; and Charles Fay. Compensation: Theory and Practice. Boston: Kent Publishing, 1983.

Chapter 12

Compensation of Administrative Personnel

CHAPTER OVERVIEW

CHAPTER OBJECTIVES

- Present models for designing pay plans for administrative personnel.
- Illustrate the use of three components (base pay, incentives, and supplementary remuneration) in compensation planning.
- Stress the use of four planning tools (position guide, organization chart, structural analysis diagram, and compensation scattergram) in designing pay plans for administrative personnel.
- Examine the importance of pay equity and its relationship to the relative worth issue.

CHAPTER TERMS

Compensation data bank

Compensation index

Compensation planning tools

Incumbent value

Position value

Relative worth

Chapter 11 focused attention on factors related to the compensation of professional instructional personnel. Now we shift our attention to problems connected with salaries and benefits for administrative personnel.

It is generally recognized that to a certain extent problems involved in compensating administrative and support personnel are similar to those relating to the instructional staff. Regardless of the three major personnel groups in a school system for whom separate pay structures are typically established, consideration should be given to the following criteria: (a) that salaries and wages paid to individuals are commensurate with their contributions to the system, (b) that compensation is internally consistent and externally competitive, and (c) that the compensation plan (and the decisions based on it) affecting individual pay are administered and communicated in such a way that personnel perceive the system to be rational and fair.

Beyond these basic concerns for any compensation plan, pay structures for instructional, support, and administrative personnel differ in several ways. The conceptual, technical, and interpersonal skills needed in an executive position are different from those required for instructional or for support assignments. Instructional personnel, for example, focus their behaviors on diagnosis, prescription, presentation, monitoring, and feedback. Support personnel to a considerable extent are assigned repetitive and routine duties that follow established rules and procedures. Administrative personnel, on the other hand, perform work demanding decisions that require specialized conceptual, human, and technical skills. At issue in compensation planning for all three groups are the age-old fundamental relationships of personnel outputs in exchange for organizational inputs. The following text examines organizational approaches to the compensation of administrative personnel, with emphasis on the basic compensation process for all personnel (as outlined in Figure 11.9).

ADMINISTRATIVE COMPENSATION

Executive compensation, regardless of the organization, is a coveted prize not only because it is a source of internal power and represents the apex of the system's reward structure but also because it enables an individual to satisfy a basic extraorganizational need. Men and women vie for executive compensation not only because of the desire to make more money but also because of the leverage it gives them in life's daily struggle. Wiseman notes, for example, that it is a goal to some, a game to others:

> There is blood money and bribe money, conscience money and stolen money, easy money and money that has been earned by the sweat of the brow, money to burn and money as the prize of merit; there is money that is a king's ransom and money that is a whore's pay; there is money to squander and so much money as will make it difficult for its possessor to get into Heaven; there is a mistress' allowance and the wife's due; pocket money, spending money, hush money and money in the bank; there are the wages of sin and the bequests of rich uncles; there is the price that every man has and the pricelessness of objects, and the price on the outlaw's head; there are the thirty pieces of silver and also the double indemnity on one's own life.[1]

In establishing the executive compensation structure, the school system has certain expectations and conditions for individuals so designated. These include developing plans for organizational viability, deciding how to achieve the short- and long-term objectives involved in position responsibility, securing voluntary cooperation to achieve system goals, providing leadership, reconciling claimant interests, introducing innovations, advocating courses of action, and taking risks that may result in personal and organizational criticism from both internal and external sources. In essence, compensation of executive positions is significant because results the organization achieves are more likely to reflect the contributions of these individuals than those in lower level positions. Executive compensation also deserves careful consideration because pay practices at higher levels are precursors of those at lower levels. With these considerations in mind, let us turn to one of the fundamental steps in planning compensation—review of the current compensation structure.

Review of Current Compensation Structure

The existing compensation structure of any institution is an amalgam of numerous and diverse decisions, some of which were made in previous generations, some by individuals no longer associated with the organization. Some administrative pay structures have been formally adopted by governing authorities, others are administered informally. Some are systematically planned and operated, others have evolved and are adjusted in the wake of pressures or crises.

Ailing pay structures do not cure themselves, nor do healthy ones stay that way without continuing examination and proper treatment. One of the first steps, then, in improving a compensation structure is to diagnose its present status.

School systems, like most modern organizations, have long resisted efforts of theoreticians, essayists, and analysts to standardize organizational terminology. An examination of organizational charts will reveal instances of:

- Absence of differentiation between *line* and *staff* personnel.
- Different titles being assigned to identical positions.
- Wide differences in compensation for positions with identical titles.
- Administrative titles being assigned to positions that are nonadministrative.
- Nonadministrative positions being included in the administrative compensation schedule.
- Titles assigned to administrative positions in one system and having an entirely different meaning in another system.
- Titles being assigned to justify salary increases.
- Personnel having titles not descriptive of the position function.

Causes for the profusion and confusion of administrative titles are not hard to come by: reorganization of school districts without a major reorganization of the total organizational structure, creation of new titles for misplaced personnel or for those approaching retirement whom the organization cannot fit into an appropriate niche, carelessness in title assignment, and adjustments to general modification of all or part of the compensation system. It is obvious that titles are important to both the organization and the position holder. The organization should be interested in standardizing titles that can help to clarify the administrative structure and that contribute to an understanding of position functions. The status and prestige of a title are also important to the individual. The manner in which the title describes position function often affects the esteem others hold for the incumbent and for the authority and responsibility attached to the position.

The relationship between systematic development of a compensation plan for administrative personnel and definition of administrative positions should be readily apparent. Inattention to a functional scheme for classifying administrative positions and to standardization of nomenclature that makes position titles meaningful is conducive to human problems that are both related and unrelated to compensation. As the following sections are intended to make clear, effective development and administration of pay plans require clarification of the relative importance and responsibility of administrative positions and the assignment of different economic values to different positions. The precision with which positions in the administrative hierarchy are described, titled, and related to each other will have a significant bearing on the acceptance, operation, and life span of the compensation plan.

Qualification for Administrative Compensation

A description of the term *administrator* is an indispensable ingredient for developing a compensation plan for administrative personnel. If the organization does not take steps to differentiate between administrative and nonadministrative personnel, it will be plagued by pleas from members who contend that the nature of their work justifies administrative compensation. In making the distinction between administrative and nonadministrative personnel, a statement by Gross on the authority of administrators may be helpful:

> The authority of administrators consists of the right to engage in certain actions needed for the guidance of organizations or units thereof. These rights may be subdivided in various ways—such as rights to: (a) receive, request, and transmit certain kinds of information; (b) make certain kinds of decisions; (c) initiate action through commands and other forms of activation; (d) allot certain types of rewards and punishments.
>
> Some of these may be exclusively held, some may be shared jointly with others. All of them may be tied together in one bundle labelled "the right to exercise power in certain situations for the achievement of certain purposes."[2]

Some additional specifications may be needed to clarify which individuals should be included in the compensation plan. An administrator may be defined as one who is certified as a professional either in the field of education or in a field of specialization other than education (law, auditing, accounting, engineering, or medicine) by the laws and regulations governing certification in the state, and:

- Who has been granted formal (written) authority to act in an administrative capacity.
- Whose work consists of a superior-subordinate relationship with adult staff members rather than pupil personnel.
- Who serves under the rules and regulations of the administrative unit.

- Whose work is under the direction and control of the administrative unit.
- Who is assigned primarily to work that provides a service for the administrative unit.
- Who is eligible for personnel benefits provided by the administrative unit.
- Whose salary is at least equal to the entrance salary for teachers in the system.
- Who customarily and regularly exercises discretionary powers.
- Who customarily and regularly directs the work of two or more employees.[3]

The length of this description may appear to be excessive. What must be said in its favor, however, is that when the compensation of administrators is based on the relative amount of responsibility they exercise, position delineation is indispensable.

Administrative Positions Comprising the Superintendency

Widespread adoption of collective bargaining by professional and support personnel groups in school systems has led to some confusion as to whether or not certain administrative positions should be included in bargaining units representing classroom teachers. This issue is one that should be resolved before the compensation plan for administrative personnel is fully developed. In brief, the issue can be stated as follows: Should lower-echelon positions in the administrative structure (principal, assistant principal, coordinator, department head, team chairperson, and administrative assistant) be included in bargaining units of their own or with those of classroom teachers? The position adhered to in this text regarding the issue is that:

- The *superintendency* and the *superintendent of schools* are two different things. The superintendency is composed of all administrative and supervisory positions in the administrative structure. This is to say that all positions created to carry out the work of the superintendency are extensions of this office. Consequently, they do not belong in any bargaining unit because they are a part of the administrative organization of the school system.
- One of the primary reasons for giving attention to the development of a sound compensation plan for administrators is the expectation that it will eliminate the need for administrators to form or join any bargaining unit to secure better provisions for their compensation.

It is apparent, then, that in the early stages of projecting a compensation plan for administrative personnel, the system should define carefully not only what an administrative position is, how many administrative positions there are in the system, and at what levels, but it must also make clear that all administrative and supervisory positions are extensions of the superintendency. The administrative compensation plan based on this concept should include all administrative and supervisory positions in order to minimize the necessity for their being considered a component of teachers' bargaining units.

RELATIVE IMPORTANCE AND COMPLEXITY OF ADMINISTRATIVE POSITIONS

It is becoming increasingly clear that exclusive reliance on national or regional salary data for judging administrative compensation is an approach considered by many to be less than satisfactory. Experience has shown that a soundly conceived organizational structure represents an appropriate basis for designing a compensation plan for administrative personnel. The objectives of a compensation plan, however well designed, will not be realized if the organization structure is faulty. Consequently, another of the key steps in developing a context for administrative compensation is an analysis of the existing organization structure. The purpose of this activity is to gather facts and observations about the structure that can be employed to (a) enhance its ability to meet organizational goals, (b) serve as a reference guide in establishment of a compensation plan for administrative personnel, and (c) facilitate appraisal of individual performance by clarifying reporting relationships among positions in the organizational structure.

Characteristics of an Organizational Structure

Every organization has a structure—a plan for linking positions and people to purposes. The structure may be one that has been formally adopted by the board of education and described by organizational charts, position guides, and organizational manuals. Or it may be an informal structure, without documentation or evidence of any kind to describe its characteristics. In any case, organizations are comprised of people who occupy positions, interact with each other, and are vitally concerned that they are compensated, in terms of both responsibilities inherent in the work they perform and in their individual contributions to organizational effectiveness.

As illustrated in Figure 1.6, elements of a structure include purposes, people, activities, and relationships. The primary reason for bringing the matter of organization structure into a discussion of compensation planning is that *equity in pay demands that all personnel should be rewarded for the level of work that they are employed to perform.* Just how the equity principle is related to the organizational structure can be understood by examination of Figure 1.7, which is an illustration of the characteristics of an organizational structure such as that outlined in Figure 1.6. The information contained in Figure 1.7 indicates that there are different levels of responsibility in the organization. The manner in which these structural levels are employed in developing a compensation plan for administrative personnel will be described in the following text.

Assuming that the number and types of positions to be included in the administrative structure have been settled, the next step involves provision of a method whereby (a) positions are grouped according to structural levels and (b) values are assigned to positions within and among levels. Position evaluation is one of several means through which the concept of equity or fair pay is applied to the compensation plan. Values are established on the assumption that some positions entail greater responsibility and are more difficult to perform than others; the more difficult and important the positions, the higher should be the compensation.

Placing relative values on administrative positions by logical means entails analysis of each position and its relationship to all other positions in the administrative hierarchy. Alignment of positions can be accomplished by various methods, none of which can be precise or infallible because of the variety of factors involved and because of the difficulties associated with pinning down the behavior expected of individuals assigned to positions. An elaborate plan of position evaluation in a small school system is probably unnecessary because the relative importance of the several positions can usually be determined by analysis of the position guides. It is essential, in any case, that all relationships among positions in the organizational structure be perceived clearly by incumbents and that any ambiguities be resolved. When administrative positions in an organization are extensive and varied and differences among them not easily discernible, a more systematic approach is in order. Regardless of the plan used to determine **position values,** the intent is not to relieve compensation planners of making judgments about position values. Before proceeding to the next section on grouping and aligning administrative positions, the reader should examine Figure 12.1, which represents a practical approach to the problem of evaluating the worth of administrative positions.

Grouping and Aligning Administrative Positions

Effective analysis of the organization structure and the **relative worth** of the positions[4] comprising it can be facilitated by the use of four structural planning tools, the *position guide, organizational chart, structural analysis diagram,* and *compensation scattergram,* each of which is discussed here in terms of the information that can be derived from its application in order to aid in making decisions about the relative importance and difficulty of administrative positions.

The Position Guide. The *position guide,* an illustration of which is given in Figure 4.8, is one of the four devices just mentioned employed to develop

Chart 1: Point Scale Used to Rate Supervisory Positions

Factors	Degrees									
	1	2	3	4	5	6	7	8	9	10
(1) Education and training	16	32	48	64	80	96	112	128	144	160
(2) Experience	14	28	42	56	70	84	98	112	126	140
(3) Scope and complexity of skills										
Conceptual	12	24	36	48	60	72	84	96	108	120
Human	10	20	30	40	50	60	70	80	90	100
Technical	8	16	24	32	40	48	56	64	72	80
(4) Responsibility										
Supervision	15	30	45	60	75	90	105	120	135	150
Funds, Equipment, and buildings	10	20	30	40	50	60	70	80	90	100
(5) Effort										
Mental	9	18	27	36	45	54	63	72	81	90
Physical	6	12	18	24	30	36	42	48	54	60
Total scores	100	200	300	400	500	600	700	800	900	1000

Notes: In this study, *supervisory* refers to such positions as principals, instruction coordinators, and such support personnel as supervisors of payroll, construction, transportation, and so on.

Chart 2: Definition of the Education and Training Factor (Expanded from Chart 1)[a]

Degree		Points
1	High school or equivalent. Vocational or commercial education. Specialized courses relevant to the job.	16
2	Postsecondary education: business or trade school. Training in a highly skilled trade, such as electrical work. Apprenticeship.	32
3	Training equivalent to two years of college. Specialized training.	48
4	Professional training requiring three to four years.	64
5	Minimum of bachelor's degree. Specialized training.	80

FIGURE 12.1
A plan for determining relative position values in an organization structure.

Source: Adapted from Kenneth W. Humphries, "This Evaluation Plan Lets You Know What Your Administrators' Jobs Are Worth," American School Board Journal 168, 5 (May 1981), 32–36. Reprinted, with permission, from The American School Board Journal (May). © 1981, the National School Boards Association. All rights reserved.

6	Advanced education and training beyond the bachelor's degree. Specialized training.	96
7	Minimum of master's degree. Specialized training.	112
8	Advanced education and training beyond master's degree (15 to 30 hours). Specialized training.	128
9	Advanced education and training beyond the master's degree (30 or more hours). Specialized training.	144
10	Earned doctor's degree. Highly specialized professional training.	160

[a] *Note:* The "education and training" factor refers to the formal education and training necessary to prepare an individual for a job.

Chart 3: Rating an Elementary School Principal

Factors	Degree	Points
(1) Education and training	7	112
(2) Experience	4	56
(3) Scope and complexity of skills		
Conceptual	7	84
Technical	8	64
Human	7	70
(4) Responsibility		
Supervision	5	75
Funds, equipment, and buildings	7	70
(5) Effort		
Mental	7	63
Physical	6	36
	Total score:	630

This Chart Rates a Specific Position

Using the point scale in Chart 1 to rate the position of an elementary school principal, the total points for that individual job might be computed as follows (Chart 3): In Factor 1 (education and training), the job requires a degree of 7, which, according to the scale, is weighted at 112 points; for Factor 2 (experience), the job requires a degree of 4, weighted at 56 points. Each subsequent factor also is assigned a degree, which carries with it a weight of a certain number of points; these points then are added up to determine the total point value for the position. In this example, an elementary school principalship, the point total came to 630 points. The final step is to assign a pay scale commensurate with the organizational value of jobs in that approximate point range.

FIGURE 12.1, *continued*

the compensation plan. Examination of Figure 4.8 indicates that the position guide is a useful tool for describing work expectations of each position, specifying requirements needed by the holder to perform the work, clarifying the authority and responsibility involved, establishing standards of performance, and explaining reporting relationships. It is also useful for determining the relative importance of each position in the administrative structure. The position guide not only commits the formal organization to a written record of the position function and status, it provides information useful in various aspects of personnel administration, such as recruitment, selection, placement, initial compensation, performance appraisal, staff development, and salary adjustments. Thus, the position guide complements the organizational chart; it can be used to examine work allocated to each position, qualifications needed to perform work assigned to the position, and position relationships. This information, along with that derived from analysis of the organizational chart, can be used to check the extent of agreement between position responsibilities and position alignment, and to provide insights concerning overevaluation and underevaluation of both position and compensation.

Position index numbers used to identify individual positions in the organizational structure are derived from the *position index system* shown in Figure 1.7. The system is designed to:

- Differentiate between line and staff positions.
- Develop a uniform system of titles.
- Simplify identification of the structural level of a position.
- Indicate reporting relationships of each position.
- Provide information for judging the relative importance of positions.

Throughout this discussion, a recurring theme has been that *organization planning is an important antecedent to compensation planning*. Establishing primary operating units, determining the work to be done in each position, specifying relationships among positions, and developing a position index system to clarify and interpret the organization structure are activities essential to getting work done effectively. These activities also provide information to be used at points of decision involved in establishing the economic value of the work performed by individuals assigned to positions in the organizational structure.

The Organizational Chart.   One way to initiate an evaluation of administrative positions for the purpose of grouping them according to structural levels is by examination of the system *organizational chart,* such as the one previously illustrated in Figure 1.7. Although it is apparent that organization charts have serious limitations in portraying the realities of an organization or its structure, they are serviceable during initial stages of compensation planning. They contribute information about the division of work, superior-subordinate relationships, and the various authority levels in the structure. Generally speaking, organizational charts do not show the degree of responsibility and authority in various positions or the operational difference in line and staff positions. For the purpose under consideration, it can be said that the chief contribution of the organizational chart is to establish the organization's views as to the functions, relationships, and levels of various positions in the administrative hierarchy. It gives those responsible for making decisions on compensation a skeletal view of the total organization, its position composition, and a general picture of the relative importance and status accorded to levels in the position hierarchy as perceived by the organization. It serves, too, as a working hypothesis of the position values to be tested against position guides and structural analysis diagrams.

The Structural Analysis Diagram.   Third in the series of structural planning tools for grouping and aligning positions in the organizational structure is a *structural analysis diagram* of reporting relationships, such as the one illustrated in Figure 12.2. The primary function of this diagram is to reveal the number of structural levels in the organization and to identify which positions exist at each level. Secondary functions of the diagram are to (a) confirm superior-subordinate roles of positions, (b) verify line and staff relationships, and (c) reveal ambiguities that might impede development of an equitable compensation structure. In effect, the structural analysis diagram is an informal organizational chart derived from analysis of superior-subordinate roles as perceived by members of the organization.

Information concerning superior-subordinate relationships on which to base analysis of the organizational structure is obtained by using a **compensation data bank** similar to the one illustrated in Table 12.1. It should be noted that the information contained in the example is governed by the nature and complexity of the compensation structure being contemplated. For example, information is sought about each position incumbent concerning reporting relationship, preparation, length of work year, experience, staff load, and time devoted to administration. The information is to be used in determining the number, types, and relative importance of components in the *compensation* structure. Reporting relationship is the key element in differentiating positions as to level in the structure. In Figure 12.2, positions 2 through 6 and position 18 all report to position 1; positions 7 through 10, 20 through 27, and 29 through 31 all report to position 5; and so on.

Determining Levels in the Organizational Structure.   The primary purpose of gathering the data in Table 12.1 is to assign a responsibility level to each position in the organizational structure. The positions can be identified by using the code employed in Figure 12.2. When data are displayed in

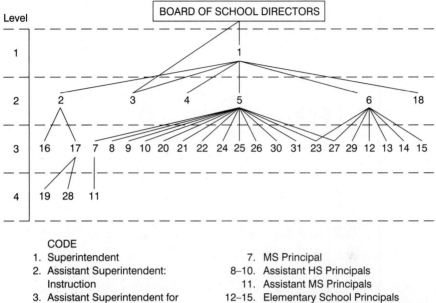

FIGURE 12.2
Structural analysis of administrative organization structure in the Goodville school system.

the form illustrated in Figure 12.2, all positions reporting to a given level are aligned horizontally. For example, positions 2 through 6 and position 18 are all grouped beneath level 1 and assigned to the second level of the position hierarchy. In the same way, the positions reporting to these second-level positions are grouped at the third level, and so on, until all administrative positions are accounted for. Use of this analytical technique results in a stratification of positions from which **position values** are readily apparent. As an additional aid in sorting the structural relationships into levels, broken lines may be used to emphasize the horizontal divisions and the segments labelled *levels* as shown in Figure 12.2. For discussion of the rationale underlying creation of sublevels in the organizational structure, the reader is referred to the discussion of sublevels that follows.

In real-life organizations, relationships among positions of various levels of the structure are seldom without some ambiguity. When such ambigui-

TABLE 12.1
Illustration of data bank for planning the compensation of school administrative personnel.

1 Position Number	2 Name of Administrator (First) (Initial) (Last)	3 Position Title	4 Individual Reports to[a]	5 Preparation[b]	6 Length of Work Year (Months)	7 Years of Experience	8	9 Full-Time Equivalent Persons Supervised	10 Present Salary	11 Percentage Time Devoted to Administration
						In Position[c]	Total in District			
1	Randolph C. Pell	Superintendent of schools	Board	D	12	15	5	525	$61,000	100%
2	John H. Laughran	Assistant superintendent: instruction	1	D	12	10	4	296	49,585	100
3	Wilmer T. Moyer	Assistant to superintendent: business affairs and secretary to board	1 Board	D	12	12	32	8	41,680	100
4	Harry C. Hancock	Assistant superintendent: personnel	1	D	12	8	24	8	41,380	100
5	John T. Lieberman	Director of secondary education and high school principal	1	D	12	10	6	152	42,925	100
6	Henry L. James	Director of elementary education	1	D	12	10	16	150	41,176	100

Position Number	Name of Administrator (First) (Initial) (Last)	Position Title	Individual Reports to[a]	Preparation[b]	Length of Work Year (Months)	Years of Experience		Full-Time Equivalent Persons Supervised	Present Salary	Percentage Time Devoted to Administration
						In Position[c]	Total in District			
7	Stephen R. Daniels	Middle school principal	5	B, M	12	9	27	52	40,458	100
8	Roland T. Knight	Assistant high school principal	5	B, M	12	12	38	6	37,510	100
9	B. Cox	Assistant high school principal	5	B, M	12	8	21	6	36,250	100
10	Clayton S. Ridgeway	Assistant high school principal	5	B, M + 15	12	8	28	4	31,300	100
11	Mark E. Lowther	Assistant middle school principal	7	B, M + 15	12	5	20	3	37,540	100
12	Richard N. Jackson	Principal, Roosevelt Elementary School	6	B, M	10	8	23	38	35,102	100
13	William W. McIllhenny	Principal, Southeast and Southwest Elementary Schools	6	B, M + 30	10	3	5	33	35,560	100

TABLE 12.1, *continued*

1 Position Number	2 Name of Administrator (First) (Initial) (Last)	3 Position Title	4 Individual Reports to[a]	5 Preparation[b]	6 Length of Work Year (Months)	7 Years of Experience In Position[c]	8 Total in District	9 Full-Time Equivalent Persons Supervised	10 Present Salary	11 Percentage Time Devoted to Administration
14	Robert C. Walts	Principal, Harrison and Hughes Elementary Schools	6	B, M + 15	10	22	10	32	34,480	100
15	John T. Malik	Principal, Hammond Elementary School	6	B, M + 30	10	10	4	26	30,700	100
16	Elizabeth N. Sutton	Reading supervisor	2	B, M	10	7	21	136	34,188	none
17	William D. Watkins	Director of pupil personnel and guidance, and department head[d]	2	B, M	12	10	24	16	36,528	none
18	Keith C. Carr	Home and school visitor	1	B + 30	12	8	10	6	33,250	none
19	Mary T. Washington	Psychologist	17	B, M + 30	12	5½	3	10	30,085	none
20	Grace T. Harker	Department head and teacher of art	5	B	9	17	19	4	28,600	50

1	2	3	4	5	6	7	8	9	10	11
	Name of Administrator					Years of Experience		Full-Time		Percentage Time Devoted to
			Individual		Length of Work			Equivalent		
Position Number	(First) (Initial) (Last)	Position Title	Reports to[a]	Preparation[b]	Year (Months)	In Position[c]	Total in District	Persons Supervised	Present Salary	Administration
21	Joseph R. Landes	Department head and teacher of business education	5	B, M	9	15	27	6	30,475	50
22	Walter N. Rosenberger	Department head and teacher of English	5	B, M	9	15	37	14	30,925	50
23	Helen M. Walters	Department head and teacher of health and physical education (K–12)	5, 6	B	9	10	23	11	29,200	50

Notes:

[a] Position to which individual reports by position number (column 1). Positions 24 to 31 (Figure 12.2) not included in this table.

[b] B, for bachelor's degree; M, for master's; D, for doctorate.

[c] Includes current year.

[d] Department head in name only.

ties obscure reporting relationships or result in confusion of function, steps must be taken toward realigning positions before position values are finally determined. Examples of structural flaws that may be identified by analysis of organizational relationships are illustrated in Figure 12.2, as follows:

- Positions 16 (reading supervisor), 17 (director of pupil personnel), 18 (home and school visitor), 19 (psychologist), and 28 (medical-dental therapist) consist of specialists who render services primarily to children. These should be excluded from the administrative organizational structure (see also Table 12.1 for position titles).
- Position 3 (assistant to superintendent: logistics) reports both to position 1 (superintendent) and to the board of school directors, *an example of dual control that frequently results in confusion of authority.*
- Positions 23, 27, and 29 (department heads) all report to two positions, position 5 (director of secondary education) and 6 (director of elementary education).
- Position 5 (director of secondary education) also functions as principal of the high school. Consequently, position 7 (middle school principal) and positions 8 to 10 (assistant high school principal) all report to position 5 and *appear to be* of equivalent value.
- The fact that secondary school principals function at both levels 2 and 3 results in assistant principals also being grouped at different levels.

Other problems evident from the structural analysis of data in Table 12.1, as depicted in Figure 12.2, are:

- Title ambiguity (titles that fail to relate to position function or status).
- Excessive span of control (position 5 is responsible for 15 positions).
- Heterogeneity of function (related activities are not grouped under the same head).
- Failure to coordinate the instructional function (elementary and secondary education) with the pupil services function.

Although it is not implied that all the structural problems that beset an organization can be resolved immediately, it is essential that long- and short-term plans as well as operating plans be addressed to eventual clarification of relationships among positions in the organization, thereby furnishing a foundation for an equitable compensation structure.

Determining Sublevels in the Organizational Structure. Values assigned to administrative positions on the basis of reporting relationships provide skeletal information for linking compensation to the relative worth of positions at different levels of the organizational hierarchy. However, there are occasions when it is necessary to assign different values to positions that function at the same reporting level. For example, some school systems employ attendance unit administrators, some of whom are employed for 10 months and others for 12 months. One way to provide for equity in compensation of these personnel is to adjust position value in such a way as to reflect differences in length of the work year. The adjusted values may be thought of as reflecting sublevels in the organizational structure because differences between them are not so great as those between levels.

Creation of sublevels in the organizational structure is justified only when there are demonstrable differences in conditions governing positions at the same responsibility level. Following are examples of conditions that might require differentiation of position values at the same reporting level:

- Difference in *value* to the organization of the work performed (e.g., direction of instruction—a line function—versus one of the staff functions—logistics, personnel, or external relations.
- Variations in length of work year.
- Part-time employment.
- Apportionment of time to nonadministrative obligations.
- State of the marketplace.

Quantitative methods for determining position values corresponding to levels and sublevels of the organizational structure are discussed and illustrated in the following text, which emphasizes linking the relative worth of administrative positions to compensation.

The Compensation Scattergram. The fourth **compensation planning tool** suggested in the previous discussion is the *compensation scattergram,* illustrated in Figure 12.3.* The technique involves analysis of the relationship between two variables: *position values,* as reflected by levels occupied by positions in the organizational structure, and *economic values* placed on those positions, as determined by the compensation of incumbents.

Each entry in the scattergram represents the compensation and operating level of a member of the administrative staff. For example, the chief executive, at level 1, receives an annual compensation of $53,500. The lowest-paid member of the organization, at level 4, receives $33,000 annually. The expected trend in relationship of compensation to position level would

---

* Salaries shown in Figure 12.3, as well as salaries shown in the previous chapter, are for illustrative purposes only. They are not intended to indicate what school system personnel are paid or should be paid.

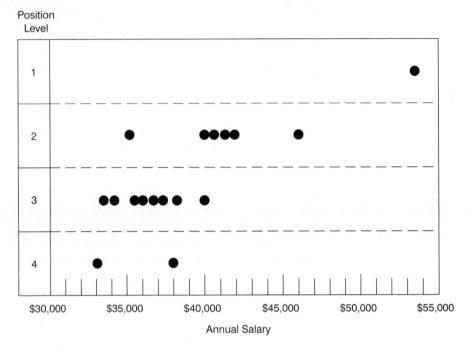

FIGURE 12.3
Scattergram illustrating distribution of compensation for administrative personnel.

be drawn diagonally from the lower left to the upper right in Figure 12.3. Visual examination of the scattergram confirms this expectation, but it also reveals several flaws in compensation practices. For example:

- The range of compensation for positions at level 2 appears to be excessive (from $35,500 to $46,000).
- Average compensation levels between position levels 3 and 4 are insufficiently differentiated.
- Average compensation levels at position levels 2 and 3 are low, relative to the practice at position level 4.

The foregoing observations reveal the degree to which compensation practices are structured in congruence with position values in an organization and suggest that, where departures from expected trends are observed, remedial action may be in order. Two remedies for inequities observed in Figure 12.3 data come to mind: (a) adjust the compensation plan to reflect more adequately position values at respective levels of the organizational structure, and (b) reclassify those positions as required to correct structural flaws.

DETERMINING THE RELATIVE WORTH OF ADMINISTRATIVE POSITIONS

Having established in the preceding sections that administrative positions in an organization can be grouped into an orderly structure designed to achieve specific purposes and that positions differ in degree as well as in kind of responsibility, it is now possible to examine them in terms of their application to a compensation structure.

Basis for the Compensation Structure

It has been shown that within the organization structure, positions relate one to another on a number of levels and that the order of each position in the hierarchy can be ascertained by examination of reporting relationships with other positions in the structure as well as by the amounts and kinds of responsibility inherent in the position. Proceeding, then, on the principle that compensation should be determined by relative importance of positions within the organizational structure, it is necessary to arrive at a consistent measure of the relative fiscal worth of positions at each level of the structure.

Basic to development of such a measure is the distinction between the nature of position and qualifications of the individual who fulfills its functions. Figure 12.4 illustrates a compensation structure that includes components relating both to (a) values inherent in the position and (b) values that reflect the relationship of the position incumbent to the position.

It should be emphasized that the compensation structure shown in Figure 12.4 illustrates the choice of possible values chosen to represent qualifications of the position incumbent. These together with the base salary represent a *decision system* designed to provide:

- A systems approach to compensation planning.
- A rational and objective basis for quantifying compensation decisions.
- Linkage of the compensation plan to the organizational structure.
- Enduring equity (fiscal consistency and fairness of treatment) for members of the organization.
- Compensation parity with external organizations.
- Responsiveness to the marketplace.
- Recognition of the individual worth of position incumbents.
- Adaptability to organizational needs.
- Linkage to staff development needs.

The compensation structure illustrated here contains components intended to link compensation both to position value and to the individual

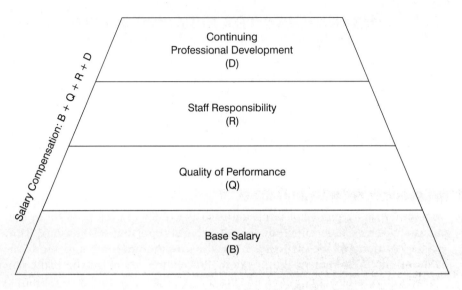

FIGURE 12.4
Conceptualization of compensation structure for administrative personnel.

worth of the position incumbent. This section is focused on linking compensation to position values, that is, to determining a base salary corresponding to each level and sublevel of the organizational structure. This component of the compensation structure is an essential part of all compensation plans.

Other components of the compensation structure consist of *addends*—chosen to establish ranges of compensation at each level and sublevel—to reflect differences in the individual worth of position incumbents. These options are intended to enhance the flexibility of the compensation structure in meeting a variety of conditions. The relative emphasis on optional components of the compensation structure, as opposed to the base salary as a determinant of total salary compensation, will vary. The number, type, and size of the addends selected may be adjusted to meet local needs and conditions. Attention is given later to procedures for selecting and incorporating addends into the compensation structure. The point to be stressed here is that in assigning values to each position in the organization, consideration must be limited to factors relating to that *position*. Even though matching the individual and the position and providing for his/her growth and economic betterment are essential concerns of the organization, *these can be considered only after position functions have been identified and the base compensation structure established.*

Linking the Compensation Structure to Position Values

Assignment of *relative values to positions* in the organizational structure for purposes of compensation rests on the following premises:

- Basic (minimum) compensation levels can be determined for positions at each level of the structure.

- The number of basic compensation levels will correspond to the number of levels in the structure (usually not more than six).

- Sublevels can be established and compensation determined, as needed, to provide for differences in value of positions found at a given level of the structure.

- Basic compensation will increase from the lowest to the highest responsibility level.

- The difference between base salaries will be progressively greater at each consecutive level in the hierarchy, from lowest to highest.

- Base salaries at each level of the organizational structure will relate consistently to base salaries at every other level through use of a **compensation index**.

- The compensation index will be based on a reference level within the administrative compensation structure rather than on some external criterion, such as teachers' salaries.

Establishing a Reference Level for the Compensation Structure

It is generally recognized that salaries of administrators are constantly compared with earnings of other personnel, both within and outside of the organization. The inevitability of such comparisons by administrators, policymakers, other members of the organization, and the general public leads not unnaturally to a desire to rationalize or to formalize linkage of compensation plans for administrators with those designed for entirely different sets of conditions.

Some compensation plans that have been devised for school administrators, for example, are linked by an index, or ratio, with salaries of other professional personnel. One consequence of this relationship is that fluctuations in salaries used for references are almost inevitably followed by adjustments in the salaries of administrators, regardless of the justification for such changes. Although the logic of these interrelationships is open to question, the practice is deeply rooted in tradition. Following are some of the bases that have been identified in the literature for determining administrative salaries:

- Average salary of classroom teachers.
- Scheduled salary of teacher with specified experience (e.g., five years).
- Highest scheduled teacher's salary.
- Minimum scheduled teacher's salary.

- Salary that administrator would earn on teachers' schedule.
- Maximum salary of teacher class for which administrator would qualify.
- Regional norms of administrative salaries.

Although there can be little argument that benchmarks such as the foregoing are useful in arriving at realistic and equitable compensation levels for administrators, in question is whether they need to be made an integral part of the plan. We propose here to develop an index salary plan for school administrators that has *internal integrity,* that is, one in which the reference base is internal and in which the elements are related to one another through an internal system of values rather than by references to unrelated criteria. Once the internal relationships within the administrative salary structure have been established, *the system can be referred directly to the marketplace* or to such external data as may be required for fiscal validation. In short, this means that adjustments to market conditions can be made for any position while maintaining the same relative values among all positions. The ultimate test of its validity will be the extent to which the compensation plan for administrators contributes to attracting and retaining an adequate supply of competent administrative personnel.

Establishing Values for Positions

When the compensation plan is linked to positions in the organizational structure, it is necessary both to establish a base and to provide for individual advancement at each level. The purpose of establishing position values is to link compensation to the organizational structure by establishing base salaries for each level, salaries commensurate with the amount and kinds of responsibility inherent in the positions at each level. It is assumed throughout this discussion that incumbents assigned to positions at each level of the organizational hierarchy satisfy specifications of the position guide as to initial preparation and to the technical as well as to the human skills required for the position. The link is maintained by use of a compensation index that expresses the relationship between the base salary at any level and the base salary at the lowest level.

The basis for the compensation index to be developed in this section is illustrated in the six-level compensation structure in Figure 12.5. As shown, the differences in position values among responsibility levels are now uniform. The difference between the fourth and fifth levels (principal and assistant principal) is twice as great as the difference between the fifth and sixth levels (assistant principal and coordinator). The difference between the third and fourth levels (director and principal) is three times as great as between the fifth and sixth levels, and so on. It should be obvious that the difference in position values at the highest and lowest levels is the sum of these differences and that at any level the amount by which the position value differs from that at the lowest level can be computed as a fraction of that total. For example, in the compensation structure in Figure 12.5, the sum of differences is 15. The difference in value between the fifth and sixth levels is $\frac{1}{15}$ of the total, between the fourth and sixth levels $\frac{3}{15}$ or $\frac{1}{5}$ of the total, and so on, until at the top level all of the differences are accounted for.

From the foregoing conceptualization it is possible to construct a model for deriving *salary indices* based on any salary range and on any number of responsibility levels. The procedure is illustrated in Table 12.2.

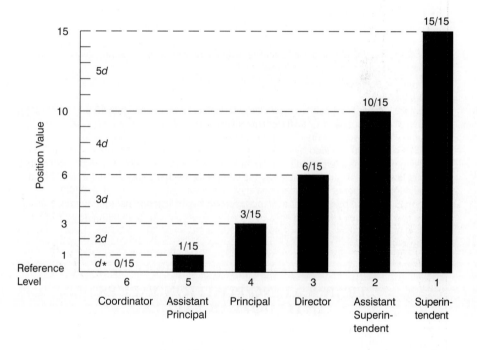

RESPONSIBILITY LEVEL

*d = difference in position values. $\Sigma d = 0 + 1 + 2 + 3 + 4 + 5 = 15$

Read as follows: Position value of Coordinator is at reference level; position value of Assistant Principal at 1/15 of position value range above reference level; position value of Principal at 3/15 of position value range above reference level. . . . Difference in position values of Superintendent and Assistant Superintendent 5 times as great as difference in position values of Coordinator and Assistant Principal.

FIGURE 12.5
Relationship of position values to responsibility levels.

TABLE 12.2
Derivation of a compensation index for determining base salaries of administrators.

(1) Responsibility Level	(2) Position Value Differential Units	(3) Cumulative Differential Units	(4) Weighting Constant	(5) Compensation Index: 1 + (Column 3 × Column 4)
1	5	15	0.0768	2.1520
2	4	10	0.0768	1.7680
3	3	6	0.0768	1.4608
4	2	3	0.0768	1.2304
5	1	1	0.0768	1.0768
6	0	0	0.0768	1.0000

Assumptions: Responsibility levels in compensation structure = 6; maximum salary = $63,500; minimum base salary = $29,500.

- Column 1 is derived from responsibility levels in organization structure, as illustrated in Figure 12.5.
- Column 2 is based on position value differentials, as illustrated in Figure 12.5.
- Column 3 represents sums of differentials between level 6 and consecutive levels.
- Column 4 is derived from the difference in base salaries at levels 1 and 6 ($63,500 − $29,500 = $34,000), divided by base salary at level 6 ($34,000 ÷ $29,500 = 1.1525). The resulting quotient is interpreted to mean that the base salary at level 1 is 115 percent higher than at level 6. This figure is divided by the *cumulative differential* for all levels (15) to relate it to the total number of differential units shown in column 3 (1.1525 ÷ 15 = .0768).
- Column 5 obtained by *adding at each consecutive level to the compensation index at level 6, the product of columns 3 and 4:* [1.000 + (1 × .0768) = 1.0768; (1.000 + (3 × .0768 = 1.2304); (1.000 + (6 × .0768) = 1.4608; (1.000 + (10 × .0768) = 1.7680); (1.000 + (15 × .0768) = 2.1520].

TRANSLATING POSITION VALUES
INTO DOLLAR VALUES

Having established base salaries for positions at the top and bottom responsibility levels of the administrative salary structure and having determined the number of levels and sublevels comprising the structure and assigned to each a relative value through the use of the compensation index, it is possible to translate position values into dollar values. The emphasis in this section is on the transformation of responsibility levels to dollar values through the use of the compensation index developed in Table 12.2. A method is shown in Table 12.3 for establishing base salaries for administrative personnel at each level of responsibility. The illustrations include computations based on differing assumptions as to the reference point, range, and number of levels in the compensation structure. Establishing *ranges of dollar val-*

TABLE 12.3
Method of transforming position values into dollar values.

(1) Responsibility Level	(2) Position Title	(3) Differential Units	(4) Cumulative Differential Units	(5) Compensation Index	(6) Base Salary
1	Superintendent	5	15	2.1520	$63,484[a]
2	Assistant superintendent	4	10	1.7680	52,156
3	Directors	3	6	1.4608	43,094
4	Principals	2	3	1.2304	36,297
5	Assistant principals	1	1	1.0768	31,766
6	Department heads	0	0	1.0000	29,500

1. Determine base salary range: $29,500 to $63,500.
2. Determine ratio of the difference to the minimum base: $63,500 − $29,500/$29,500 = 1.1525.
3. Determine number of responsibility levels and assign differential units: 6 (see Table 12.2 for an illustration).
4. Determine cumulative differential units: 0 + 1 = 1; +2 = 3; + 3 = 6; + 4 = 10; + 5 = 15 (column 4).
5. Determine weighting constant: 1.1525 (step b) ÷ 15 (cumulative total, step d) = .0768.
6. Determine compensation index: 1 + (0 × .0768 = 1.000); 1 + (1 × .0768 = 1.0768); 1 + (3 × .0768 = 1.2304); 1 + (6 × .0768 = 1.4608); etc.
7. Check compensation index: compensation index (level 1) × base salary (level 6) = $63,484.[a]
8. Convert position values to dollar values: multiply compensation index for each position by base salary at lowest level (column 6).

Note: [a] Computed value, approximates selected value.

ues for responsibility level to provide for differences in contributions of individuals to the purposes of the organization will be discussed subsequently.

As illustrated in Table 12.3, transformation of position values to dollar values is achieved by multiplying the base salary at the lowest level by the compensation index at each level and sublevel, until all position values in the organization structure have been accounted for. As a preliminary to the conversion process, a simple check of the calculation used to establish the compensation index is worth performing. Because the compensation index is based on the ratio of the highest to the lowest salary base, both of which were selected as starting points, the product of the compensation index at the highest level and the base salary at the lowest level of the compensation structure should closely approximate[5] the base salary for the highest position.

Augmenting the Basic Compensation of Individuals

Up to this point, the focus of developing a compensation plan for administrative personnel has been limited to methods of determining values of positions within the organizational structure and to devising compensation plans consistent with those values. In this section, means will be explored whereby the compensation plan can be used to provide for differences in the contribution of individual administrators to organizational purposes.

A number of reasons have been advanced for augmenting basic salaries of individuals who render service to organizations. These reasons include differences in professional development following initial preparation for the position, work load assigned, effectiveness in contributing to organizational goals, length of experience on the job, and previous service to the organization. Regardless of the bases selected for adjusting salaries of administrators in accordance with their individual worth, there is general agreement that such payments are justified by (a) increased satisfaction of the employee resulting from recognition by the organization of his/her contribution to its purposes and (b) improved capability of the organization to attract, retain, and develop those individuals who contribute to its purpose.

Once the decision has been made by the organization to provide each level of the compensation structure a systematic plan for rewarding individual contributions, questions such as the following will arise:

- What criteria will be employed as a basis for awarding addends to the basic salary?
- Which addends should be automatic? Which nonautomatic?
- What should be the number and size of each kind of addend?
- How should the number and size of addends relate to position value?
- How should the number and size of addends relate to purposes?

- How can objectivity be observed in awarding addends?
- How can the requirement of flexibility be reconciled with the requirement of equity?
- What limits should be imposed on the maximum salary? Should such limits be absolute?

After the decision has been made to provide at each level of the compensation structure a systematic plan for linking fiscal recognition of each administrator to his/her past, present, and future worth to the organization, at least three kinds of decisions need to be made. These relate to the determinants to be employed to indicate *the value of the person; the fiscal importance to be accorded to each determinant;* and *the size, number, and frequency of fiscal addends to be incorporated in the salary plan.*

Determinants of Incumbent Value

There at least four factors about which decisions need to be made in designing the measure of **incumbent value**. These factors include *continuing professional development, experience, quality of performance,* and *intralevel responsibility.* Practice varies in school systems throughout the nation with regard to the emphasis given these four factors. Which factors to include and what emphasis is given to each factor is a matter to be decided locally, but certain observations should be made on the issues involved in making decisions on the four factors.

Professional Preparation and Development Factor. The general trend in certification requirements for school administrators since midcentury,[6] community demand for greater professional effectiveness, and establishment of preparation requirements in position guides have altered somewhat the time-honored practice of placing heavy emphasis on the preparation factor as a salary determinant prior to employment. The reasoning behind this change is that the position guide calls for and the basic salary compensates for professional preparation *at the time of employment.* This line of reasoning holds that the salary plan should be so designed, especially at the upper levels of the administrative hierarchy, that salaries are adequate to reward preparation at the time of employment. Preparation, so goes the logic, is needed at the time of assignment to important administrative positions and should be paid for at that time.

This is not to contend that rewards for professional growth during service or for continuing professional development beyond the level specified by the position guide should be excluded from the compensation plan. The point is that formal education should be considered in determining addends to basic salaries only to the extent that it has not been included as a determinant of the basic salary structure developed earlier. Table 12.4 illustrates a system of addends for continuing professional development based on initial specifications set forth in position guides and on specified professional development levels beyond the maximum, which the position incumbent is encouraged to attain.

Experience Factor.   The problem of how much emphasis should be given to administrative experience as a salary determinant is as ubiquitous as the preparation issue. Most administrative positions at middle and upper levels of the structure require experience, and this element is generally written into position guides. At lower levels, opportunity should be provided for promising individuals to acquire experience in administrative positions as a means of professional development. Certainly the organization has both a responsibility and an opportunity to provide administrative experiences to further the development of potentially capable individuals. The trouble with many of the plans for compensating administrators is that the experience factor is given greater emphasis than the performance or effectiveness factor. With the advent of the ratio differential schedule, the experience factor is losing its appeal in compensation plans. One explanation for this trend is that the ratio plan appears to be more effective as a device for developing equitable and adequate administrative pay schedules than the use of factors such as initial preparation and experience.

Performance Factor.   Although inclusion of a performance factor in compensation plans for school administrators is probably the exception rather than the rule, there is growing interest in and use of performance

TABLE 12.4
Continuing professional development addends for administrative positions in the Goodville school system.

Professional Development Level	Addend (Portion of Base Salary)	Position Value (Cumulative Addends by Structural Level)						
		1	1a	2	3	4	5	6
B	—							a
M	.01						a	.01
M + 30	.01				a	a	.01	.02
M + 45	.01			a	.01	.01	.02	.03
M + 60	.01		a	.01	.02	.02	.03	.04
D	.02	a	.02	.03	.04	.04	.05	.06

Note: [a]Initial preparation specified for position.

Read as follows: Initial preparation, level 1 = doctorate, no applicable addend; addends for M + 30 credits= 2% of base salary at level 6.

appraisal as a tool for contributing to organizational purposes and individual staff development. It is an organizational expectation that an individual's performance will contribute, increasingly with experience, to goal realization. When this is the case, provision for its recognition should be incorporated in the compensation plan. For school districts that include a performance factor in the compensation plan, it is suggested that the appraisal procedure be linked to the position responsibilities specified in the position guides. Performance appraisal can be specific, objective, and relevant to individual as well as organizational needs. Essential elements in the appraisal process are (a) determining goals, (b) setting performance standards, and (c) measuring progress toward goals and realization of standards. Both goals and performance standards should be acceptable and meaningful to appraiser and appraisee and should be limited in number, unambiguous, stated in operational terms, amenable to measurement, and attainable. The emphasis here is on linking the compensation plan to the organization's goal structure through the appraisal process. Performance appraisal is focused on improving the effectiveness of each position incumbent; it is not intended as a punitive measure or as a device to hold down costs of the compensation plan.

Intralevel Responsibility Factor. Sometimes differences in the difficulty of work performed at a given compensation level require that adjustments be made to preserve equity in the salary plan. For example, the size of the professional and support staff for whom a principal is responsible may vary widely within a school system. The impact of such differences is primarily on the individual, but it relates to the capacity of the organization to attract, retain, reward, and develop those who contribute to its purposes.

One way of recognizing *differences in work loads* imposed on administrators is to provide a series of addends, graduated in accordance with the number of adults whose work they are responsible for supervising. This method of adjusting compensation is incorporated in the summary compensation plan illustrated in Table 12.8 (discussed later in the chapter), following its introduction in Table 12.5.

Another basis for awarding addends for differences in work loads consists of variations in size of the attendance unit for which the administrator is responsible. Pupil enrollment, average daily membership, and the like are indirect measures of such responsibility.

Perhaps the best method of determining differences in responsibility among administrators directly (e.g., principals) or indirectly (e.g., city regional superintendents) responsible for attendance units is the *multiple-factor measure of school complexity*. The indicator used might include factors for school size; number and qualifications of staff; social and economic condition of pupils; and pupil health, learning potential, and achievement. Although multiple-factor measures of the attendance unit work load are more difficult

TABLE 12.5
Schedule of unit complexity addends for principals in the Goodville school system.

Unit Complexity (Standard Score)[a]	Number of Principals	Addend to Base Salary (Percentage)
92 or higher	2	10%
84–91	1	9
76–83	2	8
68–75	—	7
60–67	5	6
52–59	—	5
44–51	1	4
36–43	—	3
28–35	—	2
20–27	3	1
19 or lower	1	0

Note: [a] Composite standard score, based on:
• Number of professional staff
• Number of nonprofessional staff
• Faculty experience
• Number and types of special programs
• Pupil membership
• Percentage of pupils from low-income families
• Number of non-English-speaking pupils
• Pupil turnover rate

to devise and to use than single-factor measures, they are in operation in some school districts and can be readily adapted to use in a systematic compensation plan. Table 12.5 illustrates one method whereby weighted composite standard scores derived from pupil membership, staff size and experience, curriculum complexity, and socioeconomic factors might be linked to adjustments in the base salary of attendance unit administrators.

SELECTING ELEMENTS IN THE COMPENSATION RANGE

To illustrate application of the incumbent value factors just described, let us assume that the Goodville school system plans to adopt an index compensation structure based on a reference level of $63,500 and six position levels (see Table 12.2). Principals within the system are on a uniform salary schedule and employed for 12 months. The board of education has determined that it can support total payments for administrators' maximum salaries equal to 45 percent in excess of base salaries. It has decided to preserve the values incorporated in the basic salary structure by basing the salary range at each position level on the same fixed percentage of the base salary.

In selecting the elements to be used in determining addends to base salaries, the Goodville board decides to limit its choice to those three that relate most closely to its purposes. After listing in order of importance a number of possible factors for inclusion in the plan, the three determinants of compensation for individual administrators shown in Table 12.6 are selected.

Determining the Relative Economic Worth of Elements in the Compensation Range

Having previously set a limit for individual compensation equal to 45 percent of the base salary at each position level, the Goodville board is faced with the problem of how to allocate its resources among elements it has selected for inclusion in the compensation plan. The board's decision on this problem, shown in Table 12.6, indicates the relative importance of each salary component. For example, one-fourth of the total weight ($3/12$) is devoted to addends for preparation, one-third ($4/12$) to addends for responsibility, and the remainder ($5/12$) to addends for performance. These portions, it will be noted, vary from about 12 to 18 percent of the base salary.

Determining the Size and Number of Addends Comprising the Compensation Range

The size and number of addends that the Goodville board can grant to its administrative personnel are limited by its previous decision as to how large a proportion of salary expenditures will be devoted to the compensation elements selected. Assuming a base salary of \$36,297 for principals (see Table 12.3), for example, the percentages shown in column four of Table

TABLE 12.6
Derivation of salary addends based on compensation determinants in the Goodville school system.

(1) Compensation Determinant	(2) Rank Order of Importance	(3) Arbitrary Weight	(4) Percentage of Base Salary[a]	(5) Column 4 Derivation
Performance	1	5 (a)	18%	a/d × .45
Responsibility	2	4 (b)	15	b/d × .45
Preparation	3	3 (c)	12	c/d × .45
Total weight	—	12 (d)	45	—

Note: [a] Values adjusted to multiples of 3%.

12.6 are translated in three steps into dollar equivalents, as illustrated in steps 1 through 3 of Table 12.7.

TRANSLATING A COMPENSATION PLAN INTO INDIVIDUAL SALARIES

As every administrator knows, the best of ideas and plans can be of little practical value to the organization until they are put into action. However well designed a compensation plan is, it must be adopted formally by the board of education and incorporated into the annual, or preferably the long-term, budget. Even when these steps are completed, the plan is by no means self-administering. Changes occur daily in every organization. People enter and leave the system. Positions are added and eliminated. Promotions and dismissals are to be expected. Entire salary programs, or parts thereof, become outmoded. Thus, the chief executive and staff need to view administration of the compensation plan as a cyclic operation to be dealt with anew with the preparation of each budget.

The mechanics of the plan should be simplified and quantified to the point where they are readily understood and can be utilized to calculate the

TABLE 12.7
Development of salary addends for principals.

Step 1 Select Determinants and Maximum Limits	Step 2 Select Automatic Addends and Determine Size and Number	Step 3 Select Nonautomatic Addends and Determine Size and Number
Base salary: $36,297 Maximum addends:		
A. Performance 18% Amount $6,533		Nonautomatic 6 at 3% $1,089 to $6,533
B. Responsibility 15% Amount $5,445	Automatic 5 at 3% $1,089 to $5,445	
C. Preparation 12% Amount $4,356	Automatic 6% for Doctorate[a] $2,178	
D. Total 45% Amount $16,334		

Note: [a] No addend is provided for Master's degree, which is a position prerequisite.

impact of the salaries on individuals as well as on the annual budget. Table 12.8 has been included to illustrate how data for the compensation plan under discussion might be organized and analyzed for a given school system.

To clarify the operation of the plan, the following is an example of the manner in which the salary of a given administrator would be calculated from the data and formula in Table 12.8. Part I covers the automatic elements in the plan; Part II, the nonautomatic elements.

I. *Automatic components of the plan*
- Position LA 4–1 (high school principal) is responsible for a total staff of 57, which entitles him/her to three addends of 3 percent of the base salary of $36,297 [responsibility fraction (R) = .09].
- LA 4–1 possesses an earned doctorate, which entitles him/her to two increments of 6 percent for professional development beyond the minimum (MA) specified for the position [professional development (D) = .12].
- Summing the automatic increments:

R (responsibility addend)	= $36,297 × .09 = $3,267
D (professional development addend)	= $36,297 × .12 = $4,356
total automatic increments	$7,623

II. *Nonautomatic component of the plan (Q)*
- LA 4–1 over a period of years has earned three addends of 5 percent for quality of service [quality performance fraction (Q) = .15].

Q (quality performance addend)	= $36,297 × .15 = $5,445

III. *Total Salary*
- LA 4–1 is entitled to the base salary for the position (B) plus $R + D + Q$

B (base salary)	= $36,297
R (responsibility fraction)	= 3,267
D (professional development fraction)	= 4,356
Q (quality performance fraction)	= 5,445
total salary	= $49,365

Each school organization must decide what kind of salary structure it is able to implement and maintain. Working through the design summarized in Table 12.8 using the same or a modified set of assumptions helps planners to decide whether consequences produced by the proposed structure are preferable to those yielded by the one in operation. The core of the proposal discussed here is to establish a method for determining the *relative value of administrative positions*, to establish position guides to secure competent personnel to occupy the positions, and to arrange salaries so that they are *equitable* within and among structural levels and *externally competitive* with

TABLE 12.8
Translating the compensation plan into individual salaries.

I. Assumptions:	II. Formula	
Base salary range—$29,500 to $63,500; number of responsibility levels = 6; minimum preparation—superintendent and deputy superintendent, doctorate; assistant superintendents, M + 30; all other positions, M. All administrators are on a 12-month schedule.	B = Base salary R = Responsibility fraction (total staff of 30–39 = .03; 40–49 = .06; 50–59 = .09; 60–69 = .12; 70 . . . = .15). Multiply by base salary.	B = _____ R = _____
	P = Professional development fraction (M + 30 = .06; Doctorate = .12—unless position requires either). Multiply by base salary.	P = _____
	Q = Quality performance fraction (.05 = number of awards for quality performance). Multiply by base salary.	Q = _____
	Salary = B + R + P + Q	B + R + P + Q = _____

544

III. Salary computations:

(1) Position[a]	(2) Position Title	(3) Compensation Index	(4) B Base Salary	R—Responsibility			Professional P—Development			Q—Performance			(14) Salary B + R + D + Q
				(5) Total Staff	(6) Fraction (5@.03)	(7) Addend (R)	(8) Level	(9) Fraction (2@.06)	(10) Addend (P)	(11) Number of Awards	(12) (5@.05)	(13) Addend (Q)	
LC1	Superintendent	2.1520	$63,500	—	—	—	P[b]	—	—	2	.10	$6,350	$69,850
LC1a	Deputy	1.8960[c]	55,932	—	—	—	P[b]	—	—	1	.05	2,797	58,729
SC2-1	Assistant	1.7680	52,156	—	—	—	M + 30[b]	—	—	1	.05	2,608	54,764
SC2-2	Assistant	1.7680	52,156	—	—	—	M + 30[b]	—	—	3	.15	7,823	59,979
SC2-3	Assistant	1.7680	52,156	—	—	—	P	.06	$3,129	1	.05	2,608	57,893
SC2-4	Assistant	1.7680	52,156	—	—	—	M + 30[b]	.06		—		—	52,156
SC3-1	Coord. curr.	1.4608	43,094	—	—	—	M + 30	.06	2,568	3	.15	6,464	52,126
SC3-2	Coord. P. S.	1.4608	43,094	—	—	—	M[b]			1	.05	2,155	45,249
LA4-1	HS principal	1.2304	36,297	57	.09	$3,267	P	.12	4,356	3	.15	5,445	49,365
LA4-2	MS principal	1.2304	36,297	49	.06	2,178	M + 3	.06	2,178	2	.10	3,630	44,283
LA4-3	ES principal	1.2304	36,297	35	.03	1,089	P	.12	4,356	5	.25	9,074	50,816
LA4-4	ES principal	1.2304	36,297	18	—	—	M[b]			3	.15	5,445	41,742
LA4-5	ES principal	1.2304	36,297	18	—	—	M + 30	.06	2,178	1	.05	1,815	40,290
LA5-1	Assistant principal	1.0768	31,776	—	—	—	M + 30	.06	1906	2	.10	3,177	36,849
LA5-2	Assistant principal	1.0768	31,776	—	—	—	M[b]	—	—	—	—	—	31,766
LA6-1	Department head	1.000	29,500	—	—	—	M[b]	—	—	1	.05	1,475	30,975
LA6-2	Department head	1.000	29,500	—	—	—	M + 30	.06	1,770	3	.15	4,425	35,695
LA6-3	Department head	1.000	29,500	—	—	—	M[b]	—	—	2	.10	2,950	32,450

Notes: [a] See Figure 1.7 for an explanation of position codes listed in column 1.
[b] Minimum preparation specified for position.
[c] Compensation index adjustment = $[(2.1520 - 1.7680)/3] + 1.7680 = 1.8960$.
Monetary values in Table 12.8 should not be considered as norms or standards.

those of other systems. These are among the tests any salary plan proposed to the governing body should meet.

REVIEW AND PREVIEW

In this chapter, attention has been focused on principles and methods of resolving problems connected with the compensation of administrative personnel.

Beyond the basic requirements for any compensation plan (*compensation is related to contribution; compensation is internally consistent, externally competitive; and compensation administration is perceived by personnel to be rational and fair*), pay structures for instructional, support, and administrative personnel differ in several ways. Not only do the conceptual, technical, and interpersonal skills required of these three groups differ but also the activities relating to the work performed range from manual labor to highly complex planning and decision making.

The compensation of executive positions is of significance because the results the system achieves are likely to reflect the contribution of executives rather than the contributions of those in lower-level positions.

The compensation of executive and support personnel should be considered as a part of the total reward system because pay for each individual in the organization is set relative to the pay of others. This concept is in keeping with one of the facts of compensation in organizational life: pay decisions are related to what personnel working in similar positions outside the system are paid, what they are paid for working in different positions within the system, and what different individuals working in similar positions within the system are paid.

The concept of organizational structure can be used effectively in planning administrative compensation because equity in pay demands that all persons should be rewarded for the level of work they are employed to perform. Effective analysis of the organizational structure and the relative worth of positions comprising it can be facilitated by the use of four structural planning tools: the *position guide, organization chart, structural analysis diagram,* and *compensation scattergram*. The precision with which positions in the administrative hierarchy are described, titled, and related to each other will have a significant bearing on the acceptance, operation, and life span of the compensation plan. In short, organization planning is an important antecedent to compensation planning.

Chapter 13 examines the strategic planning potential in collective bargaining through proactive approaches and avoidance of acrimonious and dysfunctional negotiations behavior.

REVIEW AND DISCUSSION QUESTIONS

1. Many salary plans include three methods of compensation: (a) automatic increases, (b) pay for performance, and (c) a combination of (a) and (b). What are the strengths and weaknesses of each method? Why is

method (b) the least popular? What values are lost by strict adherence to method (a)?

2. Prior to modifying an existing remuneration program, what consideration should be given to planning for compensation strategy? Pay equity? Compensation for individual performance? Group performance? Benefits? Special recognition for crucial skills, knowledge, and abilities?

3. List five major external environmental influences on compensation practices in education. Indicate their impact in the system in which you are employed.

4. What parties have vested influences in the design of a school system's salary, wage, benefit, and incentive provisions?

5. Does the relative worth controversy have any significance in developing administrative, teaching, and support pay plans?

6. Identify five contemporary issues that have developed regarding personnel benefits. Should administrators receive benefits that are more varied and of greater value than those that teachers receive?

7. Name three comparison sources by which personnel can assess a system's compensation fairness.

8. In what ways are compensation practices influenced by the federal government? State government? School boards?

9. Give your response to the compensation practice where all personnel on the payroll are assigned a pay grade (1, 2, 3, etc.), each pay grade is assigned a dollar value, and individuals progress through the pay structure on the basis of their worth to the system.

10. Respond to this statement: "Any administrator should be paid more than any teacher."

11. Secure a copy of a school district compensation plan for support personnel. Analyze the plan and related documents to determine:

    a. Are there indications that job analysis (skill, knowledge, abilities, and responsibilities) has been employed in determining job content? Are there indicators of methods employed to determine the values of different job categories?

    b. Develop a graphic portrayal of average pay rates for each class of support jobs in order to determine the relationship between dollar values and job values. Can you tell from the graphical portrayal that dollar values and job values are out of line (see Figure 12.3)?

12. What do you consider to be compensable factors (job content) in the following positions: teacher, principal, business manager, bus driver, nurse, curriculum supervisor, and staff developer?

13. How do these four factors affect the compensation structure of a school district: union, legal, policy, and equity? Can you identify other influencing factors?

14. Assume school district X plans to employ three new teachers for the coming school year (senior high school teachers of physics, mathematics, and computer science). Salaries of the proposed new teachers will range from 1.5 to 4 percent above those of veteran teachers. Consider the possibility of these developments:

- The long-time faculty members will file a grievance with the State Labor Relations Board charging age discrimination.
- The grievants will acknowledge that they have less preparation (in terms of degrees) but claim considerably more teaching experience.
- The grievants will claim that all faculty members are compensation equals.
- The school district will challenge the grievance, concluding that salary differentials between the newcomers and the grievants are due to competitive market salaries, not age discrimination.

- The school district will also contend that adoption of the compensation equality principle is erosive of the concept of performance rewards and incentive pay.
- Questions: Should the school district adjust the salaries of veteran teachers to those for the proposed additions? What might be the ramifications of this hypothetical grievance in terms of union support for salaries of new hires? Litigation? Compensation policy? Compensation equity among all members of the district teaching staff? What should be the stance of the Board of School Directors?

CHAPTER EXERCISE 12.1

Directions: This exercise contains statements that are designed to provide insights regarding your beliefs about compensation for administrative personnel. Determine whether you strongly disagree, generally agree, or strongly agree with each of the following statements:

- Performance increments for administrators are considered to be the most appropriate vehicle for rewarding performance.
- Pay for knowledge (e.g., for computer specialists) is an appropriate form of administrative compensation.
- The relative value of administrative positions is best determined by the job point method.
- Employees generally tend to overestimate what some administrators earn.
- The first step in designing a strategic compensation program is to raise administrative compensation.
- Individual progress through the pay structure should be based on development rather than on performance, seniority, and educational level.

- Size of the annual school budget is the best single predictor of administrative compensation.
- There is a strong positive correlation between staff size and staff compensation.
- Education and experience are good predictors of administrative compensation.
- Emphasis in administrative compensation has been shifting from the attraction and retention functions to the motivation function.
- All administrative personnel should receive the same benefits and levels of coverage.
- School systems are paying too much for dependent health care coverage in the benefit package for administrators.
- Relative worth initiatives ignore the fact that there is no definitive test of the fairness of a pay structure.
- Market forces may cause some administrative positions to be paid more than their relative worth.

- A compensation reward system will cause poor performers to leave the system.
- Women administrators receive, on the average, less pay than men administrators.
- Intrinsic rewards (achievement opportunities and recognition of achievement) have a significant impact on employee commitment.
- The most important factor in determining administrative compensation is level of responsibility.

- Length of applicable experience is an important determinant of compensation policy-making.
- Noneconomic rewards (e.g., special privileges, computers, office space, and parking space) are conducive to administrator motivation.
- Internal equity means that a supervisor should be paid the same as a high school principal because the positions are quite similar in work/effort and required skills.

NOTES

1. From The Money Motive by Thomas Wiseman. © 1974 by Thomas Wiseman. Reprinted by permission of Random House, Inc.

2. Bertram M. Gross, The Managing of Organizations: The Administrative Struggle, Vol. 1 (New York: The Free Press, 1964), 294.

3. There are exceptions to this rule of thumb. It is conceivable that some administrative assignments involve only the individual, with no other individual reporting to that position holder.

4. A *position* refers to any post in an organization to which duties have been assigned to be performed by one person.

5. The result of this calculation may not equal precisely the original value selected because of rounding errors encountered in using the index.

6. A Master's degree is now required for the principalship in a majority of the states. In many school systems, it is a minimum requirement.

SUPPLEMENTARY READING

Boe, Erling E.; and Dorothy M. Gilford, Editors. Teacher Supply, Demand, and Quality: Policy Issues, Models, and Data Bases. Washington: National Academy Press, 1992.

Boyles, Norman L.; and Denis Vrchota. Performance-Based Compensation Models: Status and Potential for Implementation. Des Moines, IA: Iowa Association of School Boards, 1986.

Cornett, Lynn. More Pay for Teachers and Administrators Who Do More. Atlanta: Southern Regional Education Board, 1987.

Dorio, Marc A. Personnel Manager's Desk Book. Englewood Cliffs, NJ: Prentice-Hall Inc., 1989.

Ivancevich, John M.; and William F. Glueck. Foundations of Personnel/ Human Resource Management,

Third Edition. Plano, TX: Business Publications Inc., 1986.

Johnson, Alan M. "Designing Total Compensation Programs." In Milton L. Rock and Lance A. Berger, Editors, Third Edition, Part 5, The Compensation Handbook. New York: McGraw-Hill Inc., 1992, 311–322.

Lawther, William C. "Ways to Monitor (and Solve) the Pay-Compression Problem." Personnel 66, 3 (March 1989), 84–88.

MacPhail-Wilcox, Bettye; and Roy Forbes. Administrator Evaluation Handbook. Bloomington, IN: Phi Delta Kappa, 1990.

Rock, Milton L.; and Lance A. Berger, Editors, Third Edition, Part 5. "Computers and Compensation." In The Compensation Handbook. New York: McGraw-Hill Inc., 1992.

Scarpello, Vida G.; and James Ledvinka. Personnel/Human Resource Management. Boston: PWS-Kent Publishing Company, 1988.

Sibson, Robert E. Compensation, Fifth Edition. New York: American Management Association, 1990.

Sibson, Robert E. Strategic Planning for Human Resources Management. New York: American Management Associations, 1992.

Sperling, Jo Ann. Job Descriptions in Human Resources. New York: American Management Association, 1986.

Tecker, Glenn H. Merit, Measurement, and Money. Alexandria, VA: National School Boards Association, 1985.

Chapter 13

Collective Bargaining: Planning, Negotiating, and Contract Administration

CHAPTER OVERVIEW

- The Collective Bargaining Condition
- Criticisms of Public Sector Bargaining
- The Regulatory Anatomy of Bargaining
- Collective Bargaining and the Human Resources Function
- Elements of the Transactional Relationship
- The Collective Bargaining Process

    Prenegotiations Planning
    Organization for Negotiations
    Shaping the Human Organization Through Contract Design
    Contract Reassessment
    Contractual Posture

- Negotiations Strategy

    Modes of Negotiating Behavior
    Scope of Bargaining
    Impasse Resolution and Strikes
    Contract Agreement

- Contract Administration

CHAPTER OBJECTIVES

- Develop an understanding of union-system relationships, which have altered practically all operational aspects of educational institutions.
- Demonstrate the capabilities of a process model for enhancing the union-system relationship.
- Put into context the strategic planning potential of the bargaining process for achieving aims of the human resources function and general purposes for which the school system exists.
- Present three approaches to contract negotiation, as well as their strengths and limitations.
- Develop an understanding of four major activities in contract administration: implementation, conflict resolution, enforcement, and evaluation.

CHAPTER TERMS

Arbitration

Collective bargaining

Collective bargaining process

Contract administration

Contract design

Grievance procedure

Impasse

Negotiating modes

Negotiations

Prenegotiations planning

Regulatory anatomy

Scope of bargaining

Strike

Working conditions

The twentieth century has been referred to as the second great transition period in the history of humankind. This period has been identified as the time of transition from civilized to postcivilized society. The magnitude, rate, and scope of change in the affairs of humans during this era have been unprecedented. Vast changes are taking place not only in science and technology but also in social institutions, including modifications in the moral, religious, political, economic, and educational aspects of life. Educational institutions have not been excluded from this upheaval.

The first compulsory public sector **collective bargaining** law in the United States was enacted in 1959 by the Wisconsin Legislature.[1] In 1962 Executive Order 10988 was issued by President John F. Kennedy, granting federal employees the right to bargain collectively. Several states enacted legislation shortly after the federal action enabling state and local public employees to organize and bargain or consult with their employers. Consequently, teacher groups began to organize extensively in protest against employment conditions. This movement has since led to widespread demands by educators for better salaries, protection from physical assault, economic and position security, freedom from paternalism, and the right to participate in decisions affecting conditions under which school personnel work. The collective bargaining movement in education is continuing to change rapidly and to bring about alterations in all types of educational institutions. Since the issuance of the 1962 Federal Executive Order, the majority of states have enacted legislation granting public personnel the right to engage in a transactional relationship with governmental units.[2] School administrators, in response to the collective bargaining movement, have become increasingly cognizant of the need for continuing education relating to collective bargaining in the public sector in order to keep abreast of rapidly changing conditions and to learn to deal more effectively with the organizational impact of collective behavior.

This institutional revolution, considered to be one of the most significant legal developments in the twentieth century, has forced school systems to master collective bargaining procedures, just as they have learned to deal with other organizational problems imposed on them by a world in transition. School boards are rapidly gaining greater sophistication and acquiring those skills essential to cope with numerous and complex issues posed by teacher unions. The initial collective bargaining movement in education found school boards and administrators generally unprepared to engage in the collective bargaining process. Some boards looked with incredulity on the use of collective behavior by teachers to resolve the conditions under which they worked. Further, they were stunned at the thought of having to deal with several types of unions or associations for both professional and support personnel. With the passage of time, however, there is increasing awareness by school officials that application of collective bargaining techniques to school personnel problems requires boards and administrators to adjust to new and changing roles in order to resolve conditions of employment for people under their jurisdiction.

In this chapter the following premises are presented:

- Collective bargaining, as one of the key processes of the human resources function, has considerable potential through intelligent direction for contributing to achievement of the system's strategic aims for its human resources.

- Existence of a high level of perceived mutual interest in human resources problems affecting both the system and the union tends to facilitate the long-term effectiveness of the organization.

- The adversarial environment that has marked the history of union-system relations must change and school officials must lead the way.

- Improvement of the design and implementation of a collective bargaining process is needed to resolve issues relating to conditions of employment in pubic education.

- Collective bargaining is and will continue to be a major factor in educational administration; new roles and responsibilities will result from and be essential to operation of the process. Attainment of organizational objectives requires a positive approach to the constant challenges posed by collective behavior of personnel.

As will be noted in the following discussion, the assumptions referred to do not embrace the view that the current state of public sector bargaining is without serious flaws. Until the present system is reformed, the school organization must continue to assume a proactive stance in using the bargaining process to develop plans that will improve personnel performance and enrich working lives.

The terms *collective bargaining* and *collective negotiations* are employed interchangeably in the literature. The term *bargaining*, as used here, refers to the *total bargaining process*, one phase of which is *negotiations*. At-the-table activities as well as those directly relevant to them are viewed as *negotiations*.

THE COLLECTIVE BARGAINING CONDITION

To understand the current direction, key issues, and continuing problems in the evolution of collective bargaining in public education, it is helpful to review some of the salient developments that have occurred since the sixth decade of the twentieth century. These changes are noteworthy, and include:

- The majority of states now permit collective bargaining for local and state government personnel, the laws for which generally follow the format found in those governing private sector bargaining.

- Membership in national organizations for educational personnel (e.g., the National Education Association and the American Federation of Teachers) has increased significantly, as have their resources and political influence.

- The negotiated agreement between school boards and teaching personnel has become commonplace.

- The growth of unionization and collective bargaining in the public sector has been accompanied by a substantial increase in strike activity.

- The collective bargaining movement in public education has resulted in legal issues that have kept legislatures, courts, school district representatives, and teacher unions constantly concerned with resolution of bargaining issues.

- The move toward administrative unionism in education is under way, spurred by (a) a concern that school boards are bargaining away the rights of middle-level school management, (b) fluctuating enrollments, (c) a desire of administrators for greater employment security, (d) affirmative action policies regulating promotion of administrators, and (e) inflationary pressures.[3]

- Efforts have been initiated to secure a federal collective bargaining law for public employees.

- Statewide, regional, council, multilevel, and multilateral collective bargaining notions have been introduced as solutions to personnel issues in education.[4]

- The scope of negotiations, whether the subjects are mandatory or permissive bargaining issues, continues to be controversial. Major trends in teacher agreements include provisions relating to compensation, grievance procedures, school calendar and class hours, class size, supplementary classroom personnel, evaluation of teachers, assignment of teachers, transfers, reductions in force, promotion, in-service and professional development programs, instructional policy committees, student grading and promotion, student discipline and teacher safety, and federal programs.

- Using a dual strategy of collective bargaining and political action, organized teachers have secured contractual gains locally and simultaneously achieved political success at higher levels of government. Although these gains are neither total nor universal, teachers have acquired a number of noncompensation items that limit the flexibility of school management and increase the cost of public education. At the same time, collective bargaining emerged as a tool for remedying decades of low salaries and arbitrary treatment by school administrators.

- One emerging pattern immediately discernible is the continually strengthening pressure for citizen involvement in the entire public school collective bargaining process.[5]

- Since 1974 there has been no dramatic increase in the number of right-to-strike laws.[6]

- The number of third-party professionals (mediators, arbitrators, or fact finders) has grown rapidly. This group has a stake in maintaining the status quo in collective bargaining.[7]

- Collective bargaining does have a significant impact on the allocation of resources in school districts. The link between inputs and student outcomes, however, is less satisfactory.[8]

- By mid-1983 the two national teacher unions were sending very different signals with regard to the educational excellence movement.[9]

- The resulting influence of teacher unions in the United States must be regarded as substantial. Its power goes beyond union membership—

union tactics and negotiated contracts are emulated across the nation, along with federal, state, county, and municipal governments helping to shape employment relations in education.

- Studies by Mitchell and Kerchner describe the evolution of union-school system relations in terms of three generations: from relaying teachers' views on policy to school officials to the realization that collective bargaining is a useful way to formulate educational policy. Negotiations ought to and do concern the way schools are run.[10]

CRITICISMS OF PUBLIC SECTOR BARGAINING

Development of collective bargaining in public education is complete enough to show that the current bargaining condition is marked by diversity in achievement among teacher personnel groups throughout the nation, diversity in opinion about approaches, and diversity in viewpoints about how to guide the future of collective behavior to make education more effective and efficient.

Clearly, collective bargaining in education has resulted in benefits as well as troublesome conflicts. The list of alleged shortcomings or negative consequences includes the following:

- Public sector bargaining is inconsistent with democratic government.[11]
- Bargaining does not have substantial impact on the compensation level of teachers.[12] Unions have promoted the principle of equal pay, or, at best, a differential pay scale that primarily takes into account educational background and seniority, thereby limiting the financial incentives available for rewarding superior professional work.
- The arbitration of grievances has become a never-ending task.[13]
- Collective agreements do not facilitate flexibility and innovation.
- Some agreements are so complicated that teachers do not understand their own working conditions.
- The right of public employees to strike gives them a power much greater than that of their counterparts in the private sector.
- Binding arbitration inhibits the rights of public agencies to make policy decisions.[14]
- A conflict exists between a double protection of statutory benefits for public employees and benefits won in bargaining.[15]
- The issue of bargaining and the constitutional rights of a system member being violated looms large on the litigation agenda.[16]
- Teacher strikes have created a chilly public climate for school personnel.[17]

- The burgeoning costs of bargaining to students, teachers, communities, school districts, and the state represent an alarming condition when viewed in terms of return on investment.[18]
- Unionization and collective bargaining are subtly altering social relations in the schools and conceptions of teaching as an occupation.[19]
- There are no standard outcomes of bargaining; considerable variation exists across schools operating under the same contract.[20]
- Unions will support reforms that coincide with the interests of teachers in their own welfare, will oppose reforms that are inimical to those interests, and will be largely indifferent to reforms that do not materially affect teachers.[21]
- In state after state, unions routinely litigate every attempted dismissal of a tenured teacher who is willing to contest it.[22]
- It is unrealistic to expect unions to support large raises for small numbers of teachers, even when all teachers receive some kind of increase.[23]

In sum, problems spawned by the collective bargaining arrangements in public education will not vanish readily. The 1990s have been witness to accelerated action in the legislatures and the courts pertaining to the interests and rights of public school employees, boards of education, and consumers of educational services.

Few will dispute the contention that the present system for governing union-school system relations is flawed and in dire need of reform. There is considerable doubt in various quarters and among many observers that reforms can be achieved in the contemporary social climate of increasing size and power of state governments, politicization of teacher unions, and the pressures for privatization of education at public expense. Those who assume that a new spirit of system-union cooperation can be developed without an adversarial environment are asking for a cultural revolution that has little basis in history or contemporary reality. Union member goals of economic advancement and position security, not proactive educational policies to improve educational outcomes, have been and will remain foremost on union agendas. The failure of unions to deal with criticisms such as those outlined above points more to a need for internal reforms than to a need for abolition of unions and adversarialism.

THE REGULATORY ANATOMY OF BARGAINING

Public employment policy in the United States is defined by specific labor laws (see Table 3.2) and enforced by administrative agencies and the courts. The nature of the external **regulatory anatomy** governing teacher union-school system employment relations, the policies by which they are shaped, the manner in which legislation is enforced, and judicial interpretations of such policy are of primary importance to the human resources function. The law must be considered by school officials in practically every personnel decision. Moreover, merging employment law into the human resources function frequently requires considerably more attention to the collective bargaining process and its derivatives than to pursuit of the organization's mission.

State public sector bargaining laws, an external factor governing union-system employment relations, encompass such activities as recognition, bargaining rights, the bargaining process, impasse procedures, the right to strike, and contract administration. These anatomical features are outlined in the following text.

The term *recognition* refers to an aspect of labor law requiring that collective bargaining cannot occur unless the bargaining unit is properly organized and certified. Most states having recognition provisions allow for exclusive representation.[24] Determination of an appropriate representation unit is decided by a voluntary democratic vote of eligible voters (members the union could represent if it wins unit determination) in a representation election. The range of *bargaining rights* encompasses (a) the right to submit proposals, (b) conferences with employers, and (c) full bargaining rights.[25] The *bargaining process* (which will be dealt with in a following section) consists of legal and quasi-legal arrangements that define when, where, and within what time frame bargaining takes place; composition of negotiating teams; authority of negotiating teams to reach a tentative agreement; proposal preparation; offers that can be both economic and noneconomic in nature; and strategies and tactics used in negotiating an agreement. *Impasse procedures* are those invoked when negotiations are deadlocked and the possibilities of reaching common ground for a new contract are unlikely. Mechanisms for breaking an impasse include mediation (bringing in an uninvolved third party to decide the issues), fact finding, and strikes. School personnel have the distinction of striking more frequently, losing more working days, and striking for longer periods than workers in other public sector levels (e.g., city, county, and special districts).[26] *Contract administration* refers to those activities involved in implementing the formal agreement. Disputes emanating from contract administration are resolved through grievance procedures, binding arbitration, and, on occasion, litigation.

The following section examines the collective bargaining process and arrangements through which it is employed to achieve system and human resources function objectives.

COLLECTIVE BARGAINING AND THE HUMAN RESOURCES FUNCTION

As we examine the relationship of the human resources function to the collective bargaining process, it is worth remembering that negotiations result in economic decisions that have considerable significance for the system, its personnel, its clients, and the community. These decisions may have a profound effect on the extent to which aims of the function can be realized.

The human resources function should be designed to facilitate the collective bargaining process and its subprocesses. Personnel administration is concerned not only with protecting the interests of the organization so that established goals can be met but also with *taking advantage of opportunities* in the collective bargaining process to satisfy needs of individual staff members and to create a framework conducive to goal achievement.

There are at least three major functions in collective bargaining that the personnel office is responsible for systematizing. The first is that of coordinating or facilitating the collective bargaining process, that is, organizing and administering the process so that problems can be identified, dealt with, and resolved. Included here is the coordination of central administration activities relating to bargaining goals, strategies, and tactics. An elusive but desirable state of organizational affairs is one in which the planning aspects of collective bargaining are linked to systemwide planning for human resources. If the central administration of a school system is committed to resolving human problems with which it is constantly confronted, chances for lessening union-system conflict are enhanced. The assumption that the antiunion prosystem dichotomy is unsuitable has been challenged by many who believe that systematic planning approaches, when applied to the collective bargaining process in the same manner as they are directed toward other facets of the organization, will minimize the need for personnel to seek assistance from unions to deal with dissatisfactions they experience while at work. The argument that the need for unions would diminish if the human resources function were properly planned and administered is not without substance.

The second function for which the personnel office exercises responsibility in collective bargaining is systematization of collecting, refining, storing, retrieving, and utilizing data essential to the conduct of bargaining. Without availability of current and relevant data, serious concession errors may result.

Next, the personnel office is centrally involved in administering the negotiated contract. This involvement includes keeping systematic records of experiences involved in contract implementation and processing grievances.

The collective bargaining process is closely interrelated with other processes included in the human resources function. Human resources planning (discussed previously) is a primary area of concern for collective bargaining because it establishes the future organization structure, the number of positions, the rules for promotion from within, transfers, staff curtailment, and the nature of the work to be performed. Similarly, matters pertaining to salaries, wages, and collateral benefits are of prime concern to both parties in the bargaining process. Security of and justice for professional personnel through tenure, academic freedom, retirement, termination, and protection from arbitrary treatment is another personnel process closely related to the collective bargaining process.

ELEMENTS OF THE TRANSACTIONAL RELATIONSHIP

Collective bargaining may be defined as a process in which representatives of school personnel meet with representatives of the school system to negotiate jointly an agreement defining the terms and conditions of employment covering a specific period of time. The following summary statements are designed to identify important elements of the transactional relationship by which conflicting demands and requirements of both parties are reconciled. It is useful to review these propositions and to show their relevance to the human resources function before going on to a discussion of various steps in the conduct of the collective bargaining process.

- Members of school systems join unions for economic, psychological, political, and social reasons. The major goal of unions is to maximize opportunities and security for the membership, including a higher standard of living, financial protection, position security, employment rights, opportunity for advancement, maintenance of individual integrity, and attainment of status and respect warranted by members of any profession.

- A major objective of the administration of a school system is to operate the system effectively and efficiently in the public interest and to attain the authority and rights it needs to accomplish this purpose. Unions seek to restrict unilateral decision making by the board of education and to modify decisions so that they are in accord with the needs and desires of the membership. The school system resists moves that encroach on its prerogative.

- The collective bargaining process in the public sector is influenced by a variety of interests that are portrayed graphically in Figure 13.1. The contract ultimately agreed to by both parties will be the result of the combined interaction of various forces, factors, and conditions. Over the years the public, courts, media, government officials, pressure groups, and students have become acutely interested in, drawn into, or attempted to influence settlement of disputes between employees and employers in the public sector. It is important to note also that the conduct of the collective bargaining process (as indicated in Figure 13.1) influences the behavior of different interest groups, each of which brings its values to bear on the process.

- Collective bargaining goes beyond willingness of a board of education to hear from, listen to, or be consulted about conditions of employment. Collective bargaining means *codetermination* of the terms of employment, which, when mutually agreed to, bind both parties to those terms. It means the end of individual and the beginning of group relations between employee and employer.

- Formal acknowledgment (recognition) by a board of education of an employee organization to represent all employees of that jurisdiction

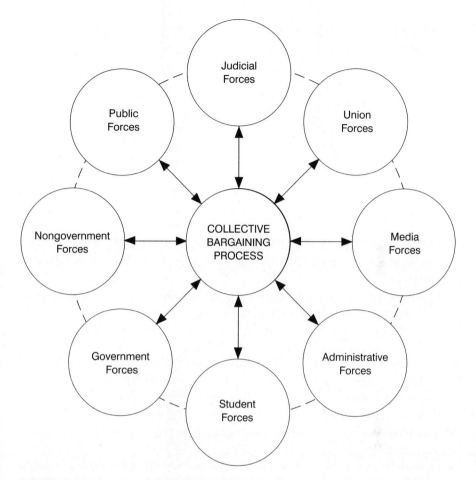

FIGURE 13.1
Forces influencing the collective bargaining process.

(members and nonmembers) means acceptance by the board of the collective bargaining principle.

- There are differences in collective bargaining situations, the outcomes of which will be influenced by relationships between the parties involved, the social context of the bargaining situation, and issues to be negotiated.
- Union behavior is likely to reflect or respond to system policies and practices. Likewise, approaches of the system to collective bargaining will determine the degree of cooperativeness of union leadership.
- The collective bargaining process involves new and emerging responsibilities for the system, modification of the administrative structure, extension of the

human resources function, and different styles of leadership to deal more effectively with emerging employer-employee relationships, the new work ethic, and changing criteria for individual effectiveness in the world of work.

- Collective bargaining in the public sector gives the public employee the right to participate through a chosen representative in determination of personnel policies and practices that affect conditions of employment. The extent of such participation and the principles and procedures governing its exercise are matters for which satisfactory solutions are yet to be reached.

- If more than one personnel association is recognized by the board of education, each of the units separately designates its bargaining representative. Large school systems, for example, may have one bargaining unit for teachers, one for maintenance personnel, and one for secretarial and clerical workers. Coalition bargaining involves a systemwide entity representing all personnel, even though they belong to separate units.

- Any negotiated agreement must be within the limits of the board's lawful authority.

- Even when the board adheres to the principles of collective bargaining, it may receive the views of individuals or other personnel groups not formally recognized as bargaining units. Agreement on the terms and conditions of employment, however, must be reached with the representatives officially designated by the recognized bargaining unit or units.

- Collective bargaining imposes restrictions on both the system and the personnel association or union. Unilateral action is prevented. The system must bargain with the official bargaining unit or units.

- The collective bargaining process, as outlined in Figure 13.2, is one of several alternatives by which a contractual agreement between two parties can be negotiated. Adherence to the process obligates both parties to initiate and maintain bilateral procedures to resolve mutual organizational problems. Each grievance issuing from the contract is an extension of the collective bargaining principle through which both parties direct their efforts to establish terms and conditions of employment.

- Acceptance and existence of the collective bargaining principle by a school system does not imply abandonment of the twin objectives of organizational efficiency and effectiveness. The investment that a system makes in its human resources is considerable. The system should, therefore, focus its attention on controlling costs and maximizing the productive contribution of each of its members in exchange for the system's investment in pay, benefits, opportunities, and position-related satisfactions.

The ultimate goal of collective bargaining is to establish a sound and stable relationship between the system and its personnel. Only by participation of both parties in resolution of disagreements and by good faith on

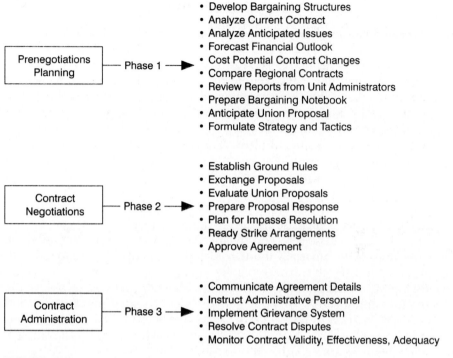

FIGURE 13.2
Model of the collective bargaining process.

either side in yielding to reasonable demands can this end be achieved. Adherence of the board to its responsibilities to constituents is another essential ingredient of harmonious personnel relationships.

THE COLLECTIVE BARGAINING PROCESS

The text that follows considers the actual steps in the **collective bargaining process** by which the board of education and the authorized negotiating unit move from prenegotiation activities to a collective agreement. The framework in which the content of this section is presented is based on a model of the collective bargaining process illustrated in Figure 13.2. This model conceives the bargaining process to embody three phases: *prenegotiations, negotiations,* and *postnegotiations.* Although the discussion that follows focuses on the various facets of prenegotiations preparation (Phase 1), reference will be made to the interrelationship of each phase to the entire bargaining process.

Prenegotiations Planning

Prenegotiations planning (Phase 1 in Figure 13.2) is a continuous activity. It begins with the signing of an agreement in anticipation of the next negotiation. One of the major reasons for the now generally recognized need for greater planning time is the complexity and number of issues to be negotiated. Although *economic issues* (such as salaries, wages, retirement, leaves of absence, group insurance, extra pay for extra work, and compensation incentives) usually constitute the core of agreement discussions, *noneconomic issues* (such as organizational justice, performance appraisal, nonteaching functions, and class size) have become equally important in the teaching profession. Moreover, the range of collateral benefits available to system personnel has increased substantially in recent years. The list of benefits provided for school personnel promises to multiply as the number and amount of benefits increase in the private sector of the economy. Finally, many recent social issues related to education now require resolution at the negotiations table, especially those involving civil rights. Integration, decentralization, transfer of teachers to ghetto schools, and community control of local school attendance units are illustrative agenda items. Accordingly, the need for sophistication at the negotiations table, based on extensive and careful preparation, is no longer debatable for boards of education; time is needed to gather facts, relate them to issues, decide strategy, and complete budget planning after contract settlement.

Planning Premises. Planning premises are advanced here to stress the importance of developing a system of plans and a planning process that will (a) strengthen the relationship between collective bargaining and student learning, and (b) lead to an organization planning culture that methodically pulls together all of the strands of collective bargaining, which when entwined lend substance to system purposes, direction, and future generation of effective educational programs and services (see Table 13.1). Planning premises include:

- *Premise 1*—The organization's information system should be designed to facilitate effective strategic planning for collective bargaining (see Table 13.1).
- *Premise 2*—Political, governmental, technological, economic, and legal factors that affect the administration of modern educational organizations are rather complex and not readily resolved by simple, short-range plans (see Figure 13.2).
- *Premise 3*—The collective bargaining process encompasses a group of activities with considerable potential for exploring the broad range of

TABLE 13.1
Outline of information related to prenegotiations planning.

Illustrative Questions for Fashioning Bargaining Strategy	Bargaining Information Subsystems	Illustrative Information Sources
What is our current school productivity situation?	Pupil, teacher, work group, and organization productivity subsystems.	Local, state, and federal achievement data (pupil, teacher, work group, and system).
How effective are our current plans and programs for student learning?	Program evaluation subsystem.	Accrediting association reports, state agency reports, and evaluations of programs and services by central administration and work units.
How effective has the current union-system agreement been in achieving strategic aims for pupils and staff?	Contract assessment subsystem.	Policy committee appraisals, reports of chief executive and staff, and system intelligence sources such as media, union, staff mediators, and arbitrators.
What strengths and limitations exist in the current contract?	Contract assessment subsystem.	Evaluations by union and system regarding actual versus desired outcomes.

opportunities and strategies in contriving to move the system from where it is to where it ought to be (see Figure 13.2).

- *Premise 4*—A collective bargaining planning structure is an effective mechanism for implementing the strategic aims of the system (see Figure 13.2).
- *Premise 5*—One of the objectives of prenegotiations planning is to generate plans for (a) development of new programs and services, (b) improvement of existing programs and services, and (c) divestment of nonproductive programs and services.
- *Premise 6*—A collective bargaining policy, as illustrated in Figure 13.3, serves as a guide to thinking, discretionary action, and decision making, and provides a common premise for action and policy implementation.

TABLE 13.1, *continued*

Illustrative Questions for Fashioning Bargaining Strategy	Bargaining Information Subsystems	Illustrative Information Sources
What changes should we anticipate in our internal situation? Our external situation?	Internal assessment subsystem. External assessment subsystem.	Community responses to contractual efficacy.
What major issues can we anticipate in the forthcoming negotiations?	Contract assessment subsystem.	Prenegotiation issue exchanges between union and system.
What do we want our future situation to be?	Strategic planning subsystem.	Strategic plans approved by the board of education.
What internal and external constraints may affect achieving the future we desire?	Internal and external subsystems.	Financial, demographic, political, economic, legal, and technological data having a bearing on system change.
What actions should we take to achieve the future situation we desire?	Strategic planning subsystem.	Strategic decisions approved by the board of education.
How shall we program the actions necessary to implement our plans?	Strategic planning subsystem.	Plans allocating responsibilities for implementing strategic decisions.

Organization for Negotiations

In the preceding section we explored the planning aspects of collective bargaining. Illustrated were activities that relate to the specification of the belief system that governs **negotiations** as well as the assembly, summary, and organization of information needed by the policy committee and the negotiating team. At the time the fact-gathering process is initiated, a concurrent decision is also needed to determine what agents will represent the system in negotiating with the teachers' association or, perhaps, the union representing custodial and clerical personnel.

Before representatives of both parties sit down at the negotiations table, it is essential that the system organize activities relating to collective bargaining; that is, that it decide what work is to be done, what mechanisms are needed to perform the work, and what the rules will be for individuals

Riverpark School System's Strategic Aims and the Collective Bargaining Process

Planning aspects of the collective bargaining process in the Riverpark School System focus on achieving strategic aims through three phases: (a) prenegotiations planning; (b) contract negotiations; and (c) contract administration. Action in each of these phases is brought to bear on these concerns:

- In the prenegotiations stage, designing a contract aimed at operating the system effectively and efficiently in the public interest and exercising authority to accomplish these aims.

- Establishing as a basis for negotiations the point of view that the strategic aims for the system as a whole, and for the human resources function in particular, can and should be furthered through the process.

- Taking the position that any negotiated contract places improvement of educational quality for every school attendee as an organization imperative.

- Stressing the premise that a negotiated contract represents an exchange in which the system creates conditions for adequate compensation, fairness, justice, opportunities for career development, and life satisfaction. System members, as partners in the exchange, are assumed to meet performance criteria; adhere to the system's code of ethics and loyalty expectations; contribute to resolution of disrupter problems noted below; and commit to realization of individual, group, and organization goals.

- Providing system members with employment rights such as position information, performance obligations, and supervisor quality; performance assistance, opportunities for career development, and upward mobility; performance recognition; and involvement in the system planning process.

- Employing negotiations to relieve conditions conducive to organization disrupters such as grievances, law suits, strikes, theft, turnover, absenteeism, abuse of benefit provisions, poor morale, alcoholism, drug abuse, and antiorganization behavior.

- Structuring the bargaining process to enhance strategic aims, including a negotiating team, good faith bargaining, resolving contract disputes, maintenance of a negotiations manual, and continuous monitoring of contract outcomes in relation to established objectives.

FIGURE 13.3
Illustration of a policy statement of intent regarding the conduct of collective bargaining.

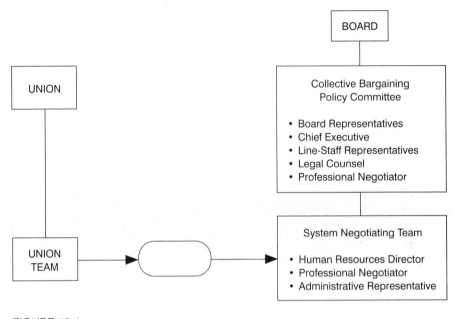

FIGURE 13.4
Model of school system organization for negotiations.

delegated to do the work. As outlined in Figure 13.4, one conceptual approach to a collective bargaining organization consists of two mechanisms: a policy committee and a negotiations team. The functions of each group will be examined in turn.

The Policy Committee.   One approach to resolving the number and complexity of modern collective bargaining issues is a central committee that develops policy recommendations for consideration by the board of education. A major function of this group is to advise the board on systemwide personnel policies related to collective bargaining, such as compensation, security, promotion, transfer, and other conditions of work. A second function is to advise the board with respect to strategies and tactics that should be adhered to in collective negotiations sessions. Related tasks might include reviewing current agreements and proposing modifications, rendering advice and service on the formulation of system proposals, estimating the consequences of either system or union proposals, studying the long-term effects of agreements, and preparing background studies on various aspects of agreements or proposals.

Composition of the policy committee may include representatives from the board of education, the chief executive, line and staff administrative personnel (such as principals, supervisors, and assistant superintendents), legal counsel, and professional negotiators or other consultants. No single model can be suggested for the policy committee. As a generalization, however, it should be noted that the board of education, the immediate superintendency team, and administrative extensions of the superintendency should have representation.

The Negotiating Team.   Much attention has been devoted in the literature to the issue of who will represent the board of education at the negotiations table. Both theory and practice suggest that the conduct of negotiations has many ramifications and requires a combination of individuals with a variety of skills to resolve what often becomes a series of complex problems. Consequently, the model in Figure 13.4 indicates that a team rather than an individual should represent the system, even though responsibility for actual negotiations may be delegated to a single individual (the prime negotiator). The reasoning justifying such a position is that there are few individuals who can fully meet the following requirements:

- Understand the operation of the system in all its ramifications.
- Possess the knowledge to conduct negotiations within the established legal structure.
- Understand the needs of personnel groups and the ability of the system to satisfy those needs.
- Discern trends in personnel policies and procedures.
- Possess the ability to retain the confidence of the system and to make decisions in its behalf.

If the system chooses to have a team similar to the model shown in Figure 13.4, one of the consequences might be that the board of education must delegate considerable authority to the negotiating team. Negotiators for the system need authority to negotiate concessions at the propitious time, without requesting board permission. Further, round-the-clock negotiations are such that a board cannot be convened readily for review of every single item that arises. An illustration of bargaining responsibilities is shown in Table 13.2.

Shaping the Human Organization Through Contract Design

By considering the collective bargaining process as a series of stages, one can identify several aspects of the first phase (planning) in which opportunities exist to develop plans for enhancing both individual and organizational effectiveness. Whether school system personnel are unionized or nonunionized, both the system and the position holders have expectations that must be incorporated into the **contract design**. The *formal contract* identifies what the individual and the organization will exchange; the *informal* (or *psychological*)

TABLE 13.2
Responsibility matrix for collective bargaining process for the Foxcroft school district.

Collective Bargaining Process Time Structure

Responsibility	Phase 1 Prenegotiations Period —to—	Phase 2 Negotiations Period —to—	Phase 3 Postnegotiations Period —to—
Board of school directors	Creates policy committee, and bargaining team. Identifies internal responsibilities and relationships. Approves alternate proposals to be designed and costed.	Approves all variances from negotiations plan. Assures that all issues are resolved at the required levels. Reviews contract prior to approval.	Ratifies agreement. Incorporates agreement elements into official budget. Directs chief executive to communicate agreement details to appropriate parties.
Chief executive	Coordinates all planning responsibilities. Assures preparations are proceeding systematically. Preparation for possible strike. Keeps Board informed about negotiations proceedings.	Serves as Board liaison agent to policy committee and negotiations team. Coordinates all system activities related to bargaining process.	Coordinates communication of contract details to administrative staff. Coordinates implementation of contract.
Bargaining policy committee	Prepares bargaining strategy and negotiating plan for Board review and adoption. Advises Board on personnel policies related to negotiations.	Counsels with negotiations team on actual or anticipated negotiations problems, impasses, and disagreements. Appoints ad hoc committee(s) as needed.	Records experiences concerning planning and negotiating the agreement.

Collective Bargaining Process Time Structure

Responsibility	Phase 1 Prenegotiations Period —to—	Phase 2 Negotiations Period —to—	Phase 3 Postnegotiations Period —to—
Bargaining team	Identifies strike issues for Board. Establishes negotiations strategy and tactics.	Continues bargaining process in accordance with policy guidelines.	Communicates short- and long-term implications of contract (chairperson submits written report).
Professional negotiator	Assesses union motivation, strategy, and goals for impending negotiations. Counsels Board on impact of union proposal in relation to system goals. Provides analyses of strengths and weaknesses of current contract. Counsels and drafts contract language on request.	Conducts bargaining process in accordance with Board objectives. Focuses negotiations on problem solving. Counsels on request. Assures all contract items are in legal compliance. Advises Board on third party utilization.	Evaluates and submits in writing report on all aspects of various negotiations (within 45 days). Reviews contract for omissions, errors, and ambiguities. Counsels Board regarding contract infractions and disputes about contract interpretation.
Director of business affairs	Provides comparative data on system's standing regarding economics, benefits, and other issues. Assesses impact of settlement costs of optional plans.	Evaluates union proposals relative to settlement costs. Renders general support service to negotiations team.	Transforms agreement into budgetary items. Administers fiscal aspects of agreement.

TABLE 13.2, *continued*

	Collective Bargaining Process Time Structure		
Responsibility	Phase 1 Prenegotiations Period —to—	Phase 2 Negotiations Period —to—	Phase 3 Postnegotiations Period —to—
Director of personnel	Prepares strike manual. Provides current and historical information pertinent to planning. Prepares negotiations handbook. Reviews prior grievance and arbitration decisions.	Furnishes negotiations team with relevant information concerning key issues. Prepares press releases as directed by chief executive.	Records experiences concerning administration of agreement (disputes, infractions, and court decisions).
Secretary	Renders secretarial service to planning committee and negotiations team. Develops minutes, records, and reports for negotiations team.	Provides support service to system negotiations personnel.	Prepares official negotiations documents to be stored in information system.

contract is unwritten, but it is constantly in operation between the individual and the system. Both parties seek to have certain conditions of work satisfied.

Assume that a formal agreement is up for renewal. Long before the bargaining begins (Phase 2 of Figure 13.2), two matters need to be considered. First, shaping a new agreement involves consideration of two kinds of contracts: formal and psychological. The formal contract may be viewed as a short- or intermediate-range plan. The psychological contract is designed to sustain the exchange concept as a way of structuring continuing mutual expectations. Schein has described the psychological contract in the following terms:

> Whether people work effectively, whether they generate commitment, loyalty, and enthusiasm for the organization and its goals, and whether they obtain satisfaction from their work depends to a large measure on two conditions:
> The degree to which their own expectations of what the organization will provide them and what they owe the organization in return matches what the organization's expectations are of what it will give and get in return.
> The nature of what is actually to be exchanged (assuming there is some agreement)—money in exchange for time at work; social need satisfaction and security in exchange for hard work and loyalty; opportunities for self-actualization and challenging work in exchange for high productivity, high-quality work, and creative effort in the service of organizational goals; or various combinations of these and other things.[27]

The second concern is that changes of one sort or another occur during the contract agreement period. Board, staff, and administrative compositions change. External and internal environments change. People change. Contract provisions need to be changed. Consequently, feedback is necessary on the quality of the existing agreement, on contemporary conditions affecting a new agreement, and on changes that should be made to progress toward idealized aims for the system's human resources (Figure 2.3). In brief, prenegotiations planning should shape plans in the formal contract to advance the system from where it is to where management wants it to be, especially on such matters as the physical work environment, economic well-being, development and utilization of personnel skills, abilities and interests, individual involvement and interest, and supervisory and work-group relationships.

Contract Reassessment

As depicted in Figure 13.2, prenegotiations preparation includes *analysis of the current contract*. This step is essential to secure information for the board, policy committee, and negotiating team relative to:

- Effectiveness of current contract provisions in achieving organizational objectives.
- New provisions needed.

- Grievances stemming from current provisions.
- Obsolescence of selected provisions.
- Clarification of contractual language.
- Elimination or modification of provisions not conducive to sound personnel administration.[28]

Figures 13.5 and 13.6 have been included to illustrate one approach to current contract analysis. Figure 13.5 capsulizes a questionnaire form sent to system personnel (board members, central staff, principals, and chief negotiator) directly or indirectly involved in the bargaining process. The intent of the questionnaire is to secure facts and opinions regarding the operational impact of the current contract. Figure 13.6 presents the response of one reviewer, who opines that Article XIX of the contract is in need of modification and the reasons underlying that point of view.

Responses to the questionnaire (Figure 13.5) from members of the policy committee provided information that formed the basis for compiling a *Policy Committee Workbook*. The workbook is conceived as a mechanism for systematizing the policy committee approach to the second phase of the bargaining process (Figure 13.2). One of the features of the *Policy Committee Workbook* of the Foxcroft school district is the inclusion of a set of strategic objectives, as well as subobjectives that are considered to be essential in the upcoming union-system contract.

Contractual Posture

Examination of Table 13.2 indicates that the policy committee in the Foxcroft school district is responsible for shaping elements of the proposed

---

A. Are there clauses in the present contract that need modification?

B. What are the reasons for needed modifications? What information has led you to support the need for contract modification?

C. Has the agreement achieved those goals the school system expected to achieve as a result of its formulation and acceptance?

D. Is evidence available to indicate violation of the terms of the agreement?

E. What difficulties have been encountered in administering the agreement?

F. Have desirable items been excluded from the agreement?

G. Does the present agreement permit the flexibility required to administer the school system effectively?

FIGURE 13.5
Foxcroft school district questionnaire for reviewing current contract provisions.

A. Yes, see page 16, Article XIX, Tuition Refund.

B. Although the Article specifies that tuition refunds will be granted only for graduate credits taken to improve professional competence in present assignment or to further a career objective, a preapproval procedure for courses taken *is not required*. This omission creates administrative confusion.

C. No. We are refunding for credits taken in areas of dubious value to the school system. Further, graduate correspondence courses have proven to be less than satisfactory.

D. Yes. Personnel records indicate flagrant abuse of this benefit.

E. Refunds are given without formal review. Administrative controls are nonexistent.

F. No. Administrative decision making is not in existence on this provision. Personnel enroll in courses without administrative controls being exercised. (Principals and central staff are not included. Therefore, course work cannot be tied effectively to staff-development plans.)

FIGURE 13.6
Respondent reaction to one contractual provision (see questionnaire, Figure 13.5).

contract, which represents, in effect, the system's approach to resolving union-system contractual problems, including matters of educational policy, economic issues, personnel appraisal, and board rights and responsibilities. There are several advantages to the system in couching its posture in verbal context. These advantages include:

- A proposal is an appropriate medium for communicating to system members the issues of concern and the position that the board plans to adopt.

- The proposal can be reviewed to determine whether the elements are legal.

- Preparation of the written proposal provides an opportunity to communicate the intent and expectations of the board's planning for human resources.

- In planning the proposal there is time to test major decisions and contemplated action both internally and externally.

- Elements of the proposal can be linked to system and unit objectives that the board hopes to attain, either on a short- or long-term basis.

- Preparation of a proposal places the board in a proactive rather than a reactive posture. It is the board's approach to designing and finding better solutions to union-system problems.

- A proposal represents a planned strategy for initiating, implementing, and administering activities related to the master plan for the system's human resources.

- The proposal is intended to emphasize the board's responsibility for achieving a fair return on the community investment in education.
- Careful analysis of clauses in the current contract, as well as those in system and union proposals for the forthcoming contract, is possible prior to initiation of the second phase (negotiation) of the bargaining process.

Contract wording can be reviewed to test the extent to which the clauses in the proposal specifically and accurately express the system's intentions and expectations in a way that the values by which the organization intends to operate are clearly reflected.

The context of the text that follows is woven around salient features of the latter two phases of the bargaining process (negotiations strategy and contract administration) portrayed in the Figure 13.2 process model.

NEGOTIATIONS STRATEGY

A *strategy* is one of the several different kinds of plans aimed at accomplishing a specific purpose. Decisions involved in developing a strategy are based to a considerable extent on anticipation of responses of those affected by the plan.

Negotiations strategy in collective bargaining (Phase 2 of Figure 13.2) is concerned with the kinds of educational services the system should deliver to its clients, procedures by which it should develop and deliver these services, and means for motivating personnel to cooperate voluntarily in accomplishing system goals. The latter should be such as to enable each individual member of the system to derive from his/her work a suitable standard of living, a sense of dignity and worth, and meaning in a complex society. Thus viewed, collective bargaining strategy is one of several kinds of plans developed by the system to guide both its long-range and daily activities. Its primary intent is not to outmaneuver the other party at the negotiations table; rather, it is concerned with determining the extent to which and the manner in which the *strategic aims of the system can be furthered through the collective bargaining process*. By way of illustration, the strategic aims of the system for its human resources may be to:

- Place improvement of the educational quality for every school attendee at the top of the priority objectives list.
- Create a performance culture that will enhance educational achievement.
- Provide the best compensation and collateral benefits possible within the ability of the school system.
- Provide incentives to enable each individual to give his/her best efforts to the assigned role.

- Provide development opportunities to aid individuals to advance within the system.
- Provide leadership that enables each individual to do his/her best work.
- Establish working conditions, position security, and personal recognition that will make the system an attractive place in which to work and plan a career.

It is hoped that these are the kinds of conditions that the school wants to achieve for its staff, regardless of the presence or absence of a teachers' association or union. Moreover, if a system chooses to engage in collective bargaining, its *strategic planning* will consist in part of considering what proposals it plans to place on the negotiations table to achieve its long-term goals for its personnel and clients. By the same token, strategic planning also involves analysis of proposals to be made by the union, especially in terms of whether and to what extent such plans will assist the institution in attaining its purposes.

The central idea behind strategic planning for collective bargaining is that it offers considerable opportunity for both parties to achieve their expectations. It should be noted also that the link between the human resources function and the collective bargaining process is a strong one—the aims of the human resources function often coincide with those contained in proposals of teacher groups or supportive personnel.

Strategy planning in collective bargaining is essentially a decision-making process consisting of four phases: (a) defining the problem, (b) finding alternative solutions, (c) analyzing and comparing alternatives, and (d) selecting the plan or course to follow. This is to say that plans for achieving system goals for human resources through the collective bargaining process must be based on a definition of what the system intends to achieve, identification of the obstacles involved, examination of alternative courses of action available, and evaluation of the consequences of each suggested plan. The same logic should be employed in evaluating proposals made by personnel groups to the system. The system is interested in judging proposals on the merits of their contribution to the strategic aims of the total operation. The collective bargaining *policy committee* is one mechanism for strategic planning. It can recommend what proposals the system should make, identify and analyze proposals unions are likely to make, and suggest alternatives to both union and system suggestions.

Strategic plans will be affected by a variety of factors, including resources of the school system and attitudes of groups who influence plans (unions, boards of education, communities, and administrative personnel). There are many types of strategies a system can adopt, such as rigid resistance to negotiations, defensive negotiation, avoiding decisive commitments, and, finally, affirmative negotiations. The latter strategy, that of keeping in advance of the other party, is the one this author advocates. This means that the best strategy for dealing with personnel groups in education is to view collective bargaining as a mechanism by which constructive steps can be taken to achieve for people working in the system those arrangements needed to integrate the individual and the organization and to achieve simultaneous satisfaction of both individual and institutional needs. The strategic plan in negotiations really boils down to how the system intends to treat the human resources in its employ. If properly planned, it can be advantageous to everyone.

Modes of Negotiating Behavior

The tactics of collective bargaining are the particular actions taken by either party to achieve strategic objectives. Some actions are taken prior to negotiations; most are made at the bargaining table. Tactics are the means by which policy goals are translated into attainable objectives on which the school system seeks to secure agreement with personnel groups.

Factors involved in choosing among three common **negotiating modes**—competitive, collaborative, and subordinate—have been described by Johnston[29] and are illustrated in Figure 13.7, which contains a synopsis of these three modes, including their dynamics, characteristics, and predicted results. Comparison of the three bargaining modes shown in Figure 13.7 leads to several observations regarding the conduct of negotiations. First, it brings into bold relief the fact that each mode varies from the other in intent, tactics to be employed, planning activities, risk calculation, and outcome predictability.

Second, it supports the premise that there is no universal method for planning and controlling the collective bargaining process. Relationships that exist between the two parties as they enter into negotiations, the economic scene, and the outcome produced by the previous agreement are illustrative of factors that will affect the negotiations mode.

Third, and perhaps most important, the type of negotiations mode to be employed is situational, which requires a careful examination of the circumstances affecting negotiations and the application of those tactics that will likely be effective in a given situation. Each or all of the modes may be utilized, depending on the circumstances. Although the shift from the competitive to the collaborative mode (minimization of conflict) is a desirable form of relationship, its attainment requires both parties to put greater emphasis on mutual goal orientation as well as value and attitude modification.

If the system adopts an affirmative strategy to improve conditions under which its personnel perform services, it is clear that this cannot be accomplished in a single agreement. Tactics may well be concerned with securing agreements on a series of subgoals that contribute to the broad strategic aims mentioned earlier. For example, it is difficult to improve a faulty compensation structure through a single agreement. Extensive improvements in the several elements that make up the compensation

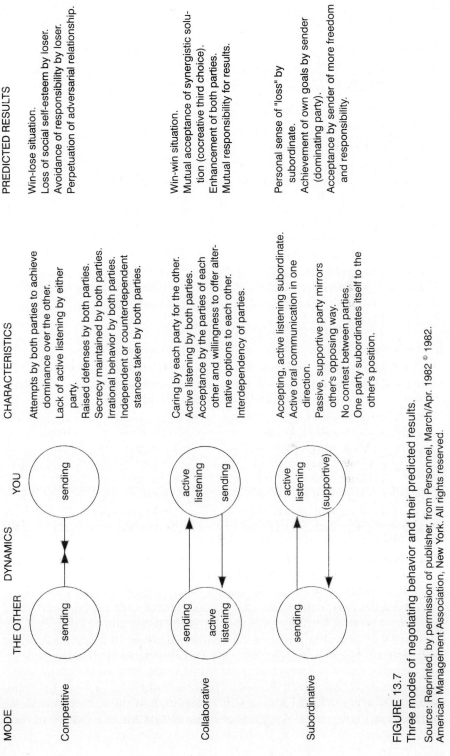

MODE	THE OTHER	DYNAMICS	YOU	CHARACTERISTICS	PREDICTED RESULTS
Competitive	sending		sending	Attempts by both parties to achieve dominance over the other. Lack of active listening by either party. Raised defenses by both parties. Secrecy maintained by both parties. Irrational behavior by both parties. Independent or counterdependent stances taken by both parties.	Win-lose situation. Loss of social self-esteem by loser. Avoidance of responsibility by loser. Perpetuation of adversarial relationship.
Collaborative	sending active listening		active listening sending	Caring by each party for the other. Active listening by both parties. Acceptance by the parties of each other and willingness to offer alternative options to each other. Interdependency of parties.	Win-win situation. Mutual acceptance of synergistic solution (cocreative third choice). Enhancement of both parties. Mutual responsibility for results.
Subordinative	sending		active listening (supportive)	Accepting, active listening subordinate. Active oral communication in one direction. Passive, supportive party mirrors other's opposing way. No contest between parties. One party subordinates itself to the other's position.	Personal sense of "loss" by subordinate. Achievement of own goals by sender (dominating party). Acceptance by sender of more freedom and responsibility.

FIGURE 13.7

Three modes of negotiating behavior and their predicted results.

Source: Reprinted, by permission of publisher, from Personnel, March/Apr. 1982 © 1982. American Management Association, New York. All rights reserved.

structure, such as salaries and wages, collateral benefits, extra pay for extra work, overtime, and noneconomic provisions, are generally not realized simultaneously. To secure incremental gains leading to achievement of a specific objective, the tactics may have to include:

- Putting into writing the strategic aims of the system and the tactical objectives to be pursued in the forthcoming session. This information should be developed by the policy committee and circulated among the system's policy and administrative groups, such as the board of education, policy committee, negotiating committee, and administrative personnel not included in these units.

- Vesting one person, the chief negotiator, with authority to make decisions for the system. (The chief negotiator is usually a professional negotiator who works under the direction of the superintendent of schools.)

- Focusing negotiations on problem solving, de-emphasizing legalism.

- Ensuring that procedural matters will not stifle the conduct of negotiations.

- Getting agreement on procedures in advance.

- Exchanging proposals of both parties prior to negotiating.

- Deciding the order in which items to be negotiated will be placed on the agenda. There is an advantage to getting agreement on issues on which it is likely that the parties will be in accord.

- Securing a thorough consideration of the facts relating to each agenda item proposed by either party.

- Following an agenda designed to facilitate a systematic approach to problem solving.

- Timing the tactics so they will have maximum effect. When to listen, speak, object, stand firm, concede, compromise, counterpropose, refute, or postpone action are tactical techniques whose application depends on the situation at the negotiations table.

- Resolving and formalizing agreement on less controversial issues, then proceeding to the more complex matters.

Much has been written about the tactics of negotiations, but there is no pattern of tactical activity applicable to every negotiating situation.[30] Let this be clear: when two parties come to a negotiations table, the facts of the situation are paramount. Neither side can choose freely the issues to be negotiated or the tactics to be employed in settling them. Different objectives require different tactics. Some problems are long standing, arising again and again. The facts or conditions pertaining to current problems and issues will determine the kinds of negotiations that take place and their final outcome.

When the formalities of certifying a union as the exclusive unit bargaining agent for any group of school personnel are completed, both parties (the union and the system) are required to negotiate collectively. Bargaining issues are commonly described as *mandatory, permissive,* and *illegal.* Mandatory issues refer to conditions of work (e.g., compensation or working periods), permissive issues are those outside the mandatory category (e.g., educational policy), and illegal subjects are those in conflict with regulatory provisions.

Modes of negotiating behavior are influenced by a variety of factors, for example, governmental restraints, economic conditions, bargaining strategies, bad-faith bargaining, dispute mechanisms, and court injunctions. The ultimate aim of collective bargaining is to arrive at an agreement to which both parties are signatories, the terms of which they are obligated to follow for a specified period. Strategies invoked at the time of negotiations determine not only the duration of the bargaining period but also the number and kinds of dispute mechanisms employed for resolution purposes.

Scope of Bargaining

The substance of what is to be negotiated at the negotiations table may be classified as economic or noneconomic issues, although they are not completely separable. Many noneconomic provisions have attendant costs, either direct or indirect. Economic issues relate to the level, form, structure, and method of compensation and collateral benefits. Noneconomic issues generally include those relating to such matters as management and union rights, nondiscrimination clauses, hours of work, vacations, sick leave, leaves of absence, seniority, grievance procedures, and terms of the contract (dates).

The **scope of bargaining** has been a negotiating issue fraught with conflict throughout the history of public sector bargaining. At the core of the matter is the question of what is bargainable, especially as it pertains to noneconomic issues. Unions have sought to extend their sphere of influence into the policy role of organizations by insisting that the scope of negotiations include items traditionally considered to be organizational prerogatives. It is not uncommon for unions to include in agreement proposals provisions pertaining to the curriculum, the instructional system, the performance appraisal system, transfer, promotion, seniority, residency requirements, discipline of union members, termination, and staff development. Institutional efforts to blunt union incursion into policy matters usually take the form of (a) a management rights clause asserting that control and operation are matters vested exclusively in management, except for those limited by provisions in the agreement, or (b) a clause listing all matters not subject to joint determination.[31]

The problem of what is bargainable is wrought with complexities. How to draw the line between mandatory and voluntary demands is not distinct and remains fluid, shifting and changing with administrative rulings, legislation, and court decisions.[32] Expanding the scope of bargaining to include educational policies (especially those that are not conditions of employment) is criticized on the grounds that it is undemocratic, constituting the negotiations of public policies with one interest group while other interest groups are systematically excluded.[33]

The last word has not yet been spoken or written on the scope of bargaining. Problems stemming from the union concept of equalizing the power of the public employee and public employer are numerous, raising questions as to whether collective bargaining in the public sector is desirable public policy, whether public policy on personnel matters should be a joint determination, and whether the present system of public sector bargaining is the best that can be devised to serve the interests of individual system members, the union, the school system, and the public. Experience has indicated that current approaches have not been able to meet all of these conflicting goals. Unless there is greater concern for a balancing of the public interest, what can be anticipated is greater public insertion into the collective bargaining process through various entries to ensure that its interests are served.

Impasse Resolution and Strikes

The collective bargaining process, as illustrated in Figure 13.2, involves two parties who make and live with an agreement in the form of a written contract. In negotiating the terms of a future contract and in living with an existing contract, disagreements and disputes are inevitable. Disagreements arise over (a) matters of interest (i.e., matters of concern to both sides in negotiating a new agreement) or (b) matters of right (i.e., those that relate to interpretation of provisions in the existing contract). There are occasions when proceedings reach an **impasse** or deadlock and neither side will move from its stated position. At this point in the process, various methods of resolving disagreements may be employed. The following text focuses on methods of dispute resolution.

Trilateralism.   When two parties are unable to resolve a dispute, either over matters of interest or matters of right, public employment policy, either in the form of federal or state legislation, provides for a third party to enter the controversy. The third party may be either a mediator or an arbitrator (often a government official), who helps the disputants to reach an agreement. Activities of a mediator center on efforts to stimulate, persuade, and influence the parties to reach an agreement; the mediator or conciliator has no authority to decide the issues involved. Moreover, the mediator's activities are centered on negotiations involving a new contract. In effect, most mediation is new-contract mediation, not grievance mediation under an existing contract.

Arbitration, it should be noted, is primarily concerned with matters of right, that is, interpreting provisions in the existing contract. When the two parties involved cannot agree on how to resolve an issue stemming from the existing agreement, the procedure most commonly employed is referred to as arbitration, of which there are two types: voluntary and compulsory. Arbitration, generally speaking, is a process that involves the use of an impartial third party who collects pertinent facts from the disputants and proceeds to make a decision, which is usually binding. Compulsory arbitration usually involves both compulsory submission of the dispute to arbitration and compulsory acceptance of the decision. Thus, arbitration is the terminal step in the contract's grievance procedure. Under voluntary arbitration, either side may initiate action to take the unresolved grievance to arbitration. Under compulsory arbitration, especially in disputes in the public sector, the dispute resolution is transferred to a government-appointed agency. Legislative provisions often establish a fact-finding procedure, which is the designation of neutral third parties to assemble facts and make recommendations based on these facts. This procedure may help the parties involved reach an agreement voluntarily, which they might not do were not such facts and recommendations set forth.

Figure 13.8 lists procedures that are available and have been employed in union-system negotiations to resolve impasses. The procedures are listed in terms of frequency use.

Mediation and fact finding appear to be procedures most frequently found and utilized in settling union-system disputes. The final impasse procedure (after bargaining, mediation, and fact finding have been exhausted) may be the right to **strike,** or it may be one of several forms of arbitration that the parties have agreed to as an alternative to a strike. Experience in

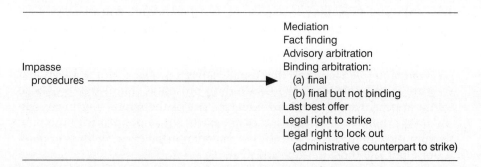

FIGURE 13.8
Procedures utilized to resolve union-system impasses.

the public sector with binding arbitration has resulted in such criticisms of its employment as:

- The authority of arbitrators to order the expenditure of school district funds with no accountability to the public is tantamount to taxation without representation.
- Binding arbitration usurps government authority.
- Binding arbitration subverts the very purposes for which government was designed.
- The arbitration process is not conducive to good faith collective bargaining.
- Permitting third parties not accountable to the electorate to engage in the process is an illegal delegation of legislative authority.
- Binding arbitration violates the one-person, one-vote standard mandated by the Fourteenth Amendment.
- Third party appointees frequently do not represent the public interest.

When an impasse occurs between the board and the teacher union in public education, state controls govern the resolution process. The following provisions are representative of state controls:

- An orderly procedure has been established by state law, setting a deadline for the commencement of bargaining, with an impasse procedure included in the legal provisions.
- Impasse resolution procedures allow for the parties of interest to come to agreement with voluntary mediation. In cases where this is not successful, or if specified deadlines are not met, state-level procedures are invoked.
- Impasse procedures include mediation, fact finding, and compulsory arbitration.
- A grievance procedure is mandated as a part of any agreement, with a definition of grievance limited to the interpretation or application of the agreement.

One of the state controls that usually governs public sector strikes is that they are lawful only when the fact-finding process is completed. Strikes, it would appear, have become an integral part of the bargaining process in the public domain. Although strikes are extremely unpopular with the public (and they are not typical results of negotiation), they and efforts to abolish or eliminate them must be anticipated.

As an alternative to the prohibition against school employees having the right to strike, the American Association of School Personnel Administrators has proposed the following resolution for states considering ways of dealing with strikes against the public and its governing representatives:

- A prohibition against retroactive contract settlements if there is a strike.
- A state procedure for a secret ballot election for all individuals in a bargaining unit to accept or reject the board's last and final offer on all issues. If accepted by the employees, the contract becomes binding on all parties; if rejected, the employees would follow the strike vote procedure or continue negotiations.
- A state-required procedure that governs how and when strike votes would be conducted and a mandatory cooling-off period. The state would select a fact finder or fact finders to hear the impasse issues and make recommendations for settlement. If the report was rejected by the parties, the strike would be allowed.[34]

Problems involved in preparing for a strike include what to do about various services, as illustrated in Table 13.3. Preparation of a strike manual by a committee assigned to the task of deciding in advance what arrangements are needed is a desirable practice. The strike manual automatically becomes the controlling document if a strike occurs, and may contain two categories of information: (a) what system procedures and responsibilities will be if operations continue during a strike, and (b) procedures to be employed if the system ceases operation for the duration of a strike. The manual may also include instructions to system administrators about their roles as well as the conduct of operations to bind the wounds when the strike is over.

The major limitation of current approaches to resolving impasse in public sector bargaining is the lack of finality, whether the third party is a fact finder, mediator, conventional arbitrator, final offer arbitrator, or mediator-arbitrator. The search continues for means different and more creative than current public sector impasse techniques that will lead to more constructive union-system relationships through satisfaction of mutual interests.

TABLE 13.3
Illustration of service areas and types of emergency prearrangements needed in anticipation of a strike.

Support Services	Instructional Services	Administrative Services
Food	Instructional plans	Public relations
Transportation	Substitute service	Record keeping
Security		Picket lines
Building maintenance		Staff meetings
Relations with suppliers		Board meetings
		Law enforcement
		Documentation of events
		Suspension of compensation, benefits

Paramount to any approach designed to correct current drawbacks in impasse procedures is the recognition of the right of personnel to negotiate the terms of employment, commitment to the public interest principle, cooperative system—union contract planning, and awareness of union-system obligation to develop a partnership of responsibility.[35]

Contract Agreement

The agreement arrived at by the school system and the personnel negotiating unit stipulates in writing the nature of the relationship that will exist between the two parties for a specified period of time. Composition of the agreement generally consists of four functional categories, each one of which has a specific purpose: (a) security or rights of both parties, (b) compensation and **working conditions,** (c) individual security, and (d) administration of the agreement. Each of these divisions of the agreement will be discussed briefly in the following text.

Security of Both Parties.   One of the first steps in collective bargaining is to settle the extent of recognition to be accorded bargaining units representing teachers or other personnel in the school system. Security clauses in agreements covering personnel groups negotiating with the school system may include such matters as the description of the bargaining unit, duration of the agreement, degree of recognition of the union or association, avoidance of discrimination based on union membership, permissible union activity on school premises, and access to school executives by union officials.

Prerogatives of the school system in the agreement are intended to affirm the rights the system must have to discharge administrative functions with which it is entrusted. Collective bargaining is a two-way street, and the system must have flexibility to administer the enterprise properly. When it bargains its rights away, the system renders itself incapable of carrying out its responsibilities. Protective clauses in agreements reserve to the system discretion in such personnel matters as size of staff, position content, teaching or work schedules, promotion, transfer, discipline, dismissal, staffing assignments, appraisal, and leaves of absence. In addition, the system may demand clauses stipulating protection of personnel from union intimidation, exercise of good faith in the use of privileges granted, restraint in publishing false or misleading information about the system, and a zipper clause that ensures negotiations will not be reopened for a specified period of time. In short, the system must clarify in the contract what it considers to be its rights and privileges.

Compensation and Working Conditions.   The core of any agreement negotiated collectively between two parties is the individual personnel contract. The school system, under the terms of the agreement, agrees to provide certain remunerations and to establish working conditions for employees in exchange for specified services. In recent years, considerable debate has taken place with respect to what is negotiable between the two parties. High on the list of items frequently considered at negotiations sessions are salaries, wages, collateral benefits, class size, consultation in setting school calendars, lunch and rest periods, adequacy of physical facilities for teachers, transfers, teacher planning time, protection of teachers from physical assault, nonteaching functions, control of student behavior, school closings at noon before holidays and vacations, academic freedom, and recruitment of unqualified personnel.

Pressures from personnel groups to increase the scope of bargaining must be anticipated as standard procedure. There is nothing wrong with conducting bargaining that includes a wide range of matters of interest to personnel. Two criteria against which the negotiability of any item should be tested are (a) its relationship to the strategic aims of the system for its human resources and (b) its impact on the prerogatives the system must retain to administer the institution effectively.

Individual Security. Figure 13.9 illustrates a response by a policy committee to a union proposal concerning class size. The intent of Figure 13.9 is to indicate one facet of a school system's manner of taking steps through bargaining by objectives to accomplish desired educational results.

Clauses in the agreement that cover the security of an individual member of the staff are designed generally to protect him/her against arbitrary treatment from the school system, the union or association, other personnel or personnel groups, and community groups. This type of security is of as much concern to the system as to the individual or the personnel negotiating group.

Protection against arbitrary acts of the system are dealt with through an appeals system or grievance machinery. As a matter of sound personnel policy and with or without collective bargaining, the system should establish grievance procedures to protect the individual against arbitrary treatment in such areas as salaries, wages, transfer, promotion, and dismissal.

Protection of the individual against arbitrary acts of the union or association is dealt with by including clauses in the agreement covering these matters. The right of an individual, for example, to belong or not to belong to the union and to be free from intimidation by the union is generally guaranteed by the system in its prerogative clauses.

Protection from pressure groups within the community needs to be guaranteed by both parties. Within recent years, during attempts to decentralize urban schools, some members have been threatened by arbitrary demands for their removal without recourse to an appeals system. As the struggle for control of education in attendance units goes on, the need for both the union and the system to join hands to protect the security of individuals should be self-evident.

Content of bargaining objectives proposal to extend personnel health care maintenance program to include provisions for employee assistance.

A. Contract bargaining item — Extension health care maintenance program for school personnel.

B. Contract proposal clause number — Article XVI.

C. Financial or nonfinancial — Financial: will increase health care benefits from 20 to 31 percent of current personnel compensation payments.

D. Contract objective — Improve measurable effects on students' learning abilities and attitude through enhancing personnel health and performance effectiveness.

E. Contract priority level — On a scale ranging from 1 to 5, this item's relative importance to all other bargaining proposals is rated at priority level 2.

F. Ideal solution — Employee assistance program would improve learning outcomes; aid personnel performance; reduce problems related to absenteeism, chronic illness, lateness, alcoholism, substance abuse, AIDS, leaves of absence, disciplinary action, and interpersonal relations; and lower long-run costs of insurance premiums.

G. Current situation — No systematic plan currently in operation.

H. Solution obstacles — Insurance premiums will increase initially, union will probably withhold participation and support, it will be difficult to manage both job-related and non–job-related problems, and selection of range and channels of assistance will be open to criticism.

I. Legal ramifications — Identification of personnel needing assistance, terminations, privacy ensurement, and challenges to use of public funds.

J. Present cost — None. No formal program in operation.

K. Change cost — Health insurance premium per employee per month will increase from $2,640 to $3,150 (19.3%). Combination of system, union, and individual contributions will make up cost.

L. Likelihood of objective attainment — Proposal is within the bounds of reality. Chances are better than even that union resistance will diminish when the social responsibility, as well as the self-interests of the individual, the group, and the organization, are fully understood.

FIGURE 13.9
Policy committee workbook planning illustration: bargaining by objectives.

In the final analysis, problems that impinge on the security of personnel are so complex that protection of the individual is not possible without cooperation of both parties. A system consists of individuals bound together, willingly or not. Accordingly, on issues such as individual security there is much to be lost by failure to agree. It is worth noting, however, that there are some things that agreement between the parties cannot achieve in and of itself. The right of an individual to progress within the system according to his/her initiative and ability cannot be guaranteed by the union. Moreover, the right of effective supervision, leadership, and exercise of individual initiative can be fostered most effectively by the system. It goes without saying that when the system is stripped of its rights to administer functions for which it is held responsible, rights of the individual are certain to be lost in the process.

Administration. Day-to-day administration of the agreement negotiated by the two parties is based on application of grievance machinery, which is intended to settle violations of the agreement promptly, deal with disputes relating to the interpretation of specific clauses in the agreement, or handle problems arising in areas not covered by the agreement. Grievance procedures, including steps to be taken, time limitations, and provisions for arbitration, are discussed briefly in the following section of this chapter.

CONTRACT ADMINISTRATION

After the agreement has been ratified by both parties, each has a responsibility to make the contract work. Although rights and obligations of both the system and the union are specified in agreement clauses, disputes are certain to arise over the meaning of the language in the agreement, as well as over methods employed to implement the contract. Because numerous disputes arise from the interpretation of contractual language, care should be taken to use language that will minimize misinterpretation, and the agreement should be reread carefully before it is signed.

It is conceivable that problems will arise from practically every provision in the agreement. When they do occur, the contractual means designed for their resolution is the **grievance procedure**. A grievance is a wrong, real or fancied, considered as grounds for complaint. The grievance procedure provides system members the right to appeal what they consider to be a violation, misinterpretation, misapplication, or inequitable or improper application of any provision of the existing union-system contract. In some contracts, a grievance is defined as a conflict arising from interpretation of a negotiated agreement; whereas a complaint is construed to be a conflict arising from the interpretation of policies, rules, and regulations not in the negotiated agreement. Practice varies with regard to grievance and complaint procedures. In brief, a formal grievance is an allegation that a provision, or provisions, of the agreement have been violated.

Characteristics of a formal grievance procedure, as illustrated in Table 13.4, include a series of steps through which a grievance may be appealed to several levels of the administrative structure for settlement; stated time limits for presentation of grievances, rendering of decisions, and taking of appeals; and provision for arbitration as the final step in settling an unresolved grievance. Actually, the possibilities for settlement of a grievance are the same as those available for settling an impasse in negotiations. These include arbitration (calling in a third party who is given the authority to issue a binding decision), mediation (using a third party to help both parties reach an agreement voluntarily), and strike (work stoppage or cessation of service).

The grievance procedure has been referred to as the heart of the agreement. This is because the practical test of an agreement lies in its day-to-day application. Either side may attempt to adjudicate through grievance machinery differences of opinion arising out of meaning, interpretation, and application of various provisions of the agreement.

Effectiveness of the grievance procedure, as with any other step in the collective bargaining process, depends on those responsible for its administration. During administration of the agreement, the personnel director or his/her counterpart is able to perform various functions essential to making the contract a positive force for advancing the interests of both parties in the relationship. These functions include:

- Recording and reporting to the superintendent of schools progress and problems encountered in administering the contract.
- Interpreting the agreement to the administrative staff.
- Providing ways of instructing line administrators to follow grievance procedures built into the agreement. Administrators at the operating level, for example, will need counseling in problems relating to work assignments, discipline, and performance appraisal.
- Recording experiences concerning administration of the agreement.
- Meeting frequently throughout the contract period with union or association representatives. The purpose is to inform each other of problems encountered, examine ways of improving the administration of the contract, discuss revision of those provisions that are ineffectual because of semantic weaknesses, or discuss failure to cope with unexpected contingencies.
- Coordinating efforts to make the grievance-arbitration process an instrument for achieving and maintaining organizational justice.
- Identifying trouble spots within the system.

It has been said that there is more to a marriage than a wedding. So it is with collective bargaining. When the high drama of negotiating an agree-

TABLE 13.4
A state-mandated grievance procedure.

	For Use in Disposing of Claims Related to Interpretation of Terms of Agreement			
Steps	Administration of Board Representation	Grievant or Employee Organization Representation	Time Limits	Comments
I	Principal or other first level supervisor	Grievant, with or without building representative of employee organization	Appropriate time limits on both parties for answer to grievance and appeal decision	*Step I* Person, or persons, initiating the alleged grievance shall present the grievance, in writing and on a form provided by the employer, to the building principal or other first level supervisor within (*time limit*) days after its occurrence. The building principal or other first level supervisor shall reply to the grievance within (*time limit*) days after initial presentation of the grievance.
II	Assistant Superintendent, Personnel Director (with Principal or others as desired)	Grievant and representative of employee organization		*Step II* If the action in Step I above fails to resolve the grievance to the satisfaction of the affected parties, the grievance shall be referred to the assistant superintendent or personnel director (or other designated person).

TABLE 13.4, *continued*

	For Use in Disposing of Claims Related to Interpretation of Terms of Agreement			
Steps	**Administration of Board Representation**	**Grievant or Employee Organization Representation**	**Time Limits**	**Comments**
III	Superintendent (with Principal or others as desired)	Grievant and representative of employee organization		*Step III* If the action in Step II above fails to resolve the grievance to the satisfaction of the affected parties, the grievance shall be referred to the superintendent.
IV	Final decision by the Board of Education except when the parties to such an agreement are required by Section 903 of Act 195 to go to binding arbitration for resolution of such a grievance.		Recommendation or decision within (appropriate specific number of) days	*Step IV* If the action in Step III above fails to resolve the grievance to the satisfaction of the affected parties, the grievance shall be referred to the Board of Education (Section 903 of the Act).
V	Final decision by arbitrator on those issues subject to arbitration as defined in Section 903 of the Act. Both parties bound to decision except where enabling legislative action is required, in which it is binding only if such legislation is enacted as provided in Section 901 of the Act.			*Step V* If the action in Step IV above fails to resolve the grievance to the satisfaction of the affected parties, the grievance shall be referred to binding arbitration as provided in Section 903 of the Act. If the grievance fails to meet the criteria of Section 903 of the Act, the decision of the Board of Education in Step IV shall be final.

Source: Pennsylvania School Boards Association, Act 195 (Harrisburg, PA: Pennsylvania School Boards Association, 1973), 57ff.

ment has passed, the problem of two parties learning to live together begins. What both parties do in the process of administering the agreement and how they do it become important to maintenance of sound relationships between the system and its personnel groups.

In summation, **contract administration** (Phase 3 in Figure 13.2) includes four elements: implementation, conflict resolution, enforcement, and evaluation. Few negotiators are blessed with wisdom to foresee every problem, every conflict, and every clause with a potential for misinterpretation. Essential to positive agreement outcomes is the establishment of a union-system plan for resolving disputes and minimizing their effect on organizational operations.

Appraisal is one of the functions of the administrative process designed to see how well performance conforms to plan. It is concerned with the effects of all plans and procedures in relation to their contribution to system purposes. Appraisal of the collective bargaining process is an absolute necessity. The system, for example, wants to know:

• Strengths and weaknesses of the existing agreement.
• Sources of disputes in administering the agreement.
• Effectiveness of the negotiating team and its individual members.
• Impact of the agreement on the motivation of personnel.
• Desirability of modifying the negotiations strategy and tactics of the system.
• Steps that should be taken to improve the bargaining process.
• Whether the contract promotes attainment of strategic goals.

Coordination of appraisal activities relating to the negotiations process, like other matters pertaining to the conduct of the human resources function, is a responsibility of the individual in charge of the function. This includes the tasks of recording experiences and gathering facts and observations vital to the preparatory stages of the next agreement to be negotiated.

In sum, the collective bargaining process is a tool by which the system and its personnel solve problems growing out of their relationship. Its future direction in public education is something only time can tell. Its strength lies in providing an opportunity for improving organizational democracy and in providing a fundamental human relations tool for the betterment of education.

REVIEW

In this chapter, we have emphasized the view that the ultimate shape of a school district's future will be determined in part by how successfully it manages a handful of key bargaining issues. Chief among them is the manner in which it envisions and links bargaining with strategic aims of the human resources function (Figure 2.3). Three subsets of bargaining strategy include *prenegotiations planning, negotiations,* and *contract administration.*

The effect of the collective bargaining performance will be shared by the system, its human resources, and those for whom it delivers educational programs and services. Unless negotiation strategies address both parties' substantive and relationship priorities, negotiation outcomes will fall short of strategic expectations.

REVIEW AND DISCUSSION QUESTIONS

1. In light of the criticisms of teacher unions identified in this chapter, should teachers be permitted to strike? Why?

2. It is widely proclaimed that because arbitrators are not responsible to the public, they should not be allowed to make binding rulings on economic issues. What is your response to this claim?

3. Form two groups of five class members each. One team will be the union and the other will be the school board. Furnish each team with data, supporting information, bargaining issues, and instructions for negotiating matters involved in an actual negotiating situation, and have the teams role-play such a negotiation. The rest of the class will critique the exercise.

4. Write a brief on the reasons underlying the rigidity of the regulatory environment in which collective bargaining takes place in the public sector.

5. Form a group of five class members to prepare for contract negotiations in a school system, and have the group share its plans with the class. Can the preparation be improved? In what way?

6. Examine a grievance procedure in a union-system contract. What are its strengths and limitations? How can its effectiveness be improved?

7. Examine a union-system contract. How many clauses relate to economic provisions? To noneconomic provisions? Commentary?

8. What is meant by "bargaining by objectives"? What are the arguments in favor of this approach? Against it?

9. Identify major clauses in a teacher-school district contract (e.g., union rights, system rights, seniority, etc.).

10. If the right of teachers to strike were abolished, what alternatives would you propose to the state legislature?

11. Choose a state where collective bargaining by teacher unions is permissible, and examine the state regulatory controls. What kinds of bargaining issues are mandatory, voluntary, and illegal?

12. Explain briefly why each of the following factors is a potential determinant of negotiations impasses: environmental factors, structural characteristics of the union and the school system, interpersonal factors, and union-system bargaining history.

13. What is the major difference between mediation and arbitration? What are the relative advantages and disad-

vantages of these procedures in impasse resolution?

14. Why are cost considerations usually ignored in public sector bargaining for resolving disputes between public employees and public employers? Consider state costs, system costs, union and union member costs, taxpayer costs, school district costs, noneconomic costs, and indirect costs. Do the costs in any state justify bargaining outcomes? Are there alternatives that are more cost efficient and cost effective than the contemporary approaches? What are the reasons for the paucity of university and governmental research on bargaining costs in relation to learning outcomes?

15. Is there a factual foundation for the allegation that school boards are less resistant and more amenable to union demands than employers in the private sector? Defend your stance.

16. "Public sector bargaining parties couldn't care less about public opinion." What is your response to this statement? If you agree with it, what do you think are the implications of this image for education reform?

17. *Group Project.* The instructor will secure copies of a teacher union-system contract and make the following assignments:

> *Student A*—Identify those items in the contract that refer to system obligations.
>
> *Student B*—Identify those items that refer to union obligations.
>
> *Student C*—Describe the grievance procedures.
>
> *Student D*—Describe the impasse procedures.
>
> *Student E*—Describe state regulatory controls in the contract.
>
> *Student F*—Examine the contract for indications of the existence of a school system human resources strategy.
>
> *Student G*—Examine the contract for (a) personnel termination procedures, (b) right to strike, and (c) clauses pertaining to noneconomic considerations.

CHAPTER EXERCISE 13.1

Directions: The following exercise contains selected union bargaining goals of a state teachers' association. Determine whether you completely disagree, somewhat disagree, somewhat agree, or completely agree with each of the following statements:

- Association members shall be paid similar salaries based on education and experience regardless of the district in which they are employed.

- The career salary should be attained in no more than ten years by every member holding an advanced degree.
- Every local shall negotiate a salary package that provides minimum starting salaries for all professional employees of $30,000.
- Employment of teachers should be limited to those who have graduated from NCATE-accredited institutions.

- During their first year of teaching, candidates to become professional teachers would be designated as *interns*.
- Teacher *licensing* and *advanced certification* should be required of all candidates in order to become professional teachers.
- Every local association shall negotiate contract language that reduces nonprofessional responsibilities.
- Every local association president shall be given released time during the student day to perform duties of the office.
- Every negotiated contract should establish voluntary and involuntary transfer procedures.
- The negotiated contract language should guarantee adequate preparation time during the school day for all teachers.
- Every local association shall negotiate contract language governing the proper induction of teachers.
- Every local association shall negotiate contract language that guarantees

- every member the right to choose professional development courses without system restrictions.
- No local association shall accept insurance caps or reduction of benefits.
- Contract language governing class size shall take into account the application of instructional technology in large and small classes.
- The financial burden of health care insurance for retirees should be treated in the same manner as insurance for active members.
- Every member shall be guaranteed fully employer-paid family dental insurance.
- Every member shall be guaranteed a fully employer-paid medical plan that provides family coverage for hospitalization and major medical care.
- Every salary package shall provide a minimum salary increase of ten percent plus increment.
- The local association should not support retention of teachers who are not serving their clients well.

CHAPTER EXERCISE 13.2

Directions: This exercise contains selected contract language from a negotiated agreement between a school system and its teachers' union. Determine whether you completely disagree, somewhat disagree, somewhat agree, or completely agree with each of the following statements:

- The Board of Education reserves the right to add or delete any position at its discretion.
- The Board of Education reserves the right to fill or not to fill any position at its discretion.
- An extra curricular contract shall not be considered part of the professional contract of any teacher.

- Unused sick leave shall accumulate from year to year and may be taken during any year without restriction.
- Membership in the school district sick leave bank shall be required of all members of the bargaining unit.
- The teacher's regular work day shall not exceed 7 hours and 30 minutes.
- No new appointment shall be made while there is a suspended professional employee available who is properly certified for the position.
- A central file on each member of the bargaining unit will be maintained by the District.

- A member of the bargaining unit has no right to review the official file maintained in the central office.
- A member of the bargaining unit shall have the right to request on an annual basis that certain materials be removed from the official file.
- Although the employer agrees to protect the confidentiality of personnel references and other similar documents, the employer or its representatives shall not establish separate personnel files that are not available for the employee's inspection.
- No employee may be permitted to remove personnel information from system files.
- After one year, the bargaining unit member may request the removal of any or all materials from the file not required to be kept by legal provisions.
- An involuntary transfer or reassignment shall be made only after a meeting between the member involved and a member of the central administration.
- No reprisal of any kind shall be taken by the Board or any member of the administration against the union or its representatives relative to participation in any grievance procedure.
- Disciplinary action shall be limited to demotion, unsatisfactory ratings, and insubordination.
- Any member of the bargaining unit may be reduced in rank and compensation when there is sufficient grounds for such action.
- Sexual relationships between bargaining unit members or between bargaining members and students shall be considered grounds for dismissal.
- Violation of provisions of the District's Code of Ethics shall be considered grounds for disciplinary action by the Board of Education.
- A grievance shall be filed by the Board for absenteeism abuse by any member of the bargaining unit.
- Criticism of the Board, administration, or any employee made in public will be considered an act of disloyalty and subject to disciplinary action.

CHAPTER EXERCISE 13.3

Directions: The instructor will furnish class members with digest copies of (a) a school system budget and (b) the budget of the teachers' union. In preparation for class discussion, students should answer the following questions:

- In regard to the system budget, what items are included in the budget for contract negotiations? Legal and/or consultant fees? Arbitration and mediation? Negotiations preparation? Conduct of negotiations? Contract administration? Grievance responses?
- In regard to the union budget, what are the sources of teacher union income? What is the percentage of total union income from system member dues? From other income? What percentage of union-budgeted income is devoted to consultant fees? State teachers' association? Political activities? Advertising? Contract administration? Grievance filing? Office expenditures? Court costs?

CHAPTER EXERCISE 13.4

Directions: According to an article in the *Wall Street Journal* (Vol. CCXIV, No. 110, December 6, 1994, A-1), firing public sector employees is cumbersome. "The Chicago Park District says it is cutting steps to fire incompetent workers from 84 to a handful." "Columbus, Ohio, has one hearing officer to handle grievance and discipline actions for 6,500 unionized workers." With this information in mind, answer the following questions:

• What are the implications of these conditions for public sector management?

• What steps should a board of education take to prevent external or internal factors from resolving personnel dismissal problems?

• Because personnel dismissal is a board function, what can management do to offset unjustified union attempts to interfere with the personnel dismissal process?

• What has been the history of union behavior in public education regarding teacher dismissal?

CHAPTER EXERCISE 13.5

Directions: Two recent developments in public school education have been (a) unfunded state education mandates and (b) the surging costs of settling and administering union-system contracts. With this information in mind, read the two examples and then answer the questions that follow.

Example A—In one state 174 state mandated regulations affect each school district; only 4 are reimbursable. The bulk of the regulations deal with school personnel.

Example B—In the same state the average yearly increase in settling

personnel contracts was 8.08 percent, nearly twice the yearly increase in inflation.

• What are the financial implications in a school district in your state for financing unfunded mandates?

• What is the dollar cost for settling a negotiated teacher contract?

• Could mandated expenditures and contract settlement costs be better redirected toward system strategic objectives?

NOTES

1. Public Service Research Council, Public Sector Bargaining and Strikes (Vienna, VA: Public Service Research Council, 1978), 1.

2. Education Commission of the States, State Education Collective Bargaining Laws (Denver, CO: Edu-

cation Commission of the States, 1984).

3. William P. Knoester, "Administrative Unionism: What Kind of Solution?" Phi Delta Kappan 58, 8 (February 1978), 419–22; see also Bruce S. Cooper and Kent F. Murrmann,

"Effects of Unionization on School Administrators," Administrative Notebook 30, 1 (1982), 1–4.

4. For descriptions of alternative bargaining models, see Phi Delta Kappan 63, 4 (December 1981), 244–48; and Vernon H. Smith, "Fuel for the Coming Battles over Public Sector Unions and Bargaining," Phi Delta Kappan 62, 5 (January 1981), 402.

5. Smith, 403.

6. Grace Sterrett and Antone Aboud, The Right to Strike in Public Employment (Ithaca: New York State School of Industrial and Labor Relations, 1982), 3–4; and Smith, 403.

7. Smith, 403.

8. Center for Educational Policy and Management, The Effects of Collective Bargaining in Public Schools (Eugene, OR: College of Education, University of Oregon, 1981).

9. Chester A. Finn, Jr., "Teacher Unions and School Quality: Potential Allies or Inevitable Foes?" Phi Delta Kappan 66, 5 (January 1985), 334.

10. Douglas E. Mitchell and Charles T. Kerchner, The Dynamics of Public School Collective Bargaining and Its Impact on Governance, Administration, and Teaching (Washington, DC: National Institute of Education, 1981).

11. Myron Lieberman, Public Sector Bargaining (Lexington, MA: Lexington Books, 1980), Chapter 6.

12. Richard Wynn, "The Relationship of Collective Bargaining and Teachers' Salaries," Phi Delta Kappan 63, 4 (December 1981), 237; and Twentieth Century Fund Inc., Report of the Twentieth Century Fund Task Force on Federal Elementary and Secondary Education Policy (New York: Twentieth Century Fund Inc., 1983).

13. Antimo Papale, "The Impact of Centralized Bargaining in Quebec," Phi Delta Kappan 63, 4 (December 1981), 250–51.

14. Lieberman, Chapter 5.

15. Ibid.

16. Ibid.

17. Sterrett and Aboud, 3.

18. Lieberman, Chapter 7.

19. Gary Sykes, "Contradictions, Ironies, and Promises Unfulfilled: A Contemporary Account of the Status of Teaching," Phi Delta Kappan 65, 2 (October 1983), 91.

20. Susan M. Johnson, Teacher Unions and Schools (Cambridge, MA: Institute for Educational Policy Studies, Harvard Graduate School of Education, 1982).

21. Myron Lieberman, "Teacher Unions and School Quality: Folklore by Finn," Phi Delta Kappan 62, 9 (January 1985), 343.

22. Ibid.

23. Ibid.

24. John A. Fossum, Labor Relations: Development, Structure, Process (Dallas, TX: Business Publications, Inc., 1982), 419.

25. Ibid.

26. Ibid. 426–27.

27. Edgar H. Schein, Organizational Psychology, © 1980, p. 99. Reprinted by permission of Prentice-Hall, Inc., Englewood Cliffs, NJ.

28. For additional information on contract reassessment, see Dale Yoder and Paul D. Staudohar, "Auditing the Labor Relations Function," Personnel 60, 3 (May-June 1983).

29. Robert W. Johnston, "Negotiation Strategies: Different Strokes for Different Folks," Personnel 59, 2 (March-April 1982), 36–44.

30. Useful suggestions for negotiations strategy are developed in Dennis A. Hawver, "Plan Before Negotiating . . . and Increase Your Power of Persuasion," Management Review 73, 2 (February 1984), 46–49; Gary G. Whitney, "Before You Negotiate; Get Your Act Together," Personnel 59, 4 (July-August 1982), 13–27; Vida Scarpello and James Ledvinka, Personnel/Human Resource Management, Third Edition (Boston: PWS-Kent, 1988), Chapter 18; and Wendell L. French, The Personnel Management Process, Sixth Edition (Boston: Houghton Mifflin Company, 1987), Chapter 24.

31. Dale Beach, Personnel: The Management of People at Work, Fourth Edition (New York: Macmillan Publishing, 1980), 113–14.

32. French, 543.

33. Myron Lieberman, Public Sector Bargaining (Lexington, MA: Lexington Books, 1980), Chapter 4; Myron Lieberman, "Teacher Unions and Educational Quality: Folklore by Finn," Phi Delta Kappan (January 1985), 342.

34. American Association of School Personnel Administrators, Trends in Collective Bargaining in Public Education (Seven Hills, OH: American Association of School Personnel, 1978), 7.

35. Phi Delta Kappan 63, 4 (December 1981) devotes considerable attention to collective bargaining topics, including compulsory binding-interest arbitration, centralized bargaining, integrative bargaining, collective bargaining, fact finding, compulsory unionism, dismantling collective bargaining, bargaining and salaries, and a critical review of teacher bargaining.

SUPPLEMENTARY READING

Asherman, Ira G.; and Sandra V. Asherman. The Negotiation Sourcebook. Amherst, MA: Human Resources Development Press, 1990.

Barling, Julian; Clive Fullagar; and K. Kevin Kelloway. The Union and Its Members. New York: Oxford University Press, 1992.

Bascia, Nina. Unions in Teachers' Professional Lives. New York: Teachers College Press, 1993.

Cheng, Charles. Teacher Unions and the Power Structure. Bloomington, IN: Phi Delta Kappa, 1981.

Dougherty, Edward J.; and Laval S. Wilson. "The Making of a Contract for Education Reform." Phi Delta Kappan 71, 10 (June 1990), 791–97.

Finn, Chester E., Jr. "Teacher Politics." Commentary (February 1983).

Freedman, Warren. The Employment Contract: Rights and Duties of Employers and Employees. Westport, CT: Quorum Books, 1989.

French, Wendell L. The Personnel Management Process, Sixth Edition. Boston: Houghton Mifflin Company, 1987.

Gorton, Richard A.; Gail T. Schneider; and James C. Fisher. Encyclopedia of School Administration and Supervision. Phoenix, AZ: The Oryx Press, 1988.

Green, Ronald Michael; William A. Carmell; and Peter S. Grey. State by State Guide to Human Resources Law. New York: Panel Publishers, Inc., 1992.

Kerchner, Charles T.; and Julia E. Koppich. A Union of Professionals. New York: Teachers College Press, 1993.

Lovell, Ned B. Grievance Arbitration in Education. Bloomington, IN: Phi Delta Kappa, 1985.

Martin, Roderick. Bargaining Power. New York: Oxford University Press, 1992.

Masters, Frank M. "Teacher Job Security under Collective Bargaining Contracts." Phi Delta Kappan 45, 7 (March 1975), 455–58.

Medcalf, Robert L. "A Successful Board Approach to Collective Bargaining." National Forum of Educational Administration and Supervision Journal 7, 3 (1990–91), 415+.

Morrison, William F. The Prenegotiations Handbook. New York: John Wiley and Sons, 1986.

Nelson, R. R. "State Labor Legislation Enacted in 1989." Monthly Labor Review 113 (January 1990), 35–36.

Rauth, Marilyn. "Exploring Heresy in Collective Bargaining and School Restructuring." Phi Delta Kappan 71, 10 (June 1990), 781–85.

Rist, Marilie C. "Teacher Empowerment and Teacher Unions." The Education Digest LV6 (February 1990), 6–9.

Seifert, Roger V. Teacher Militancy: A History of Teacher Strikes: 1896–1987. New York: Taylor and Francis, 1987.

Godin, Seth, Editor. The 1994 Information Please Business Almanac and Desk Reference. Boston: Houghton Mifflin Company, 1993.

Tuthill, Doug. "Expanding the Union Contract: One Teacher's Perspective." Phi Delta Kappan 71, 10 (June 1990), 775–81.

Watts, Gary; and Robert M. McClure. "Expanding the Contract to Revolutionize School Renewal." Phi Delta Kappan 71, 10 (June 1990), 765–75.

Wynn, Richard. Collective Bargaining: An Alternative to Conventional Bargaining. Bloomington, IN: Phi Delta Kappa, 1985.

Appendix A

Method for Estimating School Enrollment

DIRECTIONS FOR RETENTION-RATIO ENROLLMENT PROJECTIONS (GRADES K-12)

Procedures for anticipating probable future pupil enrollment for a school system involve (a) collection and organization of data, (b) analysis, and (c) extrapolation of observed trends to some future date. Information in Table A-1 is organized into three associated phases. Phase I (data formation), Phase II (ratio calculations), and Phase III (enrollment projection). Each phase is described in the following text.

Phase I: Data Formation

1. Select a *key grade* that shows promise of linkage to birth data and from which consecutive *survival ratios* can be determined. For a variety of reasons, enrollments in the lower grades tend to be unstable with respect to births. Accordingly, Grade 2 was chosen as the *key grade* from which estimates in other grades are developed.

2. Obtain *grade enrollments* for a sufficient number of years to establish a trend series. Eleven years, including the most recently available year, were selected for Table A-1.

3. Obtain *birth data* corresponding to the years when children enrolled in Grade 2 (key grade) would have been born. In Table A-1, seven years would have elapsed between birth and Grade 2 enrollments for each year of the trend series.

4. Organize *birth and enrollment data* so as to facilitate the following: (a) survival analysis from birth to Grade 2, from Grade 2 to Grade 3, and so on; and (b) establishment of ratios for deriving Grade 1 enrollments from Grade 2 enrollments, and Kindergarten enrollments from Grade 1 enrollments.

The data base illustrated in the first phase of Table A-1 consists of birth-rate and enrollment information needed to calculate pupil survival ratios from cohort to cohort, and to extrapolate those trends so as to obtain estimates of future enrollments. It is worth noting at this point that treatment of ancillary information such as nonpublic school enrollment trends, population and housing projections, population migration patterns, employment of residents, land use zoning ordinances, and plans of external agencies (both public and private), which may impact on population fluctuations, is beyond the scope of the methodology described here. Although information of the kinds shown in Table A-1 is central to the retention-ratio enrollment projection process (and may in fact reflect related demographic influences), serious consideration should be given to any additional information that might aid in interpreting the eventual projections. Credibility of the projections will be enhanced to the extent that observations based on a variety of relevant sources can be reconciled with the end results illustrated in Table A-1.

Following is a discussion of ways in which retention ratios are obtained by analysis of the enrollment data.

Phase II: Trend Analysis

The purpose of calculations during Phase II of the retention-ratio projection process is to obtain survival rates from each grade to the next, beginning with births. These are based on past experience and will be used to extrapolate observed enrollments into the future. *The underlying assumption is that those factors that shaped enrollment trends during the recent past will persist in the immediate future.*

Survival ratios based on enrollments summarized under *Data Formation* in Table A-1 consist of those obtained for each year in the series and *means* for the included period. Their derivation will be explained in Steps A to D, which follow, and illustrated in Tables A-2 to A-5. For this illustration, Grade 2 was selected as the key grade to be linked to births and from which enrollments in other grades will flow. Survival rates will be determined in the following order:

- Birth to Grade 2 (Step A and Table A-2).
- Grade 2 to Grade 1 (Step B and Table A-3).
- Grade 1 to Kindergarten (Step C and Table A-4).
- Grade 2 to Grade 3 (Step D and Table A-5).

Enrollments in Grade 2 will be linked by ratio to those in Grades 1 and 3. Survival rates to Grades 4 and beyond are each calculated from enrollment in the preceding grade.

Step A—Calculate survival ratios from birth to Grade 2 for each year of the series. For example:

TABLE A-1
Retention-ratio projection, Kindergarten to Grade 12.

Year of Birth	Number of Births	Year of School (September)	2	1	Kdg.	3	4	5	Grade 6	7	8	9	10	11	12	Total Enrollment K–12
Phase I: Data formation																
1973	211	1980	151	146	124	156	177	174	189	195	158	192	267	202	199	2330
1974	217	1981	143	145	125	142	164	168	165	190	176	169	242	230	180	2239
1975	170	1982	130	128	117	152	137	152	167	156	155	190	195	181	182	2042
1976	191	1983	128	138	113	130	148	143	148	150	145	191	215	127	114	1890
1977	180	1984	125	125	114	129	138	142	150	148	138	181	217	165	124	1896
1978	195	1985	122	112	116	128	129	142	153	146	134	171	219	203	133	1908
1979	177	1986	115	127	129	133	118	138	136	151	142	160	249	191	168	1957
1980	192	1987	125	146	155	124	133	119	140	145	132	160	199	229	153	1960
1981	202	1988	151	183	157	124	121	129	130	137	143	149	220	187	159	1990
1982	199	1989	187	185	186	161	141	117	131	133	127	161	210	184	153	2076
1983	218	1990	182	194	165	195	171	133	134	138	124	169	202	164	156	2127

TABLE A-1, *continued*

Grade 2 to Birth 7 Years Previously	1 2	K 1	3 2	4 3	5 4	6 5	7 6	8 7	9 8	10 9	11 10	12 11
Phase II: Trend analysis												
1980	.716	1.02	.86		1.05	.95	.95	1.01	.90	1.07	1.26	.86	.89
1981	.659	1.12	.98	.94	.97	.93	.99	.95	.82	1.08	1.15	.75	.79
1982	.765	1.00	.85	1.06	.97	1.04	.97	.90	.93	1.23	1.13	.65	.63
1983	.670	1.10	.90	1.00	1.06	.96	1.05	1.00	.92	1.25	1.14	.77	.98
1984	.694	1.02	1.02	1.01	1.00	1.03	1.08	.97	.91	1.24	1.21	.94	.81
1985	.626	.97	.91	1.02	.92	1.07	.96	.99	.97	1.19	1.46	.87	.83
1986	.650	1.02	.88	1.09	1.00	1.01	1.01	1.07	.87	1.13	1.24	.92	.80
1987	.651	.97	.85	1.08	.98	1.01	1.09	.98	.99	1.13	1.38	.94	.69
1988	.748	.98	.85	.99	.98	.97	1.09	.98	.99	1.13	1.38	.94	.69
1989	.940	1.02	.96	1.07	1.14	.97	1.02	1.02	.93	1.13	1.41	.84	.82
1990	.835			1.05	1.06	.94	1.15	1.05	.93	1.33	1.26	.78	.85
Average (mean) ratio:	.723	1.02	.91	1.03	1.02	.99	1.03	.99	.92	1.18	1.26	.83	.81

Phase III: Enrollment projection

1984	1991	230	166	179	198	187	199	169	137	133	127	146	213	168	133	2155
1985	1992	242	175	218	251	171	191	197	174	136	122	150	184	177	136	2282
1986	1993	296	214	276	197	180	174	189	203	172	125	144	189	153	143	2359
1987	1994	375	271	217	219	220	184	172	195	201	158	148	181	157	124	2447
1988	1995	294	213	241	219	279	224	182	177	193	185	186	186	150	127	2562
1989	1996	327	236	241	219	219	285	222	187	175	178	218	234	154	122	2690
1990	1997	327	236	241	215	243	223	282	229	185	161	210	275	194	125	2819
1991	1998	327	236	236	212	243	248	221	290	227	170	190	265	228	157	2923
1992	1999	320	231	233	212	243	248	246	228	287	209	201	239	220	185	2982
1993	2000	315	228	233	212	238	248	246	253	226	264	247	253	198	178	3024

151 enrollees in Grade 2 (1980/211 births (1973) = .716
143 enrollees in Grade 2 (1981/217 births (1974) = .659, etc.
(See Table A-2 for the preceding and remaining calculations,
including the mean.)

Step B—Descending from Grade 2, calculate the ratios of Grade 1 to Grade 2 enrollments. For example:

.146 Grade 1 (1980/143 in Grade 2 (1981) = 1.02, etc.
(See Table A-3 for the preceding and remaining calculations,
including the mean.)

Step C—Descending from Grade 1, calculate the ratios of Kindergarten to Grade 1 enrollments. For example:

TABLE A-2
Calculation of survival ratios in the Foxmoor school district from birth to Grade 2.

Live Births to Residents[a]		Grade 2 Enrollments as of October 1[b]		Survival Ratios Column 4/Column 2
Column 1 Year	Column 2 Births	Column 3 Year	Column 4 Enrollment	Column 5 Survival Ratios
1973	211	1980	151	.716
1974	217	1981	143	.659
1975	170	1982	130	.765
1976	191	1983	128	.670
1977	180	1984	125	.694
1978	195	1985	122	.626
1979	177	1986	115	.650
1980	192	1987	125	.651
1981	202	1988	151	.748
1982	199	1989	187	.940
1983	218	1990	182	.835

11-year mean ratio (Column 5 mean)... = .723

Notes: [a] Selected birth year precedes enrollment date by 7 years.
[b] A more refined measure of educational demand is average daily membership, defined as "aggregate days pupil belonged," each from the date of admission until withdrawal. The pupil accounting period selected may be other than monthly, but should be of sufficient length to sample pupil demand and consistent from year to year.
How to read this table: Data in Column 2 are births shown under Phase 1 of Table A-1. Those in Column 4 are Grade 2 enrollments in the same data base. Survival ratios derived in Column 5 become the basis of Grade 2 enrollment to birth ratios shown in Phase 2 of Table A-1.

TABLE A-3
Calculation of *retroactive* enrollment ratios in the Foxmoor school district from Grade 2 to Grade 1.

Grade 2 Enrollments as of October 1		Grade 1 Enrollments as of October 1		Survival Ratios Column 4/Column 2
Column 1	**Column 2**	**Column 3**	**Column 4**	**Column 5** Retroactive
Year	**Enrollments**	**Year**	**Enrollments**	**Enrollment Ratios**
1981	143	1980	146	1.02
1982	130	1981	145	1.12
1983	128	1982	128	1.00
1984	125	1983	138	1.10
1985	122	1984	125	1.02
1986	115	1985	112	.97
1987	125	1986	127	1.02
1988	151	1987	146	.97
1989	187	1988	183	.98
1990	182	1989	185	1.02
—	—	1990	194	—

10-year mean ratio (Column 5 mean)... = 1.02

Note: How to read this table: Data in Column 2 are Grade 2 enrollments shown under Phase I of Table A-1 for school years 1981 through 1990; those in Column 4 are first grade enrollments for school years 1980 through 1990 in the same data base. Survival ratios derived in Column 5 become the basis of ratios shown in $\frac{1}{2}$ column, Phase II, Table A-1.

.124 in Kindergarten (1980/145 in Grade 1 (1981) = .86, etc.
(See Table A-4 for the preceding and remaining calculations, including mean.)

Step D—Ascending from Grade 2, calculate the ratio of Grade 3 to Grade 2 enrollments. For example:

.142 in Grade 3 (1981/151 in Grade 2 (1980) = .94, etc.
(See Table A-5 for the preceding and remaining calculations, including the mean.)

The procedure followed in Step D is repeated to establish survival ratios from each grade to the next for the following year in the remaining grades. Means determined from the survival ratios are the cohort survival ratios to be used in the projection calculations in Phase III of the retention-ratio projection process. As calculated in Tables A-2 to A-5, for example:

TABLE A-4

Calculation of retroactive enrollment ratios in the Foxmoor school district from Grade 1 to Kindergarten.

Grade 1 Enrollments as of October 1		Kindergarten Enrollments as of October 1		Survival Ratios Column 4/Column 2
Column 1	Column 2	Column 3	Column 4	Column 5 Retroactive
Year	Enrollment	Year	Enrollment	Enrollment Ratios
1981	145	1980	124	.86
1982	128	1981	125	.98
1983	138	1982	117	.85
1984	125	1983	113	.90
1985	112	1984	114	1.02
1986	127	1985	116	.91
1987	146	1986	129	.88
1988	183	1987	155	.85
1989	185	1988	157	.85
1990	194	1989	186	.96
—	—	1990	165	—

10-year mean ratio (Column 5 mean).. = .91

Note: How to read this table: Data in Column 2 are Grade 1 enrollments shown under Phase I of Table A-1 for school years 1981 through 1990; those in Column 4 are Kindergarten enrollments for school years 1980 through 1990 in the same data base. Survival ratios in Column 5 become the basis of ratios shown in the K/1 column, Phase II of Table A-1.

Grade 2/births = .723
Grades ½ = 1.02
Grades K/1 = .91
Grades ¾ = 1.03, etc.

These calculations are summarized in Phase II of Table A-1.

Phase III: Enrollment Projection

Calculations employed during the third phase of the enrollment projection process are directed toward estimation of *future enrollments*. At this stage, *mean survival ratios* obtained in Phase II are applied to each cohort from year to year. Because Grade 2, as previously noted, has been selected as the key grade from which other enrollment estimates will flow, the sequence of calculations illustrated below in steps A to G and Tables A-6 to A-9 will be as follows:

• Project births as needed (Step A).

- Project Grade 2 (key grade) enrollments from births (Step B and Table A-6).
- Project Grade 1 enrollments from Grade 2 enrollments (Step 2 and Table A-7).
- Project Kindergarten enrollments from Grade 1 enrollments (Step D and Table A-8).
- Project enrollments for Grade 3 from Grade 2 enrollments (Step E and Table A-9).
- Project enrollments for remaining grades, each from the preceding grade's enrollments (Step F).
- Summarize enrollment estimates by desired grade organization of attendance units (Step G).

Step A—Project births beyond those most recently available. Note that those shown in Table A-1 are actual through 1990, the terminal year of

TABLE A-5
Calculation of survival ratios in the Foxmoor school district from Grade 2 to Grade 3.[a]

Grade 2 Enrollments as of October 1		Grade 3 Enrollments as of October 1		Survival Ratios Column 4/Column 2
Column 1	Column 2	Column 3	Column 4	Column 5 Retroactive
Year	Enrollments	Year	Enrollments	Enrollment Ratios
1980	151	1981	142	.94
1981	143	1982	152	1.06
1982	130	1983	130	1.00
1983	128	1984	129	1.01
1984	125	1985	128	1.02
1985	122	1986	133	1.09
1986	115	1987	124	1.08
1987	125	1988	124	.99
1988	151	1989	161	1.07
1989	187	1990	195	1.04
1990	182	—	—	—

Notes: [a] Calculation of survival rates from Grade 3 to Grade 4, from Grade 4 to Grade 5, and through successively higher grades will require use of the format illustrated. (Each enrollment in a grade for a given school year is divided by enrollment in the next-lower grade for the preceding year.)

How to read this table: Data in Column 2 are Grade 2 enrollments shown under Phase I of Table A-1 for school years 1980 through 1990; those in Column 4 are third grade enrollments for school years 1981 through 1990 in the same data base. Survival ratios derived in Column 5 become the basis of ratios shown in the $3/2$ column, Phase II of Table A-1.

TABLE A-6
Calculation of future estimated enrollments in the Foxmoor school district (Grade 1).

Column 1 Year	Column 2 Births	Column 3 Survival Ratio Grade 2/B	Column 4 Year	Column 5 Grade 2 Enrollments (Col. 2 × Col. 3)
1984	230	.723	1991	166
1985	242	.723	1992	175
1986	296	.723	1993	214
1987	375	.723	1994	271
1988	294	.723	1995	213
1989	327	.723	1996	236
1990	327	.723	1997	236
1991	327	.723	1998	236
1992	320	.723	1999	231
1993	315	.723	2000	228

Note: How to read this table: Births in Column 2 are those shown in Phase III of Table A-1. These are multiplied by the mean survival ratio, *birth to Grade 2,* shown in Phase II of Table A-1, to obtain Grade 2 estimates shown in Column 5 above. Derivation of the mean survival ratio is illustrated in Table A-2.

actual enrollments. Births shown from 1990–1993 in Table A-1 are based on assumptions as to probable trends.

Step B—Project Grade 2 (key grade) enrollments from births (birth/Grade 2 mean survival ratio) = .723. For example:

$$.723 \text{ X } 230 = 166 \text{ in Grade 2, 1991}$$
$$.723 \text{ X } 242 = 175 \text{ in Grade 2, 1992}$$
$$.723 \text{ X } 296 = 214 \text{ in Grade 2, 1993, etc.}$$

Step C—Project Grade 1 enrollments for those obtained for Grade 2 (Grade 1/Grade 2 mean survival ratio = 1.02). For example:

$$1.02 \text{ X } 175 = 179 \text{ in Grade 1, previous year 1991}$$
$$1.02 \text{ X } 214 = 218 \text{ in Grade 1, previous year 1992}$$
$$1.02 \text{ X } 271 = 276 \text{ in Grade 1, previous year 1993, etc.}$$
(See Table A-7 for remaining calculations)

Step D—Project Kindergarten enrollments from those obtained for Grade 1 (Kindergarten/Grade 1 mean survival ratio = .91). For example:

$$.91 \text{ X } 218 = 198 \text{ in Kindergarten, previous year 1991}$$

.91 X 276 = 251 in Kindergarten, previous year 1992
.91 X 217 = 197 in Kindergarten, previous year 1993, etc.
(See Table A-8 for remaining calculations.)

Step E—Project enrollments for Grade 3 from those obtained for Grade 2 (Grade 3/Grade 2 mean survival ratio = 1.03). For example:

1.03 X 182 (see Table A-1, Phase I, 1990) = 187 in Grade 3 the following year, 1991
1.03 X 166 (Phase II, 1991) = 171 in Grade 3, following year 1992
1.03 X 175 (Phase II, 1992) = 180 in Grade 3, following year 1993, etc.
(See Table A-9 for remaining calculations.)

Step F—Project enrollments for remaining grades from those obtained for each preceding grade.

Step G—Summarize projected enrollments to reflect desired grade organization of attendance units.

TABLE A-7
Calculation of future estimated enrollments in the Foxmoor school district (Grade 2).

Column 1 Year	Column 2 Grade 2 Enrollments	Column 3 Survival Ratio Grade 1/2	Column 4 Year	Column 5 Grade 1 Enrollments (Col. 2 × Col. 3)
1992	175	1.02	1991	179
1993	214	1.02	1992	218
1994	271	1.02	1993	276
1995	213	1.02	1994	217
1996	236	1.02	1995	241
1997	236	1.02	1996	241
1998	236	1.02	1997	241
1999	231	1.02	1998	236
2000	228	1.02	1999	233[a]

Notes: [a] Because of the absence in Column 2 of enrollment estimates beyond year 2000, projected enrollment for the last year shown in Column 5 will be assumed as constant for the following year, as in Table A-8.

How to read this table: Grade 2 enrollment estimates shown in Column 2 are those shown in Phase III of Table A-1 as beginning in 1992. Their derivation from births is illustrated in Table A-6. Enrollment estimates projected for Grade 1 in Column 5 above are obtained by multiplying the Grade 2 estimates by the Grades 1/2 survival ratio shown in Phase 2 of Table A-1. Derivation of the ratio used is illustrated in Table A-3.

TABLE A-8

Calculation of future estimated enrollments in the Foxmoor school district (Kindergarten).

Column 1 Year	Column 2 Grade 1 Enrollment	Column 3 Survival Grade (K/1)	Column 4 Year	Column 5 Kindergarten Enrollments (Col. 2 × Col. 3)
1992	218	.91	1991	198
1993	276	.91	1992	257
1994	217	.91	1993	197
1995	241	.91	1994	219
1996	241	.91	1995	219
1997	241	.91	1996	219
1998	236	.91	1997	215
1999	233	.91	1998	212
2000	233	.91	1999	212[a]

Notes: [a] Because of the absence in Column 2 of enrollment estimates beyond year 2000, projected enrollment beyond the last year shown in Column 5 will be assumed as constant for the following year.

How to read this table: Grade 1 enrollment estimates shown in Column 2 are those contained in Phase III of Table A-1. Their derivation from Grade 2 estimates is illustrated in Table A-7. Enrollment estimates projected in Column 5 above for Kindergarten are obtained by multiplying Grade 1 enrollments by the Kindergarten and Grade 1 ratio found in Phase II of Table A-1. Derivation of this ratio is illustrated in Table A-4.

Summary

Procedures required to estimate future enrollments are of three kinds: gathering and ordering demographic data, analyzing the information for trend indications, and projecting current enrollments based on evaluation of the findings. Table A-1 and the related illustrations are accordingly organized into three phases, with all of the base data, derived trends, and eventual projections contained in Table A-1.

In interpreting enrollment projections, it should be kept in mind that the end results are subject to decisions made during data treatment, such as which and how many years are to be used in determining average grade to grade survival rates and as to which grade to link to births. It should also be remembered that trends adopted for estimating future enrollments, however valid in the short term, are increasingly subject to unknown factors with the passage of time.

The foregoing cautions suggest that estimates of future demand for education be tempered by (a) examination of factors external to the school system that are likely to impact on the school population, (b) adjusting of

TABLE A-9
Calculation of future estimated enrollments in the Foxmoor school district (Grade 3).

Column 1 Year	Column 2 Grade 2 Enrollments	Column 3 Survival Ratio Grade 3/2	Column 5 Column 4 Year	Grade 3 Enrollments (Col. 2 × Col. 3)
1990 (actual)	182	1.03	1991	187
1991	166	1.03	1992	171
1992	175	1.03	1993	180
1993	214	1.03	1994	220
1994	271	1.03	1995	279
1995	213	1.03	1996	219
1996	236	1.03	1997	243
1997	236	1.03	1998	243
1998	236	1.03	1999	243
1999	231	1.03	2000	238

Note: How to read this table: Grade 2 enrollments shown in Column 2 are those contained in Phase III of Table A-1. Their derivation from births is illustrated in Table A-6. Enrollment estimates projected for Grade 3 in Column 5 above are obtained by multiplying the Grade 2 enrollments by the 3/2 survival ratio found in Phase II of Table A-1. Derivation of the ratio used is illustrated in Table A-5.

estimates by plus and minus an increasing percentage from year to year into the future, and (c) periodic examination and modification of extrapolations in light of experience and new evidence.

Appendix B

Health Care Legislation Proposals and Education Enactments by the 103rd Congress

Throughout this text emphasis has been given to the influence of the external environment on the human resources function in public education. A summary follows of two types of initiatives by the 103rd Congress (1994), health care reform proposals and education enactments, that have far-reaching implications for managing the human resources function.

The *health care reform proposals* represent a spectrum of approaches, and even though they were not enacted in 1994, they lay the groundwork for passage of a national program of health insurance. In effect, the kind of future health care plan adopted by Congress will have considerable impact on how health care packages are negotiated in school districts across the nation. The health care bills introduced in the 103rd Congress include:

- H.R. 3600/S.1757 (President Clinton's plan)
- H.R. 1200/S.491 (McDermott/Wellstone)
- H.R. 3080/S.1533 (Michel/Lott)
- H.R. 3222/S.1579 (Cooper/Breaux)
- H.R. 3698/S.1743 (Stearns/Nickles)
- H.R. 3704/S.1770 (W. Thomas/Chafee)
- H.R. 3918/S.1807 (Santorum/Gramm)

The *education enactments* by Congress will have considerable import in school districts on its human resources. For example, funds have been allocated for site-based decision making, recruitment and retention of highly qualified teachers, class size reduction, technology training for students and teachers, and improvement of education opportunities in rural and urban schools. Education enactments by the 103rd Congress include:

- Elementary and Secondary Education Act Reauthorization (ESEA)
- Goals 2000: Educate America Act

- Safe and Drug-Free Schools and Communities Act
- Schools-to-Work Act of 1993
- National Service Trust Act
- School Readiness Programs Under the Human Services Reauthorization Act of 1994
- Technology for Education Act
- Student Loan Reform Act

Glossary

Absenteeism formula. (Total hours of absence) ÷ (Total hours scheduled) × 1000

Academic freedom. The ability of professional personnel to exercise intellectual independence and to encourage it in the classroom without impediment or undue restraint.

Administrative rationality. Formation of organizational decisions aimed at satisfying system and member expectations, by relying on policies, programs, processes, and technology that are conformable to reason. Contrary to courses of action that appear to be obstinate, overly visionary, misguided, or fail to apply a workable approach to achieving performance effectiveness.

Administrative theory. A set of concepts that guides administrative behavior and influences choices from among alternatives for deciding courses of action.

Adverse impact. Refers to employment discrimination that occurs when a disproportionate number of a legislation-protected group (e.g., minorities, women, or senior citizens) are rejected for employment, placement, or promotion.

Affirmative action. Plans developed and actions taken by school systems to comply with Equal Employment Opportunity regulations to prevent employment discrimination against underrepresented groups regarding recruitment, selection, placement, promotion, development, and termination practices.

Age Discrimination Employment Act of 1967. Prohibits employment discrimination against persons aged 45–65 regarding selection, compensation, termination, and related personnel practices.

Americans with Disabilities Act of 1990 (ADA). Employers may not discriminate against an individual with a disability in hiring or promotion if person is otherwise qualified for position.

Application ratio. The number of applicants applying for each position ($^{10}/_1$, $^{20}/_1$, etc.).

Arbitration. Process that involves an impartial third party who collects pertinent facts from the disputants and proceeds to make recommendations based on the findings.

Archives. Storage arrangement for retention of records having historical importance.

Authority. Empowerment vested in school officials to create and modify formalized conditions of employment and to encourage and uphold adherence by system members.

Behavior tolerance zones. Zones of behavior tolerance that the organization will accept from a system member. This concept can be illustrated in terms of a continuum, arbitrarily divided into two kinds of behavior: productive and counterproductive. The line of demarcation is established to assist the organization in evaluating the acceptability of past, present, and predicted future behavior.

Benefit. Collateral or fringe benefits are certain direct or indirect forms of compensation that do not require additional services to be performed beyond those required under the basic compensation structure.

Cafeteria benefits plan. A benefit plan in which position holders elect benefits they will receive within a specified dollar amount.

Career. The sequence of positions experienced throughout an individual's working life.

Career development. Activities pursued by individuals based on specific career objectives.

Career ladder. Vertical progression from one position to another.

Career path. Movement upward, downward, or across levels in the organizational structure.

Career planning. Organizational programs to assist position holders in considering their interests, capabilities, personality, and objectives in relation to career opportunities.

Career stages. Stages through which a position holder passes from career outset to retirement. These stages have been described as establishment, advancement, maintenance, and withdrawal. Career stages have been compared to life stages, identified as early adulthood, mature adult, midlife, and withdrawal.

Civil rights. Individual rights created by federal and state constitutions, statutes, and court decisions, one element of which is employment.

Civil Rights Act of 1964 (CRA). Prohibits all forms of discrimination on the basis of race, color, religion, sex, or national origin.

Civil Rights Act of 1991 (CRA). Employer must demonstrate that educational, physical requirements, etc., are job related.

Cohort. A group of individuals having a statistical factor (e.g., age or class membership) in common in a demographic study.

Cohort survival ratio. A factor expressing variation of the number of individuals in a cohort from one accounting period to the next. For example: 550 individuals enrolled in Grade 10, having been preceded by 500 in Grade 9 enrolled during the preceding year, would yield a ratio of $550/500$, or 1.10.

Collective bargaining. The process by which a teacher union and the school system negotiate a contract for a stipulated period of time regarding compensation, benefits, work periods, and other conditions of employment. The terms *collective bargaining* and *collective negotiations* are employed interchangeably in the literature. *Bargaining* generally refers to the total bargaining process, one phase of which is negotiations. At-the-table activities, as well as those directly relevant thereto, are viewed as negotiations.

Collective bargaining process. One of the processes in the human resources function embodying three phases: prenegotiations, negotiations, and postnegotiations.

Comparable worth. Refers to discrimination against women through pay practices. Embraces the position that women should receive the same compensation as men for comparable worth as well as equal worth. Work assignments not equal in content but providing equal value to the system warrant equal compensation.

Compensation equity. Conformity to principles of fairness and impartiality in deciding the economic worth or value of positions and position holders. *Internal equity* refers to equal pay for equal work and performance outcomes under similar working conditions. *External equity* refers to internal compensation that is comparable to that of other school organizations with which the system competes for personnel.

Compensation index. A plan for establishing base salaries for administrative and supervisory personnel by transforming responsibility levels into dollar values.

Compensation planning tools. These include the position guide, organization chart, structural analysis diagram, and compensation scattergram.

Compensation structure. Interrelated provisions governing salaries, wages, benefits, incentives, and noneconomic rewards for school personnel.

Computer. (a) An electronic machine that, by means of stored instructions and information, performs rapid, often complex calculations, or compiles, correlates, and selects data; (b) a programmable electronic device that can store, retrieve, and process data.

Confidential information. Maintenance of information about system personnel within the limits of the Privacy Act of 1974.

Contingency plans. Plans established to resolve a possible but uncertain occurrence, such as a budget rejection by the board of education or community, a teacher strike, new legislation affecting the system, a court decision, and a school merger.

Contingent personnel. Temporary, part-time, and substitute professional or support personnel. Defined in general terms by the U.S. government as those who work fewer than 35 hours per week.

Contract administration. Day-to-day administrative negotiations between the union and the school system. Grievance machinery is employed to resolve contractual disputes.

Contract design. The elements of a written contract proposal concerning system-union relationships, compensation issues, and contractual disputes.

Control. Evaluation of the extent to which progress is being made according to plan (objectives). When results deviate from standards, corrective action is initiated to ensure success of the operation. Some form of control is essential to every organizational undertaking, regardless of its scope.

Criterion. A standard, benchmark, or expectation by which to evaluate personnel performance, policies, processes, procedures, and organizational outcomes.

Criterion-related validity. Agreement between a predictor measure (e.g., teacher examination test) and a criterion measure (e.g., teaching effectiveness on the job).

Culture. Shared values by system members that produce norms shaping individual and group behavior.

Data (plural of datum). (a) Known, assumed, or conceded facts developed to establish a verifiable record of some past happening or event; (b) facts or figures from which inferences are made or conclusions are drawn; (c) individual facts and statistics capable of being converted into information.

Data base. (a) A collection of organized data, especially for rapid retrieval; (b) mass data in a computer arranged for rapid expansion, updating, or retrieval.

Data processing. The conversion of raw data to machine-readable form and its subsequent processing.

Development appraisal. Designed to improve performance or potential for performance; identifies areas for improvement or growth.

Development process. A process designed to assist position holders to raise their level of performance in present or future assignments to performance expectations.

Discrimination. To treat unequally or unfairly. Employment discrimination refers to unfair or unequal treatment regarding race, color, religious or political beliefs, sex, or national origin.

Dismissal. A personnel action initiated by the system to sever an employment relationship.

Due process. A process that guarantees rights of system members or union protection against infringement on employment rights. Requires showing of "just cause" and the use of "rules of reasonableness."

EAPs. Employee assistance programs. Plans designed to assist members with resolution of personal problems (e.g., alcohol or substance abuse) affecting position performance.

EEOC. Equal Employment Opportunity Commission. Established as the administrative agency for Title VII (Civil Rights Act of 1964).

Effectiveness. The degree to which organizational, group, or individual aims or intended effects are accomplished.

Efficiency. Outcomes or results evaluated in terms of organizational resources expended.

Employee Polygraph Protection Act. Employers prohibited from requiring or requesting job applicants to take a lie detector test.

Employment communication. A two-way exchange or partaking of information between supervisors and subordinates, designed to achieve mutual understanding of roles and relationships underlying position performance.

Equal Pay Act of 1963. A federal law requiring equal pay for equal work, regardless of gender.

External environment. Forces external to the organization over which it has no control, such as federal, state, and local regulations; court decisions; public opinion; economic fluctuations; and political movements or activities influencing system courses of action.

Failure analysis. The process identifying the factor or combination of factors associated with ineffective performance.

Family and Medical Leave Act of 1993. A covered employer must provide up to 12 weeks of unpaid leave if the employee provides appropriate documentation substantiating leave need.

Feedback. Information received by position holders and/or administrators regarding position performance or planning outcomes.

Fiduciaries. Financial organizations entrusted with managing retirement funds and related assets.

File. A collection of papers or documents systematically arranged for reference.

Form. A standardized method of recording data.

Formative appraisal. Appraisals aimed at improving the performance of position holders.

Forms management. Responsibility for creating, revising, and controlling all school system forms.

Goal structure. A hierarchy of assumptions, ranging from broad to narrow organizational intent (mission, purpose, goals, objectives, and targets). Developed to identify desirable future outcomes.

Grievance procedure. A prescribed series of steps or line of appeals designed to resolve a disagreement, dissatisfaction, dispute, or conflict concerning conditions of employment.

HMO. Health Maintenance Organization. The Federal Act of 1973 requires employers to offer an HMO (medical organization) to their employees as an alternative to conventional group health plans.

Human resources function. Personnel is one of the major functions of school administration, including these processes: planning, bargaining, recruitment, selection, induction, development, appraisal, compensation, justice, continuity, and information.

Impasse. A situation existing when negotiations are deadlocked and the possibilities of reaching common ground for a new contract are unforeseeable.

Incentives. Forms of compensation in addition to base salary that link rewards to outstanding performance.

Induction. A systematic organizational plan to assist personnel to adjust readily and effectively to new assignments so that they can contribute maximally to work of the system while realizing personal and position satisfaction.

Information. Knowledge consisting of facts that have been analyzed in the context of school administration. Information consists of data that have been refined.

Information system. A systematic plan designed to acquire, refine, organize, store, maintain, protect, retrieve, and communicate data in a valid and accurate form.

In-service education. Planned programs of learning opportunities afforded staff members for the purpose of improving the performance of individuals in already-assigned positions.

Internal environment. Forces within the school system, such as mission, goals, processes, performance culture, and leadership styles, that influence organizational courses of action.

Job. A group of positions identical with respect to their major tasks.

Job analysis. The process of gathering information about how a job is performed in order to produce a job description or specification.

Job categories. Includes professionals, office and clerical, skilled and semi-skilled operatives, unskilled laborers, and support personnel.

Job evaluation. The process by which jobs are compared in order to determine compensation value and ensure pay equity.

Job satisfaction. Individual inclination, expression, feeling, or disposition relative to a work assignment and the environment in which it is performed.

Job specification. A statement setting forth the personal requirements or capabilities entailed in performing the work of a position.

Justice system. Organizational provisions by which personnel actions (individual and organizational) are determined as right or wrong. Rewards and penalties are allocated impartially according to principles of equity or fairness.

Management by objectives (MBO). Specification of objectives for all system positions and work units, linking them to broader organizational aims (especially its overall mission).

Mentor programs. Programs established by a school system to enable outstanding experienced teachers to serve as coaches, guides, and/or role models, especially for beginning teachers, teachers changing from one grade position to another or to another school, and to enhance the performance of other experienced teachers. Mentor programs entail special incentives for those serving as mentors.

Minority. Part of a population differing from others in some characteristics (cultural, economic, political, religious, sexual, or racial) and often subjected to differential treatment.

Model. A tentative description of a system or theory that accounts for all of its known properties. Models for the human resources function, for example, are conceptual frameworks designed to isolate key factors in personnel programs, processes, or procedures to show how these factors are related to and influence each other. A model helps to visualize or portray plans that cannot be visualized directly or readily before adoption.

Modeling. The use of models to create, pretest, diagnose, and monitor various kinds of school system plans (structures, instructional systems, human resources processes, pupil forecasts, and compensation designs). Models are employed frequently to design and test the reasonableness of new plans or to diagnose the worthiness of those already in operation.

Motivation. Internal or external forces that influence an individual's willingness to achieve performance expectations.

Motivation theories. Assumptions regarding determinants that influence personnel to cooperate in putting their abilities to use to further organizational aims. Among those cited in the literature are two-factor, social comparison, consistency, reinforcement, and expectancy theories. Beliefs school officials hold about motivation influence personnel decisions.

National Health Care Insurance. A variety of national health care insurance plans were introduced in the 103rd Congress in 1994 without reaching the enactment stage. These ranged from reliance on tax incentives for individual insurance purchasers to employer mandated contributions to health care costs, to establishing a national health insurance system. See list in Appendix B.

Need. A discrepancy between an actual and a desired state. Objectives are the counterparts of needs and are employed to translate problems into programs.

Negotiating modes. Three common modes of negotiations are generally described in the literature: competitive, collaborative, and subordinative.

Negotiations strategy. Plans that establish the kinds of educational programs and services the system will make available for its clients, procedures by which these programs and services will be delivered, and means for motivating personnel to cooperate voluntarily in making the delivery system effective.

Norms. Unwritten group rules or values shared by members regarding work behavior. Statistical norms are averages sometimes construed as standards (goals).

Objectives. What is to be accomplished, for what purpose and to what extent, by whom, with what resources, and within what time frame. Objectives should be measurable and linked to broad system aims and strategies.

Organization. A group of individuals systematically united to achieve a particular method or objective as a military, educational, religious, or commercial organization.

Organization chart. A graphic representation of functions, accountability, responsibility, relationships, and levels of various positions in the organizational structure.

Organization culture. Values, standards, and attitudes of appropriate conduct and fair treatment established and reinforced by the organization and system members.

Organization manual. A document (handbook) describing the formal organization structure and related policies, processes, programs, rules, and regulations.

Organization structure. A framework for assigning roles, responsibilities, relationships, and decision-making authority among system members.

Organizational development (OD). Most definitions include (a) a planned systematic intervention; (b) to shape a more desirable organization culture; (c) by improving individual, intragroup, and intergroup attitudes, shared beliefs, and norms; (d) employing theory and technology of applied behavioral science.

Organizational elements. Key elements include structure, design of positions, power, and staffing.

Organizational influences: external. Among the external, uncontrollable elements influencing the human resources function are the regulatory environment, legal precedents, political climate, federal and state legislation, community population patterns, cultural/social change, technological developments, economic change, school enrollments, and union culture.

Organizational influences: internal. Among the internal elements influencing the human resources function are system financial condition, quality of information flow, structural setting, quality and quantity of school personnel, individual behavior, group behavior, and nature of formal and informal organizations.

Performance appraisal. The process of arriving at judgments about a member's past, present, or predicted future behavior against the background of his/her work environment or future performance potential.

Performance criteria. Criteria used to measure or evaluate position-holder performance. They include trait, behavioral, or outcome criteria, or any combination of the three.

Performance culture. Established patterns of behavior deemed essential to fulfillment of agreed-on position, group, and organizational values, standards, and attitudes.

Performance effectiveness. The level of performance that the position holder is expected to achieve.

Performance effectiveness areas. Key results areas or components, specified in a position description, in which the incumbent should be investing time, energy, and talent to achieve position expectations.

Performance objectives. A statement containing information relative to what a position holder is expected to accomplish and how well it is to be accomplished.

Personnel administration. Refers to the range of personnel activities involved in achieving individual, group, and organizational aims through proper use of the system's human resources.

Personnel continuity process. A series of managerial tasks and provisions designed to retain competent personnel and foster continuity in personnel service.

Personnel development needs. Development needs that surface at various levels (organizational, unit, and individual), at different times, for varying reasons.

Personnel development process. Formal and informal activities aimed at improving abilities, attitudes, skills, and knowledge of system members.

Personnel information. Information about individuals who apply for employment and enter, work in, and leave the system.

Personnel information modules. Units of personnel information arranged or joined in a variety of ways with the specific purpose of contributing to administration of the human resources function.

Personnel information process. An organizational process through which efforts are made to achieve a desired state relative to personnel information. Steps in the process include diagnosis, preparation, implementation, evaluation, and feedback.

Personnel policy. A written statement expressing general aims and intentions of the board of education, with respect to working conditions and relationships, which are intended to prevail in the school system.

Personnel protection. Protection of persons, jobs, income, and staffing.

Phased retirement. Opportunities for personnel nearing retirement to reduce their work load through leaves of absence; part-time employment; and reduced work days, work weeks, or work years.

Planning. Deciding in advance of action those objectives to be achieved and developing strategies to achieve them.

Planning tools. A set or collection of management mechanisms that belong to or are used together. For example: (a) *mission* refers to the primary purpose for which schools are established; (b) *strategy* refers to the use and allocation of system resources to guide action toward long-range objectives; (c) *policies* are the express system intent and boundaries within which actions are permitted or expected; (d) *aims, goals,* and *objectives* refer to desirable future results; (e) *programs* and *projects* are plans designed to achieve objectives; (f) *procedures, rules,* and *regulations* are specific instructions that guide actions and performance behavior essential to attainment of objectives; and (g) *controls* are management arrangements designed to compare planned and actual results; *budgets, audits, standards, inventories,* and *research studies* are types of controls employed to compare and correct deviations from plans.

Planning vision. An idealistic image of the school system or its components in a preferred future state. A vision of the future state of the human resources function, for example, incorporates the long-run changes deemed essential to achieving the desired image.

Policy. Broad statements of organizational intent that establish guidelines to govern the scope and boundaries of administrative decisions. There are, for example, compensation policies to govern base pay, addends, benefits, temporary hires, and pay levels comparable with other employers.

Position. A collection of tasks constituting the total work assignment of a single worker.

Position guide. A statement describing both position requirements and position-holder requirements. Useful in the recruitment, selection, induction, compensation, and development processes.

Position-holder value. Economic worth of individuals who occupy positions in the system.

Position value. The relative importance of a position in the organization structure. Positions involving greater responsibility and difficulty are valued more highly and should receive more pay than those of less responsibility and difficulty.

Power. The degree to which an individual can influence others.

Power bases. Five power bases are described as reward power, coercive power, referent power, legitimate power, and expert power.

Pregnancy Discrimination Act of 1978 (PDA). Prohibits discrimination in employment practices on the basis of pregnancy, childbirth, or related medical conditions.

Prenegotiations planning. Initial phase of the collective bargaining process, which includes such activities as developing the bargaining structure, analyzing the current contract, anticipating issues, preparing the financial outlook, developing the bargaining handbook, and formulating strategy and tactics.

Privacy Act of 1974. Federal legislation that places limits on the collection and dissemination of personal information of members of affected organizations.

Problem personnel. System members who are unable or unwilling to meet organizational standards of performance or behavior.

Professional staff size index. The number of professional staff members per 1,000 students.

Program structure. Parts of an educational program arranged in some way, such as curricula; courses of study; electives; and instructional objectives, outcomes, and practices.

Psychic income. (Also referred to as noneconomic perquisites). Includes a variety of privileges incidental to regular salary or wages. Granted voluntarily, beyond position requirements, usually in recognition of, in return for, or in anticipation of some service to the school system (recognition, appreciation, status symbols, special commendations, transfers to more attractive work, psychological security, or special arrangements related to work or working conditions).

Psychological contract. A conceptual view of an unwritten employment transaction between the system and its members, in which the position holder exchanges certain types of position behavior (cooperation, continuity, and adherence to position requirements) in return for compensation and other sources of job satisfaction (rights, privileges, and position control).

Quality of organizational life. The extent to which conditions or arrangements in the school system maximize opportunities for the position holder to assume a personalized role conducive to satisfaction of position performance, growth, initiative, and flexibility.

Record. (a) A written entry or memorial for the purpose of preserving memory or authentic evidence of facts or events;

(b) accumulation and organization of data regarded as more than temporary significance.

Records center. A central storage area for school system inactive records.

Recruitment. A process employed to seek out and attract applicants who have the qualities necessary to fill positions in the system.

Regulatory environment. Outside forces that govern and influence virtually all of the personnel processes (e.g., the Constitution, congressional acts, executive orders, state and local legislation, and judicial systems).

Reinforcement. The process of behavior modification by arranging positive consequences for desired behavior and negative consequences for undesired behavior.

Reliability. Refers to those measures that give consistent results either over periods of time or among different raters.

Reports. Utilization of records to communicate information.

Resignation. A voluntary decision by a position holder to sever an employment relationship.

Retention-ratio projection. An estimate of the future number of individuals in a cohort, derived by multiplying an existing number by the mean survival ratio experienced over a selected number of time intervals.

Retroactive enrollment ratio. A factor expressing variation of the number of individuals enrolled from one accounting period to the preceding period. The ratio is derived by dividing enrollment in a grade during a given year by enrollment in the next higher grade during the following year. For example: 500 individuals enrolled in Grade 9, having been succeeded by 550 individuals enrolled in Grade 10 during the following year, would yield a ratio of $500/550$, or .91.

Salary. Compensation for work of professional and support personnel whose contract stipulates weekly, monthly, or annual compensation.

Scope of bargaining. The substance of economic and noneconomic issues to be negotiated at the bargaining table.

Security process. Arrangements designed to protect system members from internal threats and anxieties that occur in organizational life.

Selection. The process of choosing from an applicant pool those candidates deemed most qualified and most likely to realize selection criteria.

Socialization process. Formal and informal experiences through which members become adjusted to values, roles, relationships, and organization culture. A formal socialization process (induction) is aimed at assisting members to make a productive start in their positions.

Span of control. Ability to manage a given number of people.

Spreadsheet. A computer program used to analyze numbers in a row and column accounting format. Useful in budgeting, collective bargaining planning, forecasting school enrollment, and staff projections.

Staff development. Systematic means for continuous development of performance capabilities of system personnel. The philosophical underpinning of staff development is that anyone who keeps a job should keep proving and improving himself/herself every day that he/she is paid.

Standards. Criteria against which to judge or measure the acceptability of performance or service. These measures include quality, time, cost, and personnel ratios.

Strategy. Development or employment of overall plans sometimes referred to as *grand designs,* in order to achieve goals, planned effects, or desired results. Considered a technique of total planning that encompasses the overall aims of the system and establishes functional strategies (e.g., educational program, personnel, logistics, and external relations) to achieve them. Each functional area is broken into individual modules to create an overall strategic plan for the organization.

Stress interview. A recruitment-selection technique designed to identify candidates who are capable of reacting in a calm and composed manner in tense, uncomfortable, and pressure-driven situations.

Strike. To quit or cease working in order to compel employer compliance with a demand.

Summative appraisal. Personnel appraisal focused on decisions involving compensation, tenure, dismissal, promotion, and reemployment. Does not occur simultaneously with formative appraisals.

Support personnel. Employees who perform work for which no educational certification is required and who do not participate directly in the educational process.

Systems concept. A concept that embraces the interdependence among system components and the internal and external environments in which they operate.

Technical rationality. Judicious use of techniques, operations, resources, knowledge, and know-how employed to improve, sustain, and encourage effective performance.

Tenure. A system designed to provide educators with employment security during satisfactory service. An orderly procedure is followed in the event that dismissal is considered.

Termination. Severance of an employment relationship.

Termination at will. The absolute right to discharge, with or without cause, in the absence of a written contract.

Theories of learning. Assumptions regarding the process by which new behaviors are acquired.

Theory. (a) A proposed explanation to describe or account for a phenomenon; (b) an individual view, speculation, or hypotheses. Theories in the literature describing certain aspects of the human resources function include behavioral, organization, equity, motivation, administrative, and communication.

Uniform guidelines of 1978. Federal guidelines covering employee selection procedures.

Validity. The degree to which an instrument measures what it is designed to measure.

Values. Ideals, customs, and beliefs of system members toward which a group has an affectionate regard.

Variable. A quantity susceptible of fluctuating value (e.g., test scores, performance rank, and absentee rate).

Wages. Compensation paid to personnel who generally have no guarantee of employment throughout the year.

Work-force analysis. Analysis of the composition of the work force with respect to balance in the number and percentage of minority as well as male and female personnel currently employed, by level and position classification.

Name Index

Subject Index

ISBN 0-02-320201-7